W9-ASC-213

TEACHING LANGUAGE AND LITERATURE

Teaching Language

Harcourt, Brace & World, Inc.

WALTER LOBAN
University of California, Berkeley

MARGARET RYAN
University of California, Berkeley

JAMES R. SQUIRE
University of Illinois

and Literature

GRADES 7-12

Under the General Editorship of

Willard B. Spalding

Chairman, Division of Education, Portland State College

New York · Chicago · Burlingame

Library of Congress Catalog Card Number: 61-11842

Printed in the United States of America

FOREWORD

At the heart of the problem of teaching English lies the need for integrating purpose, content, and method. The *why* of English must be related to the *what* and the *how;* furthermore, neither *what's-to-be-done* nor *how-it's-to-be-done* can be determined independently; neither can be divorced from *why-it's-to-be-done.* Integrity of purpose, content, and method guides the planning of the English curriculum.

The organization of this book is designed to clarify the relations among these three aspects of teaching English. Our subject is divided into five main sections—thought, understanding, appreciation, communication, values—each an important area of concern for the classroom teacher. The initial section deals with the processes of language and thinking, both basic to understanding, appreciation, and communication; the final section assesses values emerging from the study of English. Illustrative units, showing how the content and methods discussed may be introduced into the classroom, are presented at the end of each section.

The individual chapters have also been organized to relate purpose, content, and method. In each chapter "Perspective" presents a point of view about the content to be taught—the essential subject matter, the insights needed by the teacher, the philosophical and psychological problems involved. "The Teaching Problem," in three parts, is concerned with the strategies of classroom instruction. The first part discusses ways of designing curriculum—often from grade to grade or level to level—in order to achieve incremental learning. Although our knowledge of the sequential patterns of instruction through which students learn language and literature is still far from complete, we do know that every act of learning has antecedents and consequences. Only as we are able to identify more adequate sequences of instruction will we eliminate false starts and unnecessary duplication and thereby achieve a truly articulated English program. The second part presents Suggested Learning Experiences, the instructional procedures applied to the content being considered, but equally appropriate in many other contexts. The third part suggests methods for evaluating progress toward the goals set forth.

The prologue, "Teacher and Learner," considers the ideal English teacher in relation to students who are products of a rapidly changing culture. The epilogue, "Program and Plan," is concerned with general ways of organizing lessons, units of instruction, and curricula. Thus the teacher of English can see his particular problems in broader perspective.

Teaching Language and Literature may be used in a flexible manner. It need not be read in the order of its presentation, even though the inner logic of our subject has determined the organization of the book. Depending upon his purpose, the reader may begin at any point of interest, perhaps with the analysis of planning and curriculum or with any of the statements on separate language skills. Nor is the book intended only for use in college classes on methods and curriculum in English. Other uses are readily apparent:

As a help to curriculum committees charged with reassessing their programs in English

As a guide to study groups interested in a particular aspect of English, such as grammar, unit planning, or the teaching of poetry

As a tool for the in-service education of beginning teachers of English in a particular school

As a ready desk reference for the experienced teacher

The index, the table of contents, and the locational aids within each chapter have been planned to encourage flexibility of use. The authors have attempted to write a book helpful to the beginning teacher yet of interest to the experienced teacher as well.

Because this volume relies heavily upon our own teaching experience, the persons to whom we are indebted are many. In a real sense the hundreds of teachers and students with whom we have worked have contributed substantially to our present attitudes. The manuscript was given an extensive critical reading by Willard Spalding, Portland State College, Portland, Oregon, and by Mrs. Luella B. Cook, Wayzata, Minnesota. To all these and to our friends and those at home who encouraged us in the years of writing, we are deeply indebted.

In the final analysis, of course, no book on curriculum or methods is so important in determining the caliber of instruction as is the teacher's personal philosophy, never static but growing as the teacher grows. The choices open to a teacher of English are many; each will teach what he thinks important. Thus it is essential that each individual teacher know *what* he teaches, *how* he can best teach it, and *why* it must be taught. In no other way can he foresee and utilize the teachable moments that occur daily in the classroom.

W. L., M. R., J. R. S.

January, 1961
Berkeley, California
Urbana, Illinois

CONTENTS

TEACHING LANGUAGE AND LITERATURE

Teacher and Learner

The teacher views his task

Each of us in his own way brings to the classroom an image of himself as a teacher of English. He does not always articulate his concept of the teacher's role; sometimes the image is only vaguely defined; yet he strives to emulate in his teaching those patterns of behavior which are compatible with his image and to eliminate those which are not. Whether one has taught for many years or is just beginning, his conception of the role of the teacher of English governs his expectations and determines how he acts in any school situation.[1]

Models and memories What is the source of these theoretical models? Primarily, personal experience. Many of us select English as a career because of youthful contacts with teachers we admired and respected. Such direct experiences—whether in one's family, in secondary school, in college—provide us with a certain image of teaching. Our impressions are supplemented and reinforced by observation of teachers in the community, by personal friendships, by reading, and by comments in conversation. Ultimately, of course, primary experience, first as a student teacher and later as faculty member, forces us to test our images and to modify and expand our conceptions of the role. In the beginning, however, when the new teacher attempts to approximate the theoretical model he has created, he must eliminate many inadequacies in his understanding of the nature of education and the role of the teacher.

Preconceptions are not inherently bad provided they are subject to amelioration and change with practical experience. Some conception of role is inevitable. How else can teachers establish standards against which to measure their effectiveness? A mind which reaches a professional teaching career as a *tabula rasa* is a mind lacking in purpose and dedication. But a mind which fails to change when faced with the realities of fact is one which does not grow. The role of the teacher appears quite different from the front of the classroom than from the rear.

[1] In a study of beginning teachers, Shafer found that students entering teacher education programs not only had many preconceived images of the role of the English teacher but that these preconceptions were persistent in their effect on subsequent behavior. Robert Shafer, "Concepts of Role in Prospective Teachers of English," unpublished doctoral dissertation, Teachers College, Columbia University, 1958, p. 122.

Perhaps no greater challenge faces the beginning teacher than this task of testing and modifying his theoretical model of the role of the teacher of English. Personal memories of "good" teachers are not always reliable guides. Such images become cloudy over the years, particularly when reconstructed from the recollections of a student whose very sensitivity to language and literature distinguished his observations from those of his fellow classmates. Lack of clarification of role emerges, too, from the difficulties faced by beginning teachers in distinguishing their responsibilities as undergraduate students of language and literature from those as teachers in secondary schools. Whereas a college student places stress on certain elements of content, valuable and delightful purely as a part of knowledge, the secondary school teacher must consider how content can be learned and how pupils are to be prepared. Thus the unique shifts in perception which occur as one enters the profession have a vital influence on each individual's outlook. Few serious students of the educative process pass through this period without considerable soul searching, relying often on the wisdom of experienced associates when uncertain of their own perceptions.

The ideal teacher of English The ideal teacher of English is one whose liberal education has freed him to lead a harmonious, well-balanced life. He has been liberated from those accidental restrictions—the circumstances of birth and environment—that narrow personal vision. Freed from such limitations by education, he may associate with the best minds of all centuries and of all nations, viewing perspectives which he might otherwise never have known. Such an education, moreover, extends beyond formal schooling with its primary concern for intellectual development. The liberally educated teacher of English is one whose feelings, imagination, and intellect have been fused into that stable poise which enables him to grapple with essential and ultimate questions of experience. He sees more clearly than most how ends and means are related, how outer symbols shadow forth the inner truths of existence, and how choices reflect the values, conscious or unconscious, an individual accepts.

Such a teacher clarifies in his own mind and in the minds of his students the values to be gained from studying language and literature. This requires a complex equilibrium of many qualities and skills, but four characteristic outlooks may be identified. These define the ideal teacher of English, investing him with the special sense of direction characteristic of those who truly teach language and literature.[2] In the four sections which follow immediately, the authors present their own viewpoint, the matrix which gives shape to the concepts of teaching in this book.

[2] The four points of view presented here as characteristic of the ideal teacher of English might be applied to other teachers as well. However, it is our contention that in science and mathematics, the social studies, and the fine or useful arts, additional considerations alter the relationships among these points and extend them in various directions of emphasis. These four represent a crucial quartet which must be kept in balance by the *teacher of English.*

The English teacher has clarified his viewpoint about human nature. He may be orthodox in his religious beliefs and explain man's imperfections by a fall from grace. He may be a humanist and view the evils of human behavior as partly the result of adverse environment and partly of man's heredity as a creature of the natural world. But whatever his religious or philosophical stand, the English teacher does not, like Machiavelli, accept the "deceitful, cowardly, and greedy" aspects of man as the very essence of his nature. Nor does the teacher veer to the opposite extreme, like some of Rousseau's disciples, and view man as innately good, lacking only the freedom to erase the obstacles to wisdom and virtue. Somewhere between these two extremes, teachers of English create their own over-all design and their daily strategies for guiding those they teach. Like Jefferson, they swear hostility against all forms of tyranny over the mind of man, but like Huxley, they see their work as that of a gardener in perpetual warfare with weeds and wildness, an effort never intended to eventuate in perfection. The teacher works with human beings on this earth, not with seraphs at the pinnacle of a celestial hierarchy.

But if the English teacher does not presume to promise utopias, he does expect to help pupils think more clearly, communicate more effectively, and feel more keenly. To the extent that these goals are accomplished, the English teacher believes other desirable ends of education will inevitably follow: Superstition and bigotry will diminish along with ignorance; individuals will adjust in more mature ways to the inevitable adversities of living; better relations will exist among individuals of differing groups and nations; cooperation will increase while exploitation and narrow self-interest wane; and a dynamic social stability will more often prevail. And this view—neither sentimental nor pessimistic—influences both curriculum and methods of instruction in English.

The English teacher has clarified his point of view about thinking. The cruciality of clear thinking in achieving the goals of the English program requires each teacher to sharpen his perception concerning the relationship of thinking to language and literature and thus to human behavior.

What is thinking? We know it is an activity of the nervous system, particularly of the higher brain centers, but this is not very helpful. We may get further, perhaps, by asking why human beings think. Although not the whole explanation, adjustment of the individual for the sake of survival must be considered one dominant function of thought. By thinking, an individual adjusts to his environment, both external and internal; thinking is, at its foundations, essential to human life. Bruner and others [3] have pointed out that thinking enables man to identify objects and to reduce the complexity of his environment. Thinking alleviates the necessity of constant relearning—presumably to conserve energy needed for higher levels of existing—and enables the thinker to estimate *in advance* appropriate and inappropriate actions. This future-oriented aspect of thinking allows the individual an opportunity for prior adjustment. Thinking helps him know what things are worth his

[3] Jerome S. Bruner, Jacqueline J. Goodnow, and George B. Austin, *A Study of Thinking* (N.Y., Wiley, 1957).

attention and, lest he break down in confusion, what things may safely be ignored. Thus thinking becomes a means of maintaining equilibrium. Yet this cannot be a static equilibrium: Growth and change are also part of existence, and curiosity, inseparable from thinking, prevents us from adjusting too well.

Language is not essential to thought. Thinking can be done without verbal symbols—witness Helen Keller before she learned to use words. But if language is not essential to thinking, it is a vehicle making possible infinitely more precise and rapid thinking. One way to see this relationship between thinking and language is to study man's capacity for making distinctions. Poison oak differs from maple leaves; proteins offer some advantages over animal fats. Making and using classifications is an important aspect of thinking, and language enables man to maintain his classifications against the confusion and flux of living.

According to John Dewey,[4] language, although it is not thought, is necessary for any high development of thought and communication. Dewey sees linguistic signs as *fences* which select and detach meanings from what would otherwise be a vague blur, as *labels* which retain and store meanings, and as *vehicles* for transfer and reapplication to new situations. But linguistic signs have another important aspect; they are *organizational instruments* as well. Not just indicative of a single meaning, words "also form sentences in which meanings are organized in relation to one another."

But thinking is more than the means by which the individual adjusts in order to survive. The speed and competence of language make possible such a fine state of equilibrium that human energies need not be entirely consumed in charting a course between breakdown or vegetation. It is this freedom from animal struggle for survival, this extra dividend of release, which counts most heavily in teaching children and adolescents to use language with power. Thinking becomes reason, to which Whitehead assigns a function, the art of life—to live, to live well, and to live better.[5] Through the arts of language—all based upon effective reasoning that transcends the need to outwit the adverse forces of nature—pupils assume their heritage as human beings. They can make choices among ethical and esthetic values; they can weigh and consider, sifting truth from falseness; they can help to organize society on a foundation of wisdom rather than on one of blind authority, class, or raw power.

The English teacher has clarified his point of view on the nature of his task. The secondary school teacher of English is in the classroom to help pupils shape their thoughts and experiences toward form and order. Metaphorically speaking, he acts to oppose the devil of Goethe's *Faust,* the clever Mephistopheles who wants the world and all its creatures to revert to the original chaos from which they have evolved. Mephistopheles yearns for the

[4] John Dewey, *How We Think* (Boston, Heath, 1909; rev. 1933), p. 232.
[5] Alfred North Whitehead, *The Function of Reason* (Boston, Beacon, 1958), p. 8.

primeval night, the nothingness from which matter has moved toward structure and form—and *therefore* toward meaning and significance. "I am the Spirit that Denies!" Mephistopheles announces, "And justly so: for all things, from the Void called forth, deserve to be destroyed." With such an antagonist, the teacher becomes an actor in a drama of significance, struggle, and suspense. The more clearly the teacher understands his commitment to the principle of lucid, coherent order, the more skillfully will he play his role as protagonist.

But the English classroom involves forces and tensions even more complex than this drama of chaos versus structure. If Mephistopheles cannot destroy order by direct attack, he falls back upon a substitute ruse, the lure of a dead order. Under the guise of virtuous tradition, he offers English teachers an outwardly respectable facade of drills, rules, declensions, and memorization, all of which ultimately prove to be a travesty on genuine tradition and as wasteful as the havoc of chaos. The devil knows that the outer covering, the husk, is always easier to comprehend than the living seed, and that in every human enterprise he can always tempt us to settle for a tangible ritual rather than the complex meaning. Thus, he dupes those whose instruction achieves order at the expense of vitality.

Static order can be as perilous as vitality without order. To avoid either extreme, the teacher of English must live dangerously, in the sense that all instruction is a dynamic equilibrium, a delicate harmony of many complex elements. But just as one is most aware of life when he is most in danger, so is teaching most exhilarating when it requires an alert accommodation of many unexpected or new elements. Like "infinite riches in a little room," teachers of English find before them the vast panorama of life itself. Each new discovery opens unforeseen possibilities, each new idea leads to many more. Actually there can be no one ideal English teacher because the paths of language and literature are so varied and many. What each teacher of English can attempt is to bring a reasonable sense of order to the study of a rich and complex field. Unless he does this, he stands in danger of drowning in an "impenetrable sea of knowledge."

Composers put order into the dissonance of sound and bring forth melodies and harmonies to express what cannot be put into words; scientists search for order in the universe and find structures to reduce the abrupt and the obscure; teachers of English seek to create in pupils those harmonies of clear, orderly thinking, those controlled resonances of emotional response and lucid expression that give meaning to life. Both chaos and sterile order may be combated, so the English teacher feels, by helping pupils free themselves from crooked thinking, blurred communication, and dull, sodden feeling-tone.

Finally, *the English teacher has clarified his point of view on how to relate human nature and his task.* In so doing, the secondary school teacher of English considers adolescents and how they learn. Because of his familiarity with literature and its insights into human behavior, he is unlikely to accept overly simple generalizations about learning or to expect infallible recipes. Nevertheless, the formulation of instructional principles, complex though they may be, requires a place in the thinking of every teacher who hopes to change the behavior of his pupils. Indeed, it is essential to realize the importance of selecting classroom procedures consistent with what is known about learning if one is to rise above the limitations imposed by specific techniques and is to continue to grow as a teacher. It is an intellectualization about method for which the teacher must strive—an intellectualization placing theoretical concerns central in his viewpoint. Such an achievement safeguards the teacher against blindly accepting specific techniques and definitive answers to instructional problems and invests him with the personal resources needed for creating procedures consistent with his own philosophy or theory of learning. The principles of learning summarized in the next few pages suggest the concept of method in English from which the procedures described in this book have grown. Each teacher must develop his own point of view if he is to assess procedures recommended by others and to create appropriate procedures of his own; such a point of view will come to the English teacher only as he learns to relate what he knows about learning to what he knows of the nature of language and literature.

The ways of learning

Certainly the whole domain of educational psychology cannot be summarized here, nor would the rest of this volume suffice for that growing subject. What is possible, however, is a brief statement of the basic principles influencing the choice of methods recommended in this book. This matrix of learning theory may be summarized under five headings:

Motivation and involvement
Organization and relationships
Process as distinguished from product
Sound evaluation
Individual differences

What has seemed to us of crucial importance in each of these aspects of instruction is presented below, together with a few illustrations of how we have used them in this book.

Motivation and involvement Often in this book we will speak of *will* or *volition,* terms we use interchangeably. Will power is that energy through which the individual chooses and carries out plans of action toward some goal. When strong desire to learn is part of an instructional situation, learning almost certainly occurs; when indifference or perfunctory efforts predominate, learning is always meager. Without persistent, purposeful, and selective effort, learning cannot be efficient. To be *purposeful,* the learner must accept the goal as his own; otherwise his motivation will be weak or sporadic. To be *selective,* the learner must have help in identifying those details or aspects of the situation which hold the key to understanding. Thus there is an important relation between purpose and selection, a matter of economy in learning.

The first step in economical learning is to establish a goal. The pupil will select and learn those responses which lead to the goal as he perceives it. Then after each attempt to execute the skill or behavior pattern the learner should gauge his success by references to the goal, adapting his responses in the light of this evaluation. The word *adapt* is of crucial significance.

Goals and purposes must be clearly understood, not only with respect to the broad pattern of response but also with regard to significant details of performance. Because time spent in drilling perfunctorily on exercises is mostly wasted, teachers should spend more time creating an *interest in improvement.* There can be no real development of power over language except through the general quickening, maturing, and energizing of the mind in all its aspects: interest, emotion, thought, and volition. Goals must be possible; pupils need to feel that they have a chance of success. Repeated failure to reach the goals set by teachers damages the self-confidence and affects the achievement, not to mention the mental health, of any pupil—bright, average, or dull.

We have now come to one of the most crucial of all questions in the teaching process. What is the relation between goals and pupil volition? Who is to set the goals, teacher or pupil? If the teacher sets the goals, will the pupils be apathetic in their learning? Are pupils wise enough to chart their own courses and persevere in them? In some schools these questions have often proved dilemmas, and in others teachers have taken extreme positions. Some school people have acted as if there were no alternatives between teacher domination and pupil leadership.

Resourceful teachers avoid wasting their time in such futile arguments. They realize they must make the goals of English important and worthwhile to their pupils, and to do this, they are prepared to range quite freely among possible solutions. Depending upon the maturity of their students and the particular content, they vary their own role. Research, summarized in the accompanying chart developed by Cronbach, suggests that there is no single method of class organization to be followed in all situations. Whether a class should be group controlled, teacher controlled, or organized in some other way will depend on the purposes to be achieved. Integrity prevents most teachers from pretending that the fundamental questions of what is to be learned and how it is to be learned can be decided by pupils. Most of the time, they rely upon their own ability to help students see the value of what they teach and to choose the best ways to make this clear to pupils. But often, and as ingeniously as possible, teachers draw pupils into the act of charting directions, of selecting among the various means of learning, and of gauging progress.

Effects of three control patterns: a summary *

Outcome	*Effect of undirected activities*	*Effect of teacher-controlled activities*	*Effect of group-controlled activities*
Emotional security	Disturbing because of low accomplishment.	Relieves anxiety by setting definite standards, provided goals are stated.	Frustrating if group feels planning wastes time.
Enjoyment	Enjoyable until anxiety appears.	Enjoyment depends on the work; little social satisfaction.	Enjoyable if group feels it is progressing. Promotes friendly interaction.
Effort and efficiency	Frequently wasteful of energy. Low persistence.	Effective if group accepts direction and if leadership is maintained. Group may resist direction and make minimum effort.	Leads to greater acceptance of goals and to continued effort when leader is absent. Leads to understanding of task and self-direction.
Learning of course material	No direct evidence. Probably ineffective compared to other approaches.	As good as group control.	As good as teacher control. Encourages free expression of ideas and feelings. Possibly superior for altering attitudes.
Learning skills of group membership	No better than spontaneous play.	Little opportunity for social learning.	Provides directed training in planning, teamwork, and leadership.

* Lee J. Cronbach, *Educational Psychology* (N.Y., Harcourt, Brace, 1954).

Teaching is an art, and only the teacher is prepared to practice the art. Pupils cannot possibly be expected to harmonize the delicate strategies and sensitive pacing of instruction, but they can be drawn into the dynamics through expressing their perplexities, sharing their reactions, and taking responsibilities commensurate with their vision. Throughout this book, we draw upon procedures which exemplify these relations among purpose, economy, and volition. For instance:

In teaching drama and poetry, oral participation is featured as a means of pupil involvement.

In group work, students are placed in circumstances where they can be taught to function effectively, where they can learn the skills of communication in a situation where there is someone to whom they genuinely wish to communicate.

In the program for guiding individual reading, books are chosen for their relevance to the abilities, interests, and purposes of the reader.

In the chapter on grammar and usage, ways to help students select their own errors for improvement and drill are described.

Significantly related to motivation and learning, too, is a teacher's awareness of communication as a necessary goal of language development. Controversy over the importance of acquiring skills versus having something to communicate is pointless. Clearly, improvement in language learning occurs most surely in situations featuring bona fide communication. Pupils must have something to express, a desire to express it, and someone to whom they wish to express it. Only in such circumstances does instruction have any hope of improving pupils' facility in expression. Divorced from communication, attention to the skills of expression is futile. This emphasis on communicating—on giving to another as a partaker, on making thoughts and feelings available to someone else—is reiterated throughout this book. Not only in the chapters on speaking and writing does this emphasis occur, but also from the reverse side of the cloth—in reading, listening, and the appreciation of literature, where the demand for receiving meaning is no less important.

Organization and relationships The main factor responsible for durability in learning, it is our experience, always proves to be organization. Pupils—not only the teacher—must relate what is to be learned to some coherent structure; the individual parts must be easily summoned up and sustained by some intrinsic pattern or principle of organization. What one really learns, if it is to last, is a pattern, a generalization with applications, rather than a miscellany of specific reactions. In organizing their learning, some adolescents are like a confused girl with a handful of vari-colored beads which keep spilling out of her hand and mixing with all the other colors. Other adolescents are like a girl who has sorted the beads by color and placed them in separate boxes—but who never wears the beads. The successful learners are like a third girl who wears her beads firmly strung on a suitable and well-woven cord and arranged in attractive hues of intensity.

The danger is that teachers, like their pupils, will be satisfied with placing items in proper classifications, as in naming parts of speech or in listing ten qualities of the lyric poem. But learning is infinitely more than classification; it is seeing relationships, and the ability to see relationships does not occur through mere accumulation. Detail poured upon detail ultimately results in a surfeit that drives pupils to boredom if not rebellion. In order to relate and organize their experiences, students must practice thinking about key qualities or important characteristics—whether of poetry or of usage or of paragraphing—in settings other than those in which they were originally perceived. Learning often proceeds by this noting of details which have previously been experienced in another form or pattern.

This important process of differentiation takes place within an organizing framework. Classification, so satisfying to tidy and limited minds, often proves to be Mephistopheles' dead order. No one denies the importance of classification as a first step toward bringing order out of chaos. The danger is to stop there.

> How great is the number of readers who think, for example, that a defective rhyme —*bough's, house; bush, thrush; blood, good*—is sufficient ground for condemning a poem in the neglect of all other considerations. Such sticklers, like those with a scansion obsession, have little understanding of poetry. We pay attention to externals when we do not know what else to do with a poem.[6]

And we might add, when we do not know what else to do with any significant learning problem. It is always much easier to recite rules of grammar than to apply them, or to report on an author's life than to grapple with his intention in a literary selection.

In teaching a subject as complex as English, one of the temptations is to classify the content by logical analysis of the subject and then allot to each classification a block of time. Presumably even the purist among classifiers does not intend that relationships should never occur between literature on Mondays and grammar on Thursdays, or between composition in the fall semester and public speaking or literature in the spring. Nevertheless, human behavior has not changed since Aristotle noted that the classifications into which things are arranged condition what is done with them. In the teaching of English, separate emphases on aspects like composition, spelling, and oral communication never prove as effective as their advocates envision. No matter how good a teacher's intentions, the classifications tend to be self-contained, diminishing valuable relationships and support from other aspects of English. Furthermore, the classifications, although unquestionably determined by the nature of the discipline, lack vitality for most of the learners, who have not themselves made the analysis. Psychology has shown us that the learning process in adolescents, as in all human beings, starts from interest and motive and progresses toward a comprehensiveness that enables them to perceive the logic of a discipline. This may seem perverse, but it is human.

By the integrated program advocated in this text, the reader should understand learning situations which fuse several aspects of English: Composition and discussion related to the values and concepts illuminated by the study of literature; reading and library skills taught in preparation for a panel discussion; grammar, spelling, the principles of rhetoric or logic, used as means to the effective expression of rational and imaginative thinking. Central to the entire conception of this text, then, is a firm rejection of segregated aspects of English arranged separately throughout the week or semester. Integration within the English program is more exacting, for both teacher and student—and also more interesting, more rewarding—than logical categories arranged consecutively, so alluring in their neat simplicity, so deceptive in their promise of efficient order, so disappointing in their results with young learners.

Six units are included in this volume to illustrate ways in which pro-

[6] I. A. Richards, *Principles of Literary Criticism* (N.Y., Harcourt, Brace, 1924), p. 24.

cedures discussed separately in these chapters may be integrated in the classroom. The units, intended to be descriptive rather than prescriptive, are planned for different age groups and types of classes, and each is developed in a rather distinct manner. For example, the twelfth grade study of *Macbeth* shows how language skills may be directed toward the study of a single classic; the tenth grade plan, "Meeting a Crisis," reveals the unity which may be developed out of the study of diverse literary selections. Each unit, however, is planned around basic conceptual goals which supply an underlying organizational framework. In each also are presented the various learning experiences, the materials used, and the methods of evaluation.

Throughout this book we describe procedures that exemplify and exalt organization and the relationships which the pupils achieve. For instance:

In "Oral Language," which stresses discussion as a means of integrating various learnings.

In "Listening with Discrimination," which shows ways of correlating listening skills with those in other areas of English instruction.

In "Program and Plan," which shows how teaching a thinking skill may be incorporated within a unit.

In "Imaginative Thinking," which emphasizes control and order for inspiration and range of intellectual-emotional vision.

Process as distinguished from product The English teacher concentrates his attention on the process of his students' learning as well as on the product. Sometimes pupils shrewdly guess at the answer a teacher wants or derive the proper results by uneconomical means. Sometimes pupils come to wrong conclusions but neither teacher nor pupil sees a value in determining why. To the extent that a teacher can penetrate beneath the surface of answers and outward behavior to the processes of thought, he can outwit wasteful learning. By emphasizing occasions for the pupil to analyze, synthesize, discriminate, compare, and generalize, he can decrease the amount of meaningless repetition and rote learning. Process, discovery, and problem solving are not always easy to arrange in classroom situations, but they are to rote learning what jet planes are to covered wagons drawn by oxen. The reader is urged to note in this book:

The procedure of teaching the short story described in "Literature: Basic Approaches." Here the teacher divides a story into its inherent segments and stops to discuss each segment in order, building a cumulative sureness of response at the same time that he observes the pupils' responses *during the process of reading.*

The procedure of presenting two versions of the same poem or short story, one a faithful version and the other debased, as described in "Imaginative Thinking." As the pupils discuss which of the two versions is the better and why, the teacher learns much about the decisions which lie back of their choices.

"Oral Language," which stresses the teacher's role in guiding the process of discussion and in making students aware of process as well as product.

The thesis of the first chapter that understanding language as process is basic to acquiring power over language.

The ideal teacher of English avoids the situation in which the teacher does most of the learning attended by a group of docile spectators whose parents pay the bill. The pupils must be encouraged to discover and report processes by which they gain control of problems. There must be silences for reflection, long silences of which neither teacher nor pupil is fearful. There must be time for mistakes and for muddling through and time for evaluation of such confusion in order to distill principles for streamlining the next similar situation. There must be repetition of the same skill or concept in a variety of situations wherein the pupil concentrates on the essential features which recur, transferring the key elements to new situations. Over and over again in this book, procedures for teaching composition, literature, listening, or speaking will reflect this concern for process.

Sound evaluation The teacher of English recognizes that sound evaluation produces sound learning. The experiences of many young people lead them to think of *test* and *evaluation* as synonymous. Studying the meaning of the two words, and the contrast in the emotional overtones each carries, provides a lesson in language process as well as a means of initiating understanding of the scope and the purpose of evaluation in the English class. A test is a *trial* which may or may not result in *critical appraisal.* For many pupils tests are dreaded experiences tinged with emotional crisis, preceded by cramming and followed by final and irrevocable judgments concerning personal merit. If the student learns to see tests as both indicating degree of progress and giving directions for future learnings, he can develop a healthy attitude toward evaluation. Belief that appraisal must be continual, varied, and inclusive underlies the treatment of evaluation throughout this text.

If evaluation is *continual,* the student realizes its constructive purpose. Brief, frequent appraisals give him a chance to see what he has accomplished and what remains to be learned; they allow time for him to recoup his losses before final assessment must be made. Thus, they serve for evidence of improvement, for diagnosis, and for motivation. Since the scope of each is narrow, the results are not so dire as to cause discouragement. Continual evaluation should dissipate much of the tension occasional over-all testing seems to generate.

If *various methods* of estimating progress are used, the pupil learns not to overestimate the importance of those written examinations which determine only whether the desired response is available at a given time. He learns the significance of self-evaluation and that made by his peers; he learns ways of gauging progress in oral work; he learns the difference in import of tests that call for remembering facts, that require application of principles, that demand demonstrations of skillful performance. All of these necessary learnings can receive impetus if various methods of evaluating are used.

If evaluation is *inclusive,* all goals set for learning receive proper emphasis. The procedures used for evaluation influence learning in subtle ways. Although lip service may be paid to aims never evaluated, the pupil soon learns to disregard those that "do not count" in his final grade. For example, a situation like this often arises: One of the goals for learning may be to increase skill in making pertinent contributions to a discussion. Peter writes skillfully, and he hands in all written assignments on time. However, his discussion techniques do not improve; he may maintain complete silence, he may monopolize, he may insist upon acceptance of his statements without support. If frequent evaluations do not call his attention to these deficiencies, he rightly decides that the oral goals mean no more to the teacher than they do to him. Continual, varied, and inclusive evaluation of learning is an essential part of teaching, as is illustrated in this volume in many ways:

In the suggestions for evaluating group interaction in "Oral Language."

In the procedure of establishing folders of written work discussed in "Written Expression."

In the use of cumulative reading records to evaluate growth in taste, as described in "Literature: Basic Approaches."

Individual differences In the Greek myth, the giant robber Procrustes lay in wait for unwary travelers, who were dragged into his cave and stretched or shortened to fit his bed. Sometimes the curriculum in English has been like Procrustes' bed, whittling down the brilliant and wracking those whose native abilities were limited. Unlike the citizens of Huxley's *Brave New World,*[7] human beings are not decanted from bottles according to a standard formula. They vary in many ways—in talent, in energy, in aspiration. This is a fact, and facts are stubborn things. In a nation where almost the entire population of junior and senior high school age is in school, this variation in the human family overshadows almost all other educational problems. In the English class it means great ranges in ability to read, to handle verbal symbols of any kind, to see relationships, and to generalize from principles to applications. Virtually every method in this book has been written from the authors' lives among such pupils in schools ranging from Virginia to Illinois to California. Perhaps, among all the procedures offered, the following may be cited as notable for their evolution as part of the American public schools' adaptation to mass education:

The unit method of instruction, described on p. 220 and illustrated by a series of resource units throughout the book.

The grouping of students within the classroom to handle problems of varying complexity.

Guided individual reading to supplement class instruction on a single text.

Permitting pupils whenever possible a choice among alternative ways to learn.

Methods of evaluation that provide for differing levels and for varying rates of speed in understanding.

Enrichment for able pupils; simplification and a slower pace of learning for

[7] Titles of literary works and visual aids mentioned throughout the book are listed in special bibliographies at the end of the text.

pupils who find it difficult to deal with verbal symbols, as in the lesson described on pp. 221-22.

Certainly the sequences of human development affect the variations among students found in every classroom. Before a pupil can write a long paper, he must learn how to control the paragraph; before he can summarize a panel discussion, he must learn to generalize from a relatively simple discussion. All the stages of difficulty need to be related to the levels of human development through which pupils are passing. Adolescents ought neither to be forced like hothouse plants, nor left like Topsy, who "just growed." It is the teacher's responsibility to see that young people mature as rapidly as is consistent with sound learning. Yet Rousseau had an important insight when he said, "Look at the child and see what he is like. He is not a miniature adult, and your efforts will go to waste if you begin where you, the teacher, stand instead of at the point which the child has reached." Every teacher of adolescents should bear in mind the motto, *Festina lente: Too swift will arrive as tardy as too slow.*

These, then, are crucial aspects of learning which each teacher of English must consider. Only as the content of learning and the form of learning become intimately related does teaching really become an art.

Directing English learning in today's schools

Because schools are social institutions, the teaching of any subject is affected by cultural conditions and demands. The teaching of English is strongly influenced by the surrounding world. The impact of environmental factors on language development, the statement of cultural values in literature, the high assessment placed on language proficiency in certain strata of society—such interrelationships almost require the teacher of English to view his perception of the way students learn language and literature against the social scene. Thus the teacher of English needs to consider both the general role of the school in American culture and the special ways in which society influences learning in his classroom.[8]

Effect of non-responsibility When an American teacher stands aside and tries to view his pupils with the perspective of historical detachment, he sees one strange and disturbing feature, the long false dawn between childhood and maturity. In no other era of history and in few contemporary cultures have adolescents been consigned to such a long period of non-responsibility. In most times and places, young people mature through fulfilling obligations important

[8] Teachers who have not completed some study of school and society in their preparatory programs will find the following books particularly helpful: James B. Conant, *The American High School Today* (N.Y., McGraw-Hill, 1959), pp. 1-9; Margaret Mead, *The School in American Culture* (Cambridge, Mass., Harvard U. Press, 1951); Robert Havighurst and Bernice Neugarten, *Society and Education* (Boston, Allyn & Bacon, 1957); Harvard University, Committee on the Objectives of a General Education in a Free Society, *General Education in a Free Society* (Cambridge, Mass., Harvard U. Press, 1945).

to the community. If an Afghan boy fails to guard the sheep, if a Bolivian girl does not know how to weave clothing, the community or the family suffers. Freed—or, more accurately, deprived—of such responsibilities, our own adolescents inevitably experience considerable drift that delays maturity. Nihilism, confusion, and a cynical dependence upon luck and ruthlessness characterize the values of numbers of our high school students at an age when, in other times and places, they would be functioning workers preparing for marriage and molded by the mores of their communities. We might well ask ourselves how much this lack of responsibility contributes to the adolescent's attempt to attain security and status by conforming to the standards of his peers. To what extent does this urge for conformity in youth nurture the adult who chooses adjustment to his environment, rather than the development of his inner resources, as his ultimate goal?

Impact of urbanization Another notable feature of our culture, influencing the school's growing concern with choices in a free society, is the triumph of urbanization with its detrimental impact on the primary social institutions. As the large cities grow larger and the rural population declines, the dominion of home, community, and church diminishes. In many homes both parents work, and their children are in school throughout the day; in the evening various organizations and interests frequently disperse the family again. The vastness of the city, inducing feelings of isolation and anonymity, blunts the feeling of community cohesiveness and weakens traditional ties. In the earlier rural communities the family not only was a necessary economic unit but served also to transmit values from one generation to the next. Boys, as they ploughed or milked with their fathers and uncles, absorbed the principles guiding these men in a settled, slowly changing culture; girls, as they sewed or baked with their mothers or older married sisters, talked about men and families and religion, assimilating the values by which these women lived. Most of these adults—unlike many of those today—had not the slightest doubt that their values were absolute and free from inconsistency. Birth, death, marriage, sorrow, and joy were occasions of moment to the entire community. We gain some realization of how different American life is now if we turn quickly from Salinger's *Catcher in the Rye* to Wilder's *Our Town* or contrast Arnow's *The Dollmaker* with *Huckleberry Finn.*

Demands upon the school Is there emerging a new and different society, one in which families, churches, and communities will further wither under the impact of technological advancement? We think not. But during the period of adjustment to the unsettling transformations of cultural change, schools will not be able to avoid responsibility for concern with values as well as with basic skills and information. Wisdom has always been one of the aims of education; in a time when many boys and girls are receiving fewer of their values from their parents and an increasing number from television, comics, and their peers, society will bend the school, its instrument, to a concern with value choices.

Values and the teaching of English If anyone in the secondary school is concerned with discriminating among values, that person is the teacher of English. Yet he knows that helping individuals find their values is one of the most delicate of all enterprises. The older cloying repetition of moral precepts has collapsed as surely as the more recent total rejection by the schools of all responsibility. The direction the schools may now take is a middle ground, one that serves as a conclusion to the Rockefeller Report: [9]

> We would not wish to impose upon students a rigidly defined set of values. Each student is free to vary the nature of his commitment. But their freedom must be understood in its true light. We believe that the individual should be free and morally responsible: the two are inseparable. The fact that we tolerate differing values must not be confused with moral neutrality. Such tolerance must be built upon a base of moral commitment; otherwise it degenerates into a flaccid indifference, purged of all belief and devotion.
>
> In short, we wish to allow wide latitude in the choice of values but we must assume that education is a process that should be infused with meaning and purpose; that everyone will have deeply held beliefs; that every young American will wish to serve the values which have nurtured him and made possible his education and his freedom as an individual.

This text is very much concerned with values. The final chapter is a statement of conviction about the role of the English teacher: One human being sharing with younger human beings the ethical and esthetic values which animate the teaching of English and give meaning to life.

[9] Rockefeller Brothers Fund, Inc., *The Pursuit of Excellence: Education and the Future of America* (Garden City, N.Y., Doubleday, 1958).

PART ONE

Language, Thought, and Feeling

1. Language as Dynamic Process
2. Logical Thinking
3. Imaginative Thinking

UNIT: Power Over Language

Chapter One

Language as Dynamic Process

How beautiful that first slow word
To him who found it,
To those who heard,
Back in the shadowy dawn of Time.
—AUTHOR UNKNOWN

PERSPECTIVE

"Give me the right word and the right accent, and I will move the world."[1] Thus Joseph Conrad pays tribute to the power of language to influence thought, feeling, and action. Language is indeed the Archimedian lever which allows each of us to exercise some degree of control over his individual world. By means of language we enrich and sharpen our thinking, share our experience with others, receive and transmit the great ideals of our civilization. Therefore, the fulfillment of our roles as individuals, as participants in an organized society, as members of the human race, depends significantly upon the extent of our mastery of the linguistic process.

Language, thought, and feeling are interrelated. Problems concerning all three are necessarily complex because their roots are deeply embedded in the intricate problems of individual and social behavior. For language does not "stand apart from or run parallel to direct experience but completely interpenetrates with it."[2] The development of language is man's most important accomplishment; learning to use language effectively is the most complicated task confronting an individual, because language embraces most of life.

Basic Characteristics of Language

Three basic characteristics of language account, in large measure, for both its power and its complexity: Language is a symbolism—but only a symbolism—of experience; it is highly individual, its meaning differing from person to person; it is growing and changing, never static.

[1] Joseph Conrad, "A Familiar Preface," *Personal Record* (N.Y., Doubleday Page, 1923), p. 14.

[2] Edward Sapir, *Culture, Language, and Personality*, ed. by David G. Mandelbaum (Berkeley and Los Angeles, U. of Calif. Press, 1957), p. 8.

Language as symbolism

In theory, language as symbolism is a concept readily understood; yet in practice, language, perhaps because as children we learned it unconsciously, takes on a more substantial quality, seeming almost to have a life of its own.

Speech, the primary symbolism The basis for the study of language is speech, the primary symbolism of experience. Writing is secondary. Cassirer writes, "Psychologists are unanimous in emphasizing that without insight into the true nature of speech our knowledge of the human mind would remain perfunctory and inadequate." [3] Psychologists interpret the delight that every normal child shows in learning and repeating names as his attempt to understand and control the objective world. Using the name as a focus of thought, he begins to bring some meaning and order to his hitherto vague perceptions and uncertain feelings. Language is the instrument for interpreting and organizing experience. It is the means used to control environment or, control failing, to make appropriate adjustments.

Symbol and thing symbolized Students need help in understanding the significance of language as symbolism; they need help in ridding themselves of the notion that the word is the thing. Certainly children cannot distinguish between the symbol and the thing the language symbolizes. First words, so closely integrated into the context of the total experience, seem not names to describe it but identical with it. To the child, *mama* stands not for the mother alone, but for anyone who takes care of his needs; it stands also for his satisfaction in feeling comforted and protected. This congeries of perceptions and feelings creates an aura of magic around some words that persists throughout life. Thus, although the word as mere representation of the thing wins easy intellectual acceptance, actions often belie this understanding. Only intensive study of the characteristics of language helps underline this knowledge so that it works for the student in his daily life.

Personal quality of language

Language differs with each individual. Each responds differently to what might seem to be the same environmental stimuli; each attempts to exercise control in his own particular way. Guided by his past experience and his immediate needs, he uses language to interpret and integrate present stimuli and thus forge new experiences, never quite the same for any two persons. This all-pervasive, highly individualized quality of language is a source of its power, but does create problems.

[3] Ernst Cassirer, *An Essay on Man* (New Haven, Conn., Yale U. Press, 1944); in the paperbound edition (Garden City, N.Y., Doubleday Anchor, 1953), this quotation appears on p. 169.

Source of meaning Since the word is not the thing for which it stands, there is no necessary connection between its sound and its sense. In the normal process a word derives meaning through the force of custom and convention; it gains currency because human beings have agreed, for the most part unconsciously and over a long period of time, to allow certain words to represent certain actions, feelings, things. This agreement results in an area of *general* meaning, common property of all those who have made the word their own. The *personal* meaning, however, is an individual matter, arrived at by individual routes; it gathers significance as we encounter language in different situations. Quite literally, the meaning is not in the word; it is not in the dictionary; it is in us. Our store of words, with their attendant meanings, is one of the most personal things we own.

Individual experience, unique It is easy to ignore the uniqueness of each person's experience and, consequently, the individual quality of his language. A person is likely to assume that the total meaning of a word exactly coincides with his own personal meaning, that the language he uses means the same to his listener as it does to him. While this assumption is false, the variation in any particular instance is not necessarily extensive; it cannot be, if approximately precise communication is ever to take place. Accurate communication between two persons is in direct ratio to the degree to which their experience overlaps; the greater the area of coincidence, the greater the chance for effective interchange of ideas. The accompanying diagram helps visualize the principle.

Mutual Experience and Communication

The circle represents the general meaning of any concept; the segment AEB *in each case represents the meaning the sender attaches to it; the segment* CED *represents the meaning it has for the receiver.*

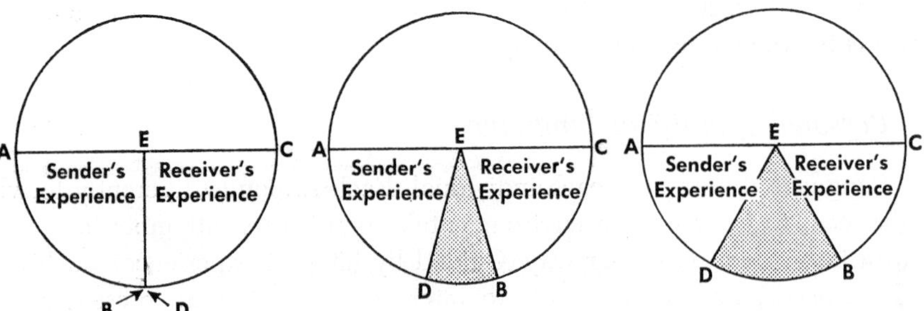

No overlapping of experience and, therefore, no communication possible.

When experience of sender and that of receiver overlap, some communication is possible (represented by segment DEB*).*

When mutual experience is greater, greater communication is possible.

Language change

Language normally changes—constantly in speech but not necessarily in writing. This change, not controlled by conscious effort on the part of man, is inherent in natural growth. No one knows how language started nor in any final sense how, in its initial stages, it evolved. We do know it came into being in answer to man's need, and as man's life becomes more complex, the language grows and alters to enable him to deal with these complexities. The same holds true for the language of each individual. Understanding change as basic to all language will help the student appreciate the importance of this characteristic in determining meaning; it will illuminate the idea that language, an integral part of life, is never static.

Change in word meaning Change can be more readily observed in the meaning of words, since alterations in the structure of language occur slowly. Direct the student to almost any page in an unabridged dictionary. There he will discover that many words arise, gain temporary popularity, and then either become an accepted part of the language or fall into disuse. Words that are attempting to gain a foothold are labeled either *colloquial* (*phone, quitter*) or *slang* (*rock and roll*), the first more respectable but both rated below the literary level; the great bulk of words are those sanctioned by present usage; the third group includes the *archaic,* those rarely used (*howbeit* for *although*), and the *obsolete,* those no longer conveying a meaning previously granted (*abandon* for *banish*). Some of the first group will undoubtedly die; others, if they gain general acceptance, will join the second group in later dictionaries.

Usage, the criterion Who is responsible for creating new words or for sending forth old ones charged with new meaning? Normally it is an anonymous process, fundamentally the same for all innovations, whether they appear first in the literary language or in the vernacular. Originators of both are motivated by the same desires—novelty or economy of expression. Someone coins a word which gains tentative acceptance; it may flourish for only a short time, or it may live for centuries. Wherein lies the difference? Why do some words quickly die, while others prosper? It is not that one is of more lowly origin than the other. Many words, standard today, began life as slang before finally achieving a secure place in the language. Every word has its chance for survival, but it must win its own way. Usage is the only criterion. Nothing can force a new term into the language if people will not use it, nor can anyone keep it out. If it satisfies a semantic need, it remains. The people are the final arbiters.

When does a word enter a language? Students can learn from the unabridged dictionary that for the vast majority the time can only be approximated. There is a close analogy between the vocabulary of an individual and that of a people. We cannot tell with any certainty when we acquired the greater part of our personal word store, but looking back, we realize that each different area of experience contributed its quota. Perhaps when we learned to drive a car, *clutch* took on new significance; if we learned to sew and cook, we may have noticed that *baste* was used for two entirely different processes. Occasionally we remember with startling vividness when we first met certain colorful words and added them to our possession, but for most we cannot be exact as to the time. This much only do we know definitely—when the experience of existence changes, either for an individual or for a people, so too does the language.

Some young people are first attracted to the study of language through the romantic story of words. Knowledge of their etymology gives glimpses of times long past. The student should know that the English language, particularly in its everyday aspects, derived from the Anglo-Saxon; that as a result of the Norman conquest in 1066 it was greatly modified in both vocabulary and structure; that its words have been borrowed from every nation under the sun. Each new experience of Britain, and later of the United States, has been mirrored in the language. Thus words give us pictures of the past; they recall the impact of constantly expanding horizons—Christianity, the Crusades, the industrial revolution, the world wars, the advances made in science and invention. Words coined today continue the picturization, giving philologists of the future glimpses of the customs, fashions, and beliefs of the present. So the change continues as long as the language lives.

Metaphorical extension of meaning Although little is definitely known about the origins of language, certainly in the beginning words were few. The number is still relatively small, yet we can talk about a multi-million things. How did the first word take on new meanings? That the chief way was metaphorical seems logical. Supposedly, the process goes something like this. Encountering a new phenomenon and having no precise way to describe it, the speaker seizes upon a word denoting something similar and uses it figuratively, the context making the sense apparent. As the process repeats itself, the concept of the word gradually grows to include more and more meanings. An unabridged dictionary furnishes specific examples.

Our own observation further substantiates the theory. Contemporary writers in describing unusual phenomena inevitably draw upon metaphorical language to make the phenomena comprehensible to the general reader. Thus, the number and kinds of atoms in a molecule are compared to the make-up of a baseball team; the minuteness of the atom is made somewhat more understandable when we are told that those in a drop of water the size of the earth would be only about as big as a basketball. One writer [4] compares scientists trying to smash atoms with boys throwing rocks at a coal pile: The atoms are pieces of coal; the protons and deuterons, rocks; the electric voltage, the arms of the boys. The cyclotron provides a "merry-go-round" to energize particles on the same principle that David's whirling of the stone gave it sufficient

[4] Robert D. Potter, *Young Peoples' Book of Atomic Energy* (N.Y., McBride, 1946).

force to strike down Goliath. Pictures are the mind's stock in trade; the unknown must be reached through the known.

Students are likely to think of metaphor as embroidery for poetical ideas; they must learn to consider it as an intrinsic part of the warp and woof of language. They need to recognize extension of meaning through metaphor as a fundamental principle of language development—in all probability, the most important means by which language has grown and adapted itself to fit our changing needs.

Role of Language in Learning

As the language of a people grows and changes with experience, so too does that of an individual. All education, whether within the classroom or without, is effected by extending the experience of the learner; in each extension, language plays a significant role. In helping the young child acquire language power, teachers are aware of the necessity, first, of providing opportunities for him to enlarge his experience, and then of helping him find appropriate words to clarify and organize it. The same holds true whatever the age or degree of advancement of the learner; understanding comes not from dealing with words alone but rather with the things for which the words stand. Each extension of experience creates new language needs and forces the acquisition of new language power. The vocabulary and concepts of geometry differ from those of algebra, those of the automobile mechanic from those of the television engineer. The person whose associates represent a wide range of backgrounds is likely to have a greater facility with language because he has been forced to use it in widely varying situations.

Wendell Johnson, exploring the relation between the mastery of the linguistic process and the development of the productive personality, places on the lowest level of development the unreflective individual who learns by rote, believes what he is told, and attempts to regulate his life by slogans and formulas; at the other extreme is the person who, possessing a richly developed language for talking about his language, is effective in thinking about his thinking, in judging his judgments, and in evaluating his evaluations.[5] An understanding of language as dynamic process offers a basis upon which such mastery can be built.

Concepts for the Student

For intelligent practice in the mastery of language, the student needs to understand four basic principles, principles he sees illustrated daily. The

[5] Wendell Johnson, "Symbolic Processes in Personality Development," *ETC: A Review of General Semantics*, Vol. 8, No. 1 (Autumn 1951). This paper was prepared at the request of the Fact-Finding Committee of the Midcentury White House Conference on Children and Youth.

concepts to be discussed here are not intended to present an exhaustive explanation of the way language works.[6] They are, however, ideas that seldom fail to pique the interest of students of both low and high intellectual caliber. Offering concrete manifestations of the symbolic, personal, and changing quality of language, these four concepts furnish a background for understanding how language functions in thinking and in communication: Language is used for a purpose; factors of context affect meaning; the statement conveys diverse meanings; language approaches accuracy only as it approaches conformity to reality.[7]

Language is used for a purpose

Language is always used for a purpose; it is intended to do specific things either for the user or the recipient. The boy on the playground who says, "I can lick you," may be trying either to bolster his own confidence or to intimidate his opponent; he may be attempting to do both. The person who upon a chance encounter exclaims, "Isn't it a beautiful day?" may be expressing his exuberance at his own feeling of well-being, or he may be trying to cement the bonds of fellowship important to all men. In short, we may use language either to clarify our own thinking and express our own feelings and ideas, or we may use it to accomplish some purpose with others.

To understand purpose in the use of language, the student needs to gain insight concerning *motivation* as well as knowledge of the *general purposes* for which men use language.

HUMAN MOTIVATION

Language is an integral part of human behavior. Therefore, an understanding of the purpose for its use demands awareness of the qualities in human beings which influence thinking, feeling, and action. What do we know about man that will help us discover what is likely to hold his interest? What are the motives underlying his conduct? We know the answer to such deeply significant questions is never simple. But we do know that the answer lies in the basic human needs—basic because they are either ingrained in human nature or have been built up by our culture. Often the two may be in conflict.

The most important concept for the student to assimilate concerning motivation is that it is infinitely complex; it can never be reduced to a formula. This complexity arises from the fact that man is both an individual and a

[6] See selected readings at the end of the chapter.

[7] Throughout this text "reality" refers to the essence of anything in all its aspects as it would be perceived by an all-wise observer. Since human senses are limited, perceptions are often inaccurate. The way an individual defines his situation constitutes for him its reality. This interpretation of events upon which the individual acts is sometimes called "functional reality," its key contained in the unique background of each participant in any situation. Thus functional reality not only differs with each person, but being partial and incomplete, differs in some degree from reality. See Earl C. Kelley, *Education for What Is Real* (N.Y., Harper, 1947).

member of a social group. Both considerations are important; although human relations are a crucial factor in any life, man lives mostly with himself. The individual's capacity for inner growth is the determining factor in his ability to maintain satisfying relationships, for if he cannot live in harmony with himself, he cannot live in harmony with others.

Because we are human, inherent in our nature are constructive forces which urge us to strive for self-realization. Because we are individual, these strivings lead to diverse goals and to different values. Both aspects of motivation—human and individual—deserve consideration.[8]

Common drives Three powerful drives common to all men are mastery, love, and freedom. In the normal personality they exist side by side; never mutually exclusive, one reacts on the other, either reinforcing or restricting. The problem is one of balance and control.[9]

Mastery We are endowed by nature with the impulses of self-assertion and with the emotions of self-satisfaction and pride.[10] Upon these, realistic self-respect and self-confidence can be built. Normally, the drive for mastery shows itself in healthy strivings for competencies to meet the challenges of life; gone awry, it may expend its force in attempts to use others for selfish purposes.[11] In achieving mastery, the individual must choose among the values in his culture; he has to decide which are worth fighting for and which merit compromise or rejection.

When given free rein, aggressive tendencies make us inconsiderate of others, resentful of restraints, impatient of attempts at guidance, determined to have our way in all matters. When under control, they make for efficiency and worthwhile accomplishment. As soon as we are emotionally able to accept the fact that we cannot be superior in all things, that we cannot fulfill all our desires, we begin to discriminate; we begin to explore our potential, to commit ourselves to the goals that seem most important. Thus the beginning of a sense of values is born.

Love Love is a profound urge to preserve and extend life in all its manifestations—a reaching out for union with all living forces that protect, comfort, and sustain. It includes love of mate, of family, of friends, of work, of humanity, of God—all the wonders of the mind and spirit. It is acceptance and affirmation of life in its totality.

[8] Since this is not a text on psychology, no attempt has been made to discuss all drives; included are only those that may be useful in helping students evaluate language and literature. For amplification of the ideas expressed here, teachers may wish to consult the references cited in footnotes 9-13.

[9] Karen Horney, *Neurosis and Human Growth: The Struggle toward Self-Realization* (N.Y., Norton, 1955).

[10] Gordon W. Allport, *Becoming: Basic Considerations for a Psychology of Personality* (New Haven, Yale U. Press, 1955).

[11] Erich Fromm, *Man for Himself* (N.Y., Rinehart, 1947), *The Art of Loving* (N.Y., Harper, 1956).

Love is all of one piece, growing out of a healthy self-regard. Fromm presents cogent arguments to support his belief that what man does to others he does to himself.[12] This spirit of mutuality, this capacity to give and to receive, is love's keynote. Unpossessive, those who truly love go about the business of living, knowing that everyone has a right to his own integrity; they know life is so infinitely varied that dependence for personal fulfillment upon any single individual or upon any one thing is a delusion. Hence rejections, real or fancied, can be borne more philosophically. Love, rightly conceived, helps us meet the demands of life.

Freedom Every person needs the freedom to develop his potential at his own rate. He needs the right to experiment, to find his own answers, to agree or disagree, to make his own mistakes, to reach his own decisions. In no other way can he acquire the independence necessary for emotional maturity. Freedom, of course, has realistic limitations and carries its own responsibility; my freedom must not interfere with yours. The wisdom of discretion insures the balance between too much and too little.

A selfish desire to be completely free may have serious consequences; it may deprive us of the healthy friction of experience, the stimulation of the give and take of social interaction. We cannot escape the fact that we exist not alone as individuals but as members of society as well. Wisely, we refrain from emotional involvement with the non-essentials in our environment, but commitment to nothing means withdrawal from real living. Such withdrawal takes its toll; it saps the energy, blunts the emotions, and dissipates zest for life. The drive for freedom, misused, obstructs the development of the human potential; rightly used, it is an invigorating force conducive to personal growth.

Varying individual motivation Since each person develops in his own particular context, general human drives lead to diverse values, and goals differ with each individual. Personality derives not only from the previously discussed drives, but is influenced by heredity, culture, and environment.[13] Each individual's potential and his degree of control over cultural and environmental factors determine the direction and the intensity of his drives for mastery, freedom, and love.

It is difficult to generalize about personal motivation because personal values are so diverse. We can, however, isolate certain incentives to behavior which seem to operate in our culture. The classification suggested here, certainly not intended as definitive, was first made inductively by high school students themselves under teacher guidance. Ordinarily an hour spent with television or magazines will yield enough examples to form the basis for organization, since appeals found in these media are often designed to achieve

[12] Fromm, *Man for Himself*, pp. 225 ff., *Art of Loving*, pp. 1-133.
[13] Allport, *Becoming*, pp. 24-28.

a specific effect. In analyzing appeals, however, students need to keep in mind that categories are made to serve the purpose of the user and that labels are merely a matter of convenience. Yet they must realize further that some motivation, however complex and difficult to classify, underlies all human action. Although six divisions are discussed in the following example, students usually do better to devise their own classifications and terminology.

Appeals to human behavior

Protection	Use of every means within our power to protect all that is peculiarly ours—life, health, comfort, opinions—and to avoid embarrassment and worry.
	Young Harcourt, confused in his sense of values, in Morley Callaghan's "The Snob"; Macbeth's later murders, actuated by a desire "to be safely thus."
Possessions	Saving money, securing property, adding to possessions, collecting—among adolescents, such things as match covers, sweaters, records, etc.; the acquisitive instinct apparent even in small children —*mine* is a word learned early.
	Tom Sawyer's propensity for trading; distorting and debasing of the drive in the madness of the sea captain and his son in *Where the Cross is Made* and in the warped natures of the principal characters in *The Little Foxes.*
Power	Desire to accomplish our aims, to maintain our freedom and independence; the pursuit of knowledge, research in science;[14] belief that we have the capacity to do a creditable job, to build a satisfying way of living.
	Necessity for confidence in the power to surmount obstacles, the theme of "The Fifty-first Dragon"; Marty's efforts to make a place for himself in his group, in "The New Kid"; the mother's efforts to control the life of her son, in *The Silver Cord;* the symbolic presentation of everyman's story of aspiration and frustration, in *The Great God Brown.*
Prestige	Desire for approval of our characters, actions, abilities, opinions, even our possessions.
	The family in *Confessional,* each member reluctant to admit his willingness to accept a bribe because he thinks he would be repudiating standards the others hold inviolable; the French peasant destroyed by the unjust contempt of his fellow citizens in "The Piece of String"; the couple in *Sham,* afraid they will lose face with their friends if the burglar finds nothing worth taking from their home.
Stimulation	Need for physical, mental, emotional stimulation: traveling, participating in sports, cultivating hobbies, attending lectures and plays, reading books, visiting art galleries, listening to music.
	Undoubtedly, this drive supplies partial motivation for persons involved in feats requiring daring and stamina—the young scientist

[14] See Bertrand Russell, "The Springs of Human Action," *Atlantic,* Vol. 192, No. 3 (March 1952).

in *Kon-Tiki,* the mountain climbers in *Annapurna.* Assuredly too, the drive is necessary for sustained learning; the English classroom offers a chance for varied intellectual and emotional stimulation as we share the excitement of the characters in *Treasure Island,* follow the devious thinking of Fortunato in "The Cask of Amontillado," relive the tragic experiences of the pilot in *Night Flight,* enjoy the humor of Ogden Nash, contemplate the wonders of life with the poets.

Spiritual Security — Need for a belief in something greater than self; the quality in man which is dissatisfied with the material only, which gropes toward the ideal; need for developing a satisfying philosophy of living, one which will recognize man's moral and altruistic aspirations.[15]

The man and his wife in *Dust of the Road,* choosing peace of mind in preference to ill-gotten wealth; the motivating force of Cordelia in *King Lear* and of Banquo in *Macbeth.*

Drives to action are intrinsically neither good nor bad; they are merely forces to be reckoned with. Those that are legitimate in our culture may have either beneficial or detrimental effects. In infancy, man's egocentric wants predominate; as he progresses toward mental and emotional maturity, his desires broaden to include the moral and the spiritual. Drives to action are good, in that striving to satisfy the fundamental wants has resulted in much of what is called progress both for the individual and for the race; they have evil consequences only when uncontrolled. One may be so overriding that it thwarts development of the human personality: in *The Scarlet Letter,* Dimmesdale's desire to maintain his reputation. One may become so strong that ruthless attempts at fulfillment may crush others: Macbeth's drive for power. The problem is one of recognition and control.

Complexity of motivation Continual emphasis on the complexity of motivation disabuses an occasional student of the mistaken idea that knowledge of basic needs gives him a quick formula for manipulating others. As he becomes more perceptive of the intricacies of behavior, he learns there is no quick formula. He can readily see that some human beings selfishly use a knowledge of powerful drives in attempts to influence others; he must develop awareness in order to protect himself. Understanding helps him guard against the unscrupulous, whether the too-insistent salesman or the unprincipled demagogue. Continued experience with literature, continued effort to understand human behavior, lead him to realize that motives for crucial action are never simple. The reasons for our behaving in a certain way are almost always complicated; often we may not entirely comprehend them ourselves. It is easy to understand motivation for action in principle; it is comparatively easy to understand it in relation to fictional characters where the author has given the necessary information and we are able to be somewhat objective; in life, however, where we are seldom in possession

[15] See Fromm, *Art of Loving;* Sapir, *Culture, Language, and Personality,* pp. 121-123.

of all the facts and where personal feelings intrude, it is extremely difficult to assess accurately the forces which determine our own behavior or that of others.

Basic needs and language proficiency Man devised language to meet his needs; he uses it to gain his purposes. Thus understanding how these needs affect both an individual's purpose and the means he selects to accomplish it is an integral part of the study of language in any particular situation; such understanding assumes an important role in achieving language proficiency. Awareness of how our motivating desires play their part in our thoughts and feelings will make us more effective as human beings. An appreciation of the force of these basic needs is vital whether we are trying to interpret the world in which we live or are attempting to communicate with others.

GENERAL PURPOSES OF LANGUAGE

Although the particular purpose for the use of language at a particular time must always be determined, the student will be helped in organizing the problem by a consideration of the general purposes for which language is used: to maintain rapport, to inform, to convince, to persuade, to communicate experience in esthetic form.[16]

The student meets the first four purposes continually in his daily use of language; they overlap, one frequently being used to support and reinforce another. The fifth pertains to literature.[17] Study of these purposes–illustrated in the following discussion by reference to those who use language with integrity–will increase the student's awareness of the part intention plays in thinking, communication, and expression.

To maintain rapport In its simplest form, maintaining rapport is exemplified by the conversation which takes place upon chance encounters with strangers and casual acquaintances when convention demands that we speak in order to avoid seeming rude. Such examples can lead students to see that this use of everyday language operates not primarily for the communication of ideas but for the establishment of appropriate social relationships. On such occasions we are careful to introduce subjects immediately establishing

[16] The terminology and classification given here represent a choice among many. Students of language, although in general agreement of its uses, select different labels and categories. Each chooses the one appropriate for his purpose, e.g., Joshua Whatmough, *Language: A Modern Synthesis* (London, Secker & Warburg, 1956), pp. 88 ff., divides language into four categories: informative, dynamic, emotive, and esthetic. Many speech texts give five: to inform, to convince, to move to action, to entertain, to impress. For some classes two purposes are often sufficient: to give information and to influence feeling. The teacher must decide what classification will make the nature of language more comprehensible to his students.

[17] Although the basic principles of language underlie all five purposes, this chapter is concerned primarily with the first four; later chapters dealing with imaginative thinking and literary appreciation are pertinent to the fifth.

a common meeting ground. Remarks about the weather, inquiries about a person's health, inconsequential comments upon unimportant topics—all of these seem trivial only if we mistake the purpose for an informative one. They are anything but trivial when we understand the real purpose—securing rapport with others.

A further dimension of this purpose is illustrated by the writer or speaker whose sole aim is to entertain, to arouse interest for the moment. If information is given, it is incidental. He may deal in humor, anecdotes, exaggerations, the strange, the incongruous—anything he thinks will genuinely please his listener or reader. Some magazines maintain regular features whose main purpose is entertainment—for example, "Post Scripts" in the *Saturday Evening Post.* Many after-dinner speakers, those conducting story hours for children, and the accomplished raconteur furnish other examples.

But this aim has wider implications; communication being a two-way process, securing rapport is basic to the achievement of the other purposes of language. Obviously, if one is irritated or distracted by such things as insincerity, tactlessness, or ineptness on the part of speaker or writer, communication may be blocked. In like manner, a speaker, sensing a hostile or disparaging attitude, is likely either to withdraw or to dissipate his forces trying to cope with the ambivalence of the situation.

While students may be intuitively aware of the desirability of maintaining rapport in any social situation, they need help in acquiring respect for that large segment of language used for the legitimate purpose of oiling the machinery of social intercourse. They can see that rapport is achieved most consistently by those who have formed the habit of considering others. Group work is one effective means of providing opportunities to foster this habit. Working in small groups on any of the problems which are a part of learning English, the student has a chance to use language in a situation which he can help control.[18] Here he can become aware of the necessity of noticing not only what is said but why it is said, of interpreting vocal tones and facial expression. Here he can assume responsibility for bringing out the diffident, for softening the too-brusque remark, for guiding discussion into productive channels. Teaching students how to work in groups is rewarded by the knowledge that the gradually increasing skills they show will be useful to them always. For sensitivity to the other person in any situation, whether formal or informal, is essential to maintaining the harmony necessary to make language function.

To inform The aim of information is to increase knowledge. If the facts are vital to the recipient, the only problem is to explain clearly; the informant uses simple language, being careful to include all necessary details. Writers of manuals telling us how to get the most out of our car or television set strive only for clarity. Even with an interested audience, however, the accom-

[18] The group method of teaching is discussed on pp. 434-35, 457-63.

plishment of this purpose is not easy. The complex nature of language makes precise communication difficult. Any English teacher is aware of the seemingly inordinate amount of time spent in many classes in helping the student say exactly what he means.

On the other hand, if the information does not seem pertinent to the listener, as often happens in the classroom, the task becomes increasingly difficult. Then the teacher, using the present interests of his students to spark curiosity, strives to extend those interests by moving from the known to the unknown, by connecting the new facts with the familiar. He tries to picture events vividly, using concrete examples to illuminate salient points. He makes judicious use of repetition and summary. In short, he tries to relate the information to the experience of his students so that the facts will seem important and thus will be remembered. Just as teachers use these principles in trying to foster the interest which will make facts vital, so too students must try to do the same in their speaking and writing.

Professional writers know the necessity for presenting facts in a way to pique curiosity. The wide appeal of non-fiction today can be partially explained by the fact that writers, knowing the widespread curiosity about many facets of the fast-changing world, offer explanations in a guise that both interests and informs—witness such books as *Conquest of the North and South Poles* and *The Sea Around Us,* such factual television programs as enlighten the viewer concerning advancements in science and medicine.

To convince One who seeks to convince is desirous only of securing agreement; the appeal is to the understanding. Any attempt to convince uses facts. Here, however, the reasoning as to what the facts mean and the language which presents this reasoning assume greater importance. From the same "facts" individuals arrive at different conclusions. Therefore, in attempting to convince, the speaker frequently meets resistance. He thus proceeds cautiously, starting with ideas he knows are non-controversial; he examines the opposing viewpoints fairly and dispassionately, admitting the strengths and showing the weaknesses; he relies heavily on facts and evidence, taking care to present a complete and logical picture; if possible, he uses testimony from competent and acceptable authorities for reinforcement.

Often, attempts to convince are but preludes to attempts to persuade. At times, however, conviction is an end in itself. For example, many post-mortems held by students after football games have no other purpose than to show how the losers might have won if the strategy had been different. The usual aim of writers concerned with an explanation or interpretation of past events—critics dealing with the works of authors no longer living or writers presenting a fresh viewpoint on an historical event—is to convince the reader of the validity of the argument. For instance, Bruce Catton's article, "Who Really Won at Gettysburg?" [19] presents evidence to show that

[19] *Saturday Review,* Vol. 40, No. 24 (June 15, 1957).

the real winner was not the North but all the American people, since the battle symbolizes "the direction of the American dream."

To persuade To persuade or to move to action is the most difficult purpose to achieve, because in persuasion the final appeal is to the volition and most human beings are reluctant to change. It is difficult because everyone has reasons, often deeply hidden and unknown, for clinging to familiar ways, and because action may mean giving up opinions lived with a long time, overcoming fears, altering habits.

Two aspects of this purpose should be considered with high school students. At times, a speaker is trying to secure action from those who are already convinced they should adopt the course suggested but fail to live up to their convictions. Most individuals believe they should be punctual in keeping appointments, do the job they are hired to do, obey the laws. The persuader does not need to convince; instead, he tries to so vitalize the recipient's sense of responsibility that the desired action will follow. Most sermons, pep talks, and "inspirational" books fall within this category.

Often, however, those who try to get others to act are faced with minds already made up to the contrary. In such cases the first three purposes must be achieved as preliminaries to the fourth: The speaker or writer must maintain rapport, inform, convince, before attempting to persuade. Such is frequently the case with the teacher trying to guide the recalcitrant pupil, the salesman trying to sell his product, the candidate trying to win votes, the writer marshalling facts and arguments for a persuasive editorial.

In introducing this purpose, the teacher would be wise to start with a familiar example and then let pupils supply their own. They will have many. Thinking back over almost any week, they can recall instances where the arts of persuasion have been tried on them. They can discern the arguments used and appraise their validity and effectiveness. Such a beginning sets the stage both for logical thinking and for evaluation of motives for action.

To present experience in esthetic form The purpose of the literary artist is to present a segment of experience in the most perfect form he can devise. His is a cultivated style. His aim is revelation; although at times he may inform or convince or move to action, that is not his real purpose. Moved by the significance of some aspect of life, he seeks to share his insights concerning human values and human conduct. The student builds his understanding of artistic purpose through continued study of individual literary works, the whole range of literature offering varied and particular examples.

Understanding the general purposes for which language is used, coupled with recognition of the influence deeply rooted needs have on language chosen to achieve specific purposes, reinforces the student's awareness of the *personal* element in thinking and in communication. The intellect does not function apart from the rest of the personality; in reaching decisions and in making choices, the student must learn to take emotional tendencies into account. Assimilation of the idea that language is used for a purpose, a purpose that cannot be divorced from the psychological aspects of human behavior, makes the concept of language as dynamic process more comprehensible to him.

Factors of context affect meaning

The total context of any language situation is a fabric of many interwoven strands, each making its contribution to the texture of the whole. Although the various aspects are treated here as if they were distinct, in practice such arbitrary division is not possible, since all interact to make a closely integrated unit. *The personal element is the unifying force.* All other factors must be seen in relation to the user of language, for only in use does language become a living thing.

We bring to any environmental stimulus not only our mood of the moment but the sum of all our past experiences, each bearing its own intellectual and emotional significance. Both influence evaluations and may at times completely block a rational response. Illustrations come instantly to mind. Teachers can bear witness that student attitudes toward a subject are sometimes influenced by frustrations having nothing to do with the particular classroom—a clash with parents, a misunderstanding with a friend. These can form part of the context and act as a hindrance to effective thinking and communication. Again, approval of a speaker's personal life or his political doctrines may create a bias which lulls listeners into unthinking acceptance of all his statements, whatever their validity; disapproval may have the opposite effect. Similarly, from one we accept a criticism, from another we reject it, even if both are stated in identical terms. The personal element necessarily dominates the context in which language occurs.

Verbal denotation Understanding the literal meaning of the verbal context is basic to exact interpretation. An isolated word is rarely significant; it must be considered in its verbal context, for words, chameleon-like, take on color from their surroundings. The number of things in existence so far exceeds the number of words in the language, that most words must assume various shades of meaning. We may, for example, listen to a musical *round,* give a *round* of applause, watch a *round* of a prize fight, take a *round* trip, climb a *round* of a ladder, fire a *round* of ammunition, speak of the national debt in *round* numbers, and so on and on. Always we consult the verbal context to ascertain the meaning intended. If the clues given there leave us in doubt, if our knowledge of etymology fails us, we then, but not until then, turn to the dictionary. It will serve as a guide, but only as a guide, to interpretation; it will not give infallible answers. The information found there requires critical appraisal. The historian of language has recorded what various words have meant in the past; he has directed attention to *areas* of meaning, since all situations in which words have been used cannot be listed. He has compiled the available data, but the final decision as to a particular meaning rests with us. To discover which definition seems most fitting, we turn again to the verbal context, because it alone contains the answer.

Degree of abstractness The degree of abstractness of language also influences meaning. The less concrete the words, the more difficult it is to determine the extent they conform to reality. Two aspects of abstractness should be noted: Some words are termed *abstract* (*dread*) in contrast with the more concrete (*chair*); others are called *general* (*food*) in contrast to the more specific (*custard*). Abstract words have no referents in the objective world; they do have a psychological core of meaning. Because they do not stand for "things" perceptible to the senses, no universally accepted standard exists for determining their meaning exactly. Sometimes called *emotive-evaluative,* such words are used in expressing feelings (joy, anger, happiness) and judgments (just, good, beautiful). We try to pinpoint meaning by giving examples, comparing with similar phenomena, describing ways of behavior. Thus, we attempt to convey what we mean by *justice* in any particular circumstance by citing actions which exemplify our idea of what is *just.* Words in the second category, arrived at by the process of abstracting, represent groups of items having something in common. The individual units making up each group may be either abstractions like those previously discussed (*fear*) or items with concrete referents (*table*). Therefore, group names may have either a psychological core of meaning (*emotion*) or an objective one (*furniture*). Study of both aspects of abstraction will prepare students for some of the difficulties of thinking clearly and communicating accurately.

The *process* of abstraction, if demonstrated by general words representing groups of items having concrete referents, is readily comprehended in principle. Even young children can understand that through the procedure we arrive at a word that emphasizes the similarities and disregards the differences, that *boys* is an abstraction which includes all the male members of the class, yet the various boys remain individuals. They can see, at least in theory, the significance of the system of indexing recommended by semanticists to remind us that boy_1, John, differs from boy_2, George, and that both differ from boy_3, Peter. Older students can recognize the danger, prevalent in fields where prejudice is more likely to enter, which the use of such a system (Jew_1, Jew_2, Jew_3) attempts to avoid.

Variance in the *degree* of abstractness can be illustrated on a continuum ranging from the more highly abstract to the more specifically concrete. Let us take a very simple example.

Food	**Fruit**	**Apple**	**Jonathan**	**This Jonathan**
still more abstract	more abstract	rather abstract *or* rather concrete	more concrete	specifically concrete

Start with *apple;* beginning somewhere in the middle makes it easy for students to see that we can move either up or down the scale, that the degree of abstraction varies with the word. Let students decide how apple should be classified. Since the thing for which the word stands remains the same whatever the decision, the terminology is immaterial. What is essential is that students realize the significance of the fact that either term, concrete or abstract, pertains to the same reality, that classifications are seldom rigid but change to suit the convenience of the one making them.

Levels of abstraction constantly shift when language is used effectively; ideas are made concrete by specific examples; details are drawn together by significant generalizations. Consider two illustrations, both from the classroom. If we allow discussions to consist only of a succession of concrete items, no matter how interesting and informative each is of itself, we remain on a low level of abstraction, nor does a generalization at the end remedy matters. Where thinking is purposeful, play between different levels is constant. There is a shuttle-like action, first throwing out loosely threads of different colors (the more concrete), then drawing them taut to construct a meaningful pattern (abstract). Only in this way do we explore the potential of any question. Conversely, "talking over the heads of pupils" usually means that we are speaking on a high level of abstraction; as far as communication goes we are vague, indefinite, and ambiguous; we have failed to make our language, however concrete it may seem to us, conform to a reality the students recognize.

The literature we study is filled with illustrations of the clarification of meaning through interplay of different levels. Cassius' speech to Brutus in Act I, scene ii of *Julius Caesar,* is an excellent example of statements descending the abstraction scale gradually; each idea, stated in more concrete terms, clarifies the one which has immediately preceded. Cassius begins, "Well, honor is the subject of my story"; highly abstract, without amplification it means almost nothing. The next remark explains, but only in a general way; Cassius feels lacking in honor because he must live in awe of a man. What man? What does he mean by awe? He immediately names Caesar, saying that by circumstances of birth, background, and stamina Caesar is in no way superior to Brutus or himself. He continues with two specific examples intended to show that Caesar not only is not superior but is in reality much weaker than he himself. Finally he concludes,

> . . . Ye gods! it doth amaze me
> A man of such a feeble temper should
> So get the start of the majestic world
> And bear the palm alone.

There is no doubt now what *honor* and *awe* mean to him in this instance; the communication is explicit.

Understanding the process of abstraction, then, is nothing so simple as recognizing the differences between two words or two statements at the opposite extremes. It is a complicated phase of experience, far-reaching in its implications, requiring discrimination in its use.

Affective overtones Many words, besides having an impersonal meaning, have also affective connotations which arouse in the listener an extremely subtle, almost unconscious, response. It arises not because of any quality inherent in the word itself but because of the association, pleasant or otherwise, which it has for us. This association is in part traditional, closely allied to the most intense experiences of humanity; it is in part personal, linked with ideas, persons, events, which have evoked either our sympathy or our aversion.

The traditional atmosphere clinging to *mother* and *home* conveys pleasant feelings to most of us. Teachers, however, at times meet children whose reaction, due to personal experiences, is the opposite. Probably to most Americans *flight* suggests air travel, the connotation pleasant if they enjoy flying; but to the displaced segments of humanity, their word representing flight undoubtedly means something totally different, arousing feelings akin to panic.

This affective power of words is readily accepted as part of poetry, for we expect the poet to be concerned with emotion, with sensory experience, and with intellectual concepts vitalized by feeling. In prose, spoken or written, formal or informal, these factors are no less important. We do not find them maintained at the same high level of intensity, but they are there. If we want to interest and move the listener, if we wish him to feel toward the ideas expressed as we do ourselves, we must use affective language; when we are the recipients, the problem is one of recognition and evaluation. Furthermore, not only do the words chosen set the tone of any discourse, the way they are combined and used may heighten it. Prose, like poetry, has its rhythm, its alliteration, its repetition of words and phrases, its comparisons, its contrasts, its variously patterned sentences—all forming part of its affectiveness. Moreover, in oral communication the nuances of the voice carry their own connotations, harmonizing with the context or striking a discordant note.

This aura of feeling, then, is not a characteristic exclusively of literature, nor a thing that occasionally intrudes. It is a part of the living tissue of everyday thought and language—yet another complexity which must be taken into account in considering language operation.

Historical aspects The historical aspects of context can be seen most clearly in reference to literature, for to understand the events occurring in any literary work, we must see them in correct historical perspective. For example, the excesses perpetrated by the common people of France in *A Tale of Two Cities* are credible only if we are familiar with the circumstances which gave birth to such intemperance. That the same kind of thing did not happen in England can be partially accounted for by an understanding of the social structure slowly evolving there, where by legislative means the lower classes were gradually acquiring more and more self-determination. Thus, the events of the novel are in accord with the contrasting political and sociological histories of the two countries. Language also has its historical context. The scholarship of a recent novel set in early nineteenth-century England has been severely criticized because of incongruities resulting from disregard of this principle. The author, by allowing the characters to speak in contemporary slang, has made them incredible to the discriminating and so disturbed the tone of the entire work. The historical context of the events is at variance with that of the language.

Evidence of the effect of national development on language is seen both in the diverse meanings that the same word has for different peoples and in the use of different words to refer to the same thing. Because of dissimilarities in experience it is understandable that *democracy* means one thing to us and another to the Russians, and that to the Athenians of ancient Greece it meant still another.[20] Conversely, British and Americans use different terms for the same thing or the same action. Our *corn* means *wheat* to the British. Our lurid paperbacks, once called *dime novels,* are to them *shilling shockers.* We say, "charge it" while they say, "put it down." We only *miss* a train, but they actually *lose* it.

This same phenomenon occurs also within our own country. Linguistic atlases chart, among other variants of language used in the United States, different terms used to designate the same thing by those living in different sections of the country. Pancakes, for example, may be called *flitter fritters, flapjacks, slapjacks, flannel cakes, griddle cakes, hot cakes, fritters, crepes,* depending upon the locality. So environment influences the semantic history of words. The historical aspect, in addition to the verbal, personal, and physical, makes its essential contribution to the totality of the context.

Language at all times takes place in an individual context dominated by the personal element. When the student becomes deeply conscious of the way various factors in that context may influence meaning, he is able to appreciate more fully the nature of language.

The statement conveys diverse meanings

Just as it is impossible to assign only one meaning to each word, it is also impossible to assign only one meaning to a statement. Students learn that the declarative sentence is used to make an assertion, but when they

[20] The difficulties encountered in securing agreements in the United Nations often spring from no "mere haggling over words" but from the wide divergence in the backgrounds of the participants. Difference in the structures of the native languages of those taking part makes communication difficult; difference in cultures makes agreement at times impossible. The following incident exemplifies some of the problems: "Some years ago a commission of the United Nations attempted to develop a universal symbol for the concept 'woman,' in connection with the labeling of certain materials for the use of illiterates. The stylized nude figure which is conventional in Western culture was indecent to millions of the world's people; indeed, any representation of a woman which did not show her veiled was shocking to many. But a veiled woman has a misleading implication to the Westerner. No single symbol could be agreed upon." Educational Policies Commission, National Education Association, *Mass Communication and Education* (Washington, D.C., N.E.A., 1958), p. 48.

try to understand how language functions, this information is of only slight significance. There are many kinds of statements, their use depending upon the intention of the speaker. Why has he chosen to express his ideas in this particular way? What is he actually saying? Here, as with the word, a knowledge of the total context is requisite for accurate evaluation.

If the student is to achieve any degree of control over the linguistic process, he must learn the kinds of statements commonly made and have practice in discerning the meaning each carries. It is his *command* of language that is of primary concern to the English teacher. Therefore it is not enough to teach that when we wish to assert, we use the declarative sentence. The statement, bearing as it does the crucial part of the load in thinking and communication, deserves intensive study.

Because language, complex though it undeniably is, is more limited than the situations with which it deals, statements will not fit neatly into rigid categories; therefore, any discussion of types of statements tends to be somewhat arbitrary. However, comprehending the diverse roles that assertions may assume proves difficult for some students; it should be attacked from various points of view. Understanding the significance of four types of statements—factual, judgmental, normative, and metaphorical—heightens awareness of the intricacies of language.

Statement of fact A statement of fact is concerned with something outside the speaker; he gives no indication of his feelings, expresses no attitude toward the object, person, or event. The truth or falsity of such a statement can be established by observation (The Times building is on the corner of First and Franklin), by experimentation (The Midget Car has a maximum speed of 150 miles), or by reference to the record (John Abel in the June 1955 issue of *Harper's* magazine, writes, ". . . . ."). Any combination of the three methods may be used. Although the assertion may not be true, nevertheless—because its falsity can be demonstrated by objective means—it is a statement of fact.

An example will clarify. Not long ago an auto supply firm conducted a contest in which participants were to estimate the number of spark plugs in a display window, the dimensions of which were given. Although thousands of estimates were made, no two were identical. Using the same information, each contestant arrived at a different number; all statements described life-facts and all of them were false, even that of the winner. In most instances, however, absolute proof is not so readily forthcoming. In such cases, if the weight of the evidence seems to indicate probability, the statement is tentatively accepted as true.

Judgment Judgment, as used in this text, refers to those statements which cannot be validated by objective means. They have no reference to anything in the external world; they refer to something existing in the mind of the author. Therefore, in attempting to validate judgments, we necessarily concentrate on the one making the statement. Who is he? Why does he say what he does? Why in this particular place and at this particular time? How does he know what he claims to know? Because the answers to such questions are hard to come by, deciding whether to agree with judgments is difficult, at times impossible.

Basically, *awareness of the distinction between statement of fact and judgment underlies all cogent thinking.* Students will find it comparatively simple to distinguish between the two if they center attention on the *referent* of the key word or words in the statement. Do they refer to something in the objective world? If so, the statement is factual (Sarah Jones is a *teacher at Redfield High*); truth or falsity can be established by objective means. Does the key word refer to something existing only in the mind of the speaker? If so, the statement is judgmental (Sarah Jones is a *liar*); after considering the reliability of the sources, one can agree, disagree, or decide more information is necessary before either acceptance or rejection is possible. The clear thinker forms the habit of quickly distinguishing between factual assertions and judgments.

Normative statement In a normative statement, the speaker is suggesting that a norm—a model or pattern—has been established which individuals try to emulate. (Some students of semantics use *directive* to describe this kind of language, because the speaker seems to be directing his listeners to think as he does.) If *should* or *ought* are used, the meaning is immediately apparent; however, if the injunction is obscured in what seems to be a statement of fact, confusion may arise. Because there is no doubt that the purpose is to persuade, normatives used in advertising, in political campaigns, in any recognized propaganda, are easily detected. If our automatic response is not one of suspended judgment, we have only ourselves to blame. "ABC Loan Company relieves you of your money worries" would deceive only the most gullible. "Our candidate has only your interests at heart" deserves at least a grain of skepticism.

Normative statements in reference to personal and social aims may not be so obvious. Like the advertiser, the user here is trying, either from selfish or altruistic motives, to influence future action. At times adults, in an attempt to impose socially accepted patterns of conduct on the young, resort to the reiteration of directives, more or less subtle. "Little boys don't cry," "Little girls don't climb trees," are evidently not factual statements. At least one little boy and one little girl seem to have those propensities.

Normative statements are an indispensable part of language. Man, committed to life in an organized society, must have some way of impressing individual members with their obligation to the group. Physical coercion, even if it were desirable, is impossible; only words remain as a weapon for social cohesion. One of the most interesting manipulations of language is its use by society as a whole and by groups within that society to enlist individual loyalty and support, to insure that each person has the "right" reaction built in. Mottoes, slogans, songs, written in affective language and repeated with almost ritualistic significance, serve to fortify ideals of behavior. Words, their persuasive overtones embedded in the memory, come back in times of tension and serve to mold action. Who knows what deeds of valor have been inspired by the marine's idea of his destiny facetiously expressed in the official hymn?

> If the Army and the Navy
>   Ever look on Heaven's scenes,
> They will find the streets are guarded
>   By United States Marines.

Who can say how many alumni have opened wide their wallets as lines from an almost forgotten college song challenge them from the masthead of official stationery?

> Loyal and true we are always to you,
>   Dear old Alma Mater.

The important thing to remember about a normative or a directive is that its purpose is not to inform but to influence action. The important questions to ask are, Is the implied goal worthwhile? Will the suggested action help me attain it?

Metaphorical statement The conscious use of metaphorical language—used here in its comprehensive sense to include all expressed or implied comparisons of the essentially dissimilar—is an act of imaginative identification. Its purpose is to shock us into attending sharply, to force our surrender to the feelings evoked. If it is to increase and intensify the connotative force of the literal, it must be both apt and fresh. Since its intention is to illuminate meaning, it cannot be so strained that the reader stops to marvel at the writer's ingenuity, nor so trite that it irritates. Each extreme diverts attention from the context and fails its purpose. Whether the metaphorical language helps or hinders understanding depends upon the taste and sensitivity of both user and recipient.

Each must decide for himself whether the intended effect is produced by such expressions as "cheese-cake," "come-in-and-drown-yourself-eyes," "steak as tough as a squad of marines," "fractured English," "tattered confidence," "her laundrybag figure," "fever of despair," "wrath exuding like an unpleasant perfume," "a crooner's voice pushing against the ear like a soft, dry sponge."

The student should be helped to see that since metaphorical language is imbedded in the pattern of language development, and since its purpose is to heighten meaning and feeling, it will be found on all levels from the vernacular to the literary.

For the purpose of studying language as it operates in use, we have isolated words and statements, but both, when divorced from the pressure of context, are lifeless things, yielding no deep secrets. Like bits of mosaic, they reveal their significance only in relation to the whole.

Language approaches accuracy as it approaches conformity to reality

Familiarity with the implications of the concepts previously developed will sensitize students to some of the difficulties of securing accuracy in the use of language. One who wishes his language to conform as closely as possible to the reality it represents must train himself to think of language as symbolism; he must be aware that when he tries to translate complex events into words he can never effect a complete transfer. The words will always be *about* the experience; the experience itself can never be communicated. In trying to clarify an event for himself, he must be conscious of the personal quality of his language, governed by his own purposes which are conditioned by his immediate needs and by his previous experiences. In communicating, he must remember that similar conditions operate with the recipient. Furthermore, both in thinking and in communicating, he must take into account the fluid, changing quality of language. In addition, if the student is to strive for accuracy, he must recognize the *sources of knowledge* and learn to use the methods of *validating evidence* from these sources—evidence upon which he bases his decisions and makes his choices.

THREE SOURCES OF KNOWLEDGE

A statement purports to originate in knowledge. How do we acquire the facts, truths, and principles that make up our personal store? If we except intuition, the world's wisdom as well as the individual's comes from only three sources. Each person gets his store of knowledge either through *perception* or from the *testimony* of others; he adds to the information gained from these two sources by *inference.* We gain direct knowledge through the senses; from this we infer—that is, we go beyond the established facts and attempt to interpret, corroborate, and correlate them to form a satisfying conclusion. From one inference we arrive at others, and then still others; the chain goes on and on. Testimony provides us with indirect knowledge from "authorities" who have received their information directly, as we have, or indirectly, from the reports, or the reports of reports, of others. Their information too is colored by the perceptions and inferences, correct or incorrect, of the individuals serving as links in the communication. Obviously, in each acquisition of knowledge language plays a significant role.

Students should know that all four types of assertions *may* be largely the products of inference, and that three types—judgmental, normative, and metaphorical—since each is in a sense evaluative, *must* be derived in part by inferring. Only the simplest statements can be based on perception alone; only the most immature personality accepts testimony automatically. Almost immediately the power of reasoning asserts itself. The student must cultivate awareness of the pervasiveness of inference in his thinking and, hence, in his acquisition of knowledge.

VALIDATION OF EVIDENCE

Just as evidence can be placed in two categories, so too can the tests of its validity: That of the factual can be established by objective means; that of the evaluative, by proof of the reliability of the source. Specific examples depicting different circumstances will illustrate the care required in testing evidence.

Degree of objectivity in inference The same stimulus may initiate different chains of inference with two individuals. Each, associating the stimulus with other experiences similar in certain respects, supplies what seems to him to be a logical explanation. Inferences differ greatly in degrees of objectivity —that is, in the extent to which they refer to something in the external world in contrast to something that exists only in the mind of the one making them. They may be true or false, valid or invalid. They are true if they express things as they are; they are valid if justified by the evidence given in their support, and then only until contradictory evidence casts doubt on their validity. The fewer the elements which have referents in the objective world, the more difficult is the validation of the inference.

An observer seeing a stranger entering the house next door may report, "Someone dressed as a policeman just went into the Todds'." This is a factual statement based on perception. If the speaker had substituted "a policeman" for "someone dressed as a policeman," part of the statement would depend upon inference. Granted, the distinction is finely drawn; but if we are to teach the student how commonly we infer when we think we are only describing our perceptions, we cannot cavil at such niceties.

Any number of inferences may be drawn from the above observation. Suppose the speaker concludes, "The police are selling tickets for their annual ball." With this factual statement validation is easy; he simply waits for his own doorbell to ring. The thinking of a different observer might take another direction, causing him to decide, "Johnny Todd is in trouble again." This has elements of the judgmental. It may be validated if the speaker produces evidence of Johnny's prior escapades and uncovers facts to prove that he is again an object of interest to those concerned with a violation of the law. The listener, in turn, can decide whether or not to agree, whether the evidence given is sufficient to warrant belief.

Suppose this observer goes further, drawing a second inference which ventures a prediction, "That boy will come to no good." Unless the speaker is gifted with occult powers, he cannot substantiate this; the judgment has neither truth nor validity. It emanates from a personal scale of values, telling more about the one who pronounces the verdict than about the situation. The more charged with emotion his tone, the more clearly does the speaker reveal himself. If the listener automatically agrees, it is probably safe to infer that he is guided by a similar set of values. See what a structure can be raised upon one casual observation? Perhaps the gentleman in uniform was only "the man who came to dinner."

Inferences of literary characters Characters from literature offer useful examples for learning accuracy both in perception and in reasoning—concepts developed in the chapter that follows. Students can discern what difficulty arises when judgments are accepted as descriptions of life-facts—sometimes because of carelessness or inability to secure information upon which validation may be made, and other times because of wishful thinking. Many literary characters have been so betrayed. Macbeth, emboldened by the belief that the prophecy of the witches has only the literal meaning he wishes to believe, rushes to his own destruction. Lear, confusing words with facts, "forsakes reason and suffers the penalty of reason forsaking him." Pip, in the Dickens novel, bases his great expectations on a false premise. Each accepts the result of his inferential process as a fact when in reality it represents a judgment. Students need to become increasingly conscious of the thinking process, more appreciative of the need for appraisal of the facts and of the reasoning upon which conclusions are based.

Distinguishing perception from inference The crucial need for discriminating between perception and inference and for validating each is nowhere more evident than in standard courtroom procedure. Here no witness is permitted to express his attitude toward the fact he describes. The representatives of the court do that; society has already decided that the crime of which the defendant is accused merits punishment. In differentiating statements of fact—both descriptions of perceptions and inferences from them—and judgments, we are in somewhat the same position as the judge, the final arbiter as to whether testimony will or will not be admitted. Only descriptive statements of firsthand experiences are accepted from most witnesses; inferences are barred. Testimony may place the defendant at a particular place at a certain time; speculation as to his reason for being there is inadmissible. One of the hazards of the courtroom is the inability of untrained witnesses to distinguish between perception and inference. The line between the two is often blurred.

An inferential statement, a deduction from evidence, is admitted only from one who first qualifies as an authority in the pertinent field. The ballistics expert may testify that two bullets have been fired from the same gun; the doctor may interpret the evidence revealed by the autopsy as confirmation of the probable time and cause of death. Although inferences made by experts are never infallible, they are accepted as factual, the closest approximations of the truth it is possible to obtain.

In the courtroom, opposing attorneys and the judge stand guard to insure that each statement is admissible in any given situation; in other circumstances we must rely on our own powers of discernment. Although it is impossible to concentrate with the same degree of intentness on the kaleidoscopic events which confront us in life, here, as in the courtroom, awareness of the nature of the statement being made is the first step in the evaluation process.

Evaluating evidence In evaluating experience, we resemble the jurors who must determine what the evidence is worth. Descriptive statements of perceptions from different witnesses may be contradictory; inferences of experts sometimes disagree. Rarely does the evidence point only one way. In most cases, as in life, much of the evidence is circumstantial—that is, "proof is given of certain facts from which the jury may infer others which usually follow according to the common experience of mankind." Inherent in the privilege of judging is the moral obligation to reject guesswork or conjecture, "a vast field in which no jury is permitted to roam." [21] A juror must give to all statements whatever weight he thinks they deserve; he must ignore those rejected. From the cumulative evidence thus accepted, he makes up his mind as to the verdict. Ideally, when we must decide what to accept, we adopt the same procedure as the jurors in the courtroom. Admittedly, we cannot submit each detail to the same minute scrutiny, but awareness of the desirability for doing so is a basic discipline in precise thinking and discriminating communication.

Language may be likened to a mirror. The image the mirror reflects, the event the words describe, both assume the semblance of reality. Mirrors may create illusions; so too with language. They may flatter, distort, magnify, minimize; language may do the same. When we buy a mirror for general use, we want one which shows things as they appear to be; for most purposes we demand the same of language. In carnival spirit we may enjoy an occasional trip through a crazy mirror house; we can laugh at the grotesque and ludicrous shapes that leer at us from every angle, for we know the purpose is to entertain. We are not tricked. Language, too, recognized as an expression of fantasy, beguiles us, but does not deceive. Only when taken as a literal transcription of fact, either in life or in literature, does it mock and delude. Language is indeed a magic mirror. Through language, we catch glimpses not only of the material and spiritual world but also of the speaker or writer, for the language that each has created for himself, his unique way of reacting to experience, reveals the man.

As English teachers we are concerned with language in the world of fact and in the world of imagination. With both logical and imaginative thinking, the role of language looms large; with both we are concerned with the degree to which language conforms to the reality it represents. How trustworthy is the perception? How accurate the memory? How relevant the inferences? How precise the words that describe the experience? How valid the judgments and insights? The two worlds have much in common; they

[21] J. A. Ballantine, *Law Dictionary* (Rochester, N.Y., Lawyers' Coop, 1930), pp. 216, 263.

are never completely separated; language is an integral part of both. Ability to cope with both is essential.

Recognition of the many purposes for which language is used, of the various factors that may affect meaning, of language as a symbolism only approximating the reality it represents, will give the student an understanding of his language as dynamic process. Continual evaluation of this process as it manifests itself in the areas of fact and of imagination will reveal to him the wonders and complexities of his language. He will see it as a living thing, changing with experience, its many facets reflecting life in all its aspects. With Whitman, he will realize that it is "not a construction of the learned and of dictionary makers, but something arising out of the work, needs, ties, joys, affections, tastes, of long generations of humanity, and has its bases broad and low, close to the ground." [22]

THE TEACHING PROBLEM

Whatever the area of English instruction, the teacher must first be thoroughly familiar with the pertinent concepts, attitudes, and skills within the area that he thinks it important for students to develop. He must also, since the durable factor in learning consists of generalizations with applications rather than a miscellany of specific reactions, be aware of the relationships existing among the desired learnings in all areas. Instruction in all aspects of English is continuous and cumulative. The teacher is simultaneously making a three-pronged attack: preparing for concepts, attitudes, and skills to be taught later; teaching those of the moment; re-emphasizing those previously taught. Understanding of the relationship the learning in one area bears to that in another and his own conviction as to what is important for students to learn are the only governing principles he can trust. Without this grounding, he cannot plan learning experiences economical of time; he cannot help students see the study of English as an integrated whole.

Organizing Instruction

Since language is the major instrument for both teaching and learning, practice in its use goes on continually. The teacher does not need to search for occasions to introduce pertinent experiences; his problem is rather one of wise choice. With any class he must decide *when* to focus on language as language, *what* that focus will be, and *how* the learning can be best accomplished. These are difficult questions to which no categorical answers can be given. However, the problem of introducing the study, of continuing its emphasis, and of selecting a time for the introduction of various concepts will be considered.

[22] "Slang in America," *North American*, Vol. 141, No. 5 (November 1885), p. 431.

Introducing the study Two methods have been used in planning the strategy for teaching language as process: units concerned with certain aspects of the nature of language; series of lessons interspersed throughout the semester or year. The first method is illustrated by the unit, "Power over Language." The second is illustrated by several examples:

A lesson on language as symbolism and the importance of context in determining the meaning of symbols, pp. 49-52.

A sequence of experiences suitable for teaching understanding of motivation of behavior, pp. 54-57.

A sequence used in teaching ninth-graders the general purposes for language, pp. 57-59.

Either method or a combination of the two provides intervals when the learning experiences may focus on language as dynamic process.

Continuing the emphasis Two ways of emphasizing concepts previously introduced are effective: incidental teaching, as illustrations of basic principles occur in language used in the classroom; and bulletin board displays. With the first, the teaching is only what might well be done in any case; however, if examples fulfilling the more immediate aim can be tied to a concept concerning the nature of language, a twofold purpose is served. The teacher merely extends the dimensions of the present learning, helping students integrate the skills and concepts which various areas have in common. For instance, if a class has studied the sources of words, three minutes spent in examining the several elements of a word found in the textbook and in allowing students to suggest other words formed on the same pattern will serve as a reminder of one aspect of language process. Ten minutes spent trying to determine why a fictional character draws an inference the reader knows is invalid can emphasize the personal quality of language. Opportunities for such incidental teaching occur almost daily. It is neither necessary nor desirable to use all.

A second plan encouraging regular attention to language as process employs bulletin board displays, frequently changed. All pupils are encouraged to contribute. The examples, given to student clearing committees for selection, are mounted under appropriate headings on large sheets of art paper. After each has served its immediate purpose as a poster, it is inserted as a page in a looseleaf scrapbook. Each contribution bears the name of the donor, his grade level, and the date. Brief discussions take place regularly; some teachers set aside a twenty-minute period each week to examine the recently acquired visual illustrations of principles studied. Classroom examples that have passed without mention offer one source; reading, conversation, and televiewing furnish others.

Many teachers, in planning the year's work, use units as well as several series of lessons; both are reinforced with incidental teaching and visual displays, which complement each other. Such a plan is productive of more lasting results than one which concentrates on a few periods of intensive instruction separated by long intervals of neglect.

Selecting what and when Advice concerning what concepts should be introduced at any particular grade level cannot be offered unequivocally. So much depends upon the particular situation. In general, the more immature—chronologically and intellectually—the pupil, the more concrete the level of instruction. Certainly it would be unwise to spend time teaching even a brilliant seventh grade class the general purposes for which language is used—not because it would be difficult for the pupil to assimilate such information, but because the time can be more wisely spent in other ways, for instance, in directing his reading. The same holds true for those with less than average ability at all grade levels; other experiences will undoubtedly prove more profitable. However, even young children use language for *specific* purposes; therefore, understanding of the particular purpose in the language he uses himself and in that used by others should be a part of the learning of all pupils. In this way the stress remains on the concrete.

Another idea—that language only *stands for* experience—must receive emphasis on all levels. Students have been helped to appreciate language as symbolism by a simple diagram showing the difficulties encountered in precise communication.

The Communicative Process

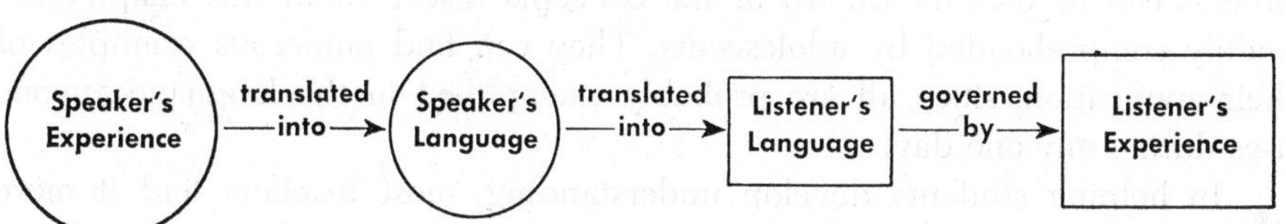

It is impossible to communicate an experience exactly. The speaker must translate his experience into word symbols, which are never capable of transmitting the whole; in turn, the listener must understand the message in terms of his own word symbols, which differ from the speaker's in some degree because the experience and needs of any two people are different.

The teacher can combine the use of a graphic device with specific examples to help pupils see the individuality of language. Such a simple statement as "I *did* the assignment" means different things to different students. How much does the meaning of the verb depend upon the conscientiousness of the individual? How much on his understanding of the problem? How much on his work habits? Stories too can illuminate the personal quality of language. What does "hundred dresses," in Eleanor Estes' story *The Hundred Dresses,* mean to Wanda, who longs for beautiful clothes? What does it mean to her classmates, who interpret as impossible pretense Wanda's reference to having the dresses?

Many selections studied in the seventh and eighth grade furnish examples of various aspects of language operation—certainly, of the effect of motives on language and of the importance of context in determining meaning. Often, too, examples can be found of different interpretations by participants of the same event, allowing stress on the distinction between perceptions and the inferences drawn from them; at times, expressions of opinions incapable of adequate support can also be illustrated incidentally. For example, the following paraphrases an idea found in a biographical sketch in an eighth grade anthology: "X's life shows that a boy can do anything he wishes if he has enough determination." Such a statement should not be passed over without considering the thinking which lies behind it. In what sense may the assertion be true? In what sense, false? How can it be reworded to express the truth more exactly? In such ways, the immature pupil can consider illustrations of aspects of the linguistic process, acquiring a backlog of concretions upon which he can later build the complex understandings required to make his language function in practice.

Starting in the ninth grade the student should begin to see relationships in the understandings he has been developing—in part unconsciously—concerning the nature of language. He can begin to realize the complexities of language, in one sense as a thing apart, and in another, as an essential ingredient of his own personality.

Throughout the senior high school years, instruction in language as dynamic process can be continuous. All of the concepts discussed in this chapter are readily comprehended by adolescents. They can find numerous examples of their application, since all are probably exemplified in the language anyone uses during any one day.

In helping students develop understanding, most teachers find it more effective to start with a subordinate idea—"Words may change their primary meaning with the context"—rather than with the major concept—"Language changes." After experience with a number of minor ideas, students may be led to devise a scheme of organization which will show the relation of the ideas to each other and to the general principles they exemplify. Furthermore, these items need not be taught in any certain order, nor is it desirable to teach one exhaustively before another is considered. Since they overlap and interact with each other, the impact is stronger when they run concurrently, as they do in life. All emphasize in some small way the larger problem: the necessity, if one is to think clearly and communicate accurately, of sensing the relation words bear to the facts they represent.

The control of language is a lifetime job; it is extremely complicated; it cannot be hurried. Students will quickly learn to recognize single aspects of language dynamics; the difficulty, as anyone can testify, comes in so integrating these understandings that they will function in use. Thus, continual practice in applying the principles is essential. The student should think of language mastery, not as something to be gained in one semester or even in many years, but as a problem that will be with him always. The methods for teaching language presented in this chapter are intended to serve as a basis for a six-year program. They are intended to promote understandings and to initiate habits on which the student can continue to build long after he has left the classroom. Committed to such a program, the teacher of English can aid the student in acquiring a healthy respect for the power, the complexity, and the uniqueness of his own language.

Suggested Learning Experiences

The learning experiences given throughout this text suggest specific procedures which teachers can use to lead students to understand and apply the principles discussed. Hence, these illustrations are concerned with the particular aspect of teaching English which has just been considered; however, they are not intended to be used solely in the context in which they appear, nor is it implied that they be used in isolation. The teaching of English is an *integrated process;* teaching one segment as an entity without relation to others or to the whole contradicts the nature of language and of life. What one really learns in English is a pattern—generalizations, skills, attitudes—applicable to many specifics of thinking, feeling, communicating. Thus, in adapting for a certain class any learning experiences suggested in this text, one should be aware of certain principles of learning: that of *relatedness,* the importance of an organizational design which helps students see the bearing present learnings have on others; that of *readiness,* the teacher's obligation to prepare students for the learnings they need to acquire. Used with this precaution, the experiences can provide not only focus on the particular subject under discussion but ways of supplementing instruction in other areas of English.

To learn to think of language as symbolism

■ *Learn the nature of symbols*

As the initial venture in arousing interest in the way language works, the teacher of a class of seventh-graders used non-verbal symbols.[23] One day after the pupils had returned from an assembly, he started a discussion by asking,

"Why do we salute the flag? . . . Yes, it's ours, but do we salute everything that's ours? . . . Where have you seen the flag flying?" (Schools, post-office, the Presidio, ships, parades . . .)

"If you were in France and saw our flag flying over a building, what would it tell you? . . . Then our flag stands for what? . . ."

He wrote on the chalkboard, *Our flag stands for the USA.*

"The flag is what we call a *symbol.* That's a new word for us. We use symbols every day. In the light of what we've been saying about the flag, let's see if we can make up a definition of *symbol.* If we cross out some words in this sentence and make a substitution, we have *A symbol stands for* . . . How shall we finish? . . . Yes, U.S.A. would still make sense, but it wouldn't help us with a definition, would it? We're trying to make a statement that will apply to all symbols. . . ." (A symbol stands for something else.)

[23] An abbreviated transcript of an actual lesson.

"Good. Now let's change this statement into a definition. A symbol is . . . ?" (A symbol is something that stands for something else.) "Now we'll try to think of other symbols. . . . Why is there a picture of a cub on your book covers? . . ." (School emblem, policeman's badge and uniform, insignia for cars, for boy scouts . . .)

"All of these symbols are things we can see. Can you think of any we can't see? . . . No? Haven't you been in classes where you haven't smelled smoke, you haven't seen flames and yet . . ." (Fire siren, signal for fire drill, emergency alert, Morse code.)

"So in addition to symbols we can see, we have those we can hear. We've seen that some symbols mean only one thing to us—the flag with the stars and stripes in a certain arrangement always stands for the USA; in this school three blasts on the horn, repeated over and over, mean an emergency . . .

"Let's look at some other symbols. What does '+' mean? . . ." (Plus, addition.) "Yes, when we see $3 + 3$ it does mean that."

Then he sketched on the board different contexts for "+".

"What does '+' stand for now?" (A church.) "And now?" (The Red Cross.) And now? . . .

Next he used the same procedure with "×". (Crossing, signature, multiplication.)

"So we've found symbols that stand for one thing and symbols that may stand for several according to their surroundings. We call such surroundings the *context*. Do you know that word? Let's define it . . .

■ *Study words as symbols*

The same teacher carried the lesson further the next day.

"Let's explore the idea of symbol a little further."

He pointed to his desk.

"What's this?"

He wrote *desk* on the chalkboard.

"Is this *desk*, the one that I've written, the same as that, the one you can see? . . . Why not? . . ."

Through questioning and securing additional examples, he led pupils to see that a word stands for something in the same way as the flag does.

"What, then, can we call these words on the board? . . . What did we say the flag was? . . . A symbol, yes . . . Language is made up of thousands of symbols. So now we see we have symbols we can write . . . And? . . ." (Read . . . Speak . . . Hear.)

"You'll remember we found symbols that meant only one thing and symbols that might mean different things. In what class shall we place words?" (Disagreement arose, one pupil insisting that *desk* would always mean desk.)

"You are partially right; *desk* is more specific in meaning than many other words. If I asked you now to come to the desk, you'd know exactly what I meant, wouldn't you? Why?" (The physical and verbal contexts were explored.)

"Suppose we were on the playground and I said, 'Go to the desk.' Would you know where to go?" (The class supplied modifiers to clarify the direction.)

"Let's take a look at some other words. What does *rich* mean?" (*Having a lot of money* met with universal approval.) "Does it mean that in the slogan, 'The richest ice-cream money can buy'? What does it mean when applied to ice-cream? . . ." (Good-tasting.) "What does rich color in a painting mean? . . ." (Vivid.) "A rich voice? . . ." (Full, pleasant.) "A rich joke? . . ." (Very funny.) "Do you remem-

slang or colloquial. Have them pool their findings. Before they report, ask the class to estimate what the percentages will be. Exactness is unimportant; the exercise will, however, emphasize both the stable and the slowly changing aspects of the language.

3. Study words which in the course of their history have changed their meanings:

	from	**through**	**to**
silly:	blessed	blessed fool	foolish
brave:	crooked	scoundrelly	courageous
nice:	ignorant	silly	pleasing, exact
villain:	serf	one of lowly birth	scoundrel
constable:	stable companion	officer of high rank	policeman

Ask volunteers to consult books dealing with language (see titles listed at end of chapter) to report similar examples to the class or to prepare for the bulletin board.

■ *Learn how to make words by combining elements in the language*

1. Ask students to consult a dictionary to discover the status and meaning of the following words—all the result of word combinations. (If the word is not labeled, it is standard; otherwise *St.* is used for standard and *Sl.* for slang.)[26]

horselaugh	applesauce (St., Sl.)
clodhopper	crackup (St., Sl.)
greathearted	grapevine (St., Sl.)
kickoff	gumshoe (St., Sl.)
killjoy	roughneck (Sl.)
bookworm	windbag (Sl.)
tipoff	greenhorn (Col.)
shoplifter	boom-and-bust (Col.)
milksop	rock-and-roll

2. Help students build words using different combinations of roots, prefixes, and suffixes. A pictorial device, representing families of words as trees, is effective if the concept of word building is new to children; they may enjoy making graphic examples for the bulletin board.

Root	postscript, description, conscript, nondescript . . .
	transport, deportation, portable . . .
	aqueduct, conduct, introduction . . .
Prefix	egocentric, egomaniac, egotism . . .
	antibiotic, anticlimax, antifreeze . . .
	anteroom, antedate, antecedent . . .
Suffix	militate, obviate, equivocate . . .
	specialist, oculist, conformist . . .
	rectify, vivify, fortify . . .

■ *Recognize other languages as a source of words*

Ask a committee of students to mark on a map of the world the geographical source of such words. Here are a few to start with; as others occur, indicate on map.

[26] *The American College Dictionary* (N.Y., Random, 1947), was consulted concerning words in this chapter. Students may use different dictionaries and discover that they do not agree; such information will emphasize the essential point being taught.

blitz—German	corral—Spanish
garage—French	kibitzer—Hebrew
hoi poloi—Greek	ski—Scandinavian
ghoul—Arabic	solo—Latin
ravioli—Italian	typhoon—Chinese
taboo—South Pacific	banshee—Irish and Scottish
goulash—Hungarian	viking—Icelandic
boomerang—Australian	bungalow—Hindu

■ *Learn the three most common ways of coining words*

1. These words derive from *proper names.* Let students work in groups, consulting the dictionary to discover the source, ascertaining if possible the approximate time the word entered the language.

quisling	pasteurize	quixotic
ampere	watt	vandalism
derringer	babbittry	titanic
martinet	derrick	bedlam
macadam	sandwich	hamburger

2. Only the first two of the *telescoped words* below are in the dictionary; discuss the meanings with students. What are the possibilities for change in status? For example, if the phenomenon represented by "smog" becomes more universal, the word will undoubtedly achieve standard usage. It would seem also that several of the other words are quite respectable colloquialisms and will soon be included in dictionaries.

radar—ra(dio) d(etection) a(nd) r(anging)
smog (Col.)
brunch, motel, Unesco, cinemaddict

Globeloney and *grismal* are examples of words, recently coined by telescoping, that have never quite caught on even as slang. Let students add those in vogue with teen-agers or coin some of their own.

3. The first time we meet words coined by *imitating other words,* the meaning is instantly clear if we recognize the prototype. The following are examples. Let students supply prototypes.

racketeer	aquacade
booketeria	beautician
iffy	realtor
bookmobile	majorette

Encourage students to make a collection of words coined in this way.

To realize the importance of motivation

■ *Recognize specific human wants*

1. Ask students to select two advertisements in which the advertiser tries to sell his product by implying there is one certain thing everyone wants; have them show the advertisement and analyze the appeal.

In giving the assignment, the teacher can illustrate by pointing out similarities in the appeals of advertisements for different types of products—for example, appeals to our love of comfort in advertisements for shaving cream, vacuum cleaner, mattress.

In discussing the appeals in the advertisements collected, the class tentatively agrees on some specific wants which seem widely emphasized. The teacher may add appeals that students miss, e.g., non-materialistic needs; perhaps he may ask for identification of the appeal in "Do you care enough? Help CARE take care of others," or "The Good Guy Gives." The class secretary should keep a list of the needs featured.

2. Next, post advertisements around the room, taking care that each category is amply illustrated, for example:

General wants	Advertisements for	Appeal
Protection	Pain reliever	Speedy relief
	Tires	Safety
Possessions	Book	Save with coupon
	Gasoline	More miles to the gallon
Power	School	Prepare for executive job
	Dancing lessons	Increase popularity
Prestige	Sterling silver	Add to your prestige as a hostess
	Car	The right car proclaims your success
Stimulation	Television set	High fidelity tone
	Travel poster	The land of your dreams
Spiritual security	March of Dimes	Give this child a chance
	Blood Bank	Someone needs your blood today

Ask students to identify the wants to which appeals are made. Add these to the list already compiled.

■ *Decide upon a classification and validate it*

1. Let students group into tentative categories the specific wants which have been discussed for the preceding assignments; through class discussion, teacher and students arrive at an experimental scheme of organization acceptable to both.

2. To cover a large amount of material in a short time, the teacher divides the class into three groups, each to investigate the advertisements in a different type of magazine—pulp, slick, elite. They are to consider appeals made to the basic wants and to determine whether the advertisers seem to be appealing to the same wants previously discussed by the class. They prepare a report on their findings. The class, with the teacher's guidance, after discussing the reports made by the groups, either decides that the classification is valid or agrees upon modifications.

■ *Discover how advertisers tailor their appeals to fit probable readers*

Using the same material brought in by students for the previous assignment, again divide the class into three groups, each containing representatives of the three different types of magazine. Ask students to compare advertisements which appeal to the same want in at least two different types, noting similarities and contrasts in the logical and emotional aspects of the appeals and in the language in which they are couched. Compare, for example, the "glamor" advertisements in *Vogue* and *True Confessions*.

Do the findings tell anything concerning the advertiser's estimate of the readers?

What effect, if any, would this estimate have on the editor in selecting stories or articles to be published?

■ *Recognize, in the behavior of fictional characters, motives for action rooted in the basic human needs*

1. Ask students to select from a recent motion picture or television program a specific action of a particular character. Explain the motives. Do they seem based on any of the fundamental drives? Discuss.

2. Plan a series of lessons using short stories and plays.[27] After the literature has been studied, ask students to review actions of the characters to find illustrations of impelling motives based on the fundamental needs. For example, we recognize the desire for power predominant in "The Secret Life of Walter Mitty," where the hero, figuratively donning the mantle of Superman, encounters in his daydreams experiences which reality denies him.

3. Ask the student to analyze the behavior of one character from the book he has selected as part of the guided reading program.[28] For the discussion of this assignment the class may be divided into groups. Each group discusses motivation for action, determines the main and contributing drives, and selects examples to be reported to the class.

■ *Determine motives for behavior in life situations*

1. Ask students to identify the drives acknowledged in news items in which individuals give reasons to explain their behavior. One week supplied the following from one daily newspaper:

It seemed a fool-proof way to make money. (Possessions)
I did it for a thrill. (Stimulation)
He embarrassed me before my friends. (Protection)
They wouldn't let me out in the evenings. (Power)
I'm out of a job and have a family to support. (Protection)
I thought I could sell it. (Possessions)
I wanted to help him. (Spiritual security)
I wanted to see the Giants in action. (Stimulation)
I wanted to impress the neighbors. (Prestige)
I never could do what I wanted to do. (Power)
I didn't want the other kids to know. (Prestige)
My first responsibility was to the passengers. (Spiritual security)

The value in an exercise such as this lies in the discussion it entails. Agreement concerning classification is less important than that students understand the difficulty of correctly assessing motivation.

2. Discuss the possible motives behind these activities:

Cheating in an examination
Owning a hot rod
Running for president of the student body
Disturbing a class
Attending a dance
Winning a game
Playing football
Entering an art contest
Belonging to a club
Winning a scholarship

[27] See the unit "Meeting a Crisis" for list.
[28] Guided reading program is discussed on pp. 247-48, 292-94.

3. Use a short written exercise, such as the following:

Analyze a recent action of your own. Are your motives clear to you? Are they based on the fundamental wants? Write a paragraph of explanation. (If these papers are to be discussed, better results will be obtained if the anonymity of the writer is preserved.)

In the above learning experiences, the series of activities suggests a sequence moving from the simple to the more difficult. Offered as an illustration of the study of motivation as it pertains to understanding language as process, this order is logical, but it may not be applicable to any particular class. In many classes, students will have studied motivation in reference to fictional characters before studying it as influencing the use of language. If so, the teacher would start with familiar examples taken from literature or from the students' experience before attempting to lead the class to see that the universality of certain drives permits a classification. The suggested learning experiences elsewhere in the text do not necessarily suggest an order for teaching. In any particular instance the teacher must decide what experiences and what order will be likely to produce the desired learning most economically. The order suggested above is built upon the following rationale:

Study of the repetitive and forthright appeals found in advertisements will give even the slow student a crude and broad basis for understanding human motives.

Study of the ordered experiences offered by literature will help him refine and interpret his knowledge.

Analysis of life situations will lead him to see the difficulties of accurately determining specific motives for specific behavior.

To understand purpose in the use of language

Again a sequence is presented, designed to show how a teacher may introduce a series of lessons on language process, reinforcing or extending concepts being developed in other areas of English instruction. This plan was used by a ninth grade teacher with a class which had read essays and stories. Notice that he did not present the categories as information to be learned; rather he moved from the specific to the general, from the known to the unknown. He had been gradually preparing pupils by helping them determine specific purpose in their reading, listening, speaking, and writing; therefore, he had many examples familiar to students.

He *started by reviewing these,* asking questions to re-emphasize purpose in material previously read, for example:

"I Meet Walt Disney": to show us that Disney is a likable person.

"Now That You're Tanned—What?": to make us laugh at a human foible.

"Leiningen Versus the Ants": to impress upon us the capabilities of the human brain, dramatized by the experiences of a self-reliant man.

He *continued,* eliciting information concerning purpose of talks given by pupils in class.

He *then asked* students to give examples of purposes for which they had recently used language:

To explain why I did not do an assignment.

To persuade my mother to let me go to a movie.

He *next asked* for examples of purpose in language directed to them:

To get me to wash the car.
To help me understand an assignment.

In some such way, a teacher may introduce any factor in understanding language as process.

■ *Realize that all language is used for a purpose*

Ask students to notice the specific purpose of particular language they use and hear; to prepare to report on five examples. In the discussion following, pupils may need help in seeing that:

A large area of language is aimed at facilitating social intercourse.

To convince may be an ultimate purpose as well as a preliminary to persuasion.

If examples of all the general purposes to be taught are not volunteered by pupils, appropriate questions will elicit those omitted: Did anyone tell a joke, something interesting which had happened to him, something unusual he had observed? Did anyone try to convince a friend that rock and roll is real music, that a certain movie is better than another? Did anyone use language without a purpose?

The discussion should clinch the idea that all language, whether we are aware of it at the time or not, has a *specific purpose.*

■ *Classify the purposes for use of language*

The teacher, using the specific purposes given above, leads pupils to discern similarities. After purposes have been placed in groups, the class can agree on names for the categories—not necessarily the ones given here.

After classification has been agreed upon, give students a list of statements suitable for central ideas for either written or oral work, for example:

The Leaping Leopards should have won the pennant. (Convince)
Give to the Community Chest. (Persuade)
A recent survey gives the following facts about the city's industry. (Inform)
Join the rooters at the game. (Persuade)
It was the most exciting incident of a long exciting career. (Interest)
More competent leadership of both industry and labor would have averted the strike. (Convince)
There are three steps in making a kite. (Inform)
This is the funniest story I've ever heard. (Interest)

Ask students to place each in a category. Discuss. Disagreement and doubt will be salutary. Discussion should point up the *complexity* of language and the need for *precision* in its use.

■ *Recognize general purposes in one's own language*

1. Ask students to select from their own use of language a specific example to illustrate each of the general categories, for example:

I tried to get my father to increase my allowance. (Persuade)
I explained an assignment for a friend. (Inform)

2. Ask students to compose four sentences, each one possible as a controlling statement for written or oral work and each illustrating a different general purpose.

General purpose	Response desired	Controlling sentence
To interest, to entertain, to maintain rapport	I enjoyed myself. or It held my interest.	Getting up in the morning is the hardest job of the day.
To inform	I understand.	The equipment needed for building a high fidelity set is . . .
To convince	I agree.	If John had obeyed the camp leader's instructions, the accident could have been avoided.
To persuade	I will do it.	Buy a ticket for the class play.

Connecting specific purpose with the response of the listener or reader will help students see that not only must the purpose of the speaker or writer be considered but also that of the recipient.

■ *Identify the purpose of language used by others*

1. Ask students to clip from a newspaper or magazine examples of the four purposes. Are they used singly or is one used to reinforce the other?

Features, stories—to interest, to inform
News items—to inform
Editorials—to convince, to move to action
Cartoons, comic strips—to interest, to inform, to move to action

Select the controlling sentence, or if it is only implied, compose one. Prepare to read the sentence, to state both the general and the specific purpose.

This exercise may launch several assignments; it can be carried further with the student analyzing the item to determine its effectiveness and the reasons for success or failure in the accomplishment of its purpose. It can be used as an assignment for all students, or the class may be divided into four groups, each to find illustrations of a different general purpose.

2. Ask students to select a radio or television program which has a combination of purposes, to decide upon the ultimate purpose, and to show how the others contribute to it.

■ *Use the knowledge gained about purpose in the use of language*

Let students draw names of other class members; each is to write a short composition for the person whose name he has drawn, selecting a specific purpose he wishes to accomplish. The composition is given to the one for whom it has been written; he decides on the writer's general and specific purpose, his degree of success in achieving it, and reasons for his success or lack of it; he makes these comments on the paper and returns it to the owner.

Use class discussion to review principles and to explore ways successful writers used in trying to accomplish their purpose. How many considered interests of the reader? In what ways?

To study contextual factors that may affect meaning

■ *Determine first-level meaning from verbal context*

1. Ask students to investigate in an unabridged dictionary the meaning of common words applicable to different objects or different areas of experience and to determine why the general meaning is appropriate for the various specifics. One method is to divide the class into groups, giving each a noun which names a part of the human body—arm, eye, face, foot, hand, head, heart, leg, neck, nose; students are to discover other areas of meaning, e.g., *arm* may be used in reference to a chair, a ship, the sea, the government, etc.

Follow with other words. Here are some suggestions:

air	book	field	range
approach	bow	fix	rate
band	box	hit	reach
bank	brush	hold	run
bar	case	idle	tack
base	cast	jack	tender
bay	catch	joint	train
beam	check	last	trap
bear	exchange	launch	trim
beat	fan	level	turn

2. Play guess-the-word for a few minutes a day. The student says, "I am thinking of a word of seven letters, beginning with 'h'; it is often used to describe heart, weapons, or taxes." (heavy) Or, "I am thinking of a word of four letters, beginning with 'b'; it is used in reference to music, clothing, or radio broadcasting." (band)

3. Give students the italicized parts of these statements—fictitious quotations—to interpret.

Senator Doe: "*The report of this committee is remarkable;* never have I seen so many errors in a single document."

Critic A: "Although *the author had access to an abundance of reliable sources,* he apparently did not use them."

Representative X: "If the witness has told the truth, then it would appear that *Mr. B. is engaged in subversive activities;* however, the witness has given no evidence to support his accusations."

Critic Y: "*Dressed in a fashionable gown, Singer C, charming and gracious, captivated her audience* until she began to sing."

Afterward, give students the complete statements; then let them write their own, meeting with a partner to select effective examples for a bulletin board display.

4. Use the same procedure with sentences out of context: Remove from a paragraph a sentence admitting several interpretations, ask students to think of possible meanings, then read the paragraph. The following sentences are given, not for use in the classroom—for that the entire paragraph is necessary—but to show how lacking in precise meaning even the simplest sentence becomes when removed from its context. The idea is often a revelation to students.

Moving was an ordeal.
One or two whiffs was all he could stand.
They had scraped and pinched.

After students have given as many meanings as they can think of, read the sentence in its context.

■ *Study the effect of abstractions on meaning*

1. Discuss with students the meanings in fictional names:

If we were to speak of someone as one of the following persons of fact or fiction, saying "He is a regular ———," to what quality would we refer? What would we disregard?

Hamlet	Munchausen
Peter Pan	Frankenstein
Job	Beau Brummel
Micawber	Quisling
Babbitt	Hitler

Let students add to the list.

2. Have students construct abstraction scales with words:

human being, American, man, doctor, pediatrician.

3. Do the same with statements:

I like to travel.
I enjoyed my trip to Europe.
France is the European country I prefer to visit.
Paris has much worth seeing.
The Louvre contains many art treasures.
One of the most famous paintings in the Louvre is the Mona Lisa.

4. Ask students to examine advertisements to determine the connection, if any, between pairs of statements like the following and the reason for shifts from the more abstract to the more concrete statements:

More doctors recommend it . . . Zylox is safe for you.
Make your children happy . . . Give them Tastie Toasties for breakfast.

5. Re-emphasize the concept whenever possible by using the literature being studied to point out examples; by asking students to select, from the books they are reading, passages where shifts in the levels of abstraction illuminate meaning. Prepare for the bulletin board or for oral presentation.

■ *Consider the emotional effect of language*

1. Have students collect a list of pairs of words (near synonyms) which have different affective connotations, e.g., plump, fat; kind, soft; courageous, brazen; frank, tactless.

2. Discuss the differences in emotional overtones of pairs of statements similar to the following:

President scuttles farm aid; President vetoes farm bill.
The Senator persists in his fanatical sniping; the Senator continues his earnest criticism.
The Tigers clobber Bears 5 to 4; the Tigers nose out Bears 5 to 4.
We can now exert positive leadership; we now have the whip hand.
I failed the test; "she" flunked me.

3. Divide students into groups. Let each group select a school problem suitable for an editorial, then write a pair of lead statements—one in the style of reporting, the other using emotionally toned words. Compare the effects.

4. Play the game introduced by Bertrand Russell on the B.B.C. called "Conjugation of Irregular Verbs." Examples:

I am firm, you are obstinate, he is a pig-headed fool.
I am slender, you are thin, she is skinny.
I am beautiful, you are pretty, she'll get by if anyone likes the type.

5. Discuss the emotional effect of such purely factual statements as

With the holiday week end only half over, the number of deaths on the highway already exceeds the number of casualties predicted by the National Safety Council for the three-day period.
A gas station attendant died this morning, shot to death by a bandit who got away with less than ten dollars.

Ask students to find in a newspaper a factual statement which has emotional impact.

6. Let students work in pairs; they are to select a mythical person and decide upon his name, sex, and age. Then one student makes a list of factual statements which, if used in describing the person, would create a favorable impression; the other, unfavorable. For example:

Mary devotes three mornings a week to volunteer work in a hospital.
Mary was arrested last week on a shoplifting charge.

With these lists the students meet in groups of six, each group representing three of the persons chosen for description; the problem is to find the implications of "Facts arouse feelings."

Follow with class discussion exploring the findings of the different groups.

■ *Investigate the effect of history and environment on language*

1. Help students account for such historical changes as

Changing the name of St. Petersburg, Russia, first to Petrograd and later to Leningrad; changing Tsaritsin to Stalingrad.
Renaming Stern Park Gardens, Illinois, to Lidice.
Approximate time of changing established place names in the United States to Roosevelt Drive, MacArthur Boulevard, Pershing Square, Eisenhower Plaza, etc.
Prevalence of *Los* or *Las* and of *San* in names of towns in California and other parts of the West.
Appropriateness of *minne* as a prefix for Minnesota place names.

2. Point out the higher degree of conformity in choice of words and in pronunciation among persons within certain regions in the eastern United States—New England, North, North Midland, South Midland, South—than among those living west of the Mississippi. Discuss the historical events that explain the high degree of conformity within each of the eastern regions and its lack in the West.

3. Investigate with students the source of place names in your community and

state. Have any been changed? What ones can be explained by local events? By national happenings? By historical background?

4. Investigate the origin of the names of the states. How many derive from Indian terms? How many are of French, Spanish, or English origin? Discuss in class.

5. Read to the class "Mother Tongue," by Richard Armour; these verses, prompted by a travel advertisement stating that no language barriers exist between the British Isles and the United States, give examples of differences in terminology. Point up the differences in British and American terminology. Mencken's *American Language* contains a list of British and American terms for the same things (pp. 232-237); ask volunteers to select examples to report to the class.

To discriminate among kinds of statements

■ *Compare factual and judgmental statements*

1. Ask students to consider statements similar to these, to decide whether they are largely factual or judgmental, and to pick out the elements in each which substantiate their conclusion.

Mary talks incessantly in order to gain attention.
The school dance will be a flop; they've hired Hal's orchestra.
Senator Doe championed desegregation in order to win the Negro vote.
To promote its own selfish ends, the Central Medical Association is opposing socialized medicine.
John is so shy that he avoids school dances.
My mother won't let me go to the party because she doesn't want me to have any fun.

2. Ask students to examine an editorial from the daily press, to underline the facts, to enclose the judgments in parentheses, and to decide whether the facts are sufficient to support the judgments.

3. Read to students a story where facts and judgments are rather clearly distinguished. In "The Adventure of the Bruce-Partington Plans," Conan Doyle is more fair to his readers than is his custom. Most of the clues and Holmes's deductions are revealed as the story progresses. Therefore, the teacher may stop before each major inference and let students draw their own.

4. Ask students to supply facts which would be needed to furnish support for the following statements:

Our team is the best in the league.
He's a good sport.
Senator X is against foreign aid.
She's a wonderful girl.
Our candidate would make a good president.
He is an expert driver.

■ *Compare factual and normative (or directive) statements*

1. Use a short written exercise such as the following:

Are any of the following factual? Remember that a statement of fact may be false and that a normative or directive may be accepted by the unwary as factual or as giving the whole truth.

The courts insure justice for all.
This magazine will keep you well informed.
"Man shall not live by bread alone."
Our candidate typifies the ideal American.
A rolling stone gathers no moss.
Let me compliment you students on the neatness of your school.
"Absent yourself from felicity a while."
This movie will give you a lift.
Frank Patterson, one of the Senators from Florida, recently left for Asia.
"Let us here highly resolve that these dead shall not have died in vain."

Analyze the ones you have selected as normative statements or as directives. Do they contain any factual parts? What is the aim of each?

2. In discriminating between informative and normative or directive statements, consider the verb "to be," more widely used than any other in the language. When we use "is" as a synonym for "exists" or "takes place," the intention to inform is clear —e.g., "The boy is on the playground," "The dance is tonight." However, three other meanings give the verb the force of a normative or a directive, since the speaker seems to be suggesting that the listener should think as he himself does.

Since these uses of "is" are often found in contexts characterized by strong emotional overtones, the need for pinpointing the exact meaning is greater.

Should be, ought to be
"The right to work is every man's privilege." This is clearly not a statement of fact but a reference to a goal.

In my opinion, appears to me to be
"He is a bully." Such statements are at times accepted by both speaker and listener as fact rather than judgment.

Can be classified as
"He is an ex-convict." This is a factual statement. The danger lies in accepting it as telling all about a person, rather than just one fact. The verb often has this implication in disparaging remarks about national and ethnological groups.

Ask students to recast the following sentences so as not to invite misinterpretation.

Blood is thicker than water. (Goal)
Mary is a wonderful friend. (Opinion)
After all, he's a foreigner. (Classification)
Robert is a Communist. (Classification)
A mother is solicitous for the welfare of her children. (Goal)
Isn't that just like a man? (Classification)
Oh well, you know how women are. (Classification)
A doctor is guided by a strict ethical code. (Goal)
He's nothing but a politician. (Classification)
He is generous to a fault. (Opinion)

3. Let students make up sentences using the verb "to be" with one of the three meanings. Call upon classmates for exact meaning. Work for accuracy, then speed. Spend a few minutes a day until the idea seems to have become rooted.

4. To show the significance of ideas underlying normative or directive statements, use the short radio broadcast, "A Word in Your Ear."

■ *Study metaphor as an intrinsic part of language*

1. A local ice cream parlor displays the sign, "Teen-Age Spoken Here." Discuss its significance with class. Let the class compile a list of slang terms in current use with students; see how many are based on metaphor.

2. *Time* magazine is a prolific source of metaphorical language. Most of the articles make use of it here and there; in almost every issue at least one or two items are built on extended metaphor. Remove pages from an old copy, giving one to each student with instructions to underline the metaphorical elements in red. Post examples.

3. Encourage students to make a collection of song titles using metaphor: hymns ("Rock of Ages"), spirituals ("Swing Low, Sweet Chariot"), patriotic songs ("Columbia, the Gem of the Ocean"), popular ballads ("Wayward Wind"). Let students make up metaphorical titles they think suitable for songs.

4. Ask students to glance through the indices of current magazines to find article and story titles based on metaphor. Encourage volunteers to write metaphorical titles for articles suitable for school or local paper and to explain content briefly.

5. The series of paperbound books of animal photographs by Clare Barnes Jr.,[29] *White Collar Zoo, Home Sweet Zoo, Campus Zoo,* is based on metaphor. Each picture represents a type of person. Mount the most appropriate for a bulletin board display.

6. To emphasize the aptness of metaphor, collect brief examples of metaphorical language; out of context, they point up more sharply the need for imaginative cooperation on the part of the reader. Type each example on a separate card. Ask students to imagine circumstances where it might be appropriate. Examples:

It was Sound itself, a great screeching bow drawn across the strings of the universe.
He received the news with his eyebrows.
The room seemed to empty like a washbowl.
The darkness was piled up in the corners like dust.
The kind of lie the bruised ego feeds upon, course after course, never sickening.
Her blue cape faded haughtily in the distance.
She was no more than a name on a Christmas card, not much of a patch to mend six years with.
His antennae were already out, feeling over this new world.
The kind of room that seemed more interested in people than in things.
She reminded him of a coil of barbed wire.
He chipped away at her self-esteem with the cruel pick of his words.

7. Ask each student to make a copy of one interesting example of metaphorical language found in his reading. Students, working in pairs, exchange, imagine the situation, check with the original. Volunteers report unusual examples to the class.

8. Divide the class into groups, giving each the name of something which could be described about a person, e.g., face, head, hands, posture, walk, voice, smile, etc. Ask each student to devise metaphorical expressions which could be used in making different kinds of faces, smiles, and so on, vivid for the reader.

[29] N.Y., Doubleday, 1950.

The next day have the students meet in groups and make a composite list. Duplicate the list, giving one to each student. Ask him to combine terms from the various categories which might be used by a writer in making a character consistent—for example, would a writer be likely to describe "a smile rippling like sunlight" across a "hatchet-face"? Or would he endow it with a "vulpine" grin? Would he give a "moon face" to an arrogant individual? If so, what might be his purpose?

To cultivate awareness of problems concerned with accuracy

■ *Recognize difficulties involved in drawing valid inferences*

1. Clip explanatory matter from pictures taken from pictorial magazines. Let students study the pictures and write captions. Compare with the original. Reexamine picture to account for correct or faulty inference. Were sufficient details given? Do they support your caption fully as well as they do the original?

2. Ask students to select a cartoon and to clip and preserve the legend. Students, working in pairs, exchange cartoons and write suitable legends. Choose some for a bulletin board display.

3. Prepare a file of series cartoons which present without commentary the steps in a story or situation. Let students work in groups preparing legends.

■ *Develop awareness of the prevalence of inference in our daily use of language*

1. Ask students to examine an issue of a magazine which uses jokes for fillers in order to determine the percentage of those in which the humor depends upon faulty inference. (In those examined by students in various secondary classrooms the range was from 25 to 50 per cent.) The inference may be made ignorantly because facts have been misinterpreted, or deliberately to cause discomfiture to one who relates facts to establish another conclusion.

2. Encourage groups of students to prepare a file of captioned cartoons where the humor depends upon inference, e.g., A man comforting a small boy: "Your mother didn't mean to run over your wagon, and what was it doing in the flower bed in the first place?" Four bridge players: "Reputations conferred in absentia."

3. Most advertisements illustrate inference in two ways. First, the writer from his knowledge of human nature has inferred that the reader wants certain things. Second, he presents what purport to be facts from which he hopes the reader will draw the desired inference. Introduce the problem by discussing with students inferences which could be drawn from sets of facts similar to those that follow.

What is the connection, if any, between the two sets of facts in the advertisement?

"The All-news Weekly is designed for people like *you*." —List of well-known persons who subscribe.

"Everyone wants a beautiful skin." —"Use Glamor Cream like Lita Lovely."

"Knowledge brings success." —Picture of boy and set of encyclopedias.

An investment firm's claim to knowledge of stocks with high growth potential. —Examples of correct predictions made in the past.

"Opportunity no longer knocks." —"It telephones."

"That smiling confidence." —Picture of a woman and child waving to a man entering a plane.

Encourage students to find other examples.

4. Ask each student to analyze one simple event in which he has participated within the last twenty-four hours, and to list the distinct perceptions he was aware of and the inferences drawn from each.

5. In the middle of a class period, allow fifteen minutes for each student to list the perceptions he has made since the class started, stating one inference arising from each. Is there any instance in which a second inference arose from the first? Discussion of such activities should bring out the difficulties in distinguishing between perceptions and the inferences based on them—the almost automatic way an inference occurs.

■ *Investigate basis for beliefs*

1. Ask the student to make two lists of things he thinks he knows; the first should contain information gained by observations and the reasoning based on those observations; the second, information gained from the testimony of others. Which is longer? Which contains more complex items? Such an investigation shows students that most individual information necessarily comes from testimony—the more complex it is, the more it is based not on one fact, or alleged fact, but on a group of facts combined with interpretations of what the facts mean.

2. Ask the student to select two beliefs he holds—one which if proved incorrect, would not matter to him; the other, which would. Ask him to account for the difference. Discussion should emphasize the significance of personal interest in determining beliefs; a wish to believe sometimes influences what is believed.

3. Ask the student to examine the sources of one of his more complex beliefs, and to consider the amount of investigation necessary to establish approximate accuracy of its sources. Does any individual have the time, energy, and means to check all his beliefs? What does such inability signify? Discussion should highlight the significance of the preponderance of *verbal* learning in what the individual looks upon as his store of knowledge, as well as the need for awareness of the inability of language to describe experience completely and accurately.

■ *Consider factors involved in validating beliefs*

1. Divide the class into three groups; each student is to select a simple fact, or alleged fact, that can be easily checked; those in the first group, a fact that can be validated or disproved by observation; those in the second, by experimentation; those in the third, by reference to a record.

Such an assignment should show it is comparatively easy, if resources are available, to check the authenticity of isolated facts.

2. Allow each student to choose a term from a list similar to the following: a football coach, a teacher of science, a farmer, a physicist, a member of Congress, a newspaper reporter, a labor leader, an historian, a president of a large corporation, a movie star. The student, instead of using the general term, substitutes the name of a person he knows, at least by reputation, e.g., not a member of the Senate, but Senator X. Then the student is to determine under what circumstances the individual might be considered an expert witness—that is, in what areas might his training and experience make him *competent* to testify—and under what circumstances he might be considered *biased.*

For instance, Mr. Z., a prominent motion picture producer, might be competent to testify on the problems involved in producing motion pictures; he might be biased in his belief that certain motion pictures were a good way of giving audiences in India an appreciation of American culture.

Besides pointing up the necessity of considering both competency and the possibility of bias in determining the reliability of witnesses, these assignments emphasize the difficulty of validating complex information based on judgments.

3. Ask each student to select circumstances in which he himself might be a competent and unbiased witness, and others in which he would be competent but might be biased. In the discussion stress the importance, in forming conclusions, of considering not only the competency and bias of others but also one's own.

To explore the difficulties of accurate communication

■ *Realize the degree to which experience cannot be communicated*

Give students a jumbled list of statements containing words with referents:

Present and concrete
This is my desk. These apples came from our orchard.
Absent and concrete
My grandfather left me his desk. The caves show unusual natural formations.
Abstract–referring to a way of acting, a manner of behavior, a process
My grandfather was a tyrant. Democracy has many advantages.
Abstract–referring to feelings
Terror gripped me. The pain mounted.

Ask students to number the items in the probable order of increasing difficulty for the communication to have maximum meaning for the recipient. Which require amplification? What form might that amplification take? Which would present the most difficulty in conveying the approximate totality of the speaker's experience? Why?

In the discussion following, these points deserve consideration:

The user of language should be aware that many words have no concrete referent, but refer to a manner of behaving, a process.

The more abstract the language of the total communication, the less effective it is likely to be.

Differences of experience of sender and recipient make support of abstractions by concrete examples necessary.

No matter how great one's control of language, there are areas of experience that are incommunicable; especially is this true of feelings–we can tell the results of our own anger; we can see the effect of pain on others; the feelings themselves can never be satisfactorily communicated.

■ *Through practice cultivate awareness of the problems of communication*

Let students draw slips, each containing a word without concrete referent: hate, love, beauty, pride, wit, cruelty, justice, hunger, odor, cold, courage, cowardice, etc.; use the same word on more than one slip, to allow for comparisons later. Each student is to write a paragraph or two in which he tries to communicate as many facets of the meaning as possible to one unfamiliar with the concept.

The next day place students in groups to listen to the paragraphs and to determine the characteristics of those that communicate most effectively. If sensations or feelings were aroused in the listener, to what extent did his previous experience contribute to them? What stimulus from the writer initiated them?

Follow with class discussion to synthesize the findings of the groups and to point up some of the major difficulties involved in communication. How many stem directly from the characteristics which make language complex?

The teacher should be aware of the interchangeability of the Suggested Learning Experiences among the various areas of English instruction. For instance, *purpose of language*, offered in this chapter as suitable for inclusion in a unit on language as dynamic process, might also be used in other ways: in analyzing and evaluating assembly and television programs, in the study of newspapers and magazines, in analysis of propaganda techniques, in teaching principles of organization for speaking and writing, in evaluating speeches of characters in stories and plays, in teaching appreciation of an author's writing technique. Such interchange allows students to see the learning in the English class not as a collection of unrelated segments but as an integrated process.

Evaluating Growth

As a basis for evaluating, the English teacher may use tests which help the student determine whether he has learned the necessary facts, whether he is able to apply them, whether the knowledge and understanding function in practice. Illustrations of each of these tests as they pertain to language as dynamic process will be given.

Evaluating knowledge The close relationship between learning and evaluation indicates that many of the activities described as Suggested Learning Experiences may be used both for teaching and for estimating progress; e.g., a list of statements suitable for controlling sentences expressing specific purpose (p. 59) may be used in teaching and a similar list employed in checking recognition after the principle has been taught. Hemingway's story "A Day's Wait" (see p. 51) can serve as a test to determine whether students recognize the significance of the personal quality of language, the characteristic having been previously presented with the help of the film "Do Words Ever Fool You?" and other activities described in the same section (p. 52 ff.). Thus, each succeeding item in a series taught in developing any idea may serve both to deepen insight concerning the concept and to evaluate progress made.

Tests of recognition using the same examples and the same language employed in instruction assess nothing more than memory and usually should be avoided. Such a question might be, Name four general purposes for which language is used in daily life. Recognition tests demanding the *use* of memory with at least a slight amount of reasoning provide a better basis for determining how well the necessary facts have been learned. The teacher may devise a test similar to the following to help the student evaluate how quickly and surely he senses the relationship between specific and general purposes.

Relationship between specific and general purpose

The column on the right contains a list of specific purposes for which language might be used. In the parentheses before each, place the number of the general purpose it illustrates.

1. To maintain rapport	(2) To explain a play in football
2. To inform	(1) To make a stranger feel welcome
3. To convince	(4) To get my friend to go to the show
4. To persuade	(2) To give directions for reaching the school
	(3) To prove I had a good reason for absence
	(1) To draw a shy student into the discussion
	(4) To get my mother to buy me a dress
	(Etc.)

Evaluating understanding A test requiring the student to apply a principle to an unfamiliar situation is standard procedure in helping him determine whether he understands the implications of any concept. The following writing assignment tests not only knowledge of specific and general purpose in the use of language but understanding of the relationship between purpose and the motives of speaker and listener:

> Select an occasion when someone tried to persuade you to do something you did not wish to do. Analyze the motives of the speaker as you interpreted them and your own for finally agreeing or refusing. Analyze the appeals used. Can you give reasons why the speaker thought they might be successful? Can you think of others that might have been more persuasive? Why? Looking back on the experience, how accurately do you think you judged it at the time?

This difficult assignment assumes considerable study of motives and purpose; it will show the student and the teacher how effective both the learning and the teaching have been.

Evaluating performance The ultimate goal of English instruction is skillful performance which makes use of the knowledge and understandings gained—changes in attitudes and behavior which extend beyond the classroom. Obviously the individual's approach to this goal cannot be evaluated accurately. Performance can be tested fragmentarily, usually when the student's attention has been directed toward specific ideas and skills; results of these show what he can do when he tries. His typical behavior cannot be so easily assessed. Here self and peer appraisal supplements the teacher's observation. Although never completely objective, all three are important. Self-evaluation, stressed throughout this text, forces the student to consider his own behavior, his typical reaction under most circumstances; it gives him practice in applying the form of assessment he will utilize most consistently all his life.

In all areas of English instruction, the teacher can observe whether the student is beginning to form desirable habits based upon understandings of language as process:

In the incidental teaching when attention is focused on the skills of reading, listening, writing, or speaking, does the student notice the emotional tone of words? Is he alert to the effectiveness of metaphorical language? Does he discriminate between fact and judgment? (Substitute any principles illustrated by the immediate language.)

Do the number and variety of the examples the student, on his own initiative, finds for the bulletin board indicate he is cultivating awareness of the way language works?

Occasional self-checks on performance help students realize the importance of remaining alert to the dynamic qualities of language. Items for two such lists are suggested below. The first is appropriate for intermediate stages of instruction; the second has been used with mature students who have had considerable experience in studying language as process. Unless used for diagnosis, such checklists should, of course, contain only concepts being developed with a class.

Reactions to communications

Underline the response that most accurately describes your habitual reactions. This check is not to secure evidence for grading, but to help you probe your thinking; the reasons are more important than the categorical answers.

Am I more likely

To agree with statements of a person I like rather than with those of one I dislike?	*Yes*	*No*	*Sometimes*
Reason: ______________________			
To be wary of factual statements rather than of judgments?			
Reason: ______________________			
To doubt ideas I want to believe rather than those I do not want to believe?			
Reason: ______________________			

Reactions to implications of the dynamic quality of language

In answering the following questions, write the numeral corresponding to the response which most accurately describes your habitual performance. In the parentheses place (1) always, (2) usually, (3) sometimes, (4) never.

When I use language either as sender or receiver, do I try

1. ( ) To determine the user's purpose?
2. ( ) To notice the appeals used?
3. ( ) To detect the feeling suggested?
4. ( ) To consider the possible sources of the information?

. . .

13. ( ) To compare alleged facts with others I believe to be valid?
14. ( ) To check the internal consistency of the language?
15. ( ) To consider, in determining the accuracy of the communication, the possible bias of sender and receiver?

Increased skill in evaluating his own use of language—logical and imaginative—should enable the student to become more effective in both his thinking and his communication. Underlying the effectiveness of both is awareness of the dynamics of language as process.

SELECTED READINGS

Ruth Nanda Anshen, ed., *Language: An Enquiry into its Meaning and Function* (Science of Culture Series). N.Y., Harper, 1957. This book, each chapter written by a specialist in his field, develops understandings significant for the English teacher.

Roger Brown, *Words and Things.* Glencoe, Ill., Free Press, 1958. A discussion relating language and the psychological principles of human behavior.

John Ciardi, *How Does a Poem Mean?* Boston, Houghton Mifflin, 1959. (Also published as Part III of Herbert Barrows, Herbert Heffner, John Ciardi, and Douglas Wallace, *An Introduction to Literature,* Boston, Houghton Mifflin, 1959.) Invaluable for the teacher of poetry, this book is mentioned here for what it has to say about language. See especially the section entitled "The Words of Poetry."

Lee Deighton, "The Survival of the English Teacher," *ETC,* Vol. 10, No. 2 (Winter, 1953).

Wilfred Funk, *Word Origins and Their Romantic Stories.* N.Y., Grosset & Dunlap, 1954. Interesting examples suitable for classroom use.

Doris B. Garey, *Putting Words in Their Places.* Chicago, Scott, Foresman, 1957. An explanation of the way language works, with exercises designed for use with first year college classes.

H. L. Mencken, *The American Language,* 4th ed. N.Y., Knopf, 1946.

Catherine Minteer, *Words and What They Do to You.* Evanston, Ill., Row, Peterson, 1953. Specific lessons for teaching basic understandings concerning general semantics to junior and senior high school students.

Mario Pei, *The Story of Language.* N.Y., Lippincott, 1949. A readable account of basic information about language—its development, structure, and social function.

Edward Sapir, *Culture, Language, and Personality.* Ed. by David G. Mandelbaum. Berkeley and Los Angeles, U. of Calif. Press, 1958. A scholarly presentation stressing the implications of language as a cultural and social product.

Chapter Two

Logical Thinking

It cannot be said too often that no one can give the learner his concepts. If he is to have them at all he must construct them out of his own experiences.
—BROWNELL AND HENDRICKSON [1]

PERSPECTIVE

Students need help in learning the steps and skills involved in logical thinking and the ways to use reason in disciplining emotion. Unchecked and unevaluated emotional responses offer no reliable guide for behavior. Research, as well as experience, has demonstrated that the planned study of methods of reasoning clearly contributes to the ability to make sound judgments and form intelligent conclusions.[2] Increasingly the findings of research in perception and social psychology seem to demonstrate that the way in which an individual thinks determines in some measure what he thinks and how he acts. Such relationships have been observed both in the behavior of individuals who lean toward rigid, authoritarian patterns and in that of those who are far more flexible.

This chapter is concerned with the structure and methods of rational and orderly thought processes in relation to the dynamics of language considered in the preceding chapter. The unique role of emotion and feeling in imaginative thinking is presented next. Together, the three chapters discuss the basic framework which underlies the use of language and is thus fundamental to all phases of the total English program.

Whether we can actually distinguish separate processes in the thinking of individuals, or whether these are intricately interrelated and an inseparable

[1] W. A. Brownell and Gordon Hendrickson, "How Children Learn Information, Concepts, and Generalizations," in G. Lester Anderson, ed., Forty-Ninth Yearbook, National Society for the Study of Education, Part 1, *Learning and Instruction* (Chicago, U. of Chicago Press, 1950), p. 112.

[2] For example, as one indication of the effectiveness of direct study, Lyman reported that twelfth grade students who received detailed instruction in reasoning during the eleventh year were clearly superior in detecting sound and unsound arguments to those who received no instruction. R. H. Lyman, "How High School Seniors Explain Common Errors in Reasoning," *English Journal,* Vol. 12, No. 5 (May 1923), pp. 293-305.

part of the totality of the person, is a problem about which researchers are not yet in agreement.[3] For the purposes of planning instruction, however, teachers find classifications to be helpful. Categorization of thinking processes, even if somewhat arbitrary, aids in considering the basic problems involved in improving thinking. This chapter discusses three kinds of thinking important in English—concept formation, problem solving, and judgment making. Imaginative thinking, a fourth type, will be dealt with in the next chapter.

Concept formation [4]

We begin to organize facts as soon as we perceive them. We sort and sift basic information, bringing order to a multitude of impressions, observations, and associations. An adolescent's first impression of a large high school is vague and generalized as he considers three floors, one hundred rooms, and a few distinguishing characteristics. Later he begins to identify separate impressions—the office suites, the industrial arts center, the English department, the areas reserved for recreation. His general impression is gradually refined as he classifies his observations. In similar ways, each of us develops concepts by differentiating and integrating ideas and impressions. To understand the role of the teacher in helping students to organize and evaluate their ideas, we must understand how concepts develop; how such forces as bias, selectivity, and emotion affect the process; and how both inductive and deductive methods may be used in the classroom.

UNDERSTANDING HOW CONCEPTS DEVELOP

To understand his role in guiding the formulation of concepts, the teacher must understand that they develop through a gradual and sequential process which varies with person and situation. This is not to say that concepts are developed through any fixed, logical series of steps which can be presented to students as a formula for logical thinking. The process is complex and subject to much variation; yet always it tends in the same direction—from the specific to the general, from hunches evolved out of similarities in past experience to generalizations which prove useful in assimilating impressions obtained in future experience.

Thus we evolve a conception of "beagle" based on observation at several kennels, e.g., a hound colored brown and white, low-slung body, height no

[3] W. E. Vinacke, in *The Psychology of Thinking* (N.Y., McGraw-Hill, 1952), leans toward the interrelated approach. David H. Russell, in *Children's Thinking* (Boston, Ginn, 1956), offers a typology. For an interesting discussion of the research on this problem, see E. Elona Sochor, "The Nature of Critical Reading," *Elementary English*, Vol. 41, No. 1 (January 1959), pp. 47-58.

[4] The terms "concept" and "generalization" are used synonomously here to designate abstract ideas which express relationships between relatively concrete objects. Some writers attempt to differentiate between concepts, generalizations, laws, principles, and rules. Little uniformity is observable in the use of these terms in psychology and education, and such distinctions seem unnecessary for our purposes here.

greater than thirteen inches. The concept assists us in identifying other dogs as beagles, but it is subject to further modification. Unless we stand ready to extend or refine our concepts, we are prone to hasty generalization and possible oversimplification. For example, our conception of the beagle must be modified when we first meet the long-legged, fifteen-inch representative of the field strain. The forming of concepts thus involves a continual grouping and regrouping of one's ideas—a reorganization influenced not only by new facts and new experiences but by our ingenuity and imagination in seeing new relationships. Each of us must recognize that his concepts, based on fairly restricted experience, are thus subject to limitation; since more complete information may force modification, never can we say we know everything about anything.

For children in school, planned learning of certain concepts may extend over several years, as crude undifferentiated initial responses become gradually more refined and full of meaning. Thus a seventh-grader's relatively simple conception of a paragraph as a loosely related group of sentences becomes modified throughout his years of instruction in English as he reads and analyzes many paragraphs, discovers a method of organization within each paragraph, and considers the relationship of the paragraph to the over-all organization of the essay or theme. Undoubtedly, the ultimate development of such understanding will vary with the abilities, experiences, and motivations of the learner, and with the nature of his instruction. In general, the basic role of the teacher at any level is to encourage students to formulate their own generalizations rather than to present the final generalization as an empty verbalization to be memorized. In attempting to develop concepts, the teacher bears in mind three important considerations: the impact of prior experiences, the gradual nature of conceptual growth, and the need for selectivity in identifying concepts to be taught.

Impact of prior experience An extensive background of experiences serves as the basis on which generalizations are built. Some students are fortunate enough to have had many broadening opportunities—travel, reading, observation of many dimensions of life. Less privileged youngsters have only the most meager backgrounds on which to draw. For such children, often those from low socio-economic environment, the teacher continually struggles to develop a basic background for understanding. Carefully planned experiences, both real and vicarious, directly related to the ideas being discussed, will facilitate the formulation of concepts. Motion pictures, recordings, excursions, and reading offer possible approaches. For example, during a unit on "Dimensions of Justice," one eleventh grade class read and discussed the conflict of human and legal justice in *Les Misérables,* analyzed the effects of just and unjust action in a film, *Due Process of Law Denied,* and observed the administration of justice in courtrooms of the local community. Out of perceptions gained through such varied activity students usually develop more mature understandings of the problems involved in humane interpretation of law than do those whose experiences are confined to reading and discussion alone.

Gradual nature of conceptual growth Concepts develop gradually and are learned through a variety of ways. Rarely will students achieve complete grasp of an abstract idea without thinking through the concept slowly and completely. Planning many varied, rather than repetitive, classroom experiences tends to deepen understanding. Even ideas which seem to emerge from a moment of insight or illumination have almost always been preceded by a period of mulling over or conscious study. In developing important generalizations, most students profit from repeated opportunities to think ideas through in different situations. For example, in attempting to increase understanding of the complete sentence, some teachers introduce several brief activities—analysis of student errors in writing, practice in rewriting sentences, oral and written drills. Continued emphasis on the same basic principle through different types of experience tends to be more effective than either repeating a similar type of exercise or extending the length of a single activity.[5] The interrelationship of purpose, drill, and economy of learning leads teachers away from lengthy, mechanistic drill periods which deaden the student's zest for learning, and toward briefer and more frequent drills and experiences with clearly defined purposes.

Selectivity of the learner Selectivity is important in identifying concepts for emphasis. Children learn thousands of ideas, in school and out. Recognition that every concept cannot be taught demands the selection of a few for emphasis. For example, in a single work of literature, such as *Julius Caesar,* the teacher emphasizes a few of the major themes or ideas rather than all those possible, letting the basic purposes of instruction control the selection. In most studies of *Julius Caesar,* for example, understanding Brutus' personal dilemma is more important than acquiring general ideas about the power struggle in ancient Rome.

Thus, in guiding conceptual development, the teacher needs to select the ideas for emphasis, to organize classroom experience which will support the development of understanding, and to plan for a gradual, thorough development of each important concept.

Organizing discussion to develop concepts Often teachers wish to structure learning situations sufficiently to encourage the development of a particular idea. In teaching *Johnny Tremain,* for example, a teacher will encourage young readers to view the novel in part as an expression of an adolescent boy's experiences in developing maturity in judgment. Insight into Johnny's development as a person will occur only if the reader considers the nature of the boy at different moments in the story, and the forces which bring about changes in his outlook and behavior. A teacher who encourages students to

[5] See Percival Symonds, "Practice versus Grammar in the Learning of Correct Usage," *Journal of Educational Psychology,* Vol. 22, No. 2 (February 1931), pp. 81-95.

construct their own generalizations can provide basic guidance through a sequence of discussion questions. The first phase of the discussion may be limited to a consideration of the narrative, since readers must understand *what* happens in a novel before they consider *how* and *why* things happen. Once basic understandings are clarified, the teacher encourages some *tentative* interpretations of the meaning of events. Ultimately he asks students to detect relationships between various passages. Thus, through a carefully planned series of thinking tasks, the student's understanding of the novel is deepened and extended. The various levels of analysis of a novel are suggested in the accompanying chart.[6]

A pattern such as that presented in the chart would develop gradually

The development of concepts through discussion
Sample Topic: The behavior of Johnny Tremain

Level 1 Grasping the narrative *Basic Question:* What happened?	**Level 2 Interpreting the facts** *Basic Questions:* What does this mean? How and why did it happen?
Sample incidents	
EARLY INCIDENTS:	
Johnny displays scorn and sarcasm in his treatment of Dove and Dusty at the silversmith's shop.	Johnny's actions reveal pride, a sense of superiority, and a lack of tolerance for those who try hard but are limited in ability.
LATER INCIDENTS:	
Through friendship with Rab, Johnny learns to think before speaking ("to count ten").	Johnny is learning to be patient and tolerant, and is developing some conception of the feelings of other people.
Johnny gives Cilla time to apologize when she soaks him with water.	
CONCLUDING INCIDENTS:	
He reacts negatively to the rigid rank-and-file relationship between the British officer and the private.	
Johnny is so worried about Rab, Cilla, and the cause of freedom, that the discovery of his own birthright leaves him unmoved.	Johnny Tremain forgets himself in his concern for other people.

Level 3 Generalizing about the whole

Basic Question: If the interpretation of incidents is valid, what does this reveal about the purpose of the entire novel?

Student-formulated generalization: Johnny Tremain is a book which reveals how a selfish, arrogant boy learns consideration of other people.

[6] For a further discussion of methods to use in structured discussions, see "Oral Language," pp. 424-84.

over several related discussion periods rather than during any single hour. Continually, the teacher would assist students in gathering, organizing, and relating facts. Although the amount of class time spent discussing the narrative would vary with the abilities of the students and the difficulty of the material, in each class some opportunity should be provided for such processes of interpretation and generalization.

STUDYING THE RELIABILITY OF OUR IMPRESSIONS

The sources of our concepts require continual classroom study. How we react depends upon what we perceive as truth; since no two persons perceive a situation in exactly the same way, no two will have exactly the same reaction. In constructing concepts, we select and organize our impressions in terms of a point of view which depends largely on our earlier experiences and on our purposes at the moment. Difficulties frequently result when ideas or action are based upon incomplete or misinterpreted evidence. No information is so persistent and compelling as that obtained first hand; yet even personal experience offers no guarantee of truth. Students who understand the following three concepts will recognize the necessity for weighing impressions carefully: Purpose controls selectivity of observations; bias may color interpretation; recall may involve sharpening and leveling.

Purpose controls selectivity of observations The orientation of any individual affects what he selects as significant. Men with differing values rarely look at objects in similar ways. In his history of art, André Malraux observes that each succeeding culture has placed new interpretations on the beauties of primitive art, and comments, "We prefer Lagash Statues without their heads, and Khmer Buddhas without their bodies, and Assyrian wild animals isolated from their contexts. Accidents impair and Time transforms, but it is we who choose." [7]

Just as cultures vary, so do individuals. A motion picture is viewed differently by a critic, a member of the audience, and an actor appearing in the film. The three reactions may be illustrated by such statements as "The mood is sustained," "The film left me breathless," and "I was better in *Trilby*." An individual attempting to base a judgment on one of these comments must understand the peculiar orientation of the speaker. The critic's analysis would excite those who value thoughtfully executed films; the viewer's, those who wish a "breathless" experience; quite possibly the actor's might discourage attendance.

By considering the diverse motivations of individuals, we can teach how purposes influence perception. Illustrations are found in every school. A series of meetings devoted to problems of student government may seem uninteresting to one student but significant to another who has responsibilities in school affairs. In deciding whether to attend, a third student (if seeking guidance from either) needs to consider possible purposes underlying such

[7] André Malraux, *The Voices of Silence* (Garden City, N.Y., Doubleday, 1953), p. 67.

points of view. Similarly, students will react positively or negatively to the rebellious behavior of leather-jacketed ruffians depending upon whether the incident threatens or supports their previous point of view toward such gangs. Purpose leads individuals to interpret impressions differently. A strong desire to see a flying saucer or a celebrated sea serpent may well lead one observer to attach significance to phenomena which would be overlooked by another. Teachers find many opportunities for introducing a discussion of selectivity in perception.[8]

Bias may color interpretation Almost all of us claim to recognize the insidious effect of prejudice in shaping the views of other people. Fewer of us allow for the operation of such affective influences in our own thinking. During the past two decades, the noteworthy and determined efforts of many individuals and groups within and without the schools have resulted in heightening our awareness of the ways in which prejudices influence thought and action. Some intellectual understanding of the effects of prejudice is probably a necessary prelude to the improvement of individual thinking; it does not insure, however, that the individual will be alert to controlling his own emotional biases. Although the efforts to destroy false concepts and stereotypes which tend to erect barriers between various social groups is essential, this work must be supported by preparing students to handle the effects of emotional bias in less inclusive, everyday situations.

Students seldom recognize that every strong loyalty or attitude may operate as a prejudice capable of blocking clear thinking. Some loyalties are important and necessary for social human beings—loyalty to family, to friends, to country. These are a cohesive force, binding individuals together for the common good and serving a necessary and important function. Deep feeling surrounds every basic loyalty, however, and deep feeling sometimes creates a bias which prevents a person from thinking objectively. An active participant in a social club does not bring the same understanding to a school directive limiting the activities of the club as does a student who is not a member. Either one may be biased. Adolescents who are themselves unskilled in social amenities may be keenly sensitive to the feelings of such literary characters as Stephen, the ungainly protagonist of "Clodhopper." The result of such deep involvement is worthwhile if it enables the reader to understand a character more fully. If not balanced by rational consideration of all observable factors, however, such emotional involvement may result in misinterpretation. Some adolescents identify so completely with the boy that they do not attempt to understand the attitudes of those who surround him. Continual study of the dimensions of emotional bias is necessary to prepare students to handle emotionally charged issues.

Recall may involve sharpening and leveling The further a report is removed from the time of occurrence, the greater the possibility of distor-

[8] A number are suggested in Chapter 1, "Language as Dynamic Process."

tion. We remember more accurately our actions of yesterday than those of a month ago. Our natural tendency to forget details is only one facet of a problem which involves shifts in emphasis and changes in point of view. Most of us have had the experience of relating the same incident on repeated occasions. Perhaps we describe a visit to Disneyland. Our first presentation may be colored with detail—a twenty-minute gem. Later we find we can compress the report without losing effectiveness. We condense; we eliminate; we drop details which no longer seem important. After repeated presentations we find we can present the "same" information in less than ten minutes. Actually we have not presented the same ideas at all. Many changes are consciously made; others, unintentionally. In reconsidering a particular event, we tend to modify our perspective. Minor observations may be sharpened to major proportions; others may be leveled. These tendencies, differing among individuals and not necessarily undesirable in their effect, are encouraged by the responses of listeners. A passing comment on the cleanliness of Disneyland which interests one group may on subsequent occasions be restructured as a major conclusion to capitalize on its audience appeal; a telling observation on the characteristics of the park's patrons may be de-emphasized or eliminated if it fails to arouse comment. Sometimes we so modify our views that we completely shift our focus.

Understanding some possible effects of sharpening and leveling helps students evaluate the comments of others. Occasionally a segment of a complete event may be so overemphasized as to distort the entire perspective. Thus an individual emotionally disturbed by the questionable refereeing of a crucial play in a football game may in time recall little about the game except "sloppy officiating," even though only one of forty decisions is questioned. Occasionally, rumors are unintentionally created, as when careless words seem to convey the unjustified impression of a causal relationship between an industrial accident and the presence nearby of a group of laborers or businessmen. Students should be encouraged to exercise particular care in evaluating reports which may be harmful to other individuals and groups. Occasional class activities focused on the effects of sharpening and leveling may awaken students to the problem.

Sound concepts are based on accurate information. A first step in improving accuracy is to lead students to examine the reliability of their own perceptions and the perceptions of their friends.

STUDYING THE WAYS OF REASONING

Beyond guiding the formation of students' concepts and providing for the study of the reliability of sources, the teacher has an obligation to provide for the study of the processes through which concepts are formed. In most secondary classes, such an approach calls less for a disciplined analysis of the principles of logic than for careful attention to crucial problems involved in using deductive and inductive processes of reasoning.

Inductive and deductive thinking Thus far the emphasis in this chapter has been on inductive thinking—the formulation of concepts or generalizations based on many examples or facts. Beginning at a concrete level, this approach minimizes the danger of verbalization—the rote acceptance of abstract ideas without an understanding of their basic meanings. Most students will assimilate generalizations developed from many examples.

Deductive reasoning—the application of concepts to specific facts and situations—is a process which becomes increasingly important as we mature and extend our experiences. Much of our knowledge is acquired deductively as we apply learned concepts to new situations; for example, we assume we understand the difficulties involved in providing shelter in Antarctic regions because of our prior reading and our personal experience with problems resulting from snow and ice in other situations. Much learning in our classrooms is of this nature. The use of teaching procedures which encourage students to apply ideas tends to be less time consuming than building concepts inductively, but is perhaps less vivid and less thorough.

Sustained thinking is neither purely deductive nor purely inductive but involves a combination of the two approaches. In searching for the answers to a single problem, we almost always shift back and forth. At the same moment that we identify the theme of a short story through inductively relating key episodes, we also test the validity of concepts deductively against our own perception of truth. Seldom do we use one or the other exclusively. Teachers rely on both approaches in the classroom. They aid students in evolving concepts and then encourage students to apply them. The maturity of the learner and the nature of the learning task determine the approach. Many understandings may be taught in either way, as in the following example:

Desired student understanding: Newspapers differ in their treatment of news, in their degree of objectivity, in the extent of their coverage.

Deductive approach

The class discusses an article which asserts that newspapers vary considerably in the treatment of news. The article may be read by the teacher or assigned to be read in a textbook. Following the discussion students decide to find illustrations of generalizations which have been discussed. Several representative newspapers are brought to class and compared.

Inductive approach

Front pages of many different newspapers for a single date are examined by the students in class. During the discussion period which follows, the students compare observations and develop tentative generalizations regarding the similarities and differences.

Because generalizing from specific instances can lead to dangerous simplification, the teacher gives students a home assignment to analyze more than one newspaper in the light of generalizations developed by the total class. Thus students are encouraged to test and further modify their observations.

Regardless of which method is introduced, genuine learning will result only if students do the reasoning. No one can do this for them. The teacher's role is to guide and assist the process. One of the important ways in which the teacher can be of assistance is to help students recognize and avoid faulty and misleading thought processes which prevent the development of sound concepts. In secondary classrooms, instruction may well be concerned with three recurring flaws: oversimplifying, avoiding issues, and assuming false relationships.

Oversimplifying The searching analysis of fact—the heart of sound reasoning—does not come easily. In our impatience for answers we sometimes accept quick and easy generalizations as carefully substantiated conclusions, even when a thorough examination of available evidence would lead us to modify our thinking. This is one mistake which Bernard Shaw's Henry Higgins made in regard to Eliza Doolittle. His initial assumption that the mere acquisition of upper-class manners and mores will be sufficient to make Eliza happy overlooks both her personal feelings and her future position in society. To help students avoid conclusions based on incomplete data and recognize these errors in the reasoning of others, we may focus on three common forms of oversimplification—the sweeping generalization, the "either-or" fallacy, and the substitution of formula statements for genuine products of thought.

Sweeping generalizations occur when individuals attempt to reason on the basis of inadequate data. Obviously such statements as "Children are no longer being taught to read" and "Teen-agers are wild drivers" involve overstatement of the facts. Such observations tend to be reported by individuals who advance conclusions after considering one or two cases. By failing to qualify such generalizations, a speaker or writer applies his conclusions to "all children" or "all teen-agers." Possibly he does so because he is not conversant with all of the facts; he may mislead himself as well as the persons with whom he is attempting to communicate. Seldom, indeed, may such inclusive observations be applied to all members of a group. Students need to learn that general statements of this type often correspond to truth only when modified by such terms as *some, many, few,* or *sometimes.* Unqualified statements which seem to have universal application should be examined critically.

The *either-or fallacy* in thinking occurs when an individual reduces to a clear-cut dichotomy an argument which will admit other possibilities. For example, the statement "Either Bob or Mary is right" is sound reasoning only if we have examined and discarded the possibility that both may be right or both wrong, or that there are other alternatives. We must particularly guard against reducing to extremes our consideration of a problem which involves many points of view. The reference to "both sides of the question" is rapidly becoming recognized as a signal heralding the possibility that an oversimplified presentation will be introduced.

Formula explanations—clichés and stereotypes—are pat judgments and conclusions. They hamper sound reasoning when individuals apply them to particular situations without thinking through the available evidence. Often they are evoked by superficial similarities between the immediate problem and the commonly accepted explanation. Here again the thinker attempts to generalize on the basis of inadequate data. Dubious behavior by the son of a disreputable father dismissed with the pronouncement, "Like father, like son"; a child's delinquency interpreted as being the result of an unhappy home, with no further attempt to examine the situation for other explanations; an "emotional block" offered to explain failure in spelling—such explanations are *sometimes* adequate but certainly not always. To immature minds such concepts seem the more acceptable because they are familiar.

Oversimplification is common in the thinking of immature persons. Students should not be reprimanded for each sweeping generalization, either-or fallacy, or stereotyped argument; rather they should be led to examine the complexity of each problem and the reasons why their thinking was faulty.

Avoiding the problem Individuals utilize many ways of evading direct consideration of specific issues. A speaker or writer who wishes to avoid committing himself may evade answering by commenting on the nature of the problem rather than the issue itself, e.g., "It's a serious situation" or "It's a very difficult problem." A pupil who neglects to submit a theme may claim that the assignment is of no value because "it's all mixed up." Sincere or not, such a student offers no real support for his argument, but simply restates his opinion in different words. In attempting to overcome any tendency to avoid issues, high school students may well concentrate on three recurring fallacies —begging the question, arguing by personalities, and responding only to exaggerated extensions of an argument.

Begging the question occurs whenever a speaker or writer assumes a conclusion which requires proof. The statement of the student mentioned above is no less a case of question-begging than such obvious reliance on unproved assumptions as "Everyone of course agrees that . . ." and "No one who has studied the problem would doubt that . . ." A special form of question-begging is circular reasoning, in which two statements are used reciprocally to prove each other; for instance: "The boys at South High are near-delinquents; you know they must be trouble makers because they go to that terrible school." "Mary is unpopular because she goes to so few dances; she doesn't go out much because she knows she isn't liked." "John has difficulty in schoolwork because he's a behavior problem; he wouldn't act up so much in class if he were really able to learn." Circular reasoning, like other forms of question-begging, is a way of avoiding the central issue.

Basing argumentation on personalities or on personal qualifications rather than on fact is a familiar occurrence in school discussion. The boy who says that he is voting for Pearl because he "can't stand" Adele, her opponent, is merely circumventing any real consideration of the factors which give rise to his decision. Similarly, when John, told by Mary that he could improve his oral report if he would speak from notes rather than a complete manuscript, replies, "You did that yourself," or "Practice what you preach," he is responding in terms of personalities rather than of ideas. Similar illustrations may be observed in many classroom discussions.

Extending and exaggerating are more difficult to eliminate than the other fallacies discussed here because students do not easily recognize gross misinterpretation as a way of avoiding a problem. For example, as a suggestion for increasing participation in extracurricular activities, a student suggests lowering the cost of admission to athletic events. Rather than consider the proposal fully, an opponent of the idea responds, "In other words you want to give tickets away." Clearly the second speaker's purpose is to represent the idea as extreme and unworthy of consideration. "From the way you talked one would think . . ." and "If you carried that line of reasoning to its conclusion, . . ." are other phrases which sometimes introduce attempts to evade objective consideration by extending a statement to a point which is untenable.

Directness and forthrightness in considering ideas reflect an individual's sense of responsibility in communication; on the other hand, evasiveness characterizes an immature thinker who avoids the disciplined analysis of issues. Many adolescents employ question-begging, argumentation in terms of personalities, and exaggeration and extension without recognizing the dangers inherent in such fallacious reasoning. Precisely for these reasons teachers plan experiences which direct students' attention to these barriers to sound conclusions.

Assuming false relationships Questionable generalizations will sometimes result when individuals assume relationships without thoroughly examining the data. Consider the following:

A. Because this is the author's latest book, it is his best.
B. Because John plays baseball, he's a good sport.
C. Because two subjects are equally difficult, they are of equal importance to the learner.

Statement A is based on an assumed causal relationship between the writing experience of an author and the quality of his work, an assumption which does not always correspond with known facts. Statement B tends to equate sportsmanship with participation in a single sport—certainly a conception based on inadequate evidence. Statement C assumes that two objects which are similar in one respect remain similar in others—a fallacious assumption of the kind we must guard against particularly in reasoning by analogy. The thinking which produces such generalizations results from a failure to identify and examine all dimensions of the relationships involved. Having noted certain connections between objects or events, we often suspect the existence of a particular relationship. Sound thinkers conceive of such inferences as hypotheses requiring verification rather than as proved generalizations. Students need to learn to reason with discrimination and care, suspending final judgment until all the evidence has been examined, organized, and evaluated.

Since unreliable and misleading methods of thinking result only in spurious conclusions, an important step in improving the student's ability to form sound judgments is to help him examine his present thinking—the reliability both of his impressions and of his methods of thought. Such examination, particularly if it occurs more or less continuously throughout the secondary school years, will heighten the student's awareness of the need to refine thought processes.

PERCEIVING THE CRUCIALITY OF RELATIONSHIPS

Basic in all learning is the ability to relate ideas; such ability is of particular significance in the English class, where students sometimes have difficulty in linking the verbal learning of the classroom to the experiences of outside life. The perception of relationships—involved in both induction and deduction—is essential if the student is to see the bearing that concepts developed in the English class may have to personal behavior.

Some students see little value in poetry. Others wonder why they must read about "all the dead people" in *Julius Caesar.* Some find *Our Town* to be "hopelessly dated." Readers will react to literature in this manner when they see little connection between the book and the experience of life itself. Unless they do perceive an essential relationship between the two, literature becomes for them a study apart from experience—an unimportant exercise, a time-filler easily forgotten. The problem of improving students' ability to relate their vicarious experiences in literature to the real experiences of life is an important aspect of our over-all program for encouraging individuals to examine all available data.

As it is with literature, so it is with other aspects of the English program. Ninth-graders may see no connection between propaganda techniques in examples presented for analysis by the teacher and the "big sell" used by advertisers on their favorite disc-jockey radio program. Seventh grade students may need help in perceiving the relationship between a class discussion on the reasons why people have hobbies and their own interest in collecting stamps or mounting botanical specimens. Such generalizations are the durable factor in learning; students must be helped to organize their experiences and to see the relationship between the activities of the classroom and the world outside.

The most important general method of helping students organize their experiences is the unit approach in planning instruction. A unit is a sequence of related classroom activities, organized around a central core of content and extended over a period of time. Suggestions for this type of planning are presented in "Program and Plan," and several illustrative units are included at the ends of the various sections of this volume. In any unit, the reading, writing, and oral activities are organized for a unified impact on the student, and each new experience is developed from work previously introduced. For example, seventh grade students studying "Animals and Pets" follow the reading of *Stickeen* with a discussion of their own pets, with reports on such related books as *Red Horse Hill, Silver Chief,* and *King of the Wind,* and with brief paragraphs describing animals. Thus the students are continually asked to sift their multiple impressions of class activities in terms of the unifying topic. They are forced to compare and contrast, to relate new ideas to those which are already known, and to apply the ideas in writing and discussion. The learner gains breadth and depth of understanding, as well as experience in perceiving relationships. Eleventh grade students consolidate these gains on a more advanced level in such a unit as "The American Imagination."

Students will form concepts of some type, with or without guidance from others. By helping them with the processes involved in this type of thinking, the teacher is more likely to find the emerging generalizations to be sound, logical, and grounded in fact.

Problem solving

Problem solving is a special form of logical thinking which individuals use in attempting to overcome an obstacle in the way of a definite objective. It is the specificity of the direction, rather than the processes themselves, that distinguishes problem solving from concept forming. This kind of thinking aims at achieving a particular goal. Confronted with a problem which demands consideration, we direct our energies to the achievement of a reasonable solution. Whether it is a question of determining action or developing a theoretical understanding, we engage in a sequence of thinking activities which lead us from an identification of the task to what seems a satisfactory solution. Thus many of the processes of reasoning discussed previously in this chapter are used in problem solving.

Using a general guide Many attempts have been made to define the "steps" involved in problem solving. Sometimes these are called the "scientific method," although it has been written that the scientific method is something talked about by people on the outside wondering how the scientist does it.[9] Generally these simplified descriptions of the process include such stages as the following:

Identifying the problem or goal as distinct from the procedures and methods to be used
Exploring the problem
Formulating possible solutions or methods of achieving solutions
Predicting probable results of alternate methods of action

[9] P. W. Bridgman, on "Scientific Method," *Teaching Scientist* (December 1949), p. 23.

Evaluating the proposed solution by analysis, experimentation, and consideration of implications

Concluding with respect to the validity of solution

This list offers little more than a hypothesis regarding what may take place as individuals reach solutions to problems. The description of formal steps is not necessarily accurate. Perhaps it is better applied after a solution is achieved as a recapitulation of what has happened, than used as a prescriptive guide to be followed during the process. Certainly many of us exhibit patterns of thinking which are less orderly and sequential. As Russell points out in an extended analysis of problem solving, such descriptions present methods more often used by disciplined adults than by immature adolescents.[10] The steps offer a general guide, not a rigid, precut pattern which can be imposed on students.

Fostering desired patterns of behavior Throughout the years of schooling, we aid students in solving their present problems and prepare them for facing those they will meet in adult society. The two responsibilities cannot be separated. Students must learn to deal with the problems of the present if they are to acquire the self-confidence and the methods of reasoning needed for attacking problems later. Fear of failure and similar emotional factors frequently interfere with these processes. Most teachers can supply from their own experience illustrations of the ways in which anxiety affects the performance of individuals in speaking situations or in examinations. By providing successful experiences in problem solving in the classroom, we encourage growth of confidence and proficiency in the skills necessary for the successful formulation of solutions.

In the English classroom, the tasks which face students may either involve action (discovering how to locate a library book) or understanding (discovering why "The Fall of the House of Usher" has such a frightening impact when one first reads it). Whether either kind of task emerges as a problem to students or as a way of solving problems depends on the nature of the learning situation. The teacher organizes instruction so that the student will acquire or modify his behavior, but the pupil learns this behavior only if he needs it to accomplish some purpose of his own. Thus, before he learns how to locate a library book, he wants to find a particular title; before he studies the effect of the short story on himself, he feels its impact and then the desire to unlock the puzzle of how Poe achieves the effect. In both situations, a specific desire leads to learning—learning a skill on the one hand, learning about the craft of the writer on the other. In either case, the teacher, in addition to improving the processes of problem solving, must encourage students to establish goals which bring about the learning of desired patterns of behavior. This means that the teacher's primary goal and the student's will often differ; but the student, to accomplish his own goal—

[10] Russell, *Children's Thinking,* p. 257.

the acquisition of a library book—must first accomplish the teacher's—perfecting certain locational skills.

Choosing problems for class study Both the nature of the problem and the situation in which it is to be solved affect the learner's solutions. Difficult tasks far beyond an individual's experience tend to provoke aimless trial and error rather than systematic analysis. For example, assigning the preparation of a panel to students who have had no prior experience with this form of organized discussion will almost always result in confusion. Similarly, teachers would not ask junior high students to consider such mature problems as the choices that Martin Arrowsmith must make between personal ideals and social success, although problems involving the same conflicts have meaning for young adolescents if related to the values of the peer group. Better than problems faced only by adults are questions like, "Should boys who violate school regulations be permitted to participate in athletics?" Issues must be real and immediate to the learner if the experience is to prepare him for more difficult situations later.

The physical, experiential, and emotional condition of the learner will also influence his solutions. A learner who is overly tired, who must work in cramped space, feels insecure, or is tortured by self-doubt and fear of failure is seldom one who will venture many imaginative solutions. On the other hand, a fresh, alert, self-confident student who finds materials available and adequate space in which to work may achieve a goal in record time. In addition, the conditions of time under which he works will often shape his willingness to begin and his ultimate success or failure. In addition to necessary work space and adequate resources—e.g., books, library tools, graphic materials—individuals need reasonable time. Teachers must recognize the limitations imposed by the rigid time restrictions in most classrooms. For example, projects involving extended inquiry by groups of students into complex and difficult problems will not seem reasonable to the learner unless adequate class time is provided for research, study, and discussion. Too often library research or panel presentation or dramatization results in failure because we do not allow time for such study. Students who have had bitter experience with such failure may well be wary of undertaking a new project unless they see how and when it can be accomplished. A plan for extensive problem solving in longer units of instruction must allow sufficient time.

Social factors also influence students' abilities in problem solving. Research indicates that groups of students often produce better results than do individuals alone.[11] A higher level of aspiration is set by the group than by the individual even though more time tends to be required for solution. Undoubtedly some of the superiority of the group approach may be attributed to the opportunities provided in the social situation for the analysis, discussion, and consideration of many potential solutions. The nature of the task should determine whether the teacher wishes to encourage group or indi-

[11] Russell, *Children's Thinking*, pp. 266-269.

vidual thinking. The group approach seems to be more appropriate when problems require the expression of various points of view or the consideration of many experiences—such as the selection of a book for reading by the entire class or the identification of the complex causes of juvenile delinquency. The citizens of a free society solve problems individually and in groups. The school needs to provide experience in both approaches.

Making judgments

In the play, *Teahouse of the August Moon,* Captain Fisby is forced to choose between building the teahouse requested by the Okinawan villagers and building the pentagon-shaped schoolhouse required by American military planners. Fisby's assigned task is to teach the Tobiki villagers to be democratic and self-supporting. Through his experiences with Sakini the captain has learned a great deal about the nature of Okinawans and the way in which they live. He must draw upon these ideas in making his decision—a task which involves comparing, discriminating, and weighing evidence in choosing between alternatives. Fisby's behavior illustrates important differences between the processes of judgmental thinking and those involved in other kinds of reasoning. In developing his ideas regarding Okinawans (concept formation), and in considering how to accomplish democratization of the village (problem solving), Fisby engages in reasoning which is essentially *productive.* However, in choosing between the teahouse and the schoolhouse (making a judgment), his action is *decisive* by nature. The processes involve somewhat different considerations.

Judgments are used in forming concepts and in solving problems, of course; for this reason, it is important to distinguish those aspects of judgmental thinking which need to be studied separately. Individuals make three types of judgments: conceptual judgments in perceiving and organizing facts and ideas, judgments regarding hypotheses in considering alternative solutions to problems, and value judgments in determining preference for objects, ideas, or courses of action. The first two types are essential to productive thinking and involve the sublimation of emotional considerations to the demands of logical necessity. Value judgments, however, involve the determination of qualitative distinctions and therefore tap the feelings. Hence, a real problem in making sound judgments of this type is the control rather than the suppression of emotion. For this reason, value judgments merit consideration as a separate form of thinking.

Considering how values develop To understand what can and what cannot be taught to students in a classroom, teachers need to consider how children and young people learn the values on which their judgments are based. In a real sense each person is both developing his values and being guided by them as he makes his decisions. Choices tend to be determined by beliefs an individual thinks important; yet not until one makes a choice and tests that choice in action, do values become operational. The complexity of this interrelationship needs to be recognized by teachers. So too does the fact that all elements in a culture may influence what one learns to prize. Awareness of how values develop over a long period of time out of the totality of a person's experience emphasizes that only carefully planned, cumulative instruction in judgmental thinking, extending over the six secondary years, is likely to have a substantial effect.

> Value development proceeds from the simple to the complex, from the specific to the general. Children first learn to observe simple rules of conduct, later to relate individual action to their total ethical behavior. Ultimately they become aware of some of the problems and dilemmas of life involving clashes in ethical values.
>
> Value development proceeds from the external to the internal. In childhood, choices of conduct are often determined by parental injunction, school regulation, or neighborhood mores. Later, individuals substitute internal regulation for the external control—a self-enforced code of behavior for the external reward and punishment.
>
> Orientation in decision making moves from the present to the future. Children consider each decision in terms of immediate satisfaction; mature thinkers, in terms of the implications of actions. Until an individual begins to base judgments on larger ideals, such as honesty, justice, or love, he is guided by egocentric pleasure-pain appeals.
>
> Values are learned from models. Through emulation, imitation, and identification, youth acquires his ethical point of view. These identifications may be with parents, members of the peer group, teachers, athletic and entertainment heroes, or even characters in fiction and biography.

Thus, the ability to make sound value judgments develops slowly, and it is best developed through actual conduct. Not until students have opportunity to consider decisions in concrete situations do they make substantial progress. To be sure, the most disturbing choices faced by adolescents occur out of school; the classroom seldom offers direct opportunities to help them with their most basic problems. Yet, the school can guide students in wrestling with problems of certain kinds, can introduce in the literature program the directed study of values held by other people, can offer analysis and discussion of decisions young people face. In every term, students should have some opportunity, within the limits of the curriculum, to choose among alternatives; the choice must be real, not one the student has reason to suspect has already been determined. The unit "Meeting A Crisis" suggests possible approaches. In discussing problems, the teacher can lead a class to see the possibilities each alternative offers, the difficulties and rewards of each; he can suggest different ways to pupils differently oriented. The choice, however, is the student's. Nor is it the better part of wisdom to offer too much protection to one repeatedly stranded in a morass of confusion as the result of impulsive decisions and rash judgments. Experience in accepting the consequences of choices freely made pays cumulative dividends.

Stressing the need for balance In making decisions, individuals try to achieve a balance between internal and external demands. Our personal wishes, needs, and ideals must be balanced against facts and realities over which we have no control. For example, in judging the worth of a classroom procedure, teachers weigh their own attitudes toward the method—the satisfactions they obtain and their enjoyment in using the approach—against objective considerations—the learning of pupils, the resources available, the various procedures they know. The extent to which we permit personal feelings to influence us varies with each task. Thus, in evaluating methodology, the teacher is guided largely by a dispassionate appraisal of the learning situation because he knows his choice affects many individuals; however, in selecting books for personal reading, he follows his own preferences. Pupils must learn to examine both internal-emotional factors and external-objective factors in each decision situation; they must learn to be aware of their personal preferences, the consequences of their decisions for themselves and others.

The identification of our personal preferences and desires is the first step in controlling them. In making the judgments involved in selecting clothing to wear, or in choosing motion pictures to attend, we base decisions largely on our feelings at the moment. More frequently, however, our wishes are balanced against outside demands. In judging the quality of *Nancy Drew, Detective,* a girl must weigh any personal reading preference for the teen-age theme against the unrealistic depiction of adolescent manners and mores presented in the novel. We need to be aware of our personal feelings, even as we consider other matters.

Any decision has both antecedents and consequences; behavior does not occur in a vacuum. Students must learn to consider the ways in which present action may influence future events. They need to recognize also their responsibility for the consequences of their decisions. Prediction of the results of behavior is not always easy. In making judgments such as those involved in choosing between college preparatory, commercial, or vocational courses of study, many secondary students recognize the importance of their decision. However, in one involving less obvious consequences—say, considering whether to accept a position on the school paper—individuals may overlook many possibilities—time, obligation to the school, conflict with other activities, learnings which may be required. Often predictions will be inaccurate, since each particular situation presents its own problem. However, continued experience in balancing internal and external demands as one estimates probable and possible outcomes tends to encourage wiser decisions.

Providing classroom experience Individuals make mature decisions based on all perceivable considerations only after much thoughtful experience in judging. However, mere participation in the action is no guarantee of growth. Adolescents are faced daily with decisions outside the classroom, yet often fail to learn from their activity. To encourage growth the teacher must plan appropriate experiences in judging. But these become productive, *thoughtful* experiences only when the processes of reasoning are later analyzed and considered. Thus the role of the teacher involves organizing both the experience and the follow-through.

As students identify with characters and become involved in situations, their emotional response is intensified. Under such conditions they can learn to weigh both internal and external considerations. Teachers generally find that involvement is likely to occur when the decision situations emanate from experiences which seem important and real to adolescents. Certainly seventh grade students can not comprehend emotionally the dilemma facing Hamlet, and they would lack sympathy with the Dane's philosophical orientation even if they could understand it. However, such students respond strongly to Tom Sawyer's skirmishes with Aunt Polly, since problems involving conflicts with adult authority are central in the developmental experiences of this age group. Many teachers capitalize on such concerns in selecting material for class presentation.

Decision situations facing young people which induce strong student empathies may be introduced by displaying pictures of adolescents facing recognizable dilemmas, by reading appropriate cuttings from stories, by presenting short films designed to confront young people with choices, or by describing verbally a problem which will admit solution by role playing.[12] In addition, the choices which students face in planning class activities will frequently provide opportunities for analysis. Once the problem is introduced, the students may be led to examine each decision by applying the questions discussed earlier, e.g., What are my personal feelings in the matter? What are the possible consequences? How will the decision affect others?

The same questions may also be applied to the decisions of characters in literature. Because literature deals with the impact of experience on the individual, it offers unique source material for studying the ways people think. Analysis of the thinking processes used by literary characters and study of the ways in which their decisions affect subsequent behavior may well sharpen students' insight into the varied dimensions of decision-making.

Literature provides illustrations of individuals who base their decisions only on their emotions. "I Can't Breathe" offers a humorous portrait of a girl completely lacking in objectivity.

Literature shows how judgments affect other people. *The Ring of the Löwenskölds* traces the effect of certain decisions on two generations of individuals. *Willow Hill* depicts the effect on a community of decisions to accept and reject new neighbors.

Literature provides experiences in evaluating difficult decisions involving conflicts in loyalties. In *The Peacock Sheds Its Tail,* the traditions of family privilege clash with the bold democratic demands of a new generation in Mexico. Caught between the quarreling factions, the American, Jim Buchanan, is forced to choose

[12] These procedures are discussed in detail elsewhere in this volume. For use of the picture stimulus, see "Written Expression," p. 514; for the unfinished story technique and role playing, "Imaginative Thinking," pp. 143-44.

between alternative courses of action. By studying the way in which Jim evaluates his personal loyalties in relation to his sense of justice and his belief in democratic procedures, students may be lead to an awareness of the complexity of choices involving two apparent rights.

Discussion of examples from literature gains in effectiveness when the teacher encourages students to relate examples from their own experiences. Thus the analysis of complex decisions in the Hobart novel may be followed by such questions as, "How would you have reacted?" or "What different results might a different decision have provoked?" "At what time in your own lives have you been faced with similar conflicts in loyalties?" Such questions tend to increase student involvement.

A study of value judgments may help students become aware of the complex nature of their own values. Recognizing the influence of personal codes on behavior can help students clarify their thinking concerning important decisions they must make. Such understanding may relieve the doubts and anxieties felt by many adolescents who discover that their desires sometimes conflict with their beliefs. It almost certainly will make them more able to interpret human behavior, both their own and that of others. Continuing appraisal, through carefully planned classroom experiences, of the ways his own values and those of characters from literature affect decisions should convince a student that the life he builds depends not only upon the values he selects but upon the volition he brings to bear in making them function in practice.

In summary, then, students learn to make wise decisions only after much experience with this type of thinking. Activities can provide experiences in judging or studying the judgments of others; teachers can carefully evaluate with students the reasoning that occurs; but only the person himself can really improve his skill.

The control of emotion by reason which has been discussed in this chapter does not embrace the total spectrum of thought. To concept formation, problem solving, and judgmental thinking, we would add at the least the processes of numerical reasoning and imaginative thinking. The former, being the province of the teacher of mathematics, is outside this discussion; the latter is introduced in the chapter to follow.

The methods discussed here for teaching students to formulate sound conclusions have three general characteristics:

The approaches provide directed experience in forming conclusions about present problems, coupled with a provision for intellectual assessment of processes used to achieve these ends.

The problems selected for consideration are appropriate to the maturity of the learner and are capable of eliciting his involvement.

The approaches provide experience and instruction in different kinds of thinking —in forming concepts, solving problems, and making judgments.

Classroom procedures sharing these characteristics will help the learner improve his ability to think logically. As an individual and as a member of a group, the citizen of a free society makes constant choices which affect others as well as himself. This is his right as well as his responsibility. The teacher in this society must prepare each citizen to make such decisions as soundly and wisely as possible. This is the teacher's obligation and his opportunity. And the teacher of English deals with language, the medium through which most decisions are made.

Do teachers overstate the importance of the task, if they, like Gilbert Highet, see this search for sound conclusions as one of the "strongest and most permanent force[s] in human affairs"? In assessing Plato's reliance on reasoning, Highet writes:

> Ask the questions. Examine the answers. Go on discussing until the reason is satisfied with the result. As you think by yourself, all alone, you should converse with Reason almost as though Reason were another person, with claims to respect at least equal to your own. When you argue with someone else, the argument should not be a fight between you two, but a hunt after Reason, in which you both join, helping each other to detect and capture the truth you both desire.[13]

THE TEACHING PROBLEM

Organizing Instruction

Clearly the program of instruction in thinking outlined in this chapter envisions the planning of curricular offerings which extend over several years of instruction. Improvement in any skill occurs only after repeated practice. Continual stress on sound reasoning, supported by brief, frequent lessons, tends to be more effective than reliance on infrequent, intensive study. Teachers will want to consider ways of incorporating in lessons learning experiences such as those described in this chapter as well as ways of insuring a sustained sequential program throughout the secondary school years.

Certainly the principle of readiness applies here as elsewhere in the English program. Learning experiences are most effectively introduced at times when students make particular errors and can be led to recognize a need for learning. For example, the sharp polarization of student attitudes toward accepting or rejecting Jerry, the orphan boy of "A Mother in Mannville," has been used to introduce a class to the analysis of dangers involved in either-or thinking; similarly, for individuals who fail to support or qualify broad sweeping statements in their compositions, some teachers provide the necessary class or group instruction. Often special correction symbols are used to direct

[13] Gilbert Highet, *The Art of Teaching* (N.Y., Knopf, 1950); in the paperbound edition (N.Y., Knopf Vintage, 1954), this quotation appears on pp. 163-164.

attention to such errors; brief personal comments written by the teacher are even more effective. The opportunities to relate instruction to need are many. Most units of instruction require students to form concepts, solve problems, or make judgments, thus providing opportunity for instruction as well as for practice.

How do we assure continuity in learning over the years? The problem is not an easy one. Ultimately it depends on each teacher's accurate assessment of the needs of the learner and the teacher's ability to build on what has gone before. From the primary level on, teachers can direct students' attention both to flaws in reasoning and to methods of thinking which lead to sound conclusions. Probably at each level a few items may be emphasized; perhaps the following, in grade nine:

Either-or thinking
Sweeping generalizations resulting from failure to qualify ideas
Seeing relationships—the difference between comparing and contrasting

Given a few such items for emphasis with a particular class, the teacher may observe student behavior in writing and speech and plan suitable learning experiences. By focusing on a few fundamental problems and processes at every instructional level, he encourages sustained development in the processes of thinking. Thus the problem for the teacher is to find for each desired learning a teachable moment in the classroom. Because individuals continually rely on their impressions of fact, and because they of necessity use the methods of thinking discussed in this chapter in formulating conclusions, the task of capitalizing on readiness and motivation in teaching the skills of thinking is less arduous than it first appears.

Suggested Learning Experiences

Here as elsewhere in this volume learning experiences are suggested to illustrate the principles and procedures which are discussed. These activities result in effective learning only when introduced at appropriate times. Many of them require more extensive preparation and follow-through than can be discussed here. Illustrations of some ways in which specific learning experiences may be integrated within longer units of instruction are developed in the illustrative units presented at the end of each section of the book.

To recognize how purpose controls the selectivity of observations

■ *Analyze situations from different points of view*

1. Present to the class a brief film involving controversial behavior, such as the "fishhook" sequence from the film, "Captains Courageous." In this episode the spoiled boy, Harvey, ties knots in a fisherman's line to make certain that his friend Manual will catch the most fish. Manual wins a bet by catching the most fish but discovers the boy's duplicity and throws his catch overboard in anger.

Before showing the film, divide the class into three groups and ask each to view the incident as one of the characters—as Manual, Harvey, or the rival fisherman. Ask each student to describe the events which have the greatest impact on the person whose role he is assuming. Students reacting as Harvey often emphasize the overriding importance to the boy of insuring Manual's victory; the second group reports that Manual's reactions are dominated by his concern for the boy's dishonesty; the third group is certain that the rival fisherman is interested primarily in the fact that he has been cheated. Students unable to maintain the assigned roles will often view the incident as "general" observers and express more concern over the "waste" of fish than over the conflict in values involved.

Experience of this type requires students to identify the emotional prejudices of three individuals and predict how these influence objectivity in viewing a particular incident.

2. Ask students to analyze the possible motives of persons in newspaper stories. Particularly useful are stories in which individuals are reporting on events which they have witnessed, e.g., Woman Sees Wild Animal in Patio, Pilot Describes Flying Saucer, Tourist Reports Sea Serpent at Loch Ness. In considering motives and the possible points of view of such individuals, ask students such questions as, "What impressions would this person stress?" "Which would he be likely to overlook?"

This experience requires students to consider some of the affective influences on the perception of persons who "witness" unusual phenomena.

■ *Study the impact of experience on purpose*

Gather twenty-five or thirty small objects in a paper carton. Include miscellaneous items, such as pencils and erasers, toy trinkets, several fruits, eight to ten cooking utensils—cookie cutter, baking dish, grater—and eight to ten small tools—pliers, screwdriver, chisel. Introduce the activity as an exercise in observation, and show the contents for about sixty seconds to the class at two separate times. After the first showing, ask the students to write the names of as many *objects* as possible; after the second trial, ask them to write the names of as many *tools* as possible. Then lead the class in a discussion aimed at explaining differences in the two lists which have been compiled. The following guide suggests principles which may be developed:

Probable result	**Possible explanations**
Students list more objects on the second trial.	The specific task of looking for tools aids individuals in organizing observations.
Boys list more tools than girls.	Familiarity with objects affects speed and accuracy.
	Greater familiarity with objects enables boys to recognize tools quickly. To test this generalization, class might refer to results on the first trial to determine whether girls listed more cooking utensils than did the boys.
	Memory of the first experience may aid in the second.

Such an activity offers a concrete way of demonstrating to pupils how experiences may affect perception in unstructured situations.

To discover how bias colors interpretation

■ *Analyze the prejudices of students*

1. Display a number of selected portraits of various persons clipped from news magazines. The personages should be unnamed but should include many "types" of individuals—criminals, humanitarians, statesmen, etc. Ask students to describe the kind of behavior they would expect to be characteristic of each person depicted. Then compare their predictions with a report of the known behavior of each person. In the ensuing discussion, lead students to see that in relating character to physical appearance they are merely reflecting their emotional biases, and that sound judgments of character must rest on more objective information.

2. Ask for three volunteers to report independently on a controversial speech or discussion to be broadcast on television or radio. Ask each student to summarize what is said and to describe the apparent purposes of the speaker. Arrange for each to report separately so that he will be uninfluenced by the other summaries. Lead the class in an examination of differences in the reports. Frequently these are great enough to suggest that each reporter has listened to a separate broadcast. A teacher who suspects that the differences will be great may wish to record the program so that it is available for reference. The success of this activity depends on the degree of the students' involvement in the issues being discussed. Adolescent problems are particularly appropriate subjects.

3. Write the following quotations on the chalkboard of an eleventh grade classroom:

(1) "To be prepared for war is one of the most effective means of preserving the peace."

(2) "Labor is prior to, and independent of, capital. Capital is only the fruit of labor and could never have existed if labor had not first existed."

(3) ". . . governments are instituted among men deriving their powers from the consent of the governed. . . . Whenever any government becomes destructive to these ends, it is the right of people to alter or abolish it."

(4) "The workingmen are the basis of all government, for the plain reason that they are the most numerous."

Then ask each student to select the author of each statement from the following list of names:

Thomas Jefferson	Joseph Stalin
Nikita Khrushchev	George Washington
Dwight Eisenhower	Abraham Lincoln
Karl Marx	

When student choices are tabulated, many statements will be attributed to Khrushchev, Marx, or Stalin. Then reveal the actual authorship:

(1) Washington, First Annual Address, 1790
(2) Lincoln, Speech, Cincinnati, 1861
(3) Jefferson, Declaration of Independence, 1776
(4) Lincoln, First Annual Message to Congress, 1861

In the discussion which follows, lead students in an examination of the reasons why the quotations are incorrectly attributed. Ultimately most students will see that they are guided by personal feelings, attributing ideas which seem questionable to disliked personalities. Then consider the implications of the finding for life situations, including illustrations of the ways in which an individual's emotional impressions –whether of fellow students, politicians, or television personalities–influence his willingness to accept or reject rumors or stories.

■ *Analyze propaganda techniques used by others* [14]

Guide mature students in the critical analyses of selected statements which are designed to influence the reader's thinking by capitalizing on his biases. False appeals and specious arguments provide excellent materials for such exercises.

Sample paragraphs from a letter which was widely distributed in a bitter election campaign illustrate one type of available material. Here the references to particular individuals have been eliminated, but the type of material will be recognizable. The kinds of questions which aid in directing student thinking are suggested by the study problems which follow.

Illustrative paragraphs from a printed letter

While We Pray the Enemy Plots Our Destruction

Dear Christian American Friends:

(1) This letter contains vital information which you cannot afford to miss–in fact, this may turn out to be the most important warning and the most practical information you have ever received through the mail.

(2) On November 3 John Jones let the cat out of the bag. He lifted the curtain and gave us a peek behind the scenes. Said Jones: "If the opposition wins this election, the other nations of the World will look to Russia for leadership. Following a brief administration, by the opposition party, America will go Communist."

(3) *The hidden hand which has directed the black political magic* for the past several years is now reaching for the jugular vein of our Party. Rats that have deserted the sinking ship are now creeping into the Party, hoping that they can rule or ruin the coming Congress.

(4) *You are to be congratulated* on being a part of this crusade which did much to help bring about the recent election victory. We endorsed 187 candidates for Congress and the Senate. Nearly 170 were victorious. In scores, yes almost hundreds of political campaigns, my name and the name of the cause you and I represent became issues. Practical politicians who only a few months ago thought my endorsement to be the "kiss of death" discovered that the support of us Nationalists brought victory. In state after state literally millions of circulars were put out by the enemy. In practically every one of these cases our man was victorious.

Illustrative study questions based on the material

Heading. What favorable connotation would the reader of this letter be expected to supply for "Christian"? For "American"? Does linking these two words carry the implication of excluding any group of Americans who are not Christians? What group in particular might be so intended here? Is this implication favorable or unfavorable to this group? What is the implication of "friend"?

Par. 1. What in this paragraph is intended to lead the reader to adopt a favorable attitude toward what will follow in the letter? Is such an attitude justified?

Par. 2. Does the secrecy implied in the expressions "Let the cat out of the bag,"

[14] Other examples are to be found in "Language as Dynamic Process," pp. 29-32.

"lifted the curtain," and "a peek behind the scenes" seem to be a secrecy concealing a pleasant surprise or a sinister, undesirable situation? What makes you think so?

Par. 3. In what ways is this paragraph related to the statement attributed to Jones? Whose is the "hidden hand"? What does the writer seem to mean by "black political magic"? What emotional attitude seems to be induced by these (foregoing) expressions? By the phrase "the jugular vein of the party"? Does the writer supply evidence to enable you to identify the "rats"? Is the implication that this desertion and creeping is participated in by many or by a few? What would be the significance in either case?

Par. 4. What is likely to be the effect of the first sentence upon the uncritical reader? Why? What affective value is provided by the word "crusade"? The implied argument is that since "we" endorsed nearly 170 candidates who were elected, the endorsement was therefore a cause of their winning. Is the argument sound? If not, where is its weakness? What is the implication of the expression "practical politicians"? If the reader of the letter deems himself a "practical politician," what effect might this phrase and this sentence have upon him? Make a list of the connotations which "Nationalist" has for you. Are all of these connotations favorable to the attitude of the writer of this letter? What is the emotional value of "the enemy"? What are the implications of this word in contrast to those of, say, "the opposition"?

The teacher can follow such detailed analyses of selected individual paragraphs by asking students to assess the over-all contentions and purposes of the author (or sponsoring organization) in the total letter. Individual students who are proficient in such analysis may be urged to locate similar examples of persuasion which they can analyze in a class presentation.

To perceive how sharpening and leveling influence recall

■ *Urge students to study their own retellings*

1. Ask students to write brief summaries of the narrative immediately after reading a short story such as Payne's "Prelude." This is the story of a troubled romance between a high school sorority girl and an unkempt boy from an immigrant family. In the story the heroine is forced several times to endure taunts from her snobbish friends and is ultimately faced with a choice between material and human values. One week after reading ask students to summarize the story a second time without the aid of review. Request a third summary three or four weeks after the initial reading. Then return the three papers to the students. By analyzing carefully chosen examples from student papers, the class will see how modification and distortion occur when events are recalled over a period of time. Appropriate selections for such an activity are those which elicit many dimensions of response. "Prelude," for example, will be recalled by some as a pleasant love story of a rich girl and poor boy, by others as a bitter, driving denunciation of high school sororities.

Such experiences force students to recognize their own tendencies to sharpen and level recollections. They may then be asked to examine the underlying causes.

2. Ask four or five volunteers to leave the room in preparation for an experiment in recall. Then display a large photograph showing a dramatic situation involving several figures. The effectiveness of this activity is increased when the photographic situation is sufficiently ambiguous to require rather extensive comment and interpre-

tation. The picture should suggest a conflict without specifying its exact nature. Illustrations depicting adults and adolescents in apparent disagreement are particularly effective in high school classes. Ask one class member to describe the situation in the photograph to one of the volunteers who returns to the room. Neither the student describing the situation nor the listener who has returned is able to view the photograph, yet the two students should be so situated that the photograph remains discernible to remaining class members. Each of the volunteers is asked to return individually. After listening to a description of the situation, he repeats the description to the next returnee. Since the picture remains visible to the class, the students are later able to discuss the examples of sharpening and leveling which occur.[15]

To improve inductive and deductive reasoning

■ *Study ways of classifying data*

1. Ask the students to "learn" the following nonsense words which are written on the blackboard:

shro	sigg	sid
sorr	shum	simm
seg	sunpt	shig

After a moment examine the various ways in which individuals attempt to impose order on the nonsense syllables. How many pronounce the words in attempting to find a phonetic pattern? How many examine structural clues? Alphabetical sequence?

The exercise shows students how individuals strive for order even in nonsense material. It also illustrates how data may be classified in various kinds of categories.

2. If students have difficulty in organizing, present a series of items such as the following, to be grouped in two or more categories:

automobile, washing machine, train, dishwasher,
orlon, wool, airplane, cotton, electric range . . .

Increasingly difficult exercises of this type may be introduced in preparation for writing activities. A class may be encouraged to list all possible facts and ideas concerning a general topic before attempting to categorize them. For example, in developing ideas for a composition on the topic, "The Impact of Science Fiction on the Imaginations of Teen-Agers," a class may suggest varied items: nightmares, television programs and motion pictures, changed reading habits, belief in the supernatural, increased interest in scientific facts, curiosity regarding the unknown. With teacher guidance, each item may then be grouped either as a potential cause of, as a possible result of, or as unrelated to the increased adolescent reading of science-fiction material. This activity requires students to perceive levels of abstraction ranging from the simple and concrete to the complex and universal.

3. Discuss with students the importance of such methods of classification as alphabetical sequence, the Dewey Decimal System, the organization of school departments under subject headings, postal delivery zones. Such a discussion points

[15] An interesting psychological experiment of this type is reported in Gordon Allport and Leo Postman, *The Psychology of Rumor* (N.Y., Holt, 1948), pp. 63-74. James I. Brown has also described a similar classroom project in "Dealing with Bias as Readers and Listeners," *Exercise Exchange,* Vol. 5, No. 1 (October 1957), pp. 9, 10.

up everyday applications of the principles of classification as well as the fact that these systems are arbitrary creations of men, rather than accurate categories inherent in the material.

■ *Stress similarities and differences in generalizing*

1. Ask students to group the following occupations into two or more categories:

> laborer, farmer, businessman, mechanic, waitress,
> white collar worker, politician, policeman, secretary,
> real-estate broker, lemon grower, bulldozer operator,
> stevedore, electrician, insurance salesman

For each category, discuss with students both the unifying characteristic and the differences which are overlooked.

2. Analyze with students the effect of categorization implied in such statements as those below. What similarities are stressed? In what ways are the statements misleading?

> Sportsmen enjoy basketball, track, fishing, hunting, and ping pong.
> Almost everyone laughs at cartoons, jokes, comedy situations on television, clowns, and the antics of young children.
> If you enjoyed reading *A Tale of Two Cities,* you will enjoy *Henry Esmond, Northwest Passage,* and *Tap Roots.*
> If you enjoyed *A Tale of Two Cities,* you will enjoy *Great Expectations, David Copperfield,* and *Pickwick Papers.*

This exercise requires students to recognize and evaluate the assumptions underlying each expressed relationship.

■ *Recognize the importance of "open-mindedness" in reasoning*

1. To illustrate how our understanding of words is extended through the processes of analysis and synthesis, ask students to explore and define the meaning of nonsense words which are used in several contexts. Example: *zupu*

> I was sick because the sea was *zupu* today.
> His skin felt *zupu* because he had not shaved.
> The *zupu* diamond was sent to the stone cutter.
> He had had little education and his language seemed simple and *zupu.*[16]
> The students talked so much they gave the substitute teacher a *zupu* time.

Exercises of this type demonstrate how understandings are deepened through experiences.

2. Discuss in a simple way the importance of thinking in terms of degrees. Consider the impossibility of determining the extent to which individuals possess such traits as the following:

beauty-ugliness	honesty-dishonesty
superiority-inferiority	goodness-badness

[16] Examples of this kind have been used in an interesting study of the development of children's understanding of verbal symbols. See Heinz Werner and Edith Kaplan, *The Acquisition of Word Meanings* (Evanston, Ill., Child Development Publications, 1952). Other classroom uses of this method are illustrated in the unit "Power Over Language" and "Reading with Comprehension."

Discuss the imperfect nature of such generalizations concerning the behavior of individuals and the use of such qualifiers as *often, sometimes, seldom, seems to, tends to,* and *appears to be.*

3. Present to students a list of twenty statements describing actions of men and women. Ask each student to indicate whether he regards each of the following actions as "work" or "play":

A lineman charging after a halfback
An author writing a short story
A woman putting up strawberry preserves
A theatre critic viewing a play
An elderly man weeding a garden
A carpenter building a boat
A young man building a boat on a Saturday

Divide the class into several small discussion groups. Ask the students in each group to compare their decisions and to attempt to identify the factors which influence each individual.

In a final discussion develop an understanding of differences in point of view regarding work and play and of the importance of qualifying the arbitrary judgments which students make.

The last two activities, above, require the learner to make certain value judgments. These judgments are based on each person's evaluation of the particulars relevant to the judgment. In the subsequent discussions, students should recognize that in many cases the initial perception of an event on which they base judgment is extremely limited.

■ *Compare inductive and deductive methods*

Ask students to develop arguments to prove such generalizations as the following:

Schools should not operate on a twelve-month basis.
Television has a beneficial effect on viewers.
The rates for baby sitting should be increased.

Ask half of the class to develop one idea inductively and the remaining students to do this deductively. Selected paragraphs may then be analyzed for logical development. Experiences of this type require students to utilize and compare the two basic approaches.

To examine oversimplifications in our own reasoning

■ *Study oversimplifications in the discussion of students*

Tape record a panel of students discussing an issue about which they feel strongly, such as problems involved in raising the minimum grades required for participation in extracurricular activities, in establishing a ten o'clock curfew for adolescents, or in abolishing high school fraternities and sororities. Play the recording and ask the class to analyze the arguments of individuals to discover oversimplified statements. Do not hesitate to interrupt the playback at appropriate times to highlight illustrations. A discussion of this type furnishes excellent material for such an analysis. Such experiences require students to apply their general understanding of the principles of sound reasoning to their own communication.

■ *Identify common forms of oversimplification*

1. Present students with a list of clichés and assumptions such as those below. Urge them to add to the list. Ask students to change, modify, or rewrite the statements to make each express an idea which they would be willing to defend.

Long ear lobes are a sign of aristocracy.
Individuals with red hair have quick tempers.
A stitch in time saves nine.
Italians make good opera singers.
Women live longer than men.
An apple a day keeps the doctor away.

In the final review, students point up the flaws in reasoning involved in each statement as originally expressed.

2. Ask students to examine statements such as the following to determine whether each may be considered as (a) never true, (b) always true, (c) sometimes true, (d) of uncertain truth (insufficient data to determine).

High school students are interested in science.
Football is played in the fall.
The first Monday in September is Labor Day.
A young child who is spoiled is seldom successful in school.
Rapid readers remember little of what they read.
Drag racing will keep boys out of trouble.
Women can shed ten pounds in thirty-six hours on a diet of yogurt and fresh pineapple.

Plan a discussion of the students' answers to develop an understanding of the importance of basing generalizations on adequate data.

Both of these activities begin with concrete statements which students are asked to examine. The choice of examples will determine whether the exercise will concentrate on various manifestations of a single problem, e.g., using stereotypes, or will deal with many kinds of oversimplification. Many teachers introduce exercises of this type after the need for such concentrated study is revealed by repeated problems in the students' writing and speech.

To detect methods of evading consideration of an issue

■ *Study the evasions of others*

1. Sections in magazines and newspapers which reprint "letters to the editor" are a fertile source of illustrative material. Examine such a letter as the following with a class:

Dear Editor:

There can be no doubt that John A. was wrong when he wrote that comic books do not cause delinquency. These so-called magazines have increased tremendously during the last few years and so has our juvenile problem. Either John A. has no children or he doesn't know how they spend their time. From the way he reasons he would permit young minds to read anything.

Sincerely,
Mrs. G.

A few key questions aid students in analyzing such letters: Why was the letter written? What is the central thought? What evidence is offered to support this proposition? Such examples may well be used to introduce study of the problem or to clinch the students' understanding.

2. Encourage students to bring to class interesting examples of evasion. Develop a special bulletin board to illustrate the methods people use to avoid answering questions. Ask students to examine the reasoning and to identify the particular error involved in such examples as the following:

"I don't know what's wrong with Mary at school. All her grades seem to be low. She got a C in Algebra and a B– in English. Her only explanation is that she gets as good grades as her friends. They don't seem to teach self-discipline in schools any more."

Man: "Do men attach as much significance to manners as they once did?"
Woman: "Well, I didn't see you offering your bus seat to any elderly ladies."

Man: "They say that many boys and girls average twenty hours a week in watching television."
Woman: "Someone should make certain that better programs are planned for youth."
Man: "Too much talk of that sort would lead to censorship."

To distinguish sound relationships from those false or misleading

■ *Examine relationships between ideas*

1. Ask students to indicate which of the supporting statements are unrelated to the argument in such propositions as the following:

Bud Wilkinson is a great coach.
- a. His teams won many games.
- b. He developed many plays.
- c. He coached at Oklahoma.

Beagles make excellent pets.
- a. They are gentle with children.
- b. They are becoming increasingly popular.
- c. They respond well to obedience training.

"Stardust" is a wonderful song.
- a. It was written by Hoagy Carmichael.
- b. Its melody seems fresh and lilting.
- c. The lyrics seem to express the feeling of the music.

2. Ask students to consider whether the relationship between such paired statements as the following may be considered to be (a) perfect, (b) pronounced, (c) slight, (d) unrelated, or (e) unknown.

The color of the hen; the color of its eggs.
The height of children; the height of parents.
The fullness of the moon; the height of the tide.
The weight of the green vegetables eaten; the curliness of one's hair.
The price of automobiles; the price of wheat.
School grades in English; school grades in geometry.

An examination of the probable reasons for linking each pair of items may increase students' perception of the causes of much fallacious reasoning.

3. Provide a list of statements such as the following and ask students to indicate whether the reasoning is *sound* or *unsound*. Discuss with students the reasons for their decision.

John claimed that Knute Rockne was a more original coach than either Frank Leahy or Joe Koharich because he was the first great Notre Dame coach.
Sound or *Unsound?* Reason: ______

A person should vote Democratic because it is the party of such great modern leaders as Franklin D. Roosevelt and Woodrow Wilson.
Sound or *Unsound?* Reason: ______

John's high grade on the test was the inevitable result of his command of the subject and his long hours of work.
Sound or *Unsound?* Reason: ______

Our neighbors the Joneses must be wealthy because they can afford two cars.
Sound or *Unsound?* Reason: ______

■ *Practice drawing sound relationships*

At a time when the class is considering how to develop ideas, ask students to identify several possible hypotheses which might be developed from sets of data like the following:

The consumption of carbonated beverages has increased since 1918.
The average height of fifteen-year-old boys appears to have increased during the past thirty years.
Mental institutions are more crowded today than after the First World War.
The population has increased considerably during the past thirty years.

What causal relationships are suggested? How many are tenable?

Jack is a sophomore in high school. During the past year Jack
has read many new books.
bought a TV set which he watches nightly.
has become friendly with a boy who is an amateur taxidermist.
joined a school club for nature study.
has had a new science teacher.

Which of these would logically explain the improvement in Jack's grades in science?

Clearly many possible hypotheses would be instantly rejected as unreasonable, yet even extreme examples may reveal to some students how spurious relationships may become accepted as truth.

To improve ability to see relationships

■ *See parallels in life and literature*

1. Encourage students to compare events in literature with events in contemporary life. Following the death of Joseph Stalin in 1953, Bishop Fulton J. Sheen aroused the imagination of many Americans by reading a portion of *Julius Caesar* on television, substituting the names of members of contemporary Soviet leaders—Malenkov, Beria, Khrushchev, Molotov, Bulganin—for the conspirators Cassius, Brutus, Casca, Trebonius, and Cinna. Bishop Sheen was capitalizing on what appeared in 1953 to be a striking parallel between events in the play and the situa-

tion in contemporary Russia. In our teaching we must be careful to avoid forcing parallels which are not justified by the facts, but we, like Bishop Sheen, can heighten awareness of the immediacy of much literature by leading the student to see similarities between the conflicts and tensions in a literary selection and similar forces in life.

2. Begin with familiar experiences in introducing the study of literature. On a breezy spring day discuss the sounds and rhythms of the wind before introducing "Who Has Seen the Wind?" and "The Wind Has Such a Rainy Sound." Share common experiences of embarrassment and awkwardness in social situations before reading "Clodhopper."

3. Plan writing assignments which encourage students to apply to their own experiences the concepts which have been developed through a discussion of literary selections. Seventh-graders who discover that *My Brother Mike* is the conscience of the boy in Doris Gates's book may later be asked to write on the topic, "When My Brother Mike Helped Me." One teacher followed a discussion of the irony implicit in the burglar's discussion of middle-class mores in *Sham* by asking tenth grade students to list examples of similar ironies which they had experienced in life.

In each of these learning experiences students are required to identify points of contact between the literature and experiences in the world today. The first and third exercises involve recognizing possible similarities in motive and situation. The second requires identification of parallel feelings and emotion.

■ *See differences in literature and life*

1. Provide opportunities for an objective appraisal of teen-age literature which deals with delinquent behavior. Not all stories concerning adolescents present valid and realistic portrayals. Swayed by a tendency to identify with youthful heroes and moved emotionally by contrived patterns of suspense, many adolescents fail to test incidents in their reading against their own daily experience. Organize a panel of students to report on representations of adolescent behavior in books of such varying quality as *Hot Rod* or *Street Rod, The Dark Adventure, Blackboard Jungle, Why Did They Kill?*, or *The Amboy Dukes*. Provide panel members with such thought questions as the following:

Study the portrayal of the leading figures in the book. To what extent are these figures presented as representative of most adolescents? To what extent are they presented as unique?

What reasons are suggested to explain the behavior of adolescents in this story?

To what extent do your own friends act in this way?

To what extent are their motives similar?

What other evidence can you find to show that boys and girls act this way?

Do you conclude that this book presents a fair portrait of adolescents today? Why or why not?

Organize similar panels to evaluate motion picture and television performances. In such an experience students are required first to identify the basic assumptions concerning adolescent behavior which seem to underlie the author's point of view, and then to test these assumptions against the reality around them.

■ *Compare the treatment of common themes in several selections*

1. The comparison of literary selections aids students to see that similar ideas may be expressed in many different ways. For example, choose a pair of selections

for class study. Normally one selection would be studied intensively, the second being read more quickly for comparative purposes. Some interesting pairings:

Seredy's *The Good Master;* Brink's *Caddie Woodlawn*
Twain's *Tom Sawyer;* McCloskey's *Homer Price*
Kipling's *Captains Courageous;* Moody's *Little Britches*
Gipson's *Old Yeller;* Rawlings' *The Yearling*
Saroyan's *The Human Comedy;* Wilder's *Our Town*
Eliot's *Silas Marner;* Steinbeck's *The Pearl*
Cather's *My Antonia;* Buck's *The Good Earth*
Shakespeare's *King Lear;* Hardy's *Return of the Native*
Shakespeare's *Macbeth;* Dostoyevsky's *Crime and Punishment*

2. When students have been reading related individual titles, ask them to compare the treatment of a topic through discussion in small groups. For example, ask tenth grade readers of books on family life to analyze the various methods used by characters in making decisions. Each is to analyze selected situations in the book he has finished and compare his findings with ideas presented by others.

Both of these experiences require learners to interpret separate literary selections and then to analyze the relation of elements in two or more interpretations. This necessarily involves assessing the understandings already possessed concerning each of the selections and then identifying those elements relevant to the comparison.

To improve skill in problem solving

■ *Develop a "questioning" attitude*

A spirit of inquiry encouraging the exploration of ideas helps individuals identify problems of personal concern. Restricted to subject matter prescribed by the textbook, a student will seldom develop initiative in identifying tasks of his own, nor will he share the excitement of finding new problems through the study of language and literature. Undoubtedly the use of multiple learning materials and the extension of learning beyond the classroom through the discriminating use of excursions, audio-visual aids, and guest speakers will broaden the student's horizons. So also will a classroom atmosphere which encourages class members to raise issues and questions. Some teachers use planned approaches such as the following in encouraging students to identify problems and to phrase questions.

1. Divide the class into several small groups for a brief discussion period. Ask the students in each group to raise questions or problems concerning the content being studied by the class or the methods which are being used in learning. Ask each group to propose one problem for consideration by the entire class. Teachers who introduce such periods frequently find them a helpful way of encouraging students to consider the purposes underlying learning.

2. During the introductory phase of a unit, ask students to formulate questions to answer through reading and study. For example, after a class has decided to study the use of humor in literature, ask each individual to list questions concerning humor in which he is particularly interested. Discussion of these personal lists culminates in the formulation of a series of objectives for the entire class.

Such class hours encourage students to think through ideas and to express opinions. Repeated experiences of this type encourage students to develop a questioning attitude.

■ *Relate new information to what has been learned before*

Success in coping with major problems depends largely upon an individual's mastery of basic skills and his ability to apply the knowledge he has previously learned. A boy applying for a job in a strange section of the city relies on his ability to read directions in reporting for an interview. A mature reader of George Stewart's *The Years of the City* must summon his prior understandings about the Greek city-state; so must an adolescent about Cortez in reading Shellabarger's *Captain From Castille.* In a real sense all classroom learnings tend to prepare students for the problems they face in the future. Yet individuals must still be taught ways of drawing upon the knowledge they possess in tackling the problems of the present. Teachers use such approaches as these:

1. Present to the class a topic for composition on which many students may reasonably be expected to have some background of information or experience—"The Fun of Large Groups" for the junior high school years, "Man's Dependence on Nature" or "Some Influences of Television on Adolescents" for older students. Many students do not believe they possess sufficient information to write on such topics. Show them that by asking appropriate questions which "tap" their storehouse of knowledge—Who? What? When? Where? Why?—they may list many facts, impressions, and ideas related to the topic and later organize these ideas in writing.

2. Plan class work over the year so that each new unit of work will be related to earlier classroom experiences. For example, seventh grade students who have studied characteristics of world folklore through reading books about Robin Hood, King Arthur, and stories from the Arabian Nights will draw upon this experience in a subsequent analysis of American folklore heroes. Similarly, *Julius Caesar* was used as a year's culminating study for tenth grade students who had completed separate units on poetry; language and the mass media; the theme, "The Nature of Truth"; and the topic, "Lost Worlds and Modern Problems." Analysis of the tragedy involved concepts which had been considered in all four units. Students were forced to re-evaluate many of these ideas.

Such activities require students to make a detailed analysis of their own experience and then to organize their ideas into a coherent whole.

■ *Learn methods and habits of thinking conducive to exploring hypotheses*

In exploring and testing possible solutions to problems, individuals must learn to suspend final judgment, to consider willingly all conceivable solutions, to predict probable results of alternative courses of action, to withhold final decisions until the consequences of actions have been examined. Faulty anticipation of outcomes is, of course, a frequent source of error in thinking, yet realistic methods of appraisal come primarily through experience in predicting. An "if-then" approach to the examination of a problem—"if" the proposed solution is assumed, "then" what are the consequences?—encourages an attitude which seems conducive to a realistic analysis of hypotheses. Such a point of view may be nurtured in school if teachers provide many genuine experiences in problem solving, and occasionally analyze with students the dangers of snap judgments and easy solutions. Such experiences as the following may suggest methods:

1. With teacher guidance the class examines the processes of thinking used by literary characters in solving problems. Caddie Woodlawn's thorough analysis of the possible consequences of voting to return to England is an excellent example

of "if-then" thinking. So, also, is Ronny Perry's consideration of how to gain acceptance at school in *All-American*. Conversely, in *Operation A.B.C.*, Tom Roerdan's attempt to avoid school tests for fear of revealing an inability to read offers a clear, if exaggerated, illustration of an inadequate solution accepted by an individual who fails to consider the consequences of his action.

2. Provide frequent opportunities for groups and individuals to plan classroom action. Following the reading of Morrow's *On to Oregon*, for example, an eighth grade class may be organized into groups for work on projects related to their reading on westward expansion. Ask each group to develop a presentation for the entire class. Whether the project involves creating a bulletin board, preparing a dramatization, explaining a model, or arranging for several illustrated talks, the groups are faced with a practical problem. Before determining action, they must consider the time allowed for planning, the resources available, and the extent to which the class audience must be prepared for the presentation. For students with little experience in self-directed activity, the teacher arranges for special guidance. Specific suggestions for directing group work are contained in Chapter 9, "Oral Language."

To refine skill in making judgments

■ *Establish the basis for judging*

1. By establishing standards for classroom behavior with the students and by evaluating progress in terms of these criteria, the teacher is able to demonstrate the importance of definite and realistic bases for evaluation. For example, ask a class to decide upon aims and goals for group work early in a semester, then evaluate subsequent group activity in terms of these standards—through discussion, through individual rating, through selected student observers, and through periodic review and reassessment of the selected criteria. Determine whether the standards should be lowered or upgraded.

2. Study the judgments of motion picture and television critics. Practice in judging is the only really effective method of encouraging students to develop discrimination in evaluating novels, motion pictures, and television programs; however, students do benefit from examining analyses written by experienced critics. One method which has proved useful in developing criteria for book reviews involves clipping professional reviews from such current periodicals as the *Saturday Review*, *Harper's*, the *Atlantic*, the *Reporter*, the New York *Times* and New York *Herald Tribune*. Allow students thirty minutes to study and exchange the printed reviews. Then ask the class to note characteristics which seem to be common to many reviews. In the discussion which follows, help students identify the basic elements of a well-written review—selection of an idea from the book which can be developed as an essay, expansion of the idea with reference to the point of view of the reviewer, and the conclusion.

3. Present to students such a list of decisions as the following. For each situation ask students to identify the factors which must be considered with respect to personal preferences, consequences of the decision, its probable effect on other people.

A sixteen-year-old boy wondering whether to purchase an automobile on time

The father of a twelve-year-old girl wondering whether to vote for or against a proposed ten o'clock curfew for adolescents

A family trying to decide whether to vacation in the mountains, at the seashore, or in a large city
The manager of an office selecting a receptionist
A high school student deciding whether to enroll in public speaking, drama, or journalism

This exercise requires students to identify elements affecting each decision and to predict the probable results of each choice.

4. Mount on a bulletin board six illustrations of men and women who appear to be successful in different endeavors. Include, perhaps, a football player, a military leader, an actress, a nurse, a statesman, and a mountain climber. The pictures should be large enough to be seen by all students. Ask each student to select the one of the six whom he considers to be the most successful and to write a paragraph explaining his choice. In the discussion that follows, develop an understanding of the various dimensions of success and the extent to which the judgments of students are based on different criteria.

■ *Improve objectivity in making inferences*

1. Ask students to write brief paragraphs describing the type of individual who is suggested by each of the following groups of adjectives:

Shy, reticent, quiet, precise, insecure, perceptive
Vital, chic, sporting, beguiling, talkative, poised
Dangerous, sharp, quick-witted, energetic, shrewd, sly

Compare student descriptions. Examine with the class the extent to which inferences are based on emotional as well as logical factors.

The purpose of such an exercise is to reveal to ourselves the extent to which we rely on stereotypes in our thinking.

■ *Evaluate authorities*

1. Ask students to evaluate carefully whether they would accept the authority of each of the following individuals on the topics indicated:

An international party hostess, on international affairs
A world traveler, on color photography
A tennis player, on tennis balls
An opera singer, on television programing
A motion picture star, on hair tonic

Follow this discussion by asking class members to suggest possible authorities on whom they would rely in obtaining information on such topics as the following:

Modern warfare	An Air Force general? A senator? The Secretary of Defense?
Hydroplane races	*Sports Illustrated?* The president of a motor company? A hydroplane pilot?

2. Ask students to select from a list of names on the chalkboard those persons whom they consider to be reliable authorities in the following three fields: nuclear

energy; American baseball; contemporary fashion. List real-life examples of people with such occupations as:

a leader in industry	a renowned humanitarian
a designer of hats	a manager of a baseball team
a motion picture star	the owner of a local woman's store
the administrator of a nuclear project	a sports writer
the Secretary of Defense	a dress designer
a physics laboratory assistant	a famous pitcher
the President of the United States	an army general
a physicist	

3. Provide experiences in choosing between authorities. Present students with a request for certain specific kinds of information (List A). Ask them to select from List B the authorities whom they would consult in obtaining the necessary facts.

List A Information desired

State parking and speeding regulations for automobiles

Directions on how to repair a leaky faucet

Information on the best location for planting camellias and rhododendrons

Suggested procedures in planning a wedding reception

List B Possible sources of information

Local nurseryman

An interested neighbor

A plumber's handbook

The classified advertisements of a newspaper

Encyclopaedia Britannica

"Popular Gardening" magazine

The state motor vehicle code

The judge of a local court

An etiquette book published in 1935

The writer of a newspaper column designed to answer questions on personal problems

An etiquette book published in 1950

The society section of a newspaper

4. Ask students to consider the biases of authorities by evaluating a series of statements on a selected topic. Ask each individual to estimate the degree of bias in such statements as the following by rating the speaker's degree of objectivity on a five-point scale. Ask students to note the reasons for each rating.

Judging possible bias

Directions to Student: How much confidence would you place in each of the following statements? Indicate your opinion concerning the possible bias of each speaker by rating each statement on a five-point scale ranging from *Objective* to *Extreme bias.* Then write your reasons for the rating. In considering the speaker's qualifications, think not only about his knowledge of the subject but his possible motivation for making the statement.

1. "This is certainly one of the greatest comedies that Hollywood has produced and one that no one can afford to miss." —Motion picture editor of a leading news service, at the Hollywood premiere.

1	2	3	4	5
Objective				Extreme bias

Reasons: ______________________________

2. "Certainly no one can resist the gay new comedy from Twentieth-Century-Fox. It is a merry romp calculated to dispel all gloom, and Katherine Drew has never looked lovelier." –Movie critic, writing in a monthly motion picture (fan) magazine.

3. "This offers further evidence that Hollywood films are successful only when they fail to come to grips with ideas." –Broadway drama critic, New York paper.

4. "I accept only roles that my fans will enjoy, and this, I am sure, is my best." –Star, making a personal appearance with the film.

5. "Some may object to the film's searching and intimate portrayal of middle-class marriage, but most will recognize the serious social criticism intended." –Executive producer, at a press interview before release of the film.

6. "I guarantee that this is one of the most compelling films which we have shown in two-and-a-half years." –Printed advertisement attributed to manager of local theatre.

7. "The stars do their utmost with stilted dialogue and inept direction and they do manage to make the affair moderately diverting, but those who have expected the ultimate in screen comedies will be sorely disappointed." –Local newspaper critic, after the film opens.

■ *Weigh evidence and varied points of view*

1. Students need much experience in weighing different points of view. Ask tenth grade students who have selected biographies for individual reading to assess the objectivity of the authors involved. With guidance lead the class to study the effect on biographical writing of the author's point of view, his particular interests, his selection and organization of incident. Then ask each student to obtain basic facts regarding the life of the individual about whom he is reading, to locate and read at least one or two interpretive articles on the person in addition to the longer book, and to compare the accounts.

When students are being introduced to the problem of evaluating the objectivity of biographers, some teachers prefer to plan some common study for the entire class. For example, students might compare the eulogistic description of Louis Pasteur by his son-in-law, Vallery-Radot,[17] with the severely critical account of the scientist by Paul DeKruif. These contrasting points of view might later be compared with that of the motion picture, *The Story of Louis Pasteur.*

2. Provide exercises for juniors and seniors which require the analysis of printed materials prepared for specific propaganda purposes. Sometimes materials published by special groups within the United States are useful. Documents published for English readers by foreign countries are of special interest since these reveal unusual points of view toward American readers. With mature readers in some school situations, teachers find that propaganda materials released by the U.S.S.R. provoke thoughtful analysis.

The following publications are presently obtainable: *USSR,* an illustrated monthly magazine similar to *Life; New Times,* a weekly journal of news commentary; *Moscow News,* an eight-page daily newspaper.[18]

[17] René Vallery-Radot, *The Life of Pasteur* (N.Y., Doubleday Doran, 1923).

[18] *USSR* is published by the Russian Embassy; the editorial offices are at 1706 Eighteenth St., N.W., Washington 9, D.C. Both of the newspapers are published by the Alliance of Soviet Societies of Friendship and Cultural Relations with Foreign Countries, and are obtainable from Imported Publications and Products, 4 W. 16th St., N.Y. 11, N.Y.

In asking students to analyze such documents, prepare a special guide which includes such pointed questions as the following:

Judging from the contents of the issue, what kinds of events and ideas seem most important? Political? Cultural? Athletic? Industrial? Military? What gives you this impression? What factors may explain this selection by the editors?

What is the dominant impression that the publication seems to convey? How is this reflected in choice of article? In illustrations? In headlines?

Select any single article which you believe would have been rewritten or eliminated if the paper had been prepared for domestic reading. Why?

3. Mature students may sometimes be asked to consider difficult decisions involving conflicting values, as in the following assignment which was introduced in a larger unit on "Loyalties." [19]

Directions to Student: The following situation poses problems in loyalties and preconceptions. Write fairly complete statements of your own position. Do not merely answer Yes or No or write one statement. Defend and explain all your points of view. Where there seems to be more than one possible approach to a problem, state all possibilities.

John Adams, Negro, using the helpful influence of his army officers, succeeded in renting an apartment in a housing project. His was the first Negro family in the project, and at first they were received coldly by the other tenants. After a period of months, through their own cheerful and courteous efforts, the Adamses won the friendship and respect of their neighbors. They were accepted in the social life of the community. At this time, a Negro friend came to John to request a favor. She was to be married and she wanted John to write a letter of recommendation which she would use in applying for an apartment in the same project. John knew the girl and felt that she would make a desirable neighbor, but he did not know her fiancé. He knew, too, that if the couple moved into the project, his own family would be judged by the behavior of the new tenants.

He began to worry about the possibility of his friends' friends having noisy parties or behaving in some way which would antagonize the other tenants. If he wrote the letter, then, he would possibly endanger his family's status in the project; and he could not forget the months of cold rejection which began their stay. If he refused to write the letter, he would feel that he had betrayed his loyalty to his principles and friends. What do you think are some of the problems John must settle before he can act? What should John do? Why?

In some communities, racial sympathies and antipathies may be so strong that classroom discussion of the problem is inadvisable. In such cases, however, teachers will introduce situations involving conflicts between other loyalties.

Problems of this type require students to marshal all their problem solving abilities. They must analyze all pertinent aspects of the problem, determine the principles involved and the possible courses of action, and predict the probable results of each alternative course.

[19] Developed by Merritt Beckerman, San Francisco City College.

Evaluating Growth

How does one evaluate growth in the ability to formulate sound conclusions? Ultimately the real test is to be found only in the learners' ability to cope successfully with increasingly mature decisions, concepts, and problems. Too seldom, however, do teachers have opportunity to see the ultimate fruits of classroom endeavor. Rather, most teachers rely on evaluating growth toward goals established for a manageable period of time—a lesson, a unit, a semester, or a year.

If lesson and unit goals are identified in terms of specific student behaviors, the task of evaluation is relatively clear. Thus, if "improvement of ability to see relationships between two literary selections" is an objective, the teacher can provide no better way of determining the effectiveness of the learning than by introducing a comparison of two poems or stories which will require students to use their newly developed skills. Similarly, if the elimination of prejudice and bias from students' thinking has received attention, an effective way of approaching evaluation is to examine individual ability to cope in speech or writing with an issue highly charged with emotional bias. Whatever the specific method, the focus will be on assessing a behavior of the learner, not on his acquisition of factual knowledge. Here we are concerned with the refinement of thinking processes which lead to sound conclusions, so we evaluate in terms of process.

To assess long-range goals—those for a semester, a year, sometimes even an extended unit—teachers find it helpful to have a touchstone against which individual progress may be assessed. Both standardized tests and informal methods have been used to obtain a general assessment of student abilities.

For teachers who like to compare student abilities with clearly defined norms, two standardized instruments are available:

Logical Reasoning Test, General Education Series, Grades 10-12. (Cooperative Test Division, Educational Testing Service, Princeton, N.J., 1939-1950.) Ten series of test questions requiring judgment and reasoning developed by the Evaluation Staff of the American Education Fellowship, formerly Progressive Education Association.

A Test of Critical Thinking, Grades 7-9. (Mary and Hugh Wood, University of Oregon Press, 1951.) Test yields seven scores on qualities, inquiry, open-mindedness, ability to relate concepts. May be reproduced.

Except for special research purposes, formal instruments of this kind are seldom used more than every two years or so. Like most standardized tests, these are as helpful in diagnosing needs as in assessing growth.

Most teachers find they must rely in part or totally on informal teacher-made tests of student growth. Here the test-teach-retest method may be used over long intervals of time. By collecting evidence of students' abilities early in a year, the teacher later has a touchstone to which he can refer. Many of the learning experiences described in this chapter may be introduced in September, then repeated in modified form in June. By comparing results on two similar exercises, themes, or even recorded discussions, the teacher gains insight into the changes which have occurred in student thinking. Often, too, the students may make their own assessments of growth by comparing their processes and procedures after receiving instruction with those on which they relied before. Often a cumulative file of sample papers and exercises for each student will be of continual use.

The purpose of the program described in this chapter is to teach students to think clearly regardless of their irrational feelings and thoughts. By analyzing the thinking of students, and by teaching them ways of forming concepts, solving problems, and making judgments, we strive to improve their understanding of the conclusions of others and their ability to form sound conclusions of their own. Ultimately then, the basic test of the program is to be found in the maturity of the students' grasp of the skills and arts of the language and in the soundness of their values.

SELECTED READINGS

Gordon Allport and Leo Postman, *The Psychology of Rumor.* N.Y., Holt, 1947. An interesting report of experiments with adults and with children and youth. Teachers will be most appreciative of the suggested exercises. Chapter 10 presents some interesting examples of rumors which may be used with secondary students. A "Guide for the Analysis of Rumor" is also included.

Monroe Beardsley, *Thinking Straight: Principles of Reasoning for Readers and Writers.* 2nd ed. Englewood Cliffs, N.J., Prentice-Hall, 1950. A handbook intended for college students, suggesting humorous exercises which can be adapted for lower levels.

Benjamin S. Bloom, ed., *Taxonomy of Educational Objectives, Handbook I: Cognitive Domain.* N.Y., Longmans, Green, 1956. A handy reference booklet prepared by a committee of college examiners who attempt to identify concrete objectives of the acquisition of knowledge and the attainment of intellectual skill. Of particular use in teaching are some of the test questions suggested to measure such complex skills as synthesizing, making judgments based on external and internal evidence, and seeing relationships.

Jerome S. Bruner, Jacqueline J. Goodnow, and George Austin, *A Study of Thinking.* N.Y., Wiley, 1956. Contains a thorough analysis of the psychological aspects of thinking, including some treatment of language and categorization.

S. I. Hayakawa, *Language in Thought and Action.* N.Y., Harcourt, Brace, 1949. This well-known volume not only contains an analysis of language and thought but suggests many activities which can be used in secondary schools.

David H. Russell, *Children's Thinking.* Boston, Ginn, 1956. A readable compilation of research bearing on the thinking of youth. Teachers will be especially interested in Chapters 12 and 13, which deal with the improvement of thinking.

Critical Thinking in Current Affairs Discussion. The Junior Town Meeting League, 356 Washington Street, Middleton, Connecticut, 1956. This pamphlet reviews importance of critical thinking, identifies "steps," and suggests classroom activities.

Chapter Three

Imaginative Thinking

> *. . . the real crisis in the life of our society is the crisis of the life of the imagination. Far more than we need an intercontinental missile or a moral rearmament or a religious revival, we need to come alive again, to recover the virility of the imagination on which all earlier civilizations have been based . . . I do not mean that I think education is wholly responsible for the flaw which has split knowledge of heart from knowledge of the head, though it has surely its fair share of the blame. I mean rather that it is principally by the process of education that the flaw can be healed.*
>
> —ARCHIBALD MAC LEISH [1]

PERSPECTIVE

John Stuart Mill's father believed in the value of mental tasks for his son. At the age of three, the child began his study of Greek. By the time he was eight, he had read numerous books on government as well as Plato and Xenophon in the original. So that his education might assume a "more serious phase," he studied arithmetic at night until fully prepared for higher mathematics. When he was twelve, a more advanced stage was added to his instruction—logic. He read through the *Organon.*

At this point, the father judged that his son's education had begun in earnest. Mr. Mill had an immense distrust of feelings and emotions. Most children were annoyingly addicted to outbursts of enthusiasm or petulance, but now logic could fortify reason, pruning away any remnants of childish weakness. And, indeed, Mr. Mill appeared to be right. His son continued to devote his mind to logical thought day and night, suppressing any tendencies toward feeling—until he was twenty.

One rainy November evening, the youth looked up from his books, aware of an intense gloom and mental depression. Sensibly, he went to bed, assuming that a good night's sleep would fortify his logical determination to eliminate this unfortunate melancholy. Sleep apparently was no solution, for the next day he collapsed completely. Up until this point he had been increasing

[1] "The Poet and the Press," *Atlantic,* Vol. 203, No. 3 (March 1959), p. 46.

his control of logic; now logic, along with consuming his feelings and emotions, had apparently lost its power.

Throughout that winter the young Mill remained in a trance of listless melancholy. His entire personality was in a process of revolt and transformation, but not until spring was there a sign indicating a break in his apathy. While reading about a boy who performed an act of kindness, John suddenly shook with violent emotion and tears flowed down his cheeks. During the next month he groped painfully toward equilibrium, turning to the poetry of Wordsworth and the music of von Weber. From these beginnings he reached out to other romantic poets, Shelley and Goethe, and to lighthearted people around him. And by 1831, when Carlyle met him, Mill was no longer merely a logical machine; he was a slender youth "with earnestly smiling eyes, modest, remarkably gifted with precision of utterance; enthusiastic yet lucid, calm." He was ready to write his famous essay, *On Liberty*.

Balancing reason and imagination

For their students, teachers of English endeavor to achieve by less dramatic means this balance of lucidity and enthusiasm. Educational efforts to develop a bare intellectuality are doomed to failure—doomed because by nature men are emotional as well as intellectual. The study of English concerns more than systematic thinking. Although the importance of logic and analysis as educational imperatives should not be minimized, students' feelings and imaginations must also find frequent expression lest the classroom become a grim intellectual gymnasium. Too heavy an emphasis upon logical thought—to the exclusion of imagination and inspiration—eliminates the zest and satisfaction of learning.

No sharp distinction between imagination and reason Reason and imagination are not, however, two distinct kinds of thinking; sometimes they are conveniently symbolized as two ends of a continuum. Dominating one end of the scale is logic, with its realistic problem solving and its objective appraisal of the actual world. At the other end? Imagination, reverie, and intuition, all those forms of mental activity nourished by man's internal needs and impulses. Thinking shifts rapidly back and forth along the scale, never completely realistic, never completely imaginative. The mature individual maintains a delicate balance, emphasizing according to the situation the requirements of outer reality or the inner needs of his personality. The danger, always, is to lose equilibrium. Evidently John Stuart Mill moved perilously close to an inhuman world devoid of feeling. Schumann, Nietzsche, Nijinsky—to choose three examples—apparently upset the balance in the other direction, disregarding the demands of objective reality. The scientist uses both kinds of thinking, often simultaneously. Systematic thinking is so often interfused with imagination that any presentation of these powers as opposite ends of a continuum (as in this chapter) risks false interpretations.

In this chapter, we urge the case for a balance that includes the imagination. Obviously, an intense classroom preoccupation with pixies and leprechauns would press all but the most docile adolescents into justified revolt and disenchantment. Nor, in the preceding chapter, do we advocate that instruction in English imitate the cold harsh logic of stern figures like John Stuart Mill's father. Respect for the whole nature of man, not for intellect alone, not for feeling alone, becomes the equilibrium the English teacher must skillfully maintain.

A definition of imagination What is this imagination, this brand of thinking so often claimed as a basis necessary for appreciation and creative expression, so often confused with the fantastic and unusual? Imagination is a mental activity which—because it is relatively free from realistic demands—enables one to summon up images, feelings, memories, sensations, intuitions. Because of the freedom from immediate practicality, the imaginative thinker can rearrange and recombine these mosaics of association in fluid fashion to create new delightful or useful relationships. The essential ingredient is the creative synthesis, the new whole made by combining elements experienced separately. These elements may be conscious or unconscious; in fact, it is the access to the unconscious which gives special power to the imagination.

But if the mental activity in imagination is freer, bolder, less dependent than logic upon demonstrable proofs, it is not irresponsible fantasy. Between imaginative and systematic thought no radical distinction exists; both are a part of imaginative intelligence, a single entity. Reason, says Santayana, is itself a method of imaginative thought, and the only valid distinction between imagination and understanding is a pragmatic one. Constructs of the imagination which prove useful in daily affairs or the work of the world are called the ideas of understanding; others, less useful in predicting the future or directing one's daily life are called imagination.[2]

The importance of the imagination may be demonstrated by returning to our emphasis upon its power to synthesize diverse elements. Among the qualities the imagination can balance or reconcile, Coleridge lists an interesting group; among them, "a more than usual state of emotion with more than usual order; judgment ever awake and steady self-possession with enthusiasm and feeling profound or vehement." He ascribes to imagination "the power of reducing multitude into unity of effect and modifying a series of thoughts by some one predominant thought or feeling."[3] This balance, this equilibrium, draws into action more of the human personality than does most

[2] This concept of the unity of imaginative and systematic thought is based upon the ideas of Santayana. See George Santayana, *Dominations and Powers* (N.Y., Scribner's, 1951), p. 463.

[3] These quotations are taken from Coleridge's *Biographia Literaria,* the close of Chapter XIV, and Chapter XV.

thinking. Whether scientists, poets, or ordinary human beings, we find that the imagination opens our minds to more expansive perceptions. "We cease to be orientated in one definite direction; more facets of the mind are exposed . . . more aspects of things are able to affect us."[4] We respond, not narrowly but simultaneously and coherently, through many ways of perceiving.

In this high state of combined alertness, flexibility, and coherence, the thinker is able to accommodate and turn to advantage a multiplicity of stimulation and richness that would ordinarily bewilder him. At such times, he feels more fully alive, achieving insight into situations otherwise confusing or opaque. From these imaginative moments he returns to ordinary living and thinking with a more stable poise. Sometimes this happy experience occurs when he reads a great book, performs an experiment, or listens to music; sometimes he achieves it in a particularly satisfying conversation with friends; sometimes this clarity and heightened insight occur in his own meditation, perhaps while he is driving to work or standing alone on a high hill. Whenever he sees more fully, not through a single response, but *coherently and simultaneously through many responses,* he is experiencing imaginative insight.

Imagination important to everyone One misconception about the imagination requires brief comment. The imagination is no trivial plaything of the dilettante. Imagination is vital to the housewife, who must make leftovers palatable, to the carpenter, who must envision spaces and stresses, and to the teacher who must devise ways to make wisdom prevail. Add to the list: the driver in city traffic, the diplomat, the young man seeking a job. To some degree, everyone must think like the poets, and the poets themselves have recognized that their subjective art is not truly divorced from reality:

> We are the music makers,
> And we are the dreamers of dreams,
> . . .
> Yet we are the movers and shakers
> Of the world forever, it seems.[5]

And the scientist must be as imaginative as the poet. Of the physicist, Michael Faraday, we read:

> . . . Faraday's first great characteristic was his trust in facts, and his second his imagination. . . . Only, it is important to remember, these two characteristics were not separate and distinct. . . . it was because in Faraday they were held together in vital tension that he became so potent an instrument of research into Nature's secrets. . . . In carrying out physical experiments he would experience

[4] This quotation and the concept of simultaneous awareness and coherence are drawn from Chapter XXXII of I. A. Richards, *Principles of Literary Criticism* (N.Y., Harcourt, Brace, 1924). Richards' discussion of the imagination has been an important influence throughout this text.

[5] Arthur William Edgar O'Shaughnessy.

a childlike joy and his eyes sparkled. "Even to his latest days he would almost dance for joy at being shown a new experiment." [6]

In all the most important acts of life, in all vocations, imagination marks the difference between success and mediocrity.

Commenting on his father's plan of education which systematically eliminated emotion from thinking, John Stuart Mill wrote in his *Autobiography:* "I was left stranded at the commencement of my voyage with a well-equipped ship and a rudder, but no sail; without any real desire for the ends which I had been so carefully fitted out to work for . . ." The methods of teaching described in this chapter are based on a conception of imaginative thinking as a necessary balance for logical thinking. Without the full range of human thought, pupils in school can also be stranded without sails, without guidance toward clear thinking, appreciation of beauty, and lives of awareness.

The language of imagination

Man is a rational being, but it is not prudent to forget that his consciousness includes emotional and volitional spheres. Feeling and will—like reason—also require expression. Yet language is an inadequate medium for expressing the whole nature of man. Language "merely names certain vaguely and crudely conceived states, but fails miserably in any attempt to convey the ever moving patterns, the ambivalences and intricacies of inner experience. . . . If we say that we understand someone else's feeling in a certain matter, we mean that we understand why he should be sad or happy, excited or indifferent, in a general way; that we can see due cause for his attitude. We do not mean that we have insight into the actual flow and balance of his feelings . . . Language is quite inadequate to such a conception." [7] Thus Susanne K. Langer sums up the limitations of language for expressing feeling.

Jespersen extends Langer's point. He believes language began to develop when communicativeness took precedence over exclamativeness. The world of objective reality is the inescapable subject matter of most communication and the content of everyday discourse is mainly that of rational concepts and facts. To be sure, emphasis, tone of voice, and other forms of vocal coloring do contribute some feeling quality to what a speaker seeks to convey, but they do so uncertainly. In writing, even with the help of italics, underlining, and exclamation points, feeling is even more difficult to express. Consequently man has developed, and is still developing, ways to express his feelings, ways to flash awareness of inner states of mind from one person to

[6] Havelock Ellis, *The Dance of Life* (Boston, Houghton Mifflin, 1929); in the paperbound edition (N.Y., Grosset & Dunlap, 1956), this quotation appears on pp. 123-125. Ellis quotes John Tyndall, Faraday's friend and fellow worker.

[7] Susanne K. Langer, *Philosophy in a New Key: A Study in the Symbolism of Reason, Rite and Art* (Cambridge, Mass., Harvard U. Press, 3rd ed., 1957); in the paperbound edition (N.Y., New American Library, 1948), this quotation appears on p. 82. In other passages, Mrs. Langer expresses her respect for the power of language.

another. These ways are those of art, symbol, and ritual. Of these, the way that most concerns teachers of English is literature.

Literature, like all the arts, uses special ways to *evoke* experience in others. True, literature uses words, but careful examination reveals that the language of literature is not the language of everyday use. Although anchored to the grammar of ordinary language, literature seeks to express realms of experience inaccessible to that ordinary language, and does so more often by symbolic than by logical statement. Lyric poetry is the purest example of the way literature accomplishes this evocation of the full response—emotional, volitional, and rational. Listen to Yeats: "Poetry bids us touch and taste and hear and see the world, and shrink from all that is of the brain only, from all that is not a fountain jetting from the entire hopes, memories, and sensations of the body." Poetry expresses more of the poet than does ordinary language; poetry invigorates more of the total human being than do the forms of everyday language. The aim of lyric poems like Herrick's "To Daffodils" and Housman's "Loveliest of Trees" is certainly not to bring us horticultural information about daffodils or cherry trees, even though both poems employ rational propositions concerning the color of blossoms and the duration of their bloom. The poets are expressing their feelings about the transience of beauty and the brevity of man's life, and are seeking to evoke in us these same feelings. If their symbols are successful, there occurs a flash of insight, stirring our entire consciousness—rational, emotional, volitional, and whatever else there may be yet hidden from psychology and philosophy.

How much poetry and imagination are akin can be understood by referring to the definition of imagination . . . *summoning up images, feelings, memories, sensations, and intuitions . . . enthusiasm and feeling profound or vehement . . . modifying a series of thoughts by some one predominant thought or feeling.* Yet the imagination is more than poetry, just as the mind of man is more than brain. The mind of man is more than either reason or feeling. It is art and science; it is conscience, morality, religion. It is music and poetry as well as chemistry and homemaking; whenever the term *thinking* is used in this book, this *entire range of man's consciousness is intended.*

The danger of logic is that it neglects the whole nature of man. Logical thinking clamps down "restrictive frames of reference upon the activity of the mind, and presently ends in impoverishing the activity which it purports to guide into creative channels. It becomes intolerant of the immediate, unanalyzed primitive abundance of the mind, and by so doing destroys its own source." [8] To understand thinking as representing the whole consciousness of man, as including all his modes of perceiving, is healthy. Lacking the flexible energy of the imagination, the classifications of logic become too neat, too rigid.

Pupils should realize that thinking is more than reasoning and that language includes both emotive and referential meanings even though it must

[8] Harold Lasswell, *Psychopathology and Politics* (Chicago, U. of Chicago Press, 1930), pp. 32, 33.

be used in special ways to feature either one. Nor is language the ultimate medium for expressing the modes of feeling. Beyond language lie music, painting, and other non-verbal arts, but these are not, directly, the concern of those who teach language and literature. The tool of language and the range of thinking associated with it—these are the commission of the English teacher.

Some approaches to imaginative thinking

Methods used to foster imaginative insight need to be closely fitted to an accepted definition of imagination. The definition used in this chapter yields five approaches which may be identified as guides to classroom instruction. Doubtless other systems of relationships could be devised, and research in the future will surely reveal more about the structure of the imagination and about any hierarchy among its elements. The five classifications adopted here represent an arrangement benefiting from research and philosophical inquiries.[9] The following categories are offered, however, not as an established taxonomy of the imagination but as a teaching guide for those who want to extend the range of classroom thinking. Their order here is based upon a progressively increasing admixture of logic.

Flexibility and fluidity of thought; the opposite of rigidity

Vitality, but a controlled vitality; the opposite of apathy

Insight, a notable bias toward searching for implications; the opposite of obtuseness, of superficial and unwary acceptance of appearances

Synthesis, the fusion of varied elements by some unifying design; the opposite of randomness

Understanding, an intellectual grasp of the nature and importance of the imagination; the opposite of ignorance concerning its nature and function

Toward flexibility, away from rigidity There are many occasions when teachers want to encourage pupils to be original, to observe freshly, and to strike out in new directions. The fluent thinking underlying such creativity appears in all studies of the imagination. As a result of his research, Barron describes imaginative persons as those who use, more than the average person, the life of the unconscious—fantasy, reverie, intuition. "They have exceptionally broad and flexible awareness of themselves. The self is strongest when it can regress (admit primitive fantasies, naive ideas, tabooed impulses into consciousness and behavior), and yet return to a high degree of rationality and self-criticism."[10] For notably creative pupils as well as everyone else in his classroom, the teacher contributes to the health of the mind by fostering a disposition to break occasionally with habit and to express feelings. The pur-

[9] See the Selected Readings at the close of this chapter.

[10] Frank Barron, "The Psychology of Imagination," *Scientific American,* Vol. 199, No. 3 (September 1958), p. 164.

pose is not to produce emotional misfits and exhibitionists; a balance of perspective will prevent such excesses. But a release from stultifying grooves of thought and a wholehearted response to life will contribute to the supple mentality which was lacking in John Stuart Mill, the logical machine.

Toward vitality, away from apathy Everyone has endured the annoyance of being involved in a limp, soggy conversation; everyone has enjoyed animated talk when, feeling joining with thought, a surge of vitality flowed from one speaker to another. Wherever imagination appears—in good conversation, in scientific discovery, in decorating a home—vitality is essential and contagious. In a classroom, this energy radiates most forcefully from the teacher himself. Important also are the connections students see between what they are studying and life beyond the school. Other elements are a classroom climate of mutual respect, clear awareness of aims, alternations of serious effort and relaxing pleasures, and times when the teacher introduces some element of surprise, challenge, or humor.

Creative people, it has often been noticed, have an exceptional fund of physical and mental energy. Note, for instance, a description of high school students during the act of creation: ". . . writing accompanied by elation, by an almost unnatural feeling of well-being; fatigue disappears; enormous quantities of labor can be accomplished; one can work for hours without a demand for rest, or even for food or sleep. Young people know all about this characteristic of the vital energy . . ."[11] How strikingly similar this is to Coleridge's description of the elements balanced by imagination: "a more than usual state of emotion, with more than usual order; judgment ever awake and steady self-possession with enthusiasm and feeling profound or vehement." Recent research also reinforces these descriptions. MacKinnon, reviewing findings at the Institute for Personality Assessment and Research (University of California, Berkeley), depicts the creative person as having access to more of his intelligence, as being more discerning, more observant, more alert, more able to concentrate attention readily and to shift it appropriately, more fluent in scanning thoughts. According to MacKinnon, he is one who does not characteristically suppress or repress, but rather *expresses.*[12]

But vitality alone is never enough. This phase of imaginative insight must be conceived as an *ordered vitality,* never an incoherent energy mounting its horse and riding off simultaneously in seven directions. From such chaos there emerges not imagination but turbulence. The vitality must be dominated either by a significant goal or a drive toward form and order. This search for order is one of the links between imaginative thinking and rational thinking. There is no sharp division between the powers of imagination and the powers of rationality.

[11] Hughes Mearns, *Creative Youth* (N.Y., Doubleday, Doran, 1925).
[12] Donald W. MacKinnon, "Identifying the Effective Teacher," *California Journal for Instructional Improvement,* Vol. 1, No. 1 (October 1958), pp. 12, 13.

Toward synthesis, away from randomness When a pupil is drawing upon imagination, he is more than usually alert and in control of his thought. Under the power of a heightened understanding, an extended mental horizon, he is able, through use of energy and insight, to impose patterns on what might otherwise be a jumble of confused ideas and impulses. The patterns vary enormously, for structures are as diverse as the universe itself. The metaphors and symbols of the poet are one way to impose order on thought; the constants and variables of the physicist are another. The poet and the physicist, like the musician working with the chaos of sound, impose order on a variety of elements that would otherwise be random and therefore meaningless. Witness this evocation of fireworks from the creative writing of a high school boy:

Rockets [13]

A genie's arm, and sleeved in gold
Was thrust across the sky. Behold
How from his smoking palm there falls
A silent chime of colored balls.

The same boy, watching acrobats, jaunty and glib at the end of their act, wonders if they've really comprehended that "They've tickled Death along his bony rib." In both poems, unlike elements are related through a sudden flash of imaginative insight. This is a high equilibrium of vitality, flexibility, and order.

Perhaps one of the most interesting findings of recent research is the evidence that imaginative persons like the challenge of disorder. Barron's subjects, both artists and scientists, preferred paintings and figures that to the unimaginative viewer might appear unbalanced and disordered, and they expressed an aversion for things that were simple and too obviously symmetrical. The illustration on p. 125 underlines some of the differences between creative persons and others selected at random. Barron relates these findings to synthesis, pointing out that

> Behind this inclination to like and to construct what is not too simply ordered there appears to be a very strong need to achieve the most difficult and far-reaching ordering. When confronted, for instance, with the Rorschach inkblot test, original individuals insist to a most uncommon degree upon giving an interpretation of the blot which takes account of all details in one comprehensive, synthesizing image. Since some of these blcts are quite messy, this disposition to synthesize points up the challenge of disorder. It also illustrates the creative response to disorder, which is to find an elegant new order more satisfying than any that could be evoked by a simpler configuration.[14]

Barron sees the most imaginative persons as those who can live with complexity because they have confidence they can meet the challenge of confusion

[13] From "Fireworks" by Tom Prideaux, from Mearns, *Creative Youth.* Reprinted by permission of Hughes Mearns.

[14] Barron, "The Psychology of Imagination," p. 155.

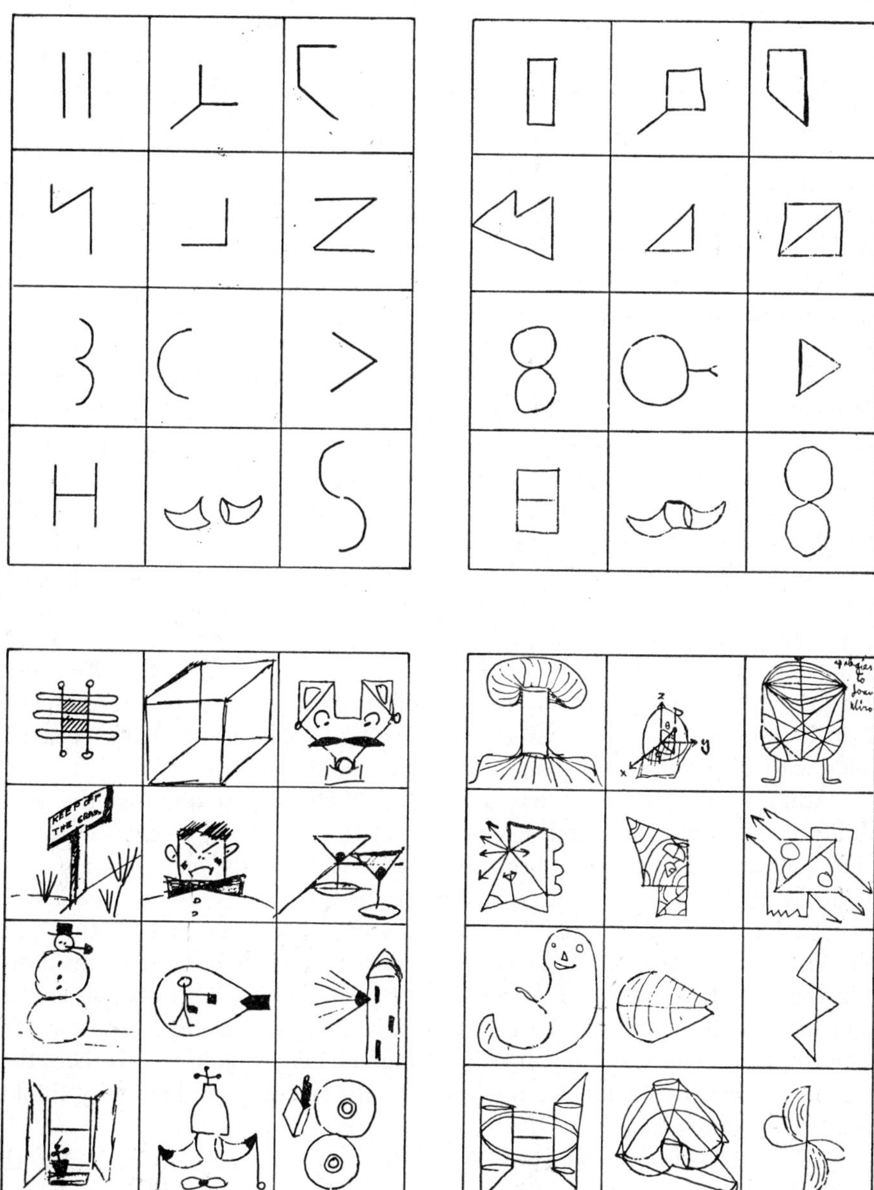

Drawing-Completion Test, devised by Kate Franck. Figures to be completed are at top left; a typical response at top right; bottom sections show drawings by creative individuals. Reprinted from Scientific American, *September, 1958, by permission of the Institute of Personality Assessment and Research, and of S. S. Dunn, Assistant Director, Australian Council for Educational Research.*

by finding the order that lies behind it. To resolve their discomfort by finding simple solutions is a temptation they resist. Thus they refuse to achieve order at the cost of excluding evidence; they realize to reject any evidence precludes the satisfaction of attaining a larger perspective and more appropriate judgments.

Synthesis, then, is part of the search for order which must be imposed upon flexibility and vitality if these traits of the imagination are not to be distractions to effective thinking. The order, however, must be appropriate to the material, taking all of it into account. Simple solutions for complex problems, mechanical structures for supple or human situations—these will fall short of the true order imagination requires.

Toward insight, away from obtuseness Flexibility, vitality, and synthesis combine to make possible the mental behavior called insight. *In*-sight is mental vision, *seeing into* the true inner nature of things. Sudden, gradual, or partial, there are different degrees of insight, varying with persons and situations. Even children can discover the essential principle in one situation and through insight transpose it to others. For instance, children three to seven years of age have been shown six toy airplanes, all colored green. Each of these planes was placed behind a door in a hangar, each door painted a different color. When the child pulled the green door which matched the airplanes, it opened and he received the toy. Most of the children discovered this principle and were able to apply it when the planes were different colors and all the doors the same color, or when both planes and doors varied in color with one plane corresponding to one door.[15]

Adult insight in chemistry, poetry, or mathematics requires the same ability to see into a situation, to understand it as a whole, and it varies with different people and different problems. Insight merges reason and imagination so firmly that one can readily understand that reason is itself a method of imaginative thought. Turned toward structures and processes in the outer physical world—as in the case of the children getting the planes—insightful thinking is called reason. Turned toward the inner feelings and desires of man himself, insightful thinking is called imagination. Both are part of the same psychic energy welling up in all human beings. Joined together, they become the way of thinking of the poet and the scientist—and of every thinker in all times and places.

The imagination is like an X-ray, penetrating surfaces, exploring the reality behind deceptive outer appearances. Imaginative insight becomes one of man's ways to strive toward deeper interpretations, for what appears on the surface does not always correspond to the truths available to the imagination. Here is the ancient riddle of shadow and substance. Teachers seek not only to make their pupils aware of this complexity of truth, but also to foster

[15] K. E. Roberts, *Learning in Preschool and Orphanage Children: An Experimental Study of Ability to Solve Different Situations According to the Same Plan,* University of Iowa Studies in Child Welfare, Vol. 7, No. 3, 1933. (Iowa City, State University of Iowa.)

a disposition to recognize implications, to look for interpretations, and to feel at home with symbols. This imaginative alertness is a valuable way of life; the obtuse person, lacking the delicate equilibrium of the insightful person, is often confused by the blows of daily existence. It is true that native ability limits the degree of insight each individual may reach, but almost everyone has the potential of more than he uses.[16] The methods described in the Suggested Learning Experiences (pp. 132 ff.) will suggest others to the reader; those listed cannot possibly exhaust the ways nor predict all the teachable moments in which insight may be underscored. Insight is, after all, a goal of all education.

Toward understanding, away from ignorance Should students become consciously aware of the main features of imaginative insight? A thin line exists between ignorance about the imagination and vague, inaccurate use of the term. Some teachers believe that in addition to the four approaches to the imagination presented so far, instruction will remain ineffective unless the student himself gains a clear awareness of what is at stake. For senior high school classes, these teachers go beyond the evoking of imaginative reactions; they design lessons intended to identify the dimensions of imagination, to fix firmly in each student's mind some of its salient features. In addition to the four approaches to imagination already presented in this chapter—*flexibility, vitality, insight,* and *synthesis*—they add this fifth approach of *understanding,* an intellectual grasp of the nature and function of the imagination.

Back of this viewpoint lies the principle that goals and purposes must be clearly understood by the learner, not only with respect to the significant details of performance but also with respect to the broad pattern of response. These teachers want their students to be fully aware of the importance of imaginative insight; they want them to clarify its key qualities and characteristics so that success will not be merely accidental—and therefore infrequent.

The haunting case history of Joey, the "mechanical boy," has come to symbolize for many thoughtful people the dangers of a civilization that tends to exalt the machine more than the human spirit. Joey, a schizophrenic child whose mental breakdown brought him to a clinic under the direction of Dr. Bruno Bettelheim, was an intelligent child whose experiences had persuaded him it was best to convert himself into a machine. He existed in a constant frenzy of building apparatus to keep himself running. To eat or eliminate food he had to plug himself into an electric wall socket. Sleep was impossible without an infinite number of adjustments to the wires and gears surrounding his bed. He avoided all feelings and emotions, all expressions of desire and will, all contacts with human beings. With time, infinite patience, and affec-

[16] Othmar H. Sterzinger, in his studies, found a few very prosaic and matter-of-fact subjects who never were able to cope with imaginative thought in which figurative language was used. His "Die Gründe des Gefallens und Misgefallens am Poetischen Bilde," in *Archiv für die gesamte Psychologie,* Vol. 29 (1913), pp. 16-91, is the source for this reservation as to the possibility of all individuals achieving insightfulness.

tion, Joey's fears of being human were gradually dispelled. Dr. Bettelheim concludes: "One last detail and this fragment of Joey's story has been told. When Joey was 12, he made a float for our Memorial Day parade. It carried the slogan: 'Feelings are more important than anything under the sun.' Feelings, Joey had learned, are what make for humanity; their absence, for a mechanical existence. With this knowledge Joey entered the human condition." [17]

THE TEACHING PROBLEM

Organizing Instruction

English teachers who perceive thought as including the full range of reason and imagination can give vitality and impetus to daily learning, and form in many pupils the desire to continue learning long after they leave the school. In view of the fact that many personal predispositions of temperament and many influences of environment shape imagination, deliberate attempts by the school to foster it might appear futile. The same defeatism could as easily be turned upon logical thinking, for some psychologists have concluded that "the intellect is used rarely by most persons in meeting the larger problems and issues of life, and few individuals are able to use their reasoning powers except in limited situations." [18] The English teacher does not share these attitudes, either toward man's imaginative powers or his rational powers. At the beginning of this book, English teachers were likened to gardeners in a perpetual warfare with weeds and wildness, an effort never intended to eventuate in perfection. But although not expecting utopias, English teachers can help pupils think more clearly, communicate more effectively, and feel more intensely. To the extent that these goals are accomplished, other desirable ends of education will follow—less ignorance and superstition, more creative living, better human relations, and more social stability. Suggested Learning Experiences like those at the close of this or the previous chapter may have little or no effect if presented as isolated exercises. However, as part of a total classroom climate where controlled expression replaces repression of thought and feeling, these suggested experiences can extend the range of thinking for most pupils.

Security fosters flexibility Insecurity can induce a rigidity of thought, stifling the expression of feelings and the production of new ideas. Young people have an immense amount of plasticity; if not too insecure, they can break with routine more easily than adults, and can envisage new alternatives, thus becoming more hospitable to originality. *If not too insecure!* The stubborn and inescapable truth, as has been pointed out in the section on

[17] Bruno Bettelheim, "Joey: A 'Mechanical Boy,'" *Scientific American,* Vol. 200, No. 3 (March 1959), pp. 116-127.

[18] Percival M. Symonds, *The Dynamics of Human Adjustment* (N.Y., D. Appleton-Century, 1946), p. xii.

the learner, pp. 1-16, is that adolescents in urban, technological cultures like ours have every reason to be insecure and therefore vulnerable to the dulling impact of peer group conformity. Schools can do much to encourage pupils to observe freshly, to think fluently, and to strike out readily in new directions of promise. Schools can foster the disposition to break with useless habits and to express feelings and emotions—all part of a release from stultifying grooves of thought. However, these goals require teachers who encourage, through their methods and their attitudes, the expression of feelings as well as ideas. Such expression withers in situations that are authoritarian, disorderly, or apathetic.

A climate for imaginative thought A classroom where imagination is respected and flourishes is also one in which teacher and students believe wholeheartedly in the significance of their endeavor. Closing his poem "Two Tramps in Mud Time," Robert Frost writes of the urgent need to love one's task, to unite one's avocation and vocation. So, too, in classrooms the work must be "play for mortal stakes." A climate of sincerity and friendliness encourages pupils to become imaginative and creative, to respect each individual, to be secure enough to value and enjoy variations of opinion and personality. In building such an atmosphere the key person is the teacher. One study of two groups of subjects shows that a threatening situation for one group increased the members' rigidity of thinking and reduced their powers of abstract thought.[19] For most people strong fears and anxieties have an adverse effect on imaginative or creative production. A number of other studies build an emerging picture of the inflexible personality, notable for unimaginative and stereotyped thought, related to considerable anxiety, conflict, and fear of ambiguity.[20] The teacher whose warmth of personality is guided by sound thinking provides both the model and the situation for an increase of imaginative insight among his pupils.

Yet even veteran teachers will ask, "How is the teacher to achieve this stimulating situation from the stubborn clay of daily experience?" How easy to advocate a classroom of imaginative pupils. How infinitely more difficult to achieve such a classroom when one teaches five or six large classes each day, numbering among the pupils many whose attitude toward school is one of distaste or indifference. All too frequently a chasm exists between the ideal atmosphere a teacher envisions and the rude reality—a chasm, the teacher surmises, not entirely caused by his own ineptitude.

For present large class loads and unfortunate pupil attitudes toward disciplined learning, no easy solution exists. But teachers who remain in the

[19] Ernst B. Beier, "The Effect of Induced Anxiety on Flexibility of Intellectual Functioning," *Psychological Monographs,* Vol. 65, No. 9 (1951), pp. 1-19.

[20] Frenkel-Brunswik, Else, "Interrelationships Between Perception and Personality: A Symposium; Part I, Intolerance of Ambiguity as an Emotional and Perceptual Personality Variable," *Journal of Personality,* Vol. 18, No. 1 (September 1949), pp. 109, 130-134; Sidney Siegel, "Certain Determinants and Correlates of Authoritarianism," *Genetic Psychology Monographs,* Vol. 49 (May 1954), pp. 187-229.

profession and continue to find satisfaction in their work often say something like this: "Many teaching situations are far from ideal. For the good of the individual pupil and the ultimate social aims of education, we are obligated to work in every way possible to improve conditions of class size, extracurricular load, and unwise expenditures of teacher time. Nevertheless, facing the situation as it is, we still choose a better path—better for ourselves as well as for our pupils—if we see the task as a challenge rather than an irritation, if we enjoy the task rather than endure it. Teaching will always be work, but the mature person would not alter, even if he could, the fact that all important tasks have a strong element of struggle."

If teachers view their work with perspective, perhaps they will feel less depletion of energy and more buoyancy. This day in the classroom is part of the life of each individual there; and for teacher as well as for learner "the work is play for mortal stakes."

There are times, to be sure, when some classes need regularity and decorum, a low pitch, and a relaxed pace to compensate for an over-stimulating world beyond the classroom. The frenetic, shallow activities of these pupils are the direct opposite of the controlled *vitality* characterizing imaginative insight. For most classes, however, experiences with language and literature should be intensely *alive,* as orderly and exuberant as Mozart's music to the trained ear. As John Stuart Mill and Joey, the "mechanical boy," discovered, vitality and zest for any task rise from deep emotional springs. Logic alone is not enough.

Literature the teacher's finest resource For fostering imaginative thinking, the English teacher's best resource is literature. Using both rational and imaginative thought, both referential and emotive language, literature requires alertness from a wide range of human response. Properly appreciated, literature requires a reader to be wide awake, lifting him toward the fullness of his powers as a human being. It promotes in him an equilibrium between reason and feeling, a harmony that diminishes the petty, narrow concerns always ready to consume his life, replacing these with a refreshing, resonant awareness of being alive.

Thus whenever a teacher succeeds with instruction in literature, he is also succeeding with instruction in imaginative thinking. In the Suggested Learning Experiences in this chapter and in the later chapters on literature, numerous ways to combine literature and imaginative thinking are described.

The total program in English contributes to imaginative thinking If literature is the teacher's foremost resource for encouraging imaginative thinking, the rest of his English program, if properly understood, is scarcely less valuable. To use oral language effectively, to write with power, to listen creatively—these, too, give scope to the life of the imagination. Instruction in them need not invariably be aimed directly toward imaginative insight. Often it is incidental—but not accidental.

For instance, a teacher may wish to organize instruction to include attention to synthesis, the fusing of varied elements by some unifying feature. Such an aim, however, may be better served if woven into a larger design rather than shaped into a separate lesson. One teacher wanted her pupils to see how a satisfying conclusion to a story must be a synthesis or fusion of the form and ideas preceding it. She chose the unfinished story as a method, but rather than introduce the method as an isolated activity she waited for an opportunity in which its use might develop naturally from some discussion with genuine issues at stake.

Such an occasion occurred during a period of time when class work centered on the concept of justice. Incidents of unjust treatment and revenge had been drawn from current news, novels previously read, personal experiences, and the literature selected expressly to illuminate this particular theme. Examined and discussed here were such topics as William Dane's cynical betrayal of his best friend, Silas Marner; the miscarriage of vigilante justice in "Due Process of Law Denied," a film based on *The Ox-Bow Incident;* and the culmination of a local court case involving perjury and revenge. The local perjury trial centered attention on the crucial importance of truth for upholding justice, whether in courts of law or elsewhere, and the danger of polluting the channels of language, as in spreading false rumors or advertising quack medicines. By a series of steps logically related to the court trial, class discussion reached the topic of revenge, a topic most teachers find to be of intense interest to adolescents. It should be noted that discussion did not begin with the abstract idea, revenge; incidents and concrete particulars were shared before generalizations could be drawn. At this point, discussion of revenge was interrupted by the close of the class period and in this interruption the teacher recognized an opportunity to use an unfinished story as a way to begin the next day's class and to provide an occasion for imaginative thinking.

"The Cruise," a story of revenge,[21] seemed an excellent lever for lifting the class discussion to a new level. The next day the teacher read this story up to the words, "After a time, Carl crawled back into the cockpit . . ." The students were then asked to write a conclusion for the story, deciding whether or not Carl scuttled the yacht of the man who had humiliated him. Here, in completing a partial design, the pupils had an opportunity to use imaginative thinking in a situation using literature, writing, and discussion.

As a method, the unfinished story requires planning, sensitive timing, and an incisive appraisal of results. Teachers find it most satisfactory when not used as a special trick to secure writing. In this case, the opportunity for an effective use of the unfinished story developed from class discussion, set in a larger context, a study of justice. Such natural timing is not, of course, essential. A teacher can introduce a topic through a discussion, a filmstrip, the reading of a poem, or in any number of different ways, following it up by reading a story relevant to the tension of the issues evoked. Thus, concern

[21] George Loveridge, "The Cruise," *Yale Review*, Vol. 41, No. 1 (Autumn 1951).

for imaginative thinking is integrated with other elements of the English program.

Incidental teaching, as in this illustration of the unfinished story, should not be confused with accidental teaching. Incidental instruction of a skill, concept, or relationship rises naturally from those most important sources of a teacher's artistry, his philosophy and his over-all design for teaching. A clear understanding of the ends of instruction and a deep belief in their significance helps the teacher foresee opportunities for incidental teaching and also helps him recognize those he has not foreseen. The teachable moment cannot always be predetermined; typically it must be seized whenever it presents itself, and the right conditions for emphasizing imaginative thinking will occur in many different activities. For instance:

Written composition may proceed from expository writing to experiments with sensory appeal and figurative language, as in the Suggested Learning Experiences on pp. 157 and 153.

Time for writing poetry, as described on p. 142, may be planned for an interlude between two units of instruction.

An activity such as the one on p. 194, in which the students listen for the tone of comments on a boy's dance date, illustrates an opportunity to stress flexibility and insight, both important approaches to imaginative thinking.

Slow-learning pupils, not yet ready to profit from the great classics of drama may nevertheless have elementary experience with imaginative thinking in the thumbnail dramas described on pp. 144-146.

By beginning with the larger activity and then analyzing its possibilities for particular processes and skills, a teacher will find appropriate occasions to weave in many effective lessons to emphasize imaginative insight.

Emerson believed that imagination was not the talent of some men but the health of every man. The teacher who conceives of imaginative thought as a pervasive influence in the entire classroom is more likely to conduct a healthy, pleasant program with learning at its optimum.

Suggested Learning Experiences

Difficult goals in English cannot be won in a single semester or year. However, most pupils can improve in their ability to think logically and imaginatively, and teachers who are patient may count on satisfying pupil growth over a period of six years in the secondary school. In examining practical suggestions such as those which follow, the teacher will need to remind himself that it is impossible to consider *How-it's-to-be-done* without relating it to *What's-to-be-done.* The practical must be related to the philosophical in the sense of understanding what it is one is trying to accomplish. The illustrative procedures should be examined in the light of basic principles such as those discussed in this chapter:

The need to balance and blend systematic and imaginative thought, rather than to distinguish too rigorously between them.

The usefulness of literature in drawing upon a full range of response—emotions and feelings as well as logical propositions.

The paramount significance of procedures to elicit flexibility, vitality, insight, and synthesis.

For as many pupils as possible, the importance of an intellectual grasp of the nature and function of the imagination.

However practical any of the following suggestions may be, the teacher must be able to invent from them still more appropriate and flexibly applicable classroom procedures. Specific suggestions, no matter how valid, do not of themselves insure instruction that fosters imaginative thinking. For such instruction, a sound theoretical position remains the only source of effective method.

Toward flexibility . . . Away from rigidity

To express moods and feelings

■ *Use music to motivate writing*

Because most music evokes emotional responses, it can enhance or support teaching for imagination. One such method varies the usual procedure of written composition by using a musical background for writing. The teacher may announce the plan in advance,[22] or on the day of the writing, say something like this: "Today, we are going to try something different. I am going to play some music. While I play the record for the first time, don't write; just listen, and try to 'feel the music.' What mood does it express? What ideas and images cross your mind? Then when I pick up the needle and start the record a second time, begin writing. Write whatever seems appropriate to you, whatever the music makes you feel. The music may suggest a story or a poem; it may merely indicate a scene or a mood you will try to capture in words; it may toss up some idea or thought you will want to develop logically. Whatever you offer, long or short, I will accept. The only requirement is that it be your sincere product in response to the music."

Answer any questions, start the music, and step from the center of the stage, returning only as the recording draws to a close. Play the record several times if necessary, and then allow the writing to continue without music. If some students request it, play the record once more before the close of the time period. Too much repetition, however, may dull the response or irritate some pupils.[23]

Unfamiliar music, not too apparent in style, succeeds better in stimulating the imagination than a composition like Rimski-Korsakov's "Flight of the Bumblebee." Famous compositions like "Clair de Lune" or the *William Tell* overture, because they elicit ready-made associations from many pupils, should be avoided. For a short recording, a composition like "Fêtes" by Debussy evokes a wide variety of reactions. Longer but equally stimulating recordings can be selected from among the works

[22] Advance planning with the class, with committees, or with student chairmen pays dividends in classroom management and effective learning. For more explicit discussion of this topic, see p. 656 in "Program and Plan."

[23] For an account of the use of music to exercise student's imaginative thinking, see Harold P. Simonson, "Music as an Approach to Poetry," *English Journal,* Vol. 43, No. 1 (January 1954).

of composers like Ravel, Satie, or Holst. Recommendations, however, are superfluous. Each teacher will have his own favorites, will enjoy experimenting with various musical backgrounds, and will select music with his particular class in mind.

■ *Display non-representational art*

An interesting variation to the method of writing to music adds or substitutes a single painting, preferably something abstract or non-representational, in color. Reproductions of paintings by artists like Tanguy and Miro, because they do not limit or direct the pupils' imagination and interpretive abilities as much as representational scenes, prove more successful.

What writing does one get? A variety of results: many stream-of-consciousness products; occasional poems; prose tinged with the dreamlike quality of "Kubla Khan"; some stories; and some compositional dough that fails to rise. On the whole, however, students like this approach to writing and at the close of the hour many worthwhile products are placed in students' folders for further revision and polishing.[24] Obviously the method is not designed for teaching logical organization or encouraging simple straightforward writing about the pupils' everyday experiences. However, its general success in *eliciting some writing,* particularly from students who have previously been somewhat reluctant to write, warrants its use several times each year.

■ *Relate reading to form and color*

To stimulate interpretation, two teachers[25] used finger painting, encouraging the students to express in color and pattern their personal reactions to one of several poems. When they were finished, each student wrote an interpretation of his painting. After the students had recorded their intentions on paper but before these papers were read, the paintings, identified only by the titles of the poems represented, were placed along the chalkboard in front of the class. This afforded an opportunity for all students to share and compare experiences in critical analysis without influencing the original interpretations. Attempting to select the most appropriate representations required an intensive and profitable examination of the poems themselves.

From these first steps, the two teachers proceeded to lessons on symbolism and the use of symbols in four dramas. Once again, the students finger-painted their reactions, this time expressing definite symbols through color and pattern. The teachers report that the method used had a major value in reducing adolescent inhibitions, helping students "to *feel* in genuine, non-stereotyped terms—to respond directly to some universal sensibility and morality." In addition to releasing student response to literature—very successfully—the method provided non-verbal pupils with a means of expressing imaginative reactions to their reading.

■ *Discuss feelings through the medium of literature*

Adolescents' problems are often too personal for open discussion. In groping fashion, young people look for wisdom on many problems about which they feel deeply: the dangers of daydreaming, how to stand against or conform to the

[24] For suggestions on organizing a class to use such folders, see p. 518, in Chapter 10, "Written Expression."

[25] James R. Squire and Merritt Beckerman, "The Release of Expression," *English Journal,* Vol. 39, No. 3 (March 1950).

ways of their age groups, the consequences of making choices. An open discussion of these problems, using characters in literature, often elicits an expression of feelings that would otherwise be too personal were the adolescent himself the topic of discussion. Try reading aloud a story like "Not Wanted," or the essay "Mary White." In advance of reading, pose one or two questions, alerting students to certain insights the story provides and offering a springboard for the discussion to follow. Sometimes the teacher leads the discussion; at other times, individuals, pairs, or panels of students direct it. For instance, one teacher reading Katherine Mansfield's "Miss Brill" used just one question: What is the best way for anyone to handle a humiliation or a blow to his feelings? An eighth grade teacher,[26] reading Mary Deasy's "The High Hill" to a low socio-economic group, used the single question: Why do people want friends?

To increase fluent thinking

■ *Pose novel problems to be solved*

Borrow some of the methods used in the research which examined the creative thinking abilities of Army Air Cadets.[27] Although developed for application to science, engineering, and invention, these methods may easily be transferred to the English class. Learning, whether by air cadets or adolescents, is more than storing bits of knowledge, and the process of reorganizing and integrating requires more than mere accretion. The methods described here can help to promote the flexibility with words and ideas which is one aspect of imaginative learning.

1. Ask pupils to list, as fast as they can, all the uses they can think of for an ordinary brick (or bricks). The average student will list such items as making a wall, a path, or a doorstop, outlining a garden border, supporting a sagging floor. More imaginative students will think of a weight to hold down papers, a wedge to place behind a car wheel on a slope, an item in a still-life composition for an artist-painter, a base for a lamp, a weight to place on the head for practicing erect walking, and the like. Let pupils score their papers twice, once for number of items and once for number of categories, such as a building material; a weight of some kind; a support of some kind; uses by volume, thickness, or abrasive quality; an unusual use. Grant extra points for unusual uses which are not unreasonable.

The first time the students try this exercise, many will not fully use their imaginations. After the exercise is completed and results are compared, they will usually be eager to try again. Other items to use: a burro, aluminum, glass, tar, a wheelbarrow, string, a pine tree, a sheet of paper of typical typewriter size.

2. Within a time limit, have pupils list as many things or actions they can think of that are impossible to do: drive a car to the top of Mount Everest; listen to Chopin playing his "Fantasie Impromptu."

3. Have pupils make sentences out of words in scrambled order. For instance, from "Beauty only this everything its has but imaginative know people," make "Everything has its beauty but only imaginative people know this."

[26] Hilda Taba and Deborah Elkins, eds., *With Focus on Human Relations: A Story of an Eighth Grade* (Washington, D.C., American Council on Education, 1950). This book, an account of an eighth grade teacher with a difficult class, includes numerous suggestions for relating literature to the full range of thought and feeling.

[27] Robert C. Wilson, J. P. Guilford, Paul R. Christenson, Donald J. Lewis, "A Factor-Analysis Study of Creative Thinking Abilities," *Psychometrika*, Vol. 19, No. 4 (December 1954).

4. Have pupils make words out of scrambled letters. For instance, *iwahia* and *aefrugript* become *Hawaii* and *grapefruit.*

5. Let students separate words run together in continuous discourse. For this activity, the teacher needs to duplicate relatively difficult passages, running them completely together, the words as well as the sentences. The students place light pencil lines between each word, heavy or colored lines between each sentence. When completed, individuals volunteer to read the passages aloud. The passages, about five to eight sentences long, should cover content varying from science to literature, from description to narration. After the first few trials, time limits may be set in order to encourage fluency rather than slow, deliberate solutions. *Caution:* Explain the time limit so that it is not a threatening element in the lesson.

6. Use mutilated words: Let pupils identify words composed of partial letters, or words in sentences, the words containing the correct letters, but arranged in erratic fashion. For instance, "Enverd si het ipacalt fo Colodaro" becomes "Denver is the capital of Colorado."

7. Try a consequences test: Let pupils list the immediate or remote and far-reaching consequences of certain hypothetical changes in the world—everyone becomes deaf; each year the world grows warmer as the sun slowly approaches; large numbers of people begin to live more than 200 years; space travel becomes common; a scientist discovers a harmless chemical which dispels feelings of anger and aggression in human beings; the laws of chance cease to operate; everyone grows two feet taller; Brazil finds a way to raise the average I.Q. of its people 50 points.

8. Present synonyms: Let pupils write several synonyms for each of ten words such as *jolly, cheap, dull,* and others suitable to the age and ability of the class members.

9. Ask pupils to suggest two improvements for each of several social institutions: the school, the courts, labor unions, large corporations, small businesses.

■ *Try a judicious use of "brainstorming"*

Brainstorming is a method of searching for solutions to problems. Its originator [28] calls it "creative collaboration by groups." When the technique is used in some business organizations, a number of people are brought together to use their brains to storm, in commando fashion, some objective in the world of ideas. These idea-producing conferences are relatively fruitless unless certain rules are understood and followed:

> *Judicial judgment is ruled out.* Criticism of ideas must be withheld until later.
>
> *"Free-wheeling" is welcomed.* The wilder the idea, the better; it is easier to tame down than to think up.
>
> *Quantity is wanted.* The greater the number of ideas, the more the likelihood of winners.
>
> *Combination and improvement are sought.* In addition to contributing ideas of their own, participants should suggest how ideas of others can be turned into *better* ideas; or how two or more ideas can be joined into still another idea.[29]

In the English classroom, students and teacher may choose some problem such as these which were used in one school: How can we have more speeches and

[28] Alex F. Osborn, *Applied Imagination* (N.Y., Scribner's, 1953).
[29] Osborn, *Applied Imagination,* pp. 300-301.

group discussions without giving up time needed for literature and writing? What could be done to reduce the criticism that this school is too much dominated by student cliques? Groups of six pupils, including one student-secretary, pour out their ideas as rapidly as they can within a fixed time limit. The secretaries then meet to organize a presentation to the class. From this presentation, the best solutions are distilled and the class evaluates both the solutions and the value of the brainstorming session. This evaluation of brainstorming itself deserves special emphasis, for many teachers view it as a meretricious device lacking soundness. Evaluation of it as a method to increase fluent, flexible thinking can, however, focus attention on the purpose of the experience.

■ *Create a shift in perspective*

1. Describe a new or different kind of world, one in which many of the customs and normal events taken for granted in our world have shifted. For instance, one teacher describes the setting for *The Machine Stops* by E. M. Forster, a world of the future in which everyone lives in underground chambers beautifully lighted and perfectly tended by a universal world machine. Taking this unfamiliar pattern, students describe an hour of life in such a situation, or work out some problems such as the kinds of television programs such people would prefer, the books such people would like to read, or how governing would be accomplished.

This exercise may be followed by one in which groups of students deal with a world which is continuously rainy or a world turned completely dry or one growing colder every year. Within the framework of these unfamiliar patterns, each group of students is to envisage the new alternatives that emerge with the shift in perception. For instance, a group imagining a world growing increasingly colder will realize that ships would cease crossing oceans, people would be driven to live underground, means of heating and of keeping warm would become crucial, resort cities with famous bathing beaches would lose their advantage. After working out these possibilities, each group tells some of the interesting shifts and changes it envisions.

2. A similar approach might be called "Utopias." The teacher describes some of the famous utopias: More's *Utopia,* Plato's *Republic,* Bacon's *New Atlantis,* Butler's *Erewhon,* Bellamy's *Looking Backward.* After discussing the meaning of utopias, students—either individually or in groups—are set to the problem of describing facets of life in a utopia of their own. In one junior high school, students worked in groups, each group drawing a map of an imaginary island and selecting a name for it. Girls described the fashions in this utopia; boys described the sports, the forms of adventure; groups devised plans for government, education, and crime control.

After such exercises, the teacher may pose for his pupils less spectacular but more exacting shifts in perspective: living in another country, in another income or racial group, or in another climate. Looking at issues from the point of view of a parent, a teacher, a small child, or a member of the opposite sex can be illuminating and challenging.

■ *Use squiggle stories in junior high school*

Ask each child to draw three squiggles—random lines—at the top of a sheet of paper. Students then exchange papers, each one to complete the squiggle lines in such a way as to create a reasonable drawing. As soon as the drawing is completed, a story is to be written about the "illustration" at the top of the page. Robert C. Wilson, who describes this method, suggests that the students "should be reminded that in a story: (a) something must happen, (b) it must happen in sequence, and (c) it should have a definite ending or a punch line." [30]

To project the familiar into imaginary situations

■ *Predict how characters in literature might react in new situations*

To extend story situations pupils must draw upon their imaginations as well as upon what they know about a character. The solutions to imaginary literary situations impose problems of seeing relationships between new situations and behavior established by an author. Here are several ways teachers have set such challenges:

1. The teacher reads or describes the imaginary dinner conversation of historical personalities in books like Landor's *Imaginary Conversations* or *Van Loon's Lives.* Students "invite" three literary or historical characters to a dinner or some suitable event and write or dramatize their conversation. In a junior high school class, pupils may imagine the boys from *Captains Courageous, Little Britches,* and *North Fork* enrolling in the same class at school. Informal dramatic skits planned in advance may serve as the vehicle for expression.

2. Another extension of this idea in grade eleven might be a discussion of pioneer experiences by characters in *Let the Hurricane Roar, The Way West,* and *Giants in the Earth.* This approach offers a variation from other forms of reporting individual reading.

3. Students describe the impressions of a book character on an imaginary visit to their school. What classes, clubs, and activities would provide the greatest interest for tomboys like Kate (*The Good Master*) and Caddie Woodlawn? For Ralph (*Man of the Family*) and Jade Snow Wong (*Fifth Chinese Daughter*)? Groups of pupils may discuss these matters and report their consensus to the class.

4. Interested students write additional entries in Anne Frank's *Diary of a Young Girl* or extend the personal journal presented in Ring Lardner's story "I Can't Breathe." At their best, such assignments achieve not only logical prediction of behavior but also maintenance of tone, mood, and style.

5. Junior high school students who have read stories about boys and girls of other lands pretend they are on shipboard or at an international airport like Shannon or Honolulu. Meeting on their way back from the countries represented in their books, they reminisce about their "travel experiences," incidents adapted from books they have just read.

These skits succeed best if groups of three pupils present them. Once the books have been completed, one planning session on the part of the trios can produce genuinely imaginative and entertaining skits for the rest of the class. Special commendation should be given to those who draw into their presentation some indication of insight into customs differing from our own or ways human beings are alike beneath superficial differences. The method has the further virtue of fostering an increase in reading. By posting the titles and authors of books involved, the trios aid those who want to draw from the school or classroom library any of the books used as source material.

[30] Robert C. Wilson, "Creativity," Chapter VI, p. 123, in Fifty-Seventh Yearbook, National Society for the Study of Education, Part II, *Education for the Gifted* (Chicago, U. of Chicago Press, 1958).

6. After a short story, a play, or a novel, plan a class exercise entitled "Grasp of Human Conduct." By setting before pupils the problem of how a certain character might behave in a situation not present in the literary selection, the teacher focuses attention on interpreting human behavior. The following is related to a group of short stories just completed by a tenth grade class:

Sample from grasp of human conduct exercise

To the Pupil: Each of the following items concerns one of the more important characters in the short stories you have read. The item also contains the description of a situation which is *not* in any of the stories. After each situation described, five courses of action are listed. On the basis of your acquaintance with the character, you are asked to check the course of action the character would most probably follow. Remember, do not check what *you* would do in the situation described or what you think the character *should* do. Rather, consider all the evidence of the story and bring it to bear upon the problem: How would this character probably conduct himself in this situation? Then place a check in front of the course of action which *best* describes that you think the character would take.

1. *Character:* Jerry, in "A Mother in Mannville" by Marjorie Kinnan Rawlings.
Situation: During a baseball game on a vacant lot in a nearby town, one of the players bats a ball through the window of a convertible passing by the lot. Jerry is playing left field at the time and is not the boy who batted the ball. The boys run away.
Courses of Action:
Jerry runs away with the other players.
Jerry pretends he was merely walking by and saunters down the street.
Jerry runs away with the other players but tries to persuade them to go back in a body and face the consequences. They won't go back so Jerry gives in to the majority opinion.
Jerry goes to meet the angry car owner. He offers to work out his share of the blame.
Jerry stands paralyzed with fear, unable to run or even think what is best for him to do.
2. [Other characters and situations from other stories]

Teachers using this method avoid rigid adherence to so-called right answers. In class discussions growing out of this evaluation instrument, the teacher willingly acknowledges that human beings do not always act consistently. However, in the light of Jerry's behavior in the story, which answer does seem most logical? The stimulus to class discussion justifies the use of such an instrument, even if no scores are recorded for evaluation purposes. Disagreements will lead to rewarding class discussion. Sometimes the teacher may test students' thinking by creating a set of "answers" no one of which could possibly be correct. Camouflaged among more respectable items, these traps for the unwary sort the docile from the alert. Either before or after such an incident, the teacher and students might agree that whenever answers appear inadequate, students may write in one of their own.

■ *Transpose the familiar into myths, fantasies, and tall tales*

After reading such myths as the account of Apollo or Pandora, students write myths of the modern world, transposing familiar events into fantasy and wonder tales. Variations of this method include the use of tall tales—such as those about Paul Bunyan, Mike Fink, Davy Crockett, Miss Pickerel, or Mary Poppins. Indian legends, both local and published, represent other materials that might be used;[31] Norse, Irish, Finnish, and Oriental mythologies have seldom been fully exploited in American schools. In some classes modern fantasies like James Thurber's *The Thirteen Clocks* and *Many Moons* will stimulate imaginative writing, as will Antoine de St. Exupéry's *The Little Prince* and Rummer Godden's *The Mousewife*.

The underlying method here starts with reading mythology, legend, or fantasy and moves to the selection of models as guides for original compositions. If the imagination is to operate, the emphasis must necessarily be on originality and ingenuity rather than imitation. The teacher aids pupils in identifying the presence of exaggeration, the ridiculous, and the elements of plausibility in a tall tale; other aspects need identification in myths, legends, and fables. To use these elements in new situations becomes the creative task for the pupil. One caution: Guard against an impression that the imagination consists solely of fantasy and the fantastic.

To release oneself from the confines of individual experience

Viewing the world through the eyes of someone else is a tremendous advantage. Each person tends to become fixed in the groove of his own habits and surroundings. Through conversing with other people and through literature he opens his mind to new slants on familiar subjects. His partial experience is rounded out.

On the millions of topics and thoughts of life, we often see only a single side—our own. Like the blind men in the famous parable who examined only the elephant's tail or trunk or ear, we judge by a single feature. Unless we have "blind imaginations," we discover how to extend our limited experiences through the minds of others, and literature is such a means of extension if we learn how to use it.

■ *Use literature with parallel and contrasting elements*

The use of parallels and contrasts in literature offers many adaptations and extensions. The attitudes of Homer, of *The Human Comedy,* and Pip, of *Great Expectations,* can be compared and contrasted; the ways two boys learn to accept responsibility can be seen in *Captains Courageous* and *Little Britches*.[32] Nor does the parallel always need to be linked to content. An aspect of form, for instance, may interest teachers presenting the short story as a type. Or the emphasis on form may represent the culmination of a planned program of literary parallels increasing in difficulty. The illustration to be used here directs attention to an author's tone, but the methods described are applicable to a wide range of literature.

For adolescents exploring the dimensions of literature, Saki's tone—tart, bracing, antiseptic—is frequently a new kind of reading experience. One high school teacher begins a study of tone with "Blue Jays" by Mark Twain and a single story by Saki, either "The Open Window" or "The Lumber Room." She first places brief samples on the board. For instance, this quatrain with its definite tone of wry protest:

[31] See, for instance, Cyrus Macmillan, *Glooskap's Country, and Other Indian Tales* (N.Y., Oxford U. Press, 1956).

[32] See also p. 152. Methods drawing upon parallels in content are further described in Chapter 6, "Literature: Basic Approaches," pp. 294-95. An excellent account of using novels for comparisons and contrast is David M. Litsey, "Comparative Study of Novels," *English Journal,* Vol. 48, No. 3 (March 1959), pp. 149-151.

A-tomic Ache [33]

My confidence in terra firma
Now I find in error
O Science, rest! I daily feel less
Firma and more terra.

At this point the teacher defines tone, and asks, "How do we 'detect' the poet's tone?" Next she reads "Blue Jays" aloud, asking students to watch for its indirect comment on the comic ways of the human family.

The teacher then assigns the Saki story as a trial of the students' insight into tone. The student must be alert and imaginative enough to read between the lines. Almost everything that is really important is deliberately left for the reader to supply.

In a subsequent lesson the parallel might be theme, point of view, or setting.

■ *Dramatize selected stories*

In stories where characters represent many points of view, one effective approach may be called the "Jigsaw Puzzle." One student is designated to interrogate or interview seven other students, each of whom represents a character in the story. The interrogator questions each character in order to elicit his version of the incident.[34] In each case the character interviewed is to present the matter exactly from his own point of view within whatever limitations the story imposes. For instance, in Saki's "The Open Window," Framton Nuttel tells his version with complete conviction that the niece was truthful, the aunt addled by her tragedy, and the state of his own nerves such that he might have been overwhelmed by the power of suggestion. The aunt presents her uncomplimentary interpretation of Mr. Nuttel, unaware of the extent to which her niece had influenced Nuttel's behavior. The husband and two brothers appear as a trio and briefly contribute their picture of the situation. If some timid or less able student is to be given a minor part, the cyclist can contribute his amazing and brief encounter with Mr. Nuttel. The final witness is the niece who is persuaded by the interviewer, after some preliminary dissimulations, to tell the whole truth—to solve the jigsaw puzzle.

Except for written questions to which the interrogator may refer, students should avoid any scripts or memorization of their roles. Impromptu and creative dialogue, based upon exceptionally careful reading and interpretation of the story, succeed best.

One of the values of all class discussion and dramatization of literature is the opportunity for the slower students or confused students to match their partial or erroneous interpretations with the more skillful or exact interpretations of their peers. Frequently enlightenment is accepted more graciously in this situation than it is when a teacher imposes or merely presents a just interpretation. Of course teachers should often lead students to reasonable and accurate interpretations, but teacher-led discussion succeeds better if interspersed occasionally with student presentations.

[33] Donald S. Klopp, in *English Journal,* Vol. 40, No. 1 (January 1951), p. 11. Reprinted by permission. A cluster of selections featuring the lighter touch of humor—the dry, urbane, and witty poetry of Phyllis McGinley or Richard Armour—also makes a good introduction to tone.

[34] See "Language as Dynamic Process," pp. 19-20, for a principle of language covering this example of individuals reacting to what may seem to be the same stimuli, reconstructing highly personal and unique experiences.

Toward controlled vitality . . . Away from apathy

To evoke feeling

■ *Make time for writing poetry*

Under favorable conditions, many adolescents will convert an amazing amount of energy into writing poetry. Teachers whose classes respond to this activity often begin by presenting poems written by young writers, poems from sources like *Scholastic magazine* or from such books as *Creative Youth* and *Young Voices.*[35] While reading a number of these for enjoyment and appreciation, the teacher directs attention to their rhythms, diction, or freshness of observation. From this point on, teachers often follow the general features of the method Mearns described in *Creative Youth.* Essentially, these features include:

Soliciting verses already written—often brought from private hiding places—and a cautious use of these for informal personal instruction, leading students to see why the feeling of the poet did or did not become the feeling of the reader

An encouraging teacher who does not prescribe or even suggest subject matter or form but who does emphasize the danger of imitation and the importance of original, personal thought (Mearns says he drives pupils back upon themselves, drives them to search within: "I can't tell you what you should write about because I don't know what you know. What sort of experience have you been having? What do you think about most of the time?")

Much sharing and enjoyment of published poetry and prose, favorite selections chosen by individuals rather than prescribed in a single text (For instance, students bring to class poems they like and read them to one another as a preface to spontaneous, informal discussion; they form literary societies and carry on programs; they present programs of "Favorites—So Far.")

An emphasis on sincerity of expression, on respect for every opinion, no matter how naive or unfledged the opinion may appear to the instructor

Teacher alertness for sincere expressions of imaginative insight—sometimes only a word or a phrase; whenever it appears, praise from the teacher and also from classmates

The spur of an attractive and regular publication for the best creative writing

Finally, one should note that some pupils in Mearns's classes were content to read poetry rather than write it. Others, writing without scaling any heights of expression, felt supported by the assurance that attempts to express imaginative insight would be respected but not received with insincere flattery.

Teachers using these methods place emphasis on originality and insight. They praise apt comparisons, flexible thinking, fresh insights, new ways of viewing experience. One chalk board or bulletin board may be devoted to Felicitous Phrases and Voluntary Verses, and another to Flat Fulminations and Stale Stereotypes. On the latter, students place clippings illustrating clichés, tired slang, overworked words, and similar hackneyed expressions. Teachers who have not previously tried to elicit poetry from students are often surprised to find students enjoying and profiting from such lessons.

[35] *Scholastic* magazine, Scholastic Corporation, 33 W. 42nd St., N.Y. 36, N.Y.; Mearns, *Creative Youth;* Kenneth M. Gould, and Joan Coyne, eds., *Young Voices* (N.Y., Harper, 1945).

■ *Maintain a balance between imaginative and analytical writing*

In writing, most students need, primarily, instruction in the organization of simple, straightforward exposition. Recognizing the disadvantages of an overemphasis on personal expression, teachers nevertheless do find a judicious use of such writing valuable. Further suggestions for motivating imaginative writing are described on pp. 504-05, "Written Expression."

To increase expressiveness

■ *Try role playing*

1. If students have never used role playing in previous schooling, explain the technique somewhat in this fashion:

> "In role playing you become another person; you try to imagine how that person would walk, talk, and think. In other words, you become that other person insofar as you can with the knowledge you have about him. Role playing is not a rehearsed play; some pre-planning is necessary so the main outlines of the action are blocked out and members taking part are sure of the roles they are playing, but you plan and play the story without memorizing lines or actions. Invent the conversation and divide the main story into a series of scenes. Determine where you will begin and what episodes you will feature; then make a study of the characters.

In one class, studying *Boy on Horseback* by Lincoln Steffens, the students decided to enact scenes to show what kind of person Lincoln Steffens was and how he matured. The setting for the first scene was an English classroom before the bell rings. Steffens comes in and talks with some of his friends. (Clues to what they might discuss can be found in the chapter "Preparing for College," where Steffens talks about his interests.) Then the instructor in the story calls the class to order and gives an assignment without much point—for instance, writing a paragraph with three compound sentences, one complex, and two simple. As the book implies, "students" in the drama should all start writing without hesitation, but the boy playing the role of Steffens should question the assignment with an inquiry such as, "What is the reason for the paragraph?"

Another scene might be an interview between Steffens and his father when the latter learns his son has been refused entrance to the university. Analysis of the role playing should be determined by the original purpose: to reveal Steffens' personality and the forces in his growing up.

2. Role playing need not always be based on reading. The teacher may describe situations in which teen-agers find themselves at cross purposes with adults. For instance, the teacher outlines a situation such as this: A girl has just been asked for a date by a boy whom she likes very much. Because of poor marks on her last report card, her parents have restricted all dating. Students block out action for the father, mother, a grandmother in the home, an older brother or sister, and the girl herself, revealing how the problem is resolved. Those who take adult parts are instructed to do their best to see the situation through the eyes of the adults.

In all classes, but particularly those in junior high, groups preparing to act out stories or situations need definite assistance from the teacher. For instance, in an eighth grade class dramatizing "The Ruby Glass" by Hugh Walpole, the teacher placed on the chalkboard these questions: What kind of a man is Jeremy's father?

Is he really cross? Why is he so sharp with Jeremy? How well does he understand his children? The teacher then helped the pupils divide the story into scenes and plan action for the first scene.

At first, role playing does not always move along smoothly; but students will improve each time they repeat a scene, gaining poise and new ideas for action or dialogue. After most scenes they should stop for criticism and suggestions. First the players themselves should have an opportunity to make suggestions for improvements; then everyone should offer advice. Sometimes it is wise to change several players and try the scene again. The teacher should watch to see whether or not the characters are reacting to one another. The main purpose—to see facts and feelings from a new orientation by stepping into someone else's shoes—should bring about a deeper imaginative involvement of the student actors. Unless this occurs, informal dramatics misses much of its value.

The same scenes may be presented by several different groups of students, providing opportunity for comparison and analysis of the same original text. Through such impromptu dramatization, the teacher can learn much about how well his students interpret their reading, and about confusions which may be remedied. The method is suitable for slow or fast learning pupils as well as for those average in ability.

■ *Act out thumbnail dramas*

1. For slow learning high school students, one teacher writes brief dramatic skits, using only 3000 basic English words and a limited number of characters. The pupils, most of them poor readers, act as they read the parts in their "Walk-on Rehearsal Book." [36] Through this method they have an opportunity for reading and speech experience, a starting point for discussing problems familiar to them, and an activity which is notable for dispelling apathy. "Shining Up the Car," printed here, is typical of the method.

Shining Up the Car [37]

Time: One Friday afternoon.
Place: Bob's backyard.
Characters: Jack and Bob, two high school boys.

(*Bob is busy washing his father's car. Jack enters.*)

JACK: Hi, Bob.

BOB: (Surly) Hi, yourself.

JACK: What you doing?

BOB: Just playing nursemaid to Dad's old car. Just giving the old crate a shampoo and a shoe shine.

JACK: Thought you washed the car last week.

BOB: Right. And the week before. And the week before that. And the week before the week before—

JACK: Hold it. Evidently this must be a weekly job.

BOB: Some detective, the way you figure things out.

JACK: You don't need to get sore about it.

[36] Effie A. Hult, "The Walk-on Rehearsal Book" (mimeographed), Oakland Public Schools, Oakland, California. Used in special education and English workshop classes for retarded readers at the senior high school level.

[37] From "The Walk-on Rehearsal Book," by Effie A. Hult; reprinted by permission.

BOB: No? That's what you think!

JACK: Say listen! I didn't come over to pick a fight.

BOB: Well, see to it that you don't then.

JACK: But I'm not. I mean I didn't.

BOB: Didn't what?

JACK: Didn't come over to pick a fight.

BOB: What did you come over for? Nobody asked you.

JACK: I came over for two things. First, I came to see what you were doing.

BOB: So you came over to see what I was doing? Well, I hope you can see that I am washing, cleaning, and polishing my Dad's car. A job I have to do every Friday afternoon after school.

JACK: Well, what's the idea?

BOB: Because my Dad is trying to sell this old wreck.

JACK: You mean—

BOB: Yes, I mean that my polishing job has to make this car look like what it isn't.

JACK: No one can do that.

BOB: Oh, yes, I can!

JACK: You must be joking. Why, that looks like a pretty good car.

BOB: Shows how little you know about a car. Why, every time we take it out, it ends up in a garage.

JACK: Kidding, aren't you?

BOB: Says you! Say, I know this car inside out. I've taken it apart and put it together a dozen times.

JACK: It's really bad, is it? The car's really in a bad condition?

BOB: I'd hate to see one in a worse condition.

JACK: I'm surprised.

BOB: Yah, you would be. You don't know a thing about cars.

JACK: But I do now. And thanks for telling me. Thanks a lot!

BOB: Say! What's it to you?

JACK: Because my Dad was figuring on buying that car. But I'll pass the word along. So long. (Exits)

BOB: Hey, you! Hey, Jack! Come back here!

The first step in any economical learning, establishing a goal, should be followed by attempts to execute the skill or behavior pattern. The students' goal in such skits is to perform successfully, entertaining and instructing their audience. The skills to be improved should be written on the chalkboard or copied in the students' notebooks—often both. In these short skits, slow learning pupils need to estimate the success of their performances by referring often to these skills, e.g., to read without hesitation or to read with an imparting tone or to use gestures and facial expressions corresponding to the meaning of the words. In the light of this evaluation, they are to adapt their behavior in subsequent trials with the same or new skits.

2. Once the method has been established, students can be drawn to more imaginative efforts such as creating their own skits. This can be followed by a series of skits developing a single theme, for example, "It is easier to be wise for other people than for oneself." A coherent and continued serial in which the same main characters reappear once a week for a semester or longer holds the interest

of classes regardless of age level or ability. It also gives scope for increasing expressiveness, an important element of imaginative growth.

■ *Present puppet dramas*

In the junior high school, with students ranging from slow to rapid learners, uncomplicated hand puppets and a simple cardboard box stage placed on a table make possible the fusion of writing, speaking, listening, and reading into a single imaginative activity.[38] Individual students or pairs write scripts to be duplicated. A cast of characters then practices its script, dividing responsibility for reading—*in a loud, clear voice* from behind scenes—and for manipulating the hand puppets. Non-verbal pupils, afraid of failing in audience situations, often gain courage behind the curtained puppet stage. On the chalkboard place standards for good audience listening.

Slow students can write brief skits in three or four scenes. For instance, one group in a seventh grade prepared an incident in three scenes, depicting a man who scoffed at the need of purchasing a hunting license, his encounter with the sheriff at the scene of the hunt, and his remorseful account to his wife upon his return home. A much more advanced group of seventh grade pupils presented an original version of a new incident for *Homer Price.* The increase in expressiveness does much to replace classroom apathy with vitality.

The spontaneous nature of puppetry is particularly conducive to impromptu creative dramatics. In the junior high school, scripts are not always necessary.

Toward synthesis . . . Away from randomness

To complete partial designs

Just as soap bubbles become perfect circles or vapor freezes into symmetrical snowflakes, so do thoughts, feelings, and actions strain toward form and design. An unfinished melody or an incomplete lesson in algebra can haunt our thoughts and mar our slumbers, for some natural law of closure apparently links our human sense of form to the predictable orbits of the planets, to the underlying orderliness of Nature. This human need to close gaps in structural systems can be employed in teaching imaginative insight.

■ *Extend moods and explanations from clues*

1. Some poems present only hints or fragments of meaning. Students often enjoy speculating on the implications of poems like "The Listeners" by Walter De la Mare and "The Skater of Ghost Lake" by William Rose Benét. Others which incompletely etch in their mysterious stories are "Childe Roland to the Dark Tower Came" by Robert Browning, "O What Is That Sound?" by W. H. Auden, and "The Erl King" by Goethe.

2. Some stories provide clues but do not interpret them for the reader. For junior high pupils, use such stories as "Boy in the Dark" and "A Mother in Mannville." For senior high pupils, use "By the Waters of Babylon" and "A Cup of Tea." In all four, the reader must make leaps of imagination in order to interpret the clues provided by the authors. Other stories requiring ability to follow the author's

[38] The film "ABC of Puppetry, Part I," presents simple methods of construction. Some teachers keep a stock of puppets, some with blank faces and others capable of being used in many roles.

implications are "The Lottery" and "Charles" by Shirley Jackson, and for junior high school, "The Nightingale" and other tales by Hans Christian Andersen. Whether poem or story, the selection may be read silently, followed by a second oral reading. Occasionally arouse good discussion by suggesting an interpretation that is obviously off balance or willfully one-sided. In rejecting such interpretations, students search for clues to coherence and at the same time have the experience of transcending an uncritical acceptance of authority.

■ *Construct meaning from incomplete and unusual situations*

Duplicate or place on the chalkboard several ambiguous story openings. Students are to develop written interpretations related to one of these and in keeping with some single mood or effect. They should be aware they are attempting mental leaps to connect data out of focus in any realistic mental lens. Praise writing that maintains the most consistency of effect. In one classroom, the teacher used these four curious beginnings and left a fifth space on the chalkboard to be filled by the best additional contribution chosen from among several volunteered by class members. On the following day each pupil chose one from among the five story openings that were thus available to them. Anyone who wished to do so was permitted to substitute an opening of his own.

Gerry stopped his car, waiting for the elegant red convertible to draw up alongside. At the wheel sat one of the ugliest old crones he had ever seen. Her thin gray hair was blown about her wrinkled face, and she held toward him something resembling a small palm tree—except that it was bluish and withered.

In the trees at the city's edge the American girl suddenly felt oddly depressed. "What," she thought, "am I doing in Portugal? Why did I leave the festival? What do I expect to find in this ruined temple by the olive grove?"

Diane looked at the odd figures decorating the walls of her playmate's room. Suddenly her eye rested on one grotesque animal. Did its eyes move just as she glanced toward it?

Looking out through the curiously shaped window, the passenger saw stars, the moon, and earth far below. To the right, in the strange twilight he viewed what seemed to be a meadow, and on it were moving sad-faced beings half horse, half human. "These," someone said, "are the ones who have been condemned to spend eternity on this distant, insignificant star."

(Additional provocative opener chosen from among any volunteered by class members.)

In accordance with the age and background of his pupils, each teacher will modify such suggested openings. At the junior high level, pupils respond better to incidents similar to their reading interests. Boys usually prefer rugged adventures in situations that imply action in sports or pioneering; girls often like fantasy, mystery, mild adventure, horse stories, and love stories.

This type of writing should be used temperately. Although student interest can be fired by such stimuli, a stress on the unreal and fantastic presents a one-sided picture of the imagination. Teachers will avoid overemphasizing lessons of this nature to the exclusion of other facets of imagination and reasoning.

■ *Devise insightful titles*

1. Duplicate poems, omitting their titles. Ask students to create titles to bind the varied elements of the poem into a single unified and imaginative essence. With

junior high school pupils, relatively simple but unfamiliar poems like "Past and Present" by Thomas Hood and "Reflections Dental" by Phyllis McGinley are suitable. For older pupils, poems by Robert Frost, Emily Dickinson, and Karl Shapiro serve particularly well. Occasionally one may use a brief poem with a considerable admixture of ambiguity: Dylan Thomas, William Butler Yeats, and other modern poets will serve to thrust students out of habitual modes of thought. (For instance, Thomas' "The Hand that Signed the Paper Felled a City" or Yeats's "The Song of the Wandering Aengus.") The purpose is to stimulate students to integrate diverse elements through combining, recombining, and reconciling.

2. Other variations of this method depend upon the teacher's presentation of art reproductions—film slides of such modern painters as Rouault and Picasso—and synopses of novels such as may be found in any book review source. Effective also, are short stories such as those found in *Literary Cavalcade* and in *Short Short Stories*.[39] As in selecting titles for the poems, the method depends upon listing some of the titles the students submit and then, with their help, selecting the best title indicated by the elements offered by the painter or writer.

■ *Talk extemporaneously on partially sketched topics*

Extemporaneous oral talks require the student to impose order swiftly on the various parts of his experience. Select somewhat unusual or challenging topics and place them on slips of paper for a class secretary or chairman to distribute. Each topic has the initial parts of an outline, indicating the direction in which the extemporaneous talk should be developed. For instance a talk on teen-age driving may be partially designed from the viewpoint of an adult such as a highway patrolman or an insurance agent. Whoever draws the slip must complete the design in the same vein. One student is given three minutes to order his thoughts—usually out in the hallway. As he enters the room to speak, the pupil chairman gives another slip of paper to the next speaker who, in turn, retires to the hallway, preparing his material while the first speaker talks before the class. A committee—or those who have finished—assumes responsibility for evaluating the presentations, using some set of standards agreed upon in advance. Some topics which require a fusion of imagination, knowledge, and insight are listed here:

If you were a citizen of Alaska, a teacher in this school, a shrimp fisherman in the Louisiana bayous, the editor of a large city newspaper, a visitor from another planet [possibilities here are endless, limited only by the teacher's awareness of those his class can handle], what thoughts might you have as you returned home in the evening?

If you were the parent of a teen-ager who was running wild, what would you do?

How would you improve assemblies in our school?

What will students in the year 2065 study in high school?

■ *Create a story from multiple authorship*

For slow learning or younger pupils, teachers may build a story by a process of accretion. Using a tape recorder, the teacher tells the opening passage of a story with a pronounced mood of mystery or humor. Each volunteer thereafter adds several sentences or a paragraph to this beginning. The tape is stopped until someone volunteers; usually time is needed for plotting the next surge of action or de-

[39] *Literary Cavalcade*, Scholastic Corp., N.Y.; William Ransom Wood, ed., *Short Short Stories* (N.Y., Harcourt, Brace, 1951).

scription, and penciled notes are required for smooth delivery. Several tapes may be produced and reviewed for consistency of mood, unity of characterization, and coherent story line. The students should be aware that they are completing a partial design and that the skill required is consistency.

To perceive the relationship of parts in an organized structure

■ *Present two versions of the same poem or story*

1. A teacher may read aloud a story—"Child Pioneer" by Honoré Willsie Morrow and "Sixteen" by Maureen Daly are typical examples of stories that succeed well at the junior and senior high school levels respectively—and then offer two conclusions, the original and one which is not true to the author's development of the story. For instance, in "Sixteen" the author's ending expresses with poignant awareness a girl's first experience of rejection by a boy. By means of a careful selection of detail, skilled description, and stylistic rhythm, Maureen Daly's ending evokes the mood of adolescent hurt. A spoiled version distorts these.

2. Another variation of this method is the comparison of two versions in different literary forms, such as the original story, "The Man Who Liked Dickens" by Evelyn Waugh and the television adaptation.[40]

■ *Locate missing parts in a harmonious design*

Present literary, musical, or pictorial experiences from which some significant part has been deleted. For instance from a poem like "Annabel Lee" or "Ode to the West Wind" some portion is omitted and the abridged version presented either as a listening or a reading experience, the student's problem being to locate the flaw and to suggest the nature of what is needed for a harmonious whole. The method may be applied also to prose, architecture, and to all the graphic arts. By splicing tapes, the same method may be applied to music.

For junior high pupils or in the initial stages with older pupils, the deletions should be quite obvious and damaging to the proportion of the work of art, e.g., the entire final stanzas of "High Flight" or "Annabel Lee," or the necessary resolution of a significant phrase in "Eine Kleine Nachtmusik." Although the English teacher will, of course, emphasize literary forms, he will find a variety of art forms useful in establishing the concept of proportion and wholeness in artistic design.

Toward insight . . . Away from obtuseness

To gain more awareness of insight

■ *Place thought-provoking questions on the chalkboard*

For a period of time, keep questions like the following before the pupils. Numerous classroom situations and occasions will arise for discussing one or more of these ingredients of insight:

Do you jump to conclusions?

Do you look for implications? Do you read between the lines? Do you look for the reality behind the symbol, the seed beneath the husk?

[40] Robert Tallman's TV adaptation of "The Man Who Liked Dickens" appeared in *Literary Cavalcade,* Vol. 6, No. 7 (April 1954). The original story, titled "À Côté de Chez Todd," appeared in Evelyn Waugh, *A Handful of Dust* (Boston, Little, Brown, 1934); paperback (N.Y., Dell, 1959). It is also available in *Survival,* James R. Squire, ed. (N.Y., Scholastic, 1960).

Are you suspicious of easy formulas, stereotypes, simple solutions, and single causation? Do you know what these are? Can you illustrate each with an example?

Do you keep in a fluid state all the clues to solving a puzzling problem? Do you let your mind hover over a matter before making an important decision?

■ *Feature lack of insight in its comic aspects*

1. On a bulletin board, display posters which illustrate lack of insight. Students may be familiar with posters depicting Dilbert, an obtuse person who wrestles on the edges of swimming pools, swims in deep water without knowing a variety of strokes, and dives before checking the depth of the water.[41] Dilbert posters may not be available, but students will enjoy drawing others to take their place and to illustrate other situations. Sunday comic sections provide many examples.

2. Let gifted and interested pupils prepare film strips showing the amusing consequences of failure to see beneath the surface. For example, depict the naive customer at the used-car lot of Giveaway Givins, who "loses his shirt on every sale."

3. Use political cartoons, brief news ancedotes, and *New Yorker* drawings.

Remind students that lack of insight is not always amusing. Behind the symbol of the swastika lay the workings of warped minds; some cynical money-seekers masquerade in the trappings of evangelistic religion or medical cures; illegal diploma mills take advantage of eager young people who want further education. The comic examples can lead into serious discussions.

To see beyond the obvious

■ *Use fables and parables*

Some students are often hesitant to interpret, to look beneath the surface. Establish the attitude that it is better to have soared occasionally to the wrong implications than never to have soared at all. In fables as in swimming, one must plunge in if learning is ever to take place. Merely to know "what happens" in most worthwhile stories is to wade in the shallows.

1. Begin with simple exercises. Have students tell—or read to them—Aesop's fable of the fox and grapes. They will easily grasp the point that it is intended to be more than an account of some animals and grapes. Press them to describe real-life situations, somewhat in detail, in which the sour-grapes attitude shows itself.

2. Next, present a more unfamiliar fable such as the following:

> A pig ate his fill of acorns under an oak tree and then started to root around the tree. A crow remarked, "You should not do this. If you lay bare the roots, the tree will wither and die." "Let it die," replied the pig. "Who cares as long as there are acorns?"

The teacher should be prepared to offer several examples of shortsighted wastefulness if pupils cannot do so. Students who offer implications that are off center or inapplicable should not be discouraged by teacher or classmates. However, assessment of the *best* illustrations is entirely justifiable and even necessary if growth in seeing imaginative relationships is to occur.

[41] Posters prepared by the Naval Training Program, United States Navy, and displayed at swimming pools.

3. From fables, move on to parables, usually somewhat more complex. Use Buddha's parable, Returning Love for Hatred,[42] and some of the Christian, Jewish, and Mohammedan parables. Once the students understand the requirements of the assignment, meaningful generalization and application may be used with more difficult materials. Encourage, also, fluidity of thought, urging as many applications as possible to a variety of situations. If more responses are forthcoming than can be handled by oral recitation, direct pupils to use some form of abbreviation or private shorthand to record their applications. Then close the lesson by asking each student to write the best application from among those he recorded. Some of the most imaginative and pertinent should be read to the class. (A committee of students to select these can often save the teacher's time for other work.)

4. If the students fare well on this exercise, scale even more difficult heights. Use aphorisms such as these from Eric Hoffer: [43]

"Rudeness is the weak man's imitation of strength."
"Fear and freedom are mutually exclusive."

or maxims like these from La Rochefoucauld:

"Hypocrisy is the homage that vice pays to virtue."
"Greater virtues are needed to bear good fortune than bad."

Poor Richard's Almanack, Will Rogers's homely wisdom, Thomas Jefferson's *Decalogue,* the sayings of Confucius, and the aphorisms from the Old Norse sagas will furnish further tightly coiled meanings for students to unravel. A pleasant variation: Place students in groups, giving all the same maxim to unfold through application. Each group then vies with the others to produce the greatest number of apt illustrations, the teacher or a committee acting as judges.

5. Gifted pupils may continue this course by using *Animal Farm, The Prophet,* or *Fables for Our Time.* All of these offer stimulation for developing an interpretive bend of mind. They assist the teacher in fostering an interpretive focus which pulls toward penetration and away from superficial acceptance of face value. Multi-leveled, and therefore suited to similar enrichment of meaning, are many children's stories, such as *Charlotte's Web, The Mousewife,* and *The Story of Ferdinand.*

■ *Use "Letter to a Fan"*

For slower classes and for younger pupils who find difficulty in penetrating beyond the literal meaning of literary selections, Howard Pease's "Letter to a Fan" [44] is exceptionally helpful. In his response to the student who had read all but two of his books, Pease asks what it means to read more than the surface elements of a story and then charts the way for many pupils who are unaccustomed to looking beneath the surface events of a story for its theme, symbols, and human values.

[42] "Parable of Returning Love for Hatred" by Gautama Buddha, from R. C. Dutt, ed., *Civilizations of India* (London, Dent, pp. 45-50); reprinted in Luella D. Cook and others, eds., *The World Through Literature* (N.Y., Harcourt, Brace, 1949), pp. 82-84.

[43] Eric Hoffer, *The Passionate State of Mind* (N.Y., Harper, 1955).

[44] Howard Pease, "How to Read Fiction," in *They Will Read Literature,* A Portfolio of Tested Secondary School Procedures (Champaign, Ill., National Council of Teachers of English, 1955).

■ *Use poems and stories in parallel*

Another method of helping pupils see beyond the obvious uses short stories or poems with parallel themes. For instance, Robert Frost's "Dust of Snow" and Sara Teasdale's "Wood Song" both assert nature's power to dispel a mood of bitterness. A boy's relation to his parents is the theme of a cluster of very teachable short stories:

"My Father is an Educated Man" by Jesse Stuart
"Mama and Nels" (from *Mama's Bank Account*) by Kathryn Forbes
"The Duke's Children" by Frank O'Connor
"The Snob" by Morley Callaghan
"The Pheasant Hunter" by William Saroyan

In reading and discussing parallel short selections like these, students can discover the value of going beyond *what happens* in a story. Although many classes will require as the first step a retelling of what happened, they can be taught to take further steps: to analyze and generalize about the motives and behavior of the characters, to seek the theme of the writer, and to note values that determine the choices and attitudes of the characters.[45] Seeing relationships between selections and discussing the significance behind the incidents require imaginative insight and creative thinking. Gifted students will handle the method of parallel selections with more intensity than other students, but even very slow pupils can relate a brief story like "The Snob" to "Mama and Nels." Here is a method that emphasizes relationships rather than simple classification.

■ *Devote time to reflection*

1. Some teachers provide time for thinking through a topic before discussion. They write a question on the board; then they ask the students to think about the question and to make notes of their thoughts. After four or five minutes, the discussion is opened with the help of some reliable student. This procedure may be varied on different days. Sometimes pupils write for five minutes on a topic, then develop an oral discussion on the same topic. Other times, written reaction will conclude a ten-minute oral discussion.

2. Occasionally a question is placed on the board for silent reflection not to be followed by any talking or writing whatsoever. To be sure, the teacher doesn't know the student is thinking, but this method often proves extremely effective. For it, teachers use more personal questions than those used for discussion. To illustrate the method, some questions for thought and meditation used with the novel *Silas Marner* are listed here. Teachers will vary the questions according to their purposes and the material they are studying.

Topics for reflection followed by discussion, writing, or both

Some people are born lucky; others never have any good happen to them. True or false? Apply your answer to Dunstan, Godfrey, or Silas.

Some choices in life stunt our growth; others help us to grow.

[45] Two books showing how to develop discussion of this sort, which gets beyond "what happened" in a story, are Margaret Heaton and Helen B. Lewis, eds., *Reading Ladders for Human Relations,* rev. and enl. ed. (Washington, D.C., American Council on Education, 1955); and Taba and Elkins, eds., *With Focus on Human Relations.*

"No man is an island unto himself." What connection does this quotation have with this story?

This novel would be a good book for parents to study. It has wisdom about how to rear children and how not to rear them.

Topics for reflection followed by no discussion

Does selfishness carry its own punishment? Is this true in *Silas Marner*? Is this true in real life?

The need for love and affection is not limited to characters in novels.

Does money play *any* part in a happy life? What does George Eliot seem to say? What do you say?

Avoid an excess of moralizing on these matters. Students often reject adult preachments if the points are too heavily emphasized.

■ *Study metaphor to illuminate relationships*

When a man's heart is compared to a shriveled, sour apple, the adolescent reader, if he is not to be puzzled, must respond with an interpretive turn of mind. Figurative language may be collected by students as an assignment. Each pupil is to search for three imaginative comparisons, copying each on a card. Groups or committees may select the most striking examples for publication in the school paper or for a bulletin board devoted to imaginative writing.[46] One class liked these:

"A lanky boy whose bolts needed tightening."[47]

"He was at that awkward age when he could walk through empty rooms and knock over furniture."

Toward understanding the imagination . . . Away from ignorance about the imagination

To develop a definition of imagination

■ *Use an inductive method of defining imagination*

1. Place on the chalkboard several contrasts between imaginative and unimaginative statements:

The helicopter came toward us.
The helicopter descended upon us like an infuriated palm tree.

That assembly program showed very little planning.
That assembly program was about as carefully planned as a hiccup.

After beginning with these simple contrasts, lead the discussion to several more complex examples of imagination:

A substitute teacher, facing an unruly class, takes one boy into the hall, sends him to the office, bangs with terrific force on the lockers, and returns to a roomful of silent, decorous students.

[46] Ways of developing skill with figurative language are described further on pp. 300-301 in Chapter 6, pp. 369-74 in Chapter 7, and pp. 235-39, in the discussion on vocabulary in Chapter 5.

[47] From Charles Brooks, *English Spring* (N.Y., Harcourt, Brace, 1932).

Tom Sawyer induces the other boys to help him whitewash the fence.
Huck Finn outwits the Duke and the Dauphin.
The Wright brothers fly their plane.

Newspaper clippings or magazine articles relating original or insightful behavior are also useful.

2. Using such examples as these as starters, encourage pupils to tell about other imaginative events, actions, or language, such as creating new recipes, tools, fashions, architecture, laws. After sufficient examples have been described, ask pupils to help in developing a definition for imagination. At first many of them will say "Imagination is when . . . ," continuing to give concrete examples. Do not criticize this at first. Say, "Good! But let's not have any more *examples.*" Point out the need for generalizing from the specific examples. Try to shape the students' contribution toward Coleridge's definition of imagination (see p. 118), helping them to discriminate between the *fantastic* and the *imaginative.* For a follow-up assignment, ask rows or groups of students to bring to class examples of

Insightful comparisons in language
Expression of profound feeling or enthusiasm admirably controlled
Multiplicity or diversity brought into order through some unifying or predominant thought or feeling
Originality of action in some situation
Remarkable insight into some situation or some other person's feelings or problems
Creative inventions or actions

The situations described in this assignment may be either actual or fictional.

3. Slow learning students will not be able to generalize rapidly in this manner. Rather than risk loss of interest in the time needed to develop a definition with them, the teacher may wish to emphasize the difference between originality and imitativeness in concrete situations. For this purpose fables, parables, and brief anecdotes are suitable. One teacher prepares a class of slow learners for a writing assignment by giving them colored chalk and art paper, asking them to draw for fifteen minutes "What Makes Me Mad," then to write paragraphs interpreting their drawings. After the students have written, the teacher reads examples of interesting papers; in the course of reading, he defines imagination, writing a definition on the board. When slow learning students are in classes of mixed ability, the teacher will, as frequently as possible, arrange multiple assignments.

All pupils can profit by a discussion of the difference between appropriate uses of the imagination and inappropriate escape into fantasy. The world of fantasy reaches out to many and the means of escape into it are often learned too easily. Certain poems and stories, useful for discussing this concept, should be known to all teachers:

For junior high
"Stolen Day" by Sherwood Anderson
"That's What Happened to Me" by Michael Fessier
For senior high
"Paul's Case" by Willa Cather
"Mrs. Ketting and Clark Gable" by Ann Chidester

"Petit, the Poet" by Edgar Lee Masters
"Miniver Cheevy" by Edward Arlington Robinson

■ *Use a deductive method of understanding imagination*

Here the teacher reverses the process described above and starts with a definition of imagination. After furnishing some examples himself, the teacher asks the students to supply further examples, both in class and as a home assignment. For example, a student might tell how he successfully used a board that was too short, in a woodshop project. This might be an opportune time to recommend certain books for recreational reading, books that stress imagination—*Engineers' Dreams; Jules Verne, the Biography of an Imagination; Kon-Tiki; 20,000 Leagues Under the Sea; The Bright Design.* These books help many boys, especially, to understand that imagination is not exclusively connected with poetry and fantasy.

To discriminate between stale and fresh expression

■ *Act out clichés*

Have pairs of students dramatize the idea of an expert on clichés who takes the witness stand and testifies in the following manner: [48]

Q. Where do you live?
A. Any old place I hang my hat is home sweet home to me.
Q. What is . . . your occupation?
A. Well, after burning the midnight oil at an institution of higher learning, I was for a time a tiller of the soil; then I went down to the sea in ships. I have been a guardian of the law, a poet at heart, a prominent club man . . . and—
Q. And you expect to live to—
A. A ripe old age.
Q. What do you thank?
A. My lucky stars . . .
Q. How right are you?
A. I am dead right.
Q. What kind of meals do you like?
A. Square meals.

Students may work in pairs to collect overworked phrases and present brief question-and-answer skits before the class. Before the exercise is concluded, devote some time searching for fresh and original ways to express the ideas the clichés represent. Make the point that one of the elements of imagination is seeing new relationships, finding new insight into similarities between unlike elements. Seeing the world in a fresh and original manner rather than through the eyes of others underlies imaginative thinking.

■ *Substitute fresh comparisons for tired language*

1. The teacher may write hackneyed descriptions like the following:

It was Dina, a vivid girl with lips like cherries and eyes like stars. [This may be continued for several more sentences.]

[48] Frank Sullivan, "The Cliché Expert Takes the Stand," *New Yorker*, August 31, 1935. A long list of clichés appeared in the *Saturday Review of Literature* for November 30, 1946. More recently, "The Cliché Expert Testifies on Baseball" by Frank Sullivan appeared in *Literary Cavalcade*, Vol. 2, No. 7 (April 1959).

Students are to write or locate a description of a girl, a description they nominate for merit on the basis of originality and power to evoke genuine imagery. Subsequent exercises may be descriptions of people, actions, scenes in nature, storms, or fires.

2. Another approach uses duplicated hackneyed comparisons with a space beneath each for more imaginative solutions. Here are a few examples. The teacher or a committee of perceptive students can expand the list.

pretty as a picture	working like a beaver
brown as a berry	dumb as an ox
fit as a fiddle	dead as a doornail
dying to meet someone	poor as a churchmouse

3. Certain tired expressions also deserve attention for their lack of originality and their frequent appearance in adolescents' writing: *dull, sickening thud; struggle for existence; bolt from the blue; cap the climax.* Before completing each of these lessons, direct student attention to their bearing upon an understanding of the function and purpose of imagination. One avoids prefabricated phrases only through the vitality and creative flexibility of the imagination. Pupils who are aware of this are more likely to let meaning determine the phrases they use rather than the opposite—an indolent blur of easy vagueness.

To examine the creation of images

■ *Give pupils training in visualizing*

During instruction in literature, the teacher may stop to discuss the pictures evoked by a passage. After volunteers have described their images, he relates his own as vividly as possible. What elements do they have in common? Why? How do they differ? Why? Thus, while stressing the importance of visualization in arriving at meaning, he underlines the fact that the same words will produce in no two individuals exactly the same mental picture since no two ever have identical experiences. Such lessons should begin in the junior high school with relatively easy and impelling selections. At each grade level thereafter, teachers plan some training in visualizing,[49] saving for this purpose passages like the description of a jungle river in Conrad's *Heart of Darkness.* Junior high pupils respond well to passages such as the arrival of the hermit mousecatcher in *Homer Price. Tom Sawyer,* stories of Robin Hood, and *Call It Courage* also furnish excellent passages for this age level.

Whether in junior high or senior high, the teacher reads the sentences aloud while the students close their eyes and visualize their responses; then they list what they actually see, making quick pencil jottings. Important at this point is the distinction between what a pupil actually visualizes and what he adds as he describes his thoughts. Discussion of these "delayed images" and of the variety of images among class members should raise a number of questions: How do words—mere guttural sounds or marks on paper—give us meanings? Why don't all of us receive identical images? Do some of us have more complete—or more highly colored—images than others?

[49] In the senior high school, the teacher will want to make clear that in reading, the nature of the material and the reader's purpose will affect the extent to which one lingers over a passage, seeking clear images. Many times a reader purposely prefers vague imagery. Such a discussion might easily relate to the reading of Bacon's essay, "Of Books."

■ *Consider sensory imagery of all kinds*

Play short unfamiliar melodies on the phonograph. Ask students to hold the melody in their inner ear to determine whether or not they have a memory for sound images. Can they repeat the sound memory by whistling the melody? Experiment with odors like geranium, lavender, camphor, peppermint, and orange peel. Do the same with images of touch—velvet, silk, stone, concrete, metal foil—and taste.[50] Much of the reporting will, of necessity, be subjective. Nevertheless, students become interested in sensory imagery and sensory memory, and the interest enlivens oral discussion. Blindfold tests with sight, sound, odor, touch, or taste will show that human beings have developed sight and hearing much more fully than the other senses.

Evaluating Imaginative Thinking

Evaluation of imaginative thinking is difficult and cannot be precise. However because evaluation helps both teachers and pupils to move in the direction of curricular aims, the usefulness of check lists and rating scales should be considered. Also helpful are collected samples of student creative production and anecdotal records of students' imaginative behavior, provided that teachers have time to collect and use them. Unless English teachers evaluate progress in imaginative thinking, they are omitting an important responsibility. The procedures that follow have been chosen for their feasibility as well as their value.

Self-inventory for pupils These self-questionnaires may be signed or anonymous. Although in the latter case they cannot be used for grading pupils, they do assist the teacher and pupils in reviewing instruction and in planning future emphases. The following questions might be typical of such an inventory:

Self-Inventory

1. Do you use original comparisons in your speech and writing? Sometimes_____ Often_____ Seldom_____ Never_____

   Examples: Her face was so long she could drink buttermilk from the bottom of a churn without using her hands. The chandelier was like a silvery fountain stopped by an enchantment. Architecture is frozen music.

2. Do you sometimes imagine and foresee what will happen if you take a certain course of action? If so, give an example.
7. Do you often see a relation between two stories, or two poems, or any two selections? If so, give an example.
8. Can you appreciate a story by a writer whose outlook on life is quite different from yours? If so, give an example.

[*Continue with progressively more difficult items.*]

[50] The teacher need not furnish these odors, touches, or tastes. An individual or a committee from among the students can attend to these. Moreover, because this is a study of sensory *imagery*, the actual presence of all the materials is not always desirable. Pupils may imagine and describe these images without the presence of the physical stimuli.

16. Can you feel yourself into a character well enough to interpret that character in dramatics? If so, name a character you could play.
17. Have you ever written a poem expressing something you felt quite deeply?

Pupil self-rating scale: imaginative insight When a scale such as the following is used at intervals throughout a semester, the pupil will become increasingly aware of the situations in which such items occur. Repetition of any evaluation instrument converts it into a reminder, reinforcing the aims of instruction.

Examples of imaginative insight	Almost always	Usually	Sometimes	Never
1. When I read a story I try to see more than what happens. I look for its theme or its deeper meanings.				
2. I avoid making snap decisions; I let my thoughts hover for awhile before settling important matters.				
3. I can *interpret* the meaning of fables and tales like "The Fox and the Grapes."				
4. As I read, I visualize scenes and characters.				
[*Continue with progressively more difficult items.*]				
11. I avoid clichés and other forms of overused language. *Examples:* As luck would have it, the happy pair, heart-to-heart talk.				
12. In most of the things I do at home or at school, I try to be inventive and to see new ways of doing things. Give one or more examples.				
13. I like to do things in new ways, and whenever possible I avoid depending on habit. Give one or more examples.				

Guess-who questionnaire This type of appraisal, first developed in research with adolescents,[51] is now used frequently in teaching. Present students with statements describing varying personalities and ask them to designate the names of fellow students who best fit these descriptions. (None of the descriptions should be derogatory.) With slow students, the teacher may read aloud and comment on each item.

Guess-who questionnaire on imaginative insight

Read each question. Each will describe an individual. Whenever you think of someone in this class for whom the description is suitable, write his name in the blank.

[51] Carolyn M. Tryon, "Evaluations of Adolescent Personality by Adolescents," *Monographs of the Society for Research in Child Development,* Vol. 4, No. 4 (Washington, D.C., National Research Council, 1939).

You may write the names of more than one person in the blank.
You may write a person's name as many times as the description fits that person.
You may leave any item blank if you feel no one in our class fits this description.
Try to be as fair as possible.
Do not sign your own name or list yourself. [optional]

1. This person has many good ideas in some specialty like art or industrial arts or creative writing. He (or she) does new, original work and does not imitate any other person's work. ______
2. This person is almost always enthusiastic and full of good ideas. This person has more interesting ideas in an hour than most people have in a week. ______
3. This person is remarkably able to understand other people and to see why they act the way they do. If this person were an author, his (or her) books would show great insight into the thoughts and feelings of the characters. ______

[*Continue with progressively more difficult items.*]

11. This person is not stiff or stubborn in his thinking and acting. He (or she) is quick to see through a situation, can change when wrong, and does not find it difficult to "take in" a situation. This person is quick to see when there is more than one side to an argument. ______

Casting characters A variation of the "guess-who" method is the following:

Suppose your class was going to produce some plays. Next to the description of each character, write the names of classmates you think best suited for each part. You may choose the same classmate more than once. If you think of several classmates for any part, write each of them down. Do *not* consider acting ability.

1. Someone who is tremendously alive—full of energy and enthusiasm but never confused or all mixed up. This person *controls* his (or her) energy and enthusiasm. ______

[*Continue with similar descriptions related to imagination.*]

12. Someone who figures out the best way to do difficult things. Someone who is resourceful enough to imagine ways to get things done when no one else can think of what to do. ______

Although these "guess-who" methods are by no means precise instruments of evaluation, they often draw upon areas of pupil experience to which the teacher does not have access and supplement measures such as those which follow.

Collection of samples Samples of imaginative writing, creative oral productions on tape, and notations about extra-class creativity in stage designing, woodworking, musical composition, new recipes for cooking, projects in agriculture, and many other areas of human imaginative activity may be kept or recorded by students and reviewed by teachers. In the final analysis, these may be the most effective evidence that the school is encouraging and fostering imaginative thinking.

Teacher check list Check lists like this one should be used two or three times each term rather than just once.

Teacher check list: imaginative insight

Behavior to be observed	*Names of students*
Insightful about other people, socially sensitive	
Flexible and fluid in thought; no evidence of rigidity or stereotypes in thinking; adaptable but not vacillating	
Interpretive; has a bent toward seeing beneath the surfaces of situations	
Uses imaginative language; figurative and original language often evident	
Inventive in some special area (such as woodworking, sewing, class leadership, etc.)	
Evidence of writing notable for imaginative qualities of form	
Uses appreciational skills in reading literature; responds to implication, mood, and style	

Testing In addition to the methods described above, teachers may use tests like the one pictured on p. 125, those developed for the Army Air Corps (pp. 135-36), or modeled on "Grasp of Human Conduct" (p. 139). The Thurstone Test of Mental Alertness [52] is a short intelligence test to measure ability to think flexibly, adjust to new situations, learn new skills quickly, and understand complex or subtle relationships. Typical research findings indicate no relationship between academic grades or standard aptitude measures and creative scientific achievement. Of greater value as indicators of creativity are certain special aptitudes (such as the aptitude for divergent thinking), certain qualities of temperament (such as independence versus conformity), and certain kinds of motivation (such as inquisitiveness of mind).[53]

SELECTED READINGS

BOOKS

Harold H. Anderson, ed., *Creativity: And Its Cultivation.* N.Y., Harper, 1959. A collection of essays by authorities in a number of fields: psychology, education, architecture, sociology, etc.

June E. Downey, *Creative Imagination.* N.Y., Harcourt, Brace, 1929. A perceptive presentation of the springs of the imagination, with special emphasis on literature.

Susanne K. Langer, *Philosophy in a New Key: A Study in the Symbolism of Reason, Rite and Art,* 3rd ed. Cambridge, Mass., Harvard U. Press, 1957. (Also in a

[52] Science Research Associates, Inc., 57 West Grand Ave., Chicago 10, Ill.

[53] *The Second (1957) University of Utah Research Conference on the Identification of Creative Scientific Talent* (Salt Lake City, U. of Utah Press, 1958).

paperbound edition: N.Y., New American Library, 1948.) Langer rejects the theory that reason and imagination are two distinct kinds of thinking. To link insight and intuition to unreason and irrationalism is to fail to see that logic and imaginative insight are only two related ways to truth. Chapter 4 deals with the language of discourse and the language of the feelings.

John Livingston Lowes, *The Road to Xanadu.* Boston, Houghton Mifflin, 1930. (Also in a paperbound edition: N.Y., Knopf Vintage, 1959.) Creative synthesis, says Lowes, is the symbolic road on which the imagination voyages through chaos, reducing it to clarity and order.

Hughes Mearns, *Creative Power—The Education of Youth in the Creative Arts,* 2nd rev. ed. N.Y., Dover, 1958. Primarily concerned with creative writing, this book has been listed by the NEA as one of the twenty foremost books in education in recent years.

I. A. Richards, *Principles of Literary Criticism.* N.Y., Harcourt, Brace, 1924. Richards defines the imagination in Chapter XXXII.

George Santayana, *The Sense of Beauty: Being the Outlines of Aesthetic Theory,* new ed. N.Y., Scribner's, 1936. This book is concerned with the origin and condition of aesthetic values and their relation to other aspects of life. Santayana examines the thought that animates both art and science, and discusses the uses of imagination.

———, *The Life of Reason, or, The Phases of Human Progress: Reason in Art,* rev. ed. N.Y., Scribner's, 1954. Santayana said that he intended this book to be a history of the human imagination. In it, he recognizes the element of imagination in science and relates it to art as part of the human activity called reason.

W. Edgar Vinacke, *The Psychology of Thinking.* N.Y., McGraw-Hill, 1952. This exceptionally interesting text includes chapters on the imagination, autistic thinking, and creative thinking.

ARTICLES

Frank Barron, "The Psychology of Imagination." *Scientific American,* Vol. 199, No. 3 (September 1958).

———, "The Disposition Toward Originality." *Journal of Abnormal and Social Psychology,* Vol. 51, No. 3 (November 1955).

J. P. Guilford, "Creativity." *American Psychologist,* Vol. 5, No. 9 (September 1950).

Robert C. Wilson, "Creativity." In Fifty-Seventh Yearbook of National Society for the Study of Education, Part II, *Education for the Gifted.* Chicago, U. of Chicago Press, 1958.

———, and others, "A Factor-Analysis Study of Creative Thinking Abilities." *Psychometrika,* Vol. 19, No. 4 (December 1954).

Power Over Language

A Word About Units: "Power Over Language" is the first of several illustrative units. A unit is here defined as a planned block of study unified by certain major concepts whose comprehension involves certain skills and abilities. There are many ways to write down such units, none sacred. In this text, the unit will usually begin with a statement of aims and major concepts. Since such aims and concepts must come alive in actual experiences for learners, the next sections will deal with launching, developing, and culminating the unit. At the close will be found suggestions for evaluating the success of instruction, and resources for both students and teacher.

Effective unit design reflects an awareness that learning is dynamic, that skills, concepts, and facts all develop together. The unit, properly understood, is a strategy for evoking understanding rather than mere recall. For further discussion of selection and creation of units, the reader is referred to the section "Program and Plan," pp. 658-75.

A Unit for Grade Seven

Overview: At some point in his life, the educated person stops taking language for granted and becomes aware of it as a marvelous and fascinating phenomenon. The seventh grade is not too early for pupils to become aware of the importance and some of the most significant features of language, which if understood, make possible increased power over it. This unit is designed to provide seventh-graders with experiences in standing off to take such an objective look at language. At the close of this unit, when they start to use language unself-consciously again, they should have the basis for greater effectiveness and precision in handling both thought and communication.

AIMS

A unit is intended to produce specific learnings. Out of many possibilities in the disciplines of linguistics and communication, the five aims listed here have been chosen as most basic and attainable for beginners as immature as the typical seventh grade pupil. For gifted pupils, the unit may be enriched and deepened as a basis for the study of foreign languages. For slow learning pupils, the unit may be kept simple, crucial activities being repeated often enough to establish only the first four aims listed here. All pupils, whatever their native ability, can profit from a sharper awareness of language as an instrument of thought and communication.

1. To become more aware of the importance of language—to individuals, and to the peoples of the world
2. To realize that human worth is not determined by the language or variation of that language a person uses
3. To note the purposes for which language is used (This will include abuses of language as well as the range of respected and commendable purposes.)
4. To identify the differences between fluent, effective language and halting, weak language, noting ways to improve one's own power over language, both oral and written
5. To observe how the English language operates—through words: how they get their meanings, how they work with other words, the interest that may be found in them; through statements: their functions and relationships

CONCEPTS AND ATTITUDES

In organizing instruction to accomplish these aims, the teacher will inevitably introduce and emphasize certain concepts. In advance of this unit the following concepts should be carefully considered by the teacher. If they are clear in his mind, he will be alert to opportunities for teaching them in language the pupils can comprehend. These concepts and attitudes, phrased in the language of the teacher, represent points of view rather than specific aims to be accomplished. Such concepts should permeate all instruction in language.

Language relies upon words, spoken and written *symbols* freed from concrete situations. Only human beings can use words in this way.

There is no evidence of animals having made the leap from signs to symbolic language, to words freed from concrete situations. A growl, a harsh command, even a green traffic light—*signs* like these, directly tied to a concrete situation, can take on meaning for animals as well as for human beings. Symbols, however, are instruments of thought, and by means of symbols human beings—and only human beings—can allude to an object or a concept in its absence.

Without symbolic language, there would be among men no civilization, no sharing or passing on of ideas and discoveries, no literature, science, or religion.

Although some of our thinking may be carried on in other ways, most of our thinking is done with word-symbols.

The deliberate use of language for falsehood weakens the foundation for communication and understanding among mankind.

Understanding words and statements requires more than a definition of each separate word or statement. It requires an awareness of the purpose behind the language, and its relationship to other words and ideas in their context.

The ability to use standard informal English is almost always a requirement of the community for those who do not wish to be limited in their economic opportunities and friendships.

People who have real power over spoken language are typically those who feel secure, being at ease with other people, respecting themselves and others, and therefore speaking easily and sincerely; have the flexibility and resilience that come from realizing how complicated the world is; are sensitive to other people and perceive how others receive what they say; have energy and therefore enter into many situations requiring the use of language with other people; use the prevailing language conventions accepted by the community in which they live; enunciate clearly and use a pleasant tone of voice; and are reasonably fluent.

TIME PLAN

This unit should last no longer than three weeks. For most seventh grade pupils examining language *as language* for the first time, a longer period of study could dissipate their initial enthusiasm. However, a great many of the aims and activities suggested here deserve to be drawn into the curriculum at later periods throughout the year. For instance, the activities for vocabulary building and those showing how words and statements operate are suitable for use in many other units and for individual daily assignments not incorporated into any unit. Inasmuch as power over language is the English teacher's concern throughout the year, this particular unit may be viewed as an intensified effort to feature attitudes and concepts to be reinforced later in many ways and in many situations. For instance, even though the concept of freedom from linguistic snobbery is presented in this unit, a teacher will undoubtedly wish to maintain the pupils' attempts to rise above narrow provincialism. To eradicate suspicion and ridicule of those using a differing language will require more than a single lesson. Thus "Power Over Language," as a unit, may be said to last for three weeks, yet it is only a preliminary focus on content intended to recur throughout the entire secondary school period.

LAUNCHING THE UNIT

Considering the nature of seventh grade pupils, the teacher will no doubt wish to open the unit with some activity designed to catch pupil interest immediately. The activities listed in this section are intended to contribute to an interest in words and how words acquire their meanings. The teacher and pupils, planning together, may choose one, two, or all of these suggested activities or others similar in nature. Through them the teacher will seek to initiate an interest in language as a whole, an awareness of its importance, and curiosity as to how one might progress to greater power in using language.

■ *Home assignment: animal intelligence*

Observe some animal—a pet dog, a cat, or some other animal. Try to decide at what points animals reach the limits of their intelligence in understanding vocal sounds. Then answer two questions, writing about one page for each:

What can animals do with vocal sounds?
What can animals not do with vocal sounds?

Be ready to discuss in class: Can animals think, remember, foresee, understand cause and effect?

■ *How words get their meanings*

Play the game "Substitute." The teacher begins the game by asking students to guess what is meant by the strange new word *gleb* in the following sentences. Students should number from 1 to 10, writing down at each number a guess as to the meaning.

1. There are many different kinds of *glebs* in the world.
2. A *gleb* does not care for music; neither does it dislike music.
3. A *gleb* needs water but it does not need steak or ice cream.
4. Some *glebs* require a great deal of water; a few *glebs* can go without water for long periods of time.
5. *Glebs* like sunshine but they do not like snow.
6. We have a *gleb* in this room.
7. *Glebs* are usually colored green.
8. A *gleb* really belongs out of doors, but people often bring *glebs* inside.
9. Sometimes *glebs* do not grow very well, especially if one does not water them.
10. The *gleb* in our room has a red flower.[1]

The game should begin with contexts that are broad and vague. Each sentence, ideally, should sharpen the focus of meaning so that the last sentence occurs in a context making possible success for almost everyone. (It is interesting to note that for some pupils early incorrect guesses often become obstacles to identification as new information appears in subsequent sentences.) The immediate purpose of the game is to determine as early as possible the meaning of the coined word that has been substituted for a word regularly established in the language.

Occasionally, the teacher should employ a word from another language in order to show students that what may sound strange to them has a meaning to other people. For instance, *krükvaxt* (pronounced *krook'vekst*), a Swedish word for house plant, might be used instead of *gleb* in an exercise such as the one above. The ultimate instructional purpose of the game is to lead students to consider how the sounds they call "words" achieve their meanings by association. If they understand the principle of association easily, the teacher may also wish to point out how the principle of reinforcement is added to association: If we use a word correctly, other people respond appropriately; thus our association of sound and meaning is reinforced by the reactions of others.

After the teacher has demonstrated the game, students who understand the ground rules may prepare similar sets of ten sentences for trial with their fellow pupils. The teacher follows the experience by helping the students to generalize from their experience and by extending the principles in four new ways:

1. He asks the students how they learned to associate meaning with words like *jet, nimble, reveille, Brazil,* and new words they have learned recently. What new words have the pupils recently learned in science? In other courses in school? How did they acquire them?

2. He teaches a new word in as many ways as possible, using derivation, root, experiences with the word, dictionary definition, examples in context. In one Wisconsin school, for instance, a mango was purchased as a part of school supplies; the students felt it, smelled it, peeled it, cut it into pieces, and tasted it. They looked it up in the dictionary and the teacher furnished examples of the word's use in literature and other writing. All words are not as concrete as *mango;* yet for words like *incubation, jovial,* and *fickle* an imaginative teacher will turn up a variety of approaches.

[1] For a note on research employing this method, and suggestions for other classroom applications of it, see Chapter 2, p. 101, and Chapter 5, p. 241.

3. He reads two passages, one about familiar matters and one about experiences highly unfamiliar to the class. The students are asked to generalize: What happens to our thoughts as we listen to the two passages?

4. He asks questions: What happens to the language of people who leave their own countries and migrate to another country where they must speak a new language? Why do they lose their facility with their mother tongue? Do they lose their native language completely? Have any students parents or grandparents or neighbors whom they can interview on this matter?

■ *How words can sometimes lose their meanings*

1. To demonstrate that the sound is not the reality, ask the pupils to choose some word. *Pickle, cackling,* or *rugged* are excellent choices to offer. Each pupil quietly repeats the word over and over enough times to hear the sound as a strange noise rather than a meaningful word. Many of the students will have the curious experience of stripping the sound almost completely of its meaning.

2. Ask which word in each of these pairs is harder to "un-mean"? Why?

father *or* atom
mother *or* fantasy
home *or* Ceylon
dog *or* puma

■ *Why we do not understand foreign languages*

1. Place on the board this Finnish sentence:

Taskukello on tehty kullasta.

Why don't we understand this sentence? Then place on the board the translation of the same sentence:

The watch is made of gold.

Why do we understand these words? The teacher must, of course, press beyond the superficial answer that we are not Finnish-speaking people. What is meant by "to learn a language"? What is the best way to learn a foreign language?

2. Summarize these four activities by helping students generalize: Words gain their meanings by the experiences we have with them. We associate meaning with words, but the word, in and of itself, has no meaning. The word is merely a strange sound, or mark—but a strange sound that becomes familiar and meaningful to those who use it in any language family, in any language system. *Taskukello* means *watch* to five million people who call their native land "Suomi." We call it "Finland."

■ *How words come into the language*

The teacher begins by asking pupils to list words that are new this year. (As we write, certain words connected with space flight are new.) Next they list words that were new during the last ten years.

Since 1900 what words have come into the language and why? Do any words ever drop out? Why? What conclusion can be drawn about language? (It is changing, at least in regard to words. Perhaps the deeper structure remains the same? Or does it? Do you suppose pronunciations change?)

Coin some mouth-filling words after examining and laughing at Alastair Reid's ideas for new words in *Ounce, Dice, Trice* (13).[2]

■ *Records, films, newspapers*

1. The teacher may pass around the class a recent foreign newspaper, magazine, or comic book. Particularly interesting are contemporary publications in Japanese, Russian, or Tagalog (Philippines) with their pictures, comics, and advertising.
2. Play a part of a recording of Chaucer's *Canterbury Tales* read in Middle English (18). Help students realize that their present language may someday sound and look strange. (If the record is not available, pass around a copy of Chaucer in the original.)
3. Show a short film in which a foreign language is used.
4. Use the film "The English Language: Story of Its Development" (19).

■ *Class discussion*

What could we study about language that would be worthwhile for us to know? The teacher lists the pupils' suggestions on the chalkboard. He asks students to group together those that are similar. If some of the important aims of this unit are not suggested by the pupils, he may ask leading questions to induce some pupils to suggest necessary concepts to be woven into the design of this unit. The purpose of this activity: to draw the pupils into the over-all planning of the unit and at the same time to focus their suggestions in the direction of significant aims the teacher envisions for the unit.

DEVELOPING THE UNIT

No teacher could carry out all the activities suggested and contain this unit within the three weeks' time limit. These suggested activities are all designed to develop the aims of the unit, but each teacher will select those which appeal to him as most appropriate for his classes according to the relative emphasis he places upon the aims previously stated or the aims as modified for a particular class.

■ *A world without language*

Ask the pupils to imagine a world in which men and women live without the use of language. After several suggestions have been made, read aloud to the class "A World Without Language," Chapter One in *The Tree of Language* (1). Let these four interesting pages serve a double purpose: to point up the importance of language and to introduce this book which is to be used throughout the unit. Conclude by having students try to express ideas without words. Give each individual such sentences as these:

Danger: sharp curve ahead.
Young people in the seventh grade begin to realize how interesting language is.
Don't scratch the chalkboard with your fingernail.
The next day we tied our flatboat to a small island off the east bank of the Mississippi River.

[2] Most of the units in this book conclude with a list of resources for the pupil. The figures in parentheses following a title refer to the numbers in this list, which gives full bibliographical data as well as information about where to procure supplementary materials.

■ *Home assignment: silence is golden . . . and difficult*

Each pupil is to attempt, from the dismissal of school until the next class hour, to speak as little as possible, holding all talk to an absolute minimum. What difficulties arise? How does one feel, not using language? How do other people react? Did anything notable or amusing occur as a result of such unusual behavior for a seventh grade pupil? What situations arose that made speech absolutely necessary? (During the discussion of these points the teacher is alert for misuses of the past tense in all verbs used, making notes for future reference but not, at the time, correcting misuses. The improvement of usage in past tense is suggested as a special task during this unit.)

■ *Oral reports*

Individual pupils may report on the following interesting matters of communication:

- scout signs and signalling
- braille
- the language of the deaf
- the Morse Code
- international communication among aviators of different countries
- slang [See the books by Ernst (7) and Pei (2)]
- road signs [A good report for a slow pupil]
- the history of writing
- strange alphabets: Arabic, Chinese, Russian, Egyptian hieroglyphics
- the mystery language: Basque
- history of the English language
- shorthand
- musical notation
- symbols in mathematics
- artificial languages such as Esperanto, Walapuk, and ITO

■ *The uses and importance of language*

How many uses of language have you noticed today?
What are some of the ways the peoples of the world use language?

These questions may seem very simple at first, but they are the means of drawing pupils to look at language, its various uses, and its importance. Ask other questions, such as:

How does language help us to be kind and thoughtful to other people?
How do we use language to make people feel welcome and to express other courtesies?
To what evil or unworthy purposes do some people put language? Illustrate.
Do we use language in thinking? Give examples.
Do representatives of nations use language to bluff one another? For instance?
List all the ways you can recall having used language for the past day or two. *Examples:* to ask questions, to tease my brother, to persuade my father, to sing while I washed my sweater.
What television programs have you viewed? Besides using language yourself through speech or writing, what reading or listening have you done?
Summarize: Language is important because . . .

■ *The abuses of language*

Initiate this activity by alternately reading aloud and telling the incident from *Huckleberry Finn* in which the bogus Duke and King attempt to swindle money from three orphaned girls (Chapters 24 to 30). Extend the class discussion to a consideration of some abuses and misuses of language: gossip, slander, libel, perjury, plagiarism, name calling and smear words, and verbalism (using words without knowing their meanings). For seventh grade pupils, most of these words will be new and will need definition. In some cases, demonstrations help to fix the meaning. For instance, two students may present reports on the early life of Mark Twain, one version to be an uncomprehending reproduction of the material in an encyclopedia, the other to be a lively report in the student's own words, in which he shows clearly by an imparting tone of voice and proper emphases that he understands every word he uses.

■ *The importance of accuracy and truth in the use of language*

The teacher forms the class into five or six teams of pupils. Each team is to have the same number of players, numbered one, two, three, etc. The teacher has all number-one players come to his desk to view a somewhat complicated picture. Each number-one player then returns to his group and quietly explains the picture as precisely as he can to player number two on his team. Number two, in turn, explains the picture to player number three. This continues until the final member of the team has received the information. He then jots down what he is going to say and comes before the class to give a description of the picture. The class notes the variations in the presentations of these final members of the teams. Then the teacher holds up the picture for everyone to view and to discuss. Consideration may be given to the problems in the relay wherein language misunderstandings occurred. This game may then be played again, with an attempt at improved precision in the use of language.

One thought-provoking variation of the game—and one which may result in much valuable discussion—can be introduced by a plot between the teacher and one pupil. Without the knowledge of the others, this one pupil deliberately distorts the information. Members of his team will be puzzled as to what has caused them to reach a final description so different from those of the other teams. When the teacher and pupil divulge their duplicity, the occasion has arrived for generalizing about the social importance of integrity in language. Further discussion should explore the seriousness of perjury in courts, the reliability of witnesses, the problems of advertising and propaganda, and the reasons people distort the truth.

■ *Home assignment: skillful uses of language*

Each pupil is to copy a passage from a book, magazine, newspaper column, or from wherever he chooses. The passage, to exemplify skillful use of language, may be notable for its beauty of phrasing, for its precision, economy, or any other virtue the pupil may wish to feature. A few students may be skillful enough to copy spoken language from a television program, and such contributions if faithfully recorded should also be encouraged. In class the students may read and discuss their choices in groups of five. The best choices from each group are presented to the class, along with comment on the qualities which deserve special note.

■ *Improving the use of appropriate language*

The teacher presents the concept that people who speak differently from us should not be ridiculed; that a man's worth is not measured by the way he speaks his language. Anecdotes and illustrations will help clinch these points.

The teacher follows this by introducing the idea of levels of usage and illustrating the realities of community pressure for appropriate and conventional usage, e.g., Why would we be surprised if the President of the United States, in a television broadcast, said, "We ain't gonna let no gol-durned furriners hog-tie us"? Pupils can present impromptu skits in which applicants being interviewed for desirable positions are disappointed in their ambitions because of insensitivity to the prevailing conventions of usage.

To avoid the scattering of attention that follows too many language considerations, the teacher should next choose a single element of usage and focus attention on its relation to accepted conventions in language. (For this unit, we have suggested attention to the appropriate use of past tense.[3])

■ *Jabberwocky sentences and the basic sentence patterns*

1. The teacher reads or presents "Jabberwocky" by Lewis Carroll and asks the students to help him create a few jabberwocky sentences on the chalkboard. He follows this with an explanation of simple subject and predicate. With the students' help, he expands sentences from "skeleton," the student suggesting ways to build up the sentence:

alligator *ate*

The *alligator ate* the scientist.

The bright green *alligator* with the sorrowful eyes *ate* with relish the rotund scientist who fell asleep by the river bank.

These extended sentences may be plotted out on the chalkboard. After each extension, the modifying words may be erased, leaving again only the simple subject and predicate to be amplified in some new way, e.g.,

The tender-hearted lavender Martian *alligator ate,* as daintily as possible, the artichokes brought to him each day by Miss Pickerel, the eccentric tourist from Earth.

2. Next, have each student write a brief anecdote using only nouns and verbs. Have some of these read aloud; despite the restriction, the sentences should communicate. Point out that subjects and predicates are the necessary elements of communication in most writing and speaking.

3. When the concepts of subject and predicate are firmly established, the teacher next presents Jabberwocky sentences for analysis:

The saleb tringes tributhed on the flust.
Arthusta was emfressed by the bibblement.

First let students practice reading sentences aloud, noticing how the pattern invites certain intonations although no specific meaning is conveyed; then guide them to note the natural clues within the sentences, such as the groupings of words and the specific signal words and word endings; from these activities draw some useful conclusions about the way English sentences operate.

4. Conclude by presenting models of the four most common patterns of the English sentence:

Pattern I John eats.
Pattern II John eats onions.

[3] A complete description of how this might be carried out is presented on pp. 671-75.

Pattern III	Onions are roots.
Pattern IV	Onions are good.

After giving several examples for each pattern, ask pupils to use it in devising sentences to be given orally. When all four patterns have been sufficiently illustrated, pupils may write several sentences imitating each. The purpose here is to introduce the concept of *common patterns of the English sentence.* Unless students have had previous instruction in grammar, technical terminology identifying different kinds of complements need not be given.

A final test of their comprehension might be one in which they write Jabberwocky sentences to illustrate each pattern, for example:

Pattern I	The shruftsa blumps griggled for their reetsnup.
Pattern II	The kulshind, gargy and stooble, treeped his snipar.
Pattern III	The eertsin was a blik goobing.
Pattern IV	An eborsch is neeby ruggily.

The teacher should help students use real words for the linking verbs as well as for the articles, prepositions, and pronouns.

To supplement this activity, suitable drills from available texts or workbooks may be used with superior classes. However, sentences which include expletives, inverted word order, or understood subjects should be omitted. These tend to confuse the pupils and should be introduced at some other time or in a later grade.

■ *Explorations in other languages*

1. The pupils may read the section called "Other People's Languages" in Mario Pei's *All About Language* (2). The teacher then helps them read very simple materials, such as fables, brief parables, jokes, or paragraph anecdotes in French, Spanish, German, Portuguese, Chinese, Russian, and Latin, or as many of these as possible. The purpose is not to teach the foreign language but to help pupils explore, in a preliminary manner, each of the major languages studied in schools. For instance, the following sources in Spanish contain suitable material: *Cuentos Y Leyendas* (15)—The Three Bears, Little Red Riding Hood, Pied Piper of Hamlin; *Leamos* (16)—The Old Woman and Her Pig, The House that Jack Built, The Gingerbread Boy, and others; *Mother Goose on Rio Grande* (17)—a collection of rhymes, riddles, and games given in both languages.

Similar books exist for the other languages. Where they are not available, the teacher may borrow a set of beginning texts, or copy brief anecdotes from beginning texts, in each of these languages.

2. Teachers find that if pupils learn only a few common expressions, such as the words for *Good Morning, I thank you,* and *Good-by,* they begin to take an interest in the foreign tongue. Interesting features may be pointed out as the teacher wishes, e.g., the Spanish say "*dar* un paseo" but is it any stranger to *give* a walk than to *take* a walk? Word order, also, is different in various languages; adjectives, for instance, come after the noun in French and Spanish but before the noun in English and German. Some languages identify all nouns as masculine, feminine, or neuter. Germans must remember that *horse* is neuter, Spaniards that *sacrifice* is masculine, Frenchmen that *venison* is feminine. For *rhubarb, atom, brick* and all the other nouns, these people must remember a classification that speakers of English do not use in their system.

The teacher may present as many of these linguistic contrasts as will hold the interest of the pupils. He may even present the need for an international language, along with examples of Esperanto, Basic English, ITO, Walapuk, and Pidgin English. Several of the books recommended as text materials for this unit contain excellent discussions and may be assigned for reading. See especially Laird and Laird (1) and Pei (2).

3. The teacher may conclude this exploration of other languages in a number of interesting ways:

The pupils may be formed into committees or pairs to investigate what languages are spoken and read in the homes represented in the school; to get information on the languages taught in the high schools to which they will go; to visit the library to find what newspapers, magazines, and books in other languages are available; to read in books and encyclopedias about the languages of the world and how widely used each language is; to make a language map of the world; to invite language teachers to come to class to describe their languages, to invite people who use other forms of communication—such as Morse Code, braille, sign language—to visit the class.

Teach the class a few words that English has adopted from other languages, such as the following:

French words and expressions used in English

à la mode	de luxe	naïve
à propos	élite	née
au revoir	en route	nom de plume
bon voyage	ensemble	nouveau-riche
bourgeois	exposé	rendez-vous
chaise longue	faux pas	repartee
chic	fiancé(e)	R.S.V.P. (Répondez s'il vous plaît)
coiffure	finesse	résumé
coup d'état	gourmet	sabotage
débris	laissez faire	tête à tête

English words derived directly or indirectly from the Spanish

adobe	bolero	enchilada	mustang
avocado	buckaroo	fandango	mosquito
adios	cafeteria	flamingo	patio
alfalfa	chinchilla	hacienda	pronto
barbecue	canyon	hoosegow	rodeo
barracuda	cinch	hombre	savvy
burro	corral	loco	tango
bronco	coyote	lasso	vamoose
	calaboose	lariat	

Individual pupils may also interview students or adults who have come to the United States from other countries. What language difficulties do they recall? What sounds, words, and ways of expression were or are difficult for them?

Examine the preface in 41 languages in *English Through Pictures* (7).

Pupils may interview social studies teachers on the topic of language. How has history been influenced by the existence of so many languages?

■ *Building an interest in words*

The teacher begins by calling attention to the odd fact that most words beginning with *sn* are unpleasant words (snap, snort, sneaky, snicker, etc.) and goes from there to a consideration of thin measly words, fat sober words, and beautiful words. Laird and Laird (1) and Lambert (3) offer excellent help in developing an interest in words and may be used for assignments. Radke's two books (4, 5) and Miller (6) are equally helpful, and should be used as the basis of a series of lessons. Particularly amusing to seventh grade pupils are the books by Reid (13) and Brown (14).

■ *Films and filmstrips*

The following films or filmstrips, or others similar to them, may be used to develop an interest in words and how they operate.

1. "Build Your Vocabulary" (20), a film demonstrating methods of vocabulary building.
2. *Words: Their Origin, Use, and Spelling* (21), a series of six filmstrips in color: "Words, Then and Now," "Roots and Shoots," "Times and People Change Words," "Words and Your Work," "The Right Word in the Right Place," "Increase Your Stock of Words."
3. *Word Study Series* (22), six filmstrips in color. Designed for language arts classes, the series includes synonyms, antonyms, word origins, and word derivations.

■ *Semantics* [4]

The teacher aims at these insights:

A word may have several meanings.

Word meanings are affected by experience, time, and context.

Words are not mechanical parts like sections of an erector set; rather they are like notes of music affected by their surroundings.

A statement may have diverse meanings.

1. *Problem*—To show how the same word may have more than one meaning and depend upon its "neighbors" (context) or the occasion when it is used. Ask students to use, in as many different meanings as possible, words like these:

run, slip, rich, box, date, table, break, sheet, glasses

Play guess-the-word for a few minutes several days in a row. A student says, "I am thinking of a word of four letters, beginning with 'd'; it can be eaten, it is a way to keep track of time, and some boys ask girls for them." (date) Or, "I am thinking of a word beginning with 'c'; some people carry one when they ride horseback; farmers gather them; a chicken has one; sheep do it to a grazing ground." (crop).

2. *Problem*—To realize that word meaning, a product of experience, differs with each individual. Tell the story of the six blind men and the elephant, or the story of the fifth grade girl who read her older brother's world history book and gained the impression that the French Revolution wrote insulting letters to the American Revolution. ("The French Revolution corresponded roughly with the American Revolution.") Discuss with students how words fool us because we have varying associations with them. Show the film "Do Words Ever Fool You?"

[4] The teacher will find many useful suggestions on this topic in Chapter 1, "Language as Dynamic Process," pp. 18-72.

Or discuss how one might explain a term such as "squeeze play" or "bunt" to a Hindu visitor to the school, who is not acquainted with sports or American customs.

3. *Problem*—To become more aware of the fact that the word is not the thing. Ask students to write a short paragraph telling why they think a rocket is called a "rocket" or a puzzle a "puzzle." In the discussion following, point up the fact that no necessary connection exists between the word and what it represents. Compare with other symbolism which may seem more concrete: Could red mean "go" just as well as "stop"? What do people in other countries call "rocket" and "puzzle"?

4. *Problem*—To appreciate the fact that in the course of time, many words change their meanings. Explain to students how these words have changed.

	from	**to**
boor	farmer	rude, ill-bred person
knave	boy	wicked person
villain	serf	scoundrel
queen	wife, woman	king's wife

Ask if juvenile, teen-ager, and adolescent seem to be changing.

5. *Problem*—To see how situations change the meaning of statements. Ask the pupils to imagine varied situations in which the following statements might have different meanings:

Isn't he a sweet child?
Everyone noticed Mrs. Doolste's Easter hat.
We have come to scalp you.
You must trust me.
He will not be home.
Her oral report was quite remarkable.

6. *Problem*—To discriminate among various classifications of statements. What is the difference between these two sentences?

Dover is the capital of Delaware. (Fact)
Dover is the most interesting of all the state capitals. (Opinion)

In similar fashion, present the pupils with pairs of statements which are literal and metaphorical, general and specific, abstract and concrete, formal and informal, in terms of usage. Ask: What value can come to us from noticing these distinctions in language?

7. *Problem*—To see how sentences depend upon context for meaning. Present several sentences alone and then in context. Examples:

Sentence: *The powder had to be used carefully.* [Face powder? Dynamite? Tooth powder?]

Sentence in context: On this journey, Livingston's life depended upon the game he was able to shoot. Also, in the jungle, he had to travel as lightly as possible. *The powder had to be used carefully.* The guns, alone, were heavy enough.

Sentence: *He was blind.*

Sentence in context: Brownie's first memory was of his mother's furry body and of his five squirming, hungry, helpless brothers and sisters. He weighed about a pound. *He was blind.* He could not walk; and he could not stand. He looked more like a rat than a dog.

After a few illustrations the teacher may set students to searching in books for particularly good examples.

The lesson may be concluded by dictating several sentences capable of various interpretations. The students compose paragraphs containing the sentences and then compare versions to see how much the sentences vary in meaning from one context to another. Here are several sentences for such an exercise:

It opened once again.
"We can't even eat him now," she wailed.
They took their time about the licking.
Don't you have any shoes, he thought.
The lady patted him on the head.

■ *The distinction between human worth and language*

The teacher may place on the chalkboard these two phrases:

People who are well educated
People with little education

He then asks: Which group is more likely to respect rather than make fun of the differences in English as it is spoken in Australia, Britain, Scotland, Canada, and the United States? As it varies in our own country from New England to the South, the Midwest, Texas, and the Far West. The teacher may then read aloud from the writings of Mark Twain to present the goodness of heart of such characters as Huck Finn, Aunt Polly, and Jim, all of whom use non-conventional patterns of the English language.

CULMINATING EXPERIENCES

1. The teacher and students select an effective speaker or actor, on television or in real life, to observe. The pupils are to note, in so far as possible, the qualities which the effective speaker manifests. If a telecast can be watched during class time by teacher and pupils together, the lesson will be even more convincing. The teacher should help pupils see that some of the important attributes of a good speaker are these:

Usage that does not distract the attention of the listener
Clear enunciation and articulation
Ability to cleave to the point without too much qualification, modification, and random associations
Moderation in speed of speech—neither too slow nor too rapid
Vitality: an awareness of, and adjustment to, the complexities and puzzles of life
Sincerity, which makes the words come more easily
Poise that comes from inner security and confidence, from feeling that others accept us
A resonant voice, varied in pitch, characterized by an imparting tone
A stable personality, free from excess timidity, self-depreciation, contentiousness, egocentrism

Discuss how one may gain these and improve upon them. Would the students add any more to these? Which ones do they consider the most important?

2. Plan a program for another class, an assembly, or a public meeting; it might be called "The Miracle of Language." Let groups and individuals prepare dramati-

zations, recitations, and tableaux. Use recordings and film slides. Have an announcer who will open the program, provide spoken commentary and continuity, and close the program. Ideas for the program should evolve from the aims of the unit, p. 163. A brief list of suggestions for such a program follows:

Who Makes Words? film (23)

Documents of America, George Washington's Farewell Address, record, National Council of Teachers of English, Number EAD-4

The Triumph of Louis Braille, film (24)

A double reading: A student reads some passage twice, first in a garbled manner and with many inaccurate and misplaced words, second in a clear and lucid version.

One student argues a point with fallacious reasoning. Three other students point out the fallacies.

Contests in which students find definitions in dictionaries, find suitable substitutes for trite expressions, answer questions over important points taught during the unit.

Dramatizations of situations in which language is used for thinking, for being considerate of others, for communicating important messages or ideas.

Some of the best oral reports listed on p. 168 of this unit.

Brief talks on "What I Want to Remember from this Unit."

EVALUATION

The most important results of this unit lie in the realm of attitudes and choices of behavior; these do not lend themselves easily or fully to paper and pencil tests. The development of an interest in studying a foreign language, increased reading skill in relating words and statements to their contexts, wiser judgment of human worth regardless of the use of language, increased effectiveness in oral communication—these are some of the important outcomes which may operate in situations beyond the teacher's province. However, although the complete scope of evaluation is not possible, the teacher should gather as much evidence as is available. The following suggestions are offered with the restrictions of evaluation fully acknowledged.

■ *List of learnings and a paragraph of recommendation*

The teacher may ask the pupils to list the most important new learnings they have gained from this unit. After making the list, the students are to write a paragraph (or, if they are gifted pupils, several paragraphs) recommending improvements and changes in the unit before it is taught again to the next class. The teacher then assesses the extent to which the important concepts of the unit have been grasped by the pupils.

■ *Check list of attitudes*

The teacher may ask pupils to check anonymously lists such as the following, perhaps by drawing stick figures in the appropriate columns. Student committees may collect the lists, tally the answers, and present the findings to the class and the teacher for a discussion on the strengths of the unit and ways to improve it.

My point of view

The view	Where I stand		
	Very true of me	*Sometimes true of me*	*Sorry, not true of me*
1. As a result of this unit, I am less likely to dislike a person who speaks with an accent different from mine.			
2. As a result of this unit, I have some definite plans for ways I can improve my speaking in everyday communication. For example:____________			
3. As a result of this unit, I am now paying more attention to the "neighbors" of words in the reading I do outside of the English class.			
4. As a result of this unit, I am paying more attention to the "neighbors" of sentences in the reading I do outside the English class.			

[The teacher tries to assess the ten most important attitudes or concepts he hoped to establish during the unit.]

■ *Completion test*

Items such as the following will give approximate samples of the extent to which some of the aims of this unit have been accomplished.

What I have learned

1. I can give examples of the differences between statements of opinion and statements of fact:
   Opinion________________________
   Fact________________________
2. Telling lies under oath is called____________________.
3. Three effective ways that good talkers hold their listeners' attention are
   a.
   b.
   c.
4. The *context* of a word or a statement is____________________.
5. Three ways I can improve my use of written language are
   a.
   b.
   c.
6. One way English and Spanish are unlike is____________________.
7. In one paragraph, explain why telling lies under oath (see question 2, above) is considered such a serious crime by the courts.

■ *Conventional use of past tense*

The real test of effectiveness in this skill may be determined by observing the pupils' use of past tense in their everyday speech and in their writing for other classes as well as for English. However, some testing may be used to determine whether or not fewer errors appear than occurred previous to instruction. Oral tests, in which the pupils listen to the teacher read a series of sentences, some conventional and some non-conventional, will furnish better insight into this problem than do the more typical paper and pencil tests. As the teacher reads each sentence, the pupils mark plus (for conventional) or zero (for non-conventional) after the number corresponding to the sentence the teacher is reading aloud. See pp. 575-76 for a full description of this method.

Materials and resources for pupils

For the purpose of this unit, the teacher should have available in the classroom ten copies of each of the following books specifically planned and written for young people:

1. Charlton and Helen Laird, *The Tree of Language.* Cleveland, World, 1957.
2. Mario Pei, *All About Language.* Phila., Lippincott, 1954.
3. Eloise Lambert, *Our Language.* N.Y., Lothrop, Lee & Shepard, 1955.
4. Frieda Radke, *Living Words.* N.Y., Odyssey, 1940.
5. ———, *Word Resources.* N.Y., Odyssey, 1955.
6. Ward S. Miller, *Word Wealth Junior.* N.Y., Holt, 1950.
7. I. A. Richards and Christine Gibson, *Spanish Through Pictures,* N.Y., Washington Square Press, 1950; *French Through Pictures,* Washington Square Press, 1960; and *English Through Pictures,* N.Y., Pocket Books, 1952.
8. Margaret S. Ernst, *Words.* N.Y., Knopf, 1950.

For slow classes or for classes with some members who read poorly, copies of the following books should be available:

9. Julie Forsyth Batchelor, *Communication: From Cave Writing to Television.* N.Y., Harcourt, Brace, 1953.
10. Sam and Beryl Epstein, *The First Book of Words.* N.Y., Watts, 1954.
11. Elizabeth Lemay Hayes, *The Tongues of Man.* Chicago, Thomas S. Rockwell, 1931.

SUPPLEMENTARY BOOKS

12. E. C. Cline, *Your Language.* N.Y., D. Appleton Co., 1930. An older text, but helpful in many ways.
13. Alastair Reid, *Ounce, Dice, Trice.* Boston, Little, Brown, 1959.
14. Marcia Brown, *Peter Piper's Alphabet.* N.Y., Scribner's, 1959.
15. Elijah C. Hills and Juan Cano, *Cuentos Y Leyendas.* Boston, Heath, 1922.
16. Hymen Alpern and José Los Martel, *Leamos.* N.Y., Oxford Book, 1941.
17. Frances Alexander, et al., *Mother Goose on Rio Grande.* Dallas, Banks-Upshaw, 1944.

RECORDINGS, FILMS, AND FILMSTRIPS

(For complete addresses of suppliers of films and recordings, see the bibliography, pp. 723-27.)

18. Chaucer, selections from the Prologue, *Canterbury Tales.* Numerous recordings are available in Middle English, e.g., The "America Listens to Literature" rec-

ords, final volume, on *England in Literature* (Chicago, Scott, Foresman, 1959); or No. RS80–1 of the National Council of Teachers of English.

19. "The English Language: Story of Its Development," film. Coronet Films.
20. "Build Your Vocabulary," film. Coronet Films.
21. *Words: Their Origin, Use, and Spelling,* filmstrip series. Long Filmslide Service.
22. *Word Study Series,* filmstrip series. Young America Films.
23. *Who Makes Words?* film. Coronet Films.
24. *The Triumph of Louis Braille,* film. Young America Teaching Films.

Materials and resources for teachers

Dwight L. Bolinger, "The Life and Death of Words." In Harrison Hayford and Howard Vincent, eds., *Reader and Writer.* Boston, Houghton Mifflin, 1954, pp. 435-445.

Charles C. Fries, *The Structure of English.* N.Y., Harcourt, Brace, 1952.

Robert A. Hall, Jr., *Leave Your Language Alone.* Ithaca, N.Y., Linguistica, 1950.

Charlton Laird, *The Miracle of Language.* N.Y., World, 1953. Also in a paperbound edition: N.Y., Fawcett, 1957.

Irving J. Lee, *Language Habits in Human Affairs.* N.Y., Harper, 1949.

Robert Pooley, *Teaching English Usage.* N.Y., D. Appleton-Century, 1946.

James Sledd, *A Short Introduction to English Grammar.* Chicago, Scott, Foresman, 1959.

Dora V. Smith, *Communication, The Miracle of Shared Living.* N.Y., Macmillan, 1955.

Louis Zahner, "The Teaching of Language." *English Journal,* Vol. 44, No. 7 (November 1955), pp. 443-445, 458.

———, "What Kinds of Language Teaching," in Edward J. Gordon and Edward S. Noyes, eds., *Essays on the Teaching of English.* N.Y., Appleton-Century-Crofts, 1960.

PART TWO

Understanding

4. Listening with Discrimination
5. Reading with Comprehension

UNIT: Science Fiction, Radar of Man's Curiosity

Chapter Four

Listening with Discrimination

The spoken word belongs half to him who speaks, and half to him who hears.

—FRENCH PROVERB

PERSPECTIVE

Listening is without question the communication skill used most often in daily living; we converse, we hear newscasts, we transact business, we ask for directions, we seek advice, we try to understand another's point of view. No doubt each one recognizes among his acquaintances both good and poor listeners—those upon whom he can count for an intelligent response and those so eager to express their own views they give no evidence of having heard what has just been said. No doubt, too, each one knows some persons whose rambling and lengthy remarks merit only cursory attention and others whose incisive comments deserve his best efforts to comprehend. In all face-to-face discourse—social, business, professional—the ability to listen with appropriate response and approximate accuracy is a valuable asset.

Recognition of the part listening has played in the development of each human being and in the transmission of culture before the written word existed points up its social and historical significance. Realization of its present role both in communication and in the mass dissemination of ideas and values makes the disciplines of critical listening important for each individual. The extent of its use in the study of all academic subjects indicates that the necessary skills and behavioral attitudes should receive attention in all classrooms where listening is used as a means to learning. The self-discipline nurtured by good listening habits can transfer to school-wide activities, as well as to all classrooms, if the faculty mobilizes its efforts for this purpose.

Listening in assemblies One senior high school which had long followed the practice of having each teacher sit with his class during assemblies to insure a quiet audience decided to eliminate such supervision. The immediate results were unsatisfactory. However, instead of reverting to the former regime of teacher-imposed discipline, the assembly committee—students and faculty adviser—decided upon a school-wide educational campaign. Realizing that both performers and audience have a responsibility, the committee planned a double-barreled attack.

First, time was spent on insuring that speakers and entertainers could be easily heard. For student participants, this meant more auditorium practice than had previously been thought necessary; for guests, it meant an explanation of the acoustical eccentricities they must contend with as well as information on the status of the audience in the process of acquiring self-discipline. Second, students were prepared for every assembly. In the homeroom preceding, they learned what to expect and discussed how to evaluate what they were to see and hear; in the homeroom following, a short evaluation was made. At times discussion was led by students; at other times, by the teacher.

Although order in assemblies improved, the discussions revealed that too many students were inclined to place full responsibility for audience control on the speaker, and seemed to equate silence, however trance-like, with listening. Consideration of this problem in student and faculty committees resulted in the decision to continue to devote a portion of the homeroom period to the improvement of listening skills, particularly as they pertained to assemblies.

To give unity to the project, the homeroom committee, composed of students and teachers, made tentative plans to cover each week—five periods of thirty minutes. After each homeroom discussion, the student-secretary gave a report to the committee, which correlated the conclusions and returned a synthesis to homeroom teachers before the next meeting. Art students used these ideas for a series of posters entitled "Are You Listening?"

After homeroom sessions had highlighted specific purposes which students recognized in their own listening, the circumstances under which such activity took place, hindrances and helps which they found, the committee formulated the following list of basic habits for good listening. Posters were made for classrooms, so that both teachers and students might have graphic reminders.

General habits of the good listener

In every listening situation
- he knows why he is listening.
- he sits where he can avoid distractions.
- he looks at the speaker.
- he concentrates, adapting to the speaker's rate.
- he is willing to share responsibility with the speaker.

In regard to the communication he tries
- to determine the speaker's purpose.
- to remember important points.
- to note reasons for illustrations and examples.
- to understand fully before he judges.

In his evaluation he tries
- to relate the speaker's points to his own experience and interests.
- to determine why he agrees or disagrees.

After this orientation, instruction emphasized the skills necessary for effective audience participation in the particular type of assembly students were to attend; the evaluation attempted to analyze the presentation and to explore reasons for the varied conclusions formed. The results demonstrated so clearly the value of teaching listening on a school-wide basis that a second project was initiated.

Listening to assignments Oral assignments formed the basis for the second attack, with instruction to be given in the English classes. Again students were asked to help with the planning. An exploratory committee, made up of representatives—one student and one teacher—of each academic subject, attempted to discover the common elements, if any, in effective assignments, regardless of subject matter.

Two sources of information were used by the committee; again both speaker and listener were considered. Students in certain classes on different grade levels and in different subject areas were asked to list helpful practices used in giving assignments, as well as those they thought needed improvement.[1] All teachers of academic subjects were asked for copies of a series of assignments which had proved effective. The writers were to remain anonymous and were asked not to mention names.

This material was divided among members of the committee. Through sifting, eliminating, and synthesizing the information given in these reports, the committee selected the following characteristics of assignments as those considered desirable by both teachers and students in all subject fields.

An effective assignment should

be concerned with only one subject, although almost always amplified by subordinate ideas.

have one controlling purpose, although subordinate purposes often contribute to the main.

give clues as to practical ways of carrying it out.

whenever possible, suggest alternate ways for its satisfactory fulfillment.

A series of assignments should offer variety in the kinds of knowledge and the types of skills demanded.

After the above standards had been accepted by teachers of academic subjects, who were asked to demonstrate the principles in their own assignments, instruction began in the English classes, continuing for a portion of the class hour for two weeks. The following points, common to purposeful listening in many kinds of communication, were stressed.

Accurate listening is based on the desire to understand.

Understanding the purpose of the communication is essential.

Accurate listening requires the ability to structure the main idea.

Such structuring includes distinguishing between principal and subordinate points; recognizing the relationship of parts and that of each part to the whole; and realizing the purpose of details and illustrations.

[1] Much of the information gained was not pertinent to the question being considered. However, a summary of the suggestions served as a basis for discussion at a faculty meeting.

The material used was selected from assignments provided by teachers at the grade level represented by the particular English class receiving instruction. Periodic evaluations were made by all classroom teachers; thus, the responsibility of the speaker for clarity and of the listener for comprehension continued to receive school-wide emphasis. The keeping of assignment notebooks by each student was adopted as a school policy.

These two experiences, which had convinced most students that skill in listening could be increased, laid the ground for instruction in all classes. Courtesy thus became not solely a mark of good citizenship, but also a means of supporting listening as a necessary instrument of learning. Disturbing pranks could no longer be considered an individual's privilege, from which he alone might suffer, but became a possible hindrance to the academic achievement of all class members. The change of emphasis had a salutary effect. Without question, the school where every teacher consistently helps students perfect their skills as responsive listeners does much to insure a climate conducive to learning.

Aspects of listening instruction

These experiences in teaching listening illustrate three aspects of sound instruction applicable to all areas of English: Teachers attempt to achieve both their own purposes and those of their students; to utilize recognized principles of learning; to employ logical steps in procedure.

Responsive and critical listening The experiences described illustrate two kinds of listening, roughly approximating those used in daily life—responsive and critical. The first requires only intelligent reaction; when our sole aim is to be entertained or stimulated, when we listen to take part in a conversation, we are concerned with the immediate; accuracy, while desirable, is not always crucial. The second demands critical appraisal; when we listen to learn, we intend to use the knowledge for future purposes; full understanding is imperative. Clearly, the two kinds of listening are not distinct, for all perception requires evaluation and results in some kind of judgment, just as correct appraisal depends upon intelligent response. In either kind of listening, the purposes of sender and receiver may differ; for instance, although those who plan an assembly may have an "educational" purpose in mind, the majority of the audience expect to be entertained. The planners take this expectation into account and strive to accomplish both goals. Understanding assignments requires critical listening. Here, too, purposes may differ; the teacher tries to gain his objectives through activities which help students achieve their own aims. Young people need to be aware that the purpose of speaker and listener may not be identical; they need to recognize that responsiveness, often the sole aim in listening, is also basic to acquiring the understandings necessary for critical appraisal.

Bases for effective instruction The two experiences also exemplify principles that must characterize instruction in listening if it is to be effective: *The material is geared to the student's ability; motivation for responsive and critical listening occurs when the learner thinks the communication important.* The first requirement was taken care of by the assembly committee and by individual teachers; each planned with particular students in mind. The second requirement was met by appealing in each instance to genuine desires on the part of the majority. In the assemblies, the appeals were to the student's wish for enjoyment and stimulation and to his determination to keep the newly granted privilege of being responsible for himself as a member of an audience. In the second instance, the realization that understanding an assignment as it is given not only saves his time but is basic to his success in school provided the student with strong motivation. Both principles apply in all learning situations.

Phases of instruction Each of the two experiences, moreover, illustrates the three essential phases of listening instruction: preparation, provision for the particular experience, and the follow-up. In *preparation* the student is helped to understand the purpose and nature of what is to come, as well as some of the techniques of intelligent listening. Why has the committee asked that applause be withheld until the close of the Christmas assembly? That clapping be restrained after each acceptance in a series of awards? How can an audience respond intelligently to the kind of presentation planned? During the *listening experience,* the student uses the information gained to concentrate on salient points emphasized in the preparation. Thus, before asking students to write down an assignment, the teacher discusses it, explaining unfamiliar terminology, reviewing necessary learnings, suggesting methods of procedure; then the more concise statement to be written can be more readily comprehended. The *follow-up* is an evaluation of three elements—speaker, listener, and speech. In the case of assemblies, it may result in a letter of appreciation to the planners or in suggestions for future programs. With assignments, allowing time for immediate questions permits exploring the reasons why further clarification has been necessary; as students learn to listen, the need for additional time gradually disappears. Whatever the subject matter, the preparation and the follow-up are as important as the listening experience itself.

In effective instruction, the listener has a purpose; he is able to comprehend the material; he knows what to listen for; he discovers the reasons for his success or failure. If each learning experience meets these requirements, the student can develop his abilities for responsive and critical listening.

The listening process

For the purpose of isolating items that may need instruction, the listening process is divided into four phases, no one discrete in itself: comprehending the literal meaning; interpreting the literal as communication; evaluating the communication; integrating the communication with experience. The competent listener does not think of these aspects as consecutive steps since they take place, in part, concurrently and one influences others. Each succeeding phase does, however, demand more from the listener.

Comprehending literal meaning Competence in listening requires the ability to direct attention first to literal meaning. What exactly do the words say? What is the fundamental meaning which anyone who understands the language will grasp? Comprehending the literal presents three problems:

Understanding the precise meaning of each assertion
Following the sequence of ideas
Sensing relationships: determining the central idea; distinguishing between the main and supporting ideas; perceiving the relation of each part to the others and to the whole; recognizing the scheme of organization

Interpreting the communication Understanding language as a dynamic process makes us aware that almost any communication is subject to various interpretations. The same words may assume widely divergent meanings for different persons. Aware that everyone's viewpoint is colored by his particular experience, we try for objectivity as we attempt to identify the speaker's field of perception. What does his use of language seem to indicate about him? What is his real purpose? In interpreting we try to

- Discern the connotative force of words.
  - Distinguish emotionally-toned from reportorial words.
  - Determine the level of abstraction.
- Recognize type of statement.
  - Differentiate between factual and judgmental statements.
  - Perceive the degree of bias in judgments.
  - Sense the relative importance of the general vs. the concrete.
  - Notice extension of meaning through the use of figurative language.
- Arrive at total meaning.
  - Recognize underlying assumptions.
  - Realize implied meanings.
  - Make generalizations warranted by information and arguments.
  - Identify the speaker's purpose as revealed by his attitude toward his subject and his audience.[2]

Evaluating the communication An honest evaluation demands an inquiring attitude concerning the worth of the communication, an attempt to discover the reality behind the language. Agreement or disagreement is not enough. Aware of his own bias, the listener uses his powers of critical analysis to make a rational appraisal. Recognition of the fact that often this can be only tentative, since he is not in a position to know all the facts, is an important aspect in learning to think objectively. So, too, is awareness of the need

[2] Pp. 29-44 give suggestions for isolating these characteristics of language and communication.

for checking, to the limits of available resources, the reliability and possible bias of the speaker.[3]

Integrating with experience Effective integration with experience is the ultimate purpose for which we comprehend, interpret, and evaluate communication. In taking the first three steps, the competent listener has correlated and checked the ideas presented with what he already knows. To complete the listening process, he makes use of this knowledge in his daily life. This does not mean that each experience must have a "utilitarian" purpose. Often understanding is its own reward; the stimulation of a challenging idea or the flash of deepening insight, its own satisfaction.

The listening process is manifestly complex. The necessity for assimilating the significance of many stimuli simultaneously, the need for concentrating to avoid a loss in meaning that may well be irretrievable, combine to make the mastery of this instrument of intake worthy of anyone's mettle.

Implications of research

Compared to the amount done in other areas of English, research on the subject of listening is meager. Of course, teachers have long known that listening skills reinforce oral skills, that the two are complementary essentials of both speech and interpretation; they have for some time realized that accustoming the ear to the appropriate form is an effective way of teaching English usage. Besides underscoring the potential of the aural aspects of such situations, the results of recent research, inconclusive though they may be, do have further implications for the teaching of English.

Findings	**Implications**
1. Listening can be taught, and gains in particular skills can be measured.[4]	1. Isolation of various skills for instructional purposes should result in more effective listening.
2. Studies exploring the rate differential between thinking and speaking conclude that	
a. The mind has the ability to receive spoken language faster than a speaker can or does produce it.[5]	a. Language spoken faster than normally produced (100-125 wpm) should make concentration easier and thus increase comprehension.[6]

[3] See pp. 79 and 97-98.

[4] Ralph Nichols and Robert Keller, "The Measurement of Communication Skills," *Junior College Journal,* Vol. 24, No. 3 (November 1953); Ursula Hogan, "An Experiment in Improving the Listening Skills of Fifth and Sixth Grade Pupils," unpublished seminar study, University of California (Berkeley), 1953.

[5] Ralph Nichols, "Ten Components of Effective Listening," *Education,* Vol. 75, No. 5 (January 1955).

[6] Observation of different student teachers, teaching the same class at different rates (the pace each normally sets for himself), supports this conclusion. Wiser use of time seems

b. With relatively simple recorded material, maximal listening efficiency is secured at 282 wpm.[7]
c. With fairly difficult material, comprehension is significantly greater at 175 wpm than at 200.[7]
3. There is a positive, but relatively low, correlation between skill in reading and skill in listening.[8]
4. Neither auditory nor visual presentation can claim to be more effective than the other in the matters of recall and of attitude shift; however, both together are superior to either alone.[9]

b. The rate of listening to speech might be improved through training.
c. The rate of speaking must be adjusted to the difficulty of the material.
3. One skill can be used to reinforce the other, but students will need help in effecting the transfer.
4. Various avenues to learning must be offered; listening experiences should be correlated with reading and writing.

Both the experience of teachers in the field and the findings of research indicate that the techniques of effective listening can be taught. Indiscriminate listening leaves the individual vulnerable not only to misinformation but to subtle attacks upon his attitudes and values. Thus it seems imperative that students become more responsive and more critical listeners.

THE TEACHING PROBLEM

Organizing Instruction

Instruction in listening[10] will be considered in four parts: occasions for classroom listening; integration of experiences; understandings for the student; skills for the student.

Occasions for classroom listening In giving instruction in listening, teachers make use of the situations occurring naturally in almost any classroom. First, the student is daily expected to listen to directions, explanations, facts, ideas, opinions, given by the teacher or other class members. Each oc-

the crux of the matter: awareness of the need for projecting ideas and noting whether or not they hit their mark.

[7] Grant Fairbanks, Newman Guttman, Murray S. Miron, "Effects of Time Compression Upon the Comprehension of Connected Speech," *Journal of Speech and Hearing Disorders,* Vol. 22, No. 1 (March 1957).

[8] H. Goldstein, "Reading and Listening Comprehension at Various Controlled Rates," *Contributions to Education Series,* No. 821 (N.Y., Teachers College, Columbia University, 1940); Robert Larsen and D. D. Feder, "Common and Differential Factors in Reading and Hearing Comprehension," *Journal of Educational Psychology,* Vol. 31, No. 4 (April 1940); Maurice Lewis, "The Effect of Training in Listening Upon Reading," *Journal of Communication,* Vol. 3, No. 2 (November 1953).

[9] Charles P. Dickey, "A Survey of Literature on Listening," unpublished graduate thesis, University of California (Berkeley), 1955, pp. 30 ff.

[10] The part listening plays in teaching literature is discussed in Chapters 5 and 6. Here we are concerned with simple narration, exposition, and argument.

casion offers opportunities to emphasize the need for listening skill. Second, realizing the value of varying the approaches to learning, teachers often utilize aural activities to reinforce concepts and skills being developed in reading, writing, and speaking. Since listening is a tool subject with no necessary content of its own, all areas of English instruction may be enriched with experience which can increase the student's ability to listen purposefully. Finally, listening may substitute for reading. Often used in heterogeneous groups to provide a common background, aural experiences are especially important in classes of pupils of strictly limited ability. Here, information needed by all must be given at times by the teacher, often aided by visual stimuli—chalk board, motion pictures, filmstrips, and graphic displays. The teacher of slow classes, too, must rely largely on oral presentations or on recorded stories and poems to furnish firsthand experiences with those literary works otherwise denied to all but the competent readers. Important in all classes, the teaching of listening is essential for those pupils who will probably never become sufficiently proficient in the art of reading to seek the written word as a means of securing information, enjoyment, and stimulation.

Integration of experiences The integrated program recommended throughout this text assumes that the usual classroom activities offer the most effective springboard for helping students acquire listening skills. Thus teaching can be continual and related to problems as they arise. The discussion of oral language emphasizes the part listening, as a complement to speaking, plays in helping build the necessary language skills; it recommends attention to one aspect at a time, with frequent opportunities for the pupil to practice combining the skills he is trying to develop; it suggests ways of helping students transfer those applicable to their writing. In like manner, as any single factor of the communicative process becomes the focus of intensive instruction, students can learn the contrasts and similarities in the skills required by the various media of communication. Many of the learning experiences suggested elsewhere in the text use the oral approach and thus provide opportunities for teaching the techniques of listening; others, with slight adaptation, can be made to serve the same end. The teacher saves time and does a more effective job when the work is so integrated that the student sees the relationship which the listening skills bear to those of reading and writing as well as to those of speaking.

Understandings for the student The student should quickly develop two understandings basic to improving responsive and critical listening. *Appreciation of the complexity of the process* will disabuse him of the belief that listening demands no effort; recognition of the many elements combining to make communication effective alerts him to the concentration needed for immediate synthesis. *Recognizing that many listening skills have their counterparts in speaking, reading, and writing,* shows him the possibility of integrating those common to all. Both understandings, based on a knowledge of language with its roots deep in human behavior, undergird the ability to listen purposefully.

Skills for the student Skills in listening accrue gradually; planned instruction necessarily focuses first on single aspects of the process. Students must then effect a synthesis of these learnings and, if responsive and critical listening is to become habitual, must be helped to make use of these skills in everyday situations. In the classroom the pupil is prepared for each experience; in contrast, he encounters most life situations not knowing what to expect. Whether in the informalities of conversation or in the speaker-audience context, the listener usually has little foreknowledge of what he is to hear. The Suggested Learning Experiences which follow isolate different phases of the listening process for instruction; provide practice in synthesis; suggest ways of applying the skills in life situations; show how the listening experiences may be fused with other aspects of the English program.

Suggested Learning Experiences

In planning instruction, the teacher at times introduces a listening activity in its own right, in order to teach the necessary skills; at other times, listening may be but one aspect of a more extended experience involving practice in reading, writing, and speaking. In either case, as he adapts any of the following suggestions for a particular class, he is careful to insure readiness on the part of his students and to fortify the learnings with appropriate follow-up.

To appreciate the complexity of listening

■ *Realize the many elements that make oral communication effective*

The Columbia "I Can Hear It Now" series of recordings—"Spoken history covering the years 1933-1945 . . . an era for the ear, the first and perhaps the last"—furnishes a mine of material. Almost any band can be used, depending upon the teacher's purpose at a particular time; bands 6 and 7, volume 1, starting with the Willkie-Roosevelt campaign for the presidency and ending with the D-Day invasion, have many uses. The total playing time is nine minutes; portions of each band may be replayed as many times as necessary to isolate the particular element being considered.

1. After an appropriate introduction giving the information necessary to set the scene, play the recording. Write on the board the names of the speakers as they speak. In the discussion following, let students bring out as many facts, in sequence, as they can recall, checking each other for accuracy; e.g., Does Murrow say that Willkie received more popular votes than any other candidate for the presidency?

Discuss the feelings evoked by the different speakers. Ask students who have definite feelings to try to determine how they were aroused, telling them they will have an opportunity, during a replaying, to check the accuracy of their analysis.

Consider the total effect of the communications as selected and arranged by the editors. The majority of listeners usually agree that the feeling is one of excitement. Determine what causes it. Suggestions made by students may mention only the obvious: sound effects, change of pace, climactic nature of the content. Then replay the recording, asking a few individuals to check points which aroused controversy. Divide the rest into groups, each to watch one aspect the class has mentioned as contributing to the feeling, to jot down specific examples.

Follow with discussion. In considering the climactic nature of the content, the teacher may wish to emphasize selection of material as a problem affecting both speakers and writers. Students are impressed by the fact that the editors, after listening to over five hundred hours of old broadcasts, selected one hundred hours to be retaped. From this they chose the forty-five minutes of "I Can Hear It Now." The following has served as a skeletal guide for such a discussion.

What principle of selection in the chronically arranged events strengthens the unity?

How does each event contribute to the climax of the total sequence?

What does the climax gain by Eisenhower's quiet manner in announcing the invasion?

2. In the next replaying, students might turn their attention to the contribution which choice of words, dramatization of events, and repetition of phrases make to the total effect. The teacher asks appropriate questions to point out the means the narrator uses to bring the listener "into" the event.

Use of words that call up visual and auditory images, evoke a mood:

Willkie's "hulking Midwestern frame, his shock of rumpled hair, his big gesturing hands . . ." (Why are Roosevelt, Churchill, and Eisenhower not described?)

Willkie's "hoarse but vibrant voice." (Why *but*, not *and?*)

"The shimmering wail of a hundred sirens bouncing off the echo chambers which are a bombed city's dead buildings and deserted docks." (Murrow says the sound can never be imitated. How well do his words call up both the sound and the effect?)

"When a howitzer shell explodes, the jungle screams back." (How does the jungle reference heighten the effect?)

Description of specific events, with repetition of the phrases *Where were you?* and *If you were* . . . (What different purpose does each series of phrases serve?)

3. Other replayings can be used to highlight further elements of this particular communication, e.g.,

Effect of length of sentences and phrases on both pace and mood.

Effect of balanced sentences and phrases.

Examples of sarcasm, determination, exuberance, etc.

Contrast in accents—Willkie's, Midwestern; Roosevelt's, Eastern; Churchill's, English; Murrow's, shall we say cultivated American?

Effectiveness of variety—pause, force, inflection, change of rate—to secure emphasis.

It is not implied that all these things should be done with all classes or with any class all at one time. The recording has served as the basis for a listening experience as many as six times over a period of three days without exhausting its possibilities. Some classes have asked to have other segments of the recording played several times, without intervening comment, to see how many different aspects of the communication they can discover for themselves. Even without further work, three periods such as are described above will convince most students of the need for listening alertly if they wish to evaluate accurately any complex communication.

■ *Realize that purposeful listening demands the ability to assimilate the meaning from various stimuli simultaneously*

1. Either of the films "Fiddle-De-Dee" or "Begone Dull Care" can be used to emphasize the ways looking and listening complement each other in determining meaning. Each attempts to coordinate music with abstract color forms in motion. Show first without sound; discuss the various interpretations of the visual elements. Then show the film with sound. The integration of music, form, color, and rhythm communicates meaning and emotion. Have original interpretations been changed? Reinforced? Why? Is there more general agreement concerning meaning? Why? Is the emotional effect weakened or strengthened? Why?

2. To show that visualization is necessary to alert listening, the teacher may use any appropriate band of "I Can Hear It Now" with which students are unfamiliar. After the necessary explanation, play the recording; answer any questions that may arise. Then divide the class into groups, each one to concentrate, as the record is played again, on a different speaker and the lines that introduce him.

Ask students to describe what they saw as they listened. Take the contributions of each group separately, comparing the images of one member with those of another. Discuss possible reasons why they differ in vividness (habitual visualization?) and in kind (individuality of experience). If all members of any one group retain no images, or only irrelevant ones, help them determine the reasons. Lack of concentration? Content too foreign to interests? Too few concrete suggestions from the language?

3. To stress the need for visualization in reading, ask students to listen to a selection written to be printed, one characterized by the use of specific examples expressed in vivid language, such as "This Land and Flag," an editorial from the New York *Times,* June 14, 1940.[11] Compare the images which the same words evoke in different persons. References to California will probably be more meaningful to children in the West; historical allusions, to those interested in history, etc. How do images aroused by the same example differ? Why?

4. Often a student who retains particularly vivid images from one example misses what immediately follows. Why? When does such an omission matter? If ten examples are given, is it necessary to remember all? Would such omissions be as likely to occur if he were reading the editorial silently? Why? Such a discussion can underline these facts:

Visualization, the calling up of bits of mosaic lodged in the memory, is governed by individual experience.

The more closely related the experience of two listeners, the more similar the images evoked in them by the language.

The need for relating the new to that already known is essentially the same in listening and in reading.

In reading, we can stop to savor and reflect; in listening, we must keep up with the speaker lest we miss a point necessary to the total meaning.

■ *Develop awareness of the significance of tone in communication*

Listening experiences in which voice quality and intonation are of particular importance offer opportunities to introduce students to the nuances of language tone. They can easily recognize the part *vocal* tone plays in meaning; this understanding

[11] Reprinted in William R. Wood, et al., *Fact and Opinion* (Boston, Heath, 1945), p. 10.

can be used as a basis for helping them form the concept that language itself, whether used in speaking or in writing, has its own distinctive tone.

Vocal Tone

1. Start simply; in a brief discussion, feature the difference between statements and questions. What in vocal tone tells the listener which is which? Is the difference always evident in the structure of the sentence? Discuss the meaning of "We'll see you Sunday" and "We'll see you Sunday?" What causes the difference? Discuss the significance of tone in training animals, and in a baby's accurate interpretation of mood and intonation.

2. Experiments with a single sentence will help students discover how logical meaning changes as different words are stressed. An example—"I think he is a good workman."

I (but others may not)
think (but I'm not sure)
he (but I don't know about his partner)
is (he is proficient right now)
good (but not outstanding)
workman (I know nothing about him as a person)

As an assignment ask students to compose a sentence and be prepared to read it aloud, conveying several different meanings through emphasis on different words. In the follow-up, let them work in groups, interpreting meaning as conveyed by vocal tones.

3. Help students experiment with a single sentence to discover how emotional overtones are conveyed by the voice; use an example like the following:

Mary discovers that Bob has asked Sally to the school dance. Pretend you are Mary; imagine several total contexts in which the remark "Bob has asked Sally to the dance" might be made. Repeat the sentence, trying to show several different attitudes toward Bob, Sally, the event, or yourself.

Approval tinged with relief—I thought I'd never get him to ask her.

Gloating, triumph—I knew I could swing it.

Joy, excitement—Sally and I with two big wheels!

Disapproval tinged with scornful amusement—Bob will have a time for himself with stumbling Sal.

Anger—That square! How can Bob fall for her flattery?

Regret, disappointment—If I'd kept my mouth shut, he'd have asked me.

As an assignment ask each student to compose a sentence appropriate for several contexts, and prepare to say it in each, conveying a different attitude each time. The discussion growing out of such assignments can lead students to see that vocal tone is an important aspect of oral communication.

Language Tone

4. Explore language tone in commercials. Ask students to listen for commercials with an obvious language tone; the following, similar to some now on television, will serve as examples.

What do we want for those we love best? Don't we all want the good things of life? . . . Take home a case of Wonder Brew.

Because she walks in beauty, because she is the essence of spring . . . Give her Dainty Razor.

No other ________ contains XYZ.

Chemists have worked for years trying to bring you ________.

Ask students to find two examples of tone in commercials—one to which they respond favorably, the other, unfavorably. They are to analyze each and to be ready to justify their choices.

5. Consider television skits satirizing or burlesquing ideas other television shows have presented seriously. Illustrate the assignment by playing "Green Christmas," Stan Freberg's burlesque on the commercialization of Christmas by advertisers.

6. Contrast different attitudes toward the same subject, to help students appreciate the importance of tone in literary works. Comparison of Richard Armour's light verses with the news items which inspired them makes a good beginning. Read the news item and determine its tone; then read the verses, noting how the tone changes. *Light Armour* contains examples suitable for classroom presentation.

■ *Realize how a communication passed orally from one person to another may change en route*

1. Give students an opportunity to see what is likely to happen when messages are relayed. Write out a fairly difficult message and keep the copy for reference. Divide the class by rows into two or three teams; let one student act as the captain of each. Take the captains into the hall and let them listen to the message once. Each captain whispers the message to a member of his team, who relays it to the next; this continues until all have heard it; the last member reports the message to the class. Compare the final versions with each other and then with the original. Which team has the most accurate reporters and listeners?

2. Use *Spreading the News,* by Lady Gregory. This short play shows how a communication can be garbled as it is relayed from one person to another. Trace the change in the original communication; notice how the words move further and further away from the reality they are supposed to represent. Reasons? Improper listening habits? Deliberate exaggeration in order to tell a more "interesting" story? Malice? (If the Irish dialect makes this play too difficult for students in the English class, ask the drama teacher to make a tape recording, or make a recording using volunteers.)

3. The filmstrip "Rumor Clinic" has been used with the above play to emphasize the part preconceived ideas may play in our interpretations of what we see and hear; the film "Whispers," to show how false rumors may be deliberately planned and used.

To recognize interrelation of skills

■ *Understand the three instruments of intake—listening, listening and looking, and reading*

Students are oriented to an aural-visual world. Listening cannot be divorced from the visual; nor can reading. If visual images are not given us, as they are in television and in motion pictures, we supply our own. What are the advantages and limitations of each method? To stimulate student interest, one teacher uses any one of three approaches, or a combination, depending upon the make-up of the class.

1. The *first approach* considers difficulties met and solutions tried in broadcasting via different mediums. This approach was first tried in a class where students had recently seen one of the early silent movies. In working with other

classes lacking such experience, the teacher found the opposite approach, starting with television, equally effective. Concentrating on each medium, students were able to identify its limitations and to suggest ways in which they might be overcome. Such an introduction can bring out the following points:

> Makers of silent motion pictures tried to compensate for the lack of dialogue by exaggerating facial expression and action; what could not be told by pictures was flashed on the screen in print; subtlety, except for a few pantomimic artists, was impossible.
>
> When radio became a means of transmitting language, the situation was reversed; even competent authors writing for the new medium were unsuccessful at first; writing for the ear, they were forced to place primary emphasis on language that would help the listener visualize.
>
> Synchronization of picture and speech, taken for granted today, is the result of a series of experiments by those who recognize the importance of both the aural and visual elements in communication.

Granting that the simultaneous broadcasting of the visual and the aural represents a great refinement in the application of technical knowledge, are we handicapped in any way by having the visual image presented to us? What restriction does it place upon our imagination?

2. The *second approach* presents a puzzle—a series of questions to stimulate thinking. Here the teacher gives students ten minutes to consider the following, asking them to jot down ideas that occur to them as they try to form a conclusion:

> Consider a certain individual; you know only that he prefers
>
> to use his leisure primarily for reading rather than for watching television.
> to read a book *before* seeing a motion picture based on the book.
> to avoid seeing a motion picture based on a book that has moved him deeply.
> to get the news from radio rather than from television.
>
> Give one reason which will explain all four preferences.

Notice that the statements definitely do not imply that this person does not like television or motion pictures. Students usually have difficulty with this exercise, but it seldom fails to intrigue them. If no one comes up with a satisfying answer, the teacher starts the discussion by asking students to identify the methods of intake compared in each statement. The person described shows a preference for reading and listening. Have the two methods anything in common? The discussion can develop the idea that both methods allow the recipient to create his own mental pictures without assistance or hindrance from an outside source.

3. The *third approach* is to consider the meaning and significance of statements about the instruments of intake. The teacher divides the class into groups, giving each one statement.

> "Better listening, better world." [12]
>
> "Books have to be read; . . . it is the only way of discovering what they contain. . . . The reader must sit down alone and struggle with the writer." [13]

[12] Slogan of the Wisconsin Association for Better Radio and Television, Madison, Wisconsin.

[13] E. M. Forster, *Aspects of the Novel* (N.Y., Harcourt, Brace, 1927), p. 28.

"In a lifetime one is lucky to meet six or seven people who know how to attend; the rest . . . have for the most part fidgety ears; . . . they seem afraid to lend their mind to another's thought, as if it would come back bruised and bent." [14]

A word is not letters on a page nor sound waves vibrating in the inner ear; it is a shape in the mind.

". . . in the movies the camera not only sees for the audience, it selects what is to be seen and, in a way, pays attention for the audience." [15]

"The listening ear implies humility, for it assumes a readiness to accept upsetting ideas. The listening ear . . . also implies an eagerness for the participation of others, both in discussion and action." [16]

Ask the groups to determine the meaning. Is the statement completely true? Partially true? Completely false? Think of specific examples to support your conclusion. Follow with discussion to clarify meaning and to give students a chance to consider different points of view.

■ *Explore contrasts and similarities among the three instruments of intake*

After stimulating interest in the problem by methods similar to those described above, the teacher may proceed through discussion to point up the advantages and difficulties of each process of intake. Students already have the information summarized below; the teacher, by asking appropriate questions, brings it to the fore and helps the class organize it.

The listener	**The reader**
Contrasts	
Has to keep pace with the speaker	Can proceed at his own rate
Has no opportunity for rechecking except with recorded material	Can review as often and to whatever degree is necessary
Gets the meaning from vocal intonations as well as language	Gets the meaning from language alone
May be influenced by audience reaction when listening takes place in groups	Can arrive at his interpretation without help or hindrance from others
May not have ready access to material he wants	Is permitted wider personal choice
Is dependent on time, place, and a collaborator	Is practically unrestricted

Similarities

Subject matter—there may be no significant difference, although material for reading can be more complex. Any subject can form the basis for either a listening or a reading experience.

Skills—almost every listening skill has its duplicate in a reading skill; we have to learn to transfer.

Process—essentially the same.

[14] Jacques Barzun, *Teacher in America* (Boston, Little, Brown, 1944); in the paperbound edition (Garden City, N.Y., Doubleday Anchor), this quotation appears on p. 177.

[15] Gilbert Seldes, *The Public Arts* (N.Y., Simon & Schuster, 1956), p. 10.

[16] Charles P. Taft, "Attuning the Listening Ear," in Edward P. Morgan, ed., *This I Believe* (N.Y., Simon & Schuster, 1952), p. 177.

What happens when we are absorbed in a book? Or in listening? Does a book for the reader exist on the printed page? Do any two individuals ever read exactly the same book? Is the knowledge or stimulation entirely in the communication? Do any two listeners ever receive exactly the same communication? The answers to such questions should lead to the conclusion that each reader creates his own book out of his inner needs and past experience; that each listener relates the communication to his experience, taking from it only what fits his needs of the moment.

Listener and Viewer—After a realization of the part the picture in the mind plays in both listening and reading, students can more readily distinguish the two main areas in which the presentation of a ready-made image is an advantage:

In situations relating to the objective world where the listener's image must be exact; for example, maps in newscasts dealing with areas which may be unfamiliar, diagrams in explanations of complex processes, sketch of a route to take in reaching a certain destination, etc.

In films, where the director organizes and unifies the experience for the viewer by forcing attention upon images in planned sequence.

An understanding of the similarities and contrasts among the instruments of intake should help students see the possibility of using skills acquired in one medium as a basis for gaining skills in another. For instance, in the unit "Meeting a Crisis," the reading builds on the listening experiences introduced in launching the unit.

To develop simple comprehension skills

■ *Listen to remember particular items*

1. Conversation on the simplest level requires remembering names and items for conversational leads. In communities where members of the class do not know each other, ask students either to introduce themselves or to work in pairs introducing each other; after a dozen introductions, call on volunteers to name in order all who have been introduced. Where students know each other, ask each to answer roll call with an interesting fact. Follow the same procedure.

The next day, let volunteers recount as many items as they can remember, giving the name of each contributor. Students like to have the teacher take his turn in demonstrating his ability to remember. This is a good way for him to learn 100 to 150 names.

2. Selecting what to remember is important in both conversation and discussion. When using oral reports in connection with any phase of the work, ask the reporter to prepare a listening test for the class. Evaluate the test; did the reporter select the points for testing wisely or did he expect the listeners to remember unimportant details? Vary the procedure by delaying the test until the day after the report. If students have difficulty recalling items, explore the reasons; does the fault lie with the reporter, the listener, or with the questions asked?

■ *Listen to improve vocabulary*

1. Before reading a selection or playing a recording, list on the board words that are likely to be unfamiliar; ask students to determine their meaning from the context; check with dictionary when necessary.

2. As they listen, ask students to list all unfamiliar words. Let volunteers consult the dictionary for alternate meanings. Reread the selection, asking students to determine which meaning best fits the context.

3. Open class for a week with a sentence containing a word whose meaning can be determined from context, such as, He put off the job from day to day but finally had to pay the penalty for his procrastination. Ask one volunteer a day to prepare a similar sentence; add words to personal vocabulary lists.

■ *Listen to follow sequence of ideas*

1. Practice giving and following directions. The teacher asks seventh-graders to listen to directions for reaching his home: "Go down Grove Street two blocks to 57th Avenue; turn left; walk three blocks until you come to a brown wooden church; turn right and go one block to an oil station on the corner; turn left on Dover Street; my home, a green bungalow, is the third house from the corner." Ask students to list landmarks in order; analyze reasons for success or failure.

Discuss the need for clarity and specificity in giving and in listening to directions. Have you ever failed to reach a destination you have been assured you cannot miss? When anyone gives such directions, what assumption is he making? Ask pupils to write directions for reaching their homes; working in pairs, they listen to each other, trying to remember items in sequence and to determine in case of failure where the fault lies—with the sender or receiver or both.

2. For practice in remembering steps in a process, use short talks or "how-to" paragraphs read aloud. Accustom students to being asked to recall main points of a speech in order.

3. To help students recognize conversational leads, and provide continuity,[17] ask for volunteers—one each for as many groups as the size of the class demands; each volunteer is to prepare to relate an event he thinks will interest the class. As he speaks to his group, each member jots down ideas which could be appropriately introduced into a conversation on the subject. These may be no more than a question; they may be something that has only a tenuous connection with the matter at hand, so long as an introductory remark can make the connection clear. For example, the narrator may be telling an incident concerning skin diving; the responses may vary from, "Isn't it dangerous?" to references to pictures in a magazine, to a spot on a recent television program, to other water sports, to the expense of needed equipment, and so on. After the narrator has finished, each member tells how one of his ideas could be introduced.

After this trial run, repeat with a second group of volunteers. In each group, after the prepared talk has been given, students converse, introducing their remarks into the conversation as smoothly as possible.

4. For further practice in conversational listening, play the game, "That Reminds Me." Ask students to prepare to tell an anecdote and to decide possible ways of introducing it into a conversation. Place students in small groups, one member starting the conversation. The problem—to bridge the gap between contributions—demands careful listening.

■ *Listen to determine the main idea*

Read a short news item; ask students to write appropriate headlines. Read a longer news item; have students summarize it as a news flash. Plan a series of listening experiences based on paragraphs developed by different methods—specific details, examples, comparison and contrast; ask students to devise appropriate titles.

[17] See the descriptions of role playing, pp. 143-44, 446-47.

To develop organizational skills

■ *Sense relationships in aural contexts*

Initially, examples are read by the teacher; later, volunteers may prepare and read original material illustrating the principle involved. Two minutes daily for a week show pupils they can train themselves to concentrate. Start simply; read only once; recognition of relationships will be instantaneous if pupils are listening.

1. *Among items in a list:* Ask students to detect irrelevancies among items belonging for the most part in the same category: sparrows, thrushes, wrens, robins, nightingales, tigers, eagles. Gradually increase the length of the lists and the number of irrelevant items. Other categories: flowers, trees, fish, sports, vocations, professions, parts of an automobile.

To help students recognize coordination and subordination of items, read a list of specifics; include a general term applicable to all, e.g., substitute *birds* for *tigers* in the above list. Gradually build the list to three or four categories with several items under each.

2. *Between clauses:* Read complex sentences to the class, omitting the conjunctions; let students supply those that show appropriate relationships: He could not go (until, before, although) he had bought his ticket.

3. *Between sentences in a passage:* Ask students to supply the connecting links:

> The Lord is my Shepherd: (therefore) I shall not want. (for, because) He maketh me to lie down in green pastures; (and) He leadeth me beside the still waters . . .

4. *Between paragraphs:* The secretary lists on the board all transitional phrases the class can name—in the second place, on the other hand, finally, in contrast—as well as devices such as repetition of key words and phrases. The teacher helps students group those denoting time, cause, contrast, etc., and discusses the use of such devices by speakers and writers as aids in directing thinking. Then he reads a passage in which students are to note these aids.

■ *Distinguish main ideas from subordinate*

1. Before reading a passage to students, say, "The author makes these two points." State them. Ask students as they listen to determine the central idea the points develop. Reread, asking students to listen for the support of each of the two points. After practice with such specific aids, students may be asked to determine the main points without help.

2. Prepare a jumbled list of ideas, facts, and illustrations used by an author. Read aloud the selection from which the list is derived. Then give the list to students, asking them to separate the main ideas from the subordinate, placing the latter under the correct headings and arranging the points in order. This procedure may be used several times, the material becoming gradually more difficult.

■ *Predict conclusions and recognize conventional patterns of organization*

1. Occasionally have student speakers stop before the conclusion; ask listeners to predict a logical one. Analyze the reasons for their success or failure. Do the same with recordings.

2. Introduce articles which employ different methods of organization—chronology, series, analysis-solution—so that students will become familiar with those in

common use. Ask students to determine the patterns of assembly speeches, certain radio speeches, etc. Compare plans, trying to determine reasons for discrepancies. Was speaker or listener at fault? Was a plan discernible? Did the listener try to fit the speech to a formula the speaker did not use?

■ *Learn to devise a meaningful structure for different forms of presentation*

Since speakers frequently do not use conventional patterns of organization, experiences with both structured and unstructured presentations should be provided for the capable student. Thus, in listening to lectures, speeches, and discussions, the student will realize he must decide early in the speech whether outlining or note-taking is the more appropriate method for getting down the speaker's ideas.

1. In presenting *outlining*,[18] use well-organized material of increasing difficulty: Give students supporting points, let them supply main ideas. Give them main headings and the number of subpoints under each; let them fill in the support. Give the skeleton form (correct lettering and numbering) which the speech follows: let students fill in both main and subpoints. After sufficient practice with these methods, let the student make the outline without help; start again with simple material and move to the more complex.

2. Material lends itself better to *note-taking* if the organization is not immediately apparent. Although students who are planning on college will undoubtedly have to take notes, relatively little can be taught about note-taking per se. Teachers can spend time to greater advantage trying to teach the student to think more clearly, so that he is more able to take useful notes, whatever the material. Everyone must devise his own system, but teachers can give students a few pointers and spend a limited amount of time in practice.

Through discussion, bring out the following points:

Note-taking calls into play all the techniques learned concerning organization—discovering speaker's purpose, main points, etc.

Competent note-takers
- strive for accuracy and brevity.
- concentrate on careful listening and alert reaction, rather than on writing.
- try different methods, adapting to the material, e.g., they jot down words to suggest key ideas, and fill in after the speech.
- reflect upon notes as soon as possible to clinch ideas and help later recall.
- make up their own scheme of abbreviating.

For practice material select interviews, discussions, question-and-answer periods after panels. First, use material that allows students to be told the general plan the discussion is to follow, for example, recordings and loosely structured magazine articles. Then, use material where students receive no advanced help, e.g., radio and television panels and debates.

3. The listener in both formal and informal situations must structure the idea for himself; the better organized the speaker, the more completely does he convey the design the idea has for him. However, the worth of the communication to the listener depends upon the structure of the idea he himself evolves; this may or may not agree with the speaker's. For example, speaker and listener may disagree on the

[18] "Oral Language" suggests that students learn the principles governing outlining more easily by devising plans for their own short talks and by evaluating the plans evident in the talks of their classmates. Such practice increases ability to determine the design in longer and more complicated material.

relevancy or the relationship the parts have to each other or to the whole. Comparisons of the various structures students make of the same presentation will show the direct dependence of evaluation on the way the listener "sees the design" of the central idea. What reasons might a speaker have for deliberately trying to confuse with a blurred design? [19] Discussion can stress the fact that one who wishes to use language with integrity must structure his communication so as to give it meaning and stability.

To test the internal consistency of a communication

Much of the information upon which we base opinions and decide upon action comes to us through the aural sense; help students develop alertness to irrelevancies and contradictions within the communication.

■ *Use sentences*

Read a list of sentences, asking students to mark a numbered list with "+" if the sentence makes sense, "0" if it does not. In a group of sentences whose meaning is instantly clear, include one or two that are ambiguous, contrary to life experience, or ludicrous because of malapropisms or faulty constructions:

The father told his son that he would have to leave.
We walked toward the setting sun, our long shadows bobbing before us.
He greeted me with an angry epitaph.
Driving due west from Chicago, you can reach New York in two days.
Swimming around the bend, the land came in sight.
He told me an antidotal story that made me roar with laughter.
I don't care for anesthetic dancing.
In the distance I heard the crack of a rifle; I ducked as a bullet whizzed past my ear.
The stars were so bright they put out the sun.

In exercises such as this, do not warn students to look for discrepancies. Most of the above are so obvious they can be spotted immediately *if the listener is alert.* The activity is helpful in pointing up the need for accuracy in listening; the role of past experience in interpreting what we think we hear; and man's need for meaning, his wish to impose order on chaos.

■ *Use paragraphs*

Take any well-written paragraph with a clearly stated topic sentence; insert a sentence connected with the topic but irrelevant to the aspect being developed. Ask students first to listen for the topic sentence. As they listen a second time, they check to see whether each sentence is pertinent.

■ *Use outlines* [20]

Tell the class you will read a skeletal outline for a speech; the first sentence will state the central idea; all those that follow will represent supporting points. Read the central idea sentence. Then give this direction: "Listen to each sentence as I read; if you think, when adequately developed into a paragraph, it will lend support to the statement that governs the speech, mark plus; if not, mark zero." Then read each supporting sentence slowly, giving a few seconds for reflection:

[19] See "Logical Thinking," pp. 82-85.

[20] Compare with speech plans in Chapter 9, "Oral Language," pp. 472-73.

I enjoy watching television.
  I find several programs consistently entertaining.
  I especially like the sportscasts.
  Repetition of the same advertisements becomes boring.
  Many old movies are shown.
Our assemblies should be improved.
  Often speakers cannot be heard.
  The talent assembly was the best of the year.
  We should have more student performers.
  I didn't like the talk on science.
C_______ is the best school in this vicinity.
  It has an excellent basketball team.
  Its building is modern.
  Its classrooms have the latest equipment.

One outline is sufficient for a lesson. The exercise can be used repeatedly, the problems becoming more complex. At this point students should not be concerned with the truth or falsity of the statements; neither should they confuse proof with support. They should decide whether the supporting statements are coordinate; which, if any, should be deleted; and which, if any, could be revised to support the argument. For each governing statement, they should consider what method of development is required. For example, the key word in the third outline is *best;* hence none of the statements is pertinent since support demands comparisons. Let volunteers prepare similar listening tests.

To develop ability to evaluate critically

■ *Judge newscasts to find those that give the greatest return in coverage and accuracy for the time spent*

1. As a *preliminary,* take a poll of the class to see how many regularly listen to newscasts of fifteen minutes or longer, how many read daily papers, how many have a weekly news magazine in their homes. Ask the secretary to keep a list of the exact news sources mentioned. Have volunteers list all newscasts at times available for student listening. Seek help from the promotion manager of the local paper; editors have been willing to supply a class set of daily papers to classes studying the news.

2. *First listening experience:* Divide the newscasts among students, so that, if possible, all are followed by several individuals. Ask each student to keep brief notes as a record of his listening for a week; he should attempt to list the news items, with a rough estimate of the amount of emphasis allotted each and the number of days it receives mention. A rating of 1 (low) to 5 (high) is sufficiently accurate.

Record of listening

Dates_____ Time_____ Station_____ Announcer_______

Item	*Emphasis*	*Days mentioned*
A.	5	3
B.	3	1
. . .		
J.	1	1

Your name_______________

At the end of the week, ask each student to consult a reliable news weekly and to star on his list of broadcast news items those which seem to have been considered important by the magazine editor. Then divide the class into groups according to the newscasts followed. Ask them to select the items from the newscasts that have received emphasis in the news weekly, to try to determine what principles seem to have guided the editors in their choice, and to prepare a report on their findings. (These reports have shown wide differences among newscasts, some having as few as 9 items, others as many as 38 items included in weekly news magazines.)

Discuss the findings, using such questions as

What significance, if any, is there in discrepancies between the two sources?
Do any of the newscasts represented by conspicuously fewer items deserve commendation for more complete coverage within a limited area?
Upon what basis do you think the editor of the weekly excluded events mentioned in the daily newscasts?
Can any newscasts be selected which seem to pay higher dividends for listening time?

3. *Second listening experience:* Let the class select as many newscasts as the students think are worthwhile. Ask each student to follow two for a week, taking careful notes only on those items that receive emphasis and comparing the treatment of the event each day with that given in one daily paper. How well do the accounts agree? Are both true reports—i.e., Does unemotional language predominate? Do both give the facts without comment? Does either source omit details needed to clarify the picture, or overemphasize unimportant aspects? Are both needed for understanding?

After re-evaluation of various broadcasts as to coverage and accuracy, encourage students to select two newscasts for consistent listening.

■ *Judge news commentaries to become familiar with leading commentators*

In the experience suggested here it is desirable that each commentator be represented by a sufficient number of students, with some of the best thinkers in each group.

1. Discuss the role of the news commentator. Use questions such as:

How does his function differ from that of the newscaster?
Have you any favorites you listen to regularly?
If we are to rely on commentators for interpretation of facts, what must we know about them?
Since a commentator must point out the historical, economic, and/or political significance of events, what aspects of his background will be of interest to the listener?
What personal qualities should we look for?
What do you know about your favorites?

2. As an assignment, ask for volunteers to investigate the backgrounds of selected commentators—their education, special interests, abilities, and experience in gathering news, the reputation of papers for which they have worked,[21] travel, time spent

[21] Consult the *Readers' Guide to Periodical Literature* for articles; *Current Biography*, published monthly, is also helpful. (Maxine Block, ed., N.Y., Wilson.)

in foreign countries, their experience with broadcast networks, special honors or awards, reputation among other commentators.[22]

Ask a second group of volunteers to follow the broadcasts of these commentators for a week, taking brief notes on several of the more important items discussed in order to report what help was given to insure listener understanding—comparisons, historical reference, examples, etc.

Ask the rest of the class to select two events of national or international significance with which the average listener will probably need help and to prepare, for each, one question he would ask the commentator if he could meet him.

After oral report on a commentator's background, ask students who have listened to commentator's broadcasts to make their contribution. Call on those who have questions they think this commentator might be able to answer. Why should he speak with authority on this subject?

■ *Recognize the techniques a news commentator uses to insure immediate comprehension of literal meaning*

1. Discuss what help the listener needs

To understand facts

Identification—"Senator _______, chairman of _______"; "You will recall a similar episode occurred . . ."
Relationship—"If . . . then"; "equally important is . . ."
Judicious repetition—"We repeat . . . we have no confirmation."

To follow the line of reasoning

"His record . . . seems to indicate . . ."
"We should watch for these immediate effects . . ."
"Now this does not mean . . ."
"The only evidence we have is . . ."

2. Ask students to listen to three broadcasts of the assigned commentator, listing specific examples of help given both in understanding facts and in following reasoning. After the discussion of the results, help students rate commentators on their consistency in giving help; rough groupings are sufficient—almost always, often, occasionally, never.

■ *Develop guide lines for choosing a reliable commentator*

The following represents the final form of such a guide as it was developed in one class over several weeks of listening.

Judging the reliability of a commentator

Does he	*or does he*
1. Deal principally with events that deeply affect many persons?	Indulge in gossip, trivialities, sensationalism?
2. Present ideas matter-of-factly?	Use them to play upon fears, special interests?
3. Help the listener think along with him?	Confuse the listener by strong emphasis on every point?

[22] Newspaper men stress "public service, independence, impartiality, and providing expression for honest, intelligent minds," as ideals which should guide the press. Quoted, together with a list of highly rated newspapers, in *Enjoying Radio and Television* (Madison, Wisc., Wisconsin Association for Better Radio and Television, 1952), p. 11.

Does he	or does he
4. Show the relationship of facts, giving sufficient evidence for the listener to draw his own conclusion?	Merely make assertions, asking acceptance on the grounds that he's invariably right?
5. Frankly admit he hasn't all the answers?	Assume oracular powers?
6. Give specific sources?	Intimate possession of a private line to the all-knowing?
7. Present opposing viewpoints fairly?	Give only his own version of a story?
8. Use a sincere, straightforward tone?	Use an emotional one?

In short, does he give the impression he is primarily interested in communicating the truth as he sees it or in building himself up as a personality?

To make critical listening habitual

■ *Develop a plan for listening throughout the year*

Without question, most of the information on which the majority of people base opinions and decide upon action comes through listening. Even if only facts were presented, the complexity of the world today makes these facts more than any one individual can cope with. Therefore, students must be helped to form the habit of listening critically to the informational and controversial material that comes over the air. Any plan devised to meet such an objective must encourage consistent practice; it must, to be feasible in most English classes, require a minimum of class time.

Two variations of such a plan are described here. Research on the history of the Peabody Award, given to newsmen for courageous and outstanding reporting, served as the inspiration for one; a series of assignments concerning individuals facing a cross fire of questions from panels, the other. Both have been used with various kinds of classes.

1. *The Peabody Award:* Each student selects two news commentators whose broadcasts he will follow regularly; all supplement their listening with newspaper and magazine articles. The class is divided into groups, each concerned with several commentators. The equivalent of one period a month is devoted to evaluative meetings: Each group meets to name a specific broadcast for commendation; representatives of each group meet to rate all commentators on the month's broadcasts.

The Peabody Award section of the bulletin board is kept supplied with material pertinent to the important events in the news and to the favorite candidate of the month. At the end of the year, after the most distinguished commentator has been chosen, teachers have used culminating activities such as the following:

A panel of students review the highlights of the year's news, modeling their reports on the "looking backward" roundups appearing on radio and television.

One student is chosen to present the award to another who acts as proxy for the commentator.

Students write letters to the commentators, telling them of the project and giving examples of broadcasts chosen to exemplify the principles of good reporting; they choose the best letter to be sent to each.

2. *Valor under Fire:* To judge how well individuals stand up under cross-questioning by panelists, use broadcasts such as the current "Meet the Press" and "Face the

Nation"; those that center on controversial figures should be chosen. Tape a broadcast for demonstration purposes.[23] Through discussion, help students understand the nature of such programs: what does the interviewee know about the panelists?

> He knows they are well informed, expert in the art of interviewing–selecting probing questions, sensing when they've touched an exposed nerve, returning to the same point by devious routes–and quick to catch inconsistencies and evasions.
>
> He recognizes their responsibility for bringing out facts in his background that seem to explain the attitude he is likely to take toward public issues.
>
> Panelists help the listener in much the same way as the camera helps the motion picture audience; they focus attention on significant points.

Play the recording, asking students to make a general evaluation of the performance of the person interviewed. Through discussion, explore reasons why ratings are favorable or unfavorable. Develop with students a listening guide similar to the following:

Does (name of interviewee)
- support his assertions with facts?
- use sound reasoning?
- state his opinions frankly?
- give seemingly valid reasons for refusing to commit herself?
- remain even tempered under personal questions, repetitious and probing remarks?
- admit the truth of evidence that does not support his point of view?
- refrain from making derogatory remarks about opponents?

On the whole, does he create a favorable or unfavorable impression?
Jot down specific examples to support your opinion.

Divide the class into small groups, each to choose one broadcast to which they will listen; these broadcasts are spaced throughout the year. After the broadcast the group meets to pool their opinions and to decide on a composite rating (1 to 10) for the performance; they prepare a bulletin board display which includes (if possible) a picture of the individual, a summary of the facts brought out in the broadcast, and the rating given by the group. The finished bulletin board serves as summary of the work.

In those classes where it is not possible to enlist the enthusiasm of all members, such projects serve as rewarding experiences for volunteer groups. Even if only a few students from the majority of classes throughout the country form the habit of listening critically to significant discussions, the audience for radio and television will gain a substantial number of intelligent listeners.

■ *Learn a formula for quick evaluations*

1. Isolate a few basic essentials:

   Find the main idea.
   Discard the irrelevant.

[23] Such a tape recording has also been used as a single listening experience, with groups assigned to pay particular attention to the various interviewers and to the person being interviewed; it could also be used as preparation for a writing assignment.

Determine whether purpose is mainly to inform or to persuade.
Determine whether assertions are mainly factual or judgmental.

Such streamlining of an intricate process cannot insure correct appraisal, but the habit of concentrating on a few essentials does give a basis for approaching accuracy on the spur of the moment.

2. Practice evaluating by formula. Evaluate student talks in groups, talks before the class, speeches in assemblies, and communications received via radio and television.

3. Evaluate personal communications. Give students a week to select a segment of one particular conversation to evaluate. They meet in groups, trying to appraise the strengths and weaknesses of the formula as an instrument for quick evaluation. Class discussion synthesizes results.

To emphasize the interrelation of forms of communication

■ *Use audio-visual material*

Informational sound films, recordings, and filmstrips offer opportunity to stress such basic principles as need for organizational design, continuity, selection of details, use of supporting examples, symbolism, etc.[24]

1. Provide incentive for discussion and writing. There are a number of sound films suited to this purpose, including "The River," "The Loon's Necklace," and "The Suicide of Society: Van Gogh." In one school, a *supplementary* English course for twelfth-graders was organized around films, which served as a basis for discussion and writing. Films of general interest were shown—biographies, historical and scientific presentations—as well as those posing problems pertinent to contemporary society.

2. Help retarded readers think through problems; the *What Do You Think* series, six short films, is useful, as well as films such as "How to Judge Facts," "How Honest Are You?" and "The Good Loser." For an illustration of the use of films in this context, see "Oral Language," Chapter 9, p. 454.

3. Supplement readings in biography; a wealth of material includes "Story of Dr. Carver" (film), "Oliver Wendell Holmes" (film), "Public Life of Abraham Lincoln" (film), "Paul Revere" (recording), "Johnny Appleseed" (filmstrip), and "Thomas Jefferson" (film).

4. Supply background information; a few aids are "Master Will Shakespeare" (film), "Introduction to William Shakespeare" (filmstrip), "Washington Irving" (film), and two recordings concerning Mark Twain—"Splendid Legend" and "Mark Twain Tonight."

5. Secure necessary information for particular units; for a unit on newspapers and magazines, for example, the following would be useful: "Newspaper Story" (film), "You and Your Newspaper" (filmstrip), "Getting the World's News" (filmstrip), and "Magazine Magic" (film).

6. Reinforce concepts:

"The Story That Couldn't Be Printed" (film)—individual integrity, freedom of the press.

[24] The *National Tape Recording Catalog* (Dept. of Audio-Visual Instruction, 1201 Sixteenth St., N.W., Washington 6, D.C.) lists the best programs selected by various educational organizations, and suggests many recordings appropriate for teaching listening. A teacher may select any program, send a blank tape, and receive his own recording for a minimal charge. The catalog also lists state tape recording libraries.

"No Man Is an Island" (records)—the interdependence of man.
"In the American Tradition" (records)—the continuity of ideals that have inspired Americans.
"The Literature of Freedom" (filmstrip)—the theme of freedom as an inspiration to writers.
"America Was Promises" by Archibald MacLeish (records)—the necessity of working to make the promises come true.
"The American Dream," Series 11 of *Lest We Forget* (records)—meeting the problems of human relations.
"Stories to Remember," Series 12 of *Lest We Forget* (records)—intercultural understanding.

■ *Use the aural method to aid writing* [25]

1. To develop sentence sense, read with proper vocal intonations a list of sentences, fragments, run-together sentences, etc., taken from student papers. Ask pupils to indicate on paper the number of sentences in each item:

Running down the street with a many-colored balloon in his hand. (0)
John and I have many things in common we both like to play football we enjoy the same television programs. (3)
Starting mostly with scrap material and with discarded parts of cars, Dick, with his father's help, has built a highly individualized jalopy. (1)

After students understand the method, throw the responsibility for reading on them. Use their own written work; while correcting it, enclose in brackets and number consecutively the items you want the class to hear. After the papers have been returned, have the students read the items aloud according to the numbers called. If the sentence is misread, ask for repetition; each student is to make a list indicating the number of sentences in each item. After the class record their answers, reread for them any items which received a varied response so that they may check the accuracy of their first impressions.

Have students who persist in misreading or who cannot hear their own vocal intonations read their paragraphs into the tape recorder. (Often a responsible student can be placed in charge.) Excuse, from a writing assignment, those who do not respond to mass teaching; while the class is writing, work with them individually, trying to help them hear what they read.

2. Help students form the habit of testing their writing by ear; this is an effective device used by professional writers. In the beginning, give students class time to read their writing aloud before handing it in. Sometimes they can do this in pairs; at other times, in groups; sometimes, each can whisper the words to himself.

■ *Integrate the communicative skills*

Students, with teacher guidance, choose a subject, decide upon its various aspects, do the necessary research.[26] The teacher conducts discussions as the research progresses. After the final discussion, ask each student to select one aspect of the subject as a basis for a composition with a strict time or paragraph limit. The time limit has two advantages: It gives practice in eliminating extraneous material and select-

[25] See also Chapter 11, "Grammar and Usage," pp. 575-76.
[26] See pp. 428-33, 490-91.

ing the appropriate, and it gives more time for attention to organization and sentence structure, since content is no problem.

To secure motivation through exchange programs

Teachers find that the exchange of tapes between classes in different schools or in the same school provides strong motivation for improvement of communication. The programs are planned, written, and spoken by students. One idea is to have the students make arrangements with a school that offers contrast with their own—a class in a large city chooses one in a small town, one in the North chooses one in the South, etc. Classes in the two schools exchange a series of tapes, acquainting each other with facets of life in their respective communities.[27] Subjects for the tapes are numerous; a few are

Newscasts of school events
News commentary on selected school problems
Descriptions of extracurricular activities
Descriptions of recreational opportunities offered in the community
Descriptions of community projects
Unusual personalities of school or community

A few of the many other possibilities are:

Two classes that have studied the same literary work exchange tapes of a class discussion.
Two classes agree on a topic for a panel discussion, exchange tapes.
Two classes exchange programs of poetry read by students, each poem preceded by an appropriate introduction.
Two classes exchange lists of books they have read or intend to read as part of the guided reading program; later, the duplicates form the nucleus of a round table discussion; the discussion is recorded and tapes exchanged.

Opportunities for acquiring the skills necessary for effective listening occur almost daily in the classroom. Since these skills are complementary to those needed for effective speaking, and since many are applicable to reading and writing, an integrated program facilitates transfer from one area to another.

Evaluating Growth

As has been stressed throughout this chapter, frequent evaluation of success attained in specific listening experiences is a necessary characteristic of both the teaching and the learning process. When extended attention has been given to certain skills, a more comprehensive evaluation can be made by using more formal tests—both those made by the teacher and those available from publishers.

[27] Teachers who think their students would be interested in exchanging tapes with students in foreign countries may secure, at the present time, a list of schools cooperating in the International Tape Exchange Project from Mrs. Ruth Y. Terry, 834 Ruddiman Ave., North Muskegon, Mich.

Teacher made tests. Suppose a teacher wishes to check class improvement in ability to recognize logical support of governing statements for expository writing and speaking. Ten items similar to those on p. 203 might be used as a diagnostic test before instruction; ten items which duplicate the problems might be used as a test after instruction, to measure growth.

Published tests. Three standardized instruments are recommended:

Brown-Carlsen Listening Comprehension Test. (World Book Co., Tarrytown-on-Hudson, N.Y., 1953.) This test, available in two equated forms and designed for grades 9-13, provides an objective measure of five listening skills: immediate recall, following directions, recognizing transitions, recognizing word meanings, and comprehending a lecture.

Sequential Tests of Educational Progress: Listening Comprehension. (Cooperative Test Division, Educational Testing Service, Princeton, N.J., 1957.) Based on oral presentation by the teacher, these test simple comprehension, interpretation, evaluation, and application. Divided into two sections of 35 minutes each; available for four levels—grades 4-6, 7-9, 10-12, 13-14.

Diagnostic Reading Tests. (Committee on Diagnostic Reading Tests, 419 W. 119th St., New York 27, N.Y.) Section II, Part 2 is an auditory test, designed to measure comprehension skills.

SELECTED READINGS

Gertrude Elliff, "A Direct Approach to the Study of Listening." *English Journal,* Vol. 46, No. 1 (January 1957). Describes an experiment in classroom listening; the discussion of procedures should be helpful to teachers planning similar instruction.

Enjoying Radio and Television and *Let's Learn to Look and Listen.* Madison, Wisc., Wisconsin Association for Better Radio and Television, 1952. Two inexpensive pamphlets published by an organization interested in securing better radio and television programs. Written concisely, with many specific examples to illustrate the principles discussed, these are outstanding in the amount of help they give teachers who are interested in encouraging students to develop standards of competency and taste in listening.

Alexander Frazier, "Making the Most of Speaking-and-Listening Experiences." *English Journal,* Vol. 46, No. 6 (September 1957). Gives suggestions for specific listening activities suitable for both junior and senior high school.

Olive S. Niles and Margaret J. Early, "Listening." *Journal of Education,* Boston University, Vol. 138, No. 3 (December 1955). Brief discussion of listening skills with suggestions for teaching and a selected list of source material.

Paul Witty, *Studies in Listening.* Champaign, Ill., National Council of Teachers of English, 1959. This monograph, with reprints of several articles from *Elementary English,* reviews and interprets experimental studies on listening as a way of learning and gives many suggestions for teaching.

Chapter Five

Reading with Comprehension

> *Understanding a paragraph is like solving a problem in mathematics. It consists in selecting the right elements of the situation and putting them together in the right relations, and also with the right amount of weight or influence or force for each. The mind is assailed as it were by every word in the paragraph. It must select, repress, soften, emphasize, correlate, and organize, all under the influence of the right mental set or purpose or demand.*
>
> —EDWARD L. THORNDIKE [1]

PERSPECTIVE

"You are barking at print," says the British teacher when grade school children fail to understand the words they call out, often with glib perfection. As teachers in all nations realize, reading is infinitely more than sounding out words. Reading *with comprehension* is indeed a very elaborate procedure, involving a balance of many elements in a passage and their organization in the proper relations to each other.

No easy formula possible As in all the arts of language, reading improvement depends on an intricate network of perception and learning. Nevertheless, human beings have an understandable but hopeless yearning to find simple solutions for complex problems. Adults no longer pluck daisy petals to determine fortunes in love, but they often transfer their petal-plucking simplification to new problems. No machine, no book of instruction, no simple three- or five-step technique will ever provide the exact recipe for teaching reading. Yet sometimes people continue to seek an easy formula; they rest their hopes on a reform of phonics in the second grade, a new machine for the junior high school, or the Schartz-Metterklume method for the low Z group in grade ten. We are all very human; we still pluck petals long after childhood.

No panaceas are offered in this book. Some pupils find all language situations difficult; neither threats of hell nor hopes of paradise can force them to

[1] Edward L. Thorndike, "Reading as Reasoning," *Journal of Educational Psychology*, Vol. 8, No. 6 (June 1917), p. 329.

read beyond their limits. Money, materials, and classes small enough for individual assistance could improve many inadequate situations, but our classrooms are not located in Utopia. The methods presented here will, therefore, avoid formulas and golden visions from the New Jerusalem. However, when the quest for simple answers is abandoned, many problems of comprehension do yield to instruction.

Improving comprehension

In this chapter we are mainly concerned with helping pupils make literal meaning from straightforward prose passages. This level of comprehension precedes any independent voyages to the realms of gold. Poor readers may take some stimulating literary excursions with a teacher-pilot at the helm. They may even venture a few short trial runs by themselves, but any sustained solo voyages leading to a lasting association with literature must wait apprenticeship in reading comprehension. It is this apprenticeship with which we are concerned here.

Demand for meaning is central Throughout time and in all places, people have read either for enlightenment or enjoyment—often for both at the same time. Whatever the purpose, the skills necessary for comprehension are basic. To understand, to grasp with the mind—this is the ultimate goal of all reading improvement. The precise meanings of words, the relations among words in sentences, and the hierarchies of main ideas in a total structure of prose or poetry must all be balanced. Yet none of these skills flourish unless the learner's volition is operating. Without a demand for meaning on the part of the learner, a teacher's efforts are wasted and the pupil's skill is not increased. How the will to understand drives people to read better than they usually do has been described by Adler: [2]

> When they are in love and are reading a love letter, they read for all they are worth. They read every word three ways; they read between the lines and in the margins; they read the whole in terms of the parts, and each part in terms of the whole; they grow sensitive to context and ambiguity, to insinuation and implication; they perceive the color of words, the odor of phrases, and the weight of sentences. They may even take the punctuation into account. Then, if never before or after, they read.

Fortunately or unfortunately, the materials for improving reading in the schools cannot be a series of love letters, but the principle is clear. When strong purpose with its attendant desire to understand is part of an instructional situation, learning almost certainly occurs; when indifference or perfunctory efforts predominate, learning is meager. Thus in reading, the comprehension problem centers on students' determination to receive the writer's

[2] Mortimer J. Adler, *How to Read a Book* (N.Y., Simon & Schuster, 1940), p. 14.

communication. Everything teachers can do to create a demand for meaning will increase learning efficiency.

Two pillars of comprehension Beyond the critical factor of motivation, comprehending communication—written or spoken—requires two basic skills. Students themselves may be led to see that understanding the words and perceiving their patterns of relationship are the two main pillars upon which comprehension rests. These fundamentals, discussed at length in the preceding chapter on listening, will not be elaborated here. Reading and listening, both instruments of intake, necessarily have elements in common. (The reader will note, too, that many of the learning experiences suggested in these two complementary chapters are interchangeable; only slight adaption in material or method is needed to make them suitable for teaching either listening or reading.) The integrated program stressed throughout this text indicates that reading and listening should be so taught that students will see their parallelism and thus be helped in transferring to one area skills gained in the other. Whether in listening or reading, understanding words and their structural relationships is the basis for comprehension.

Literature an added dimension The more subtle challenges of literature lie beyond the fundamental skills of comprehending simple prose structures. Like all the fine arts, literature uses special ways to *evoke* experience in others. By particular uses and arrangements of words, it seeks to express realms of experience inaccessible to ordinary language. Such uses of language account for much of the distress unskilled readers experience when they try to comprehend literature as if it were a series of matter-of-fact statements. Without training and imagination they cannot understand the special language of literature nor enter the domain it charts. The special skills required in reading literature are discussed elsewhere in this text.[3] Here we wish only to make the point that basic comprehension rests upon the two pillars—understanding words and perceiving correct relationships—and on such basic comprehension are built the deeper insights and keener perceptions that literature demands.

Problems unique to reading

As in listening, comprehension in reading depends upon knowing the literal meanings of words in various contexts. Like the listener, the reader must also be able to distinguish between the main idea and supporting ideas and perceive the relation of each part to the others and of each to the whole. Beyond lie even more complex kinds of thinking—grasping the significance of what is heard or read and judging its value, for example. However, several problems of comprehension specifically related to reading, rather than to listening, require inspection in this chapter.

[3] See Chapter 6, Chapter 7, and the units "Macbeth" and "The Consequences of Character."

Adapting rate to purpose and content Speed, the first of these problems, is a variable the reader can control whereas the listener cannot. To improve reading speed, the best approach proves to be an indirect one, through improving comprehension. Except for a few able students who have fallen into habits of undue slowness, emphasis upon speed itself should usually be avoided. Both natural and artificial methods have been used to improve rate and comprehension of reading, and a considerable amount of controversy continues to surround their use. Natural methods depend upon helping pupils through the use of reading reflecting their interests and through heightened awareness of ways to increase speed; in the process the learner competes with himself. Mechanical methods depend upon external means. They include tachistoscopes, films, accelerators, and other devices. Using such devices, as the Controlled Reader, some teachers offer evidence of having produced improvement in both rate and comprehension.[4] Mechanical aids frequently do prove to be good levers for motivating improvement; particularly does this seem true for boys with a deep interest in mechanisms. But two reservations about machines occur to many teachers: Their expense scarcely seems justified when more books are needed in a school; and even more serious, they tend to oversimplify, in the pupils' minds, the real task of adjusting speed to the nature of the material and purpose in reading. Competent readers adapt their speed and depth of attention to the nature of the material and their purpose in reading, whereas poor readers take in everything at the same rate and with the same exactitude or lack of it.[5] Teachers should, therefore, guide students to read along lines of personal interest and, choosing a range of reading materials, teach students to vary their speed.

Relating reading to interests and needs When they sense a purpose in their reading and want very much to accomplish that purpose, learners select more readily the meanings that hold the key to understanding. To increase reading skill, therefore, teachers plan many reading experiences appealing to the pupil's interests and needs.[6] Such reading is intended to bring about an efficient fusion of reading skills, a fusion occurring most dramatically when a reader's demand for meaning is so intense he can scarcely wait to read the next paragraph or turn the next page.

Linking reading to reality Some pupils tend to read as if words had no connection with reality, as if symbols were names without meanings. In the

[4] The Controlled Reader, Educational Laboratories, Huntington, N.Y. This machine presents reading materials of all levels of difficulty and regulates the speed with which these materials appear before the individual reader.

[5] Paul Blommers and E. F. Lindquist, "Rate of Comprehension of Reading: Its Measurement and Its Relation to Comprehension," *Journal of Educational Psychology*, Vol. 35, No. 8 (November 1944).

[6] A teacher need not underestimate the capacities of youth; students can be stretched toward the thoughts and experiences of maturity. However, ignoring the needs and interests of adolescents can be as unwise as determining subject matter solely on the basis of their present interests. See Chapter 6, "Literature: Basic Approaches."

secondary school, this verbalism often increases with the pressures to read more and to read it faster. Methods to counteract verbalism depend very much upon the teacher and his perspective. A judicious use of textbooks rather than a determination to cover them often helps. Showing pupils how to make applications and grasp implications is another way to improve the comprehen-

Courtesy True, The Man's Magazine

sion level of most readers. Beyond all specific methods, however, lies the crucial matter of classroom climate; when a pupil feels absolutely free to say, "I'm sorry, but I just don't understand this," verbalism has little hope of surviving. That pupil and his classmates are developing reading consciences.

Improving oral reading Silent reading has necessarily received so much attention that some teachers have begun to ask, "Should we do anything about oral reading? Does it slow down a pupil's rate of reading?" The answers are not difficult. Of course teachers should do something about oral reading. The emphasis on silent comprehension, crucial though it is to much learning, was never intended to eliminate oral reading. That reading aloud might slow the rate of silent reading is an unfortunate fear borrowed largely from the results of ineffectual practices in the primary grades, where some teachers misused oral reading in groups. Children who read aloud without any awareness of meaning–and those who listen to their stumbling performances do indeed make poor gains in silent reading.[7]

Oral reading, practiced to a high level of competency, can contribute substantially to comprehension in silent reading, for through oral reading the

[7] Luther C. Gilbert, "The Effect on Silent Reading of Attempting to Follow Oral Reading," *Elementary School Journal,* Vol. 40, No. 8 (April 1940).

learner can develop an "inner ear." He can become aware of the emphasis of italics, the tone of printed conversations, nuances of style, modifications of a main idea, and interpolation of subsidiary related elements.[8]

Locating information in books and libraries The skills of using books and libraries are often included in reading instruction. Any assumption that most students will somehow "catch" this kind of knowledge is unwarranted. Often the librarian will provide the actual lessons. The teacher will cooperate, planning the periods in the library and reinforcing the lessons with filmstrips, movies, and continued practice.[9] For most pupils, the important knowledge to be gained is how titles are arranged in the card catalog; how books are arranged on the shelves; and how dictionaries, encyclopedias, and any reference books in the library may be found and used. The *Readers' Guide, World Almanac,* and atlases deserve special attention.

Whenever a textbook is introduced in a classroom, the teacher has an opportunity to show how skilled readers take advantage of its organization. From time to time, the student needs to be reminded of the function and usefulness of the title page, foreword, table of contents, chapter headings, glossary, and index. The teacher should also point out the help to be gained from format—significance of italics, different sizes of type to indicate parallelism and subordination, use of boldface, etc.

Thus the use of books and libraries, like speed of silent or oral reading, constitutes a problem not found in listening. Although both reading and listening are receiving skills of communication, some aspects of teaching them differ because sound and print differ.

THE TEACHING PROBLEM

No effective program in reading can begin without a knowledge of student needs in reading. Nor can any program produce results if hasty or impromptu action mars the plans. At least a year in advance, survey testing and diagnosis need to be started, preferably as an administrative action of the school rather than by a teacher working alone. Such an appraisal of the situation yields certain important clarifications:

> Four kinds of readers will be identified: average readers of average ability, reading approximately at their grade level; accelerated readers, usually of average or better ability, reading above grade level; retarded readers of average or better ability, reading below grade level; poor readers of less than average ability, doing the best they can.

[8] For an extensive discussion of oral reading, see "Literature: Drama and Poetry," pp. 338-41.

[9] For a practical guide to library lessons, see Jessie Boyd, *Books, Libraries, and You* (N.Y., Scribner's, 1949).

The tests and diagnosis show which students may be handled in the regular classes and which ones should be given special instruction, if at all possible. Details about such tests and diagnoses will be described more fully later in this chapter (pp. 222-28, 251-55).

This classification of readers points, in turn, to a benefit in counseling pupils and their parents. Since reading cannot be viewed in isolation but must be related to native ability, intelligence must be considered in the reading program.[10] Because true native ability is very difficult to determine, several tests are better than one, and caution in their interpretation is necessary, particularly with pupils from the least favored socio-economic backgrounds. However, if a low intelligence quotient is found in combination with poor reading ability, the knowledge helps the school to guide pupil and parents.[11] A child who does not have this one kind of ability—verbal ability—undoubtedly does have other kinds; without verbal ability, however, he is unlikely to find high school easy or college possible, and his plans for the future should take such factors into account. This point of view accepts the broader definition of intelligence that Allison Davis proposes in *Social Class Influences on Learning*,[12] but does not minimize the importance of language power in secondary and higher education.

Finally, such testing and diagnosis will reveal that pupils at any single level of the secondary school range from very low to exceptionally high reading ability. Human variation being what it is, a grade spread of six or seven years—sometimes even more—should surprise only the naive. Elementary school instruction cannot prevail over native ability nor completely nullify home background. Furthermore, as children become older, individual differences become even greater, as a result of the increase in range of mental age and individuals' interaction with their unique environments.

With these kinds of knowledge about students' needs in reading, a sound program to meet each local situation is entirely possible.

Remedial and developmental reading Facts are stubborn things, and the facts of individual differences in reading need to be faced. Inasmuch as grade placement is on the basis of pupils' chronological age, the spread of reading ability will be very great—and superior instruction in the elementary school will only make it greater. It is unlikely that schools will ever be organized on the basis of reading level; if they were, the startling spread of chronological age would cause educational problems even more serious than those resulting from age grouping. To accept the facts of human linguistic variability, seeking to bring each individual up to his maximum performance,

[10] In addition to native ability, other factors often need to be considered—social and emotional maturity, the child's self-concept and aspirations, and his physical health.

[11] Reading comprehension and reading rate have been shown to be positively correlated both with verbal and non-verbal intelligence in the research of Dean S. Hage and James B. Stroud, who tested 800 ninth grade students. "Reading Proficiency and Intelligence Scores, Verbal and Non-verbal," *Journal of Educational Research*, Vol. 52, No. 7 (March 1959).

[12] Allison Davis, *Social Class Influences on Learning* (Cambridge, Mass., Harvard U. Press, 1955). If a student's cumulative record shows a decreasing IQ, he may come from a culturally deprived home and be able to learn to read much better than present IQ indicates.

is a sensible solution. This concept of teaching each individual to read in accordance with his maximum capacity is usually termed *developmental reading*. Teachers distinguish it from *remedial reading,* a term reserved for the help given pupils whose skill is clearly below the level their mental ability indicates they should be able to reach. This is a highly important distinction; when it is observed, schools do not place students of low native ability in remedial classes and then expect miracles. Remedial reading is for pupils whose handicaps *can* be remedied. Developmental reading is for all other pupils—brilliant, average, or dull—who need help with the skills required for reading at their individual stage of development.

Organizing Instruction

Reading programs vary depending upon the size of the school and the curriculum offered. No single plan of organization can be offered as a perfect universal model, but the most desirable is one in which the entire school system provides instruction in reading skills for all pupils from kindergarten to grade twelve. In many situations, however, the English teacher may be thrown upon his own resources. Organizing classroom instruction to improve reading will center, for him, around two problems: maintaining a flexible learning situation and diagnosing students' needs.

MAINTAINING A FLEXIBLE LEARNING SITUATION

Whether or not an all-school program exists, the English teacher will find that a departure from an exclusively formal organization is one of the more effective steps toward improving reading in his own classroom. By reducing the amount of single-text recitation and increasing the amount of time for guided study and individual conferences, a teacher can often turn a tide of mounting reading difficulties. He can, within limits of time and library facilities, help not only poor readers but average and capable ones as well. With a variety of reading materials ranging from easy to difficult, he can improve the reading of all pupils, seeking to help each individual reach his maximum reading capacity.

Such an increase in flexibility of method and materials does not, of course, imply complete rejection of similar content for all pupils. Instruction of this latter kind perpetuates traditions familiar to the public, the pupils, and most members of the teaching staff. But like all forms of organization, the traditional classroom carries its own particular dangers. Beneath the surface efficiency, gifted pupils often become bored, slow learners lose heart, and dreamers hide behind attentive facial masks. Yet identical content and common activities have many advantages. What is needed is a modification, not a revolution, in classroom strategy. A better balance among the ways of instruction frees the teacher to work with pupils who most need help in reading—some of them stumbling, others so gifted they lose interest under confining routines.

Organizing a more flexible classroom, accommodating individual patterns of learning—these too, have their dangers and require even more careful planning than more traditional teaching. In poorly planned classes, group work and individual conferences collapse into ineffectiveness. Obviously a first consideration must be the standards of order and decorum necessary to flexible organization. Elementary school teachers achieve these standards with children notably more active and far less aware of the purposes of instruction than are junior or senior high school students. Typically, the elementary teacher plans for three groups several times during a day and helps many individuals with reading problems. This amount of group work is, of course, not recommended as a standard plan on the secondary level, but here too, the teacher finds that with training in group processes, efficient planning, and attention to discipline, flexible organization proves to be equally possible and equally effective.

Using multiple materials Under such circumstances the teacher may use differentiated materials to advantage. For instance, one eighth grade class was formed into groups to read about youngsters whose experiences led them to mature responsibilities: *Little Britches* for average readers, *Captains Courageous* for superior readers, *Smuggler's Island* for poor readers, *Swiss Family Robinson* and *Mountain Laurel* for girls who disliked boys' books. Five pupils not identified with any group read individually books like *Boy on Horseback*, books whose content also related to the general theme of responsibility. Seniors, having completed Galsworthy's play, "Justice," extended their reading to thirty-five different novels, dramas, and biographies, all bearing on the same theme of justice and ranging from the easy to the very mature. Through sharing this extended reading, the students applied the general concepts of responsibility or justice to many particular incidents and in turn new generalizations were related back to each individual's reading.

Using the unit method The unit method offers one effective solution to many problems of pupil variation. It need not be used exclusively throughout an entire school year, but its advantages as a way of integrating content and providing for individual differences recommend it as a frequent approach. In the junior high, units may be topical and quite broad: "Boys and Girls of Other Lands," "Wagons Westward," or "Myths and Legends." In the senior high, the units should usually be more sharply centered: "The Meaning of Courage," "The Dimensions of Success," "What Is It To Be Aware?" When instruction is organized topically or thematically, the teacher is able to guide slower students to reading which is not as demanding as that being done by more able pupils, but which is still related to the over-all design. For examples of this individualization of reading through unit instruction, see the units "Science-Fiction: Radar of Man's Curiosity" and "The Consequences of Character."

Grouping according to ability Another plan to allow for individual differences is to group students according to reading ability. Ability grouping is one of the unsettled issues of American education. Almost everyone reading this book has been in a college class or a conversation where this topic has been discussed. If English classes number twenty-five pupils or less, a teacher can accept any reasonable spread of reading ability and adapt the curriculum to the situation. However, as soon as classes increase beyond twenty-five, many teachers prefer ability grouping, not because of any illusion that students will be markedly similar, but rather because time-consuming extreme cases of reading ability and disability need not be handled in the same class. Any reduction in the spread of reading ability helps somewhat in planning for all pupils.

Within a single class, grouping by reading ability is entirely possible and if certain qualifications are observed, very successful. Reading ability grouping should be only one method of teaching, and frequent changes in group membership should provide variation within that method. Often these groups will study separate assignments; at other times weeks may go by without such group work. Students with meager language facility should realize the teacher is as sincerely gratified over their limited progress as he is over more rapid progress in other groups. Grouping within the class is a resilient method and, in the hands of an imaginative teacher, one of the most effective in providing for differences in the skill of reading.

Differentiating assignments Not always does a teacher have time to design lessons and units that include such a variety of materials—nor should all instruction be differentiated to such a degree. It is often possible to provide for a range of reading abilities within the frame of a common assignment. Just as the works of Shakespeare and Mark Twain elicit various levels of understanding, so also can many of the reading assignments a teacher presents to the entire class. Students with reflective powers and superior reading ability may be challenged with more difficult problems while poor readers may at the same time be set to less complicated questions. In one eighth grade class, the teacher assigned a story about a boy and his prize steer. At the close of the story, the text included seven questions for study. Before assigning the story for silent reading in the classroom, the teacher told his students they would read better if they would concentrate on some one problem in the story. Consequently, there were to be three groups in the class; each group would be alert to a single problem. On the board the teacher wrote:

Q Group—arrangements of events in the story. Keep track of the order in which the events happen; answer questions 1, 4, and 7.

R Group—understanding characters. Be able to explain why the father and sister think and act as they do; answer questions 3, 6, and 7.

S Group—main character. How does the author make Johnny seem a real person? Answer questions 2, 5, and 7.

As the pupils began their silent reading, the teacher moved quickly down the aisles writing *Q*, *R*, or *S* lightly in pencil on the margins of their texts. In general, he assigned to the *Q* Group those pupils whose reading abilities were poor; the best readers received *R* assignments and the average, *S* classifications. After the reading period, the answers were discussed orally, each group contributing to the questions suited to its powers and all grappling with the important seventh question, which concerned a relationship between the story and life beyond the story.

By the same principle but on a more comprehensive scale, a teacher may plan for different levels of understanding over longer periods of time and with more complicated selections. For instance, the conclusion to the study of *Macbeth* (p. 411) is designed to accommodate a range of student abilities. Note that in the final written composition, students choose from a list of topics which call upon understandings gained at different depths of penetration in reading the play.

Using student helpers Occasionally, insightful and able readers may help other pupils in the class. The teacher makes the same classroom reading assignment for everyone, but as soon as each of the selected helpers completes the assignment, he receives from the teacher a set of duplicated study questions and sets up shop in a designated corner of the room. As other students complete the assignment, the teacher sends them to join one of these skilled readers, trying to match personalities for good working solidarity. Poor readers are placed with the best possible student teachers. Each group is to probe the selection with the help of the study questions and the group leader. Fifteen minutes before the close of the period the teacher asks the entire class to discuss or write on several questions selected from the study guides. If this method is not overused, there is no danger of exploiting superior readers and they, as well as those whom they help, profit from the experience.

Using programmed learning In schools where teaching machines have been purchased, individual students may work on comprehension problems, proceeding at their own rate. The new electronic machines make it possible to present problems in reading in such a way that the individual student proceeds step by step in the learning task and cannot go on to more difficult material until he has mastered all the sequential steps for comprehension or application. At each step in the learning process he is given immediate knowledge of results so he will not continue in confusion.

These various patterns of organization for flexibility accommodate easily activities such as those presented in the Suggested Learning Experiences on pp. 234-50. A teacher may select for emphasis several reading skills most needed by the least able readers. In the course of assignments, unit instruction, or group work, the teacher may stress any one of these skills, presenting them only to those who need them and relating them to the larger concerns of reading, whether within school or without. The process is always one of weaving back and forth between the larger whole—the activity, unit, or lesson—and the specific skill on which the pupils' attention is to be temporarily focused. A teacher should not be fearful of stopping the larger activity to improve the skill, a process much like stopping basketball scrimmage long enough to concentrate on some special aspect, such as dribbling.

In selecting skills for emphasis, the teacher is fortunate if his school has studied the reading problem and has developed a guide to the skills to be emphasized throughout each of the six years of secondary education. When such a guide is not available, he must select those skills which appear to have the highest priority for his class.

DIAGNOSING STUDENTS' NEEDS

Whatever method he employs to provide for differences, the teacher needs to know the reading difficulties existing in his classes in order to organize instruction competently. In classes where pupil reading ability varies widely, an approach through multiple materials and differentiated assignments such as has been described represents one possible solution. Other classes present completely different pictures: three very slow readers, third grade, at best, in the midst of thirty-two average and good readers—and in a small school with no other tenth grade class in which to place them; five gifted and nine poor readers in a class supposedly average and grouped homogeneously with the greatest of care; another class with pupils of fairly uniform reading ability. How is the teacher to know? Before sailing off in what may be a wrong direction, he must chart the situation.

In schools where standardized reading or achievement testing programs exist, cumulative folders provide reasonably valuable data. If there are no records or if they tell nothing about reading, the teacher will need to plan some strategy for survey and appraisal. Therefore three aspects of diagnosis will be considered: survey testing; testing to determine more accurately the level of reading ability; and testing to locate the particular disabilities impairing reading efficiency.

Survey testing Survey testing gives the teacher some idea of the reading ability of all his students and forms a springboard for the later study of as many individuals as time permits. For this initial appraisal, either standardized or teacher-made tests are possible.

Standardized tests If the school budget permits, reading achievement tests such as those listed at the close of this chapter should be examined. In making a selection, teachers new to such testing will wish to consult someone with experience—someone in his school, in the county schools' office, or in the state department of education. Local situations vary in this respect; larger schools have guidance personnel whose training includes test selection, whereas smaller schools must depend upon the teacher's knowledge or his contacts with someone whose advice is sound. If there is time to examine a number of survey reading tests, making the final choice will be a valuable learning experience for the teacher.

Standardized reading tests do not tell anything about a pupil's interest in reading or his disposition to read outside the classroom, nor do they measure all the critical and appreciational skills needed for reading literature. But when administered carefully and interpreted sensibly, these objective measuring instruments do improve upon rough estimates, and their norms provide comparisons with larger numbers of pupils throughout the nation. However, it is well to remember that national norms do not provide all the answers one wishes. A school in a slum area cannot usually expect to equal the performance of children in favored socio-economic circumstances; a wealthy suburb may be above the national mean without occupying the position its pupils should and could reach. Because national norms are not the only standards to guide teachers, many school systems keep their own local norms on these standardized tests. Recorded over a period of several years, such norms enable a teacher to know how his pupils perform in relation to the local junior or senior high school population.

Teacher-made tests The teacher may prefer—or lacking funds, find it necessary—to gauge the reading situation through informal testing. Drawing materials from reading planned for the English course, he constructs questions over the paragraphs selected for this purpose. The art of questioning may not be one of a beginning teacher's skills, but he may study models in published materials and first try his own questions on a few selected pupils, using the result as a guide to revision. If care is taken to insure that the questions cover the material which has been taught, a teacher's tests can be valid. Even though they provide no comparison with norms established for large groups of pupils, informal tests of this kind are highly useful.

Whether survey testing is standardized or home made, the secondary school teacher will usually find pupils ranging from very low to exceptionally high reading ability. Numerous surveys of reading in all parts of the country repeat the same spread of achievement and lead to the same conclusion: Pupils need to improve their skills of reading at their own level of development and at their own rate. The evidence also shows that students whose survey tests place them at the same grade level still vary widely in the nature of their reading difficulties.[13] Although the teacher may not have time to retest and diagnose more than a few students in each class, the survey testing will help him choose those in need of further study. The next two sections will consider the retesting of individuals and the locating of particular disabilities.

Retesting individuals In a further analysis of the reasons a student reads poorly, the student's cooperation should be elicited. He should know what is being attempted, but it is enough that he realize the teacher is trying to establish the "level of difficulty" he can handle best. For many a student, it is discouraging to be told he is reading at the "fourth grade," a term associated with

[13] Constance McCullough, "What's Behind the Reading Score?" *Elementary English*, Vol. 30, No. 1 (January 1953).

small children. He is not yet secure enough to handle such information, nor does he know, as the teacher does, that the average reading level in America falls somewhere between the seventh and ninth grades,[14] and that the unfortunate classification of reading abilities by school year grades has occasioned a vast amount of confusion. Fortunately, many of the newer materials are not labeled as to grade level. To improve the pupil's attitude and to avoid unnecessary threats to his self-respect, the teacher should explain the importance of diagnosis. "If you went to a doctor for a health examination, you would not try to mislead him by holding ice in your mouth just before he took your temperature. Here in class I will often try to locate sore spots in your educational anatomy. You will want to help me find them so I can prescribe the right remedies for you."

Once again, having to devise one's own means of individual retesting need be no occasion for regret. The familiarity gained from developing such materials has distinct advantages; insights, hunches, and certainties occur which might become blurred by more regulated procedures. For instance, the teacher may plan an assignment to occupy most members of the class while he works in one part of the room with readers who have measured low in the general testing program. For them he selects materials with the grade level of reading difficulty already established. He may use the SRA *Reading Laboratory*,[15] beginning with the easiest selections, using several in this category before moving on to the next difficulty level. Each brief selection includes comprehension questions. The teacher locates the level at which the pupil reads comfortably with genuine comprehension. To do this it is best to use several selections, including some at grade levels above and below the level located.

Other useful materials similar to those of the SRA *Reading Laboratory* are increasingly available. The *Reader's Digest Reading Skill Builders*[16] and the *Gates-Peardon Practice Exercises in Reading*[17] have been widely used. An oral reading test made up of twelve paragraphs ranging from grades one to eight is Gray's *Standardized Oral Reading Paragraphs*.[18] In using this test, many teachers ask the pupil to examine the paragraphs and to select the one he believes he can read aloud with the best understanding. Thereafter, as a check, the teacher asks the pupil to read a few paragraphs just above and a few just below the selected passage. Although the estimate finally secured

[14] In 1935, William S. Gray and Bernice E. Leary reported a study of 1,690 adults which revealed a mean score of 7.8, an average proficiency in reading equal to the normal expectation of pupils in the eighth month of the seventh grade. *What Makes a Book Readable* (Chicago, U. of Chicago Press, 1935), p. 77. In 1956, Gray reported a later study showing that half of the adult population in this country still reads below the ninth grade level. Of this number, approximately one-third are functionally illiterate, that is, unable to read at the fifth grade level. *Adult Reading*, Part II of the Fifty-fifth Yearbook of the National Society for the Study of Education (Chicago, U. of Chicago Press, 1956), p. 52.

[15] Available, as are all other SRA materials mentioned, from Science Research Associates, 57 West Grand Ave., Chicago 10, Ill.

[16] Available from *Reader's Digest*, Pleasantville, N.Y.

[17] Bureau of Publications, Teachers College, Columbia University.

[18] For data on this and other reading tests, see the list on p. 253.

in this manner may need to be supplemented, it does offer a useful initial appraisal.[19]

Where materials designed specifically for testing are not available, the pupils' level of ability can still be determined through the use of short selections in basic and supplementary readers from the elementary schools. Teachers, having no access to elementary readers or fearing adverse reactions from pupils who might surmise the source of the material, use short books for which the reading level is known. *The Sea Hunt* and *Treasure Under the Sea,* for instance, are books in the Deep-Sea Adventure Series with a second grade level of difficulty. The Cowboy Sam Series reaches down to the primary level. Other titles in the same or similar series may be selected for third, fourth, and higher grades.[20]

Whatever materials are used, the teacher asks the pupil to read until his frustration or loss of comprehension is apparent. If he is reading aloud, the teacher asks questions at the close of each selection to determine whether the pupil is comprehending or merely "barking at print." If he is reading silently, the questioning may, of course, be either oral or written. The number of selections used, the number of occasions the student is tested, and the extent of questioning depend upon the teacher's time and the number of pupils he feels he can help.

All such diagnoses should be tentative. Obviously, the teacher would like to bring to bear upon the problems as much information as possible. However, under the pressure of time, this ideal can be only approximated; what we have described is practicable rather than complete.

Locating particular disabilities Locating the specific reading difficulties underlying poor reading ability involves additional diagnosis. Once again, the English teacher must frequently proceed on his own initiative, without expert help or elaborate apparatus. If such is the situation, he will be wise to select only a few pupils, presumably those in greatest need of help, and begin a search for their particular problems. Using materials similar to those described above, he must provide some means of recording his observations.

Some teachers have found check sheets like this Short Diagnostic Guide both feasible and helpful. They interview informally each pupil chosen for diagnosis and ask him to read aloud and then to read silently. As he reads, they fill out this sheet to the best of their ability. When the reading can

[19] If these materials are too difficult, the teacher resorts to simpler ones. For instance, students below second grade reading level can be so classified by their inability to recognize the 220 words in the *Dolch Sight Vocabulary List* (Edward W. Dolch, Garrard Press, Champaign, Ill.). Some teachers type special sheets of brief sentences in which all the words are easy.

[20] A list of these materials is available in print. See Edward Fry and Warren Johnson, "Booklist for Remedial Reading," *Elementary English,* Vol. 35, No. 6 (October 1958), and the entire issue of *Journal of Education* for December, 1956 (Vol. 139, No. 2). The title of the issue is "High Interest–Low Vocabulary Reading Materials, A Selected Booklist," by Helen Blair Sullivan and Lorraine E. Tolman. Even more recent is *Aids for Selecting Books for Slow Readers,* American Library Assn., Chicago, 1959.

be taped, repeated listening has revealed weaknesses not noticed in the initial observation. Later, on the basis of what has been gleaned from several diagnostic sessions, the teacher makes tentative plans for helping the pupil. These check sheets show that poor reading is almost always a result of multiple causes. Single causation and simple solutions, apparently, have nothing to do with reading.

SHORT DIAGNOSTIC GUIDE

Based on oral and silent reading sessions

Name______________________________ Date________________

Word attack and word analysis	*Does use*	*Does not use*	*Comment or example*
Context clues			
Vowels and vowel combinations			
Consonants			
Blending (fl-, br-, -tch, etc.)			
Guessing			
Use of syllables			

	Knows	*Does not know*	*Knows partly*	*Comment*
Letter names and sounds				
Prefixes, suffixes, roots				
Sight vocabulary (Use about 200 words like *boy, home, see,* etc.)				

Problems	*Difficulty*	*No Difficulty*	*Comment*
Repeats words			
Reverses words, substitutes or omits words, becomes confused			
Reverses letters, confuses, substitutes, or omits letters			
Does not think of whole sentence meaning while reading (voice betrays "word calling")			
Cannot handle three-syllable words			
Does not isolate and recognize units of thought (phrases, clauses, sentences); does not use punctuation			
Vocalizes, moves lips, during silent reading			
Reads too fast for comprehension			
Very slow rate			

Eye movement	
Finger pointing and/or head movements	Often______ Sometimes______ Rarely______
Eye-voice span	Satisfactory________ Unsatisfactory________
Loses place	Often______ Sometimes______ Rarely______
Voice problems	
Speech defects	Sounds________________________
Enunciation	Satisfactory________ Unsatisfactory________
Voice control	Satisfactory________ Unsatisfactory________
Eyes (Is there a recent test showing normal vision?)	
Hearing (If audiometer testing is not available, try speaking to pupil in a low voice.)	
Any indication of emotional difficulties or poor social adjustment	
Intelligence Quotients *	

* Several are better than one. Scores on the *Wechsler-Bellevue Intelligence Scale* are particularly helpful.

For a thorough diagnosis in schools where money is available, the *Diagnostic Reading Tests* (see p. 252) may be recommended. The survey section measures more than short paragraphs. It presents some material that continues long enough for readers to establish a pace of reading and to encounter relationships among ideas. It also presents material from texts in literature, science, and social science. Four other parts provide for detailed study of individuals whose reading skills are poor as indicated by their scores on the general survey. The last of these four sections diagnoses word attack both in oral reading of paragraphs ranging from third to twelfth grade in difficulty and in silent reading that searches for weaknesses in phonics, syllabication, and other fundamental techniques. Teachers interested in improving their informal diagnoses of individual reading might ask their schools to purchase several of these diagnostic tests for evaluative trial. On the basis of this tentative use, a teacher can decide whether or not these long and somewhat expensive aids are feasible for his purposes.

Because a single session may be deceptive, a teacher should plan diagnosis for a series of occasions. The child's physical condition or mood on any one day may be responsible for an erroneous impression. Spreading diagnostic sessions over a period of time not only results in more accurate data but avoids discouraging pupils at the beginning of the school year, making them feel even less competent than they are.

Although the methods described here lack the thoroughness of ideal diagnosis, they will help teachers locate the reading levels and problems of pupils in distress. Skill to do will come with doing, and if a little knowledge is a dangerous thing, the teacher can comfort himself with Huxley's reaction, "Where is the man who has so much knowledge as to be out of danger?"

READING IN ALL SUBJECTS

English teachers need to be wary of the assumption that improvement of reading is the sole responsibility of the English department. To be sure, general reading ability and achievement in subjects like science and social studies are positively related, even when intelligence is constant.[21] But this does not imply that teachers in subjects other than English may relax responsibility for teaching reading. Reading in the various disciplines requires more than general reading ability.

The issue is not one of saving time and effort for English teachers but rather one of placing reading instruction where it will be most effective. The nature of reading content heavily influences the way students must read; thus, the various reading skills require different emphases in different subjects. From research we know that competent readers learn readily to adjust their rate of reading to varied levels of difficulty and that in certain fields like science and mathematics, students who slow down and read carefully are higher achievers than those who do not.[22] Specific reading instruction in each subject is therefore essential if students are to apply general reading skills to the requirements of different subject disciplines.

Organizing a school-wide reading program is a complex strategy. In approaching the problem, English teachers must be tactful; it is easy to antagonize busy instructors of science or homemaking by seeming to imply that they are not fulfilling all their responsibilities. However, when signs of interest are noted, colleagues may be encouraged to consider what might be done about the reading problem. For instance, teachers of English may recommend that all teachers check their texts for vocabulary not included in the first 5,000 words of the Thorndike and Lorge list of words classified according to frequency of use.[23] A *dart* in home economics is very different from a *dart* in physical education; simple words like *source* and *correspond* trouble many readers in history; *bisect* and *integer* often remain vague in the minds of pupils having difficulty in mathematics. Teachers who take time to establish vocabu-

[21] Esther J. Swenson, "A Study of the Relationships among Various Types of Reading Scores on General and Science Material," *Journal of Educational Research,* Vol. 36, No. 2 (October 1942); A. Sterl Artley, "A Study of Certain Relationships between General Reading Comprehension and Reading Comprehension in a Specific Subject-matter Area," *Journal of Educational Research,* Vol. 37, No. 6 (February 1944); William E. Young, "Recent Research on Reading in the Social Studies," *Education,* Vol. 62, No. 1 (September 1941).

[22] Blommers and Lindquist, "Rate of Comprehension of Reading: Its Measurement and Its Relation to Comprehension," *Journal of Educational Psychology,* Vol. 35, No. 8 (November 1944); Eva Bond, *Reading and Ninth-Grade Achievement,* Teachers College Contributions to Education, No. 756 (N.Y., Columbia U. Press, 1938), pp. x, 62.

[23] E. L. Thorndike and I. Lorge, *The Teacher's Word Book of 30,000 Words* (N.Y., Teachers College Bureau of Publications, Columbia University, 1944).

lary pertinent to their own subject fields reap a harvest of greater satisfaction and pupil achievement.[24]

Inservice education enrolling one or more teachers from different departments has some advantages; involvement of the entire staff secures even better results. Some secondary schools have featured reading instruction in meetings and bulletins, with many applications to classroom instruction and evaluation. Some of these programs have lasted for a year, others even longer. Librarians have often aided teachers in encouraging students to extend their reading in special subject fields: *The Wonderful World of Mathematics* might be recommended by the teacher of general mathematics; *Lou Gehrig, A Quiet Hero,* by the coach; *Blueberry Muffin* or *Linda Takes Over,* for some non-gifted homemaking student; and *No Other White Men,* a carefully documented account of the American past, for some interested seventh grade pupil.

Where the entire faculty is not yet ready for a school-wide reading program, English teachers may sometimes take the initiative in discussing the matter with administrators. In one district, the administrators of the secondary schools organized a series of meetings devoted to reading. At the first session, one teacher discussed reading in the content fields and passed out this statement:

Every Teacher Teaches Reading

You are already teaching reading

if you teach your students how to use the textbooks in your class by discussing the title, the table of contents, the subject headings, and the index. Do you do this?

if you use the study part of the hour to analyze various levels of reading ability, to locate slow learners and those having difficulty understanding the meaning. Do you do this?

if you select textbooks that are not too difficult for most of the students in your class. Do you do this?

if you assign an article or a section in a book and give a certain number of guide questions to direct the students' understanding of the subject matter content. Do you do this?

If you show by your assignments when you expect the students to skim, scan, analyze, or read for details. Do you do this?

if you require students to summarize content. Do you do this?

if you ask students to outline in such a way as will cause them to select the important from the unimportant. Do you do this?

if you encourage students to read about your subject for their leisure time reading. Do you do this?

The following year all secondary teachers in this district considered the reading problem in a series of meetings. Lists of reading skills and teaching methods for each subject were developed, and many teachers read these three pamphlets:

[24] Hemphill Reid, "Improving Linguistic Ability as a Factor in Solving Problems in Algebra," in Kansas Studies in Education Series, *Abstracts of Doctoral Dissertations in Education,* Vol. 2, No. 6 (Lawrence, Kansas, U. of Kansas Publications, 1941).

Five Steps to Reading Success in Science, Social Studies, and Mathematics. (Metropolitan Study Council, New York, 27, N.Y.)

Teaching Reading in the High School. Kansas Studies in Education, Vol. 10, No. 1 (February 1960), University of Kansas, Lawrence.

Improving Reading in the Junior High School, edited by Arno Jewett. Health, Education, and Welfare Dept., Education Office Bulletin 1957, No. 10, Washington, D.C.

There are many ways to help all teachers realize how the reading problem transcends instruction in English. Whatever can be done to widen the base of concern about reading will improve the quality of the total instructional program.

READING IN SPECIAL CLASSES

Slow learners reading as well as they can be expected to read, gifted pupils indifferent to the realms of gold, reluctant readers linking reading with all that is repulsive about schools, retarded readers whose inadequate skills do not match their good native ability, students with emotional, physical, or social problems—not infrequently the reading problem becomes more than an individual teacher can solve. Some strategy, more direct than classroom modification, is demanded. What are the possibilities of remedial classes? Special provision for gifted readers? Electives designed for developmental or recreational reading? Reading laboratories for a variety of problem readers? English teachers cannot be expected to provide the services of reading specialists, but often in curriculum development they are expected to play a major role in deciding school policy on special classes in reading.

Unless special reading classes are part of a *coherent* plan for the entire school, they seldom succeed. Unless they have status with students, their success is almost always doubtful. They are most likely to justify their existence whenever their addition to the curriculum has not been ill-conceived or hasty. If they are considered dumping grounds for problem pupils or slow learners, the strategy fails. If, after a semester or a year of drill, the "remedied" pupils return to inflexible classroom situations like those which contributed heavily to their reading misfortunes, the strategy fails. The value of special reading classes can usually be determined by the answer to a single question: Do the students in these classes view them as an opportunity or a cross to be borne?

Attitude important Most poor readers require, before anything else, a primary revision in attitude. Defeated and discouraged, they have learned to protect their egos by adopting either ingenious substitutes for reading or attitudes of indifference. Not infrequently they insist they don't need to read. Special teachers keep a handy list of reading necessary in typical vocations—signs, questions required for drivers' licenses, the state vehicle code, and notices of general import such as those in public buildings. All people in our highly organized civilization require reasonable reading competence in their profession, to say nothing of their need as citizens or as individuals seeking the good life and avoiding exploitation by unscrupulous persons.

Every outwardly defiant non-reader needs the support of a teacher who believes in his ability to learn to read with reasonable competence, a teacher who is sincerely willing to help him. However, priority lists of patients are often necessary, based on considerations of greatest need and greatest response to therapy. Like one of Dickens' characters, the teacher who accomplishes anything in reading must have affection beaming in one eye and calculation shining out of the other.

Laboratory for retarded readers For those students who can profit from remedial instruction, one approach is a reading laboratory, a room fitted with a number of varied practice areas:

At one table, many word games, phrase cards, phonic wheels, and sight-word cards

At another table, the SRA *Reading Laboratory* with its selections varied in difficulty and its keys to the comprehension questions

In several booths, accelerators [25] (the one reading machine a school with limited funds might consider) and Controlled Reader, if funds permit

On one table, a tape recorder and several audographs [26] ready with plastic discs

Copies of skills workbooks, like the SRA *Better Reading Books* and the *Gates-Peardon Practice Exercises in Reading*, stacked upon a desk ready to be passed out

Present in abundance, copies of *Read,*[27] *Scholastic,*[28] *Hot Rod,*[29] *Reader's Digest Skill Builders,* SRA *Life Adjustment Booklets,* vocabulary books like *Word Wealth,*[30] and up-to-date booklets on vocations.

On the teacher's desk, a copy of *Fare for the Reluctant Reader* [31] and *Book Bait,*[32] and to assist him in this book-bait angling, a classroom library of at least one hundred appealing books with colorful covers—ranging from the simple *River Ranch* to *The Pearl.*

Within this realm, the teacher moves about from groups to individuals, helping them carry out plans organized at the beginning of the period. On some days the entire class works together on skills needed in common; on others, individuals and groups work on the specific skills they need. On some days the teacher reads aloud while the pupils follow with their eyes; on others, every pupil is reading a different book chosen from the voluntary reading library. With classes of fifteen and careful budgeting of each class period so that everyone knows what he is to accomplish, a reading teacher can usually

[25] Also available from Science Research Associates. (See note 15.)

[26] Audographs are sold by Gray Audographs, 445 Bellevue Ave., Oakland, Calif.

[27] *Read,* American Educational Publications, 1250 Fairwood Ave., Columbus, Ohio.

[28] *Scholastic* magazine, Scholastic Corporation, 33 W. 42nd St., New York 36, N.Y.

[29] *Hot Rod* magazine, Petersen Publishing Co., 5959 Hollywood Blvd., Los Angeles 28, Calif.

[30] Ward S. Miller, *Word Wealth* (N.Y., Holt, 1958).

[31] Anita Dunn, et al., *Fare for the Reluctant Reader* (Albany, State U. of N.Y., 1952).

[32] Elinor Walker, ed., *Book Bait* (Chicago, American Library Assn., 1957).

salvage more than eighty per cent of the remedial cases who attend for a single half year.

The only students who belong in these remedial reading classes are those whose reading skill is markedly below their intelligence quotients or teachers' estimates of their native intelligence. Customarily, the reading ability is two or more years behind measured or estimated native ability. Such students—and only such students—are capable of being "remedied"; the term *remedial* is misused when applied to classes for students of low mental ability who are probably already standing on tiptoe in reading achievement. To press and harass students who are reading as best they can, albeit not at their chronological grade level, is to raise false hopes for child, home, and other teachers.

Special classes for the gifted All gifted children need two kinds of experience: association with all kinds of children in common endeavors, and association with other able minds in special pursuits. In many schools the policy will be to handle the able pupils in subgroups and in individual projects which offer special enrichment. Indeed, in smaller schools with no more than three or four exceptional pupils, special classes are not feasible, and plans for grouping able pupils must cut across chronological and grade-level barriers. Some schools offer electives in drama, journalism, and creative writing, and in the future many schools will probably offer several courses in English, among which students with varying abilities and talents will make guided choices.

A number of emphases deserve attention in these special classes, or in regular classes where gifted pupils form occasional subgroups. Listed below are typical approaches teachers have used successfully:

Research projects on topics that interest pupils. The witchcraft trials of Salem eventuate in a study of superstition and the psychology of creating scapegoats; the battle strategy of modern warfare leads to the reading of *War and Peace* with its ultimate discussion of determinism in history and freedom of the will in personal living. Gifted pupils enjoy reaching generalizations and are able to distill the philosophical or empirical essence of a vast amount of difficult reading.

Library use. Gifted readers, especially, need to spend much time in libraries, exploring the resources and learning how to locate material pertinent to their interests or projects. They like to use the two-volume *Syntopicon*, the dictionary of ideas that accompanies the set of fifty-four *Great Books of the Western World*, published by the Encyclopaedia Britannica.

Decision making. Direct teaching of the bases for making choices is possible with these students. With teacher guidance through the discussion of the choices and value systems of people in novels and biographies, gifted readers may be brought to see the differences between decisions based on whim, custom, authority, and rational choice.[33]

Drill to increase reading rate without loss of comprehension. Gifted pupils sometimes read more slowly than necessary. Lacking challenge, a good reader can gravitate to a slower reading rate. With or without machines like the Controlled

[33] Teachers will find very helpful the symposium on making choices in the *California Journal of Secondary Education*, Vol. 33, No. 4 (April 1958).

Reader and the accelerator, he can be taught to read more rapidly, to slow down on difficult important content, and to skim or skip the trivial or examples illuminating generalizations already grasped.

Experience with a variety of reading. Instruction in the reading of poetry, drama, satire, humor, science, history, and mathematics pays dividends with these readers. Literary criticism and polemics of all kinds elicit their complex, discriminating response.

For junior high school pupils, reading and evaluating Newbery medal award books and each year's near winners of the award.[34]

Special teachers for non-readers What can be done for those pupils who, although in the junior or senior high school, classify as non-readers? Tragic though it is that some could have benefited from help received earlier, their problem must be faced when it arises in the seventh or eighth grades. A special teacher, familiar with reading problems, should work with these pupils. For cases whose causes are not primarily emotional or physical, techniques and methods must be adapted from the primary grades. The pupils will dictate short simple stories about matters close to their interests, stories the special teacher will type or print as the basis for each pupil's reading. These "experience stories" need to be supplemented by the use of sight-phrase cards, picture-word games, and basic-sight cards such as those included in the Dolch materials.

Usually word recognition through phonics must be added to sight recognition and meaningful association with experience. Like word games, helpful phonetic word wheels, phonetic drill cards, and phonics games may be purchased. Of course, when these devices are taught as drills bearing no relation to meaningful reading passages, they fail to achieve their purpose. Other helpful materials are booklets and materials prepared for adults learning English for the first time. Particularly useful have been *English Through Pictures* by I. A. Richards and Christine Gibson[35] and the Deep Sea Adventure Series.

Special classes do have their place, since reading is stressed so heavily in contemporary education, and every possibility to improve it must be employed. Although English teachers may not teach these special classes, they need to be more informed about them than most teachers.

Suggested Learning Experiences

Recognizing that reading and thinking cannot be separated, the teacher of English does not expect infallible recipes to improve comprehension. As best he can, he selects classroom activities, similar to those suggested here, in the light of what is known about learning. A teacher must place theoretical concerns central in his viewpoint; rather than blindly accepting techniques, he must create procedures consistent with his own philosophy and

[34] Information on Newbery Medal awards may be secured from the Children's Division, American Library Association, Chicago, Ill.

[35] N.Y., Pocket Books, 1954.

theories of learning. He must assess procedures such as are recommended here, adopt and adapt those which he approves, and devise more of his own.

To improve vocabulary

An English writer, discussing the schools of Britain, regrets that many teachers do not realize that words are of less importance than ideas, that a stock of words is of little value unless one knows how to use them. "Yet the practice still exists among teachers of aiming at the enlargement of vocabulary by means of formal exercises, as though such enlargement were in itself of value. It is the mind that needs enlargement. The enrichment and illumination of experience by observation and discussion is a surer way to the genuine enlargement of vocabulary than can be secured by concentration on formal exercises in the correct use of words the need for which is not personally felt." [36] The following suggestions for vocabulary development are intended to encourage interesting excursions into *thought.* They accept the plausible truth that the meaning of a word like *mango* is more likely to persist if one has picked and eaten a mango, and that similar forces are involved in comprehending such concepts as *bland* and *stolid.* Successful vocabulary study—growth that is retained—rests ultimately on enlargement of experience.

■ *Extend vocabulary lessons over an entire term*

Spaced vocabulary discussions, recurring throughout the school year, succeed better than concentrated attack. The ultimate aim, to develop an interest in words, becomes firmly fixed only if the teacher himself is intrigued by language and words. Vocabulary discussions often arise spontaneously: "He was hurt to the quick." Now, where is the quick? "She was left in the lurch." What an odd expression! Where do you suppose the lurch is? How could such an expression have originated? What do you mean, he was in the pink of condition? Can you say a word over and over until you divest it of all meaning? Thinking only of its sound, say *shrub* or *cellar door* until you begin to hear it as it must sound to a Dane or Samoan hearing English for the first time. (Frenchmen have been known to say that *cellar door* has a charming sound.) Ideally, every teacher should have the poet's combination of exuberance and exactitude with words. But even if he is not Keats or Tennyson, a teacher interested in language may still acquire enough zest to embroider planned instruction with many an interesting spontaneous excursion.

Vocabulary lessons, like lessons in other skills of reading, may be both incidental and planned. Whole-part-whole learning means that an activity may be stopped at appropriate points for concentration on a skill. Then the ongoing experience starts up once again with the application of the skill as a part of the whole situation. Procedures for dealing with vocabulary, here and in the succeeding suggestions, are not intended to be taught as ends in themselves. Their proper use occurs as parts of some larger whole—a lesson, an activity, a unit—to which they belong, like individual tiles in a patterned mosaic.

■ *Urge a balance between using context and dictionary*

Point out that one of the purposes of vocabulary study is to acquire flexibility in the approach used in acquiring new words. One important way competent readers

[36] A. F. Watts, *The Language and Mental Development of Children* (Boston, Heath, 1947), p. 58.

learn a word is by context.[37] Make clear the importance of balance: Learning all words by context is certain to promote sloppiness and fuzziness; likewise resorting to the dictionary for every unfamiliar word is as foolish as it is time-consuming.

■ *Vary the approach*

Listed here are a few of the many facets of word study, all deserving exploration during the school year. They should be distributed over a semester or year rather than grouped as a single unit. Sometimes they may be related to an assignment or a reading lesson; at others, the teacher may introduce one of them for special focus in its own right. Brief but pleasant, they often serve to fill in the extra ten minutes at the close of some class hour or to take the chill off Monday morning before settling down to the major plans of the week. The ideas suggested here might be used as teacher reminders. During the course of a semester, a teacher could check off each as it is used, adding others not listed here, making certain of interest and variety.

Interesting word origins Give students a list like the following, only longer, and commend those who find the origin of the greatest number: curfew, tantalize, tawdry, bedlam, sardonic, sinister.

Malapropisms The bride's guardian gave her a new torso. He took two cigars from his cuspidor and gave one to me. They went to Mexico to photograph a total collapse of the sun.

Words with multiple meanings: moor, run, slip, bank, crop.

Word structure Prefixes, roots, and suffixes related to words frequently used, such as portage, porter, report, import, deport, export, portmanteau; or to words whose spelling will be made easier, such as *accommodate.*

Words whose meanings have shifted: villain, knave, silly.

Place names Begin with Stewart's *Names on the Land* [38] and extend to your own locality and state.

Subject matter words Group students according to interests and have them report on the meanings and origins of interesting words in subject matter fields: republic, soviet, fascist, and isolationist in social studies; similar words in chemistry, astronomy, mathematics, biology, shop, and homemaking.

Connotation and denotation The meaning of winter to a Hawaiian, to an Alaskan; the association of names for cars (The Riviera Townsman), housing developments (Oak Manor), fabrics (Allure), motels (The Townhouse).

Snarl words and *purr words* My wife is stubborn but I am firm of will? She is skinny or slim or svelte? [39]

Language and prejudice The use of names intended to hurt or belittle other groups: kraut, kike, wop, greaser.

Idioms Be on hand, see a thing through, try your hand at this.

Games For instance, this game of homonyms: Supply the correct sets of homonyms for these definitions:

1. (a) no (b) cry of a horse (nay, neigh)

[37] Constance McCullough, "Learning to Use Context Clues," *Elementary English Review*, Vol. 20, No. 4 (April 1943).

[38] George Stewart, *Names on the Land* (Boston, Houghton Mifflin, 1958).

[39] S. I. Hayakawa, *Language in Thought and Action* (N.Y., Harcourt, Brace, 1949), contains many other examples like this one, and countless ideas for use in studying words.

2. (a) guided (b) a metal (led, lead)
3. (a) female sheep (b) evergreen tree (ewe, yew)

Word sources Words deriving from Arabic like sherbet, zero, algebra, almanac; words from music: rhapsody, oboe, concerto, symphony; words from the sea: scuttlebutt, bosun, gunwale; words from mythology: jovial, martial, echo, cereal, plutocrat, atlas, Wednesday.

Abstract and concrete words Courage, democracy, scarlet tanager.

Word immigrants List words in English borrowed from other languages; make a world word map.

Imaginative comparisons Begin with common usage like iron will, shadowing a suspect, a bitter disappointment; next consider more imaginative comparisons like "The snows of moonlight came drifting on the town." Concentrate on the aptness of comparison, not on terminology. Continue on to other imaginative, fresh comparisons.

Synonyms, antonyms, heteronyms, and homonyms Stress not only the likenesses but also the differences in synonyms. In what contexts would ominous, sinister, and portentous be appropriate?

Phonetic analysis of words Emphasize long and short vowels and the blending of letters.

Crossword puzzles Students can be taught to devise these.

Onomotopoeic words Murmur, tinkle, growl, whisper, rattle, click.

Words not common in speech but often encountered in reading Stolid, bland, alacrity, myriads, resplendent.

Slang, its use and misuse

■ *Use films*

Several films feature the uses and values of a superior vocabulary. Some of these might be made part of the year's plan for conquering the English language: "Build Your Vocabulary," "Do Words Ever Fool You?" "Words: Their Origin, Use, and Spelling." Each year other films and audio-visual aids appear.

■ *Replace colorless verbs*

Write on the chalkboard sentences like the following:

The gang of boys *went* down to the lake to swim.

The strange man *walked* across the street.

Ask students to find replacements for the verbs. For *went,* more vigorous verbs like *dashed, sprinted, raced,* or *streaked* might be suggested. Students may think of *ambled, lurched, strolled, dawdled, sauntered, trudged,* and *shuffled* to replace *walked.* Junior high pupils should volunteer to imitate these various ways of walking, noting contrasts and similarities.

■ *Plan an experience to develop new concepts and therefore new vocabulary*

1. If the class can visit any unusual place—a naval ship, a tannery, or a museum of science and industry—the excursion may become a base for "enlarging the mind" through new concepts to be discussed afterwards. The teacher should, of course, prepare students for the experience, helping them identify these new concepts and discover words to express them. This "growing edge" expands most rapidly and permanently when students consciously realize they are to be alert to certain features of the forthcoming excursion.

2. The same advantages and the same principles of method apply to any planned use of television, films, and recordings.

■. *Use direct instruction and specific practice*

None of the emphasis on motivation, experience, or spontaneity is intended to diminish respect for planned lessons in vocabulary study. One research study of developing meaning vocabularies in reading [40] found such direct planned study more effective than incidental methods, and more effective for those with inferior native abilities than for superior pupils. Books like the following may be used effectively in planned vocabulary study:

Frieda Radke, *Living Words* (N.Y., Odyssey, 1940), and *Word Resources* (N.Y., Odyssey, 1955); Charles E. Funk, *Thereby Hangs a Tale* (N.Y., Harper, 1950); Margaret S. Ernst, *More About Words* (N.Y., Knopf, 1951); Henry L. Christ, *Winning Words* (Boston, Heath, 1948); Joseph T. Shipley, *A Dictionary of Word Origins* (N.Y., Philosophical Library, 1945); and Lee C. Deighton, *Vocabulary Development in the Classroom* (N.Y., Teachers' College, Columbia University, 1959).

There are other good texts, not listed here, and during this last half of the twentieth century, many more will come from the presses. A vocabulary text, imaginative and well organized, can be a most useful adjunct to the teacher's aims, saving valuable time for other planning.

2. Many teachers devise programs of individual pupil vocabulary lists. They help pupils set up forms for recording new words encountered in reading. As they read, the pupils check unfamiliar or vaguely understood words. They then copy each word and enough of its context to make possible a suitable dictionary definition. For instance, the opening page of one student's notebook might read like this:

Words I Have Subjugated (I have vanquished, drubbed, surmounted, and gained ascendancy over these words.)

from "The Heathen," by Jack London

stolid "The natives fell into a condition of dumb, *stolid* fear." dull, impassive, showing no emotion.

dissipate "The hurricane will *dissipate* the . . . horde (of sharks)." scatter, disperse.

Student diligence in persisting with these vocabulary lists may be considerably bolstered by teachers who inspect the lists, commend them, and use the inspection as one element in grading pupil effort. If these individual vocabulary lists are to succeed, the teacher must help students initiate the project and establish the form. Students do not always understand the importance of including the context, and they may also need instruction featuring sound judgment in selecting appropriate dictionary definitions. Although such matters seem obvious to adults, many students have not yet reached this level of sophistication. At some point they must learn

[40] William S. Gray and Eleanor Holmes, *The Development of Meaning Vocabularies in Reading: An Experimental Study*, Publications of the Laboratory Schools of the University of Chicago, No. 6 (Chicago, U. of Chicago Press, 1938). Although this study uses subjects in the intermediate grades, experiences with junior high pupils and slow senior high pupils indicate its implications are also valid for adolescent learners.

that words do not have a single, pushbutton meaning. *Dissipate,* in the exercise above, is a good example of this versatility in words; the dictionary definition *squander* will not suffice. Ask students why it is wise to avoid learning words in isolation. Although they will not know the psychology of learning or Thorndike's Law of Meaningfulness, some of them may be able to explain that we learn the meanings of new words by associating experience with them.

To see relationships

Vocabulary growth alone will not solve the reading problem. Even though the teacher has clearly underscored the fact that word meanings vary with context, many students still hope to read sentences and paragraphs as if they were constructed like parts of a toy erector set. But language, subtle and resilient, eludes such rigid molds. Reading requires accurate recognition of words; it also necessitates fusing words into larger patterns of related thought. As Thorndike has pointed out, such processes of thought require selecting, repressing, emphasizing, and organizing. Comprehension demands a dynamic balance of all the elements in a passage.

■ *Emphasize relationships of words within sentences and passages*

1. Have someone play a familiar melody on the piano or other instrument, deliberately ignoring the musical phrasing. Every note is played as if it were completely unrelated to all the others. The teacher, or a selected student, then performs a parallel mechanical reading of a passage in a book available to everyone. Reading aloud, the performer ignores punctuation, makes no attempt to group words by cadence or meaning, and avoids all such aids as stress on key words or contrast for qualifying or parenthetical elements. The demonstration concludes with meaningful performances of both the music and the prose passage. Class discussion, followed by practice, both oral and silent, completes the sequence. Such exercises need to be pointed toward the reading to be done in English, in other courses, and in adult life. The teacher chooses prose in which the content is relatively appealing to the majority, and he also asks, "Where now and in adult life will you use these skills?"

2. Place on the chalkboard sentences similar to this model:

Yes, we're going to the bowling alley however
if
nevertheless
after
although
and
but

Discussion and completion of the sentences should illuminate the ways that relationships are expressed.

3. In sentences prepared by the teacher practice inserting the missing transition words, finding the word that spoils a sentence, finding the phrase or clause that is out of place in a sentence, and finding the sentence that is out of place in a paragraph.

4. For slow learning classes, prepare a study guide stating the essential meaning of passages in selections being read by the class. Knowing in advance the general import of the passage, poor readers often show more confidence in reading aloud the segment when they locate it. An example, for an eighth grade class:

Find the passages that show:
Bertie was uncertain of himself.
Bertie was *not* a thin boy—far from it!
Bertie liked Marcia Dale better than Hyacinth.

By having pupils read aloud the passage they locate, the teacher may emphasize careful reading and call attention to the weight of various words and the relationships among them.

On a more mature level, the same type of exercise can be used for poor readers. For a novel (in this case, *Silas Marner*), an example is:

Find and read aloud the passage (or passages) that tell us:
Dunstan had no sympathy for other people.
Molly Farran evades responsibility by transferring it to others.

Such exercises give teachers many opportunities to point up the importance of vigilance, of being alert to every word in a passage, and of screening the various words, phrases, and sentences against the total meaning. With the average adolescent reader the influence of context and the importance of relationships cannot be stressed too often. Carelessness and awkwardness of performance need frequent attention in every learning situation.

5. In the junior high school, research has shown, typical comprehension difficulties arise from failure to see relationships—failure, for instance, to see parts of sentences against the total context.[41] Eighth grade pupils have a tendency to disregard or misconstrue certain parts of the sentence, such as the initial phrase in "*Aside from the fireplace,* the candle was the chief source of light." Many of them also consider the reading process as merely verbalizing words regardless of meaning. They need to suppress previous knowledge having no application to the reading at hand, and they need sensitivity to the structures of language. Methods such as we have described are intended to help such pupils rise above the mechanical concept of reading, to see reading as reasoning, and to make vocabulary growth a permanent gain.

In teaching sentence relationships, the teacher may sometimes stop in the reading of a selection to analyze its sentences and paragraphs. What is the significance of this word or this phrase to the meaning of this passage? Is there any plan by which this paragraph has been put together? Is any sentence the topic of the paragraph? Which sentences are examples? Which add significant details? What word is likely to mislead the reader if he doesn't take into account the rest of the sentence? What inappropriate association might the reader bring to this phrase if he isn't alert? Occasional halts to stress the need for careful reading can be highly effective. Particularly is this true when the analyses are means to understanding selections in which the students' interest is wholehearted.

Caution: The effectiveness of direct methods like those described above depends upon motivation. Unless a student sees the value of what he is doing, unless his will is involved, the impact of all such instruction is negligible. The teacher must often ask, "Why are we doing this, class? Who can remind us?"

[41] J. C. Dewey, "A Case Study of Reading Comprehension Difficulties in American History," University of Iowa Studies in Education III, Vol. 10, No. 1 (1935).

■ *Encourage flexibility of interpretation*

Let the teacher ask himself, "Am I doing anything to encourage that suppleness of mind, that freedom from rigid snap decisions, which counts for so much in reading skill? What can I do to help these students become impressed with the enormous importance of a tentative hovering above *all the elements* in a sentence or paragraph, of modifying and shifting perspective in a highly complex equilibrium of all the forces involved in a passage?"

One effective method, developed by Werner and Kaplan,[42] interests students because they first view it as a game. However, its value transcends this initial appeal, and through the technique of artificial words a teacher may demonstrate to students the need for an alert and resilient response to all reading. The teacher presents students with sets of six or more sentences, each one containing the same artificial word, and each one contributing an additional clue to correct interpretation.

It was only seven, but the light was *soldeving.*
We felt unsafe because the road seemed to *soldeve* into the foggy dimness.
The older it gets, the sooner it will begin to *soldeve.*
People like a bright flower better than one that is *soldeved.*
Putting the dress on the sunny lawn made the color of the cloth *soldeve.*
"Old soldiers never die, they just *soldeve* away."

Each teacher will develop his own collection suited to concepts within his pupils' range of understanding. He will soon discover that some pupils fix upon a certain meaning—such as *bad* or *dawning* in the first sentence above—and then cling tenaciously to that concept despite all the evidence, in subsequent sentences, that *bad* or *dawning* are erroneous. These pupils need to become less desperately "certain." Often they need help in becoming more secure, both in the classroom and in all of their school experiences. Through such help they may become readers who can reason and adapt, who do not expect words to perform like player pianos.

■ *Keep individual charts of improvement in comprehension*

Although slow learners respond especially well to this method, most human beings show a pleasure in charting their own progress on any skill. The charts, kept in individual notebooks or folders, may represent the per cent of comprehension questions answered correctly on a series of reading materials. Whatever variations may characterize the method, the one essential is the integrity of the comprehension questions. They must measure understanding of *significant* content and the relation of parts of a passage to each other and to the whole. Both students and teacher should discuss frequently what is important to notice and remember in a given selection, and how the selection is organized. Very often the comprehension questions should measure pupil ability to correlate several parts of a reading selection or to see how a writer's purpose leads him to include or exclude certain things.

[42] Heinz Werner and Edith Kaplan, "Development of Word Meaning through Verbal Context: An Experimental Study," *Journal of Psychology,* Vol. 29, No. 2 (April 1950); and *The Acquisition of Word Meanings* (Evanston, Ill., Child Development Publications, 1952). The exercise described here is adapted from those in this research. See the unit "Power Over Language," p. 165, and Chapter 2, p. 101, for other suggestions for classroom use of this method.

■ *Distinguish between main and supporting ideas in paragraphs*

1. Whereas successful readers effortlessly recognize degrees of potency in words and sentences, others read as if every word were of equal importance. For the latter, instruction in differential "loading" is necessary. The teacher may demonstrate by reading passages aloud twice; the first time in a voice which grants equal significance to every word and sentence; the second time, overemphasizing the difference between major and subordinate elements. After such a demonstration, the practice must be transferred to the students, and the lesson may conclude with their own generalizations written on the chalk board.

2. Choose from an assignment or unit a passage in which the author has effectively subordinated some ideas to others. Rewrite the passage, blurring the distinctions between important and subordinate elements. An effective way to do this is to change subordinate clauses into main clauses; shift principal ideas into phrases or dependent clauses; flatten emphasis through coordination rather than subordination. Present both passages for discussion and evaluation. Focus on this question: Which passage does the better job of emphasizing important ideas?

3. From current classroom reading, select well-constructed paragraphs exemplifying the use of topic sentences. The sentences are then rearranged indiscriminately and senior typists prepare them for class use. Students rehabilitate the "deranged paragraphs." Retention of specific lessons like this will, however, be slight unless the lesson is linked to something larger—reading that has interest or significance for the learner.

4. Not every paragraph, even in writing of acknowledged merit, exemplifies the classic sequence of generalization, detail, and summary. Since paragraphs vary enormously, teachers will avoid exclusive attention to the classic model with a topic sentence near the very beginning. Nevertheless a realistic study of actual paragraphs will sharpen students' awareness of the importance of unity and coherence. Key words and topic sentences will occur often enough for useful instruction. Students may be set to searching for a set of "prize-winning paragraphs." Each pupil copies his choice of a model paragraph and beneath it states his reasons for admiring it. An able student or committee may be assigned to cull the best of these contributions and fit them into a notebook for future use as models. Where opaque projectors are available, a teacher may project several paragraphs for reading and commendation. Some of the best should be drawn from students' voluntary reading of non-fiction and from current magazines.

■ *Employ the SQ3R method*

Some students like the security of a definite technique, such as the SQ3R method:[43] Survey the material, *Q*uestion the material, *R*ead, *R*ecite, and *R*eview. There is a memory-sticking rhythm to the abbreviation, and if pupils do not view the five steps as an easy and infallible formula for solving reading difficulties, the behaviors fostered by the method can be beneficial. Using several kinds of material, the teacher demonstrates how to emphasize *relationships.* Students often need help in seeing that *why* is often a more important question than what, when, or who.

[43] For a comprehensive discussion of this method by its originator, see Francis P. Robinson, *Effective Study* (N.Y., Harper, 1946), pp. 13-41.

■ *Outline passages of exposition*

1. Outlining often produces impressive student improvement in ability to see the relationships between main ideas and supporting ideas. The teacher chooses some portion of a text his students are using in science or social studies classes. For the first phase of the method, he prepares an outline in which he states the main topics of the passage, leaving a blank line for each of the subordinate points. For instance, the first duplicated exercise for the class might read as follows:

The Great Depression (pages 133-141)

I. The crash in the New York stock market caused a chain reaction in many parts of the nation.
   A.
   B.
   C.
   D.

II. The depression in the United States had world-wide effects.
   A.
   B.
   C.

The outline continues in this fashion for as many Roman numerals as are required by the content. As he passes out the outline, the teacher tells the students that this is to be a test for him, the teacher. How well can he teach them to discriminate between main ideas and supporting ideas? This is to be the first in a series of four lessons to test his teaching skill. He has identified the main ideas of the passage and also the *number* of subordinate points supporting each main point. *Can they locate and fill in these subordinate points?*

2. On the following day, as on the first day, the teacher prepares and duplicates an exact outline for the next portion of the text, but this time only the subordinate points appear and the students are to fill in the main ideas—or main headings—of the outline:

The Breakdown of Democratic Action (pages 142-153)

I.
   A. The German people were confused by the large number of political parties.
   B. The incompetence and selfishness of weak political leaders discouraged many industrialists and investors.
   C. The Reichstag, supposedly representing the people, had become an incompetent debating society.

II.
   A. Poverty in Italy made the common people desperate.
   (Etc.)

3. On the third day, the teacher presents only a skeleton outline with no words whatsoever. However, the outline corresponds faithfully to the content it represents.

4. On the fourth day, the teacher presents only clean white paper. The students are to prepare the complete outline, both main points and subpoints, for a limited

portion of the text.[44] Some teachers, at this point, ask the students not to sign the papers. These final papers are collected by a committee, chosen either by the teacher or the students. The committee's threefold assignment: to agree upon the ideal outline for this final set of papers, discuss the outline with the class, and assign scores to the papers. The composite score of the class, reported by the committee, is to be the teacher's "grade" on teaching students to discriminate between main and subordinate ideas. This feature of a "grade" for the teacher often increases pupil interest.

■ *Compose headlines for newspaper clippings*

From newspapers or magazines, clip short articles that will cover no more space than an ordinary sheet of typing paper. Remove the headlines and paste each one on one side of cardboard or colored art paper; paste the article itself on the other side. When enough clippings are available for the entire class, pass out the sets, requesting students not to read the headlines on the reverse side. Each student studies his article with a view to composing a headline emphasizing the main ideas. After the student headlines have been completed, the cards may be turned over for a period of class discussion. Some of the articles are read aloud to determine whether the student or the original headline editor most nearly approximates an ideal statement of the article's essence. For a variation of this method, assign pairs or groups of students to work on a single article. Through comparison of ideas, students often modify their own partial grasp of the article's structure and central significance.

■ *Recognize the structure of sentences*

Whatever issues exist concerning instruction in grammar, teachers acknowledge the importance of recognizing subjects of sentences and their predicates. Edward Sapir, the eminent linguist, once noted that no language exists which fails to distinguish subject and predicate, whereas of the other parts of speech, "not one of them is imperatively required for the life of language."[45]

A blurred awareness of subject-predicate relationship in a sentence inevitably lowers the reader's understanding. Thus comprehension increases if a reader becomes more keenly alert to the relationships between these two universally necessary elements of expression.

If profit is to come from this study of grammar, students must clearly understand the goal. Suppose the teacher assigns an exercise in a reading workbook. Few explanations are given, the lesson is not related to student interest in better comprehension, and no provision for applying the skill is planned. Under such conditions the chances are meager that any learning which may occur will transfer to new situations.

Some teachers prefer to connect all such lessons in comprehension to interesting materials the students have just finished. "Suppose," they say, "a student wanted to be a good reader. How should he unlock the sentences beginning at the top of page 45?" In such instruction the teacher will need to gauge the extent to which grammatical explanation and common logic require blending. With most classes, identification of the simple subject and its simple predicate should be sufficient grammar *for this reading purpose.* The aim is to establish the *feel* of the English sentence rather than to carry out a detailed grammatical analysis.

[44] For this entire exercise, do not require an outline so detailed it includes Arabic numerals or small letters. See "Oral Language" for further suggestions on teaching outlining.

[45] Edward Sapir, *Language,* 1921 (N.Y., Harcourt, Brace, Harvest Books), p. 119.

■ *Summarize passages requiring close reading*

Discuss Schopenhauer's maxim, "Do not read, *think!*" After writing it on the board, choose a passage in a selection students are about to read. Show how the total passage influences the relations among its parts and how the parts contribute to the whole. For similar intensive analysis assign other passages in which important things are said compactly and in well-organized form. After practice with short passages, assign a longer selection. Various methods of summarizing the longer selection may be used:

Expressing the theme of a story in one sentence
Writing a précis of non-fiction
Finding examples to support generalizations the teacher presents
Finding generalizations for examples the teacher presents

To adapt reading methods to purpose and content

Students often understand an analogy between reading and driving an automobile. The same engine—general reading ability—travels the highways of mathematics, poetry, homemaking, and science, but the driver shifts gears and changes speeds according to the terrain. The nature of the material one reads affects the speed and concentration with which he proceeds; so, too, does his purpose in reading. Science, mathematics, and poetry cannot be read like *Yea! Wildcats!* To skilled readers, these elementary points are obvious. Not so to the average adult reader, nor to most of those whom we teach. In the English class alone, pupils encounter many kinds of reading; in the school at large and beyond the school they meet an even greater variety and find more diverse reasons for reading.

■ *Demonstrate how to read selections of varying difficulty*

Ask two girls to bring to class the mirrors from their purses. While the others watch, the two sit at the teacher's desk. While one is reading, the other, placing her mirror in a position to reflect the reader's eyes, reports her observations to the class. She notes that eye movements are by no means a smooth flowing process; rather they are a series of stop-and-go movements with occasional reversals to the left. Teacher and students ponder and discuss these observations:

The value of an eye-span that takes in as many words as possible at a single glance—provided the words are understood

The importance of reading by phrases and word groups rather than word-by-word—provided the word groups are comprehended

The importance of the stop or fixation in the stop-and-go movement of the eyes, when the mind takes in as much as can be comprehended

The futility of trying to increase reading power through eye-movement exercises, eye movements being efficient or inefficient in relation to understanding

The crucial significance of what takes place between eye and brain, not between page and eye, indicating that ways to improve comprehension are more important than ways to improve speed

The importance of the reader's will to understand as a basis for increasing comprehension during the moment of fixation

Next, list on the chalk board the titles and page numbers of four selections in the literature anthology, typically, an uncomplicated short story, some non-fiction with closely packed meaning, a light humorous poem, and a more difficult poem with

In Square Span,
which you are now reading,
each unit is read
as a whole,
not as separate words.
Notice how easily

these units are visualized.
The eyes are permitted
to focus quite naturally,
not strained by lines
of narrow print.
Fewer shifts

at the end of lines
result in fewer
interruptions of thought.
Also, thought groups
are seen in word groups,

making for speedier comprehension
and longer memory.

The ideal size
for a standard reading unit
in Square Span
has not been accurately determined.
For example,
units which are

two, three, or even four
lines in depth
might be used.
A critic
has suggested
Square Span may be
the "Model-T"
of future reading power.

Square Span: A drastic, but imaginative rearrangement of the traditional presentation of printed words. Do you think your eyes would function better this way than moving like a weaver's shuttle along one line, then another?

Devised by Robert B. Andrews, reprinted from *The Texas Outlook.* Copyright 1949 by The Reader's Digest Association, Inc.

inverted sentences, some symbolism, and effective but unusual imagery. Using the complete poems and only portions of the prose, read each selection aloud, then ask pupils to help analyze the thought processes necessary for comprehension. Stress the importance of clarifying one's purpose in reading. At the close of the lesson, place on the wall a prepared placard to remain there for several weeks.

LEARN TO SHIFT GEARS IN READING. YOUR OWN PURPOSE IN READING AND THE DIFFICULTY OF THE MATERIAL SHOULD AFFECT HOW YOU READ.

With senior high classes, assign Bacon's essay "Of Studies" on the day the placard is to be taken down. The class gives examples to illustrate that "some books are to be tasted, others to be swallowed, and some few to be chewed and digested." Then remove the placard from its place of prominence, saying, "You cannot always have this advice before you. I hope I have taught you well enough to make such a crutch unnecessary."

This method may be converted to use with younger pupils. After the use of mirrors and the discussion which follows, demonstrate with suitable content the adjustment to purpose and the nature of the material. The placard, too, may be used, but instead of all of Bacon's essay, only the famous quotation is presented and discussed as an occasion for the removal of the placard.

■ *Construct a chart of reading rates*

Ask the pupils to suggest names for four different reading rates, names that correspond to traveling by automobile. The names and descriptions might look something like this as they materialize on the chalk board:

Whirlaway gear	Skimming
High gear	Fast, easy reading
Intermediate gear	Slower reading for more difficult material
Low gear	Painstaking and careful reading, as in mathematics or for some kinds of modern poetry

These four rates may then become the basis for a chart, listing kinds of purposes for each rate and specific selections to illustrate each purpose. The chart might begin in this fashion:

Gear	When to use this gear	Where to use this gear
Whirlaway	To skim for the main idea	Reading the newspaper when the headline doesn't clarify Searching for material on our projects in this unit on "Lost Worlds"
	Reading for further information on something we already know very well	Looking through biographies of Thomas Jefferson for additional material on his life when we have just read his biography

Continue the chart so as to include all four rates of reading.

■ *Skim material for main ideas*

1. This lesson should be used for a practical purpose. For instance, when a class is searching for materials to use in a unit or project, the teacher demonstrates this skill, using some text or book the class has in common. Pointers for skimming should be copied in the students' notebooks and several "trial runs" with classroom material should occur before the class adjourns to the magazine table or the library.

2. Prepare paragraphs into which irrelevant sentences have been inserted. Students search the paragraphs to cross out the non-essential elements. The lesson should conclude with a discussion of what has been learned and how it can be applied to all reading.

To relate reading to interests and needs

A teacher can grant a position of importance to individual reading. Instead of calling it "outside reading" or "recreational reading" or "free reading"—terms indicating that teacher and school consider such activity peripheral—he labels it Guided Individual Reading or Voluntary Reading and uses it effectively as a fundamental part of the developmental reading program. To share this reading the teacher chooses methods such as are suggested here and, in more detail, on pp. 292-94 in Chapter 6, on teaching literature.

■ *Let students recommend books to each other*

1. Some teachers use file boxes, in which pupils place cards for favorite books. The usual content of such cards: title, author, and a recommending statement which avoids divulging the crucial developments of fiction. The students sign their names and over a period of several years a substantial and useful file accumulates. The best of these cards may be organized into mimeographed reading lists or booklets

to be used both in library and classroom. These lists may even become a worthwhile project of some magnitude. The Illinois English Teachers Association has published a monograph called "Books We Like" in which students from all parts of Illinois recommend worthwhile reading. In Detroit, Hutchins Intermediate School printed two brochures in which seventh and eighth grade pupils reviewed favorite books under the titles "We Circle the Globe" and "We Meet Interesting People."

2. Assign to a class a sum, allotted from the library budget, for purchasing ten books. Let students set up committees to review books, choose among the best not yet in the library, and prepare a list for purchase.[46]

■ *Stage a series of book reviews*

Occasionally someone may present a book review prepared with special care. The reviewers should vary: the teacher, the librarian, older students in the school, students in the class, the coach reviewing a book on athletics.

■ *Base discussions on inventories of reader response*

To motivate good discussions featuring the implications of reading, check sheets like this excerpt are often highly effective. They induce reflection and response *in advance* of discussion so that almost everyone has something to say.

Inventory of reader's response for
"That's What Happened to Me"

Directions: Please answer these questions as carefully as possible. Place an X beside the answer closest to the way you feel. There are no right or wrong answers. Write comments whenever you wish.

I have had things happen to me that make me realize just how Bottles felt.
________This is very true.
________To some extent this is true.
________No, I would say this is not true for me.
________Definitely not true.

I think it is a person's own fault if he or she isn't popular. Bottles is a good example of this.
________I definitely agree.
________I agree a little.
________I definitely disagree.
________I disagree somewhat.
________I am undecided.

Anna Louise shouldn't be expected to include a boy like Bottles in her crowd.
________I definitely agree.
________I agree a little.
________I definitely disagree.
________I disagree somewhat
________I am undecided.

Comments: Write here any sentences that will make clear your point of view on Bottles Barton.

[46] A complete description of such an activity may be found in Mabel Jackman's article, "Class Book Selection," *Wilson Library Bulletin,* Vol. 26, No. 1 (September 1951).

A useful guide to discussing short stories and other literary materials is *Reading Ladders for Human Relations.*[47] The authors suggest that a teacher keep notes on discussions of stories, thus learning much, not only about the students' comprehension and application of reading, but also about the students themselves.

To link reading and reality

At some time in his career, almost every teacher has cringed as some pupil has read verbatim a report he has copied from an encyclopedia, revealing by his presentation that he comprehends not at all the sentences and words he is uttering. The problem of an empty verbalism persists in all education, often increasing as the school's pressures to read become greater. The fundamental problem rests upon the curriculum and the reasonableness of the school's expectations for each individual child; but there are also specific actions a teacher may take to point up the necessity of a demand for meaning in all reading. Such suggestions as the following may be incorporated into individual lessons and unit activities.

■ *Apply generalizations to the students' reading*

1. By urging pupils to name people, actions, and circumstances to illustrate generalizations, the teacher indicates his interest in helping students see relationships between words and their referents in reality. Instruction may include many exercises like the following:

Applying ideas

Directions: As a means of indicating that you understand their meaning and significance, apply the following ideas from Saint Exupéry's works to your own life:

Men's words wear out and lose their meaning. With what words or phrases does the author illustrate his point? With what words associated with school life can you match them? How might the term *school spirit* run the danger of losing its meaning?

There is but one means of building that something more vast than oneself: the free gift; the gift that demands nothing in exchange. What in the selection itself was "that something"? Where in school life is it exemplified? What would the "free gift" be in the study of the arts? science? literature? Wherein does the student who works for marks miss the joy to which the author refers?

2. Poems often require bridges; for instance, "The Slave" by James Oppenheim expresses the thought that men can be enslaved by chains of ignorance and superstition fully as much as by manacles of iron. Questions like these help most students in home study or class discussion:

Putting meaning into words

What does the phrase "chained to servility" mean?

Describe some situations to explain how a servile person might behave.

Under what circumstances could a person be said to be "manacled to indolence and sloth"?

Give three circumstances in which fear, superstition, or ignorance enslave a person. What, then, is a slave?

[47] Margaret Heaton and Helen B. Lewis, eds., *Reading Ladders for Human Relations,* rev. and enl. ed. (Washington, D.C., American Council on Education, 1955).

■ *Relate reading to A-V materials and excursions*

The principle of reading readiness, in which the words and concepts of a reading selection are tied rather closely to a preliminary experience, may be utilized. Thus reading may sometimes be chosen because of its local interest: farm stories in rural areas; mountain stories in Colorado; holiday materials in grade seven for Halloween and Thanksgiving.

Before reading *Giants in the Earth* or *My Antonia,* students might view the color film, "The Prairie." Recordings and excursions, carefully designed to illuminate reading, represent still other possibilities for classes who need to diminish habits of empty verbalism. For very poor readers at the secondary level, film-and-story series like *It's Fun to Find Out* may be helpful.[48]

To improve oral reading [49]

■ *Read aloud to small children*

Pupils work in groups, practicing reading children's stories like *Charlotte's Web, Madeline's Rescue,* and *Millions of Cats.* When the group pronounces a member ready, a student representative of the class arranges with the teacher of an appropriate elementary school group and the secondary school reader makes his debut as a reader to youngsters. Wherever this has been carried out, the results have been encouraging and well worth the careful arrangements. Where the plan is not feasible, encourage students to read aloud to younger brothers, sisters, or relatives and report their experience to the class.

■ *Use tape recorders and records*

1. Let pupils tape and listen to playbacks of their oral reading. As an assignment each pupil should make recommendations for his own improvement. Although the teacher will not have time to listen to each tape, he may identify in advance some of the main speech problems as a guide to self-criticism: lack of the variation of voice needed for an imparting tone, word-swallowing, pauses at inappropriate places.

2. Practice prose for which good recordings exist: "Three Days to See," Helen Keller's statement read by Nancy Wickwire, or E. B. White's "Irtnog," read by Hiram Sherman, both from the *Many Voices* record series. First, several students take turns reading; then the recordings are played. Repeat the process until the ear begins to aid the voice in imitating the models. Interpretations of materials not on record might be a culminating activity.

■ *Use students to read announcements and explanations*

The student should prepare the material he is to read and the class should be aware of the purpose of listening. When they read before a group, many students feel exceptionally self-conscious and fear the laughter of their peers. Train pupils to listen attentively and to understand the effect of laughter, good-natured though it may be.

[48] *It's Fun to Find Out,* film-story books. Each book (Boston, Heath), is based upon a sound motion picture of the same title, produced and distributed by Encyclopaedia Britannica Films, Inc. (Wilmette, Ill.) Some of the titles in this series are too elementary for junior and senior high school pupils but others, such as "The Airport," have proved to be highly useful.

[49] For further ideas on oral reading, see Chapter 7, pp. 338-41.

Evaluating Growth

In this chapter, reading comprehension has been stressed; reading speed has received only incidental mention. This has been deliberate, for it is our experience that the public—and many school people as well—place rate of reading in a much higher position of importance than it deserves. Early reading tests used in the schools were so designed that a high correlation between speed and comprehension was inevitable. This artificial result of these early tests led the unwary to conclude that fast readers were necessarily the best readers. We now know that when speed and comprehension are measured in such a way that the scores are not dependent upon each other, the correlation is positive but low.[50] Improvement in comprehension is more important than gains in speed.

Evaluating Comprehension If the primary aim of reading instruction is effective comprehension, those who evaluate such instruction will choose means suited to this aim. This implies that where standardized commercial tests are used for testing before and after a semester or year of instruction, the test used should feature comprehension of paragraphs, or even longer selections, rather than word recognition or sentence understanding. The directions and questions for the comprehension section of a test deserve scrutiny also. Sometimes the diction is so difficult that the test becomes an intelligence-vocabulary test before the reader ever arrives at any trial of his comprehension.

Many teachers feel that the present commercial tests of reading, although helpful, are limited. They agree with Davis [51] that most reading tests usually measure word knowledge and comprehension of literal meanings in isolated statements. These teachers, convinced that their home-made evaluation creates no more pitfalls than commercial testing, plan their own battery of appraisal. They record scores on comprehension questions for a series of reading selections on which no time limits have been set. Usually these selections are spaced over a period of three or four weeks toward the close of the semester, and they represent the kind of material the teacher considers important for his students to understand. In addition to such evidence, these teachers may also include in their evaluation some or all of the following kinds of appraisal:

1. Questionnaires and inventories which deal with attitudes, interests, and behavior. Samples:

I am doing better in reading my assignments for other classes now. True _______
Uncertain_______ Not so_______.
This past week, I have been reading____________________.
I would read more if____________________________.
The reason I read better now is that I have learned________________.
My biggest problem in reading seems to be____________________.

[50] Blommers and Lindquist, "Rate of Comprehension of Reading: Its Measurement and Its Relation to Comprehension," *Journal of Educational Psychology,* Vol. 35, No. 8 (November 1944), pp. 449-73.

[51] Frederick B. Davis, "What Do Reading Tests *Really* Measure?" *English Journal,* Vol. 33, No. 4 (April 1944).

Such inventories and questionnaires require judicious interpretation, but at least they throw more light on the reading problem than do mere low scores on a standardized test.

2. Progress charts and graphs kept by students and teacher. These may be growth charts such as those provided in the SRA *Better Reading Books* or the SRA *Reading Laboratory*. They may be home-made charts based on the answers to comprehension questions in *Reader's Digest Skill Builders* or teacher-devised questions for materials in local textbooks.

3. Self-appraisal by students, who evaluate their own reading by writing answers to such questions as these: How have I improved in reading? What have I learned that helps me to comprehend better? What can I do to improve my comprehension?

4. Case studies, diaries, or anecdotal records kept by teachers or counselors. In most schools, of course, it is not feasible to do this for more than a few crucial cases.

5. Item lists checked by all the student's teachers, showing whether or not any improvement has been noted. Tact must be used in asking busy teachers to co-operate on such a venture.

Many schools, of course, do administer standardized reading tests at the beginning and close of a period of reading instruction. Some of the tests often used are the following:

Sequential Tests of Educational Progress: Reading Comprehension. (Cooperative Test Division, Educational Testing Service, Princeton, N.J., 1957.) These tests measure a number of abilities from grades 4 through 14: understanding direct statements made by the author; interpreting and summarizing passages; seeing the motives of the author; observing the organizational characteristics of a passage; and criticizing the passage with respect to its ideas, purposes, or presentation.

Cooperative English Tests. (Cooperative Test Division, Educational Testing Service, Princeton, N.J., 1960.) Test C1, for grades 7-12; test C2, for grades 11-12 and college. Measures vocabulary, speed, and level of comprehension, with more emphasis on literary appreciation than most tests. Separate public school and independent school percentile norms. (40 mins.) The Cooperative Reading Comprehension Tests may be used separately.

Diagnostic Reading Tests, higher level, grades 7-14. (Committee on Diagnostic Reading Tests, 419 W. 119th St., New York 27, N.Y.) Survey section of forty minutes (this part of test is available now through Science Research Associates, Chicago, Ill.) and separate diagnostic sections. The usual tests of vocabulary and comprehension. Special features: test of auditory comprehension, tests of reading social studies and science, and a silent and oral test of word attack. Many subsections have no time limit. (For further comments on this test, see p. 228.)

Gates Reading Diagnostic Tests. (Bureau of Publications, Teachers College, Columbia University.) These are individual tests requiring from sixty to ninety minutes; the norms are for grades 1 through 8, but the tests are useful for slow readers in high school. The manual is very helpful with diagnosis.

Gates Reading Survey Test for Grades 3 to 10. (Bureau of Publications, Teachers College, Columbia University.) This measures vocabulary, power or level of comprehension, speed of reading, and accuracy of interpretation. Useful where many slow readers are to be tested.

Gilmore Oral Reading Test. (World Book Co., Yonkers, N.Y.) For grades 1-8, this measures comprehension, speed, and accuracy. Useful in high schools for gauging level of slow readers. Two forms which may be used for before-and-after comparisons.

Gray Standardized Oral Reading Paragraphs. (Public School Publishing Co., Bloomington, Ill.) An oral reading test for grades 1-8; paragraphs of increasing difficulty.

Iowa Every-Pupil Test of Basic Skills, Test A. (Science Research Associates, Chicago, Ill.) Paragraph comprehension, reading details, organization, vocabulary, and total meaning. Grades 6, 7, and 8 are considered high in reliability and validity due to careful and sophisticated test construction. (78 mins.)

Iowa Silent Reading Tests, New Edition. Advanced Test. (World Book Co., Yonkers, N.Y.) For grades 9-12; many subsections. (45 mins.)

Nelson-Denny Reading Test. (Houghton Mifflin, Boston.) Short, easy administration, and easy scoring for comprehension and vocabulary. If local norms are established, this test may be used without the stated limitations of time. In such a case, it is useful in diagnosing comprehension.

Traxler Silent Reading Test. (Public School Publishing Co., Bloomington, Ill.) Measures reading rate, story comprehension, word meaning, and paragraph comprehension. Reading rate and comprehension are measured on several consecutive pages of connected narrative, a notable and valuable feature of this test. Forms for grades 7-10 and 9-12; percentile norms for public and independent schools. (45 mins.)

Good descriptive discussions of the various commercial tests and their values may be found in *Remedial Reading,*[52] *How to Increase Reading Ability,*[53] and *Problems in the Improvement of Reading.*[54] Buros' *Mental Measurements Yearbook*[55] reviews the tests a teacher may wish to examine. The following chart presents tests used and gains recorded by two schools evaluating instruction in reading through such testing:

School	Nature and duration of instruction	Test used	Amount of gain
Mexico H.S., Mexico, Mo.	Reading instruction integrated with English; regular English classes; no homogeneous grouping; in-	(a) *Cooperative Reading Comprehension Test,* C1; (b) *Diagnostic Reading Tests,*	Mean percentile score gains: vocabulary 5.0, comprehension 7.0, speed 13.5,

[52] Maurice D. Woolf and Jeanne A. Woolf, *Remedial Reading* (N.Y., McGraw-Hill, 1957), pp. 85-87.

[53] Albert J. Harris, *How To Increase Reading Ability* (N.Y., Longmans, Green, 1956).

[54] Ruth Strang, Constance M. McCullough, and Arthur E. Traxler, *Problems in the Improvement of Reading* (N.Y., McGraw-Hill, 1955). Chapter 13 is entirely concerned with the appraisal of students' reading ability through tests.

[55] Oscar K. Buros, *Fifth Mental Measurements Yearbook* (Highland Park, N.J., Gryphon, 1959). Buros covers all commercially available tests and all measurement books published in English-speaking countries. The reviews by well-qualified experts are informative, evaluative, and thought provoking.

School	Nature and duration of instruction	Test used	Amount of gain
	struction aimed at improving word attack, vocabulary, comprehension, speed; duration of one year	Section IV, Word Attack, Part 2, Silent	word attack 15.5
Cole Jr. H.S., Denver, Colo.	Small reading groups; duration of one year.	(a) Nelson Silent Reading; (b) Stanford Reading Test.	2 to 2½ years in reading grade level for all except lowest IQ's, whose gains were about 1½ years.

A limitation of all such reports: Information about the pupils' retention of reading growth is seldom available. Do the subjects remain at the higher level or is their encouraging gain only a temporary result of their recent instruction? *After a year's lapse of regular school work, do they still retain the advantage gained?* Eventually, evaluation of reading progress must include evidence on retention, and schools should plan to carry out repeated measures over a fairly long period of time.

The use of the mean or median to indicate progress is another limitation, for it obscures the changes in individual pupils. Some may regress, others progress, and yet the mean improves. Teachers can, for instance, raise a mean score by working intensively with pupils who are just below the mean on the first test. A chart of the scores of individual pupils tells more about real gains than does the rise in mean score.

Like most evaluations in the arts of language, appraisal of improved reading skill ultimately rests upon a broad base. Genuine evidence of success must take into account important but complex results like these:

The average number of books and other materials drawn from the school library—figured on a per pupil basis in order to avoid increase due merely to school population growth

Evidence of increased participation and interest by teachers throughout the entire school system

Accurate evidence that the number of students dropping out of school is declining

Improved average achievement of pupils on the same or similar test materials over a period of years

Nothing that has been said here is intended to discredit the useful but limited range of standardized testing, and some recent published tests show an immense improvement in value to curriculum improvement. Teachers will do well to use such tests when money for them is available. But the best evidence will always be students who read eagerly and comprehend what they are reading. Students voluntarily checking out books from libraries, students buying books they actually read—these actions diminish all other forms of appraisal. Some circumstantial evidence is very strong. When a tree bears apples, we can be quite certain it is a fruit tree.

A final word This chapter began by stating that no simple formula will ever be discovered for improving reading comprehension. Reading, like all the arts of language, can never be improved apart from the energizing and maturing of the intellect in all its functions; the intellect can never be fully separated from imagination, feeling, and volition. In our first section on Language, Thought, and Feeling we emphasized precise thought and controlled feeling as dynamic processes. In this chapter on reading comprehension we have concluded the second section on Understanding. *Receiving* communication, the focus of both chapters in this section, also depends upon more than mechanical abilities. Nothing less than effective logical and imaginative thought will lead to clarity and power in what might, at first examination, seem to be a mechanical skill. Reading is, indeed, a very elaborate process involving "a weighing of each of many elements in a sentence, their organization in the proper relations one to another, the selection of certain of their connotations and the rejection of others, and the cooperation of many forces to determine final response. . . ." [56]

SELECTED READINGS

BOOKS

A. J. Harris, *How to Increase Reading Ability,* 3rd ed. N.Y., Longmans, Green, 1956. This book has long been considered one of the most useful of aids.

Ruth Strang and Dorothy Kendall Bracken, *Making Better Readers.* Boston, Heath, 1957. This book, exemplifying very clearly the developmental concept in the teaching of reading, is notable for practical suggestions which obviously derive from actual and recent classroom experience. There is an excellent section on reading in subject fields other than English.

Maurice D. Woolf and Jeanne A. Woolf, *Remedial Reading.* N.Y., McGraw-Hill, 1957. This book is exceptionally complete, both as to technique and as to the theoretical base which keeps technique from becoming aimless and self-justifying. The appendix contains a lengthy list of easy books for retarded readers and non-readers.

PERIODICALS AND PAMPHLETS

Improving Reading in the Junior High School. Health, Education, and Welfare Dept., Education Office Bulletin 1957, No. 10. Washington, D.C. This inexpensive pamphlet considers research, how to start a developmental program, objectives, materials, what to do, remedial reading, and appraisal.

V. E. Leichty, "How Slowly Do They Read?" *English Journal,* Vol. 45, No. 5 (May 1956). Leichty believes that the teacher should emphasize careful reading.

[56] Edward L. Thorndike, "Reading as Reasoning," p. 329.

Through discussing meaning and worrying less about speed and quantity of reading, the teacher makes his greatest contribution to the pupils; without understanding of literature, no appreciation is possible.

Constance M. McCullough, "What Does Research Reveal About Practices in Teaching Reading?" In *What We Know About High School Reading,* a brochure. Champaign, Ill. National Council of Teachers of English, 1957-58. This article considers the implications of research for developing vocabulary, comprehension, speed, tastes and appreciations, and means of evaluating. The article is notable for its temperate applications of research and its balancing good sense.

Wallace Z. Ramsey, "An Experiment in Teaching Reading in High School English Classes," *English Journal,* Vol. 46, No. 8 (November 1957). In a program adopted at Mexico, Missouri, High School, emphasis was placed on comprehension, vocabulary, word attack, and speed—in that order of priority. Evaluation showed gains in all the areas, and equal benefits for students in the upper and lower thirds of mental ability.

Science Fiction: Radar of Man's Curiosity

A Unit for Grade Nine

Overview: At its best, science fiction may be compared to a ship's radar, scanning distant shorelines shrouded in fog and darkness. This imaginative method of exploring new frontiers of space and time appears to be emerging as a category of literature. Like earlier genres, the Gothic and the Pastoral, science fiction also has its themes, its typical devices, and its basic intentions. Sometimes it predicts the direction of certain applications of science, as did the novels of Jules Verne. Sometimes it features social criticism, exploring the gap between man's advancing scientific knowledge and his lagging social attitudes. At other times, science fiction is merely adventure, mystery, and suspense, or pure fantasy, delightful and refreshing, without any pretensions of predictive value or social reform. But at its best, science fiction expresses man's age-old quest to reach beyond his limitations, to fuse the powers of intellect and imagination into daring thrusts against darkness and the unknown, against fear, superstition, and ignorance. Serious writers of science fiction are struggling toward a form worthy of the intellectual curiosity we honor in Socrates, Leonardo, and Einstein. Such writers help us to understand Bacon's comment that supposition is greater than truth.

This unit for grade nine is intended to place certain important educational goals in a new context that will appeal to many adolescents. Our pupils belong to an era that respects science while many old superstitions persist. To discriminate in the world of thought between authentic and spurious, between deep and shallow, between stale and fresh—these are timeless and necessary aims in educating the young. These aims may be linked to a study of the new directions of man's search for knowledge in the last half of the twentieth century. Thus science fiction becomes another variation of the Promethean theme. By using it as a way to achieve fundamental educational goals, we acknowledge the significance of motivation, of the pupil's volition, as a factor in learning.

AIMS

The following aims, stated in the language of the teacher, are those which shape the unit. Subsidiary aims might well include those of increased reading enjoyment for pupils and the increased facility with the reading skills that such enjoyment promotes.[1]

To appreciate the significance of curiosity and intelligence enlisted in the quest for truth.

To discriminate between literature of distinction and writing of inferior merit. (Particular emphasis is given to writing that is imaginative in its style and faithful to scientific truth.) To become familiar with some influential authors of science fiction, both past and present, and to set up standards for choosing reading in this category.

To become aware of the social criticism that often appears in science fiction.

To understand certain mutually supporting values of science and the humanities.

MAJOR CONCEPTS

In organizing instruction to accomplish these aims, the teacher will introduce certain concepts to undergird the aims of the unit. In advance of this unit the following concepts should be carefully considered by the teacher. If they are clear in the teacher's mind, he will be alert to occasions to teach them to the pupils in language they can comprehend.

Man is a searching creature, endowed with intellectual curiosity. He wants to see and to understand the universe surrounding him. He does this both for the sake of controlling, in order to insure his own survival, and for the sake of knowing, in itself a desirable and sufficient aim.

The challenge of the unknown beyond the horizon is an enduring search which links men of all ages together—Marco Polo with Tenzing, Columbus with those today who want to conquer outer space by 1975.

If knowledge is to be a blessing and not a curse, concern for mankind must dominate all scientific advances.

Science deals with facts and their implications, and for that reason is of great importance. Literature deals with human values, and for that reason is also important to everyone.

Poor fiction depends heavily upon stock characters and situations, stale humor, prefabricated phrases, and static characterization. In fiction of merit, the writer is original and precise. For instance, his characters grow and change with the action of the story. Science fiction, like all fiction, may be judged by standards like these.

FUNDAMENTAL SKILLS TO BE EMPHASIZED

In this unit, certain skills of writing are featured. Other skills in writing, as well as in reading, speaking, and listening, will naturally demand attention and will usually be handled when the occasion arises. However, the exercises in this unit will be *focused* on the writing of carefully planned paragraphs.

GRADE LEVEL AND TIME PLAN

This unit is planned for grade nine. With modifications, it could be adapted to grade eight or moved up to grades ten or eleven. As it appears here, the unit should

[1] Many teachers developing this unit may prefer the threefold classification of aims into knowledge and understandings, skills and competencies, attitudes and appreciations. How-

require approximately four weeks. By eliminating the last two aims and the activities designed for them, the teacher may reduce the time span of the unit. On the other hand, if the unit fares well both in terms of pupil growth and enjoyment, it can be expanded to cover five weeks. In the total plan of a year's English program, five weeks is probably as much time as this content deserves, even though the unit proves to be an important vehicle for teaching fundamental writing skills and for motivating reading.

In preparing to teach this unit, the teacher will find it helpful to plan with the pupils a tentative over-all schedule as a foundation for more precise weekly and daily plans.

DESIGN OF THE UNIT

This unit is a flexible one. The activities are arranged in a sequence corresponding to the four aims controlling the unit, but in classes where pupils help to select their goals, the arrangement may follow other emphases. The desirability of drawing students into some of the planning, and the clear fact that certain activities contribute to more than a single aim will necessitate modifications of the plan as presented here. The composition of the class will also affect the sequence and choice of activities. Even more influential will be the new ideas and contributions of each teacher using this outline. In making choices and substitutions among activities, the teacher will wish to consider, among the factors that must be balanced, the skills of speaking and listening, for as the unit is now planned, reading and writing are already heavily emphasized.

Whenever pupils show a need for a particular skill, the teacher must decide whether or not to take time for instruction and drill. If most members of the class need the help, the teachable moment is often at the time the problem arises. However, since pupils need help on such a multiplicity of skills, there will be some problems which do not, in the teacher's estimation, deserve as high a priority as others. Low priority skills can be noted for future consideration. And certainly, few skills are so crucial their lack in them should interrupt some successful activity at a time when communication of ideas is foremost. As has been noted, special priority in this unit is granted to certain skills in writing, and these should receive the primary attention.

LAUNCHING THE UNIT

To involve the pupils' interest and volition, and to turn their thoughts to the general aims of the unit, introduce one or more of the following activities.

■ *Television programs*

Assign as homework several science and science-fiction programs on television. After class discussion, ask a series of summary questions:

What useful knowledge can we gain from these programs?
Why are people so very much interested in science today?
What are the dangers and what are the benefits of scientific knowledge? How do you think mankind might act in order to diminish the dangers and increase the benefits?

ever, the four aims listed, representing as they do the animating forces which form the design of activities, are recommended as the central structure of this unit.

Some people say that we are just as superstitious as the men of old, only nowadays we are superstitious *about science.* For instance, are we easily led to believe in something of no value if the advertising says that "three out of four doctors recommend it"? What do you think of this criticism of twentieth-century men and women?

What is science fiction? Why do people read it?

■ *Checklist*

To draw the students into thinking about reasons for studying a unit on science fiction, devise an opinion questionnaire. It should be filled out anonymously and a committee should tally the results and report to the class. After their report, the committee should conduct a class discussion on the results of the tally. Items on the questionnaire might use the same form as the two examples given here:

To the student: There are no right or wrong answers. Please give your opinion by checking the response that most closely agrees with your opinion. Your comment in the space provided after each question will be greatly appreciated and will help in charting the course of this unit.

1. No good and only harm can come from wanting to explore the space beyond Earth.
   strongly agree_______ agree_______ uncertain_______
   disagree_______ strongly disagree_______
   Comment:
2. Most science fiction is written by authors who are also scientists. They carefully check all their facts before they include such facts in a story.
   strongly agree_______ agree_______ uncertain_______
   disagree_______ strongly disagree_______
   [*Further items as designated by the teacher*]

■ *Application of poem's meaning*

The teacher places on the chalk board these lines from "The Explorers" by Humbert Wolfe.[2]

The Explorers

They steer beyond the evening star,
And challenge their own dream
To overtake the things that are
Behind the things that seem,
And do not care if death should be
The price of curiosity.

The teacher suggests Columbus and Marco Polo as representatives of the men referred to by the poem and asks the pupils for modern counterparts, seeking to elicit the names of those who scaled Mount Everest, sailed the *Kon-Tiki,* or now seek to travel into outer space. What values have come to mankind as the result of such dreams and such curiosity? Could the unit use as a motto the lines "To overtake the things that are/Behind the things that seem"?

[2] From "The Explorers," in *Cursory Rhymes* by Humbert Wolfe, copyright 1927 by Humbert Wolfe. Reprinted by permission of Doubleday & Company, Inc.

DEVELOPING THE UNIT

■ *Recording*

Play "Beyond the Ranges" by James Ramsay Ullman, as recorded by Arnold Moss (37).[3] Prepare students for this listening experience through discussing why men risk their lives. Anticipate not only difficult words in the selection but also several concepts which may be new to the pupils. Feature the concept that men seek adventure and struggle, not as an escape *from* reality, but as an escape *to* reality. How can this be? This will be a challenging listening experience. Prepare students for it fully, but do not expect everyone to respond with equal understanding. Some glimpses of Ullman's meaning will be of value even to the slow learner. The rich meanings will challenge the ablest pupil.

This listening experience is designed to shape the class interest more directly toward science fiction and also to introduce the first strains of social criticism and the relationship between science and human values.

■ *Short story*

Read aloud a suitable story such as "Report on the Barnhouse Effect" by Kurt Vonnegut, Jr. (25), introducing the story by some such statement as this: "Radar is an instrument for determining the distance and direction of unseen objects by the reflection of radio waves. The word is short for *ra*dio *d*etecting *a*nd *r*anging. Science fiction is like a radar scanning the new frontiers of space and time, locating the solid headlands along unknown, mystery-shrouded shores. Science fiction predicted submarines, jet planes, and guided missiles, all weapons of war. Can it predict a weapon of peace?"

After completing the story, the teacher leads a discussion both of its plain meaning and its implications, underscoring those parts of the discussion which relate to the aims of this unit.

For classes of ninth-graders for whom Kurt Vonnegut's story is deemed too difficult, the teacher might use "Robot's Return" (29) or "The 32nd of May" (12). For classes with many slow students, a more suitable story may be found among those in *Every Boy's Book of Science-Fiction* by Donald Wollheim (30). Each teacher may have other selections he prefers to any of these.

■ *Writing paragraphs*

Below are sample topics for paragraph compositions; students should choose five of the seven suggestions.

One Thing I Wonder About
One Aspect of a Visit to the Planet ———
One Aspect of a Visit to the Future
One Topic from an Interview with a Space Pilot
If I Could Have One Science-Fiction Wish
One Aspect of a Time-Machine Visit to the Past
A Single Paragraph Review of a Book Read for this Unit

These five paragraph compositions are to be spaced fairly evenly throughout the developmental part of the unit. In each case the teacher requires a single paragraph organized around an idea carefully stated in a topic sentence. Able students

[3] The figures in parentheses following a title refer to the list of resources for the pupil at the end of the unit.

and students who wish to do so may be encouraged to write more than one paragraph, provided that all paragraphs meet the requirements—related and carefully constructed sentences built around a single topic. The teacher will plan carefully in order to prepare pupils for each writing session. Although the unit calls for five different paragraphs, more topics have been listed here in order to provide choice both for teacher and pupil. Some teachers may have classes where even more writing is desirable, and the choice of paragraph topics may be extended.

In *seeking to motivate writing,* the teacher may choose from among these suggestions, suiting the motivation to the particular composition, or he may carry out other ideas not considered here:

1. Show a film such as "New Frontiers in Space" (34), "The Medieval Knights" (33), or "The Aztecs" (31) to inspire compositions about the past or future.
2. Pass around and discuss colored pictures of the moon and the planets. In recent years many magazines have presented dramatic illustrations of other worlds as science envisions them. Books like *The Conquest of Space* by Willy Ley (15) contain pictures of remarkably evocative effect.
3. Play a recording of "The Planets," by Gustav Holst (32). This suite consists of seven movements: Mars, Venus, Mercury, Jupiter, Saturn, Uranus, and Neptune. One or two of these may be used to accompany writing. Neptune is particularly eerie.
4. Discuss interesting events of the past such as the Children's Crusade; read aloud vignettes about cave men, knights and ladies, the Aztecs, the American Revolution. So that pupils will see the relevance of past events, remind them of how often science-fiction writers use a time machine to carry readers back into past times.
5. Prepare able students to read aloud selected excerpts from conjectures about the future. Many writers, including H. G. Wells, Philip Wylie, Aldous Huxley, and Stephen Leacock have imagined life in the centuries to come.
6. Use models, either compositions written by pupils in classes where this unit has been previously taught or literary materials from the library. *Caution:* urge pupils to be original; weaker pupils tend to imitate the models too closely.

In *selecting skills for emphasis in this unit,* the teacher will, although numerous aspects of writing may deserve attention, feature single paragraphs, clearly organized and thoughtfully expressed. Therefore instruction, practice, correction, and review should emphasize the following abilities:

1. The unification of the paragraph around one sentence that states definitely what the paragraph is about.
2. Consideration of methods for developing or arranging the materials of a paragraph. These methods are not to be memorized as a list, but are to serve as functioning guides for writing during this unit.
3. Careful attention to construction of sentences, avoiding especially sentence fragments and run-on sentences.

Difficulties with other fundamental skills—problems in punctuation, spelling, and capitalization, for instance—will be noted by the teacher. Whenever a difficulty is general, the teacher will make plans to offer instruction at some early appropriate time. In some classes or situations, a teacher may consider certain problems crucial enough for immediate attention. However, the three abilities listed here should receive primary attention. Future lessons for class (or individuals) can deal with the many other writing difficulties certain to emerge. The principle employed here is one of avoiding any dissipation of learning; by not attempting to cure too many difficulties in a limited period of time, the teacher achieves success with a few.

In *handling compositions,* teachers find these practices helpful.

1. Have pupils keep all paragraphs and combine them into a booklet at the close of the unit.

2. Encourage able, creative, and interested pupils to write more than one paragraph (but do not require this of all pupils).

3. Teach through the use of the paragraphs written by the pupils. Select two or three good paragraphs with excellent unification through topic sentences. Read them aloud, view them with an opaque projector, or duplicate them. Ask, What makes this paragraph especially clear? . . . especially effective? . . . an example of one of the ways of developing paragraphs listed on the board?

4. Have paragraphs written in class, first as rough drafts and then copied as final drafts; use these periods to help individuals and groups with similar problems.

5. Share paragraphs in as many ways as possible—read them aloud in groups for selection of good models, display them about the room, exchange with other classes, collect them in scrapbooks for use in the library and for the teacher's use with future classes.

6. Require a final draft in ink but do not, in this unit, require all pupils to revise final copies that still contain errors. For some individuals such a procedure may, of course, be valuable, but for everyone, revision may be more valuable in some other writing situation.

7. Use drill material on sentence fragments and run-on sentences, excusing from such drill pupils who do not make such errors. Plan the drill so that it can be closely related to students' writing of their own ideas in the paragraphs. Also place on the board some examples, proper and improper, of pupil sentences. Discuss these sentences—why they are excellently written or how to improve them. Do not hesitate to review the concept of subject and predicate.

8. In some classes, offer for composition a larger number of topics than has been listed here. Some pupils respond better if they have a greater choice. Be flexible with individuals who wish to vary the topic of a paragraph.

9. Encourage the better students to use conversation with quotation marks and to place special emphasis on variety of sentence structure. Refer them to textbook help on the use of quotation marks, paragraph division in written conversation, and varieties of sentence pattern.

10. For the single paragraph book review, have students expand a topic sentence selected from among eight or ten placed on the chalk board. Examples:

(Title of book) has everything I like to find in a book.
After (a certain event in the story) there is only one possible outcome.
I learned something from reading (title of book).
Some things that happened in (title of book) stretched my imagination.
(Title of book) includes some highly improbable events.
If I could rewrite (title of book), there is one thing I would change.
(Name of author) relies too much on lucky accidents to carry his story along.

In addition to the paragraphs, pupils will also write book cards for each book read. For information about these book cards, see the following section, "Guided Individual Reading."

■ *Guided individual reading*

Each pupil should read one or more books related to the unit. Interested and gifted pupils should read from three to seven. Suggestions to guide the reading:

1. Motivate interest in reading by placing book jackets around the room, by reading incidents from the books in the manner of *Book Bait,*[4] and by reviewing several full length books, both fiction and non-fiction. Whenever individual pupils have already read worthwhile books of science fiction or fantasy, arrange to have the pupils recommend or review them.

2. Make arrangements for selection of books, either by bringing a collection to the classroom or through class visits to the library. After pupils have chosen titles for their individual reading, arrange directly for a class hour in which everyone reads quietly. This will help pupils make a start with their books. From time to time throughout the unit allocate class hours for the same purpose. Use these hours, also, to recommend further reading to individuals and to work with others on writing their paragraphs.

3. Take some action to steer poor readers to easier books and even, in some cases, to short stories in place of books. Use non-fiction for some pupils who prefer this type of reading. For some pupils who do not want to read science fiction, recommend books of fantasy such as *Alice's Adventures in Wonderland* (10), *Gulliver's Travels* (23), *Lost Horizon* (14), or *The Borrowers* (20). Steer gifted pupils to literature such as E. M. Forster's *The Machine Stops* (13).

4. In advance, plan with pupils how they are to share their reading. There may be oral reports before the class, or discussion groups may be formed according to the similarity of the content of their books or the author they are reading—e.g., usually enough students are reading books by Robert Heinlein or Willy Ley to form groups based upon these authors' books.

5. Each student should prepare one written card to be placed in a card file devoted to science-fiction reading. These cards should be large (5″ x 8″) and should be written in ink after a rough draft has been prepared. The purpose of making these cards is to build a reference file for use both by pupils and the teacher. This file is to be saved and used whenever this unit is taught again. Pupils should be guided to present the necessary information: title and author, where the book can be located by another pupil, and enough information to indicate the nature of the content and the kind of reader who might presumably enjoy the book, without divulging the development of the plot in such a way as to take away the next reader's pleasure. (In the case of non-fiction, other considerations may be more important.) In developing the writing lesson for the book card, the teacher will probably wish to use models and in some classes teach a lesson which includes reading book review sections of local newspapers and student magazines like *Literary Cavalcade.*

■ *Round table and panel discussions*

After the guided individual reading has gained momentum, pass around a clipboard or in some other way provide sign-up sheets for pupils who want to improve their power over oral language by participating in informal panel or round table discussions of topics such as these:

[4] Elinor Walker, ed., *Book Bait* (Chicago, American Library Association, 1957).

What are the Sober Prospects of Space Travel?
What Are Some of the Facts about Mars and the Moon?
Some Facts about Mental Telepathy
Why People Tend to Believe in Flying Saucers and Hoaxes like "The Invasion from Mars"
Artificial Satellites
Time Teasers: Are time and space like a doughnut? Could you fly around the earth fast enough to get back in time to see yourself take off? (Other questions the students propose)
The Important Knowledge about Radar and Electronics
The Geophysical Year

■ *Book map*

Instead of the usual map of the world with titles of books located in appropriate geographical locations, students prepare a map of the universe with titles of space story books located on the various planets and galaxies. (A "Map of the Heavens" appeared in the *National Geographic* in December, 1957.)

■ *Book sets*

Some teachers may wish to teach a single book to the entire class or to divide the class into a number of groups, each group to read and discuss a different book.

Recommended for study by entire class:
- Use one or both
- Mark Twain, *A Connecticut Yankee in King Arthur's Court* (24)
- Willy Ley, *Engineer's Dreams* (16)

Recommended for study by groups:
- Both of the books listed just above
- Isaac Asimov, *Building Blocks of the Universe* (1)
- Katherine Shippen, *The Bright Design* (22)
- André Norton, *Star Born* (19)
- Willy Ley, *Conquest of Space* (15)
- Homer E. Newell, *Space Book for Young People* (18)

■ *Films and reprints*

Films suitable for supporting the purposes of this unit are numerous. Two that have been used are listed here, but each teacher will wish to consult the audio-visual sources available to his school.

"A Phantasy" (35)—In a dreamlike landscape, inanimate but familiar objects come to life and move about dancing to background music.
"Solar Family" (36).

Reprints available include "Space Satellites" (40), "Rockets and Satellites" (39), and "Adventures in Science at the Smithsonian" (38).

■ *Word study*

The teacher plans special lessons to extend vocabulary:

New words: satellite, radar, light years, celestial, ionosphere, galaxy, and others
Words from mythology: Saturn, Venus, Mars, aurora borealis, and others

Prefixes, suffixes, roots: *tele*scopes, *spectro*-scopes, *lun*ar, *luna*tic, stereo*phonic,* and others

■ *Discussions*

Class discussions, usually led by the teacher, may grow out of many facets of the unit. In all cases, the pupils should be led to look upon these discussions as occasions for improving power over the spoken word, for learning courtesy and tact, for listening attentively to the ideas of others, for respecting differences of opinion, and for cleaving to the heart of a discussion without wandering aimlessly. For some topics, the teacher may wish to use group discussions in which each group has specific goals to accomplish and a clearly limited amount of time. However, for the three topics which follow, it is intended that the teacher will lead the discussions, and in preparing to do so, will develop, in line with his own preference, lesson plans carefully designed to accomplish the purposes.

Judging the Quality of Science Fiction. The teacher introduces these points:

Scientific values: accuracy, clarity of presentation, fidelity to known facts.

Literary values: logical relationship between character and plot; freedom from imitativeness, stock characters and situations, clichés and stale metaphor; characters whose motivations are clear and probable; selectivity of incidents that serve the purpose of the story; a theme, something worth getting that is beyond the surface events of the story.

The success of this discussion depends almost entirely upon the specificity of its application. Values such as the above are meaningless to most ninth grade pupils unless presented in relation to actual readings. The teacher should read aloud or procure copies of two stories, one representing literature of distinction and one representing writing of inferior merit. For a representative of distinguished writing, either "By the Waters of Babylon," by Stephen Vincent Benét (4), or "The Portable Phonograph," by Walter Van Tilburg Clark (11) might be used. For inferior writing, use some selection from one of the pulp magazines devoted to science fiction. So much of science fiction is poorly written that the teacher will have no difficulty in locating an example.

At some point in the discussion, note the dangers as well as the pleasures of reading science fiction. How is one to recognize fantasy and sift it from truth so as not to be confused? How can a reader comprehend the purpose of a writer?

Social Criticism in Science Fiction. Read aloud or, if available, assign for class reading one or more selections like the following:

"The Highway" by Ray Bradbury (6)

"Report on the Barnhouse Effect" by Kurt Vonnegut, Jr. (25)

"By the Waters of Babylon" by Stephen Vincent Benét (4) (His poem "Nightmare Number Three" (5) describes a revolt of machines being used for petty and evil purposes by human beings. Some teachers may wish to use this poem in addition to the story.)

"Robot's Return" by Robert Moore Williams (29)

"The Pedestrian" by Ray Bradbury (8)

Pertinent excerpts from the last two chronicles in *The Martian Chronicles* by Ray Bradbury (7)

"Pilot Lights of the Apocalypse" by Louis Ridenour (21)

A suggestion is to form a mock committee on censorship. Assemble three or four volunteers to act as a "committee to eliminate all writing that is dangerous and hostile to the established order." Let them stage a meeting before the class in which they discuss several stories like those listed above, eliminating "dangerous" elements or revising them in order to take out the sting of social criticism. Following this mock committee meeting, class discussion led by the teacher should consider the advantages of social criticism in a democracy, even when one finds such criticism unpleasant. Through concrete examples, the teacher may emphasize the values of differing points of view and the obligation of those in the minority to present their views in order that the group may have access to all sides of a question. These points may be illustrated with examples from school life. Finally, the teacher should try to draw out from the class the thought that those in the majority should welcome rather than resent opinions that differ from theirs. Ask why England and the United States tolerate political parties not in power.

Note: Some of the social criticism in science fiction may not be read thoughtfully by ninth grade pupils. Because much of the world's literature has involved social criticism, helping students to recognize it is a proper aim of teaching. However, because for many this will be the first experience with such content in literature, the teacher will need to go one step further. Help them realize, in "Report on the Barnhouse Effect," for instance, that the problem of war is not as simple as they might infer from the story. Obviously the problem involves forces more complicated than a black-and-white division between good "little people" and bad "people in power." Pupils often tend to see problems in terms of "the good guys and the bad guys."

The Relation of Science to Human Values. Duplicate and distribute copies of the following excerpt from "The Chief Interest of a Scientist" by Albert Einstein.[5]

> Why does this magnificient applied science which saves work and makes life easier bring us so little happiness? The simple answer runs—because we have not yet learned to make sensible use of it.
>
> In war it serves that we may poison and mutilate each other. In peace it has made our lives hurried and uncertain. Instead of freeing us in a great measure from spiritually exhausting labor, it has made men into slaves of machinery, who for the most part complete their monotonous day's work with disgust, and must continually tremble for their poor rations.
>
> You will be thinking that the old man sings an ugly song. I do it, however, with a good purpose, in order to point out a consequence.
>
> It is not enough that you should understand about applied science in order that your work may increase man's blessings. Concern for man himself and his fate must always form the chief interest of all technical endeavors, concern for the great unsolved problems of the organization of labor and the distribution of goods—in order that the creations of our mind shall be a blessing and not a curse to mankind. Never forget this in the midst of your diagrams and equations.

In the discussion which follows, use such questions as these to stimulate thought:

What does Einstein mean in saying that we have not learned to make sensible use of applied science?

[5] Reprinted by permission from the *Sigma Xi Quarterly* (now *The American Scientist*), Vol. 26, No. 3 (September 1938), p. 128.

Einstein believes the scientist's obligation to society is not fully met by inventing new devices to increase the comfort and ease of living. What else might the scientist contribute?

What do you think is meant by "concern for man himself and his fate"? How can the scientist concern himself with man's fate outside the laboratory? Einstein names two problems which he says must be the concern of scientists. What are they? Do you think these problems can be solved in scientific laboratories?

Has any of the science fiction we have read presented, in any way, a point of view similar to that of Einstein?

The teacher may wish some record of pupil participation and contribution during these discussions. One method: Select three different students during each period of class discussion and furnish them with a list of pupils in the class. Each time a pupil makes a contribution, the committee members, working separately from each other, place a tally after the pupil's name. For contributions deemed outstanding in value to the discussion, the committee members circle the tally. Teacher and class discuss in advance a suitable definition of "value to the discussion." Classes where this method has been tried find that any initial effect of inhibiting discussion disappears fairly quickly. As soon as interest in ideas sets in, self-consciousness fades away.

■ *Stale writing*

Read the following list of cliché speeches.[6] Have pupils search for similar examples of unimaginative writing in the materials of this unit and in the pulp magazines devoted to science fiction. For positive value, have them identify passages and speeches they consider good writing.

"Slade, me and some of the other small ranchers have decided to band together to stop the Ringo Kid."

"But doctor, you can't innoculate yourself with this untested serum!"

"Reckon there's going to be trouble. Wade Kincade's headed for Lucky's place!"

"Guess this is the end of the trail for old Pop Phoenix. Let the wagon train roll on without me. But do me a favor, Buck—when you git out West, name a town after me."

"Sorry I had to knock you out, Major, but you've got a wife and kids. I'm taking that plane up myself!"

"There's something strange about this place, Nora. This town isn't on the map—and look how little all the people are."

"You can't ask me to shoot this dog, Judge! I tell you it's a wolf that's been getting at McCready's sheep!"

■ *Individual and/or group reports*

There are innumerable possibilities for reports: The biography of Houdini and his lifelong attempt to persuade humanity to be less credulous; Orson Welles's radio hoax, "Invasion from Mars" (26), and its later repetition in Chile; famous forerunners of science fiction, such as More's *Utopia* (17), Bacon's *New Atlantis* (2), Butler's *Erewhon* (9), Bellamy's *Looking Backward* (3), Wells's *War of the Worlds*

[6] Reprinted by permission of Jerry Lewis Enterprises.

(28) and *The Time Machine* (27). The teacher will think of many possibilities and the more able students will also be able to contribute suggestions.

■ *Tape recordings*

Interested pupils may prepare "on the spot" broadcasts. A commentator who has a good speaking voice and a willingness to work should head the group. He may supervise a plan to interview each pupil who has read an interesting book, acting out the interview as if the reader had actually experienced the incidents of the book. For instance, the interview might begin:

> "Good Evening, ladies and gentlemen, this is your daily "on the spot" broadcast originating wherever there is news. We switch you now to the Planet Venus where (name) is waiting with a big story *on the spot!*"
>
> Commentator: Good evening from the Planet Venus. It is June 5, 1988, and this evening we have with us *on the spot* the leader of the space expedition which . . ."

Interviews of this kind may be developed on tapes, either during the class time of the developmental part of the unit or outside of school as a special project. The tapes may be played for the class during appropriate days within the unit, or used as final projects at the end. Special acclamation should be awarded individuals or groups who introduced elements of scientific accuracy, impressive presentation, or both.

■ *What is a scientist?*

Have pupils write down their mental picture of a scientist: his appearance, his way of life, his outlook on other people. Combine the pupils' word portraits in order to show inconsistencies. The teacher may follow quite closely the directions for such an activity that were used in a study of student images of a scientist. Margaret Mead and Rhoda Metraux carried out such a study in 1957, using 35,000 high school students. Their questionnaire and their results are reported in "Image of the Scientist Among High School Students—a Pilot Study" (p. 272).

■ *Bulletin board and information file*

Use a bulletin board committee to list the names of all students who bring clippings, pictures, and other materials for the bulletin board. Several times a week a member of the committee reports to the class, calling attention to some of the most useful materials, requesting more information or material on certain subjects. In addition to the bulletin board, the committee keeps material filed in manila folders, and makes these collections available to pupils during the current instruction of the unit, turning them over to the teacher for repetitions of the unit with other classes.

■ *Excursions*

A trip to a planetarium or an observatory might serve a double purpose. If the purposes of such a trip are clearly discussed in advance, the knowledge gained can be of value in itself. Motivation for discussion, reports, and compositions may also be one of the values of such an excursion.

CULMINATING EXPERIENCES

A good unit should do more than expire. It should draw to some kind of a close. Ninth grade pupils will feel a greater sense of achievement and satisfaction if they draw together the different facets of the unit and summarize the main features that deserve to be remembered. Among the possible concluding activities are the following:

Preparation of a special issue of a duplicated classroom news sheet, reviewing the unit and what has been learned

Preparation of a space patrol guide, a class-constructed booklet to be used as a guide and orientation for classes the teacher will later guide through this unit

Students' writing during a class period on the topic, Three Things I Have Learned During This Unit

Two guests—other teachers, parents, a school board member, the principal—invited in to question the pupils on what they have accomplished and learned during this unit

Interview of pupils by five members of another class taught by the teacher (The results of these interviews are to be summarized by the outside interviewers. This activity benefits both interviewers and class.)

Preparation of a check list of the goals of the unit, to be filled out anonymously, then collected, tallied, and summarized by a committee of class members

> *Directions:* Please answer thoughtfully. Your sincere, honest appraisal of this unit is what will help most. Do not sign your name. Comment, if you wish, in the space provided.
>
> During this unit, I learned to appreciate the men who adventure for the sake of learning more. strongly agree ______ agree ______ uncertain ______ disagree ______ strongly disagree ______. Comment:
>
> During this unit, I learned how to write a well-constructed paragraph.______
>
> During this unit, I . . .

EVALUATION

The teacher will have the following kinds of evidence to help him in evaluating student growth toward the goals set for this unit: number and quality of books read and recorded on cards; five compositions; records kept of pupil contributions to oral discussion and the quality of the contributions; special contributions by groups and individuals. In addition, each pupil should check some sheet such as the following:

During this unit

I wrote the following compositions:

Title or Topic Sentence . . . Grade . . .

I read the following books:

Title . . . Author . . .

In class discussion I . . .

From this unit, some of the important things I learned and will want to remember are . . .

Materials and resources for pupils

BOOKS

1. Isaac Asimov, *Building Blocks of the Universe.* N.Y., Abelard-Schuman, 1947.
2. Francis Bacon, *New Atlantis.* Princeton, N.J., Van Nostrand, 1942.
3. Edward Bellamy, *Looking Backward.* N.Y., Harper (Modern Classics), 1959.
4. Stephen Vincent Benét, "By the Waters of Babylon." In *Selected Works of Stephen Vincent Benét.* N.Y., Rinehart, 1937. (Also in *Adventures in Appreciation,* Mercury edition, 1952, and *People in Literature,* 1948. N.Y., Harcourt, Brace.)
5. ———, "Nightmare Number Three." In *Burning City.* N.Y., Farrar and Rinehart, 1936.
6. Ray Bradbury, "The Highway." In *The Illustrated Man.* Garden City, N.Y., Doubleday, 1951; N.Y., Bantam Books, 1952.
7. ———, *The Martian Chronicles.* Garden City, N.Y., Doubleday, 1958; N.Y., Bantam Books, 1959.
8. ———, "The Pedestrian." In *The Reporter,* August 7, 1951. Also in Ray Bradbury, ed., *Timeless Stories for Today and Tomorrow.* N.Y., Bantam Books, 1952.
9. Samuel Butler, *Erewhon.* N.Y., Dutton (Everyman), 1927.
10. Lewis Carroll, *Alice's Adventures in Wonderland.* N.Y., Macmillan, 1923.
11. Walter Van Tilburg Clark, "The Portable Phonograph." In *Watchful Gods and Other Stories.* N.Y., Random House, 1950.
12. Paul Ernst, "The 32nd of May." In Groff Conklin, ed., *The Best of Science Fiction.* N.Y., Crown, 1946.
13. E. M. Forster, "The Machine Stops." In *Collected Tales.* N.Y., Knopf, 1947.
14. James Hilton, *Lost Horizon.* N.Y., Morrow, 1933.
15. Willy Ley, *The Conquest of Space.* N.Y., Viking, 1949.
16. ———, *Engineer's Dreams.* N.Y., Viking, 1954.
17. Sir Thomas More, *Utopia.* N.Y., Dutton (Everyman), 1951.
18. Homer E. Newell, *Space Book for Young People.* N.Y., McGraw-Hill, 1958.
19. André Norton, *Star Born.* Cleveland, World Publ., 1957.
20. Mary Norton, *The Borrowers.* N.Y., Harcourt, Brace, 1953.
21. Louis Ridenour, "Pilot Lights of the Apocalypse." In *Fortune,* January, 1946. (Also in *Pleasure in Literature.* N.Y., Harcourt, Brace, 1949).
22. Katherine Shippen, *The Bright Design.* N. Y., Viking, 1949.
23. Jonathan Swift, *Gulliver's Travels.* N.Y., Dutton (Everyman), 1952.
24. Mark Twain, *A Connecticut Yankee in King Arthur's Court.* N.Y., Grossett & Dunlap, 1945.
25. Kurt Vonnegut, "Report on the Barnhouse Effect." In Walter Loban et al., eds., *Adventures in Appreciation.* N.Y., Harcourt, Brace, 1958.
26. Orson Welles, "Invasion from Mars." In H. Cantril, ed., *Invasion from Mars.* Princeton, N.J., Princeton U. Press, 1947.
27. H. G. Wells, *The Time Machine.* In *Seven Famous Novels.* N.Y., Knopf, 1934.
28. ———, *War of the Worlds.* In *Seven Famous Novels.* N.Y., Knopf. 1934.
29. Robert Moore Williams, "Robot's Return." In Egbert W. Nieman and George E. Salt, eds., *Pleasure in Literature.* N.Y., Harcourt, Brace, 1949.
30. Donald Wollheim, *Every Boy's Book of Science-Fiction.* N.Y., Crown, 1956.

FILMS AND RECORDINGS

(For complete addresses of suppliers of films and recordings, see the bibliography, pp. 721 ff.)

31. "The Aztecs," film. Coronet Films.

32. Gustav Holst, "The Planets." Good recordings available on Westminster, Camden, and London labels.
33. "The Medieval Knights," film. Encyclopaedia Brittanica Films.
34. "New Frontiers in Space," film. McGraw-Hill Films.
35. "A Phantasy," film. International Film Bureau.
36. "Solar Family," film. Encyclopaedia Brittanica Films.
37. James Ramsay Ullman, "Beyond the Ranges," from *The Age of Mountaineering* (N.Y., Lippincott, 1954). The recording will be found in *Many Voices,* 4B, Band II. N.Y., Harcourt, Brace, 1958.

REPRINTS

38. "Adventures in Science at the Smithsonian." Washington, D.C., Colortone Press.
39. "Rockets and Satellites." N.Y., Collier's Encyclopedia, Library and Educational Division.
40. "Space Satellites." N.Y., Collier's Encyclopedia, Library and Educational Division.

Resources for the teacher

Margaret Mead and Rhoda Metraux, "Image of the Scientist Among High School Students—a Pilot Study." *Science,* Vol. 126 (August 1957). A complete reprint of this article will be found in Paul F. Brandwein, Fletcher G. Watson, and Paul Blackwood, *Teaching High School Science.* N.Y., Harcourt, Brace, 1958, pp. 452-463.

Basil Davenport et al., *The Science-Fiction Novel, a Symposium.* Chicago, Advent Publishers, 1959. Four writers of science fiction criticize it as entertainment and as social criticism. The teacher will find particularly useful the article of C. M. Kornbluth, who considers science fiction as social criticism and concludes that none of the major works such as *1984* and *Brave New World* have had any effect on social change.

Ten Steps Into Space, Monograph No. 6, Journal of the Franklin Institute. Philadelphia, Franklin Institute, 1958.

Elinor Walker, ed., *Book Bait.* Chicago, American Library Association, 1957.

Kingsley Amis, *New Maps of Hell.* N.Y., Harcourt, Brace, 1960. Based upon Amis' lectures in a seminar at Princeton University, this is a thoughtful and sometimes amusing survey of the new form of literature, science fiction.

The following titles are typical of books suitable for guiding individual reading in this unit. The teacher and the librarian will have other suggestions and the pupils will help to extend this bibliography.

Robert Heinlein, *Farmer in the Sky.* N.Y., Scribner's, 1950.

Willy Ley, *Space Travel.* N.Y., Simon & Schuster, 1958. The fourth book in the highly successful Adventures in Space series.

André Norton, *The Time Traders.* Cleveland, World Publ., 1958. Space-minded men of tomorrow trespass the world of yesterday, struggling not only with a primitive people but a modern day enemy as well.

Jules Verne, *Twenty Thousand Leagues Under the Sea.* Cleveland, World Publ., 1946.

PART THREE

Appreciation

6. Literature: Basic Approaches
7. Literature: Drama and Poetry
8. The Popular Arts

UNITS: Macbeth; Fortitude, the Backbone of Courage

Chapter Six

Literature: Basic Approaches

The human values of a particular literary experience are to be determined finally in relation to the needs of individual human beings.
—THOMAS CLARK POLLOCK [1]

PERSPECTIVE

Proficiency in comprehending expository writing may be sufficient to insure understanding of a scientific treatise, an article on foreign affairs, or a passage from the encyclopedia, but such proficiency will not guarantee adequacy of response to a poem or a play. A young reader may be able to understand *what happens* in "The Pied Piper of Hamelin" without *feeling* ". . . the grumbling grew to a mighty rumbling; And out of the houses the rats came tumbling," but to what avail? Older readers who fail to perceive the relationship of form to content in "My Last Duchess" miss much of the subtlety and the impact of the selection. Beyond the basic search for information, beyond rational comprehension of facts and ideas, reading with appreciation demands emotional as well as intellectual perceptiveness—a totality of response in the individual, who must comprehend, interpret, and respond.

Appreciation of literature can result only from the reading of many books which have a genuine impact on the individual. The teacher's major goal is to guide the selection of books and to help adolescents read literature as human experience—not to teach a fixed number of books, a smattering of biographical data, or a miscellaneous collection of historical fact. Such information may support and extend, but can never supplant, the reader's perception of experiences communicated by the author. This chapter discusses in turn the significance of literature in the educative process, the kinds of reading material having great impact on young people, and the attitudes and abilities needed for appreciation.

[1] Thomas Clark Pollock, *The Nature of Literature in Relation to Science, Language, and Human Experience* (Princeton, N.J., Princeton U. Press, 1942), p. 203.

Literature as an active experience

Because literature offers a distillation of human experience, we find in it a significance comparable to that found in life. As an art form, literature achieves unity and order which evoke in the reader an emotional response. But its unique characteristic is the author's attempt to communicate imaginatively his insights concerning individual thought and action—insights into the meaning of experience. As Henry Alonzo Myers writes,

> Other qualities of poetry and prose are important, but insight—the writer's personal view and his ability to see others as he sees himself, from within, his ability to estimate those inner values which cannot be checked by measuring rods, weights, clocks, and thermometers—is the indispensable quality, the distinguishing trait of literature. Literature may offer more than insight, but it cannot offer less, it cannot lack insight without becoming another kind of writing.[2]

The scientist and the social scientist look on life externally; they consider individuals in terms of the group, in relation to measurable truth or to social values. The literary artist searches for truth internally, viewing the human situation in relation to the individual and through the individual. As David Daiches writes, "Fiction enables us to explore the recesses of man's head and heart with a torch; history allows us only the natural light of day, which does not usually shine into such places. Literature is Man's exploration of man by artificial light, which is better than natural light because we can direct it where we want it." [3] Thus Winston Churchill the historian lucidly describes the Allied occupation of Italy during World War II in terms of global strategy and social implications, but we need John Hersey to interpret its impact on individuals in books like *A Bell for Adano*. Both ways of looking at life are important; both must be taught to students; but the way of literature is the internal way, and it is in literature and through literature, almost exclusively among secondary school subjects, that the student learns the humane approach to examining thought and action.

To share the insight of any author, an individual must respond actively as he reads. Emotionally and intellectually he enters the conflict between Huck Finn and his father or identifies with the misery of Silas Marner. And whenever the reader so enters the experience of art, the work may have greater impact on him than does any experience of life. At various times he shares an intensity of feeling, identifies with a diverse personality, looks on life through foreign eyes, becomes involved in a problem situation. It is this creative two-way process—the author attempting to communicate the experience, the reader reaching out to share it—that is the essence of literature.

[2] Henry Alonzo Myers, "Literature, Science, and Democracy," *Pacific Spectator*, Vol. 8, No. 4 (Autumn 1954), p. 337.

[3] David Daiches, *A Study of Literature for Readers and Critics* (Ithaca, N.Y., Cornell U. Press, 1948), p. 24.

Values in literature

Many perceptions and understandings acquired from primary experience may also be attained through literature. One person discovers the gnawing pains of self-incrimination by being unkind to a friend; another reaches similar insight by sharing the anguish of the unthinking protagonist in Robert Coates's story, "The Need," or, if a child, of Maddie in *The Hundred Dresses.* Such experiences do not automatically result from reading, just as they do not automatically occur in life, but they may happen whenever literature touches a reader deeply. In describing what individuals gain from such literary experiences, we emphasize various things. We speak of the power of literature to delight, to humanize, to develop sensitivity—or we in some other way identify important outcomes of the literary experience. Most teachers, however, agree on at least three major goals—self-understanding, imaginative illumination, and a balanced perspective on life. Illustrated here in the reading of young people, these occur no less frequently in adult reading.

Literature for self-understanding Literature can reveal the significance of our emotions and actions, and reveal it in many ways. A child sharing the companionship of Charlotte and Wilbur in *Charlotte's Web* may sense for the first time the meaning of loneliness and the obligations of friendship, just as an adolescent may measure his own loyalties against the relationship of Jim Hawkins and Long John Silver in *Treasure Island* or an adult find similar illumination in *War and Peace.* Tarkington's *Turmoil* offers young readers a chance to compare moral and material values in a context fraught with immediacy, just as Salinger's portrait of Holden Caulfield's search for stability offers more perceptive youth an illumination of the turbulence of adolescence within a changing society. Through evaluating and sharing different images of life, each reader builds his own sense of values and alters the way he looks on himself and his world.

Literature as imaginative illumination The whimsical nonsense of *Mary Poppins,* the richness of "The Eve of St. Agnes," the unrelieved suspense of "The Tell-Tale Heart"—such selections offer enjoyment, variety, and escape. Some literature exists primarily to stimulate flights of fancy, to delight us with the brilliance of its execution. We are swept by the adventure of Rogers' Rangers in *Northwest Passage* or the harrowing ordeal of *Boon Island;* we travel to Queen Anne's court in *Henry Esmond;* we revel in the eastern splendor of the Arabian Nights. Some readers find pleasure in the rolling cadences of "The Charge of the Light Brigade" or the magical rhymes of "Jabberwocky," while others delight in the deftly turned phrases of Kenneth Graham, the economy and control of Conrad, the imagery of Emily Dickinson. Certainly it is more than a naive pleasure in the obvious for which teachers strive in attempting to develop appreciation. It is rather toward an appetite for different kinds of beauty, toward a heightened perception of an artistic excellence which may be discovered in the most subtle ways, so that a single person may rejoice in many kinds of literary experience.

Literature for a balanced perspective Through literature we test life by sharing experiences with many individuals. We feel sympathy and antipathy for persons quite different from ourselves and find more opportunities for choosing among different emotional responses and courses of action than life itself can offer. We may accept or reject the compassion of Peggotty in *David Copperfield,* the pride of Mary Lou Wingate in defying Northern soldiers in *John Brown's Body,* or the self-centeredness of Becky Sharp; in doing this we comprehend the needs of personalities quite different from our own. By evaluating different modes of conduct we deepen and extend our consciousness of the richness of life.

Through literature we can achieve freedom from the penalties and restrictions of singularity. Suspending our own values, we look at life through the eyes of Austen, Twain, or Henry James. The bitterness of Thomas Hardy forces us momentarily to consider life in ways we normally might reject, as do the romanticism of Emily Brontë, the controlled realism of Edith Wharton, or the frightening insights of Nelson Algren.

This capacity of literature to permeate thought and emotion makes possible its ultimate impact. Some books shape our thinking slowly and subtly; some influence it not at all. A few selections affect us momentarily during critical periods in our life while others serve as continuing sources of influence.

Selecting literature for adolescents

What literature will provide significant experiences for adolescents? Not necessarily the same books that provide literary experiences for adults. *Faust,* for example, is a great book; its profound analysis of good and evil offers insight to mature readers, regardless of time, place, condition, or philosophical orientation. But *Faust* is *not* a great book for most immature readers, who lack points of contact with the ideological struggle between Mephistopheles and Faust. For many, *The Bridge of San Luis Rey* or *Our Town* are better literary experiences, even though these works may fail the supreme tests of quality. In reacting to genuine, but less demanding, literary selections in terms of his peculiar personal experiences, the adolescent may learn how to read literature so that ultimately he can respond to the challenge of Goethe, Melville, and other great authors; whereas the direct classroom imposition of difficult selections like *Faust* may result in no reading experience at all. Indeed permanent damage to the reader's attitude may result if teachers disregard the level of maturity and experience of adolescents. For example, Annis Duff relates clearly how her daughter, even though nourished on a rich diet of books at home, responded to Coleridge in the eighth grade:

We were made very much aware of a situation that developed at school when a young teacher, still not accustomed to the temperament of boys and girls at this age, undertook a detailed study of "The Rime of the Ancient Mariner." Simply read through as the wonderful adventure of a ghostly ship and its crew, it would probably have been well liked. But discussion of its mystical and metaphysical aspects went against the grain because it was neither understandable nor interesting to eighth-graders, and they refused to take it seriously. . . . It was a wise man who said, "There are poems whose fineness and delicacy are of such a character that in forcing them prematurely on the attention one runs the risk of rendering them permanently distasteful, or vulgarizing them by incongruous association." (W. J. Alexander in the Preface to *Shorter Poems* . . .)

Six years after this dreary little eighth-grade episode a group of our daughter's classmates were talking about their work in English literature in college. When one of them spoke of reading "The Ancient Mariner" there was the immediate question, "How did you like it this time?" The girl hesitated before answering, and then said quite seriously, "I really tried to like it because the others thought it was so wonderful. But I still kept feeling upset the way I did when Mr. T. talked about guilt and penance and all that . . ." [4]

The place of classics Does this suggest then that all classics be eliminated from our program in literature? Not at all. Testimony from teachers and evidence from research indicate clearly that many major works continue to transmit meaning to the young.[5] Few will claim, for example, that a well taught *Macbeth* does not excite some youthful readers. Not too many years ago Norvell studied the reading preferences of 50,000 students and found that many standard selections possess genuine appeal. Selections like *Huckleberry Finn, David Copperfield,* "The Deacon's Masterpiece," "A Dissertation Upon Roast Pig," received unusually high ratings; among those with lesser appeal were the *Odyssey, The Vicar of Wakefield,* and *As You Like It.*[6] Clearly such studies suggest that the choice of literary material be based on the characteristics of boys and girls.

Any book offering genuine insight into the significance of human thought and action can provide a literary experience. Much writing for and about adolescence, like *Seventeenth Summer* or *Old Yeller,* will strike a reader with telling impact only during a brief interval in his life. Lacking the universality of major writing, these stories can offer the youth a moment of insight into his own world as only literature can. From such active participation in a literary experience, mature appreciations may grow. The girl who this year responds to Maureen Daly may next year discover Charlotte Brontë and later Willa Cather and Jane Austen. Such growth occurs slowly over a long period

[4] Annis Duff, *Longer Flight* (N.Y., Viking, 1955), pp. 113-115. Teachers of English will be interested in this warm, book-length discussion of family reading experiences.

[5] See Esther Anderson, "A Study of the Leisure-time Reading of Pupils in Junior High School," *Elementary School Journal,* Vol. 8, No. 5 (January 1948); Phyllis Lenner, *The Proof of the Pudding* (N.Y., Day, 1957); George W. Norvell, *The Reading Interests of Young People* (Boston, Heath, 1950).

[6] Norvell, *Reading Interests,* p. 86.

of time, but there is a close affinity between the girl who perceives meaning in Maureen Daly's work and the adult who turns to Jane Austen for insight into human relationships.

The role of the teacher The teacher can do much to help young people find meaning and experience in literature; he can do much to help them develop appreciation for literary form. He can lead students to see parallels between the greed of Silas Marner's world and that apparent today, between the fear of the unknown expressed by Henry Fleming in *The Red Badge of Courage* and the adolescent's own ambivalence before uncertainty. He can also help them see how the artistry of Eliot and Crane creates the impact of the literary experiences. Helping readers relate literature to life is one responsibility of the teacher, but such interaction is possible only if the elements of a book actually touch elements in the reader's experience. Helping students understand how an author achieves artistic unity is another of the teacher's responsibilities, but such understanding builds slowly, requiring experience with literary works varying in degrees of excellence. Appreciation of both content and form can be fostered; it cannot be imposed by royal edict.

Students can learn more easily to recognize universality of subject matter than to savor niceties of style; naturally their first reaction is to characters and the story. This interaction between book and reader may not always be favorable. Parallels which stir unpleasant relationships can sometimes cause books to be rejected. Anxieties awakened by Murray Heyert's "The New Kid" may prevent identification by a boy experiencing problems in group acceptance. When aware of potential problems, teachers can plan appropriate introductory activities. For example, Jessamyn West's story "The Hat" (from *Cress Delahanty*) deals with an adolescent girl's attempt to impress a boyfriend. Boy readers are sometimes made uncomfortable by Cress's antics and their reactions can block free discussion. One imaginative teacher assigned for reading at the same time "That's What Happened to Me," a story in which a boy wished to impress his peers, and read aloud another short story in which a boy wishes to impress a girl, "I'm A Fool." The resulting discussion focused on the desire to impress others. By relating the problem of Cress Delahanty to a widely experienced human need, the teacher made it possible for most readers to respond to the literary experience.

In selecting literature, teachers avoid yielding to the ephemeral and the meaningless. Not all books written for adolescents attempt to communicate genuine experience. Not all are stylistically acceptable. Many—too many—are trite, contrived commercial ventures feeding on stereotyped preconceptions existing in the adolescent's mind. In selecting literature, teachers will want to encourage the reading of the best books *to which immature readers can respond.* Realistically, teachers recognize that the level of quality will not always be as high as is desired and that here as elsewhere in the program they can raise the student's level of response only through *sound and organized guidance.*

Reading interest There is danger, too, lest teachers misunderstand the student's actual interest. Most find it helpful to examine a few studies of reading preference [7] as well as to determine the particular interests of the students in their classrooms. Who can say whether the continued popularity of animal themes among readers in grades seven and eight is a reflection of a widespread concern for pets or an indirect expression of the thirteen-year-old's desire to assume the responsibility of caring for a dependent? Who is certain that the world of *Great Expectations* is not closer to some boys than the America of Howard Pease or Stephen Meader? Certainly teachers must be careful to examine the reactions of each individual and to interpret them in relation to his total behavior.

Undoubtedly consideration of taste and propriety must also affect the selection of all reading materials. No one will maintain that the adolescent be permitted to read in school books that he must hide at home. Can we not discourage the reading of brutal, sordid exploitations of human misery, yet urge students seeking "strong" fare to consider *Mister Roberts* or *The Execution of Private Slovik*—books with "earthy" qualities which possess other values, such as authenticity of character or concern for human dignity?

Ultimately the improvement of taste must start with the students' level of appreciation. This necessarily demands that young readers be taught to evaluate and reject both saccharine portraits of an artificial adolescent world as well as the synthetic drug store potboilers. Over a period of time the immature reader can learn to distinguish between genuine and contrived experiences. The teacher's job is to find the level of active response and then to build upon it and extend it.

Skills and attitudes needed for reading with appreciation

Skills involved in literary analysis must be taught, but the way the reader approaches a selection is important, too. Certainly critical reading of literature can occur only if the reader is skilled in interpreting both the form and content of a literary selection. Beyond the basic competencies of comprehension, students must acquire advanced skills in reading which enable them to explore the full richness of literature. The development of these special competencies is so properly an integral part of our literary program that most instruction is introduced in relation to the reading and interpretation of specific selections. Among the more important abilities to be developed are those involved in seeing relationships between form and content, in perceiving the development of character, theme, symbol, and in detecting the multiplicity of meaning. Young readers need these skills to understand the over-all impact of a selection and to read literature more fully on their own. Thus instruction needs to emphasize the use of each skill in understanding a complete selection, rather than the development of the skill in isolation.

[7] Some of the more interesting studies of reading preferences are listed at the end of this chapter.

Moreover, teachers need to remember that basic understandings concerning literary forms are developed over the six years of secondary school. Most skills are acquired slowly, at different times, and in relation to many diverse selections. Most of the important skills fall into three categories:

Those needed to perceive the beauty in form which closely parallels content: the author's selection of media; his uses of rhythm and balance; the interrelationship of setting, tone, and point of view.

Those needed to perceive development: the structure of the narrative, the logic of the characterization, the relationship of incident and theme.

Those needed to explore meanings below the surface: the basic theme, the connotative effect of words, the use of imagery, the signs and symbols, the satire and irony.

Procedures for teaching the several skills are described in detail in the Suggested Learning Experiences presented later in this chapter.

Immature readers also need to overcome many inadequate kinds of responses which interfere with their ability to interpret literature. Anxious to encourage factual comprehension or stylistic understanding, teachers can place too restrictive an emphasis on the literary selection itself and too little on the way in which literature is best approached—on *how* the reader looks at and responds to a story or a poem, rather than on the poem itself. Indeed the way in which a reader learns to approach a romance like *Ivanhoe* and the attitudes he takes away from reading will have a more lasting influence on his appreciation of literature than will the specific understandings derived from the Scott opus.

To emphasize ways of approaching literature which produce intelligent and appreciative reactions, teachers focus on improving the processes which each individual undergoes in responding to a poem, a play, or a work of fiction, rather than on the development of knowledge about a single work or on the refinement of discrete reading skills. In doing this, teachers become, at least momentarily, less interested in teaching "The Sire de Maletroit's Door" or in increasing the student's ability to detect rising and falling action than in considering the over-all methods which the younger reader employs in approaching, responding to, and evaluating any literary work. Among the more helpful attitudes to be cultivated are responding with genuineness, suspending judgment, weighing evidence objectively, searching for a plurality of meanings, and fusing intellectual and emotional reactions.[8]

Reacting with genuineness Real appreciation develops only through honesty. We need to think for ourselves even if our judgment is not always the best. We reject or accept, like or dislike, are scornful or enthusiastic about a poem, a character, or a passage because of the effect produced on us as we

[8] This analysis is based on a special study of adolescent response to reading. See James R. Squire, "The Response of Adolescents to Literature Involving Selected Experiences in Personal Development," unpublished doctoral dissertation, University of California, Berkeley, 1956.

read. Many subtleties of idea and image will escape us until we become keenly attuned to the complexities of fine writing, yet if literature is ever to work its magic, we must learn to be honest with ourselves. If a young reader finds pleasure in the poems of Emily Dickinson, well and good; if not—if he finds pleasure only in "Casey at the Bat"—let teachers accept him at this level and try to help him find pleasure in other kinds of poetry. Too often adolescents seem to mistrust their own feelings and ideas and substitute instead the pronouncements of their teachers or the standards of their peers.

Teachers expect and welcome a range of response to any selection, but perhaps need to avoid placing too high a premium on enjoyment *per se* and place more on understanding. Isn't this a great poem? should be less the question for a class than What is the poet attempting to say? What effect does the poem have on you? What are the satisfactions which *some* people find in this selection? Once students find that they are required neither to wax eloquently over every selection nor to reflect standard literary judgments, they become more willing to express and analyze their basic feelings.

Genuineness in response can be encouraged or discouraged through such approaches to instruction as the following:

Classroom approaches which tend to stultify genuineness	Classroom approaches which encourage genuineness
Offering students prejudgments on a selection before reading and urging them to find out why the selection is "good"	Evaluating a selection with students after it is read and understood
Making students feel that there is only one "acceptable" response to a selection	Accepting a range of responses to any selection, providing that these do not conflict with verifiable facts
Overemphasizing the externals surrounding literature, such as the author, the period in which he lived, etc.	Emphasizing the literary experience—what a selection says or what it does to the reader

Suspending judgment Mature readers approach interpretation with a spirit of tentativeness and delay final judgment until they search for possible meanings throughout a selection. Most of us learn through experience that real understanding develops slowly and that people and situations are not always what they initially appear to be. Young people must discover that in the well-constructed story the inexplicable behavior of persons like Miss Haversham or Rochester ultimately becomes clarified; more important perhaps, they discover that at times characters who may initially seem clear-cut and understandable—Mrs. Penn in "The Revolt of Mother," Mattie in *Ethan Frome*—are later revealed to possess unsuspected complexity.

What can teachers do to help students develop tentativeness in interpretation? Certainly they may teach students how meaning is discovered—that to detect character, for example, readers examine an individual's statements and actions as well as what others say about him. To understand the necessity for such evaluation, students need only study a selection in which a character's analysis of himself departs radically from the views of others as, for example, the boy's in "A Mother in Mannville." In such cases the reader is forced to assess the basic nature of the person.

Certainly young readers can be encouraged to withhold final judgments regarding elements other than characterization, such as the symbolic meaning or the basic intent of the author. Usually these cannot be determined completely until the total selection is weighed. At the secondary level, much of the danger of rash, thoughtless prejudgment occurs in assessing characters, since it is with respect to people that many students tend to "jump to conclusions."

Searching for meanings Young readers need to learn ways of exploring the complexity of literature. Skill in detecting irony, satire, or symbolism contributes to the perceptiveness of readers, but the development of a basic orientation which fosters this searching attitude extends beyond the acquisition of specific skills. What is to be encouraged is an interest in detecting hidden nuances and an appreciation for richness and complexity.

Weighing evidence objectively Readers have been known to react so negatively to the girl in "I Can't Breathe" that they miss the humor of the story; others, enraged by the adolescents who call Stephen "clodhopper" in Sara Addington's story, view the selection primarily as one depicting injustice and snobbery rather than compassion and understanding. Indeed a sympathetic identification with Stephen may prevent understanding the actions of the girl in the story. Still other readers respond so favorably or unfavorably to the theme or the imagery in poems like "To an Athlete Dying Young" or "Richard Cory" that they accept, reject, or misinterpret because of their strong emotions. With such a statement as "He must have been crazy to shoot himself with all his money," they dismiss "Richard Cory" without seeing the irony implicit in the poem. Boundlessly optimistic in viewing the future, few young people will express anything except sympathy for the death of a young athlete and either overlook or repudiate Housman's solace in seeing the "man" pass before the "name." Thus, emotional predispositions often color reactions to literature and block sound perception and interpretation.

Insisting that students substantiate their judgments encourages them to weigh impressions and evidence. If a reader wishes to deny that Housman finds solace in the death of a youthful hero, let him find documentation and let the teacher and other students be alert to point out ideas and images which cannot be reconciled with such interpretation. Many situations and motives arouse strong feelings, and unless the incidents are studied carefully, readers may accept only their initial emotional reactions.

Fusing emotional and intellectual responses Any successful attempt to improve response to literature recognizes the importance of emotional as well as rational reactions. To a considerable degree, the reader relies on his emotions as a guide in entering the literary experience, else he does not respond actively and vitally. However, the analytical study of literature is a valuable and necessary supplement to emotional experience and one which often follows it. Jarred by the impact of a Poe story, a reader may try to discover how the effect is achieved. Individuals can sympathize with Amelia in *Vanity Fair* without consciously analyzing their feelings, yet a study of passages to which they react may clarify and even heighten their understanding and appreciation. There is strength in responding to the emotional impact of the whole as well as in relying on a detailed textual analysis of the parts; to help pupils acquire both habits, teachers avoid overstressing either.

There is only one sure way for students to learn to appreciate literature and that is by reading. The teacher's responsibility is to encourage wide reading throughout secondary school years and to supplement this effort by instructing students in *how* to read literature. In teaching any selection, however, the teacher does well to remember that it may be an attitude toward reading—toward Shakespeare, toward poetry, toward "The Rime of the Ancient Mariner"—that the pupil will retain long after he has forgotten the particular lesson.

THE TEACHING PROBLEM

Organizing Instruction

Certainly there is no royal road to the organization of significant classroom experiences in literature. Beyond recognizing that instruction in literature, as in the skills of communication, is most effective when organized by units of instruction, teachers find different kinds of arrangements to be appropriate at different times. Many units are based on literature, since poems, essays, stories, and the like provide content for discussion and writing. Within each unit, important reading experiences may be introduced for individuals and groups as well as for the total class. Thus several problems in planning must be considered.

APPROACHES TO TEACHING LITERATURE

The sound approaches to teaching are those emphasizing literary experiences rather than the facts surrounding literary works. Ultimately the teacher's basic competence is more likely to determine his effectiveness than any method of organization; yet certain kinds of units appear to be appropriate for particular groups.

Thematic and topical arrangement Thematic or topical units deal with values, ideas, and human experiences. To compare the treatment of similar ideas, readers direct their attention to the content of literature in such thematic units as "In Sight of Maturity" (*Johnny Tremain, The Yearling, Swiftwater*); "Justice" (*Mutiny on the Bounty, Les Misérables, The Caine Mutiny*); "The Meaning of Love" (*Romeo and Juliet, Cyrano de Bergerac,* "The Eve of St. Agnes"). In well-organized thematic units, the central experiences with which each selection deals are closely associated with the unifying theme.

Topical units also provide opportunities for contrasting similar selections, although usually on a much broader basis. Such topics as "The Pioneers Move West," "Survival," or "Meeting Successful People" are of interest to younger adolescents and offer a framework for relating diverse literary pieces, but clearly the organization here is less intimately related to the central ideas expressed in the selections than in most thematic units. Whereas the themes normally illuminate universal human experiences, the topics tend to be general categories for grouping related ideas. For example, *The Yearling* reveals certain patterns of family life in depicting the Baxter family's struggle for existence in the Florida interior and has sometimes been taught in units on "Family Life" or "Back Country America"; yet the novel is basically a study of Jody's struggle to assume adult responsibility. When introducing such a selection to illuminate a topic, teachers can see that readers perceive the unique experiences of the story before introducing the elements related to the general topic being studied. Thematic units, which often deal with basic aspects of human experience, seem to be increasingly appropriate during the later years of secondary schools; topical units are perhaps best stressed during the junior high school years.

Arrangements by type and by literary genre Units based on any form of literature permit concentration on literary craftsmanship; however, except for poetry, which does seem to require special attention, typological study *per se* need not receive considerable stress within the total curriculum. The skills and information needed for reading a particular form of literature can usually be studied within the context of a different kind of unit. Certainly students require special help in learning to read plays, just as they respond favorably from time to time to the concentrated study of folklore, science fiction, or travel stories. However, when attention is directed to modes of literature, the particular ideas and experiences communicated in each selection are still central. Probably any detailed analysis of the artist's craft is wisely delayed until the college years.

The study of a single classic Major works of literature offer such a rich tapestry of interwoven themes and experiences that they are difficult to study within a thematic, topical, or typological unit. During each school year, many teachers provide for the common study of one or more longer classics which seem to possess significance for most adolescents in the class. Certain modern classics, such as *Our Town* and *Johnny Tremain,* are often taught in separate two- or three-week units, as is such standard literary fare as *Macbeth, Julius*

Caesar, and *My Antonia*. Intensive concentration on a single work permits the study of many interrelated concepts in terms of the unified purpose of an entire selection.

Arrangements which overemphasize the externals Clarification of the teacher's role in helping students learn how to respond to reading leads to a recognition of the limited value in methods of organization which stress the learning of facts about literature rather than the experiences of literature. Approaches which enable the teacher to place primary emphasis on the critical reading of the selections themselves provide the most compelling literary experience.[9] Through the considered use of almost any approach, of course, an intelligent teacher may direct continuous attention to the experiences conveyed by literature. The exploration of significant ideas, values, or themes may be confined to works written during a single literary period or even by a single author. However, too often units stressing historical backgrounds or lives of authors degenerate into little more than factual surveys of incidents and social settings more appropriate to the social science classroom than to the English. The necessary background information to support the study of a given selection can be presented even in units focusing on ideas and literary experiences. Concentrating primarily on biographical detail—such as in using *Huckleberry Finn* to advance a unit on the life of Mark Twain rather than to illuminate understanding of human dignity and freedom—misdirects the focus of the reader. Such emphases seldom encourage growth in appreciation and tend, according to one professor of English, not "to teach what literature is about, but only about literature—or perhaps we should say, around literature." [10]

Increasingly, teachers are recognizing the value of approaches which stress ideas and themes. In a recent survey of 4,005 high school teachers, preference for the chronological approach and for studies organized by authors were reported less frequently than any other type of preference, except for blind reliance on the textbook. In the same study, presentation by theme was reported as the preferred method.[11]

[9] Burton found that concentration on themes resulted in as great a measured growth in literary appreciation as did instruction which emphasized style. Dwight Burton, "An Experiment in Teaching Fiction," *English Journal*, Vol. 42, No. 1 (January 1953).

[10] James J. Lynch, "The English Teacher's Greatest Resource," *English Journal*, Vol. 45, No. 10 (October 1956).

[11] *English Language Arts in California Public High Schools*, Bulletin No. 7, California State Department of Education, Sacramento (September 1957). The methods of teaching literature in grades eleven and twelve, as ranked according to per cent of 4,005 high school teachers' preferences, were as follows:

Teaching method	*Per cent preferring*	*Teaching method*	*Per cent preferring*
Presentation by themes	61	Chronological approach	32
Study by literary types	49	Study by authors	30
Study by culture-epoch	46	Follow textbook	25
Free reading	34		

Totals exceed 100 per cent since many teachers expressed several preferences.

TEACHING LITERATURE TO THE ENTIRE CLASS

Selecting worthwhile literature for presentation to a heterogeneous group of pupils poses such a major challenge that some teachers advocate meeting the problem through the almost exclusive use of group and individual reading. Each of these procedures is considered later in this chapter. While both offer sound and manageable ways of providing for individuals, in most classrooms students need to share a few common literary selections. Such unifying experiences provide an underlying core of ideas—a point of contact between the intellectually able and the intellectually limited—on which a subsequent program of guided group and individual reading may be based. Such common study also permits the teacher to provide the intensive help students need when confronted with difficult selections. Few would claim, for example, that any but the very superior pupils be encouraged to read Shakespeare without careful guidance from the teacher, or even that the very superior are ready for such independent reading until after a carefully planned program of instruction. Teachers can organize classrooms to present special lessons to groups of students, but much direct instruction is usually presented through common class activity.

Selecting literature for reading by the entire class Not all plays and novels elicit responses with various dimensions of meaning. Many difficult, reflective selections, like *Hamlet, Moby Dick,* and *The Scarlet Letter,* must properly be reserved for mature readers, since both in content and form they possess obstacles which discourage any but the most persistent youngsters. Other worthwhile selections, however, captivate both the gifted and the slow and involve many readers within a single classroom. Some junior high school readers, for example, react only to the adventurous narrative of *Johnny Tremain,* while others recognize the symbolic association of Johnny's physical handicap with his warped and restricted outlook on life; a few perhaps grasp the intimate parallel between the boy's growth toward maturity and the colonies' struggle for independence. All students read the book with profit but at different levels of meaning.

Certainly provision needs to be made for some teacher-directed study of books which interest the least able and yet tax the gifted. Probably one or two classics, either standard or modern, should be introduced in most classes—at least one novel and, beyond the ninth year, one long play in addition to numerous short selections. Certain familiar works continue to be taught successfully. For example, *Macbeth, Tom Sawyer,* and *Our Town* are taught to complete classes; in contrast some teachers reserve such selections as *Idylls of the King* and *A Tale of Two Cities* for special groups. The identification of the specific books to be taught to heterogeneous classes and those to be assigned only to special groups is a task that requires both understanding of literature and understanding of the students to whom the literature is to be taught.

Presenting literature orally Many common experiences in literature may be introduced through oral readings by the teacher. Slow learners often respond to the emotional appeal of verse, particularly when it is presented in a dramatic oral interpretation. When students possess scripts so that they can follow the reading, their understanding usually increases. Similarly, short stories which tax beyond endurance the silent reading abilities of some individuals can be made understandable when read aloud by the teacher. For example, a ninth-grader reading at fourth grade level, who finds "Leiningen Versus the Ants" an almost insuperable forty-page obstacle as home reading, may listen enthralled to a teacher presentation of the story. Such readings provide opportunity for all students in the class to share and discuss a common selection.

Providing for variation when teaching a single selection Much can be done to provide for individual differences, even in teaching a single selection to a total group. In leading a discussion, teachers can ask questions which encourage students to respond at various levels of interpretation. Basic factual problems can be directed to students responding only to the narrative; others will seem ready to consider the meaning of the action and events; a few may be able to assess form in relation to content or to delve into the basic significance of a selection. Since teachers usually ask some factual, some interpretational, and some critical questions in the study of each literary work, they can see that each member of the class has opportunity to make a contribution.[12]

Students require differing amounts of teacher help in reading any selection. Some teachers circulate casually around the room during reading periods to provide needed guidance. Others meet with four or five students while the remainder of the class is occupied. Thus, in directing a study of *Great Expectations*, the teacher would provide for periodic discussions by the entire class—probably emphasizing the significance of Pip's changing attitude toward the social scene—and supplemental discussions with slower readers or absentees. Usually these special meetings stress understandings of the narrative as a supplement to the interpretational emphases developed with the total class. The more able readers, who complete the novel well before their fellows, could participate in all class activities but might be encouraged to read other books by Dickens or books with similar themes, such as *Point of No Return* or *Arrowsmith.*

Some teachers find success in teaching a single work to four or five groups functioning at different levels of learning. For example, the teacher plans a series of discussion meetings to follow the reading of specific segments of

[12] Gordon believes we have five levels of questioning to consider: 1) to remember a fact, 2) to prove a generalization that someone else has made, 3) to make one's own generalization, 4) to generalize from the book to its application in life, and 5) to carry over the generalization into one's own behavior. Edward J. Gordon, "Levels of Teaching and Testing," *English Journal*, Vol. 44, No. 1 (September 1955). An important discussion of this method is also included in the introduction to Margaret Heaton and Helen B. Lewis, eds., *Reading Ladders for Human Relations*, rev. and enl. ed. (Washington, D.C., American Council on Education, 1955).

The Red Badge of Courage. The first six students to finish reading the first assignment meet with the teacher for discussion, while others continue to read; the next group to finish the first section meets with the teacher during a subsequent class hour; the slowest students, who require specialized help, make up the final group to consider each reading assignment. Despite similar content, each discussion varies. Such a plan permits individual guidance, yet provides common reference for the class so that discussion, panels, audio-visual and other total class experiences may be introduced in relation to the novel.

Teacher-planned abridgements, condensations, and summaries are useful and appropriate in certain classrooms.[13] Long and difficult descriptions or explanatory passages discourage some youthful readers in such books as *Treasure Island* or *Silas Marner.* Often slow moving content may be condensed and presented by the teacher to encourage reluctant readers to move forward to more compelling chapters. When, after several days of study, a teacher finds some students falling behind the remainder of the class, he may summarize the important events prior to a particular reading assignment and then encourage slow readers to continue from that point. This must be done judiciously, of course, for certain new dangers accompany the method. Some teachers ask the more able students who have read ahead to prepare summaries or even informal dramatizations of the chapters which may be difficult for some to read. Unlike printed adaptations, such condensations and summaries are made by a particular teacher with the needs of a special student group in mind.

These suggestions have dealt with ways of organizing instruction with a heterogeneous group so that the single selection may be read by all. For the most part the longer works, the novel and play, should be read rapidly rather than painstakingly. As a committee on reading development suggests, teachers need to avoid acting as if they are "marooned on a desert island, with only one volume to last until help arrives." [14] Seldom do students retain interest in a single work for more than three or four weeks. When a longer period is allowed for reading, many fail to see the whole as a unified presentation. The students should grasp the story first and with reasonable rapidity; then scheduled rereadings, careful analyses, and some intensive study can follow.

DIRECTING GROUP READING

The use of multiple materials and grouping procedures offers a manageable way of providing for the diversities which face teachers in large classes.

[13] These should be distinguished from the adapted or completely rewritten "classics" which offer the shell of a literary work without the essential content. To study a version of *Gulliver's Travels* rewritten for fourth level readers, is merely another, more objectionable, way of teaching *about* literature rather than teaching literature itself. Curiously, such adaptations are sometimes defended as presenting cultural experiences for the slow reader, yet few of the volumes contain anything but the names, events, and most obvious narrational features of the original book. Fortunately, the supply of genuine books for slow readers is increasing and teachers need no longer accept these ill-conceived substitutes.

[14] Jean Grambs, *The Development of Lifetime Reading Habits* (N.Y., National Book Committee, 1954), p. 7.

Before selecting literature and organizing group activity, teachers do well to identify those situations in which they plan to *teach* literature to groups as well as those in which they intend to provide for student reading and sharing while offering only general guidance. Both require sound and careful planning, but they serve differing purposes.

Providing general guidance Many books can be profitably discussed and analyzed by students without immediate assistance from the teacher. Often group reading assignments of this type develop during a unit of instruction, such as when class members choose the most interesting of three or four topics during a unit called "Lost Worlds." Following the common study of a few selections to provide a basic core of ideas, students, with teacher help, select several interesting areas for group reading and study: the destruction of civilizations of the past, imaginary worlds of the future, distant worlds of the present, etc. In each of these groups, students may read and share ideas gleaned from such titles as the following:

Ancient civilizations	Distant lands	Imaginary worlds
Last Days of Pompeii	Kon-Tiki	Earth Abides
Quo Vadis	Out of this World	Animal Farm
Voyages of Richard Halliburton	People of the Deer	Erewhon
Scrolls From the Dead Sea	Conquest of Everest	When Worlds Collide
Digging in Yucatan	Annapurna	The Time Machine
Gods, Graves, and Scholars		Lost Horizon
		A Connecticut Yankee in King Arthur's Court
		The Machine Stops

When the reading is completed, each group meets to discuss insights gained and to plan a presentation or report to the entire class. Some reports stress basic ideas through an organized panel—for example, a discussion of the motivation of men in primitive societies; other groups find dramatic or graphic presentation to be effective. The teacher's role in such activity is essentially that of consultant; having assisted in the planning and in selection of books, he remains in the background ready to assist as needed.

A similar kind of situation occurs when students select titles rather than topics for reading. For example, during a seventh grade unit called "Animals in Literature," pupils are asked to choose among *Silver Chief*, *Stickeen*, *National Velvet*, or *Lassie Come Home*. Again, units on biography may involve the study of five or six different persons by separate groups. Opportunities for such experiences may be found in almost any unit.

Occasionally teachers prefer not to organize the discussion sections until much of the reading is completed. In such cases, a teacher brings into the classroom trays of fifty or sixty anthologies of short stories and, specifying little more than a minimum assignment, permits students to choose and read a number of selections. Sometimes thirty or so may be specially recommended. After several days the rapid readers perhaps have completed seven or eight stories, while slower readers have read only one or two. The stories most frequently read, and thus of the greatest interest to the class, serve as the content for discussion. The units "Meeting A Crisis" and "Fortitude, the Backbone of Courage" illustrate this procedure.

Teaching by groups Special considerations are involved when instruction is necessary because the literature being read by groups is unusually difficult or challenging. Some teachers successfully organize class periods so as to meet separately with each group for twenty or twenty-five minutes every two or three days. For example, groups may be taught various plays over a three-week period. The more able readers study *The Silver Box;* intermediate groups read *The Admirable Crichton* or *The Barretts of Wimpole Street;* the slowest readers, studying *Teahouse of the August Moon,* may require much teacher help to understand even the basic situations developed in Patrick's play. Often class work can be organized to permit independent group meetings led by the teacher, as illustrated in the unit "The Consequences of Character." In rooms provided with adjoining conference cubicles, meetings can be scheduled away from the class; otherwise a corner of the room may be utilized. In any event, students must be provided with ample study and reading materials before the teacher attempts to meet separately with a group. To facilitate such small group discussions and to aid reading, teachers prepare students with guides in advance of each meeting so that individuals will be prepared to raise questions and issues. This plan has been adapted in such ways as the following:

> Teaching four novels: *Les Misérables, The Good Earth, Turmoil,* and *The Count of Monte Cristo* were read by diverse groups and students encouraged to search for points of contact between the novels.[15]
>
> Teaching four short stories: Separate group discussions were used with Joyce's "Araby," Cather's "Paul's Case," Daly's "Sixteen," and Fessier's "That's What Happened to Me."[16]
>
> Teaching various types of literature within an over-all topical or thematic framework: During a unit called "The American Dream," one group of students examined dreams of liberty (Benét, Whitman) while others read selections concerned with economic development (Steinbeck, Poole, Sinclair), with social equality, etc. Some groups require more help than others, since the subtlety and implications of difficult selections undoubtedly escape students without expert guidance.

Teachers also can provide instruction for groups while the remainder of the class is working on regular assignments. This method is often used in providing for gifted individuals within the heterogeneous class. While most stu-

[15] See detailed description in Margaret Ryan, "Achieving Unity With Diversity," *English Journal,* Vol. 40, No. 10 (November 1951).

[16] See description in James R. Squire, "Individualizing the Teaching of Literature," *English Journal,* Vol. 45, No. 9 (September 1956). Also, see various suggestions in Arno Jewett, ed., *English for the Academically Talented* (Washington, D.C., National Education Association, 1960).

dents are completing the reading of *Medea,* for example, a few advanced readers meet with the teacher to discuss "The Lottery," a mature story with overtones similar to classical tragedy. Or, in the seventh grade, some children are excused from the assigned reading of poems and stories on family situations for a special study of the ways in which patterns of family life differ in various countries around the world. At appropriate times such groups meet with the teacher as well as separately on their own.

GUIDING INDIVIDUAL READING

Wide independent reading contributes to the development of both skill and appreciation. Through extensive reading the child learns to apply the skills of comprehension and word analysis in many kinds of situations; through wide reading he explores interests and ideas and learns how to choose those which satisfy his own peculiar needs; through it he discovers and builds touchstones and standards against which he is able to evaluate selections. He thus develops attitudes toward literature and the perceptions it has to offer. A sound individual reading program offers solid support for the entire curriculum in reading and literature.

Importance of guidance The values of wide reading are not achieved unless careful guidance is provided. The observations of experienced teachers and the results of careful research indicate that unguided, *free* reading results in little change in student behavior. Without assistance, many adolescents remain at a fixed level of interest[17]—a boy who enjoys mysteries may read nothing else, a girl who responds to one adventure of the Bobbsey twins may devote six months to thirty other titles. In the large classes they face, teachers need somehow to develop more appropriate ways of assisting individuals.

Many teachers reserve regular times for individual reading—for example, every Tuesday or twenty minutes on Monday and on Friday may be reserved for such activity. On these occasions students bring volumes from outside or plan to read a book from the classroom collection. Some teachers reject the rigidity of fixed reading periods but attempt to reserve an equivalent amount of time each week, depending on a flexible schedule. Others report that slower readers respond to daily reading periods, ten to fifteen minutes in length. When books are available in the classroom, such students can enjoy unassigned reading during the opening minutes of every class hour. For some groups such regularized activity aids in establishing a quiet studious atmosphere.

Classroom libraries are helpful in offering teachers an indirect way of guiding reading choices and of increasing interest in books. With a balanced collection of forty to fifty books available, students often turn to reading when they finish other activities. Some teachers change the selections every few weeks to maintain continual interest; many obtain books on long term loan from public, county, or school libraries. Most of these selections should not

[17] See Bertha Handlan, "The Fallacy of Free Reading as an Approach to Appreciating," *English Journal,* Vol. 35, No. 4 (April 1946).

be overly demanding, since students will be reading on their own. However, both new books and standard titles may be included.

Fixed lists of books from which individuals are asked to make their own selections have been criticized in recent years, but it is the rigidity with which such lists are used rather than the list itself which is to be avoided. Those intended primarily to suggest titles which can be supplemented by individual arrangement prove helpful and offer a convenient way of organizing reading guidance in large classes. Often teacher and class together may prepare a list of appropriate titles, or the teacher may suggest ten or twelve books which previous groups have enjoyed. Students may also search for interesting selections in standard annotated bibliographies, such as *Books for You* or *Your Reading*, the continually revised booklets prepared by the National Council of Teachers of English. Any procedures which encourage the reading of varied and challenging titles are appropriate in the classroom.

Providing for sharing When individuals become really excited about a book, they want to discuss it, and out of such sharing may emerge a clarification of the experiences and value of the reading itself. The standardized "book report," whether submitted orally, on a mimeographed form, or as a two-page composition in which separate paragraphs are devoted to the plot, theme, character, and "the most interesting episode," certainly does little to quicken interest.[18] Most students would read less, not more, if faced continually with the unpleasant task of writing or of standardizing their responses on a form, and the endless procession of five-minute formal talks is enough to deaden any spark in all but the most lively groups. Informal grouping of students within a single class encourages greater student participation, results in more animation and interest, and provides for practice in oral communication. Each student is asked to discuss a particular book in a smaller group, and the more interesting presentations are repeated for the class.

More and more, teachers are attempting to bring "outside" reading "inside," to relate the guided reading to the unit in progress. Opportunities for such experiences occur not only in planned situations but spontaneously as the students are able to contribute incidents and ideas from their reading during class discussion of many topics. In considering the ordeals endured by the pioneers, for example, some use illustrations from *On to Oregon* while others tell how Lewis and Clark are depicted in *No Other White Men.* The extension of a unit to embrace the guided reading program thus affords adolescents an opportunity of deepening and extending understandings developed through class discussion.

[18] Traditionally, directions for "book reports" ask students to write separate sentences on the author, the title, the main characters, the setting, and the most interesting incident. These widely accepted directions for a written book report encourage students to violate basic principles of organization by asking for separate paragraphs or sentences on six or eight different items. More often the student should select and develop a controlling idea in relation to the book he has read.

The approaches used in the classroom will reflect the purposes of instruction. If literature is taught as human experience, those procedures compatible with this goal will be selected. If the varied tastes and abilities of students are considered, provision will be made for individuals and groups. Most teachers will seek a balance among the various activities.

Suggested Learning Experiences

The program in literature envisioned on these pages can be accomplished only through carefully selected learning experiences. Most teachers prefer to create their own lessons with the needs of particular pupils in mind; for them the section which follows will serve as a source of suggested classroom activity to which they may turn for ideas. They will know that any particular activity should be introduced only when it is related to the other work of the class, to the ultimate goals of instruction, and to the unique purposes of the learners.

To respond actively to the literary experience

■ *Relate literature to personal experiences*

1. Try to stress parallels between literary selections and the lives of young readers by asking appropriate questions in discussions or in writing assignments. For example, *Ginger Pye* includes a vivid sequence on how the loss of a pet affects boys and girls. Seventh grade readers may be asked to discuss or write about the topic, "When I Lost a Dog." In making such an assignment, recognize the uniqueness of each individual experience. Not all children in a class will have had the experience. These students may write on "How It Feels to Lose a Gift," or perhaps on some completely different experience.

2. Follow a reading of "Descent into the Maelstrom" or a similar imaginative selection by asking each student to sketch "Things I Have Imagined." When chalk or charcoal are used, little time is required for sketching and most of the hour can be reserved for follow-up activities. Ask students to write brief paragraphs describing their pictures. In the seventh grade try asking students to sketch "What Makes Me Mad" after reading about Jancsi's exasperation with cousin Kate in *The Good Master*. Activities of this type encourage readers to respond to the feelings of characters or to react to the emotional overtones of a selection.

3. Walter Van Tilburg Clark's story, "The Portable Phonograph," portrays a Debussy nocturne and a rusty phonograph as the final remnants of Western culture following a devastating world conflict. While the impact of the story is still fresh in the minds of class members, the teacher may ask students to listen imaginatively to "Nuages" in an attempt to "recapture" the thoughts of characters listening to the nocturne under the conditions described by Clark.

■ *Create puppet plays and other dramatizations*

Junior high school students enjoy producing puppet plays based on stories they have read. To minimize the effort involved in puppet construction, some teachers keep stock puppets available for students to redecorate, or teach students to use paper bag puppets or shadow plays. More elaborate presentations may involve experience in reading, writing, constructing, rehearsing, and revising a play, as when seventh-graders prepare a puppet dramatization of *Jungle Book* for a school assembly. Experiences in dramatization are most fruitful when students have examined the characters and literary situations with care and attempt to reproduce these faithfully.

To develop skill in relating form to content

■ *Compare the form of diverse selections*

Try contrasting such different stories as "The Gift of the Magi," "Araby," and "The Great Stone Face." Note that all three stories are built upon "surprise endings." Compare the purpose and effect of the revelation and the extent to which each is foreshadowed. Consider how a change in selection and organization of incident, in the nature of characterization, in setting or atmosphere would affect each story. Through discussion fill in at the chalk board such a chart as the following:

Story	Purpose of ending	If ending had differed
"Gift of the Magi"	Supplies ironical twist to plot, underscoring theme of selfless love.	Would not have altered characterization or theme, but story would have seemed flat and maudlin.
"The Great Stone Face"	Supplies essential insight into theme of story.	Theme would have been altered; parallelism of the separate episodes concerning general, statesman, poet, and Ernest, and their relationship to the life span of man, would have been affected.
"Araby"	Supplies insight into the nature of character.	Would destroy purpose of a story which exists primarily for this moment of insight into character.

■ *Direct attention to the author's selection and use of his media*

1. Discuss the principles of significant inclusion and significant omission. Why are certain purposes best achieved through the use of particular images, incidents, or literary forms? Questions like the following can be considered as different works of art are introduced:

Would "Loveliest of Trees" be more effective as an extended personal essay?

Discuss reasons for the lack of stage setting in *Our Town.*

What is the purpose of a narrator in a short story? To what extent is the device used to encourage the reader to "suspend disbelief" in Poe's "The Fall of the House of Usher"? How does the use of a narrator increase the dramatic irony of Browning's "Soliloquy of the Spanish Cloister"? Would the impact of Ring Lardner's "Haircut" differ if the story were told in the familiar third person?

2. Compare and contrast the diction of authors, or of the same author in attempting to achieve diverse effects in two or more selections. Ask gifted students, for example, to compare the diction and tone of Shirley Jackson in her powerful symbolic study of human relationships, "The Lottery," and in her delightful character portrait of an errant kindergartener, "Charles."

3. The reading of parodies often points up the more telling characteristics of an author. Some students may follow their reading of parodies of such widely copied rhythms as those in "Hiawatha" or "The Raven" by writing their own spoofs. Less well known, but eminently usable, are John Steinbeck's parody of "Murders in the Rue Morgue" and "The Tell-Tale Heart" in "The Affair at 7, Rue de M–," and the parody of *Macbeth* and other Shakespearean plays in Richard Armour's *Twisted Tales from Shakespeare.*[19]

4. After reading and studying intensively the prose styles of several authors, classes may be interested in considering how the selections would fare in the hands of diverse authors. What would Poe do with Hawthorne's "Ethan Brand"? How would Hawthorne introduce symbols of evil into Ring Lardner's "Haircut"? Would Lardner have handled "A Municipal Report" as did O. Henry? Some students may even want to try rewriting stories in the manner of another author.

To develop skill in perceiving narrative and characterization

■ *Explore the structural development of a fictional selection*

Select a relatively direct yet carefully constructed story, such as Wilbur Daniel Steele's "Footfalls," and review with students the basic structural elements: exposition, conflict, rising and falling action, climax, moment of revelation, denouement. A linear outline such as the following may help students perceive the directness of narrative development:

Exposition	*Development of conflict*	*Climax*	*Revelation*	*Denouement*
Characterization of Boaz Negro; his indulgent attitude toward his son.	Events of the evening, the aural clues; the fire; the long wait; the changes in Boaz Negro.	Boaz' moment of revenge.	Discovery of the identity of the murderer.	Resulting changes in Boaz Negro.

Once students grasp the basic pattern of narrational organization, show how authors achieve special effects by departing from the normal pattern, as in the following:

Frank Stockton, "The Lady or the Tiger?"; story purposely ends at moment of climax.

Situation	*Development of plot*	*Climax* (moment of choice)

[19] Teachers along with their students will also enjoy Armour's parody of study questions which often accompany textbook editions of the play, for example, "Continue and bring to an interesting conclusion Lady Macbeth's unfinished poem: 'The Thane of Fife had a wife . . .' "

Walter C. Brown, "The Puzzle-Knot"; story introduces basic conflict before exposition, so as to maintain suspense.

Cham Tai's problem *Exposition and development* *Climax* *Denouement*

Robert Coates, "The Need" which consists of a series of self-contained episodes, each of which includes rising and falling action. Meaning and total impact result only from the accumulated insights developed through all episodes.

■ *Encourage students to record significant impressions*

Introduce aids which enable students to record the significant details suggesting themes in characterization, plot development, or situation.

1. The systematic recording by students of their impressions of Martin Arrowsmith's problems, attitudes, and concerns helps them to summarize the novel and to be aware of the changes in Arrowsmith's perception. Such a chart as the following may be filled in by students in their notebooks:

Periods of Arrowsmith's life	Major influences	Details to be remembered
Adolescence	Dr. Vickerson	Gift of microscope; early interest in science.
College and university days	Dr. Gottlieb; Leora	Gottlieb's interest in Martin; his scorn for Martin's first attempts at research; Martin's desire to be a "genius."
Rural doctor in the Dakotas	Death of Leora's baby; death of Novak child; Dr. Winter	Dissatisfaction with country life; loss of yearning for research as "sanctuary."
Public health work	Dr. Pickerbaugh's insincerity; Angus Dauer	Incidents involving public relations; emphasis on the practical.
McGurk Institute	Dr. Gottlieb; Dr. Tubbs	Concern for "reputation"; the "great" experiment which seemed too late.
St. Hubert Island	Leora's death; Joyce	Problems of maintaining scientific detachment during epidemic.
McGurk Institute	Director Holabird	Joyce's dedication to material values.
Research, Vermont	Terry Wickett	Martin's realization he is just "beginning work."

In reviewing responses of students to each episode, the teacher is able to build on differences of opinion so as to develop a real understanding of the conflict within

Martin Arrowsmith. Use of such a chart should ultimately make clear to a reader Martin's continuing search for truth, his singleness of purpose, and his lack of strength to face the world alone, as well as Lewis' use of scientific research as a symbol for truth.

2. Ask students to record in their notebooks significant quotations revealing some facet of character. When a number of such revelations have been identified concerning the protagonist in a drama or a novel, a review of the items will aid students to see changes in such characters as Pip in *Great Expectations,* Jody in *The Yearling,* or Eustacia Vye in *The Return of the Native.* (See a similar approach used in teaching *Macbeth,* pp. 407-08.)

■ *Use outlines to guide the reading of difficult selections*

Even mature readers benefit from using an outline as a guide through the narrative labyrinth of *War and Peace* or the rhetorical tapestry of *Areopagitica.* Similar aids to understanding can direct younger readers to important purposes of the author and to shifts in point of view which otherwise might pass unnoticed.

1. Some outlines may be little more than informal notations concerning a poem, placed on the chalk board to guide students' reading in class. For example, such notations as the following may serve to aid juniors or seniors studying Tennyson's "Ulysses."

Lines 1-5	Ulysses contemplates his present circumstances.
Lines 6-18	He explores the significance of past travels.
Lines 19-24	He generalizes on the nature of life and experience.
Lines 24-32	He pledges to continue his life of activity.
Lines 33-42	He bequeaths his throne to his son.
Lines 43-49	He considers his ships and his mariners.
Lines 50-70	He reaffirms his desire to search until the last.

2. Outlines of longer selections can be detailed or can direct students to consideration of important incidents and relationships, as in the following sample developed for ninth grade readers of *David Copperfield.*

I. The Early Boyhood of David Copperfield
   A. The contrast in David's relationship to Peggotty and to his mother.
   B. The circumstances of family life at Peggotty's.
   C. Changes wrought at home by Murdstone.
   D. The impact of Salem House on David.
   E. Changes in Murdstone's treatment of David following his mother's death.

An outline is helpful, too, in studying those essays in which ideas are developed logically. Some teachers assign comprehension exercises by presenting the major points of an outline and asking students to supply the details. Others reverse the process and ask students to supply the author's conclusions.

■ *Use adjective checklists in developing understanding of characters*

Present checklists of adjectives which require the responder to identify the more salient characteristics of a fictional personality; disagreements often form the basis of stimulating discussion. Some teachers ask students to rate a character on an adjective checklist after reading only a portion of a long work, and then file the list for future use. Days later, when the reading of the work is completed, students are asked to rate the characters again. A comparison of the checklists may emphasize several important understandings: the ways in which characterization develops, the dangers of judging behavior on only ambiguous clues. Imagine a rating of Becky Sharp based on only the first fifty pages of *Vanity Fair.* Following are two illustrations of adjective checklists:

1. *Junior high school* The following descriptive terms have been applied to Johnny Tremain. Indicate those which you consider to be his desirable qualities by marking plus (+); mark those which seem negative by marking minus (−); for those characteristics which seem neither positive nor negative, mark zero (0); draw a line through any words which do not seem to apply. After reviewing your judgments, describe a passage from the novel which reveals both admirable and regrettable characteristics of the boy.

________awkward	________deliberate	________mischievous
________aloof	________energetic	________masculine
________ambitious	________honest	________methodical
________changeable	________intelligent	________opinionated
________conventional	________insensitive	________obliging
________courageous	________ingenious	________(Etc.)

2. *Senior high school* Check on the following lists each of the adjectives which you believe applies to Antonia. Then for each adjective checked, try to indicate at least one incident or statement in Willa Cather's novel to support your judgment.

________contented	________diffident	________resourceful
________changeable	________efficient	________simple
________courageous	________energetic	________steady
________coarse	________patient	________shrewd
________conventional	________practical	________vital
________cautious	________reliable	________sensitive

To develop skill in exploring meanings which lie below the surface of literature

■ *Consider how meanings are revealed through theme, plot, and characterization*

1. After junior high school students have read such books as *Swiftwater, And Now Miguel,* or any equally good selections which will stand careful analysis, read aloud Howard Pease's "Letter to a Fan."[20] Apply Pease's concept of levels of meanings to the book which has been read.

2. Compare three short stories in which plot, theme, and characterization receive different degrees of emphasis. "The Most Dangerous Game" is primarily a story of suspense in which plot is of paramount significance; "The Dead Dog" exists largely for its revelation of character; theme is of major significance in "A Success Story." Such a selection as "Leiningen Versus the Ants" may be introduced to illustrate the harmonious balance which is achieved when the emphasis on plot in a tale of suspense is strengthened by careful and necessary characterization of a protagonist and by the over-all unity achieved through an underlying theme.

[20] Howard Pease, "How to Read Fiction," in *They Will Read Literature,* A Portfolio of Tested Secondary School Procedures (Champaign, Ill., National Council of Teachers of English, 1955).

■ *Consider the use of imagery*

1. In studying poetry in particular, help readers see how a writer selects a vivid concrete image to express an abstract idea. What overtones are there in Shelley's image of the west wind sweeping summer dreams from earth? Why does the "crystal moment" of Robert P. Tristram Coffin suggest more to the reader than might be expressed in several sentences?

2. Bring to class a print of Millet's painting while reading Markham's "The Man With the Hoe." Here students have the opportunity to view the stimulus to the poet's imagination.

Why does Markham direct attention to the man "leaning on the hoe" as if bowed by "the weight of centuries" rather than by the labor of the day?
Why does he see the "emptiness of ages" in the workman's face rather than the absence of thought?
What does the poet suggest in his image of the man carrying the "burden of the world" on his back?
How does the poet wish his reader to feel?

3. Examine with students selections in which the poet relies on aural imagery, such as "The Pied Piper of Hamelin" or "Break, Break, Break."

4. Consider with students the effect of color imagery. Which colors suggest gaiety? Which depression? Which would be most appropriate in a painting depicting Jim Hawkins and his mother hiding under the bridge near the Benbow Inn? Which best suggest the mood of "Loveliest of Trees"? Brief discussions of this type not only emphasize the overtones of a selection but offer students an understandable and impersonal approach to identifying and discussing their own emotional responses to a selection. Music may also be considered in the same way—e.g., describe the kind of music which you would select to accompany a reading of "To Night."

■ *Consider the use of metaphorical language*

1. The teacher may introduce students to the expression of ideas through figurative language by directing attention to terms used in colloquial speech and writing:

souped up
hot rod
a veritable jewel of a play
like a granite wall at left tackle
going over the hill
peaches and cream complexion

What is the literal meaning of each statement? What are possible meanings? What elements are being compared?

2. Try helping students to identify tired, overused allusions which no longer convey original images by asking them to fill in such a series of phrases as the following:

As dark as_______	As green as_______
As hot as_______	As mad as_______

3. Select obvious examples in introducing students to the use of figures of speech, such as "There is no frigate like a book." Again ask students to consider pos-

sible implications. In what way does Emily Dickinson see books and frigates as similar? What is her emphasis? Ultimately, introduce students to the more subtle uses of figurative language including selections which may be considered to be an extended metaphor, such as "The Chambered Nautilus" or *The Ivory Door.*

■ *Consider the use of signs and symbols*

1. Direct students' attention to obvious uses of symbolism in the titles of books, poems, motion pictures, and plays—"A Man Can Stand Up" (in *Johnny Tremain*), *The Yearling, The Corn Is Green, Long Day's Journey Into Night, The Chalk Garden, A Raisin in the Sun.*

2. Discuss familiar signs and symbols that are important in communicating ideas in everyday life—legends on maps, road signs, the symbols of various holidays, symbols and signs used in advertising. A student group may enjoy preparing a bulletin board display.

3. Compare uses of different symbols to convey similar ideas. Heinrich Heine saw "The Lorelei" as expressing the same hypnotic pull toward beauty and escapism that is expressed in the popular song "Bali Hai."

4. Compare the crumbling statue of "Ozymandias" as a symbol of the futility of faith placed in material values with vivid photographs of ruins created by air raids during the recent world conflicts.

5. Read with students a story which strikes the reader as bizarre and wildly implausible if the meaning is accepted literally. An excellent example for secondary students is "The Bound Man," Ilse Aïchinger's description of the beauty and meaning which an individual can discover in living within the confinement of binding ropes and of the unwanted sympathy which his constriction arouses. Although interested in the initial image, students soon find they must grope for many implied meanings. To aid in their search, divide the class into four or five groups and ask each to consider the thoughts suggested in the following representative quotations:

> "In that he remained entirely within the limits set by his rope, he was free of it —it did not confine him, but gave him wings and endowed his leaps and jumps with purpose."
>
> "The antics [of others to release him] amused the bound man, because he could have freed himself if he had wanted to, whenever he liked, but perhaps he wanted to learn a few new jumps first."
>
> "He felt a slight elation at having lost the fatal advantage of free limbs which causes men to be worsted."

During the teacher-led discussion which follows, the presentations from each group may be examined and analyzed. The use of groups to analyze such selections is particularly helpful if the purpose is to identify a multiplicity of possible meanings. However, students need to learn that any potential interpretation cannot conflict with facts and details presented in the story.

■ *Consider the uses of satire and irony*

1. Students may be introduced to obvious uses of irony in casual conversation and in the dialogue of stories and plays. Frequently the ironical intentions are made clear when readers consider the tone of the speaker. How would these lines be spoken by Antony: "For Brutus is an honorable man"?

2. Introduce more advanced readers to the irony implicit in such situations as the following :

A thief lecturing the middle class couple on social values in the one-act play *Sham.*

The butler possessing major resources for survival and emerging as the true leader of the island society in *The Admirable Crichton.*

The humane, sentimental attitudes of the gambler and the dance hall hostess in "The Outcasts of Poker Flat."

The nobleman Pierre receiving his greatest lesson from the peasant Platon Karataev in *War and Peace.*

Social satire is involved in many of the ironical situations suggested above. Once students are sensitive to the meanings of such selections as *Sham* or *The Admirable Crichton,* consider the possible intentions of the authors. For what purpose would Barrie wish to show Crichton as the peer of British social leaders? Questions of this type may lead students to see that true satire usually reflects a desire to influence change.

3. Introduce the better readers to some memorable satirical writing by contemporary writers, e.g., *Animal Farm, Point of No Return, Babbitt.* Encourage individuals to report good examples of satire to be found in political cartoons, comics, and newspaper editorials.

To develop attitudes facilitating reading with appreciation

■ *Read and interpret with students*

The most helpful approaches usually involve the teacher reading with students and interpreting literary selections. An oral reading by the teacher which the students follow in their books permits the teacher to demonstrate how a mature reader approaches a selection. Unlike an oral interpretation designed primarily as a listening experience, these readings by the teacher may be interrupted momentarily after key words and passages to give students an opportunity to consider meanings and effects. Help with challenging selections should be offered at the time of reading, not only at the end of reading, so that the student learns how to discover the significance of clues on which sound interpretations are based. Is it surprising that we discover many problems in the ways in which young readers approach literature when most of our help is offered only *after* reading is completed?

■ *Study responses to separate segments of stories*

Divide such a story as "The Bet" into several segments to be studied independently. After reading each segment, ask class members to share their feelings and ideas about the situations and characters. The analysis of the early passages may be reconsidered after reading of the story is completed. Why were some readers able to predict behavior? How did others go wrong? A comparison of such responses offers a rich source of information on how individuals respond.

Occasionally reactions may be written and compared; on other occasions, the teacher may lead students in an informal discussion of possible meanings. Such specific events as the changes in the kind of books requested by the prisoner during his fifteen years internment—or changes reflecting materialistic, spiritual, and philosophical concerns—will evoke various comments. Some will grasp Chekhov's apparent intent from the beginning, while others hazard wild, implausible guesses, indicating that they have not yet learned to test for possibility. Sometimes the teacher may wish to approach a discussion of a segment of a story by referring to the interpretation of a single reader. For example, the following reaction to the exposition of "The Bet" has been read to students:

> I think that the lawyer will be sent to prison where he decides that he's been tricked. He will dig his way out with his hands. Incognito he will establish a business firm and ruin the banker financially before he reveals himself.

After listening to the reaction, the students consider whether any elements in the exposition of "The Bet" justify such a romantic, melodramatic solution to the conflict, whether such behavior is consistent with the character of the lawyer, indeed whether an individual who finds it so easy to "ruin" the banker would subject himself to fifteen years imprisonment to gain great wealth. Such an analysis leads to an explanation of the situation as presented in the story:

The banker—Compulsive (offers bet); lacks understanding of behavior; superior (feeling of power)
The lawyer—Avaricious (desire for gain); intellectual (intellectual bet)
Situation—Detailed delineation of character and incident, despite improbable nature of event.

At any level of instruction, such guided experience in analyzing literature permits the teacher to overcome barriers to sound interpretation and to develop the favorable attitudes discussed earlier in this section. Literary selections which reveal meaning only gradually through a carefully plotted series of ambiguous clues and symbols are appropriate for such class activities.

■ *Begin with the reader's initial response*

Ask students to write their impressions immediately after reading selections like Saroyan's "Locomotive 38" (junior high) or a poem like "My Last Duchess" (senior high). The papers may then be set aside as the class studies the selections intensively. After meanings are clarified through analysis, compare the final judgments with initial impressions to point up the importance of searching for a plurality of meanings.

To teach a selection to the entire class

■ *Prepare students for reading a work of literature*

Recognize the importance of readiness. Develop interest before passing out new books, by using varied approaches: bulletin board displays, previewing excerpts read aloud by the teacher, listening to tape recorded dramatizations of scenes prepared by another class, relating the new work to reading which has been completed. Try to prepare students in advance for special obstacles in reading, such as the unfamiliar names in the Arabian Nights or the dialectal terms in *The Yearling* or in much of Mark Twain's writing. Recognize that presentation of the background material *before* reading is the teacher's responsibility and that student research, as on the French Revolution during the time of *A Tale of Two Cities,* better evolves *after* the reading. Usually the background which students need before beginning a selection may be presented in less than a full class period. Short reports by students can be introduced at appropriate times during the reading of the book. For example, a description of the guillotine better comes while the class is discussing the executions in the Dickens novel than before the group begins the book.

■ *Encourage rapid reading of longer works*

1. To help encourage rapid reading, divide a novel into four or five long segments (fifty pages or more) to be read by certain dates. Preparatory to each discussion, present a few leading questions or ideas related to the reading to help students organize their thinking. Individuals can thus be encouraged to consider a selection in terms of major conflicts and patterns rather than specific details, as sometimes occurs when discussion is planned on a chapter-by-chapter approach.

2. Encourage students to read as rapidly as they wish by providing a generous portion of class time for silent reading. Help students make a start on the book by reading the first chapters aloud. Especially in classes with many mediocre readers, such a beginning is wise.

3. Consider keeping an accurate estimate of each student's progress in reading by a Chapter Record. It is often better to ask a student to keep this record than for the teacher to keep it himself. Not only does this save time, but individual pupils, if they are reading slowly, may be more likely to report accurately to one of their trusted peers. For this record, each pupil has a pseudonym, and the chart is marked each day by the chosen recorder. When the daily lines have been drawn, the recorder shows the chart to the teacher so he can gauge how far to carry the discussion. A few students will have read beyond the many, and some pupils will be considerably behind the others. Experience with this chart has been favorable in many classes. A typical chart:

Daily progress chart—sixth hour class

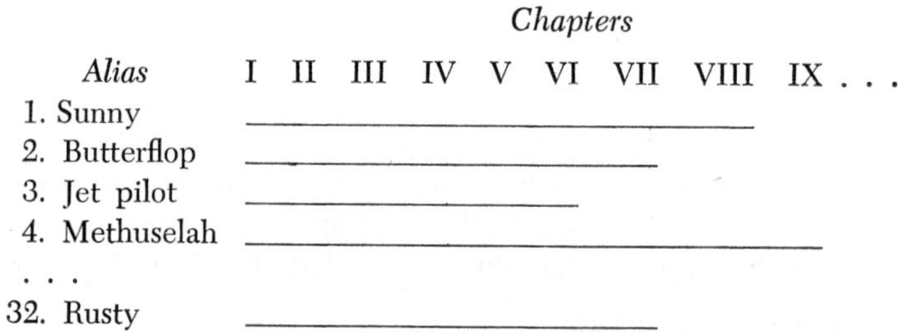

	Chapters								
Alias	I	II	III	IV	V	VI	VII	VIII	IX . . .
1. Sunny									
2. Butterflop									
3. Jet pilot									
4. Methuselah									
. . .									
32. Rusty									

Teachers who realize that a closer control on the reading would be in the best interests of a particular class may easily keep a chart like this for themselves, using actual names. Their students report progress daily during the reading part of the hour. The names and reading positions of individuals should not be made public, however. Such publicity tends to embarrass the slow reader and sometimes mars the faster reader with a taint of smugness. Sometimes, too, such publicity promotes a race to finish the book among some students, and their reading is superficial. The advantage of this approach is that it encourages students to read rapidly but at their own rates.

■ *Provide aids to assist comprehension*

1. Keep a list of basic information on the board, along with some identifying phrase or sentence. As the reading progresses, add to the list. In a class without an

assigned room, have the pupils keep these and similar records in their notebooks. For *Silas Marner,* such cues as the following are useful:

Place: Raveloe, a village in central England
Time: About 1810-1812, during the Napoleonic Wars and the Industrial Revolution
Characters: Silas Marner, a lonely weaver; Jem Rodney, a mole catcher (Add characters as the plot progresses.)

In order to keep time relations straight, list William Dane, Sarah, and Silas in a separate place on the board, like this:

Flashback: Fifteen years earlier
Place: Lantern Yard, a short street in a large manufacturing city, possibly Birmingham
Time: Around 1795 (just after the American Revolution)
Characters: Silas Marner, Sarah, William Dane

2. Occasionally introduce some regularized task permitting students to organize their reactions to the book. For example, after each discussion ask students to summarize in notebooks the major generalizations which have been drawn. Similarly, ask students to record "important" ideas which the class discovers in a play or novel. Some teachers prepare a general outline or series of questions to guide the reading of difficult selections and ask individuals to think about or even to write answers to questions after reading designated sections of longer works. The following study questions were used in teaching *The Human Comedy.*[21]

The Human Comedy, Chapters 1–9
Theme of discussion: "The experience of death"

1. *Ulysses*
   Relate the incident in which Ulysses first confronts death.
   Does he understand what death means?
   Does the thought disturb him? How does he react?
2. *Homer*
   Relate the incident in which Homer brings news of death to another. (Chapter 5)
   What do you know about Mrs. Sandoval?
   How did Homer feel about delivering the telegram?
   What was the author's comment? ("This woman was not to hear of murder in the world and feel it in herself." Chapter title, "You go your way, I'll go mine.")
   How does Homer relate the incident to his mother when he returns home? Has the incident affected him?
3. *Mrs. Macauley*
   How does Mrs. Macauley react to Ulysses' question concerning his father?
   How does she explain "life" to him?
   How does Mrs. Macauley react to Homer's feeling?

[21] Adapted from a plan by Jean Gringle Pirner, formerly of Las Lomas High School Walnut Creek, Calif.

Mrs. Macauley comments upon "loneliness"—what does she say? Does what she says make sense to you? Is loneliness a part of growing up? What is the meaning of change?

3. Slower readers profit from activities which direct attention to the meaning of specific events. Study outlines, such as the following for *Les Misérables,* are helpful because they tend to stimulate active response by utilizing a comparative approach to generalizing:

Direction: For each point select at least two incidents which illustrate the attitude of the character.

	Valjean	*Javert*
Attitude toward fellow men	1.	1.
	2.	2.
Attitude toward the law	1.	1.
	2.	2.
Attitude toward human justice	1.	1.
	2.	2.

Answers to such study questions would of course be reviewed in teacher-led discussions so that misunderstandings could be clarified.

To direct group readings

■ *Develop group assignments within larger units*

1. Following the reading and study of *Our Town,* ask students to select four basic quotations or key ideas as themes for further study. Organize groups around the basic ideas and plan with the students a series of appropriate readings with each group ultimately required to report back to the class on the points of view examined. Such themes and suggested reading as the following were chosen by one class:

"We don't have time to look at one another . . ."
The Human Comedy, Death of a Salesman, Arrowsmith.
"Do any human beings ever realize life while they live it?"
Helen Keller, *The Story of My Life;* biography of Albert Schweitzer; poetry of Emily Dickenson; *Nansen.*

2. Ask students in an advanced class to study various interpretations of a single theme, such as the theme of love. Form separate interest groups to pursue the analysis in such selections as "Tristan and Iseult," *Cyrano de Bergerac, Lilliom,* and *Jane Eyre.*

■ *Provide for special groups of gifted or slow students within the heterogeneous class*

1. Provide opportunities for individuals and groups to listen to recorded literature. During a study of the conflict between the individual and society, a group of gifted students in the twelfth grade may listen to the Siobhan McKenna recording of *Saint Joan.* In a similar manner, slow readers unable to pursue at length the reading of legends may be permitted to study the recording, "Tales from the Olympian Gods." In the seventh grade, one teacher planned a series of experiences in listening to story telling records for eight able learners who did not need the special instruction on spelling designed for the other twenty-five students. Although group listening assign-

ments of this type are easily arranged when a soundproof listening room adjoins the classroom, teachers also find that earphones may be attached to a phonograph to permit individuals and groups to listen to recordings without disturbing other class members.

2. Ask mature students to conduct special research projects related to the ideas being discussed. For example, during an eighth grade analysis of humor in literature (slapstick, farce, folk humor, incongruity, etc.), five students planned a special investigation into the kinds of humor preferred by junior high school students. The group developed a special questionnaire, presented it to selected seventh and ninth grade groups, analyzed the results, and prepared a report for the class and for the school paper.

3. Urge rapid readers to survey contemporary literature, possibly by reading and reporting on current best-selling fiction and non-fiction. A report of recommended reading may be prepared for the school newspaper or posted in the library on a special bulletin board.[22]

To provide guidance for individual reading

■ *Encourage pupils to prepare book lists and plan displays*

1. Ask committees of gifted pupils to review current publications and suggest books to be purchased for the school library.

2. Toward the end of a year encourage students to list books recommended for future classes, e.g., a seventh grade group may select "Ten Books Too Good for Seventh-Graders to Miss."

3. Organize a special weekly book club. One junior high teacher provided for three students to be selected to prepare a bulletin board display which included their photographs, their favorite books, and special recommendations.

■ *Organize "literary sampler" periods*

1. Introduce students to books which have been added to classroom and school libraries. Show the books, read selected passages, permit children to examine the books. When such "sampler" periods are followed by reading periods, many pupils will seize the opportunity to begin reading the stories that have been presented.

2. Try introducing junior high pupils to new books through playing "musical books." Place a variety of unfamiliar books on tables throughout the room. Have a phonograph available. Urge children to skim through a book until the music stops, then exchange the book for another. Permit three or four minutes for each skimming and four or five exchanges as a maximum. At the end of the experience, divide students into small groups and ask each individual to describe the most interesting book that he has seen. Permit individuals to "sign out" books immediately after this activity. Some teachers find this approach to be helpful in motivating reluctant readers.

■ *Refer to similar titles*

Capitalize on the current reading preferences by referring pupils to similar books. For some popular books teachers have developed such recommendations as the following:

[22] See A. J. Beeler, *Providing for Individual Differences in English* (Champaign, Ill., National Council of Teachers of English, 1957), pp. 4-5.

If you liked *King of the Wind*, you'll enjoy *Silver Chief, Lassie Come Home*, and *National Velvet*.

If you enjoyed *Strawberry Girl*, try *Blue Willow, Sensible Kate, The Wonderful Year*, and *Understood Betsy*.

Recommendations of this type may be dittoed and passed to individual readers or displayed on bulletin boards.

■ *Write papers comparing books*

Encourage an advanced student to select a topic which interests him, to read several books on the subject, and to write a paper presenting insights gleaned through such reading. Teachers have used such topics as the following: "The Solace of Religion," "The Impact of War on the Individual," "Responses to the Sea," "The Face of Evil."

■ *Encourage graphic displays*

1. Charts and other graphic displays interest students and direct attention to stories and books. Children respond well to a pocket chart where each child has a pocket in which he files a separate card for each book read, including a brief review that may be examined by others.

2. Some pupils enjoy designing illustrated book jackets for the stories they have read. "Reviews" may be written on the leaf of each jacket.

3. Encourage the reading and reporting of stories of Western adventure by developing a Western mural. For each story read, a student may add an appropriate symbol to the mural (cactus, horse, tombstone, etc.) on which is written the title and author of the selection and a one-sentence summary of the story.

4. A gallery of characters from books read during the semester sometimes serves as a bulletin board display in the classes of one teacher.[23] Students are asked to keep notebooks in which word pictures of characters are written, sometimes accompanied by sketches. Late in the semester the class gallery is displayed.

■ *Provide for the sharing of reactions to books*

1. Where all pupils have read similar types of books (animal stories, adventure books), divide the class into groups and ask each to answer specially prepared questions. For example, seventh grade students may be asked to list the various things which characters find amusing in their books (possibly as a part of a larger study of humor) or the problems people have in communicating with each other, e.g., misunderstandings, inadequate means of communication, etc.

2. Encourage pupils to read aloud brief, interesting excerpts. Preparation is necessary for such oral interpretations. Some teachers arrange for readings to be presented informally in small groups with the "best" reading from each group selected for presentation to the entire class.

3. Arrange occasional panel discussions by pupils who are reading similar books or even the same title. For example, students reading *Homer Price, Caddie Woodlawn, The Moffats*, and *The Saturdays* discuss the problems that people their age face in "getting along" with adults.

4. Dramatics appeal to certain pupils who enjoy formal experiences in acting out scenes from books. Junior high students will often respond well to the dramatic

[23] Vincent Leonard, Polytechnic High School, San Francisco.

situation of the "book trial," in which a defendent is accused of reading a dull book. Bailiff, prosecuting attorney, and judge add to the effectiveness, and some students are hard pressed to convince a student jury of three members that they are not "guilty" as charged.

■ *Organize individual reading records*

1. A cumulative reading record maintained throughout school years offers information valuable in studying the development of taste, and should be maintained whenever possible. Commercially printed records are available; [24] some school systems design their own folders.

2. Many junior high teachers encourage students to maintain "pie charts" of their reading in their notebooks. The circular pie is sliced into sections for various kinds of literature—adventure stories, poetry, science books, and so on. When a pupil finishes reading a book, he pastes a star in the appropriate section and writes a brief summary of the book in his notebook. A glance at this chart shows the individual and the teacher whether he is reading many types of literature or is concentrating on only one or two types.[25]

Evaluating Growth

To discover whether or not young readers are learning to enter the experience of literature and to find meaning, order, and beauty in works both simple and complex, methods of evaluating must involve the testing of more than factual recall. The basic guide in determining the method of evaluation will be the teaching objectives. Against these goals student growth may be measured, although often the goals are more basic or far-reaching than conventional methods of evaluation permit teachers to assess. Standardized and teacher-made comprehension tests are helpful, but clearly offer no substitute for legitimate attempts to measure the really important goals of the literature program. Beyond failing to offer the teacher insight into the progress and needs of students in responding to literature, tests emphasizing comprehension alone may mislead readers into placing undue emphasis on recall of facts. The ways teachers evaluate influence the learning which occurs in their classes. From texts, quizzes, and similar instruments, the student can perceive whether his English teacher is concerned with the subtleties or the superficialities of literature.

Much experimentation in measuring the ability to interpret and react has been attempted in recent years. The factors affecting response to literature are so varied that teachers certainly will never achieve the same refinement of measurement they can approach in testing rate of comprehension or ability to spell fifty assigned words. However, some teachers report considerable success in using rough devices to obtain information on student reactions when tests are constructed to measure progress toward specific outcomes. Suggestions are offered here for evaluating growth in four important areas: ability to interpret

[24] One is published by the National Council of Teachers of English, 508 South Sixth St., Champaign, Ill.

[25] Printed "pie charts" are available as "My Reading Design," from the *News Journal,* North Manchester, Ind.

behavior; sensitivity to form and style; grasp of theme and idea; extension of personal tastes.

EVALUATE ABILITY TO INTERPRET BEHAVIOR

1. A simple but effective way of assessing the reader's grasp of characterization is to present an examination in which the student is asked to identify the subjects of several rather precise descriptions of persons written by the author. Such an approach becomes little more than a prosaic exercise in recall if the cameo descriptions offer anything less than vivid etchings of personality. In studying accomplished novelists, such as Charles Dickens or Willa Cather, these tests can direct attention to important elements of characterization. The following exercise was planned for readers of *Pride and Prejudice.*

Matching test on characterization

Pride and Prejudice—Jane Austen

1. Mrs. Bennet
2. Jane Bennet
3. Elizabeth Bennet
4. Mary Bennet
5. Catherine Bennet
6. Lydia Bennet
7. Carolyn Bingley
8. Georgiana Darcy
9. Lady Catherine de Bourgh
10. Mrs. Gardiner
11. Charlotte Lucas
12. Mrs. Phillips

________There was a mixture of sweetness and archness in her manner which made it difficult for her to affront anybody. . . . She had hardly a good feature in her face, . . . [but] it was rendered uncommonly intelligent by the beautiful expression of her dark eyes.

________She was a tall, large woman, with strongly marked features, which might once have been handsome. Her air was not conciliating. She was not rendered formidable by silence; but whatever she said was spoken in so authoritative a tone, as marked her self-importance.

________[She was said to be] exceedingly proud; but . . . she was only exceedingly shy . . . there was sense and good humor in her face and her manners were perfectly unassuming and gentle.

________She was a woman of mean understanding, little information, and uncertain temper.

________[She] was a stout, well-grown girl of fifteen, with a fine complexion and good-humored countenance. . . . She had high animal spirits, and a sort of natural self-consciousness, which [had] increased into assurance.

________[She] had neither genius nor taste; and though vanity had given her application, it had given her likewise a pedantic air and conceited manner, which would have injured a higher degree of excellence than she had reached.

________[She] united, with great strength of feeling, a composure of temper and uniform cheerfulness of manner which guarded her from the suspicions of the impertinent.

2. Present a series of quotations or descriptions of incidents which reveal character; have students arrange them in chronological order and then interpret

the meaning. For example, only a student who understands the progression of Macbeth's downfall can rearrange series of quotations as suggested on p. 412.

3. Ask students to predict the behavior of a literary character in a new situation. The following could be introduced after the reading of *The Old Lady Shows Her Medals*.[26]

> Two young men have applied for a scholarship loan of $2,000 and Mrs. Dowey (Barrie's "old lady") is asked to submit a recommendation on the award, as she is acquainted with both. One, a personable young high school track star, spent a summer as caretaker of Mrs. Dowey's yard and passed many hours listening to her reminiscences. He claimed to be well acquainted with the owners of a vineyard which Mrs. Dowey was eager to visit and promised to drive her there, but the trip didn't materialize, as the boy kept making excuses. Later, when Mrs. Dowey did visit the vineyard, she learned that the owners had never heard of the lad.
>
> The other boy, a student body officer in the local high school, has a strong academic record. A neighbor of Mrs. Dowey, he brought her cherries and grapes from the trees at home. However, his visits became less frequent after he borrowed $50, which he has not repaid, and he seems to be avoiding her.
>
> Only one loan can be given. Which boy do you believe that Mrs. Dowey will recommend?

The discussions which follow tests of this type may be among the more stimulating in any classroom. Having thought through (or felt through) the reactions of characters, students will be ready to express divergent views, many of which will add spice to the analysis. The teacher will of course accept all reasonable explanations and through studying the comments obtain an estimate of each reader's perception and understanding of the character.

4. An "opinion poll" can be used to survey the reactions of individuals to characters and events in a short story as well as to indicate the intensity of each response. In the "opinion poll" the reader is asked to react to a series of statements on a five-point scale, indicating which of the positions most closely represents his own.

	Explanation box
________Strongly Agree (SA) ________Agree (A) ________Uncertain (U) ________Disagree (D) ________Strongly Disagree (SD)	(In this space, the student gives the reason for his opinion.)

Statements like the following were presented after a reading of "The Snob."

> 1. John Harcourt did not recognize his father in the store because he thought the meeting would embarrass the father.
>
> 2. John was angry at Grace because he recognized that she was a snob.

The positive wording of incorrect or undesirable responses, such as in the second sentence, helps to identify unthoughtful readers who accept John's

26 For additional suggestions on using this approach in teaching literature, see Chapter 3, "Imaginative Thinking," p. 139.

rationalization of his behavior. (Adequacy of the response recorded in such opinion polls depends both on the individual's perceptiveness while reading and on his analysis of each statement.) Most teachers consider such exercises to be learning experiences and plan directed discussion once the student answers have been collected.

5. Assign questions requiring readers to evaluate particular characters or selections in terms of questions like the following:

> Do people really act the way _______ does?
> Can we detect the motivation for _______'s actions?
> Is _______ only a stereotype? Does the author rely on common clichés concerning behavior?[27]

Students may be asked to examine such questions in assigned compositions, group or panel discussions, or teacher-led class discussions. Some teachers rely on comparisons in which students are asked to compare superficially drawn and multidimensional characters. For example, junior high school students may contrast the development of the city boy in Stephen Meader's *Red Horse Hill* with the portrayal of Jody in *The Yearling*. Older readers could compare some of the portraits of women drawn against the soil: O-Lan in *The Good Earth*, Beret in *Giants in the Earth*, Caroline in *Let the Hurricane Roar*, Leslie in *Giant*.

EVALUATE SENSITIVITY TO FORM AND STYLE

Able students easily learn to memorize definitions or to pluck figures of speech from sentences and stanzas supplied by the teacher. Fewer perhaps become sensitive to hearing, feeling, and responding to the beauties of the author's craft. Evaluating sensitivity to form may encourage readers to be a bit more responsive to the emotional effects of fine writing.

1. Readers may try to identify the effect the author is attempting to achieve. Adolescents will experience difficulty in answering such questions if they have had little instruction in this area. Such tests resemble classroom experiences in which students select appropriate musical accompaniment for the oral reading of a poem or discuss the color imagery to use in reproducing a work of literature in graphic media—approaches mentioned earlier in this chapter. In this example, a group of tenth-graders were asked to distinguish the mood suggested by a series of paragraphs from *Oliver Twist*.

Suggested test of ability to detect mood

Directions: In the left column are listed passages from the novel in which Dickens attempted to convey a certain mood or atmosphere. Select from the list of terms at the right the word which best describes the pervading mood of each paragraph. If a passage should suggest two moods, select only the more appropriate term.

[27] Some excellent questions for such exercises are to be found in G. R. Carlsen's "The Dimensions of Literature," in *They Will Read Literature* (Champaign, Ill., National Council of Teachers of English, 1955).

________The chilly mist rolled along the ground like a dense cloud. The grass was wet. The damp breath of an unwholesome wind went languidly by, with a hollow moaning.	1. Peacefulness
________An unfinished coffin on black trestles, which stood in the middle of the shop, looked gloomy and deathlike. Against the walls were ranged, in regular array, a row of boards cut into the same shape, looking like high-shouldered ghosts with hands in their pockets.	2. Hate
________The fog was much heavier than it had been in the early part of the night. A faint light shone at intervals from some bedroom window; the hoarse barking of dogs occasionally broke through the silence of the night. They cleared the town as the church bell struck two.	3. Coldness
________It was a dark, quiet night. The stars seemed, to the boy's eyes, farther from the earth than he had ever seen them before. There was no wind, and the somber shadows thrown by the trees upon the ground were deathly still.	4. Dimness
	5. Loneliness
	6. Fear
	7. Eerieness
	8. Filthiness

2. Try testing responses to language by asking advanced readers to distinguish fresh from faded styles. The opinion poll approach can be used and students asked to judge twelve to fifteen selected sentences, rating each on a five-point scale ranging from highly effective or vivid to ineffective or colorless. Once initial ratings are made, students may be asked to select the word which best explains each of their reactions (trite, vivid, awkward, pretentious, rhythmical).

Justification

________The sidewalk flower stands exuding such clouds of heavy perfume that their owners should be arrested for fragrancy.

________The traveler on his happy journey, as his foot springs from the deep turf and strikes the pebbles gaily over the edge of the mountain road, sees with a glance of delight the clusters of nut-brown cottages that nestle among those sloping orchards, and glow beneath the boughs of the pines.

________The tiny white pebbles of the clean pathway swept down to the azure lake, which, when it was full, seemed to glisten like sparkling crystal, and when empty, revealed the mud and muck of the shore.

For groups of older students, complete paragraphs may be substituted for the sentences and more complete justifications required.

3. Follow some of the leads of research in devising "measures" of ability to visualize—a skill found to be related to general appreciative factors in at least two studies.[28] After reading *My Antonia*, for example, students may be given thirty minutes to describe those situations which they most clearly recall. The

[28] Earl Forman, "An Instrument to Evaluate the Literary Appreciation of Adolescents," unpublished doctoral dissertation, University of Illinois, 1951; Henry C. Meckel, "An Exploratory Study of Responses of Adolescent Pupils to Situations in a Novel," unpublished doctoral dissertation, University of Chicago, 1946.

teacher may study the papers to identify the readers who appear to recall events with the greatest and least degrees of vividness.

EVALUATE GRASP OF IDEA AND THEME

1. Teachers need to assess students' understanding of the purpose of a selection as distinct from comprehension of the narrative. Many teachers examine students through questions which require interpretation and generalized thinking on the part of the reader as in the following examples:

In "Leiningen versus the Ants," Stephenson is attempting to say:
a. That dauntless courage will always win against insuperable odds.
b. That flashes of inspiration will frequently save lost causes.
c. That man will always overcome brute force by using his power to reason.

I believe that statement ——— best expresses the theme of the story because . . .
To what extent are the ideas in the two poems, "Mother to Son" and "Nancy Hanks," similar? Compare the two in a paragraph.

2. A difficult assignment—which may seem ridiculously obvious to the untutored—involves asking students to summarize the significance of a short story in *one* sentence. This assignment requires compression of ideas. A review of sentence summaries written over a period of several weeks offers important insights into each student's growth in perceptiveness. As reading, discussion, and writing of sentence summaries continues, students can be led to see that the essential elements of many selections are not to be found in plot alone.

3. To offer immediate information on the reader's responses to a selection—to character, situation, incident, even style—follow the reading of a story with a request that individuals complete such open statements as the following, based on "Reflections of Luanne":

I think that this story . . .
Luanne . . .
The thing that interested me most was . . .
I did not understand . . .
I think that Janet Buck . . .
This story is about . . .

If such responses are to have any meaning, students must write freely and recognize that there are no perfect answers. Such an exercise should not be considered more than a sampling of opinion. The responses may reveal those aspects of a selection which are best understood as well as those misinterpreted. Often the reactions will suggest important instructional needs, such as when an adolescent reveals a tendency to overemphasize the author's physical description of place and character and overlook clues embedded in dialogue and action.

4. Unstructured free-response "testing" is useful after the reading of a selection which has a particularly strong impact. Before any attempt is made at discussion, urge students to write their "first thoughts" or to describe "how

the story impresses them" or "whatever occurs to them about the people, the plot, or the ideas." These responses present teachers with material which can be analyzed for clues to each reader's personal reactions. On occasion, special methods of content analysis may be applied. For example, some teachers try checking the elements mentioned by each student in his free response against a list of elements to which sensitive and mature readers (at the age level of students) may be expected to react. For example, the free responses of eighth- or ninth-graders to "The Restless Ones" could be checked against the following hoped-for reactions:

Items involving content

Jerry's unwillingness to assume responsibility for his actions.

Jerry's restlessness being caused by a lack of personal resources as much as by the shortage of avocational opportunities.

Pending military induction as a factor contributing to the boy's failure to consider the future.

Comic books and motion pictures being possible causes of delinquent behavior.

Jerry's demand to be accepted as an adult conflicting with his unwillingness to assume adult responsibilities.

Items involving form

Inadequacy of character motivation. (Do comic books really affect youngsters in this way?)

Questionable realism of the dialogue. (Awkward wording, clumsy slang expressions.)

Contrived nature of the situation. (Use of flashback technique and boy's misconception concerning death of storekeeper to maintain suspense.)

Use of common stereotypes. (Comics, movies, and TV as a cause of delinquency; military induction as a cause; the use of "blind" parents who see their son as a problem only after the crime is committed.)

Use of fresh and original elements. (Ironical use of juvenile authorities to arrest the boy, thus adding to his resentment toward adults; paradox implied in use of seemingly childish behavior—crying—as a sign of newly found maturity.)

These rough approaches to studying responses to literature do not offer numerical scores which can be accepted as precise and valid measures, but do suggest ways of gaining some understanding of the complex emotional and intellectual experiences of literary response.

EVALUATE GROWTH IN PERSONAL TASTE

1. *Consider over-all growth* Since the program in literary appreciation is intended to refine personal taste and discrimination, an accurate gauge of accomplishment may be found in records of individual reading. Teachers must remember, of course, that appreciations change gradually over long periods of time and that seldom can they expect to bring about important and permanent shifts in perception during a single semester or school year. On occasion, all teachers enjoy working with an adolescent who suddenly discovers a literature which he has not known existed—a girl whose first acquaintance with modern

drama results in the reading of fifteen or twenty plays, the boy who transfers from a school with limited library facilities and celebrates by attempting to satisfy almost overnight a nearly insatiable appetite for reading, the students who become excessively interested in the Civil War, or who so enjoy *Arrowsmith* that they must read all other Lewis novels. Such impressive splurges are heady experiences in the reading careers of gifted pupils, but they tend unfortunately to be rather rare. More often teachers see trends and tendencies develop over many semesters.

2. *Maintain reading records* Most teachers attempt to maintain some kind of reading record, as has been discussed earlier in this chapter. To measure growth in personal taste, cumulative information maintained over several years and passed from teacher to teacher offers invaluable data. For example, such cumulative records reveal whether an individual's experiences with first rate literature has been confined only to selections "studied" or "assigned" in the classroom.

3. *Plan individual conferences* Teachers concerned with what a student sees in his reading know that the mere recording of book titles offers little information. They often schedule regular reading conferences, each fortnight or month depending on the teaching loads, and attempt to record on individual cards the ideas discussed, the books mentioned, the insights gleaned. Such a form as the following has been used:

Sample record of reading conference

Name of student____________________________ Grade 8

Date	*Books read*	*New titles suggested*	*Comment*
9/28	Lassie Come Home Silver Chief	National Velvet Call of the Wild	Interest in animal stories continued from 7th grade. Concerned largely with plot, suspense. Discussed plausibility of Lassie's return—what made it seem realistic.
10/20	Return of Silver Chief	Call of the Wild	He noted absence of theme in Silver Chief, inferiority of the book to Lassie in this respect. Some interest in Alaska and primitive areas.
11/16	Call of the Wild White Fang	Biography of Jack London	Very interested in London. Discussed humanization of animals. Noted foreshadowing of London in building suspense—a possible application of classroom study of foreshadowing in O. Henry.

4. *Use self-evaluation* Teachers of Wichita, Kansas, ask students to complete the following evaluation form at the end of each semester. The questions vary, of course, with the aims of the teacher and would be very different for

grades 7, 8, and 9. Reproduced here are questions and answers of a boy in a tenth grade class:

Summary of voluntary reading

Name_______________ English_______________ Date_______________

An evaluation of your voluntary reading program should show that you have improved during the second semester in the reading that you select for yourself. Check below those ways in which you feel you have benefited from this program. Below each section that you check, write in the names of three books that have helped you reach that goal.

__√__ 1. I enjoy reading several different types of books, i.e., biography, drama, poetry, history, etc.

Home Country Anna and the King of Siam Lost Boundaries Story of the F.B.I. Modern Architecture

__√__ 2. I enjoy reading books with varied geographical backgrounds.

Home Country (U.S.) Anna and the King of Siam (Siam) The Wooden Horse (Germany)

__√__ 3. I enjoy reading books whose stories take place in various historical periods.

Anna and the King of Siam Autobiography of Ben Franklin Hot Rod

_____ 4. I have matured to the extent that I can read a long book of 500 or more pages.

__√__ 5. I have read at least one book that has influenced my life (my conduct or my thinking, or helped me solve a problem).

Lost Boundaries Modern Architecture

__√__ 6. "My Reading Design" shows that I have read books in 13 sections (list one title in each section).*

Home Country The Wooden Horse Dashiell Hammet Omnibus Huckleberry Finn Modern Architecture Hot Rod Lou Gehrig, Iron Horse of Baseball Inside Story of the F.B.I. We Die Alone Drums Lost Boundaries Anna and the King of Siam Autobiography of Ben Franklin

__√__ 7. I like the book whose title appears below the least of those I've read in the second semester.

Captains Courageous

__√__ 8. I like the book whose title appears below the best of those I've read in the second semester.

Anna and the King of Siam

__√__ 9. How do you account for the difference in your opinion of the books in 7 and 8?

In Captains Courageous the setting was the same and the different events didn't vary enough. In Anna and the King of Siam something new was always coming up and some events were entirely different. The things that happened were hilarious and worth reading.

* Section refers to categories agreed upon by teacher and students.

___√___10. Do you like to read books about grownups and their problems? If so, name one or two such books.

Yes. Lost Boundaries Anna and the King of Siam

5. *Prepare examinations which measure appreciative abilities* Some teachers include questions which assess student abilities to interpret as well as to comprehend. For example, one teacher in Kansas [29] prepares three-part tests for her students. Part One of the test, the "C" section, consists of rather obvious factual questions. Students who complete only this portion of the tests receive grades no higher than "C." Sections "B" and "A" of her tests deal with interpretive questions. To receive higher grades, students must complete all sections of the test satisfactorily. The following sample questions, taken from an examination on *Abe Lincoln in Illinois*, show the range in difficulty:

Sample three-part test for Abe Lincoln in Illinois

This is a kind of test designed to show not only your knowledge of the facts connected with the play we have just read but to reveal your skill in interpreting what you read, and your ability to relate a literary experience to the life about you.

C Section

1. In what village and state does the play open?
2. Why did the professional politicians want Lincoln?
3. What political party asked him to run?
4. Which of these words best characterizes the Whig party: conservative, radical?

B Section

Choose one of the following and write specifically and fully about it.

1. What did each of the following scenes contribute to your knowledge of Lincoln's character?

 Scene 1—The grammar lesson with Mentor Graham.
 Scene 2—Lincoln invited to run for assembly.
 Scene 3—Lincoln after Ann's death.

2. The following is the text of the prayer for Seth's son, ill of swamp fever in a covered wagon. Sherwood says in his notes that "The prayer which Lincoln gives for a sick boy is, in effect, a prayer for the survival of the United States of America." Show in your discussion how this prayer could take on that meaning.

[Here is printed the prayer from the play.]

3. Here are five statements by Lincoln recording his gradual change in attitude toward slavery. Arrange them by numbering them from 1 to 5, from the most conservative position to the most radical.

________"And as to slavery, I'm sick and tired of all this righteous talk about it. When you know more about law, you'll know that those property rights you mentioned are guaranteed by the constitution. And if the Union can't stand on the Constitution, then let it fall."

________"This government cannot endure permanently, half slave and half free."

________"That Freeman's League is a pack of hell-roaring fanatics. Talk reason to them and they scorn you for a mealy-mouth."

[29] Miss Lucille Hildinger, Wichita, Kansas.

_______"It's made me feel that I've got to do something, to keep you and your kind in the United States of America."

_______"I am opposed to slavery. But I'm even more opposed to going to war."

A Section

Abe Lincoln in Illinois is a play dealing with pioneer life and the development of one of our national heroes who lived nearly a hundred years ago. The external action of the play seems remote and far away but the inner life of the people, the motives that drove them toward happiness or tragedy are the same that form our lives today. Has this play helped you to understand some types of human behavior or to feel differently toward it in any way? Consider the following questions carefully. Choose ONE and write a discussion of 150 to 200 words.

1. Do you know a Clary boys' gang who, in trying to impress others, show only their own crudities? On school occasions have you ever observed any East High Clary boys who make spectacles of themselves as successfully as the Clarys did in Scene 2? [The short questions are merely prompters.]

2. Lincoln apparently always hated slavery; his determination to do something about it took years to develop. Have you, on a much smaller scale, found belief in a principle difficult to translate into action? Have we, as a school, had any experience of this kind? Does cheating come in here? Is there racial prejudice in this class?

3. Do you know people like Mary Todd Lincoln? Are they driven by some ambition? Do they drive others? Are they satisfied when they get what they want or have they destroyed part of their happiness in reaching their goal? Is there something of Mary Todd in the teen-agers who throw over old friends for new?

6. *Use the forced-choice approach* A different approach to evaluating growth in personal taste is suggested by the test of contemporary literature developed by Dora V. Smith many years ago.[30] In this test, students are asked to rate familiar adolescent books of inferior and superior quality. Half of the eighty questions on such tests deal with worthwhile literature for younger readers, books like *Johnny Tremain* and *Caddie Woodlawn.* The other half concerns books of inferior quality like the Nancy Drew mystery stories. The items are arranged so that those referring to superior and inferior books are scrambled. For example, the following items might be included on such a test:

> *The Lance of Kanana* is a story of 1) a south sea shipping vessel's encounter with whales; 2) a famous weapon handed down for three generations; 3) an African boy hunter; 4) a native of India; 5) a boy who gave his life for Arabia.
>
> *The Blackboard Jungle* is a story about 1) hobos in a shanty town; 2) the growth of an American industry; 3) incidents in a vocational high school in New York City; 4) the life of students in Africa.

As Dr. Smith has suggested, teachers can prepare such forms for their own classes using popular contemporary titles which appeal to a range of tastes—from Mickey Spillane and the corner newsstand potboilers to good standard adventure fiction like *Shane* or superior books for students in the age group, such as *The Bridges of Toko-Ri* or *The White Stag.*

[30] Dora V. Smith, "Test of Contemporary Reading," Forms I and II, University of Minnesota, College of Education, Minneapolis, 1936.

7. *Use a plot completion test* Some years ago a special plot completion test was developed by Sara Roody. This test presents ten plot situations. Students are asked to choose the probable ending to the situation from the five which are given. For example, here is plot 3: [31]

> Donald was a bright, intelligent boy with high ideals of honor. His scholastic rating was very important to him. One day in a ten-weeks' examination in English he came to a question that called for detailed information about the *Atlantic Monthly,* including the name of the editor. Though he did not remember the name, he had a copy of the magazine in his desk. Since the boy in front of him was tall, Donald was able to open his desk and look at the magazine without being observed by the teacher. He did so. The next day, ashamed of having cheated, he told the teacher, whom he knew to be a fair-minded person. What do you think happened?
>
> Read the endings that are listed below, keeping in mind the facts of the case, the personality of the boy, and that of his teacher. Then number the endings in the order of their probability . . .
>
> a. The teacher told the class what happened and gave Donald a zero on his examination. Since that test was counted as one third of his ten-weeks' average he received a failing grade on his report card. "Let this be a lesson to all of you," said the teacher.
>
> b. The teacher said, "Thank you for telling me. I reward you for your honesty. I will give you full credit for all the answers on your paper, including the one that you copied." Donald received the highest grade in the class.
>
> c. The teacher told no one else, but gave Donald another set of questions to answer. He made a high score.
>
> d. Donald did not copy the answer from the magazine. He left a blank space on his paper.
>
> e. The teacher allowed Donald to take another examination. The questions were more difficult for him than those on the original test. Though he did well, his grade was somewhat lower than his score on the first test.

Although the complete test is not presently available, the sample item suggests an approach which individual teachers may use in their own classes. A similar instrument has been developed by Burton.[32]

STANDARDIZED INSTRUMENTS FOR MEASURING APPRECIATION

In addition to devices introduced in the classroom for instructional and evaluative purposes, teachers occasionally wish to use printed measures of general growth in appreciation rather than instruments designed to concentrate on specific abilities. Among the more interesting printed tests which have been developed are these:

1. Herbert A. Carroll, *Prose Appreciation Test.* (Educational Test Bureau, Minneapolis.) Graded tests for various secondary levels, requiring students to discriminate the quality of prose selections.

[31] Reprinted with permission of Sara Roody, Nyack High School, Nyack, N.Y.

[32] Dwight Burton, *Literature Study in the High School* (N.Y., Holt, 1959), pp. 143-156.

2. Mary C. Burch, *Stanford Test of Comprehension of Literature.* (Stanford University Press, 1929.) Forms of the test include examinations on ability to detect character and emotion.

3. Tests of literary appreciation evolved in an eight-year study, reported in Eugene R. Smith and Ralph Tyler, *Appraising and Recording Student Progress* (N.Y., Harper, 1942).

4. E. F. Lindquist and Julia Pederson, *Ability to Interpret Literary Materials,* Test 7 of the Iowa Tests of Educational Development. (Science Research Associates, Chicago, Ill.) Contains literary materials and related multiple choice questions.

5. Mary Willis and H. A. Domincovich, *Cooperative Literary Comprehension and Appreciation Test.* (Cooperative Test Division, Educational Testing Service, Princeton, N.J.) A standardized multiple choice test of four literary skills.

The introduction to this chapter suggested three important goals of the literature program—self-understanding, imaginative insight, and a balanced perspective. The suggested methods for organizing class, group, and individual instruction or for teaching and evaluating growth in important attitudes and abilities contribute to the attainment of these ends. Only when teachers actually think through the underlying rationale of programs in literature can they really hope to plan a sequence of reading experiences which will foster the development of permanent appreciations. Providing materials for individual reading which satisfy only the momentary interests of students is no more sufficient for a total program than is relying on intensive, detailed analysis of a few mature classics which are often closer to the teacher than to the students. Programs can have significance for both today and tomorrow only if young readers are continuously able to gain from their experiences the real values which literature has to offer—insights concerning themselves and their peers, imaginative release, and a rich and ever-widening perspective on life.

SELECTED READINGS

ON THE TEACHING OF LITERATURE

May Hill Arbuthnot, *Children and Books.* Chicago, Scott, Forsman, 1957. Junior high school teachers will find this a delightful source of suggestions for selecting and teaching.

Dwight Burton, *Literature Study in the High School.* N.Y., Holt, 1959. A recent general reference on literature for adolescents, which contains many helpful teaching suggestions.

Edward J. Gordon and Edward S. Noyes, eds., *Essays on the Teacher of English.* N.Y., Appleton-Century-Crofts, 1960. Especially valuable for essays on teaching *Huckleberry Finn, Silas Marner,* "The Rime of the Ancient Mariner," and *Julius Caesar,* this volume also contains help on organizing individual reading.

Jean Grambs, *The Development of Lifetime Reading Habits.* N.Y., National Book Committee, 1954. Interesting discussion of ways to create permanent reading tastes and ways not to.

Margaret Heaton and Helen B. Lewis, eds., *Reading Ladders for Human Relations*, rev. and enl. ed. Washington D.C., American Council on Education, 1955. The introduction to this excellent annotated list of books presents many suggestions for leading discussion in the classroom.

Lewis Leary, ed., *Contemporary Literary Scholarship*. N.Y., Appleton-Century-Crofts, 1958. A helpful appraisal of recent scholarship dealing with literary periods and literary genre. Includes a discussion of the literary audience.

Walter Loban, *Literature and Social Sensitivity*. Champaign, Ill., National Council of Teachers of English, 1954. Discusses ways of extending human sensitivity through the teaching of literature. Presents many suggestions for class work.

Louise Rosenblatt, *Literature as Exploration*. N.Y., D. Appleton Century, 1938.

———, "The Acid Test for Literature Teaching." *English Journal*, Vol. 45, No. 2 (February 1956). Both book and article offer valuable insights into ways of increasing the contacts between book and reader, of providing for experiences in literature rather than information about literature.

Edwin H. Sauer, *English in the Secondary School*. N.Y., Holt, Rinehart, Winston, 1961. About half of this volume is devoted to the teaching of literature. The material on advanced placement programs is not widely available elsewhere.

Jane Stewart, Frieda M. Heller, and Elsie J. Alberty, *Improving Reading in the Junior High School*. N.Y., Appleton-Century-Crofts, 1957. Describes the work of a core teacher and librarian in promoting the growth in reading of an eighth grade class. Helpful in suggesting ways of organizing the guided individual reading program.

Hilda Taba and Deborah Elkins, *With Focus on Human Relations, The Diary of an Eighth Grade*. Washington, D.C., American Council on Education, 1950. Describes in detail the developments in an eighth grade class in which the teacher experimented with individual reading and group work.

ON THE READING PREFERENCES OF ADOLESCENTS

Margery R. Bernstein, "Relationship Between Interest and Reading Comprehension." *Journal of Educational Research*, Vol. 49, No. 4 (December 1955). Demonstrates the relationship between interest and understanding.

G. Robert Carlsen, "Behind Reading Interests." *English Journal*, Vol. 43, No. 1 (January 1954). Suggests some of the motivations for the preferences expressed by individuals.

Arno Jewett, "What Does Research Tell About the Reading Interests of Junior High Pupils?" In *Improving Reading in the Junior High School*. Health, Education, and Welfare Dept., Education Office Bulletin 1957, No. 10. Washington, D.C. Summary of research on the interests of early adolescents.

———, "Research Concerning Reading Interests of Secondary School Pupils." Health, Education, and Welfare Dept., Education Office Circular No. 386, August, 1957. Washington, D.C. A mimeographed circular, periodically revised, which presents a summary of important studies concerning reading preferences.

George Norvell, *The Reading Interests of Young People*. Boston, Heath, 1950. Reports a survey of the reactions of 50,000 young people in New York State to many standard literary selections, usefully suggesting those classics to which adolescents respond and those to which they do not.

David H. Russell, "Some Research on the Impact of Reading." *English Journal*, Vol. 47, No. 7 (October 1958). Examines research on the effects of reading on the individual.

Robert Thorndike, *Reading Interests*. N.Y., Bureau of Publications, Teachers College, Columbia University, 1941. Provides a summary of prior studies and an analysis of changing interests of young people between the ages of 10 and 15.

Chapter Seven

Literature: Drama and Poetry

Magic may be real enough, the magic of word or an act, grafted upon the invisible influences that course through the material world.
—SANTAYANA [1]

Although drama and poetry have much in common with other types of literature, each calls for facets of appreciation not necessarily required of other forms. Both are concise, suggesting much more than they say; both are written to be heard. Thus in presenting either a play or a poem, the teacher relies primarily on an oral approach. This chapter will be concerned with the teaching problems arising from the fact that both drama and poetry convey meaning and feeling more by implication than by statement; that both gain much from competent oral presentation. Each of the two forms will be discussed separately.

DRAMA—PERSPECTIVE

To read dramatic literature with emotional response, one must be able to sense quickly the possible implications of the dialogue, to visualize both the setting and the speaker, to hear the shades of meaning and feeling, as they would be revealed if heard in the theater. The novelist permits a more leisurely manner of interpretation; the playwright depends upon the reader *to interpret multidimensionally as he reads.*

Purpose in teaching drama As with all literature, the study of drama has both immediate and long-range objectives. The immediate aim is to help the student appreciate one play as a record of human experience presented in a unique literary form. The purpose of reading many plays over a period of six years is to help him develop his capacity for appreciating dramatic literature so that he will select it more wisely on television, screen, and stage, and thus find richer delight in what he does select. A quickening of perception and a refine-

[1] George Santayana, *The Realm of Spirit* (N.Y., Scribner's, 1940), p. 283.

ment of discrimination for this type of literature is particularly important because so many of our students will give more time to the spoken word in the mass media than to reading. The cultural heritage, significant social concepts, and values for personal living may reach them through film and television, even though plays in printed form may appeal to only a comparatively small percentage of any population.

New skills required for drama Everyone is interested in a story. Drama, like fiction, tells a story but in its own distinctive way. Children in elementary school are accustomed to reading stories for themselves; they have had some experience in the oral presentation of dialogue. In teaching drama, the secondary school teacher builds upon this foundation. A reader accustomed to the narrative style of fiction needs additional skills if he is to develop appreciation for the dramatic form. The student acquires such skills through a sequential program which includes the study of plays over the six secondary school years. Because each tells a story, fiction and drama have some things in common; it is the manner in which the story is told that makes the reading of a play frustrating for the inexperienced reader. An understanding of the nature of drama as manifested concretely in the play—the vehicle for teaching—underlies the planning of instruction in all aspects of the dramatic form.

Nature of drama

The word *drama* signifies action. Action, originating in some human or superhuman will and moving toward the accomplishment of a purpose, is a necessary ingredient of drama. It forms the framework of any play. Within this framework the playwright depicts his basic idea which gives the play its roots in life. Creating characters and providing them with dialogue to evoke emotional response, he weaves the total fabric of the dramatic illusion.

Drama a collaborative art form While writers of other literary forms rely entirely on their own imaginative efforts, the playwright is essentially a collaborator. True, "the stirring of the idea; the gradual feeding out of information; the shock and countershock of circumstances; the flow of action; the interruption of action; the moments of allusion to earlier events; the preparation of surprise, dread, or delight—all that is the author's and his alone." [2] Nonetheless, whether writing for the stage, the motion picture screen, or television, he must consider the possibilities and the limitations of his production medium; he must take into account the part others will play in bringing his play to life.[3] He depends upon designers to fashion, not backdrops, nor pictures, nor cos-

[2] Thornton Wilder, "Some Thoughts on Playwriting," in Augusto Centano, ed., *The Intent of the Artist* (Princeton, N.J., Princeton U. Press, 1941), p. 95.

[3] For similarities and contrasts among the media see "The Popular Arts," pp. 384-85; in this chapter we are concerned primarily with writers for the theater.

tumes, but an image—an image creating an environment in which action and character will have their being. He looks to the actors to convey by voice and body the nuances of meaning and feeling. He relies upon the director to fuse the various elements of light and shade, sight and sound, repose and movement, which evoke the complete dramatic experience. Is it any wonder that many students find the silent reading of a play baffling? To substitute one's own imagination for that of playwright, designers, actors, and director requires long experience with the complexities of the dramatic form.

The time element in drama Both the external and internal time elements of drama contrast with those of fiction. With no restrictions as to length, the novelist can pile up details allowing gradual assimilation of meaning; by entering the minds of his characters as they explore the byways of memory or go forward in anticipation into the future, he can take as much time as he needs to portray events long past or to reveal the hope or dread of what may come. The dramatist can do none of these things; the more rigid time limits of his medium permit revelation only by vivid etching or by brief allusion; brevity demands action and dialogue fraught with implication and suggestion.

The internal element of time in drama assumes even greater significance than does the external. Although any story is forward-moving, fiction moves toward the present but concerns itself with what is past; its events have already happened; we know they have because one who knows has said so. In contrast, drama achieves the semblance of reality through the immediate responses of human beings to situations as they occur; we believe because we see these events happening before us. Drama looks toward the future; "it deals essentially with commitments and consequences." [4] The dramatist must so order his material as to give the illusion of life unfolding before us; the past and the future must be explicit in the present. Drama takes place, as Wilder has said, "in a perpetually present time." Within this present, pregnant both with a past which has created the situation and with a future containing the seeds of the past, the tensions of drama are created.

When a play is seen on the stage, the audience has the aid of the playwright's collaborators to summon intellectual and emotional response. Seeing events as they happen, feeling the surges of emotion, sensing the ebb and flow of the action, absorbing implications from voice and gesture—all induce spontaneous reaction. Oral presentation of plays in the classroom offers a poor substitute for the vitality of the theater. Silent reading does even less. However, oral reading by the teacher, opportunities to listen to recordings, re-creation of scenes through classroom productions, can release the imagination and attune ear and voice to shades of meaning and feeling. The study of dramatic literature, with comparisons and contrasts of plays seen by students on stage, screen, and television, can quicken discernment of the subtleties of the dramatic form.

[4] Susanne K. Langer, *Feeling and Form* (N.Y., Scribner's, 1953), p. 307.

The structural elements of a play

Young people gain appreciations of drama through the study of concrete examples—a sequence of plays illuminating dramatic literature as a distinctive art form; and through continual evaluation of those available on stage, screen, and television. Although advanced students in drama may be interested in the details of play construction, students in English classes may well be concerned with only a few aspects—setting, theme, conflict, language. Appreciation of these factors will give a basis for deeper understanding and keener discrimination applicable to all literature and pseudo-literature presented in play form.

The setting On the stage a play begins with the opening of the curtain, whether or not lines are spoken. No important conversation takes place in the first few minutes. The audience needs time to become familiar with the scene, so that, the details having been assimilated, the impression may sink below the conscious, serving its purpose as background for what is to come. For the reader the same is true; with the details of setting, the author has provided the environment for his characters and their story.

If the reader is to follow the essential movements of characters, the need for *visualizing* the setting—the physical surroundings in which overt action is to take place—is apparent. More important, such visualization helps establish the mood and meaning the scene is intended to convey. In what colors do we see it? Is any particular emphasis given to angled lines? To curved? To horizontal? To vertical? Does it suggest the familiar? The exotic? Does it express joy? Sadness? Strife? Foreboding? Is the light bright and gay? Shadowy and somber? Calm and soothing? Angry and disturbing? What is the total impression?

Skilled playwrights rigorously follow the rule that an audience should see nothing extraneous, that everything should have its purpose. Therefore, the reader must be alert to the clues given in the setting. We can expect the scene to do more than fix the physical limits of action; it will reflect something of the inner life of the play—at some times, suggesting very simple things; at others, ideas grasped by only the most perceptive. Even seventh-graders see the significance of these details describing the interior of a log hut in the Antarctic, in *The Brink of Silence:*

> No windows, an oil stove burning, packing boxes serving as chairs and cupboard, a pile of battered books and magazines. The teacher may have to direct attention to *battered* to elicit the fact that the men have been there some time.

They will also see the connection between the various items in the handsome office scene of *Salt for Savor:*

> On desk are a carafe of water, a glass, a bottle of pills; on back wall a sales chart with a heavy black line zigzagging across it, ending in an abrupt nose dive; on side walls, numerous placards—THINK, DO IT NOW, BOOST, DON'T KNOCK.

More experienced readers recognize the symbolism in these details of the setting for *Death of a Salesman:*

> The salesman's house—a "fragile-seeming home" hemmed in by "a solid vault of apartment houses"; "the blue light of the sky" falling on the house, "an angry glow of orange" on the surrounding area. "An air of the dream clings to the place"—the skeletal house, "partially transparent, the roof-line one-dimensional."

Pertinent details of settings noticed by students in movies and on television can serve as a bridge to the more difficult art of sensing clues on the printed page.

The conflict Conflict, an essential of dramatic action, is based upon an issue—something the protagonist wants to attain or to avoid. Around this issue the contest is waged. Because of the conciseness of the one-act play, the elements of structure are more easily comprehended by junior high pupils through this medium than through other literary forms. In a play the struggle is starkly etched; the close reading demanded increases awareness of the series of crises making up the action. Thus young people discover concrete examples of steps in a particular conflict as a particular person meets a sequence of minor triumphs or defeats; they recognize the factors working for him and those hindering him; they realize why he wins or fails. Continued study of short plays builds, more or less unconsciously, understanding of the significance of the play form without the need of technical terminology.

The theme Theme is strictly idea—the idea that gives the play its roots in life, the idea that pervades and gives universality to the action. It is the overriding truth behind the story, the comment the author wishes to make on human values and human experience. Any number of plays may be concerned primarily with *greed,* each with a different theme determined by the attitude the writer takes toward his subject. Occasionally, lines from the play may state the theme to the reader's satisfaction—"That is all of wisdom, the wearing of crowns before the eyes of life," from *The Slave with Two Faces.* At times the title gives specific direction—*You Can't Take It with You, They Knew What They Wanted.* More often it stirs the imagination by suggesting a clue to tie events to the underlying idea—*The Green Pastures, Journey's End, The Little Foxes.* In any case, the playwright trusts his theme to be revealed by the unity of his dramatic design. What does the play, always greater than the sum of its parts, say about human beings and their struggles to achieve their aspirations?

The language Action may be basic to the play, but it is with language, giving substance and spirit to the action, that the dramatic spell is created. Whether a line alludes to the past, foreshadows the future, advances action, exposes feelings, highlights facets of character, clarifies motives—whether it is understatement, exaggeration, or evasion—the words are primarily evocative rather than descriptive; they must be if the audience—or the reader—is to be aware of each instant as it passes. The playwright, as he shapes his ideas and delineates action, tries to hear the words as his audience will hear them, to picture the images that may come to mind. Story and theme are essential, but it is the language that reveals the subtleties of both.

From the qualities that belong to drama as distinct from other literary forms, the teacher derives the principles for organizing instruction to build the basic understandings and to foster the necessary appreciations.

THE TEACHING PROBLEM

The nature of drama determines the core of the teaching problem: helping students visualize, read for implications rather than for description or statement, hear the words as the character would speak them, see the play as a whole. These problems concern the teacher as he plans instruction in dramatic literature.

Organizing Instruction

In planning for any class, the teacher first tries to learn as much as possible about the previous experience of his students. While those teaching a play in junior high school can safely assume that knowledge of this literary form is slight, even here some students will read better than others, some will have participated in plays both within the classroom and without, some will have acquired a degree of discrimination in selecting motion pictures and television programs. A brief survey covering their experiences with plays presented in the different media—experiences pupils have found meaningful—will give some indication of the level of sophistication of individuals and of the group. Thus enlightened, the teacher may make plans for instruction. Instruction in any class takes into account the learning experiences desirable during the secondary school years. Therefore, the following discussion will suggest guide lines for four major concerns of an over-all program—content, the study of an individual play, oral interpretation, and the teaching of Shakespearean drama.

Content

In the English class, experiences with drama should center on the study and interpretation of dramatic literature. Types of plays, history of the drama, the lives of famous actors, Shakespeare's life and times, the latest news of television personalities—all such peripheral information should remain peripheral. It can too easily substitute for the real thing—the play itself.

Establishing a sequence The guide lines for a six-year program will take into account the nature of drama and the difficulties entailed in understanding and interpreting this unique literary form. Probably all English teachers would agree that one ultimate goal should be the appreciation of those Shakespearean plays appropriate for inclusion in the secondary curriculum. Such appreciation requires a long apprenticeship with simpler forms—one-act plays for seventh- and eighth-graders, a three-act modern play for the ninth grade, and Shakespeare reserved for senior high students.[5] With a thorough grounding in the complexities of drama in its simplest forms, the student has a basis for acquiring the reading skills necessary for Shakespearean plays—skills upon which to build genuine appreciation.

Providing for varying abilities Helping students of widely varying abilities attain desirable objectives requires three groupings of material, each demanding progressively more initiative and skill on the part of the student: at least one play to be studied by the class, plays on different levels of difficulty to be studied by groups, plays to be read by individuals. The first can serve as the main vehicle for teaching the necessary skills; students can then apply what they have learned to similar problems encountered in group and individual work.

Maintaining a flexible grouping The following grouping of plays is not fixed, any one in different circumstances being suitable for different purposes. At some times an entire class may profit from the study of *Winterset;* at other times, only five or six students; at still others, only one. The list below is not intended to be exhaustive; it contains only some of the plays used successfully with junior and senior high school students. Each teacher will have his own favorites. The labeling as to comparative difficulty represents personal opinion.

Difficult

An Enemy of the People Henrik Ibsen
Antigone Sophocles
Beyond the Horizon Eugene O'Neill
The Corn Is Green Emlyn Williams
Death of a Salesman Arthur Miller
Death Takes a Holiday Walter Ferris
The Emperor Jones Eugene O'Neill
The Glass Menagerie Tennessee Williams
The Green Pastures Marc Connelly
The Little Foxes Lillian Hellman
Medea Robinson Jeffers
Outward Bound Sutton Vane
Pygmalion George Bernard Shaw
R.U.R. Karel Capek
Saint Joan George Bernard Shaw
She Stoops to Conquer Oliver Goldsmith
State of the Union Howard Lindsay and Russell Crouse
Winterset Maxwell Anderson

SHORT PLAYS

A Minuet Louis N. Parker
The Old Lady Shows Her Medals James M. Barrie
Trifles Susan Glaspell
The Window to the South Mary K. Reely

[5] For gifted and able pupils, this sequence may be telescoped into less time.

Less Difficult

Abe Lincoln in Illinois Robert Sherwood
The Admirable Crichton James M. Barrie
The Barretts of Wimpole Street Rudolf Besier
Cyrano de Bergerac Edmond Rostand (Brian Hooker translation)
Elizabeth the Queen Maxwell Anderson
The Hasty Heart John Patrick
Holiday Philip Barry
Journey's End R. C. Sheriff
Justice John Galsworthy
Liliom Ferenc Molnár
Loyalties John Galsworthy
The Old Maid Zoe Akins
The Silver Box John Galsworthy
The Silver Cord Sidney Howard
Teahouse of the August Moon John Patrick and Vern Sneider
What Every Woman Knows James M. Barrie
The Winslow Boy Terence Rattigan
Yellow Jack Sidney Howard

SHORT PLAYS

Beauty and the Jacobin Booth Tarkington
Confessional Percival Wilde
The Twelve Pound Look James M. Barrie
Where the Cross is Made Eugene O'Neill

Least Difficult

*Life with Father Howard Lindsay and Russell Crouse
Ah, Wilderness Eugene O'Neill
The Far Off Hills Lennox Robinson
*The Ivory Door A. A. Milne
*I Remember Mama John Van Druten
*The King and I Richard Rodgers and Oscar Hammerstein II
Our Town Thornton Wilder
*The Piper Josephine Preston Peabody

SHORT PLAYS

*The Brink of Silence Esther Galbraith
*Dust of the Road Kenneth Sawyer Goodman
*The Eldest Edna Ferber
*Exchange Althea Thurston
*The Fifteenth Candle Rachel Field
*Finders Keepers George Kelly
*The Finger of God Percival Wilde
*The Man Who Married a Dumb Wife Anatole France
*Romancers (Act I) Edmond Rostand
* Sham Frank G. Tompkins
*The Slave with Two Faces Mary Carolyn Davies
*Spreading the News Lady Gregory
*The Stolen Prince Don Totheroh
*The Valiant Holworthy Hall and Robert Middlemas
*The Will James M. Barrie
*The Wonder Hat Kenneth Sawyer Goodman and Ben Hecht

* Suitable for junior high.

The teacher will find *A Guide to Play Selection,* listed at the end of this chapter, an invaluable aid. It not only describes individual plays but lists those included in various anthologies. Although these descriptions are helpful, direct knowledge of the play itself is of course essential for the teacher to determine its suitability for any class.

Extending experience in play reading After the class has studied one play, the teacher can provide further experience in play reading through group and individual work. In suggesting plays for groups, he will be guided not only by the caliber of the students but by the amount of time he can give to each group. Student opinion should have weight in selecting those for group study; letting students choose the play encourages more reading on the part of individuals and insures better group morale.[6] If the individual guided reading of plays is started at the same time, students will be occupied while the teacher is busy with groups. School and public librarians, dedicated to the promotion of lifelong reading habits, will help in making available the resources at their command. A classroom library is an invaluable aid.[7] Once initiated into the techniques of seeing with the inner eye and listening with the inner ear, many young people, reluctant to embark on a long novel, have found plays a less formidable venture. Lured, at first, by drama's comparative brevity and its rapid development of action through conversation, many have come to realize the pleasure such reading can bring.

The study of a play

If the class has had very little experience with dramatic literature, a play will require special attention; better learning results if teaching is so planned to provide the needed instruction for this literary form. The study of a play usually begins with an initial reading accomplished as quickly as the difficulty of the material permits; this first reading is then reinforced by discussing and rereading key lines and scenes to delineate the design of the action and the idea that controls it; oral presentation of scenes follows—always desirable, it is essential for those inexperienced in reading plays. If recordings are available, listening to skilled actors present the play makes a stimulating finale for the total experience.

The first reading The first reading stresses visualization and clues to deeper meaning in setting, lines, and action. As far as time allows, students should hear the play read aloud, at first by the teacher and the more capable readers. The teacher may read the first scene *as the class follows the text.* After the opening scenes have filled in the background and clarified the initial situation, the teacher may ask for volunteers, selecting only those he knows will give an adequate reading. If the scenes to be read orally the next day are announced, interested students may select characters and, through individual oral practice, prepare for reading. Those who cannot be taught quickly to read aloud should not be forced to at this time, since they distract others from the flow of the action. However, after instruction in oral interpretation, all should have a chance to read parts suited to their abilities.

[6] Buying ten each of four different plays rather than forty copies of the same play makes some choice possible.

[7] The following magazines which contain plays should be available to the teacher: *Theater Arts* (208 S. La Salle St., Chicago 4, Ill.); *Literary Cavalcade* (Scholastic Corporation, 33 W. 42nd St., New York 36, N.Y.); *Drama Magazine for Young People* (8 Arlington St., Boston 16, Mass.).

Walt Whitman once said, "I seek less to display any theme or thought and more to bring you into the atmosphere of the theme or thought—there to pursue your own flight." The playwright strives in similar fashion. The teacher, as intermediary between author and reader, tries to bring students into the atmosphere of the play. Thus it is almost always essential to start a play with oral reading of the opening scenes. Suppose the play chosen for study is *Death of a Salesman.* The shadowy setting establishes the mood for the entrance of the salesman with his heavy packs.

The setting

What is the effect of seeing the salesman's home as skeletal? What different impression would a firmly built structure give?

Why not have the salesman return when the room is lighted, or when the sun is shining?

Why are the tall buildings so close? Why not have their tops showing in the distance?

Why the contrasting blue and orange light?

The salesman's entrance

What do we learn from the lines of his body even before we see him clearly? How do you think he would walk?

What hint does the author give the actor to suggest the weight of the packs? Can you feel that weight?

The first few pages of the opening scene, a conversation between the salesman Willy Loman and his wife Linda, give background information and present the immediate situation. The reader learns that Loman, a man of sixty, lives in his own New York home, paid for by a lifetime of work. For years he has been the New England representative of a Manhattan firm, traveling back and forth by automobile. He has two sons; before leaving on his selling trip, he has quarreled with the thirty-four-year-old Biff, who has recently returned home. The father is worried because his son's plans for his life work have always been erratic and ineffectual. Loman has turned back without completing his business because he finds himself blacking out and the car repeatedly leaving the road. He plans to ask for a transfer to the New York office and to have another talk with Biff. These are the facts; the implications in the way the author has ordered his lines are left to the reader to discover.

The purpose of questions so early in the play is to stimulate thinking and feeling, to underline the need for close reading, not to find categorical answers. Initial questions probe for meanings, as yet only vaguely suggested, to be clarified as the play unfolds.

Assured by her husband that "nothing has happened," Linda still asks, "You didn't smash the car, did you?" Why not, "Did you smash the car?" How do the connotations differ?

Willy boasts of his early record with the company. Why is this significant? Why does he say he is vital to New England?

What is the purpose of Willy's line, "some people accomplish something?"

Willy says Biff is a lazy bum; later he contradicts himself. Why does the author have this happen? Which does Willy believe, or does he know? Why does he reminisce about Biff's early days? When has he been touched by nostalgia before? Is it significant these two instances occur so early in the play?

Linda seems at present an almost neutral character; her lines with the exception of "life is a casting off" are unrealistic, almost glib. Is she shallow? Dull-witted? Or has she been forced to bolster her husband's belief in himself so often her response has become automatic?

For most classes analysis of the first few scenes of any play is necessary. The same procedure is suggested for the entire short play read by immature students. With the more competent, working on longer plays, particular scenes can be examined and a study guide provided for the portions of the play they will read as assignments. Class discussions can insure understandings. Careful reading and penetrating analysis of the lines make form, structure, and total meaning more apparent.

The second reading The first reading of any play promotes understanding of certain human beings and their story. As the class reviews key lines and scenes, they come to realize with what economy the author has depicted his characters and built the action—the lines, written to reveal the individual's attitudes and values, his deep-seated fears and hopes; the action, created to portray situations showing him as a particular kind of person confronted with particular problems. The significance of details in the setting—the skeletal home, the angry orange light that intrudes, the harsh actuality of the encroaching buildings—has also become apparent. Now the reader realizes that none of the opening lines have been thrown away; they fill in background, but in a way to suggest Loman's dilemma. His nostalgia for the days when he envisioned material success—the only kind which had seemed important—becomes poignant as the dream contrasts with the reality. So too does the father's fear that his son's life will repeat the pattern. The significance of Willy's rejection of Linda's belief that "life is a casting off" is now clear. His life-long refusal to cast off his illusions prepares us for his final inability to perceive the truth about his son and himself.

This compression of both lines and action essential to drama helps students recognize the basic structure. As Loman relives events in his past, the commitments he has made, with their attendant consequences, delineate the steps in the conflict. The forces working for and against him, as well as the deciding agent, which has been present in the play from the beginning, become evident. All these can be stated in broader terms as the reader realizes they exist under different guises in all lives. The accompanying chart, using well-known plays, illustrates how the elements of a particular dramatic conflict reveal their universality when translated into general terms.

Perception of the elements of conflict in their universal aspects leads to an understanding of the idea or theme the drama exemplifies. The teacher, not belaboring the point nor insisting upon acceptance of any one statement, should try to help even young pupils recognize the idea that so stirred the author that he tried to translate it into the concrete situations that make up the play. At

Conflict in drama

TITLE	*Issue*	*Forces*	*Deciding agent*
Death of a Salesman	Loman wants to continue to believe in his success.	His illusions versus reality.	Recognizing he can no longer face the reality.
The Bishop's Candlesticks	The Bishop wants to give Jean Valjean a chance for rehabilitation.	Jean's attempt to secure his freedom versus the attitude of society toward convicts.	The wisdom and humanity of the Bishop.
The Ivory Door	Perivale wants to discover the truth behind the door.	An inquiring mind versus superstition.	Perivale's courage.
Elizabeth the Queen	Elizabeth wants to keep both her throne and Essex.	Elizabeth's pride and ambition versus Essex's pride and ambition.	Essex's objective appraisal of the situation.
The Little Foxes	Regina wants to possess the wealth at any cost.	Regina's greed versus her husband's efforts to protect himself.	Regina's ruthlessness.

times the beginning teacher is distressed because he cannot root out the heresy that theme and moral are synonymous. Doesn't it mean only that the readers have had too little experience to see the difference? Granted, the purpose of art is not to teach a lesson; however, its subject is humanity in all its aspects; if the immature reader thinks the lesson he gains epitomizes the author's meaning, the play still has had impact. Ability to recognize a theme consistent with the total context comes only after varied experiences with literature and with life.

The third reading Ideally, the study of a play should end with the oral presentation of key scenes. Presumably, unless the class is composed of students experienced in the play form or the teacher has assumed most of the presentation himself, oral interpretation up to this time has been negligible. Most classes need instruction in translating the printed symbols into vocal sounds which convey meaning and feeling. However, all classes, since they now understand the design of the play, should be able to select the scenes which will give an audience the highlights of the drama. In fact, this selection is a test of their understanding of the play as a whole. Insofar as time allows, teachers plan some oral interpretation as the final experience with any play the class studies.

Presentation of plays

The classroom presentation of plays is essentially a reading and listening experience. While children may benefit from the impetus that costumes and props give *if appropriate,* usually such paraphernalia, hastily collected and oddly assorted, serve only to defeat the real purpose—participation in an imaginative experience. Even stage movement, unless adequate rehearsal time has been allowed, can be a detriment. Students, seated at a table before the class, can very effectively convey the meaning and the spirit of a play through voice and facial expression. Time allowed for preparation can be more profitably spent in working on interpretation of lines and character portrayal, with students continually changing their roles from listener to reader. Helping students present a play in the classroom falls naturally into two parts: teaching interpretation and preparing a shortened version for oral presentation.

TEACHING INTERPRETATION

Since time for teaching oral interpretation in the English class is limited, the teacher, after the play has been studied, can develop skill in both appreciative listening and oral presentation by concentrating on a few scenes. A play need not be on the level of sophistication of *Death of a Salesman* to illustrate the nature of drama as a distinctive form. Even the simplest play can do this; even the briefest scene in that play presents many problems for beginners. Suppose, for example, a junior high class has studied *The Bishop's Candlesticks,* the Norman McKinnel dramatization of the well-known incident from *Les Misérables.* Two short scenes—the opening one between Persomé, the Bishop's sister, and the maid, and a later one between the Bishop and the convict—may serve as material for intensive instruction and practice. They give both boys and girls a chance to participate, and they present problems found in any dramatic scene: portraying characters, interpreting lines, projecting total meaning.

Portraying the characters By appropriate questions the teacher will review what the play has revealed about the characters. *The Bishop's Candlesticks* has two problems of balance as related to characterization. The emotional opening scene can easily be overdone, with a portrayal of Persomé as a shrew—a concept the total play does not support. Understanding the play as a whole brings into proper focus the incident in which she discovers the silver salt cellars have been sold. They mean more than pieces of silver to her; they symbolize all the refinement of living she and her brother once enjoyed. The Bishop's attitude toward her reveals much; he recognizes in her a fundamental kindness her speeches belie. The key to a sympathetic interpretation of her character in the opening scene lies in all the facts the play has disclosed.

The second problem concerns the relationship between the Bishop and Jean Valjean. Reading the melodramatic and volatile lines given the convict with all stops out will disturb the harmony of the play, which must be dominated by the quiet strength of the Bishop. Thoughtful interpretation of the characters as delineated by the author avoids striking a discordant note and thus throwing the play off balance. Young people can learn much about oral presentation, as well as more about the drama itself, by reading and listening to various interpretations of these two scenes. In like manner, with scenes chosen from any other play, students, listening to voice quality, intonation, and suggestion of feeling, can decide who best preserves the delicate balance between too little and too much, who best conveys the inner spirit of the character as conceived by the playwright.

Interpreting the lines Instead of reading and rereading any scene from any play, center attention on individual lines. All students should have an opportunity to read; all can judge the quality of the performance. Although students focus on what the lines are intended to convey, the teacher may feel that some technical knowledge concerning interpretation is helpful.

Logical meaning is conveyed by *phrasing* and *emphasis*. No fixed rules can be given for either; both are vocal expressions of mental activity on the part of the reader. Through phrasing—the division of a passage into thought groups—the reader helps the listener focus on the sequence of ideas; through emphasis—the highlighting of significant words and phrases and the subordination of others—he points up relationships and thus reveals total meaning. Phrasing sometimes causes difficulty because the thought groups the interpreter must use do not coincide with the marks of punctuation, which are guides to the meaning but highly fallible guides for the voice. Beginners tend to pause at every mark of punctuation and nowhere else; the experienced reader knows that such pauses, as in the following, are not always necessary: "Not yet, madam . . ." "Ah! You thought . . ." and that often pauses, at times so slight as to be almost imperceptible, are essential where no punctuation is indicated: "But you had no right/to do so//without asking me." When problems in phrasing arise, let students compare several readings to determine which gives the sense. Almost never is there *one right* way.

All forms of emphasis—force, duration, pause, change of pitch—are inherent in the normal pattern of intelligible speech, for the most part learned by imitation and employed unconsciously. However, the student needs help in transferring to the words and thoughts of another a technique he has heretofore used automatically. Expressive speech is marked by variety. Any form of emphasis may be overused—duration, for example, by the affected "gusher"—but force, the most obstrusive, is perhaps the worst offender with the beginning reader.[8] Let students try different ways of stressing words to bring out meaning. Thinking of what the lines say will result in variety without the need of technical terms. Continued attention to careful listening will enable students to select the interpretation which conveys the total meaning, yet avoids monotony and unpleasant vocal quality.

In teaching the very minimum of interpretation, the teacher has a chance to show some of the distinctions between oral and written language. The latter, a symbolization of the former, is inadequate for indicating to the reader how lines should be spoken. For instance, unless given to an overly precise person, such expressions as "it is rude" and "that is no reason" usually should be trans-

[8] The Suggested Learning Experiences in "Listening with Discrimination," pp. 191-95, are pertinent here.

lated into conversational idiom—"it's rude" and "that's no reason." Symbols showing states of mind or feeling—"ahem" and "ha! ha!"—are hints for interpretation, not lines to be read. Though obvious to the competent reader, these helps for reading need to be recognized by the inexperienced for what they are. Practice in transferring the printed symbols to the vocal calls attention to an important aspect of language.

Conveying emotion presents for some students a difficult problem; they may not be able to project themselves into the feeling of the character. For instance, in the opening scene described above, Persomé moves from irritation to horrified amazement, to sorrow tinged with fear. The student who reads the scene too matter-of-factly may be helped by questions to aid her either to recall occasions when she felt the same emotion or to conjure up imaginary ones. What makes you irritable? How do you act? How do you think you sound? If questions do not bring results, it is often worthwhile with beginners to turn aside from the play momentarily and allow a few minutes' practice on another sentence, first to convey the meaning pleasantly, then in an irritable manner: "I'm sorry, but you can't borrow my sweater; I'm going to wear it myself." However, too much time should not be spent on such devices; the real problem may be inhibition in expressing the emotion. Thus, repeated unsuccessful trials bring only embarrassment and make future attempts less likely to succeed. The teacher needs a light touch in teaching interpretation and must be guided by the belief that frequent brief attempts are likely to secure better reading ultimately than prolonged sessions which aim at acceptable standards for all.

Projecting total meaning After practice in interpreting lines, students are ready to attempt the projection of the scene as a unit. Any scene selected will have its own aspect of the conflict and its own crisis, however minor in reference to the total play. Through reading the scene and through discussion, students will discover that the main considerations concern tempo and climax. With beginners, maintaining proper tempo is largely a matter of forming the habit of picking up cues. Interpretation has taken care of tempo within speeches. Young people have difficulty learning that each speech, even if it is to be spoken slowly, must follow *immediately* the one that precedes. Speeches that interrupt present a nice problem, since the first word must be spoken almost simultaneously with the last word of the previous speaker:

Madam said I was not to chatter, so I thought—
Ah! You thought!

If the scene chosen does not include an example of interruption, it is often well to have the class make up one and let pairs of students practice the timing; the next scene attempted may present such a problem. The first few minutes of a class period before scenes are to be read is a good time for such an activity. The matter of timing, crucial in all drama, deserves special attention in practice; whatever the prevailing tempo of a play, the flow of action is lost unless readers are capable of conveying the feeling of continual onward movement.

The crisis of any scene must be viewed in relation to the total play. For instance, the opening scene of *The Bishop's Candlesticks* builds steadily from the beginning to the end with two minor peaks between. It cannot be read on as high an emotional level as the lines in isolation might seem to suggest. Such a reading would destroy the effectiveness of later events and disturb the balance of the play. Other scenes from other plays will present similar but different problems. Each scene, from whatever play, must be considered not only for its internal unity but in its relation to the play as a whole.

The two plays discussed—*Death of a Salesman,* appropriate for the twelfth grade, and *The Bishop's Candlesticks,* suitable for the eighth—are examples, nothing more. They demonstrate that certain problems are characteristic of all drama; the procedures suggested are applicable to all plays. Any play requires close study; any play needs oral presentation to bring it to life. Continued attempts to interpret lines and to portray characters, continued experience in trying to judge the effectiveness of classroom presentations, establish a basis for discrimination in listening, in viewing, and in reading dramatic literature.

PRESENTING THE ORAL VERSION

The limited time for teaching interpretation is the reason for having inexperienced readers present a few scenes rather than the entire play. A sequence of brief scenes is likely to provide a more satisfying experience for both performers and listeners.

Preparing the script The preparation of a script may progress in some such manner as is described here. A time limit, rigidly adhered to, should be agreed upon—perhaps no more than fifteen minutes for the one-act and thirty for the long play. Through a total class experience in preparing a script the teacher can smooth the way for similar procedures students will later undertake on their own initiative.

Selecting scenes to be read The scenes should represent some of the highlights in the play. They may include one of exposition, one presenting a minor crisis or the major climax, one illustrating some salient characteristic of the play—its humor, its dramatic power, the vivid portrayal of a character. The literary work itself determines the choice. It is well to ask each student to review the play and to select the scenes he thinks will give the fullest understanding to a listener unfamiliar with the play. After advocates present their arguments for including certain scenes, the class may make the final decision, keeping within the over-all time limit.

Writing narrative to connect the scenes Since the presentation should be clear to listeners who do not know the play, the class must plan narrative to connect the scenes. This activity, as well as the arguments advanced for the selection of the scenes, shows how well students understand the play. The secretary may list on the board items individuals think should be used to introduce each scene. After the class eliminates all but the essential points, a volunteer or a committee may write the narrative. This writing is an exercise in compression and discrimination; with clarity and brevity the narrators try to preserve as far as possible the style and the spirit of the play.

Deciding upon necessary stage direction Stage directions within the chosen scenes are kept to a minimum. Only descriptions of significant movement and of pantomime the listener must visualize in order to understand the lines should be included.

Rehearsing and casting Each scene may first be read by volunteers, followed by discussion to bring out the problems it poses. Then various interpretations of difficult lines and ways of suggesting attitudes and feelings deserve attention. After this preliminary work, the class may chose two casts for each scene; practice for this assignment does not require group meetings, although interested students often arrange for rehearsals on their own time. The following day, after listening to both presentations of all scenes, the class selects one cast, a narrator, and someone to read the stage directions for the final performance. Since all have had a chance to read during the preliminary work, teachers should not feel obligated to use as many students as possible for this final reading. When one person portrays the same character throughout, a more convincing performance, one which does justice to the play, is possible.

Presenting the final reading The final presentation furnishes testing ground for the skills and appreciations acquired by both listeners and readers. A tape recording will be invaluable in checking evidence to substantiate critical judgment and in permitting the reader to determine whether his spoken lines sound as he had hoped they would.

All characters One cannot expect a professional performance from young people; one can, however, accustom both readers and listeners to center attention on the play rather than on the performers. Some discussion of the support one actor gives another in preserving the unity of plays seen on television will stress similar needs in the classroom. All readers, even those with only a few lines, should follow the script closely. Thus, avoiding distractions, students are better able to maintain the tempo and to convey the mood to the limit of their potential.

The narrator Teachers should help all members of the class realize that every part is important. A play can be spoiled *as a play* by a single line as effectively as by many. In the kind of presentation recommended here, the part of the narrator is particularly significant; without him, the production would lack unity. His reading, requiring as much skill as that of the actors but of a different kind, should be as vital as he can make it, since it carries the action forward as definitely as do the scenes.

The reader of stage directions This student describes the setting, making it as simple or as dramatic as the details warrant. He reads the directions within the scenes quickly and matter-of-factly, subordinating these items to the sweep of the action.

The listeners Those who are not reading do not follow the text; they listen to enjoy, to appreciate, to evaluate.

Obviously, students differ in the natural equipment they bring to the art of listening or of interpreting. However, intensive instruction based on a limited amount of material, with ample opportunity for all to take part and with the less able learning from the more talented, provides a foundation upon which each can build according to his interests and native endowment.

Extending interpretive experience Further experience in interpretation can come from the plays studied by groups and from those selected for individual reading. After a group has studied a play, they may follow the procedure suggested above—select a few scenes, prepare the necessary narrative, and give the shortened version of the play as a round table reading before the class. Often teachers find ways to use these presentations outside their own classrooms: *An Enemy of the People* or *Teahouse of the August Moon* for a class in social problems; *State of the Union* for a group studying United States history; *Abe Lincoln in Illinois* for an invitational assembly; an eighth grade reading for seventh- and eighth-graders taking English at the same hour; a presentation by advanced students for a tenth grade class. When two classes are studying the same play, exchange of oral readings forms the basis for interesting comparisons. If a recording has been made, these tapes can be used, without disrupting school schedules, in any class where the teacher thinks the material suitable. In fact, the opportunities for providing further oral experiences are so abundant a teacher can use only a few of those offered.

Teachers may encourage competent oral readers to present brief passages from the individual plays read. The selection, one that can be adequately handled by a single reader, should furnish the key to one of the essential factors of the play. If the student selects a scene, it will require an introduction; if he selects several brief excerpts, connecting commentary is necessary. In any case, he avoids telling the story; instead, the selection should represent an exercise in discriminating judgment. The student should ask himself, What one impression of the play do I want to give? What passages will best express it? He may decide to stress lines presenting a decision affecting central action, depicting the resolution of the conflict, showing a character's philosophy, reflecting the theme. These individual presentations may be given in small groups, with listeners selecting those that best accomplish the purpose each reader has set for himself. Those chosen can later be given before the class.

The study and oral interpretation of drama by the class as a whole can arouse the interest of the student and help him acquire some of the skills needed for appreciation. Group and individual experience in reading and interpreting plays provides the necessary time and impetus for him to explore on his own—an exploration essential if he is ever to enjoy reading plays for himself or to become a more responsive and discriminating participant in those he sees presented.

Teaching Shakespearean drama

Shakespeare wrote his plays to be acted, to be seen, to be heard. Of course the ideal experience for appreciating his drama would be for students to attend a Shakespearean festival and to see professional actors in a series of plays. But this utopian dream is far from the reality teachers face. We can, however, approach a Shakespearean play as living theater, not as an academic chore. Stripped of his language and verse, Shakespeare is not Shakespeare. Since one of the English teacher's aims is to inculcate in as many students as possible a respect for the beauty and power of their own language, we should use the most perfect vehicle in the curriculum to disclose that beauty and power. Students should visualize the action, hear the lines read, see the play unfold. They do not need a mimeographed synopsis of the story to mediate between them and the playwright; they do need the vitality, the insight, and the expressive voice of the teacher.

Presenting the play orally Few secondary students are prepared to read Shakespeare silently on their own. The problems posed by the poetic form with its inverted word order and figurative language, the archaic expressions, the convention of the soliloquy, the multiplicity of characters and scenes, the absence of description of setting and of stage directions—all these often evoke negative attitudes even in superior students who, with diligent attention to footnotes, may ultimately fathom the essential meanings. The answer to the challenge that resistance to *Julius Caesar* or *Macbeth* creates is not the elimination of Shakespeare from the curriculum but rather the provision of more assistance to students *when difficulties occur as they read.* Oral reading by the teacher as students follow in their books is likely to spark more understanding and enthusiasm than will lengthy home reading assignments. Such a reading can convey both the essential conflict of the play and the power of the language. Moreover, the teacher can stop after an important scene or a moving speech to encourage the necessary understanding and reflection. Most plays can be read aloud in this manner in seven or eight class hours, with intensive analysis postponed until students have grasped the drama as a whole. Assignments requiring the rereading of scenes out of class or calling for exploration of passages in writing may be given to supplement the oral reading.[9]

This suggestion for oral presentation is not a plea for the teacher to outherod Herod. Reading is not acting; it is the mere suggestion of meaning and feeling to bring life to the printed page. Anyone who understands a play can learn to read it aloud acceptably; a little private practice does wonders. Then, too, so few Shakespearean plays are taught on the secondary level that it is not

[9] See the unit "Macbeth," pp. 405-13.

an impossible task for a teacher to learn to read them aloud. Occasionally class members will volunteer to read; such interest should be encouraged, but unless the teacher knows the reading will be competent, he is wise to reserve for himself the major lines carrying the meaning of the play. It is important at this point to distinguish the basic difference between teaching students *how to read Shakespeare* and providing experiences in oral interpretation. Students' readings are perhaps best rehearsed and presented after the play has been read and understood.

Supplying necessary information Consideration of background material should be limited, particularly before the plays are read. An understanding of the political turmoil in eleventh-century Scotland, inviting invasion by foreign powers, is necessary to the reading of *Macbeth;* some conception of economic and political conditions in ancient Rome, to *Julius Caesar;* for *Henry IV, Part I,* a cursory grasp of the circumstances which brought Henry to the throne: the help the Percys gave him in deposing Richard II, the contrasts between Henry and Richard as young men. Such information is necessary but can be quickly supplied by the teacher. He can fill in further background as the reading proceeds. He needs to resist the temptation to plan extended research projects on the history of the times, on the Globe theater, on the Elizabethan Age; to refrain from assignments on the introduction, no matter how delightfully written. Shakespeare should speak for himself—and as soon as possible. After a play has been read, if student interest remains high, supplementary reports on pertinent topics may well be encouraged.

Another help teachers can give concerns the names of characters and their relationships, particularly when geneologies are mingled and confused. A few minutes with the help of the chalk board will show how near and yet how far Macbeth was from becoming king legally, will explain why Duncan favors him over Banquo. Sometimes it is wise to suggest that students direct attention initially to motives and actions of only a selected group of characters: Caesar, Brutus, Antony, and Cassius in *Julius Caesar;* Henry, the Percys, Hal, and Falstaff in *Henry IV*. Such suggestions may prevent conscientious but confused adolescents from becoming overly apprehensive and yet offer direction for basic understandings which can be broadened as the play is read.

Stimulating imaginative response Begin the study of any Shakespearean play with enthusiasm and some device to spark the imagination.[10] For instance, the day before introducing *Julius Caesar,* place some large printed headlines on the board. Done in color, they should get every student's attention as soon as he enters the room:

Patriots Combine Against Dictator
Assassins Attack Noble Leader
Plot Involves Trusted Officials
Chaos Reigns in City

[10] For the use of music to introduce a play, see "Macbeth," p. 408.

The headlines should not reveal time, locale, or whether the attack was successful. Ask students to look them over carefully to see just what is revealed, to suggest to what event and to what country they might apply. Be on the alert for suggestions that some might pertain to either Germany or Italy during World War II, to the Hungarian revolt of 1956, or the Cuban Revolution of 1959. After students have discussed possible times and places, ask if there is any contradiction in the headlines; they will spot the first and second as being opposite in point of view. Practice of such slanting can be referred to later as the play is read. Then tell students these headlines never appeared, not because the events did not happen, but because newspapers had not yet come into being; supply the year 44 B.C. After establishing that the place was Rome and the attack upon Caesar, begin the introductory material for the play. With students so familiar with the curriculum that they know Julius Caesar is next on the docket, such a device may not prove a very good guessing game. However, the discussion should stress the timeliness of the themes they will discover as they read the play.

Planning specific tasks Planning specific tasks which point out significant lines and passages will aid in directing attention to the meaning of the play. Such exercises as the following have been used as assignments to help students examine action and character in *Julius Caesar:*

After reading the first scene, find the lines that show
  Pompey had formerly been as popular as Caesar.
  Not all Romans were ready to renounce Pompey.
  Caesar's growing power was considered dangerous.

After reading Act I, examine the different points of view toward Brutus reflected in the following quotations:

> I am not gamesome. I do lack some part
> Of that quick spirit that is in Antony.
> —Brutus, sc. ii
>
> Well Brutus, thou art noble; yet, I see,
> Thy honorable metal may be wrought
> From that it is disposed. . . .
> —Cassius, sc. ii
>
> Oh, he sits high in all the people's hearts;
> And that which would appear offense in us
> His countenance, like richest alchemy,
> Will change to virtue and to worthiness.
> —Casca, sc. iii

What picture of this man seems to be emerging? Application of this principle is illustrated on different levels of sophistication in the *Macbeth* unit at the end of this section.

Using instructional aids Instructional aids of various kinds prove particularly valuable in the teaching of Shakespearean drama. Those solely visual—filmstrips of stage and screen productions—prove the least basic experience but, after the reading has been completed, can help less able pupils quickly review the plot. Motion pictures with sound—film adaptations and kinescopes of television presentations—provide a more provocative experience. The Evans *Macbeth*, for instance, has been used with success in many classrooms; even less competent versions can stimulate worthwhile discussions. The many recordings of plays usually taught on the secondary level are perhaps of greatest assistance; used either in part or in their entirety, they may serve various purposes. They offer a novel approach to character study; for instance, the student may consider which rendition of Macbeth's plotting of Duncan's murder most nearly coincides with his own impression. Orson Welles's? Maurice Evans'? Alec Guinness'? What differences are apparent in the Hamlet soliloquies recorded by Laurence Olivier, John Gielgud, and Maurice Evans? An evaluation of varying interpretations encourages the reader to reassess his own point of view. Invaluable as a finale after all study has been completed is the recording of the full play, allowing listeners to sense the flow of action and to savor the beauty and power of the language. Helpful as these aids are, they are nevertheless supplemental; students derive the greatest satisfaction from a professional reading of a difficult play only after previous study has prepared for its appreciation.

A six-year curriculum, beginning with the study and oral interpretation of simple plays, continuing with those of gradually increasing difficulty, and culminating with the more challenging modern as well as Shakespearean drama, provides a program which can develop appreciation for literature and for plays presented via the various media.

Suggested Learning Experiences

Classroom experiences to increase understanding and appreciation of drama are concerned with plays students read and see.[11] Thus, the following merely suggest ways of emphasizing various aspects of such understandings and appreciations after a play has been studied by the class and while students continue reading individually and in groups.

To learn to interpret clues in the setting

■ *Realize setting may convey both facts and feelings*

1. Introduce plays for group and individual study by reading descriptions of settings and asking students to predict something of the nature of the play. The following show some of the facts and feelings that settings may suggest.

Locale

Two Blind Men and a Donkey, Mathurin Dondo—foreign, medieval atmosphere
A public square; to left, an inn with the sign of The Green Dragon, to right, the shadowy arch of a monumental gate. Stone bench under a little shrine; in background, a glimpse of tortuous streets and protruding gables.

[11] The suggestions in this chapter should be considered in relation to those given in "The Popular Arts." Student viewing does not and should not pertain only to plays and dramatizations of stories.

Dead End, Sidney Kingsley—modern, with psychological overtones

A city street ending in wharf over river. To left, a high terrace and white iron gate leading to the back of exclusive apartments. Hugging the terrace and filing up the street, a series of squalid tenement houses.

Time—Season

Uncle Jimmy, Zona Gale

By the steps grow flowering almond and bleeding heart. Trellis covered with blooming wisteria; at the back, lilac bushes in a riot of bloom.

Cyrano de Bergerac, Edmond Rostand (Last act)

All the foliage is red, yellow, and brown; heap of dead leaves under every tree. Leaves are drifting down.

Time—Era

The Little Foxes, Lillian Hellman

The room is lit by a center gas chandelier and painted china oil lamps on the table.

The Will, James M. Barrie

An engraving of Queen Victoria, later replaced by one of King Edward, then by one of King George.

Mood

Mary of Scotland, Maxwell Anderson (Opening scene)

The half-sheltered corner of a pier; sleety, windy night. Tall piles in background and planks underfoot shine black and icy with their coating of freezing rain. Two iron-capped guards.

The Wonder Hat, Kenneth Sawyer Goodman and Ben Hecht

A park by moonlight; formal fountain. Backdrop represents a night sky with an abnormally large yellow moon.

Symbols of theme

The Ivory Door, A. A. Milne

A door, hidden by tapestry. (Fairly obvious, as the real meaning of the door is grasped by the perceptive tenth-grader early in the play and the significance of the fact that it is hidden, only a little later.)

Craig's Wife, George Kelly

Room reflects fanatical orderliness and excellent taste of the mistress, who enters, appearing to have been dressed for this particular room. (Meaning sinks in gradually as play unfolds, not reaching full import until "drifting rose petals fall unnoticed to the floor" as the final curtain closes.)

2. Place in groups students who have individually read different plays; ask each to give details of setting and determine how well the group can interpret the clues.

To learn to draw implications from lines

■ *Realize single lines and passages may serve several purposes*

Ask students to find lines combining two or more of these purposes:

To refer to a significant event of the past
To foreshadow the future
To reveal a character trait of the speaker

To show the speaker's opinion of another's character
To help create mood
To show an attempt of the speaker to evade the issue
To show an attempt of the speaker to conceal his thoughts or feelings
To show the speaker's attempt to persuade by appeal to another's needs or weaknesses.

■ *Select evidence to support conclusions*

After the play is well started, ask students to begin collecting evidence for a final writing assignment requiring quotations from the play in support of conclusions. As they read, students should copy, either on cards or in their notebooks, references pertinent to the problem they are investigating. Give them a choice of purpose:

To show the gradual development of a principal character. Show how the author has developed the character of one of the principal personalities of the play; for each stage of development, supply evidence.

To explain the role of a minor character. Select a minor character; show why he is necessary to the play.

To show mood as conveyed by lines. Analyze the mood of the play, giving examples of lines that help to change or intensify it.

To reconcile conflicting evidence. Select a character whose actions often contradict his words or whose words and actions are at variance with what is said about him; justify your opinion of him by reconciling the conflicting evidence.

To develop awareness of conflict as basic to drama

■ *Realize that life has its dramatic moments*

1. Ask students to clip a news item describing a conflict between two individuals or two groups—something that might serve as the basis for a scene in a play—and to determine the issue and the opposing forces. If it is resolved, what is the deciding agent? Let students consider the problem in groups; later use class discussion to clarify controversial points.

2. As a basis for writing, ask students to think of a conflict in which they themselves have been involved, to decide upon the separate factors in that conflict and to list them in specific terms, and then to write a few paragraphs conveying to the reader the clash of purposes and the final resolution.

■ *Recognize the fundamental factors of conflict in screen plays*

1. Ask students to determine the factors of the conflict in one motion picture or one television play they have enjoyed. Divide the class into groups, where each member is to report briefly on issue, opposing forces, and deciding agent; conduct a class discussion to answer questions the groups have not settled to their satisfaction.

2. Use the same material and the same groups to explore these questions: Do all the plays follow the same formula or do some stand out as being different from the others? If they are very similar, in what do the likenesses consist? If one is different, what makes it so? Take the reports from each group; then conduct a discussion leading the class to see the amount both of repetition and of original touches in the plays students have viewed.

To become more aware of the idea the action illustrates

■ *Realize that every dramatic story has a unifying idea*

Show a short biographical film—"The Great Heart" or "The Story of Dr. Carver"; in such biographies author and director through selection and arangement have ordered the events to sustain interest; analyze with students the conflict and the idea depicted. Give the class fifteen minutes to write as many specific conflicts as they can think of which might be used by a playwright in developing the same idea; conduct a discussion in which the class is helped to see that the same theme may be delineated in many different conflicts; devise a definition of theme.

■ *Recognize that ideas governing conflict differ in significance*

Have students hand in the title and time length ot one motion picture or television performance they have seen; ask them to state in one sentence the idea unifying the events in the story. Give the papers to a committee to list the themes; use the list as the basis for a discussion of ideas being depicted in the mass media: Do some seem more basic than others? Do basic ideas predominate? If so, why? If not, why not? How much repetition appears? What are some ideas which seem of interest to many, if we can use these presentations as criteria? Can we? Why or why not?

To recognize the advantages of planned viewing

■ *Be aware of television programs you would like to see*

The teacher may call attention to coming programs that sound promising; each summer the networks give advance notice of some of their special programs for the year. Some based on plays and stories are appropriate for classroom study; when such study is impossible, brief suggestions citing points to notice give some direction and encourage viewing: If a play originally written with a tragic outcome is scheduled, ask students, without disclosing the original ending, to notice if the events lead inevitably to the conclusion. As far as teaching purposes are concerned, it does not matter whether the ending is changed or not—preservation of the original will evoke one kind of discussion; distortion another.

■ *Keep informed about community plays*

1. Encourage interested students to act as a committee to keep the class informed about planned productions; little theater groups and nearby colleges will be glad to furnish students with information about plays young people may enjoy.

2. Allow students who see productions to substitute reviews for other writing assignments; these reviews should be concerned with the unified impression of the total play, or its lack. What contributed? What detracted? Attention should be given to setting, character portrayal, the building of the action, the theme, and the language. Regular play-goers can learn to discriminate between faulty writing and faulty portrayal.

To evaluate personal television viewing

■ *Determine the character of plays habitually viewed*

1. Ask each student, for a period of two or three weeks, to keep in his notebook a chart similar to that on p. 334, listing the plays he has seen and the time limit of each; call these in each week to gain information for planning follow-up experience; at the end of the period ask the student to use his chart to write an evalu-

ation of the time spent in terms of value received. What similarities does he find among the plays selected? Does the total viewing represent a variety or do most of his selections follow the same pattern? Is there variety among his choices in subject matter or does the total lean heavily toward one type—Westerns, mysteries, serials of family life?

2. Plan a discussion based on characters portrayed in the plays. In preparation the student is to select two characters—one who seemed true to life, another who did not; for each he is to present evidence for his opinion. In the discussion the secretary may briefly list on the board the evidence given for each type. Then help the class organize the material, drawing up a list of practices that make for stereotyping of either situation or character, then those that make character and situation believable. Encourage students in their television viewing to look for credible characters in credible situations which seem true to life as they understand it; tell them the subject will come up again.

■ *Develop standards for selective viewing*

Ask individuals, using their charts and evaluations, to list the qualities which made some of these plays worth watching, and to add other factors they think should be included in their ideal play. Using only what students suggest, help them organize tentative standards as a guide. The teacher should make it clear he is not interested in the quality of the play selected; he is concerned with the evidence produced in support of their judgment guided by criteria they themselves have set.

Taste for the best on television is acquired slowly. Like appreciation for any art form, it grows from within through experiences in which students weigh the merits of the superior and the inferior; it does not come from paying lip service to external standards. The process is hindered rather than helped by blanket disapproval of any type of fare—for instance, Westerns or mysteries. Television offers quite respectable examples of each, and adults with sophisticated taste in drama enjoy both occasionally. Teachers can encourage comparisons, but the individual must see the contrasts for himself. This takes time. A developmental program through which students learn to appreciate better and better plays as they themselves present them in the classroom offers the most promise for improvement of taste.

Evaluating Growth

Development of appreciation for the play form, both on printed page and on stage and screen, is the ultimate goal in teaching dramatic literature. Such growth cannot be charted semester by semester with mathematical accuracy. The teacher does, however, have several methods of appraisal—some precise, others tenuous but practical enough to be useful.

Evaluating understandings Understandings are comparatively easy to evaluate. For instance, it is possible to determine with a certain degree of exactness how much students have learned concerning the various aspects of the structure of drama.

Interpreting clues from settings. Give students mimeographed copies listing the details of settings of several unfamiliar plays—largely factual details for immature pupils and those with psychological overtones for the more advanced. Ask them to determine what atmosphere the playwright seems trying to create; what kind of play they would expect from such a setting.

Reading for implications. Give students a copy of the opening scene of an unfamiliar play. Ask them to select and explain lines which seem to suggest more than they say. (Students cannot be expected to infer exact meanings; they can recognize lines that hint at things of the past, portend the future, etc.)

Analyzing conflicts and determining themes. Show a short dramatic film, as suggested on p. 347. Follow with a brief test, asking students to determine the issue, the opposing forces, and the deciding agent; then to state the idea exemplified by the action.

Such devices give sufficiently exact information for judging understandings of the structural elements of drama.

Evaluating oral reading Progress made in the skills of oral interpretation is more difficult to appraise precisely. Besides the continual assessing and reassessing as students present scenes in groups and before the class, a final evaluation benefits individuals, although it should not weigh too heavily in determining grades. Much depends upon the time the teacher has been able to give for instruction and upon the personal temperament and endowment of the student. All pupils, though, should be able to learn to maintain tempo and, if not to convey the spirit of play and characters adequately, at least to do nothing to detract from it. A comparison of tape recordings of brief scenes, one made at the beginning and another at the end, will supplement the teacher's observation and provide a means for students to note the gains they have made in ability to convey meaning and feeling through vocal expression. A written self-evaluation, comparing the two readings, usually reveals the student's attitude toward the experience and his feelings as to its worth for him; it gives material for a personal conference in those cases where one seems necessary.

Evaluating appreciation Appreciation can be gauged only indirectly. Does the student voluntarily select plays for individual reading? If so, what does he choose? Do his comments as they arise spontaneously in class discussion show he likes the better plays appearing on television? Do writing assignments asking for comparisons of films he has seen show he is developing standards for judging? Not precise, to be sure, such observations do give some indication of growth.

Many teachers give students a list of various blocks of learning experiences presented during a semester or year, and ask them to rate them anonymously, placing first in order those from which they have received the most benefit. This furnishes material for fruitful discussion as students review the course. Reasons for choice or rejection give the teacher insight as to whether the study of plays has approximated its desired objectives, and direction in planning for future classes.

A procedure similar to the following gives some help in judging the impact of instruction on the growth of appreciation. Early in the semester ask students to write a paragraph:

> The best television play I've seen recently is ______. I choose it as the best because . . .

Long enough after completing the study of plays so it will have no direct connection to dramatic literature, repeat the assignment, asking for an additional paragraph:

> The worst television play I've seen recently is ______. I choose it as the worst because . . .

The reasons given in each case will be more significant than the choice of play.

When this same assignment is repeated once a year, with student folders being passed from one teacher to the next, the sequence of choices with the supporting opinions provides basis for evaluation of growth in appreciation. For any improvement shown, the English teacher can assume only part of the credit. Appreciation for the best in any art form grows slowly and many factors contribute to its development.

POETRY—PERSPECTIVE

If any province of literature requires response from the whole nature of man, that province is poetry. "Poetry bids us touch and taste and hear and see the world, and shrink from all that is of the brain only . . ." [12] All literature shares this potential of invigorating the entire personality; poetry, when it succeeds, merely does so more completely. Because the paramount characteristic of poetry is its power to dispel dullness and confusion, methods of using it with adolescents necessarily emphasize delight and vitality.

On one level, teachers define the objectives of studying poetry in an operational way: to help pupils find genuine pleasure in reading poetry, to extend their ideas of what poetry is and what it can do for them, to help them understand the special language of poetry. But on a deeper level, teachers know that poetry, more than any other kind of literature, can make pupils more aware of being alive. If it succeeds, poetry lifts those who respond to it above the petty or narrow concerns that consume the lives of dull, unimaginative people. Poetry stabilizes one's whole experience—thoughts, feelings, and sensations. These deeper harmonies represent the goal of all efforts to help pupils respond to poetry. What teachers really aim at, then, is a heightened sensitivity to experience, a sensitivity so pleasant and rewarding that pupils will continue, beyond the class, to seek more of this thrilling form of literature.

Like all other arts, poetry can be enjoyed by those who do not have a

[12] William Butler Yeats, in his famous dictum, is asking for a more complete definition of the brain than that given by the logic of John Stuart Mill's father. To the analytical intellect, Yeats adds the powers of imaginative thinking.

scholarly knowledge of its formal qualities. However, the enjoyment is greatly increased by knowledge, and teachers, especially, need this trained awareness. They need not know all the poet's craft; but to appreciate it, they must cultivate sensitivity to the connotation of words, to figurative language, and to the artistic use of sound. They need to understand how imagery, symbols, and the entire tonal pattern serve communication.

Poetry, like music, is written to be heard. With both art forms the printed page is meaningless to the untutored unless brought to life by voice or instrument. Only after much experience can the reader of either medium hear the musical pattern without the production of actual sound. To arouse his interest, the student must hear poems read often and hear them read well; to nourish a gradually maturing taste for poetry, he must be able to read it for himself.

In the poetic form, the teacher has almost unlimited resources for reaching students of diverse interests and abilities. More than any other literary type, because of its brevity and its many-faceted appeal, poetry offers in one sitting the direct impact of a literary experience which can be encompassed by each student to the limit of his own potential. Because of the many short poems with something for almost everyone—ranging, perhaps, from simple enjoyment of melody or story to full appreciation of the poet's art—this literary form is particularly suitable for all types of classes.

In the study of poetry, both sense and sound are important. Although the two combine to form an artistic whole, we shall consider them separately here as the *language* and the *music* of poetry.

The language of poetry

Poetry exists in the language of imaginative insight. Through its language, poetry so sharpens our senses and freshens our awareness that we understand, almost intuitively, what would otherwise be impossible to express. Through images and metaphor, closely allied with the symbols he creates, the poet attains the rich suggestiveness of his language, evoking the most subtle emotions.

Imagery Just as no reader can give a completely rational description of his personal re-creation of the vision the poet communicates, no poet can explain the creative ferment that brings forth a great poem. However, poets who have tried to make the creative process comprehensible to the layman all agree that it is a blending, through the writer's image-making faculty, of his intellectual, emotional, and sensuous experiences; thus, he arouses imagination, enabling each reader to fuse what he himself has known and felt and thought. The poet, perceiving relationships between things essentially unlike, clarifies or intensifies for the reader different aspects of life, and in so doing, evokes for him a completely new experience.

Imagery vivifies sensory impressions for the reader or the listener. The poem helps him see, hear, touch, taste, and feel. In "A Wanderer's Song" we hear "The clucking, sucking of the sea about the rusty hulls." In "The Eve of St. Agnes" we almost taste the "lucent syrops, tinct with cinnamon"; we feel the cold—so bitter the Beadsman fears "the sculptured dead . . . may ache in icy hoods and mails." Thus, the right word, vivid and alive, summons up sensations lying fallow in the memory. The reader, surrendering to the power of the poetic language, vitalizes the feeling the poet attempts to convey. He savors the language freighted with rich associative value. Through the images, fully realized, he recaptures moments of his past; he sees "the gray dawn breaking," hears "the sea-gulls crying," feels "the wheel's kick" under his hand, the wind "like a whetted knife" across his face. In some such way he arouses within himself "the first fine careless rapture" which quickened the poet's spirit and brought the words to life.

If the student is to re-create the sensory impressions *as he reads,* the teacher must help him cultivate a sharpened awareness of this aspect of poetic language. A teacher may begin by showing how the poet selects words to evoke associations and, thus, to control the reader's mood and to direct his expectations. One teacher asks, Why does the perfume maker label his product "Evening in Paris" rather than "Evening in Brooklyn"?[13] Another asks why Poe chooses a raven and opens his poem with these lines:

> Once upon a midnight dreary, while I pondered, weak and weary,
> Over many a quaint and curious volume of forgotten lore

Why not a crow arriving at high noon just as Poe was stirring up a tasty snack of pork and beans?

This single feature of poetic language should be presented in a simple situation, where the concept is obvious and encumbered with few or no side issues. Thus it is possible to demonstrate quickly one way the language of poetry draws upon the vast resources of the imagination, how the poet, by *selecting,* releases the enormous force of a few words.[14] Once the concept is clear, students watch for the poet's intention in a number of poems: in junior high, poems like Masefield's "Sea Fever" and Coffin's "Hound on the Church Porch"; in senior high, poems like "Chicago" and "The Eve of St. Agnes."

Metaphor and symbol Metaphor, in which we include all figurative language, is the most crucial of all the concepts needed for reading poetry. Here one comes most nearly to the heart of poetic language. The value in teaching most students to discriminate among the various figures of speech is highly dubious. Instead the typical boy or girl must come to see, through many examples, how any apt comparison of two disparate and logically unrelated things flashes meanings from poem to reader, meanings that long

[13] Edward J. Gordon, "Teaching Students to Read Verse" in *They Will Read Literature,* A Portfolio of Tested Secondary School Procedures (Champaign, Ill., National Council of Teachers of English, 1955).

[14] Emerson's definition of poetry.

paragraphs of exhausting explanation becloud as often as they illumine. Our delight at the sudden insight and our awe at this daring leap of the imagination ranging over time and space give metaphor a central place in the language of poetry.

Metaphor, with its accompanying image, is nothing strange to the student; continually he thinks and speaks in figurative language, commonplace for the most part. It is the function of the poet to discover metaphors that release feeling and meaning. They may be as simple and straightforward as the likening of one concrete thing to another, or the concrete to the abstract, or the abstract to the concrete; they may be infinitely more subtle, woven into the very texture of the poem to unify the theme. Teachers present this concept inductively, beginning with the metaphor our everyday language uses to communicate ideas sharply or vividly.[15] Students can illustrate with the slang currently in favor. Just now they are likely to describe each other by such pungent epithets as *a honey, a knock-out, a dream-boat, a drip, a riot, a card, a grind, a brain.*

Symbols may be viewed as part of metaphor. Teachers begin with easy symbols: the stars and stripes, Santa Claus, the grim reaper, the dove of peace, the cornucopia of plenty, the school colors. Next they note the cross of Christianity, the wheel of Buddhism. Inductively the students build a definition: A symbol is a representation of something else—often something difficult to explain. The final step is to note how words can represent concrete symbols and convey a wealth of meaning.

When the concept of the ramifications of metaphor begins to take shape for pupils, the teacher turns to poetry.

> O Captain! my Captain! our fearful trip is done,
> The ship has weathered every rack, the prize we sought is won, . . .

With older students he may turn to life as a "dome of many-coloured glass," to the climbing of birches as a symbol of human aspiration, to the Moving Finger that writes,

> . . . and having writ,
> Moves on: nor all your Piety nor Wit
> Shall lure it back to cancel half a Line,
> Nor all your Tears wash out a Word of it."

As students unlock a poem like Robert Frost's "Birches" or Shelley's "Ode to the West Wind," they learn the power of symbols to represent complicated thoughts, to create the enormous force of a few words.

The music of poetry

If the study of poetry is not to be an exclusively intellectual pursuit, the student must be taught both to listen appreciatively to poems and to read

[15] Chapter 1, pp. 22-23, stresses the importance of helping students see metaphor not as a device used by poets but as an integral feature of language development.

them aloud for himself. In the beginning, he should have contact with much poetry where the listening experience is complete and satisfying in itself—where all the study necessary can be done in class under the direction of the teacher. Later, after instruction in oral reading, he can provide worthwhile listening experiences for others.

Much of the charm of poetry comes from the patterns of sound devised by the poet to intensify the images and thus to heighten emotion and vitalize meaning. Therefore, ear training plays a tremendously important part in helping students develop appreciation. Through purposeful listening, they can sense the significance of the rhythmical language, woven inextricably into the total meaning as the servant of thought and feeling. The first step in making them active participants is to involve them emotionally in any given poem. In the junior high grades, poems like "High Flight" and "America the Beautiful" usually succeed; in the senior high, such poems as "The Bugle Song" and "When I Was One-and-Twenty." The next step is to shift the pupils to reading poetry aloud for the pleasure of themselves and others. The rest of this chapter is primarily a guide to the accomplishment of this all-important aim.

Coleridge defines poetry as "the best words in the best order." The words of a poem—every one the best the author can devise—largely determine the tone color. The best order, varied by repetitions and omissions, accented by rhyme, determines the rhythmical pattern. Appreciation of *tone color* and *rhythm,* each an integral part of meaning, makes for greater enjoyment of poetry.

TONE COLOR

The poet in selecting the best words for his purpose is swayed by their tone color, the evocative power of their sound. He knows that, quite apart from their intellectual and emotional content, the sounds of certain words can affect feeling. That much of this power may stem from associative ideas does not alter the fact that even nonsense syllables can evoke a mood, convey meaning.

It is well to begin casually with the words themselves—perhaps with *brillig* and the *slithy toves* and the *whiffling, galumphing* Jabberwock. We may ask students to think of the many *-ump* words giving a notion of heaviness and clumsiness: clump, dump, stump, hump, bump, lump, rump. We look for lines of poetry where successful sound words exist. We may read Elinor Wylie's "Pretty Words," which suggests certain categories, and ask students to add others. We may read and note in the shivery "Daniel Webster's Horses" the repetition of consonants

Rattling the trees
Clicking like skeletons'
Elbows and knees.

and play Saint-Saëns' "Danse Macabre" to see how music suggests similar effects. In some such way we attempt to show how poetic language appeals to the ear as well as to the mind.

Although the poet will frequently use rhyme, alliteration, assonance, onomatopoeia, such devices will account for only a small proportion of the words that create the musical pattern of his poem. The tonal quality of every syllable is part of the total fabric of sound, just as each pigment selected by the painter is an essential element of the finished picture. Both artists can run the gamut of color from the light and gay to the dark and somber.

The tone color of a word is analogous to the timbre of a musical instrument, easy to recognize, at least in its broad distinctions. Although the listener may never have heard the oboe and is unable to identify the instrument producing the music, he cannot fail to sense the difference in the characteristic quality of its tone and that of the violin—a difference which derives from the variance in the physical make-up of the two instruments. In like manner, qualities in the sounds of words come from their construction, from the juxtaposition of the vowel and consonantal elements which compose them.

Various tonal values The music of the voice is carried, for the most part, by the vowels—the more open the sound, the more sonorous the quality. The range extends from the long *o*, leading all others in tonal depth, through the other long vowels and those of intermediate length, diminishing to the light quality which characterizes all the short vowel sounds. Consonants, too, although their chief function is to provide the stops, differ in tonal value—some, such as *l, m, n,* being noticeably softer and more flowing than the breathy or guttural sounds of *g, j, k.* Thus we notice that the open vowels and liquid consonants give depth and dignity to

Roll on, thou deep and dark blue ocean, roll

that the succession of short, bright sounds lends brilliance and grace to

How they tinkle, tinkle, tinkle,
In the icy air of night.

that the doubling of hard consonants produces the harsh tonal quality of

Listen to the quack horns, slack and clacking!

An appreciation of tone color helps the student develop an interest in the sound of words, an important quality in the magic the poet casts.

Tonal qualities compared Students have learned to appreciate the differing tonal qualities of words with the help of such a record as Benjamin Britten's "The Young Person's Guide to the Orchestra," designed to help the listener distinguish the different musical instruments.

Examine with students the contrast in tonal values of the first two stanzas of "The Highwayman" by Alfred Noyes. The brooding, liquid melody of the first, characterized by full-bodied tones, sets the eerie mood; the quickening excitement of the second, with its short, crisp sounds, presents the glitter and dash of the swashbuckling highwayman. Substitute *maroon* for *claret, throat* for *chin;* accent the last syllable of *forehead* and give *breeches* the long *e* sound—both pronunciations acceptable according to some dictionaries—and notice the different effect. Then play the record, asking students to select the instrument which best represents the tonal quality of each stanza. Invariably, the majority pick the poignant timbre of the cello to establish the haunting mood of the first and the brilliant, agile notes of the trumpet to express the lively, staccato quality of the second.

One such experience shows the student that the poet chooses words for the tone color appropriate to the emotion in much the same way that the symphonic composer writes his music for the instrument which will best transmit the feeling the music intends.

RHYTHM

To teach rhythm, the teacher can again use music. He may play excerpts from a Virginia reel, "Bolero," "Ritual Fire Dance," "The Swan," a march, a dirge, a waltz, a polka. The selections are not identified; instead the students are asked to suggest suitable titles or appropriate associations. The application to poetry is never difficult; poets, too, avail themselves of this same powerful device for influencing the listener's imagination. However, as students read "The Highwayman" in junior high school or, in later years, "General William Booth Enters into Heaven," they note that rhythm in poetry cannot be so pronounced as in music. It must blend with the ideas; it must not intrude.

The teacher may use different rhythm patterns to show how a poem suggests speed and excitement or evokes peace and tranquillity. He may intersperse the reading of poems with questions about the place of rhythm in life: in typing letters, sawing logs, good style in swimming and tennis, work songs, waves of the ocean, the seasons—and the latest popular dance forms. He may read poems representing a variety of rhythms, usually starting with the obvious rhythms imitating physical movements and gradually introducing the more subtle uses of rhythm in poetry.

Variations Attention to repetition and to the omission of sounds and words helps students understand the poet's practice of establishing a basic rhythm from which he is free to depart and to return. The teacher reads several ballads, noting their refrains intended for audience participation. Some pupils know this method from group experiences around camp fires. On a more complicated level, students discover the ironic importance Sandburg grants to the three lines he repeats so often in "Four Preludes on Playthings of the Wind." Once again music can demonstrate how composers repeat phrases or set a pattern of rhythm only to vary it with syncopation or silent "breaks" to increase the listener's pleasure. Just as musicians, to hold their listeners, must avoid a metronomic regularity, so must poets.

Rhyme as a factor While all poems have rhythm, many also have rhyme. Here, since recurrence of like sounds at regular intervals delineates the pattern more sharply, the difficulty in maintaining the correct degree of initimacy between sound and sense is accentuated. The tendency to use force on the rhyming syllables and to end each line with a downward inflection, followed by a pause, is often characteristic of the beginner. Such a reading usually distorts both rhythm and meaning. How can we teach the student to give the rhyme its just due and no more, to allow the listener to hear echo and re-echo, not as something important in itself, but as one of the devices used to integrate sounds with rhythm and meaning, thus binding all elements into a unified whole? Here the principle of sustaining tone and of blending one with another becomes important. Understanding clearly observable phenomenon of language—the fact that some syllables can easily be prolonged while others cannot—lays the foundation for intelligent practice.

Prolongation of sounds The long vowel sounds (ā, ō) can be sustained almost indefinitely; the intermediate (â, ô), somewhat; the short (ă, ĕ), almost not at all. Consonants show the same variation. They differ greatly in the degree of decisiveness with which they can terminate the vowel sounds. For example, *b, d, p,* and *t* are short, dying as soon as they are uttered; it is, consequently, difficult and usually inappropriate to prolong such words as *pop* and *tidbit.* On the other hand, *l, m, n, ng,* and *w,* being comparatively long, permit words like *full, calm, moon, hung, now* to be prolonged at will. The poet, although he cannot arbitrarily assign a definite time length to one word in comparison with others, as the conventions of musical notation permit the composer to do, nevertheless works on the same principle. One reading music knows that 𝅝 is equal in duration to 𝅗𝅥𝅗𝅥 or ♩♩♩♩; one reading poetry must be just as alert to the less exact suggestions of the poet, who through the combination of meaning and sounds in any word, phrase, or sentence also indicates a time value relative to the whole.

Blending of tone Any tone that can be sustained can be blended imperceptibly with the one following. The poet, probably for the most part unconsciously, makes use of this characteristic of language. In his ordering of clipped and prolonged syllables, he might be compared to one who writes for the piano. The composer may exploit either the vibrating or the non-vibrating qualities of his instrument. In the former case, the notes, sustained and blended by the pedal, produce a singing tone; in the latter, where the sound dies as soon as the finger is lifted from the key, a crisper, more brittle effect results. The poet, in building his melodic and rhythmic patterns, exploits the characteristics of the sounds of words in the same way. Three illustrations, using lines with problems of increasing complexity, will clarify for the pupil the principle of sustaining and blending sounds.

Rhyme causes almost no problem in maintaining rhythm in those occasional passages where *each line expresses one complete and distinct thought,* as in these lines by Wordsworth:

Ne'er saw I, never felt, a calm so deep!
The river glideth at his own sweet will;
Dear God! the very houses seem asleep;
And all that mighty heart is lying still!

Here the reader need not resist the temptation of the downward inflection and the marked pause at the end of each line, since both are in keeping with rhythm and meaning. His only problem is to show how the poet uses rhyme to help bind the elements of sound into an integral pattern. He does this by slightly prolonging the rhyming syllables, thus insuring the echo of *deep* with *sleep* and *will* with *still.* The tones lingering in the air emphasize the melody as do the vibrations of recurring notes from a musical instrument.

The last stanza of Bourdillon's simple lyric, "The Night Has a Thousand Eyes," furnishes examples of the other two problems: lines containing separate but closely related ideas; lines that are an integral part of those following.

The mind has a thousand eyes,
  And the heart but one;
Yet the light of a whole life dies
  When love is done.

In the above stanza, the first two lines, representing *two closely related but separate ideas,* present a problem slightly more complex than do the lines from Wordsworth. As in the Wordsworth passage, a gradual downward inflection on the last word will denote the completeness of the first thought; prolongation of the tone will take care of the rhyme. Here, however, proper blending of the lines becomes important. The pause is briefer, and "eyes and the heart" is treated almost as if it were a word of four syllables, with the first and last sustained and the second and third pronounced rapidly. The *run-on line* is still more difficult to read. However, the blending is practically the same here as in the previous example, although more pronounced—almost an elision. This necessary mingling of tone is effected by sustaining the rhyming syllable with no noticeable inflection and by making the break between it and the next imperceptible. Again, think of "dies when love" as one word with a clipped second syllable.

Understanding these simple principles has proved helpful to the student in learning to make the pattern of sound a subordinate but integral part of the thought and feeling. Of course, these principles of interpretation must be taught to reinforce the meaning behind the words. If the poem is fully understood by the reader, most of the interpretive problems are solved, and such matters as blending and inflection are readily learned as means to an end.

THE TEACHING PROBLEM

Organizing Instruction

Dependent as it is upon the artistry and enthusiasm of the teacher, successful instruction in poetry will vary considerably with each individual instructor. Some teachers prefer to arrange a sustained period of poetry with one day reinforcing the next. Others like several brief and separate samplings, teaching a few poems each time, with intervals for other activities, before entering into much more extensive development. Some teachers draw poetry into thematic units, stopping to examine aspects of form as each poem is studied and then fitting the total experiences of the poem into the larger theme of the unit. This text will recommend a number of short lessons devoted solely to poetry, but some teachers may find this unsatisfactory. Obviously, planning how poetry will be taught is a very personal matter, depending upon the personality of the teacher, the particular class, and the plans for the rest of the English course. Because of these considerations, this section will emphasize practices that stimulate interest in poetry and touch only lightly upon the organization of instruction, seeking to remain as free as possible from any prescription or dogma.

Need for balance The need for balance in teaching students to read poetry cannot be overemphasized. One who hopes to establish poetry merely by reading builds on quicksand. Equally dangerous is the so-called "scholarly" approach, in which close analysis belabors each poem as if it were an intellectual puzzle. The teacher walks a razor's edge, in danger always of leaning too far in either direction. But there are ways to maintain a positive poise. First, the teacher must be genuinely appreciative of student response; he should welcome reactions and suggestions, no matter how banal. Startling and naive levels of appreciation make clear to him where he must start with the learner. Second, he must teach the language and music of poetry without forcing these considerations into a central position. Content or some other basis of relationship may frequently decide the organization: "Not Exactly Serious," "Freedom's Ferment," "Poems by Youth"—these groupings or clusters may hold a central position in the pupils' attention. Within such clusters, the formal elements of appreciation may make their appearance. Even so, the teacher moves cautiously, stressing only one aspect of poetic form at a time, holding the others in check until another propitious moment. Perhaps symbols can be handled best during a unit on "The Dimensions of Courage," when the class reads "Mother to Son," by Langston Hughes:

> . . . Life for me ain't been no crystal stair.
> It's had tacks in it,
> And splinters, . . .

Perhaps imagery may very well be presented during "Poems with a Touch of a Shiver." However these aspects of form may be woven into the course, a restrained teaching of form in relation to content supports rather than weakens the pleasure of poetry. Reading poetry solely for what it says is to miss the route to discovering what it actually does say.

From simple to complex In planning lessons for adolescents, the teacher should not be lured to his college anthologies to find something he has learned to like. Eighth grade pupils, for instance, are not adults; because of their emotional immaturity, they will respond better to "The Highwayman" than to *The Waste Land.* James Thrall Soby, who is commended in the *Saturday Review* for his taste in art, admits he received his first impetus to enjoyment from a print of a colorful, yet ordinary, picture bought from an itinerant salesman. Taste for the best in poetry often springs from such humble beginnings.

Developing taste slowly Lovers of poetry agree that, although it requires close, careful reading, it should be taught with a light hand. The purpose of the first presentation of a poem is not to exhaust its possibilities but to whet the appetite for more. When, under the teacher's direction or of his own accord, the student returns to a poem, he begins to see that great poetry reveals its power only after many rereadings. Poetry works its magic, if at all, in small doses over a period of time.

Although for most classes it is better to focus on the various aspects of poetic form one at a time, pupils should realize that any poem has more than one simple feature. A poem should always be presented as a poem—a work of art—letting the class sense it as an entity, each student taking what his experience permits. After the class has enjoyed it in this way, the teacher may through questioning bring out one of its most salient characteristics as poetry. As soon as the various aspects have been taught, students can learn to fuse these separate qualities. However brief or lengthy the discussion, with short poems the teacher should allow time for a rereading. From the beginning, students should realize that analysis of poetry is a means to an end. The poem itself deserves the final word.

Stimulating interest The teacher, attempting to stimulate interest in any literary form, tries many avenues of approach. Because of its conciseness and its suitability as basis for a listening experience, poetry lends itself to various modes of presentation. Through this variety teachers are often able to involve students by one method when another has failed. The following recommendations, distilled from classroom experience, are intended to support and nourish interest in poetry.

Read many poems incidentally

Keep on your desk a file of typed copies of poems—not to be used as part of a unit or as a lesson illustrating an aspect of poetry, but merely some you enjoy reading and think students may like. Ready at hand, these suggest occasions for poetry that might otherwise be overlooked. Once the practice of reading from this file is started, invite students to add to your collection. The star of one teacher's file is an illustrated copy of James Weldon Johnson's "Creation," prepared by a senior class as their favorite. A close second is Sandburg's "Primer Lesson," given by a boy in apology for a pert remark.

Relate to group feeling Choose high or low moments of the school year as opportunities to read poetry aloud. On the morning of a heavy snow read Wylie's "Velvet Shoes" or Frost's "Stopping by Woods on a Snowy Evening." When spring fever strikes, try Richard Le Gallienne's "I Meant to Do My Work Today." After an assembly or film has left everyone in an exalted mood, "If" or "I Had No Time to Hate" may be appropriate. On a day of jangled nerves, limericks or the verse of Ogden Nash may contribute a needed laugh.

Use the extra minute Read poems not only for special occasions but when a disrupted program causes unavoidable delay or when scheduled work is finished sooner than expected. If only one student asks to borrow the copy of the poem or takes down the name of the author because he is interested in reading more, the time has not been wasted. Watching the reactions of the class, noting what poems are asked for repeatedly, helps determine the level on which the next unit of instruction in poetry may begin.

Accommodate diverse personalities

Granting that some aspects of poetry should be taught to all and that some poems should be read in common, teachers plan other ways to take into account the variety of temperaments and interests among their students.

Select favorite poems A poetry collection prepared for future classes; a booklet to which each student contributes one of his favorite poems; days on which everyone brings a poem he likes and reads it aloud to a group, a few of the best-liked to be selected for class enjoyment; mimeographed lists of topics and themes with several titles listed under each and many spaces for addition by students who locate suitable poems from a wide selection of books and magazines; occasional recitals by groups or individuals reading poems centered on one theme—all these are ways of accommodating varieties of pupil response to poetry.

Study prosody Although a few classes may benefit from a thorough investigation of the techniques of versification and the variety of forms employed by poets, usually only a limited number of individuals in the regular English class react favorably to such complete study. For this group, a knowledge of the mechanics of verse not only may be fascinating in itself but may be helpful to those seriously interested in trying to write poetry. Usually the teacher asks for volunteer committees to investigate and report to the entire class. These committees choose poems to present as examples of stress patterns and verse forms with which the class has had no contact. Since such work is voluntary and appeals only to a small group, students are not held responsible for the information.

Write verse Since poems, or even respectable verse, cannot be written on order, attempts to write in metrical form should also be voluntary. However, some students gain a more secure basis for appreciation of the poet's craft by trying their hand at writing limericks or parodies, the easiest forms for the beginner. Ask each student to compose only the first line of a limerick; let the class pick the line they prefer to work with as, under the teacher's guidance, they write the rest of the limerick together. Testing the merits of alternate lines suggested by individuals results in a certain non-technical understanding of some of the simpler elements of meter and rhyme. Volunteers may then compose limericks starting with a line suggested by the teacher or students. The following written by a tenth grade girl acted as a spur for some students to extend their efforts to other forms of verse.

> There once was a student at Tech.
> Desirous of saving her neck,
> She walked on her knees,
> All teachers to please
> And now she's a physical wreck.

Use art Reproductions of paintings aid in sparking the imagination; they occasionally inspire poems, but more often flashes of metaphor and rhythmic lines. Teachers use this approach as a stimulus for brief writing periods, asking students to jot down vivid words and phrases descriptive of what the picture makes them see or feel. To some, nothing will come; to others, only the trite; but a few will respond with the germ of a poetic idea. The teacher takes contributions from volunteers, considering alternate phrases, sometimes letting the class decide whether the light or serious line is more in tune with the mood. The intensity and vitality of El Greco's "View of Toledo," with its threatening movement and awesome gloom, has released expression in some; the tranquillity of "The Wheat Field" by Jacob van Ruisdael has moved others to creative reflection; the shimmering iridescence of the drifting cloud shapes and elusive light of Monet's "Argenteuil Bridge, 1874" has secured a fanciful response from still others. Bonnard's "The Checkered Tablecloth," Daumier's "Third Class Carriage," Cézanne's "Still Life with Apples," have called forth the beauty and the drama of the commonplace.

This type of work does not lend itself to probing; images and illuminating fragments come spontaneously or not at all. Hence, brief, frequent exposures are best. A few apt expressions each time, a few students inspired to extend the experience to voluntary writing, make the activity worthwhile. The results need not be used as a basis for grading.

Choose the "best" Many students like to defend their choices of the best. A teacher may learn something of his success in teaching poetry, and may be guided somewhat in selecting poems to be taught again, by an activity similar to the following. At the end of the semester, list most of the poems that have been taught. Ask each student to select from the list the three poems he thinks should unquestionably be taught to incoming classes, giving brief reasons for his choice. A variation is to ask for the first poem to be dropped from the course. If there is considerable agreement, try to discover the reason. Does it lie in the poem or in the way it was presented?

Experiences in which the listener tests his sensitivity to the emotional and intellectual elements of poetry appeal to many students. One way, because it can be repeated as often as seems profitable and because it works well on all levels, is excellent for teaching different aspects of poetry. Write several different versions of one line from a stanza of an unfamiliar poem—one line with clumsy rhythm, one changing the prevailing mood, one substituting a trite for an apt metaphor, one replacing simple language with pretentious. Write the original and the alternates on the board. (With some classes, start with only one substitution.) Read the stanza aloud, each time with a different line; ask students to pick the original. Discuss each of the rewritten versions, trying to draw from students how each detracts from the poem. What makes the rhythm intrude? Does word choice or rhythm or both disturb the mood? Why does the rejected metaphor lack communicative power? How does the connotation of the poet's words differ from that of those substituted? After the discussion, read the entire poem. The teaching done with the class can be reinforced for volunteers, working in groups, each member making his own selection and rewriting the line chosen.

An effective technique for evoking imaginative responses to literature is called the Connoisseur's Choice or the Spoiled Version. Based on principles of contrast and comparison, it offers the student two versions of a literary creation—one authentic and one spurious. In deciding which of the two versions he prefers and the reasons for his decision, the student must consider the relationship of parts to the whole. Here, for instance, the method is applied to the Rockets stanza from Tom Prideaux's "Fireworks." [16]

Rockets

A genie's arm and sleeved in gold,
Was thrust across the sky. Behold
How from his smoking palm there falls
A silent chime of colored balls.

Rockets

A ghost's hand, we were told,
Was put into our view. Behold
How from his big fist there drops
A hundred red chimney tops.

When the teacher first introduces this method, he will find it best, as in the example above, to present one version so obviously and grossly spoiled that almost everyone in the class can detect the differences in quality. As students become skilled at critical reading, the differences may be increased in subtlety.

[16] From "Fireworks" by Tom Prideaux, from Hughes Mearns, *Creative Youth*. Reprinted by permission of Hughes Mearns.

Working with unfamiliar passages, students will discover and put into words the very concepts the teacher wants them to learn. This shift from passive to active learning stimulates their full response.[17]

Teachers who use this method frequently include some pairs of equally unworthy versions for the same "poem"; this practice has the merit of keeping students on their mettle. Once they have become aware that a defensible choice requires thinking, that it does not permit settling into comfortable routines, students bring more alertness to the exercise and to similar succeeding exercises.

Use different stimuli

Invite guest readers Guest readers have an impact so beneficial that their appearance should be staged several times each semester. However, they should be carefully selected; frail or eccentric personalities can easily harm the cause of poetry. Community poets and representatives of speech and English departments of nearby colleges have served as impetus to enjoyment in many high school classes. Perhaps the most successful guests are those only a little older than the listeners: a recent graduate; two upper class boys and a girl, seated at a table before the ninth grade, reading "The Listeners," "Lone Dog," and "The Pied Piper of Hamelin"; or a similar trio of seniors before the eleventh grade, reading poems of more delicately balanced imagery–Sarett's "Wind in the Pine," stanzas from "The Rubáiyát," "The Death of the Hired Man." The excellent long playing records now appearing on the market make it possible to have as guests, at the teacher's and pupils' own convenience, the authors themselves or skilled actors reading the poets' lines.

When poetry is read aloud, the listeners should frequently have the printed words before them, the meaning reaching the mind both by way of eye and ear. As they hear repeated performances of poems they like, most pupils will discover their need for visual support disappears.

Select background music Students may also prepare their favorite poems and read them aloud in small groups. Then each group selects a poem read effectively; all members of each group search for a musical recording that will provide the perfect background for a reading of the chosen poem: "Pomp and Circumstance," "Finlandia," or "Largo" from *Xerxes* for Kipling's "Recessional"; something by Debussy for "La Belle Dame Sans Merci"; an instrumental version of "Nobody Knows the Trouble I've Seen" for "Mother to Son." These are actual choices; another class may find more suitable correspondences. The following day, with the help of several boys as technicians, the six or seven effective poems are read aloud before the class while the musical recordings are played quietly in the background.

[17] Some teachers have reservations about presenting to their students gross distortions of fine literature. They prefer to use this method with poems of lesser merit or to prepare two versions for poems of their own devising. They believe the latter course prevents any danger of permanently fixing unpleasant associations with fine poetry.

Use tape recorder One of the English teacher's best allies is the tape recorder. The first time anyone hears his own voice, amazement and ego-deflation result. However, a supportive teacher can convert the disappointment into an incentive for deeper study and for more oral practice. The second recording almost invariably shows commendable improvement, arising from more thorough understanding and better voice control. One of the most satisfying projects for an English department is the building of a collection, either on tape or records, of students' readings, not only of poetry but of other literary forms.

Experiment with choral reading

Although students enjoy hearing teachers read, as soon as possible they should begin reading for each other. Choral speaking will help bridge the gap between interested listener and solo reader. Here, where attention centers on the group rather than the individual, the reluctant participant can submerge himself until he gains confidence. Adapting his voice to the tempo and rhythm decided upon through general discussion, at first he may effect control only through imitation, but ear and voice are being subconsciously trained. Soon he should be willing to read bit parts, until gradually he loses the fear of his own voice. Then he is ready for individual readings, at first for small groups, perhaps later before the class.

Aim The reluctance of beginning teachers to attempt the choral approach to the study of poetry may be due in part to the fact that much of the writing on the subject has been directed to those preparing choirs for public performance. Consult these books, by all means,[18] but remember that the English teacher's aim is to foster an appreciation of poetry through accustoming ear and voice to respond to the nuances of poetic language. Begin casually, emphasizing only the need for pleasant voice quality and crisp enunciation to bring out the meaning. Have sections of the class listen at first, to point up the complementary aspects of reading and listening. Soon students learn to listen to themselves in practice; finally, they learn that if, after sufficient practice, attention during the reading is focused on the meaning, the poetic elements will usually take care of themselves. Even if they do not, nothing is gained while reading by concentrating on the sound pattern, devised only to communicate thought and feeling. The English teacher need not fear the technicalities of choral speaking. Moved by the desire to infect his students with his own enjoyment of poetry, all he needs is willingness to experiment.

Initial experience In teaching students who have had little experience in interpretation, the teacher starts with a poem which will disclose some of its

[18] Marjorie Gullan pioneered the work first in England and later in the United States. *The Speech Choir* (N.Y., Harper, 1937), written with students of this country in mind, gives invaluable suggestions both for suitable poems and for their interpretation and arrangement for choral groups.

values quickly. Knowing that the response to pronounced rhythm is universal and that stories have wide appeal, he usually selects a poem which exemplifies either one or both of these characteristics. Perhaps he may decide to use "Columbus" by Joaquin Miller, since the meaning is apparent upon the first reading and the verses themselves may be familiar to the students. At this point, such foreknowledge is a help rather than a hindrance; the simple problems in listening and in interpretation offered by this poem can lay the foundation for more complicated work to come later. Problems concerning mood, characterization, tempo, and climax—almost always aspects of any narrative poem—can be studied within these five stanzas.

The following steps are suggested as a method of procedure. Although the method here is applied to "Columbus," it can be adapted to any suitable poem.

The teacher reads the poem to give a unified first impression.

The first four lines—Purpose? (To establish a mood of loneliness.) How achieved? (Long vowels and sounds capable of prolongation produce a slow moving, mournful sounding line.) The teacher suggests reading the lines together, trying to convey the feeling; groups of students take turns listening. (Even the slowest tempo should never drag. Work for a light attack on each syllable.) Repeat several times until voices convey both the mood and the flowing rhythm.

The characters—Notice contrast between the two characters, which must be shown through voice; a mere suggestion is sufficient. Let students decide on the voices which best suggest the quality. (Probably the deeper, fuller voice will better convey the determination and strength of the Admiral.) Select several readers for each part.

Climax—The excitement and suspense of the story moves from the feeling of loneliness, through mounting anxiety, to the deep fear of the mad sea, and finally to the joy at sighting land. Let the selected readers take just the lines of the mate and the Admiral, trying to intensify the feeling with each question and answer. Select two boys to read the parts.

Tempo—The tempo increases, although some lines offer contrast ("They sailed. They sailed" suggests the hopelessness of the quest), until the beginning of the last stanza, where it slows to suggest the darkest hour but picks up again when land is sighted. Readers, like musicians, often retard the last phrases of a poem to prepare listeners for the end.

Casting (one possibility)—Boys for Admiral and mate; girl for narrator who takes straightforward lines such as "The good mate said," etc. All girls for "The words leapt like a leaping sword." One girl for the first three lines of the fifth stanza. Four groups (all but characters and narrator), starting with one group and adding the others one at a time, for the line "A light! A light! A light! A light!"

Reading—Work for clear tone, crisp utterance, maintaining mood and rhythm.

Since first attempts at choral reading can be expected to lack the niceties the rendition of great poetry requires, a story in verse which cannot be spoiled by mass attack makes a good beginning.

Arrangements While the arrangement for choral speaking of some poems seems inherent in their patterns, many lend themselves to a variety of effective readings. Students can make valuable suggestions; in reaching agreement, they deepen their understanding of poetic principles. As they try both appropriate and inappropriate versions, they become more sensitive to the close relationship between form and meaning. The following, all used successfully with secondary school students, will suggest others to the teacher. (The asterisks mark poems that have been used with junior high students.)

Poems with refrain

*The Owl and the Pussy Cat Edward Lear
*The Pirate Don Durk of Dowdee Mildred P. Meigs
*Jesse James William Rose Benét
*A Swing Song William Allingham
*Macavity, the Mystery Cat T. S. Eliot
*Pioneers! O Pioneers! Walt Whitman
*The Wind Robert Louis Stevenson

Poems with dialogue or antiphonal passages

*Who Has Seen the Wind? Christina Rossetti
*Ballad of the Oysterman Oliver Wendell Holmes
Invocation, from *John Brown's Body* Stephen Vincent Benét
*The Raggle Taggle Gypsies Old Ballad
Chevy Chase Old Ballad
*Sir Patrick Spens Old Ballad
*The Song of the Mad Prince Walter de la Mare

Poems effective in various arrangements

There Will Come Soft Rains Sara Teasdale
*April Rain Song Langston Hughes
* African Dance Langston Hughes
*Jazz Fantasia Carl Sandburg
*I Hear America Singing Walt Whitman
Beat! Beat! Drums! Walt Whitman
*The Potatoes' Dance Vachel Lindsay
The Santa Fe Trail Vachel Lindsay
The Barrel Organ Alfred Noyes
The Creation James Weldon Johnson
Work, A Song of Triumph Angela Morgan
The Force that Through the Green Fuse Drives the Flower Dylan Thomas

Poems for small groups

Poetry of great delicacy or of intense feeling sometimes can be read effectively only by small groups; many lyrics, of course, are suitable only for solo reading.

*Four Little Foxes Lew Sarett
A Vagabond Song Bliss Carmen
Four Preludes on Playthings of the Wind Carl Sandburg
*O Captain! My Captain! Walt Whitman
The Freedom of the Moon Robert Frost
Uphill Christina Rossetti

*Stars Sara Teasdale
*The Sea Gypsy Richard Hovey
To His Father Robinson Jeffers
The Express Stephen Spender
I Have a Rendezvous with Death Alan Seeger

The above list, both as to selection and categories, is suggestive only. Perhaps the greatest values come when students find poems they like and then decide upon appropriate arrangements. Therefore, a corner for poetry anthologies, reserved for browsing, is almost indispensable. A weekly-changing bulletin board, "Poems I Like," with selections made by students, is another source for both individual and group work. Since we cannot all like the same poems, and since we know that even great favorites are not companionable for all moods, presenting a range wide in interest appeal is necessary if poetry is to offer stimulation for all.

Encourage memorization

In every reasonable way, memorization should be fostered, for phrases of beauty and the concepts they embody live on into adult life. Use praise and your own example. Keep a corner of the chalk board for brief poems students might find worth memorizing; do not comment; see how many take the bait. Occasionally set aside a portion of a period for those who wish to "read" poems from memory. External pressures such as grades or requirements are a hindrance. Will there, then, be students who will avoid memorization? Assuredly. But better none at all than that done under duress. Certainly, nothing kills a poem more quickly for the listener than to be forced to endure a halting, glassy-eyed reading of lines that are supposed to soar and lilt. There seems no good reason for the student to perform publicly—certainly not until he has made the memorized lines his own—and that takes time.

Aid in memorizing Suggest ways others have found helpful in committing lines to memory. The best methods stress the gradual, unforced aspects of the process, the concentration on meaning rather than on words, the re-creation of the sensory images each time the lines are repeated. Give volunteers instructions like these:

Copy material in notebooks where it is readily accessible.

Memorize the sequence of ideas or images.

Read over several times a day so that memorization comes naturally; such a plan yields greater returns than does the same amount of time spent all at once.

Avoid memorizing one line at a time; the relation of parts to the whole proves the best basis for memory work.

Concentrate in each reading not on memorization but on bringing out thought and feeling; vivify the images; hear the lines.

Keep your copy before you, using it less and less, until the poem "says itself."

Developing discrimination Help volunteers establish some standards for their expenditure of time. Over the years Robert Frost and Emily Dickinson wear better than Edgar Guest and Robert Service. However, each must find this out for himself. Continue to point out notable passages and poems worthy of memorization, but leave the final choice to the student. Undoubtedly, he will select some that seem of little value, but this tendency should not worry the teacher unduly. Like many popular tunes which run in one's head to the point of exasperation, commonplace lines soon pall for one who is becoming sensitized to the language and feeling inherent in great poetry; before long he will find others of greater worth to replace the trite. In this way he acquires discrimination—one of the most important values to be derived from memorization.

Suggested Learning Experiences

These suggestions should serve merely as ideas that readers may alter and modify into activities suited to their own artistry of teaching. In general, the learning experiences presented here have been chosen because they illustrate basic principles of teaching poetry: the importance of balancing both enjoyment and analysis; the acknowledgment that taste, highly personal, develops slowly; and the importance, the inescapable importance, of appreciating form and the pattern of sound as an integral part of meaning.

To learn to listen to a poem

■ *Listen for the story*

Start with something which requires no analysis for at least superficial appreciation, e.g., an exciting narrative with vigorous rhythm. Before reading, give sufficient explanation to make the poem easily understood. Browning's "How They Brought the Good News from Ghent to Aix" might be introduced something like this:

> A horse, Roland, is the hero of this poem, which tells the story of three riders—Dirck, Joris, and the speaker—who are sent with a message from Ghent, in Belgium, to Aix, in West Prussia. The poet describes the ride but does not tell us what the good news is. We do sense the urgency of the message.
>
> The fact that the message is sent by riders indicates what about the time of the story? There are several words which further suggest the medieval, foreign atmosphere—*postern* ("behind shut the postern") Meaning? *askance? aye and non? burgesses?*
>
> Notice how the poet shows the passage of time—moonset, twilight, cock's crow—and the progress of the ride by giving the Belgian towns through which they pass—Lockeren, Boom, Düffield . . . Dalhem.
>
> Listen to the way the author suggests the headlong, breathless speed, the echoing hoofbeats of the galloping horses.

Finally, read the poem aloud.

■ *Examine the rhythm*

1. Reread the first two lines to show how the short, hard syllables suggest the sound and the speed of the plunging hoofbeats.

2. Let volunteers try reading them to emphasize the need for crisp, clear-cut articulation, the fact that to maintain the rhythm in poetry every syllable counts.

3. Let volunteers, trying to maintain the tempo, read some of the lines describing the passage through the towns.

■ *Discover some of the characteristics of poetry*

1. Poetry suggests more than it tells. Is it effective to leave the details of the message to the reader's imagination? Why, or why not?

2. Poetry is not concerned with factual material. The poet mentions the names of real towns. Does this mean the story recounts an actual event? What then is the author's purpose? (To tell an exciting story, to commemorate an heroic act.)

3. The rhythm the poet selects is an important factor in conveying the emotional charge.

■ *Listen again to enjoy the way tempo, rhythm, and story are integrated*

Other narrative poems suitable for an initial experience are "The Highwayman," "Ballad of East and West," "Lord Randal," "King Robert of Sicily," "Danny Deever," and "Lepanto."

To appreciate sensuous imagery

■ *Notice appeals in specific poems*

1. Read poems composed mainly of images:

"To ———" (Music, when soft voices die), Percy B. Shelley. In eight lines, the poet presents three images—music, odor of violets, rose leaves—each appealing to a different sense.

"Cargoes," John Masefield. In each of the three stanzas we have a picture of a different era, from ancient times to the present.

"A Birthday," Christina Rossetti. Two stanzas composed primarily of images—the first, a series of comparisons; the second, a list of exotic images appealing to sight.

2. After a browsing period, ask students to respond to roll call by reading lines containing one image.

■ *Consider the effectiveness of imagery*

1. Reread any of the poems used before. Consider reasons for the imagery, and its effectiveness. Of what value is compression in the Masefield? Does the extravagance of the Rossetti images help or hinder the desired response?

2. Encourage volunteers to try making a familiar object vivid through comparsions which create an image—a deserted house, a football, a schoolroom desk.

To respond to metaphorical language

■ *Notice the difference between the imaginative and the trite*

Ask students to substitute trite expressions for the poet's metaphorical language. Coleridge, in "The Rime of the Ancient Mariner," describes phenomena of nature we all recognize and portrays emotions we have all felt—but in images which vivify such experiences for us.

We might say	*Coleridge says*
"A broiling sun"	"All in a hot and copper sky, The bloody Sun, at noon, Right up above the mast did stand, No bigger than the Moon."
"Dying of thirst"	"And every tongue, through utter drought, Was withered at the root; We could not speak, no more than if We had been choked with soot."
"Scared to death"	"Fear at my heart, as at a cup, My lifeblood seemed to sip!"

■ *Sense the symbolism unifying metaphorical elements*

1. Read poems where the same symbol signifies different things: "Fog" and "Wind is a Cat"

2. Read poems where different symbols are used for the same purpose: "Lincoln, the Man of the People" and "O, Captain, My Captain!"

3. Read poems with fairly obvious symbols:

"Blow, Blow, Thou Winter Wind" Ingratitude—the sharp bite of the wind.
"Barter," "Dream Pedlary" Attainment of spiritual values in terms of the market place.
"How Can One Ever be Sure" Confused thinking—tangled hair.
"My Love" Unspoken love—hidden grass.
"Loveliest of Trees," "To Daffodils," "The Falling Star," and "Unlost" Fleeting quality of life and beauty—cherry blossoms, daffodils, a star, a candle flame.
"Nature" Nature's discipline—a mother's discipline.

4. Read poems where the use of symbolism is more subtle:

"November Night" and "Warning" Death—falling leaves, flight of a moth.
"The Tiger." Evil—brute force and fascinating beauty of the tiger. Good—the lamb.

Through the use of imagery, metaphor, symbol, and choice of language, the poet synthesizes his experiences and opens up new worlds for those who have learned to appreciate his art.

To study the effect of tone color

■ *Discover how words gain tone color*

1. Compare music and poetry (see p. 355).

2. Investigate the effect created by different combinations of vowel and consonantal sounds (see p. 355). Divide the class into two groups for five minutes; students in one group are to write words lending themselves to prolongation; those in the other to write words difficult to prolong. Call on students to respond quickly with several words they have listed, demonstrating the characteristic orally. Then give a few minutes for each student to write a line, using words from his list. Consider those volunteered, noting different effects. Finally, discuss association of meaning as contributing to tone color.

■ *Discover how poets use tonal values to help convey total meaning*

1. Read "The Old Song." Compare the two stanzas, noticing how within an unchanged rhythm different tempos and moods are created. Lead students in a unison reading.

2. Study Poe's "Eldorado." Notice how tempo changes with mood. Discover how the poet effects this change.

3. Read "Swift Things Are Beautiful." How is the difference in the slow and swift movements accomplished? How does this difference give total meaning?

4. Study "The Patriot." Ideas in the opening lines usually describe a gay scene. How does the poet achieve the opposite effect?

To respond to different rhythms

■ *Read poems where the reason for the rhythm is obvious*

Walking
Carefree—"Tewkesbury Road," John Masefield
Mournful—"Marching Pines," Lew Sarett
Desperately monotonous—"Boots," Rudyard Kipling

Riding
"Cavalier Tunes," Robert Browning
"Charge of the Light Brigade," Alfred Tennyson
"Sweetwater Range," Lew Sarett

Skating
"The Skaters," John Gould Fletcher
"Skating," Herbert Asquith

Rocking
"Sweet and Low," Alfred Tennyson
"Indian Sleep Song," Lew Sarett
"Lullaby," Christiana Rossetti

The Sea
"Break, Break, Break," Alfred Tennyson
"Neptune's Steeds," William Crittendon

The River
"Song of the Chattahoochee," Sidney Lanier
"How the Waters Come Down at Lodore," Robert Southey

■ *Read poems where the reason for the rhythm is more subtle*

Inner Strength
"Invictus," William E. Henley
"Requiem," Robert L. Stevenson

Tranquility
Sonnets by William Wordsworth:
"It is a Beauteous Evening, Calm and Free"
"Composed Upon Westminster Bridge"

Gentleness
"The Blind Girl," Nathalia Crane
"Four Little Foxes," Lew Sarett

Delicacy
"Silver," Walter de la Mare
"To a Snowflake," Francis Thompson

To learn to read poems orally

■ *Re-create the images as you read*

In order to experience the emotional impact and to heighten it for his listener, the reader must vivify, *as he reads,* the sensations conjured up by the words of the poet. Help the student who reads a line too matter-of-factly to gain the correct emotion by asking appropriate questions to stimulate his imagination.

Roll on, thou deep and dark blue ocean, roll!
Ten thousand fleets sweep over thee in vain.

As you try to get the feeling that Byron intends, what are you thinking of? Is the scene you visualize wholly imaginary or do you recall a specific experience? Where are you? On the shore? On a ship? How would you differentiate the sound of waves against a beach from the sound of those against a ship? Can you feel the spray on your face? Taste the salt? What colors do you see in the water? Is the sun shining? Is the sky overcast? Are there threatening clouds? Can you possibly visualize ten thousand fleets? If not, why does the poet use this expression?

Such questions help students realize that if the poet is to have a chance to work his magic, both listener and reader must take an active part.

■ *Learn to stress rhythm rather than meter*

Understanding the intricacies of metrical form is unnecessary for reading poetry. Even with no knowledge of scansion, the inexperienced reader often finds it difficult not to capitulate to the insistence of the metric beat.

1. Demonstrate for students, using a few lines of poetry. Read first, stressing the accented syllables to produce a jerky, sing-song rhythm.

"*Dárk brówn* is the *ríver,*
Gólden ís the *sánd.*
It *flóws alóng forév*er,
With *trées* on eíther *hánd.*"

Read again, combining inflection and slight prolongation of sound on the italicized words to produce a smooth-flowing rhythm. Let students decide which best suggests Stevenson's river; let them try to determine what caused the two different effects. Then lead students in a unison reading to accustom ear and voice to rhythm reinforcing meaning.

2. Explain the difference between meter and rhythm. Meter, a convention of prosody, exists on the printed page; rhythm exists in the reader. A product of thought and emotion, it results from the tension set up between meaning and meter.

3. Stress the necessity for concentrating on meaning while reading. These rough diagrams have helped students understand the problems a reader faces:

What is one who reads like this doing?

(Overemphasizing meter.)

One who reads like this?

(Completely disregarding the sound pattern, probably giving a prosy, matter-of-fact reading.)

One who reads like this?

(Trying to make rhythm reinforce meaning.)

■ *Learn to make rhyme contribute to rhythm*

Adapt the suggestions on p. 357 to help students read rhyming syllables effectively.

■ *Practice making the sound pattern reinforce meaning.*

Nursery rhymes, with their regular meter and simple rhyme, make excellent material for practice. Ask students to select one, to practice reading it, to prepare to read in groups. After work in groups, let students record their readings. Have the class listen to recordings to select examples of readings in which the sound pattern supports meaning.

Even this much attention to rhyme and rhythm should result in enough acceptable readings to serve as motivation for better interpretations of poems to be studied later. Since the problem is ever-recurring, students will have further opportunities for practice. Skill in stressing rhythm to bring out total meaning develops slowly.

Evaluating Growth

Recognizing that growth in appreciating poetry cannot be tested like increased speed or accuracy in typing, the teacher may be tempted to avoid all evaluation. This would be a mistake, for within their acknowledged limitations, several methods of appraisal have value enough to be used.

Two versions of the same poem, or similar poems on the same subject. The teacher, periodically using the ideas on pp. 363 and 364, may learn much about his pupils' growth in sensitivity to the significant aspects of poetry.

Reading poems aloud. The teacher may present students with several poems to be studied individually and recorded on tape. Poems similar to each other may be used before and after studying poetry—e.g., two similar poems by the same author. The tape recordings will help considerably to reveal whether or not the students have made progress in interpreting poetry.

Behavior of students. Students who begin to read more poetry, who want to write poetry, who choose poetry for voluntary projects, who list poetry on their individual reading lists, who purchase recordings of poetry and share them at school—all are giving the teacher some basis for evaluating the impact of his instruction. He must, of course, avoid wishful thinking and biased observation.

Rating by students. Teachers may ask pupils to rate, anonymously, the topics studied during a semester. If poetry is consistently ranked at the bottom of students' preferences and judgments of worth, the teacher should review his procedures.

Selecting the missing lines. From the four choices offered them, students are to write in the lines that are omitted and explain the bases of their choice. Example:

Moonlight [19]

by Berta Hart Nance

My father hated moonlight,
And pulled the curtains down
Each time the snows of moonlight
Came drifting on the town.

He was an old frontiersman,
And on their deadly raids,
Comanches rode by moonlight
In stealthy cavalcades;

And took the settlers' horses,
Or left a trail of red—
____
____

Choices for last two lines:

(1)
And stole the settler's harness
While they were fast abed.

(2)
The women cowered in the darkness
And shivered at each new tread.

(3)
He came to love the darkness,
And hate the moon, he said.

(4)
The curtains like women's tresses
Symbolized my father's dread.

Unwary pupils, seeking to please the teacher, will often choose 4; students who have gained little will continue to choose 1 or 2.

Identifying symbols. From a group of poems studied, the teacher may use a matching test to discover whether or not pupils comprehended the symbols used. Example:

How are the following symbols used? What, in other words, does each one stand for? On the line at the left place the number of the phrase which correctly identifies the meaning of each symbol.

________A broken sword	1. The joys of childhood
________The moon	2. Death
________Old swimmin' hole	3. The land of heart's desire
________Sherwood Forest	4. The leader of a nation
________Eldorado	5. Modern man's power
________Captain of a ship	6. Wonder and romance
________The Elf-King	7. Man's eternal quest for adventure
	8. The will to win in spite of odds
	9. Man's source of strength
	10. Life's challenge to youth

[19] "Moonlight," from *Flute in the Distance* by Berta Hart Nance. (Dallas, Kaleidograph Press, 1935.) Reprinted by permission.

Identifying themes. It is usually more important to be able to match poems with their themes than poems with authors, metrical feet, or literary movement. Example:

A. The Elf-King
B. The Broncho That Would Not Be Broken
C. Lee
D. Little Giffen
E. Old Christmas Morning

On the line at the left place the letter of the poem referred to in the following brief descriptions of the underlying theme:

________ 1. The invincible hero, great even in defeat.
________ 2. A proud spirit that would not be subdued.
(Etc.)

Poetry, appealing to our imagination by using language in a special way, gains the power to sharpen the senses and thoughts so that we see the world around us with heightened perception. Like all literature, poetry lifts us to a new equilibrium; if it is truly appreciated, it makes us more aware of life. It "stabs us broad awake." That is the ultimate justification for teaching poetry to adolescents, and evaluating should not violate that aim.

SELECTED READINGS—DRAMA

Otis J. Aggertt and Elbert R. Bowen, *Communicative Reading.* N.Y., Macmillan, 1956. A discussion of the principles underlying interpretive reading, with suggestions for the oral reading of prose, poetry, and drama.

Susanne K. Langer, *Feeling and Form.* N.Y., Scribner's, 1953. "The Dramatic Illusion" is a brilliant discussion of drama as a distinct art form.

Augusto Centano, ed., *The Intent of the Artist.* Princeton, N.J., Princeton U. Press, 1941. Thornton Wilder, in "Some Notes on Playwriting," describes the nature of drama seen from the playwright's point of view.

D. A. Traversi, *An Approach to Shakespeare,* 2nd ed. Garden City, N.Y., Doubleday Anchor, 1956. An analysis of Shakespeare's development as a playwright, with stimulating evidence to show how his maturing experience is reflected in his language and in his poetry.

Margaret Webster, *Shakespeare Without Tears.* Original edition, 1942. N.Y., Fawcett, 1957. Background material concerning Shakespeare and his theater, with comments on many of his plays.

A Guide to Play Selection, 2nd ed. N.Y., Appleton-Century-Crofts, 1958. An NCTE publication, this is a description of full-length, one-act, and television plays, a list of anthologies with the plays contained in each, and a list of references on various aspects of play production.

SUGGESTED READINGS—POETRY

BOOKS

Elizabeth Drew, *Poetry, a Modern Guide to Its Understanding and Enjoyment,* N.Y., Dell, 1959. The author writes with wisdom and depth of insight. She keeps a clear balance between meaning and form, not losing sight of either one in her enthusiasm for the other.

I. A. Richards, *Practical Criticism.* N.Y., Harcourt, Brace, 1939. This reports Richards' famed experiment with students at Cambridge. He presented them with poems of assorted merit, not revealing the authorship. The students commented upon the poems as best they could, and with complete anonymity returned their comments to Richards.

Lawrance Thompson, *Fire and Ice.* N.Y., Holt, 1942. In presenting the aims and accomplishments of Robert Frost, Mr. Thompson succeeds in his larger purpose of awakening in the reader "a more penetrating method of understanding and appreciating poetry."

Cleanth Brooks, John Thibaut Purser, and Robert Penn Warren, *An Approach to Literature,* rev. ed. N.Y., Appleton-Century-Crofts, 1939. This collection of prose and verse, with analyses and discussions, includes an excellent section on poetry. Numerous poems are analyzed, among them "My Last Duchess," "To a Skylark," and "Sir Patrick Spens." The introduction to the section deals in a most helpful manner with figurative language and meter.

Louis Untermeyer and John Davidson, *Poetry: Its Appreciation and Enjoyment.* N.Y., Harcourt, Brace, 1934. The introduction on poetry related to everyday life is helpful to teachers.

ARTICLES AND PORTFOLIOS

James Steel Smith, "Some Poetry is Popular—But Why?" *English Journal,* Vol. 46, No. 3 (March 1957). This article is an unflinching and hard-headed examination of the kind of poetry that is genuinely popular, poetry that "gives in monotonously repetitious and elementary forms a set of platitudes so general and bland they almost lack meaning." Teachers should read this article, uncomfortable though it may be to their egos.

The entire issue of the *English Journal* for March, 1957, features articles on the teaching of poetry. It includes articles on finding the right poem, introducing poems, evaluating the reading and study of poetry, and a symposium on poems in the classroom.

National Council of Teachers of English, *They Will Read Literature,* A Portfolio of Tested Secondary School Procedures. Champaign, Ill., NCTE, 1955. This portfolio includes two reprints on teaching students to read verse.

Harold Simonson, "Music as an Approach to Poetry." *English Journal,* Vol. 43, No. 1 (January 1954). Music as a useful approach to poetry has been emphasized in this text. This article offers further ideas.

Chapter Eight

The Popular Arts

There is a great deal that is mediocre, repetitious, and patronizing in television or the movies. Yet in closing their eyes to the significant contributions of the mass media, the detractors encourage the very banality they purport to despise.

—DAVID MANNING WHITE [1]

PERSPECTIVE

Listening and viewing are clearly the most popular means of receiving communication in contemporary culture. This recognition neither depreciates the value of reading and the permanence of the printed word, nor ignores the fleeting nature of much that appears in radio, television, and motion picture. Rather it admits that adults devote far more time to these media than they spend with books, magazines, and newspapers. High school students alone pass from fourteen to twenty-four hours a week before a television set; junior high, twenty-five to thirty.[2] Since the communication of ideas is a major instructional concern, teachers of English cannot ignore the impact on modern minds of these carriers of idea and image.

Much good has resulted from the revolution in communication. Children scarcely leave swaddling clothes before being transported visually and aurally to other times and places. However questionable may be the influence of some programs, the vicarious extension of experience surely contributes to basic growth in listening and speaking vocabularies. Through these media, too, the problems of South Africa and South America become almost as real as those of our South, effecting an improvement in international understanding only just beginning to be felt. Indeed, the heightened sensitivity of the American people during recent years to the problems of intergroup relations may well be a re-

[1] David Manning White, "Mass Culture in America: Another Point of View," in Bernard Rosenberg and D. M. White, eds., *Mass Culture* (Glencoe, Ill., Free Press, 1957), p. 16.

[2] Robert Hogan, "A Survey of Selected Research and Critical Writings on Television and Its Relation to School-Age Children," unpublished M.A. thesis, University of California, Berkeley, 1959, p. 16; see also Paul Witty, "A Tenth Yearly Study and Comments on a Decade of Televiewing," *Elementary English*, Vol. 34, No. 8 (December 1959).

flection of the growing involvement in mankind which has been fostered by our screens and our public discussions of world affairs. Then, too, at their best these media bring us the most eloquent expressions of humanity—the music of Beethoven and Mozart, the wisdom of Schweitzer and Churchill, the writings of Chekhov and Shaw. More than twenty million Americans witnessed Laurence Olivier's portrayals of Henry V and Hamlet on motion picture screens; an estimated fifty million tuned in on the television premiere of *Richard III*. Certainly the popular arts increase the common experiences of Americans. Teachers of English can do much to increase understanding and appreciation of these massive instruments of communication.

The term *popular art* is applied here to all mass entertainment—not solely to television, radio, and motion pictures, but, insofar as they offer forms of art, to recordings, periodicals, and newspapers. Our need to educate students to examine critically the media as conveyors of information is discussed elsewhere in this book.[3] This chapter is concerned not with improving skills in viewing and listening but with ways of increasing understanding of the popular arts and of upgrading student tastes.

No clear-cut dichotomy need be established between popular art and other kinds of art for the purposes of teaching; both must be considered together. Our job in the classroom is to teach students to understand and to respond thoughtfully. To move students from uncritical assimilation to careful discrimination requires no major upheaval in curriculum. This is a continuing task for teachers of English, not one to be accomplished in a single three-week unit or assigned capriciously to the elective program. The values and understandings which support intelligent reactions to the stage and screen are similar to those needed for intelligent reactions to literature. Yet if a transfer of habits from reading to viewing is really to take place, appreciations and skills must be taught so that students can see their applications. Clearly this calls for the serious study of such art forms in the classroom. A complete program involves a threefold approach—the analysis of the popular arts as commentary on contemporary culture, a study of the conditions under which these arts are created, and the analysis of the forms in which they are expressed.

Popular art and contemporary culture

Popular art both reflects and influences the society from which it emerges. Interaction between popular expression and culture is always difficult to assess, especially in a society like ours in which rapidity of change in both media and culture creates blurred and uncertain perspective. Yet if students are to consider seriously the ideas presented through the media and the ways in which the ideas are presented, they must understand something about the context from which these ideas flow. A minimal program will consider the popular arts

[3] See Chapter 1, "Language as a Dynamic Process," pp. 37-45; Chapter 2, "Logical Thinking," pp. 97-99; Chapter 4, "Listening with Discrimination," pp. 203-08.

as commentary on contemporary culture, as products of important industries, and as responsible instruments of expression in our society.

Contemporary ideas and attitudes In popular art are expressed the responses of serious artists to the problems, values, and conflicts of our world. Carefully attuned to the nuances of contemporary opinion, these arts are quick to reflect ideas prevalent in our culture. Whether indeed radio, television, and the motion picture are more instrumental in shaping and molding opinion than in reflecting changes caused by other factors is a problem which may well be studied carefully by teachers of English as well as by their mature students. The facts indicate, however, that when Americans feel deep patriotic convictions, such as during years of war and global conflict, the media attempt to communicate stirring human experiences in which love of country is weighed against other loyalties; when Americans are disturbed by intergroup relations within the democratic scene, scenario writers address themselves to such problems. Not all these timely products are works of art—few indeed may possess permanent value—but the attempts themselves must be seriously considered. In weighing values, the writers for these media perform one of the basic functions of the artist; our students can learn to recognize many of these offerings as valid social criticism and to see in the recurring themes some major concerns of contemporary American life. It is no accident, for example, that as this chapter is written two "hit" motion pictures, the national non-fiction best seller, and several recent television programs have dealt with the ruthlessness required of individuals in climbing the social ladder.

The popular arts contribute to the spirit of conformity in contemporary culture as much as they reflect it. Many similarities of concerns and behavior in our national culture are fostered, if not actually created, by the new mass media. Many provincialisms—in dress, in language, in thought—once characteristics of the American scene have given way before the standardized portrait of life generally depicted in these popular art forms. If concern over intergroup relations is a problem in New York and Hollywood, it is not long before television helps to create similar concerns in Shreveport and Kalamazoo. Our students need to look on these offerings as both probable results and potential causes of much current opinion.

Multi-media expression Students can learn to contrast depictions of contemporary problems in various modes of communication. Research suggests that persons alert to the presentation of ideas in one media are responsive to their presentation in another.[4] A problem play on television concerning the responsibilities of the ruling to the ruled directs attention to an issue long since considered in *Julius Caesar;* a motion picture analysis of the effect of fear on

[4] Carl Hoveland, in Gardner Lindzey, ed., *Handbook of Social Psychology* (Cambridge, Mass., Addison-Wesley, 1954), pp. 1801-1802. Also relevant are Witty's findings that younger children, if anything, read more now than before television appeared. Witty, *A Tenth Year Study.*

the human personality, perhaps presented in the guise of a serious western adventure story, may echo *Lord Jim* or *The Red Badge of Courage;* a radio panel's attempted answer to the eternal questions of being and becoming may differ from the suggested answers in *Everyman* or "Elegy Written in a Country Churchyard." The popular arts offer students a bridge to literature of every kind. Conversely, the study of literary works may introduce a discussion of television or motion pictures. Is a criminal background still the problem for rehabilitated men that it was in John Galsworthy's day? Students reading *Justice* may turn to a contemporary film or drama for an answer to the question. Similarly, seventh grade readers of *And Now Miguel* may compare the problems of shepherds in New Mexico with those of other pastoral people depicted in a television play. By helping students relate the important expression of popular art to literary selections, the teacher can vividly demonstrate the permanence of ideas and the interdependence of art forms.

Economic conditions and the arts To react intelligently to motion pictures, radio, or television, one must understand certain economic forces which shape these purveyors of popular culture. The amount of class time devoted to such matters should be limited, however. Just as the study of facts about literature—literary history, biographical data, and the like—must be carefully introduced only to support the student's ability to read with appreciation, so the consideration of facts about the media of mass communication needs to be intelligently limited to the significant few which really help him understand. Too often units on television or the motion picture stress extended studies of motion picture history or of the mechanics of TV production, rather than analysis of communication through the media. Student attention can be restricted to a limited number of understandings. The economic dependence on vast audiences, the continuing experimentation and discoveries in electronics, the widespread concern for regulating and controlling the instruments of communication—such developments influence even obscure judgments of broadcasters and writers. In the classroom, such considerations may best be introduced gradually, in relation to the analysis of special broadcasts or current problems rather than as subjects for special study. For the most part, too, the analysis is particularly appropriate for mature students who have been educated in rigorous methods of logical thinking and language interpretation, as discussed in the first chapters of this volume.

The popular arts are keenly sensitive to the nuances of social opinion. Indeed so readily do the industries respond and appeal to mass interests that they are often accused of cretinizing tastes. In striving for vast audiences they seem to perpetuate the superficialities of our culture. Yet it is important that students do not think of producers of the popular arts as linked in a giant conspiracy to undermine the mores of Americans. Rather they should understand that broadcasters and film-makers, economically dependent on vast audiences, attempt to create a product which mirrors prevailing attitudes and interests. For this reason, broadcasts skirt controversial issues not supported in the culture; witness, for example, during the pre-World War II era, the dearth of programs and pictures exploring intergroup relations as compared with the flood of such analyses during the socially sensitive Forties and Fifties. Twenty years ago, opinion on such matters was indecisive and few producers would risk alienating the public. For economic reasons many industries that create or sponsor popular art fear offending any recognizable segment of our society, whether war veterans, taxicab drivers, or even dog lovers. Evidence of this is found in attempts of broadcasters or film-makers to avoid scrupulously any situations or characters which could offend a particular racial or national group. Only attitudes widely supported by popular opinion are safe.

Inevitably the result of any attempt to placate a vast audience is a substitution of the comfortable for the unsettling, the bland for the meaty, the trivial for the thoughtful. Not all expression in these media is compromised, but much reliance on the stereotyped situation and the stock figure can be so explained. Indeed those few broadcasters and film-makers who brave prevailing public attitudes often tend to be either subjected to harsh criticism or to be virtually ignored. The latter, of course, can result in economic strangulation through "low ratings" on television or radio or by "box-office failure" in motion pictures. Specific instances are occasionally reported in magazines and may be examined with classes.

The commercial world influences the selectivity of the media in other ways. Some interesting evidence of direct censorship by industrial sponsors is apparent from time to time, e.g., the clumsy attempt of a gas company to suppress references to "gas chamber" during a TV dramatization of the Nuremberg war crime trials. More pervasive, but certainly unplanned, is the consistent point of view toward American life depicted through so many of these media and the closeness of this image to that held by the business world. Cleanly scrubbed children, modern homes out of *Better Homes and Gardens,* fashionable mothers, two-car families—this is the picture of the American family too often created. Observers have noted the inadequate coverage of American labor as well as the failure of the media to sustain serious criticism of the business community itself.[5] However great this selectivity may be, it seems born less from deliberate motives than from compatible points of view. The popular arts are products of the business world. The producers and directors—often the writers too—are willing participants at the market place and share many commercial values. As distinct from the popular folk art of many past cultures, one of the distinguishing features of contemporary popular art is that it emerges from great commercial enterprises.

The effect of the audience Students can be led to see, too, that the vivid, outspoken commentary on the values of our society often found on the contem-

[5] See Educational Policies Commission, *Mass Communication and Education* (Washington, D.C., National Educational Association and American Association of School Administrators, 1958), pp. 26-27.

porary stage is not the result of accident. Writing for a minority audience and seldom subject to the extreme pressures of popular taste, except in creating major musicals which demand return of an investment of several hundred thousand dollars, the dramatist is comparatively free to examine explosive issues. Interesting changes have occurred in radio and motion pictures as television established itself as the major media catering to popular taste. Influenced by an economic need for audiences even larger than those which sustain radio and motion pictures, TV tends to be less venturesome and "offensive" than the other media. At the same time, however, the onset of television frees motion pictures and radio in some degree from the restrictions of mass opinion and permits greater experimentation. Recent effects of this development have resulted in the introduction into motion pictures of more "adult" themes and the relaxation of censorship controls; in radio, in the increase in good music and public affairs programs. The pronounced tendency of some local radio stations to cater increasingly to the tastes of teen-agers in popular music is another less fortunate manifestation of greater attention to the interest of minority groups. As Riesman notes, "The coming of TV has given new possibilities back to radio in the bedroom, for the TV audience is now the mass audience, and the medium can appeal to the wish for privacy, and to specialized tastes and minority audiences." [6]

Social responsibilities of the media Understanding the influence of economic factors is not enough; students also need to consider the function of the media in our society. What are the responsibilities of TV broadcasters for informing the public on contemporary affairs? Should film-makers be permitted unlimited freedom of expression and choice of subject matter—even in films distributed in foreign countries? What methods of censorship, if any, should be adopted? Is freedom of broadcasting guaranteed by the First Amendment, much as freedom of the press—even though the stations are licensed by the Federal Communications Commission and agree to operate in the public interest? Or, as Gilbert Seldes indicates, must we forge new definitions of freedom and restriction because of the potential power of these media? [7] Such controversial questions need careful consideration. They are not easy to answer in the classroom, because society itself has still to resolve them. In studying such problems, students may form intelligent opinions by weighing many points of view.

If students learn to recognize the impact of public opinion and commercial pressures on the media, and if they further begin to consider the legal and ethical responsibilities of producers and broadcasters, they are on their way to learning as much about the conditions under which the popular arts are produced as they will need to know.

[6] David Riesman, *The Oral Tradition, the Written Word, and the Screen Image,* Antioch College Founders' Day Lecture No. 1 (Yellow Springs, Ohio, Antioch Press, 1956), p. 16.

[7] Gilbert Seldes, *The Public Arts* (N.Y., Simon & Schuster, 1956). The ten brief chapters which end this volume present an analysis of the problems and opportunities of the media.

The varied forms of popular art

Just as an intelligent analysis of poetic form contributes to an understanding of what the poet attempts to say, so the study of form in radio, television, and motion pictures can deepen appreciation of popular art. The analysis need not be long and detailed; some understandings developed during the study of literature, particularly dramatic literature, apply equally to these newly created methods of expression. In the dramas presented on the screen or broadcast over air waves, characters are created, conflicts developed, scenes and settings created to convey particular moods. Form in literature is often compared to

Some differences in drama presented

	Stage drama	*Motion picture*
Unity	Restricted to selected scenes. Much action occurs off stage. Physical limitation in number of settings.	Virtually complete freedom of movement in space and time.
Setting	Sharply limited, even with contemporary experimentation involving composite settings which rely on lighting to smooth transitions.	From 150 to 500 separate settings in average film, with perhaps twice as many separate camera shots. Few scenes of long duration.
Revelation of meaning	Speech and action of characters conveys meaning within the over-all setting. Dialogue is chief instrument for highlighting meaning.	Greater reliance on movement than on auditory clues, although musical effects are used to advantage. The camera often focuses on key impressions. Most literal of media.
Continuity	Division into scenes and acts.	Elaborate methods for photographic transitions between scenes—pans, dissolves, abrupt changes, montages—depending on effect desired.
Content	Much variation. Tendency to rely on the impact of a unified effect rather than a series of visual or auditory impressions. Compression within sharply defined time and place.	Much reliance on visual scope; crowds, massive sets, many characters, pageantry, trick effects. Fluidity of time and space plus potential length of feature films make possible treatment of complex subject matter.

mood, unity, or climax in these popular media of entertainment. Thus teachers almost automatically develop student awareness of the similarities and contrasts between literary works and the offerings of the popular arts. In addition, some special study of the better plays written for these media may be introduced. Selected viewing of television dramas and the reading of a good motion picture script, together with frequent listening to recorded plays, are resources for the direct study of drama as presented in several media.

Teaching differences in forms If students understand some factors influencing various art forms, their ability to evaluate different kinds of presenta-

through four media of communication

Radio	*Television*
Most fluid of all media. Virtually complete freedom of movement in space and time.	Usually restricted in time and setting as is drama, although filmed programs gain some of the freedom of motion picture.
Unlimited number of scenes. Narrator is often used as cohesive force. Setting suggested by dialogue or music.	Limited to few scenes unless filmed. Fragmentary, suggestive. Viewer must "fill in" partial clues. Author must allow for costume changes, restrictions in settings, unless program is taped in advance.
Complete reliance on auditory clues —dialogue, narration, music.	Combines attention to movement as on screen, with attention to dialogue of stage. Selective camera controls direct viewer to significant objects or persons.
Reliance on music in fade-ins and fade-outs between scenes. Because of time restrictions, scenes advanced by suggestion rather than carefully plotted detail.	Combines division into episodes or acts of stage play (allowing for commercial and station breaks) with many visual shifts of the motion picture. Frequency of breaks establishes unique form.
Number of characters usually limited because of audience inability to differentiate voices. Short plays limit characterization; characters more comprehensible types.	Fairly limited subjects. Concentrates on problems of few characters, often emphasizing character revelation in familiar situations and short episodes, not in long continued action. In this limitation can be much strength.

tion will be heightened. For example, the problem of selectivity is common to all media. The poet selects sounds and images; the novelist, particular incidents and a point of view; the dramatist, key scenes and moments of revelation. The organization of the selected images and impressions contributes both to the ongoing rhythm of a work and to its over-all unity. Such problems affect the screen and television writer in surprising ways. Selection and arrangement of scenes are as important as they are on the stage. Moreover, the way in which incidents are presented visually must be considered. Should the camera shoot from a distance or close up? Should the lens focus on a significant object, revealing its import immediately to the viewer—as on the dusty, dirt-filled corners of an untidy boarding house—or should the nature of the scene be referred to through dialogue or merely suggested by the background as the camera concentrates on the actions of the central characters? In the motion picture a total scene may be presented; on television the size of the picture limits the presentation to only a fragmentary suggestion. In this, the media are entirely different. Similar choices occur in radio and recorded drama, where the suggestive value of music and sound effects must be weighed against the possible contribution of a narrated description.

Physical restrictions in each medium also influence the form and content of presentations. Obviously radio relies on the auditory image; the vastness of the motion picture screen makes possible visual spectacles which cannot be reproduced on the stage or on television. Video presentation seems particularly well adapted for intimate dramas which demand a close affinity between audience and actor, since the limited size of the picture tube and the easily exhausted patience of the sponsor tend to check any tendency of the playwright to rely on the excesses of spectacle.

Other differences are less obvious to the casual observer. The rigid timing of radio and television forces writers to tailor expression to the demands of fixed periods of time—the fifty-minute hour, the twenty-two-minute half-hour, the seventy-five-minute hour and a half. Inevitable results of this rigidity in timing are padding and cutting, the one often resulting in the introduction of extraneous material, the other in loss of continuity. Other practices have also emerged. Radio writers concentrate on narrative elements since short dramas seldom permit much attention to character development. Less restricted in time, and concerned with the kind of impressions which emerge most effectively on small home screens, the creators of television drama show interest in plays of character, or at least in intimate, realistic episodes similar to the "slice of life" stories revealing a single dimension of character. Indeed TV drama has developed such easily identifiable characteristics that one newspaper critic complained not long ago that all such writing "was about little people in small situations coming to no conclusions and without hope in action or nobility in frustration." [8] Certainly the demands of each medium shape and mold both content and form.

[8] Quoted by Seldes, *The Public Arts*, p. 183.

In introducing the analysis of methods of dramatic presentation, teachers may begin with characteristics of the stage play which have been studied during the reading of one-act and longer plays. The accompanying chart summarizes in somewhat simplified fashion a few of the differences which may be considered.

THE TEACHING PROBLEM

Organizing Instruction

Once teachers recognize the importance of studying the popular arts, they face three difficult tasks: determining how to introduce the new media in the classroom, locating information about the media, and organizing instruction to improve student tastes. Each will be discussed briefly.

Planning a program of study

The same principles of clarity and purpose apply to communication in the popular arts as to communication elsewhere. Our teaching programs must recognize the students' need to see the integral relationship between many ways of expressing ideas.

Recognition of the importance of a unified approach means that teachers plan no separate programs for instruction in the popular arts; rather it means that experiences in studying and assessing particular achievements will be introduced throughout the six-year program. Four principles can serve as a guide:

Use the products of popular art in the same way other esthetic expression is used—to motivate, to study, to enrich.

Recognize that a single community of ideas involves all forms of expression; use many avenues of extending breadth and depth of the classroom study of ideas.

Study examples in popular culture of language and thought in operation; use illustrations to illuminate the study of language operation, logical thinking, and emotional thinking.

Study facts about popular arts only to deepen understanding of communication; place emphasis on the ideas, not on the conditions or the form.

Any program based on these principles provides for continuous serious study related to other phases of communication. Teachers need not refrain from introducing occasional units on "The Periodical," "The Mass Media," or "Appreciating Motion Pictures," since such concentrated study sometimes helps a student draw together and consciously organize many concepts about a particular medium. However, teachers who recognize the integral relationship of all communication will understand that the basic learnings must be embedded in the mainstream of the English program, not in isolated units.

Obtaining advance information

In using the popular arts, teachers face a troublesome problem in identifying useful films and broadcasts. The motion picture, by nature of its system of distribution, creates few real problems since the teacher can either preview a film on his own or depend on the informed reviews of persons whom he can trust. Except for summer reruns, television and radio programs are infrequently rebroadcast, and only a few educational programs, such as full-scale productions of Shakespearean works, are made available to schools through kinescope recordings. To a considerable degree, then, the teacher will have to rely on post mortem discussion, reconstructing situations and statements for the guidance of students who have not witnessed the events. To minimize such difficulty, the teacher may obtain advance information on programs. At least five possible sources can be considered:

Bulletins on forthcoming programs of educational interest distributed by local radio and television stations. Many stations publish mimeographed bulletins offering background information. Most educational television stations release schedules of this type.

Advance information on national broadcasts published by the leading networks. Requests to be placed on mailing lists for such publicity may be sent to the headquarters of each network.[9]

Weekly or monthly previews of productions of unusual interest are reported in professional journals, such as *Elementary English,* the *English Journal,* the *Clearing House, Audio-Visual Guide,* and the teacher's edition of *Scholastic.* Most of these have a regular column on the mass media.

The special monthlies, *Studies in the Mass Media,* National Council of Teachers of English, and the *Newsletter,* published by Edgar Dale at the Bureau of Educational Research, Ohio State University. These journals are designed to bring teachers regular information on the mass media.

Information obtained from national organizations designed to improve the quality of the mass media.[10]

Extending interest and improving taste

Underlying appreciation of all esthetic expression are basic standards of taste. Although the evaluation of any form of art requires considerable understanding of the medium as well as command of criteria against which to measure the expression, an individual's ability to appreciate and judge seems

[9] American Broadcasting Company, 7 W. Sixty-Sixth St., New York 23, N.Y.; Canadian Broadcasting Company, 140 Wellington St., Ottawa, Ontario, Canada; Columbia Broadcasting System, 485 Madison Ave., New York 22, N.Y.; Keystone Broadcasting Company, 111 W. Washington St., Chicago 2, Ill.; Mutual Broadcasting Company, 1440 Broadway, New York 18, N.Y.; National Broadcasting Company, 30 Rockefeller Plaza, New York, 20, N.Y.

[10] Among those presently active are: Wisconsin Association for Better Radio and Television, Madison, Wisc.; Film Council of America, 600 Davis St., Evanston, Ill.; The National Association for Better Radio and Television, 882 Victoria Ave., Los Angeles 5, Calif.; National Educational Television and Radio Center, 10 Columbus Circle, New York 19, N.Y.; National Association of Educational Broadcasters, 14 Gregory Hall, Urbana, Ill.

to develop as part of his over-all outlook on life rather than as a fragmentized series of attitudes toward separate fields of endeavor.

The close parallel between the methods of literature and those adopted in the popular arts—the fact, indeed, that these modern instruments of communication often fulfill in society a function almost identical with the historical role of literature itself—suggests that to a considerable degree we may build discriminating habits of viewing and listening as we teach students to value and appreciate literature. The boy who responds to Teasdale and Frost, who chooses books about a score of subjects, and who begins to reject the contrivances of Zane Grey and Erle Stanley Gardner, almost certainly will become increasingly selective in his preferences for motion pictures and television programs if he learns to apply appropriate standards. Recognition of this close relationship between reading and viewing-listening interests should encourage teachers to teach for transfer if transfer is to occur.

In attempting to refine the tastes of our pupils in the popular arts, teachers can be modest in their goals. To all Americans these media offer popular, convenient, and inexpensive entertainment. The school cannot possibly confine students' experiences to those few truly significant productions which are released each year. Let teachers recognize that much that students choose themselves will be ephemeral, superficial, and unworthy of analysis. The real goal is not to eliminate such trivialities, but to extend the range of interests so that individuals will find pleasure and see qualitative distinctions in many kinds of expression. As novelist W. Somerset Maugham writes:

> I am not so stupid as to mean that all people have such a naturally good taste that they will always prefer what is best to what is of no great value. After all, we none of us do that, and few of us are so delicately constituted that we can put up with nothing but the first rate. I know for my part I can get a great deal of pleasure out of an opera of Puccini's, but it is a different sort of pleasure from that which I can get out of an opera of Mozart's. There are times when I would rather read the stories of Conan Doyle than Tolstoi's *War and Peace*.[11]

Certainly both Puccini and Doyle are hopelessly high minimums for many secondary school students, but Maugham's basic principle applies. Individuals find pleasure in both Agatha Christie and in Katherine Mansfield, in farcical comedy and social documentary, but the pleasures are of different kinds; they read diverse authors and view diverse programs for diverse reasons. Students need criteria for judging varied books and broadcasts—some to judge a situation comedy designed merely to mesmerize audience sensibilities, others to consider serious dramatic presentations presenting a commentary on our culture.

Applying standards Standards developed through the study of literature may be applied to other media of expression, but the fit is not entirely perfect. A group, agreed on the characteristics of a "good" novel, may use their standards to judge a representative film or drama and the attempt will usually yield some criteria which apply to almost any art form, such as: The work pre-

[11] W. Somerset Maugham, in the introduction to *Great Modern Reading* (Garden City, N.Y., Doubleday, 1943), p. xiii.

sents real insight into human action, rather than a synthetic point of view; the incidents are well selected, truthful, and unbiased; the plot develops logically, with reasonable attention to motivation, characterization, and the demands of probability; meaning is supported and re-emphasized by atmosphere, setting, and symbol. But to such lists must be added certain standards of performance: The acting is convincing; the setting aids in establishing tone, place, mood; the photography supports, rather than distracts from, the theme of the story.

Thus the class must consider the peculiar demands of each form of expression. The comparative approach is helpful because it can be developed in relation to the total curriculum in literary appreciation. However, teachers using this approach need to avoid suggesting that the reading of books is *ipso facto* more cultured or more highly valued—or even necessarily "more active"—than the viewing of television or motion pictures. If the choice is between reading the pap in many women's magazines or viewing a distinguished film, valid argument clearly supports the cause of the motion picture. What is important is to encourage in students an ability to evaluate as well as appreciate many kinds of presentation.

Studying standards directly One way of encouraging students to assess the popular arts is to study standards directly. Increasingly, materials on evaluation are being included in textbooks; also, a few separate textbooks have been developed.[12] For the most part, however, students develop criteria by evaluating particular presentations. From the seventh grade on, appropriate films may be discussed in class. Reference to the standards used by reviewers in local newspapers may be helpful. Occasionally, too, advanced students gain insight by reading and reporting on—or listening to the teacher read—short, arresting articles interpreting the media.[13] Clearly, mature standards of appreciation depend in part on clear understanding of the form of expression.

Comparing media One effective way of helping students apply standards of literary judgment is to encourage them to compare the treatment of a story in different media. For instance, junior high readers find *Johnny Tremain* to be a gripping, humane portrayal of the experiences a young boy faces in assuming adult responsibilities. The struggle of the American colonists forms a rich, reinforcing background, but the novel essentially illuminates the experiences of an individual. Students who compare Forbes's book with the motion picture adaptation find little but superficial resemblances between the two. Gone in the film is the inner struggle of Johnny, the development of his sensitivity to others, the rich personal relationships. Symbols of Johnny's conflict like

[12] William Lewin and Alexander Frazier, *Standards of Photoplay Appreciation* (Newark, N.J., Educational and Recreational Guides, 1957), is now available as a student text. Study guides for forthcoming films, broadcasts, recordings, etc., are found in *Studies in the Mass Media.*

[13] Such as the symposium, "The Film: Survey of the Craft and Its Problems," in the *Saturday Review*, Vol. 59, No. 51 (December 20, 1959).

the scarred hand remain, but they have been divested of meaning; motivation of character is overlooked. What remains may be a compelling re-enactment of many events of the Revolutionary Period, but certainly no unified work of art. Opportunities for comparisons are rich with possibilities for teaching. Fortunately not all adaptations are as bland and unpalatable as is that of *Johnny Tremain.* Indeed some, like the play *Teahouse of the August Moon,* the motion picture "The Bridge on the River Kwai," or the light opera *The King and I,* may possess greater clarity, unity, and impact than do the original stories.

Reviewing films and broadcasts Just as teachers provide for reviews of books, so they can assign reviews of motion pictures, television, and radio programs. Some teachers require one review of a film, motion picture, or stage performance during each six- or eight-week grading period; others permit students to substitute two such reviews for one conventional book report. Some class time may be reserved regularly each month for the presentation of oral reviews, and on the slated day students may be divided into small groups for informal sharing of reports. Groups may be organized for each of the popular arts or formed so that TV, motion pictures, and radio are discussed in each section. Whatever the method, such assignments can encourage thoughtful viewing and provide opportunity for careful assessment.

Before preparing reviews, students may need special instruction. If standards for reviews of books have been discussed in the literature program, the student may be led to discover that the essential principles of good reviewing are similar for books and broadcasts. The particular value of reviews which communicate information to readers or viewers who have not shared the primary experience can be illustrated in the writing of professional critics. Different reactions to a single film may be contrasted, and the standards of each reviewer assessed. Such assignments not only introduce students to new reading experiences and to many unfamiliar magazines, but stress the integrity and reliability of critics in such periodicals as the *Saturday Review*, the *New Yorker*, and many leading newspapers, as contrasted with the indiscriminate reporting of writers for some fan magazines.

Sound instruction in the popular arts focuses on developing of understanding the new media and on improving student taste and discrimination. These goals are not achieved through a separately organized program but through the application to the popular arts of understandings and insights developed elsewhere.

Suggested Learning Experiences

Too often the consideration of popular art in the classroom, divorced from the study of language and literature, becomes little more than superficial, unrewarding comment. This eventuality will not occur if teachers insist that each experience be carefully planned in relation to the continuing intellectual interests and needs of the learners. Here as always purposes need to be identified with clarity and learning activity related to previous instruction in skills of thinking. If this happens, the activities suggested on the following pages can be modified by teachers to add depth and breadth to the study of English.

To study contemporary attitudes in popular art

■ *Relate ideas in popular art to ideas in literature*

1. Initiate a discussion of the ethical choices faced by the young business executive in a television drama and on the clash of values in our contemporary business world as reflected in the writing of Sinclair Lewis, John Marquand, Cameron Hawley, and others.

2. Use television productions like "Peter Pan" to interest junior high school students in reading selections treating the youthful desire to evade responsibility, e.g., "As Ye Sow, So Shall Ye Reap" by Jesse Stuart, "Goodbye, My Lady" by James Street.

3. Prepare a special book list of titles related to forthcoming broadcasts so that students can follow their viewing with good reading experiences. Junior high school teachers will find several printed in *Elementary English* during 1957. Annotated readings related to television were prepared on "Popular Music" by Clara Kircher, "Science" by Don Herbert, and "Ballet" by Rose Minicieli, Ethna Sheehan, and Elizabeth Lockhart.[14]

4. Collect products of popular arts which may someday be useful in the English classroom. Develop a personal library of tape recordings, consisting of five to ten minute "bits," e.g., a reading of a poem by Robert Frost, a talk on interpretive reading by Charles Laughton, a discussion on the nature of language change between John Mason Brown and Bergen Evans.

■ *Extend ideas in literature by referring to other media*

1. After discussing instances of prejudice found in stories like "One Friday Morning" or books like *My Antonia*, study ways in which prejudice against individuals may affect an entire culture, as shown in the historical film, "The House of Rothschild," a depiction of the Jewish banking house during the Napoleonic era.

2. Use the transcription of "When Greek Meets Greek: A Study in Values," an imaginary conversation between Athenian and Spartan youths, in a unit exploring the universal problems resulting from conflicts in cultures. Preparation for listening —or follow-up—may involve reading and discussing such books as *A Bell for Adano*, *The King and I* and *Teahouse of the August Moon*. (The transcription is one of the programs in the "Ways of Mankind," a series of thirteen discs produced by the National Association of Educational Broadcasters.)

■ *Provide intensive study of worthwhile presentations*

1. In advance courses which include some study of contemporary literature, introduce analyses of provocative current works. Such ideas as the following seem repeatedly illuminated in contemporary art and are of interest to student groups: the effects of any breakdown in communication in the modern world; the irony of individual loneliness within large, complex industrial cities; the survival of human values in the holocaust of atomic war; the power of ideals in shaping human action.

[14] Patrick Hazard's column in *Elementary English* contained the following lists on the following topics: "Ballet," Vol. 34, No. 3 (March 1957); "Science," Vol. 34, No. 4 (April 1957); "Music," Vol. 34, No. 5 (May 1957).

2. Important contemporary broadcasts and films which achieve a considerable degree of artistic integrity deserve analysis on their own merits. Outstanding offerings of each season, or classic productions like *The Defiant Ones* or *The Little Kidnappers,* which are often reshown on television or in theaters, may be analyzed with students for the theme, the development, and resolution of the conflict. The content of each offering may be considered in determining the grade level of the classes in which it should be discussed. However, many films and broadcasts provide excellent viewing for seventh and eighth grade students, even though a few are best reserved for senior high school students.

3. Study with students a recording of Kurt Weill's one-act folk opera, *Down in the Valley.* Show how the artist has expanded the simple situation implied in the folk tune into a strong, unified conflict. Encourage students to emulate Weill by selecting a similar situation in another folk song and expanding it to short story length.

■ *Prepare students for worthwhile experiences in viewing and reacting*

When an important dramatic event is scheduled—whether on the stage, on television, or in the motion picture theater—prepare students for viewing either by a brief teacher "preview" of the work or, on occasion, by a thorough study. Brief lessons are particularly important in preparing for viewing works posing problems in comprehension. Immature, unprepared adolescents will seldom attempt to derive much meaning from Shakespearean productions, or from performances of plays like *High Tor, The Corn is Green, Cyrano de Bergerac, The Cradle Song,* or *The Old Lady Shows Her Medals.*

To understand social and economic conditions affecting popular art

■ *Study how the mass audience affects communication*

1. Examine selected films or broadcasts adapted from another media. Consider the apparent reasons for changes in racial or religious identification of a character in a film adaptation of a novel or a stage play, or the basic "refinements" in narrative which are designed to bring about "acceptable" denouments. Read selections from contemporary articles which discuss these compromises. Perhaps some student would be interested in reporting on Lillian Ross' *Picture,*[15] which describes the mutilation of the filmed version of *The Red Badge of Courage* when producers attempted to "redo" Crane's story in terms of their image of popular taste. Follow this report with an examination of a superior adaptation such as "The Diary of Anne Frank," to illustrate how differences in each media necessitate changes in form, some of which can add to a drama's effectiveness.

2. Examine the broadcasting industry's attempts to appeal to different interests at different times of the day. Compare the programs presented on TV and radio during the following hours: before 3 P.M.; 3 P.M. to 7 P.M; 7 P.M. to 10 P.M.; and after 10 P.M. Even more startling differences may be seen by comparing broadcasts on Saturday and Sunday afternoons. This activity has been used with both junior and senior high school groups.

3. Develop understanding of the ways in which audience images in the different media of entertainment affect offerings. Ask junior high students to list their "favorite" television channel, then explore the reasons for their choices. What dif-

[15] Lillian Ross, *Picture* (N.Y., Rinehart, 1952).

ferences are observable in the programing of the various networks? Are differences observable in type and kind of programs? In musicals? Dramatic fare? Public affairs programs and the like?

Extend the study to a consideration of radio, popular magazines, perhaps motion pictures. Encourage advanced students to study the more subtle differences—the social class of the heroes, the conception of family life presented through illustration or setting, the nature of the advertising and what it suggests about the advertiser's conception of his audience. Try also presenting an audience image and urging students to plan suitable programs. What type of a program would have appeal for the tired businessman returning from the office at 5:30 P.M.? For the housewife who is confined to her home to care for young children? For the adolescent on a weekend evening?

A few gifted students may be encouraged to select a magazine and study a number of issues to determine the topics and values presented. Alert students will perceive important distinctions between such magazines as *Life, Good Housekeeping, Living for Young Homemakers, Reader's Digest, True Confessions, Photoplay,* and the *Saturday Evening Post.*

4. With a senior class, select several highly controversial social problems and an equal number of unresolved social problems about which Americans are generally in agreement. Examine with students the extent to which recent offerings in the popular arts deal with each of the problems, e.g., racial discrimination, control of government by labor or business, private power vs. public power, the destruction of war, evils of narcotics, the blindness of mob rule. Students may speculate over probable explanations.

5. Ask students to select a continuous three-hour period during the day or evening and to classify all TV or radio broadcasts available during the interval according to the nature of their appeal. For each program, ask students to indicate the over-all purpose, the possible reasons for listening, the audience for whom it is intended. A comparison of the findings will reveal the nature of audiences responding to these media at different times as well as the nature of the broadcasts prepared for limited groups.

■ *Study the effects of financial conditions*

1. Write on the chalk board the following average costs:

3 to 5 million dollars to start a magazine
1.3 million dollars for a Grade A motion picture
up to $100,000 recurring costs for thirty minutes of TV time [16]
10 billion dollars spent by advertisers in the popular arts during one year [17]

Ask students to suggest how such figures help to explain the shortage of creative ideas in these industries.

2. Circulate copies of *Variety* and *Billboard* magazines in a junior or senior high class. Direct attention to the ways in which products of the popular art industries are assessed—motion pictures in terms of gross income, television by audience ratings,

[16] These figures are reported in Wilbur Schramm, *Responsibility in Mass Communication* (N.Y., Harper, 1957), p. 270. Similar figures, increasing yearly with the rising inflation of the American economy, are obtainable in occasional reports in weekly news magazines.

[17] 1956. See Bradford Smith, *Why We Behave Like Americans* (Phila., Lippincott, 1957), p. 238.

recordings according to sales. Ask a group to draw conclusions concerning the nature of the industry.

3. Ask a group of mature students to prepare a panel discussion on the ways in which advertising affects presentation in the media. In preparation for the panel, require students to read "What We Read, See, and Hear" by Harry Overstreet, a chapter in *The Mature Mind.*[18]

4. Read to students an appropriate segment from *The Mechanical Bride* by Herbert Marshall McLuhan,[19] a volume presenting a series of highly amusing illustrated analyses of the appeals of selected aspects of contemporary culture—advertisements, key comics, radio serials, and the like.

■ *Analyze evidence of introspection and self-criticism*

1. Consider the cynical attitude toward television or other popular arts portrayed in such films as "A Face in the Crowd," the study of the rise of a demagogue. Try to determine the point of view of author Budd Schulberg toward the American public; toward advertisers, politicians, and members of the broadcasting industry. To what extent are the persons represented as typical or atypical?

2. Read aloud interesting excerpts from articles which satirize aspects of the popular arts. Ask students to explain the basis of humor. For example, use the following statements from *Punch:* [20]

> "TV does not change the adult fundamentally. Seven out of ten people recover almost completely when no longer exposed to television."
>
> "Four out of ten suffer only slightly from channel sickness, and a relatively insignificant proportion of viewers go gaga."
>
> "At first TV causes adults to read less, but after a time the consumption of print is more than made good by increased perusal of *Radio Times* and *TV Times.*"

3. Read aloud the following satirical stanza by Phyllis McGinley. Discuss the poet's purpose. Appoint a volunteer to locate Miss McGinley's complete poem, which is part of the series called "The Jaundiced Viewer." Encourage others to write stanzas of their own. Eighth, ninth, and tenth graders have enjoyed this activity.

Reflections Dental [21]

How pure, how beautiful, how fine
Do teeth on television shine!
No flutist flutes, no dancer twirls,
But comes equipped with matching pearls.
Gleeful announcers are all born
With sets like rows of hybrid corn.

■ *Weigh the responsibilities of the popular arts*

1. Assign individual reports or panel discussion on one or more of the following topics. (Those starred are particularly appropriate in the junior high school, p. 396.)

[18] Harry A. Overstreet, *The Mature Mind* (N.Y., Norton, 1949).
[19] Herbert Marshall McLuhan, *The Mechanical Bride* (N.Y., Vanguard, 1951).
[20] *Punch*, Vol. 235, No. 6176 (December 24, 1958), p. 819.
[21] From "The Love Letters of Phyllis McGinley" by Phyllis McGinley. Copyright 1953 by Phyllis McGinley. Originally appeared in *The New Yorker.* Reprinted by permission of The Viking Press, Inc.

Major issues and problems concerning the media of mass communication

The Influence of Audience Rating Systems (Trendex, Nielson, etc.).* To what extent are these methods of determining popularity valid and desirable?

The Impact of Advertising on Broadcasting.* The cost of TV commercials; programing influences; the desirability of pay-as-you-go TV; methods of financing used in other countries, e.g., Britain, Canada, Switzerland.

The Influence of the Federal Communications Commission. Its purpose, authority, regulatory and licensing power. How the FCC maintains engineering standards. Send to the Superintendent of Documents, Washington, D.C., for the pamphlet, *Rules of the Federal Communications Commission.*

The Regulation of the Mass Media. Evidence of their influence on morality. Voluntary and involuntary censorship, such as the motion picture code, state controls, the Legion of Decency.

Responsibilities of the Media to Provide for Minority Tastes. Provisions made for children, for various cultural groups.

Use of Media to Influence Thought. Propaganda techniques, responsibilities of broadcasters, use in political campaigning, provision for equal time for candidates of political parties.

Program Awards.* The selection of "bests," their purpose and meaning.

The Production of Films and Broadcasts. The function and contribution of various individuals—writer, director, actor, producer, editor, cameraman.

The ten biggest "box-office" films of all time.* Why were they popular? What do these films suggest about popular taste? Compare with the ten "best-sellers." Information of this kind is included in trade journals, in almanacs devoted to the various industries, in occasional articles in current periodicals.

2. Compare production codes developed to guide television, motion pictures, radio, and the comic book publishers with the newspaper code. Note the heavy emphasis on prohibitions for broadcasters. Summaries of these codes and a helpful analysis are presented by Wilbur Schramm in *Responsibility in Mass Communication.*[22] This is a worthwhile activity for able junior high school readers who may report back to their friends.

3. Ask students to react to controversial comments concerning the mass media taken from current publications. Such quotations as the following are almost certain to provoke a considerable diversity of opinion:

"If television and radio are to be used to entertain all of the people all of the time, we have come perilously close to discovering the real opiate of the people." —Edward R. Murrow [23]

"There will be no cultural programming that is not fought for, and that goes for programs of any kind. Sponsors are not going to ask for cultural programs. They are going to have to be sold it all the way."—Pat Weaver, then Chairman of the Board, NBC [24]

"At one extreme, one might even consider it wise educational policy to lock

[22] Schramm, *Responsibility in Mass Communication,* pp. 287-295.
[23] Edward R. Murrow, quoted in *Time,* Vol. 70, No. 3 (July 15, 1957), p. 66.
[24] Pat Weaver, in *Saturday Review,* Vol. 29, No. 11 (March 17, 1956), p. 66.

children up (at sometime before their majority) in a good library with good food and drink, alone with paper and pencils but no other entertainment."—David Riesman [25]

"Those who make the news cannot in a free society dictate to broadcasters to what extent, whether, and how they should cover the news. Television and radio . . . are not mere conduits which must carry everything which the newsmaker demands. We insist . . . that we are, and must remain, free to exercise our news judgment."—Frank Stanton, President of CBS, after being criticized for not screening a portion of the nominating convention of a political party.[26]

Such statements will elicit considerable discussion from thoughtful students and may be used to introduce a careful analysis of each problem.

4. Discuss public controversies which surround discussion of the responsibilities of the media. For example, Americans are not yet in agreement concerning whether the presentation on television of Congressional committee hearings represents an invasion of the privacy of witnesses or reflects a right of the public to see its government in action. A few years ago 200,000 persons viewed a televised jury trial in Waco, Texas. Many felt the trial gave viewers an opportunity to better understand judicial processes: Their point of view was supported by the fact that the audience included both high school classes and groups at Baylor University. Others argued as strongly that the presentation of trials on television hampered legal procedures, distracted attention from the "truth-gathering" functions of courts, forced attorneys to perform for the viewing audiences, and made witnesses reluctant to testify. Some teachers used the Waco case to motivate a thorough study of the rights and responsibilities of broadcasters. Student groups identified the issues, assigned fact-finding tasks, discussed parallels in the broadcasting of committee hearings, cabinet meetings, and nominating conventions. Through carefully directed analysis, these adolescents greatly expanded their basic knowledge and points of view as to the responsibilities of the mass media in contemporary society.

To understand the forms of popular art

■ *Compare treatment in diverse media*

1. Ask students to analyze the treatment of a work in several media. A study of superior adaptations—Edward Chodorov's screenplay for *Yellow Jack;* Brainerd Duffield's television drama based on "The Lottery"; Howard Estabrook's scenario for *The Human Comedy*—directs attention of students less to the mutilation of a work of art than to the differences which arise when a selection is presented well in two media. Similar comparisons have been made between *Anna and the King of Siam* and *The King and I; Cry, the Beloved Country* and *Lost in the Stars; Mama's Bank Account* and *I Remember Mama.*

2. Present motion pictures which demonstrate the differences in media. The experimental film "Four Ways to Drama," although overly long, demonstrates the changes occurring when a play is presented in several media. "The Photographer," an exquisite depiction of the photography of Edward Weston, demonstrates the problem of selectivity in any visual medium. Many short films are available to use in identifying characteristics of the various media.

[25] Riesman, *The Oral Tradition, the Written Word, and the Screen Image,* p. 26.
[26] Frank Stanton, in *Saturday Review,* Vol. 29, No. 36 (September 8, 1956), p. 36.

■ *Provide some direct study of form*

1. Use reviews of current programs and films printed in current newspapers and periodicals to introduce the study of form. For example, in criticizing the lack of unity in a broadcast on contemporary events, Robert Lewis Shayon wrote:

> The chief error of the current trend in TV feature-reporting is its failure to narrow down really to a 'feature interpretative piece.' Consider feature-writing in newspapers; for example, Walter Lippmann, Arthur Krock, Joseph C. Harsch, the Alsops do not attempt to 'cover the waterfront' on a news story. They set forth an angle, and they develop it progressively, in depth, to a conclusion.[27]

Introduce by such means an analysis of news interpretation on television, radio, and other media. The class may also study outstanding documentary films, such as "Yours is the Land," and follow these viewing experiences by reading selected articles by Walter Lippmann, James Michener, and others available in high school anthologies. Through such study, students may develop a better understanding of how incidents are selected and organized to create a total effect.

2. Use television screenings of old motion pictures as source material for studying historical development of motion picture form. At intervals throughout the semester ask students to watch such performers as John Barrymore, Greta Garbo, Katharine Hepburn, Rudolph Valentino, and others, or such distinguished American and foreign films as *It Happened One Night, Shoeshine, Great Expectations,* and *The Little Kidnappers.*

To extend student interests in popular arts

■ *Survey prevailing interests*

1. Use a questionnaire to survey prevailing attitudes and tastes. Ask students to answer such questions as:

> What are your three favorite TV programs?
> What are the three best motion pictures you have seen?
> Approximately how many hours a day do you spend watching TV? On week-days?_______ On weekends?_______
> On the following list, place a plus before the type of TV and radio programs which you prefer. Place a minus before those types which you dislike. _______news _______western _______variety _______comedy _______mystery _______sports _______drama _______dance music

There are decided implications, of course, in the differences between ninth-graders who prefer only western films and those who choose sophisticated drama, and certainly only rough distinctions can be identified through this method. The approach offers a superficial, but sometimes helpful, portrait of the level of interests of an entire group, with little accompanying insight into the reasons for the expressed preferences or the personal evaluation of students. However, tabulations of the preferences can occasionally be used as a springboard to a more considered study of the mass media.

2. Use a "listening log." For a single week ask students to record on individual charts the amount of time they spend in viewing or listening to different kinds of

[27] Robert Lewis Shayon, in *Saturday Review,* Vol. 39, No. 22 (May 26, 1956), p. 26.

programs, as in the accompanying chart. This approach has been used at both junior and senior high school levels.

Suggested log for recording time spent viewing and listening

	Hours									
	1	2	3	4	5	6	7	8	9	10
Program types										
Serials										
Westerns										
Mystery										
Music										
Comedy										

Striking contrasts in the number of hours spent in viewing programs of different types may startle some adolescents into reassessing their own uses of leisure time.

■ *Direct attention to worthwhile, overlooked offerings*

1. With junior high school classes, survey the kinds of television and radio offerings which are not widely viewed. Using their own expression of preferences as a starting point, one group identified the following categories: children's programs, serials, drama, crime-mystery, westerns, situation comedy, quiz programs, popular music, variety, sports, news, panel discussions, miscellaneous. Use a bulletin board to indicate the "outstanding" program in each classification and those considered as "mediocre." Before agreeing on a qualitative rating for each broadcast, review with students some criteria for evaluating each kind of offering.

2. Spotlight special offerings. When, through reviews, magazines, or special announcements, advance information is obtained on broadcasts or motion pictures of extraordinary merit or interests, share the information with classes. Often young people can be directed to the unusual or off beat which otherwise would be ignored, such as the presentation of a Bernard Shaw play on TV or an outstanding foreign film in a local theater. One junior high school class appointed a voluntary committee to construct a weekly graphic display on the "TV Program of the Week." The students studied scheduled offerings, agreed on the most promising, and posted appropriate clippings and photographs. A similar project can be instituted for the "Film of the Month."

3. Try reserving regular times in class for previewing the programs with students. A well-planned ten-minute talk each Friday on "TV Broadcasts Too Good to Miss" or "Fine Films Coming Our Way" will whet the appetite of student viewers just as do teacher comments on library books. Needless to say, the teacher's information must be accurate and the wares not oversold. Students come to regard highly only those recommendations which seem consistently honest and dependable.

■ *Plan individual projects requiring special study*

1. After classifying a list of the ten most popular TV programs according to audience ratings, ask a student to locate in magazine files a report on the ten most popular radio programs of the Thirties. Compare the type of programs on both lists (mystery, western, quiz, etc.) and consider the probable reasons why popular taste has changed so little that broadcasters can rely on the same basic formulae. The list of "most popular" programs may also be compared with lists of highly rated motion pictures published frequently in weekly magazines.

2. Increase students' awareness of the limited range and questionable quality of much of the content of the popular arts by encouraging interested groups of volunteers to analyze the treatment of particular subjects on TV or in motion pictures. For example, in a unit on biography, study the treatment of "heroes." By checking on the weekly reviews in news magazines, students may obtain data on the subjects of biographical films during the preceding year. An analysis of programing schedules for TV and radio will yield comparable data. The great emphasis on athletes and entertainers in the popular arts may be compared with the greater range of subjects in recent biographical writing by checking findings against a year's list of non-fiction best sellers.

3. For a special project, possibly included in a longer unit, ask a student to select one of the popular arts, to review recent developments in the area, and to report on current trends. In addition to motion pictures, radio, and television, include among possible topics the dance, contemporary music, the popular book, the modern stage.

4. Survey with students the entertainment offerings of a community. Often the activity is introduced in relation to the study of the community in social studies, sometimes as early as the seventh grade. Provide for evaluating the quality of each by using the survey to prepare an annotated list of entertainments or examples of popular art which should not be missed by visitors from foreign countries. Consider:

Motion picture theaters—types, offerings
Theatrical events—commercial, little theater
Broadcasting centers—TV, radio
Art exhibits
Musical events
Museums
Libraries—permanent collections, exhibits
Community centers—recreation departments, art stores, centers for certain ethnic groups
College and university events

5. Encourage individual reports on major contributors to contemporary art. When appropriate, students may examine biographies of these leaders as well as their original creations. Such assignments are particularly appropriate for gifted students whose curiosities often lead them to pursue interests in the various media. Teachers will be able to identify individuals worth studying in each of the media, as suggested below:

Screen
- A director known for a particular type of film, e.g., spectacle, realistic drama, comedy
- An actor whose selection of roles indicates great versatility

Stage
- An actress whose involvement for several decades in the Broadway scene make the study of her life a good introduction to the contemporary stage
- A playwright whose works are suitable for high school reading

TV
- A news analyst noted for his objectivity
- A network executive whose plans for programing influence current offerings
- An actor whose success demonstrates the impact on television of popular appeal (especially appropriate for junior high)

Music and Dance
An outstanding composer or artist of interest to students who are specially talented

To develop standards of judgment

■ *Provide experiences in judging*

1. During the annual discussion each spring of potential "Oscar" and "Emmy" award winners, encourage students to nominate and vote for their own "best" program and pictures. Individuals may wish to present brief statements supporting the choice of a particular documentary or public service program, and will thus need to identify appropriate criteria for judging.

2. Urge students to write letters commending broadcasters for outstanding productions which do not elicit widespread popular support. Ask them to request that special kinds of programs be considered. Individuals who have studied the economics of TV, radio, and the motion picture will recognize the sensitivity of producers to such appeals. Serious letters of this type require that writers think through their own attitudes and values.

3. When possible, assign to committees the task of recommending records for classroom purchase or for school use. The group may select available albums and discs (poetry recordings, recorded drama, radio transcription, etc.), preview, survey educational needs, and make recommendations to the school.

4. Some junior high school classes enjoy producing "fan" magazines. With guidance such projects can be productive if magazines include thoughtful reviews of current productions, critical comments on the nature of broadcasting or motion picture production, and basic information on the function of the media in our society.

■ *Evaluate the judgments of others*

1. Introduce students to Russell Lynes's famous charts depicting the changes in highbrow, middlebrow, and lowbrow tastes during the past 100 years.[28] Construct with students a similar chart on the tastes of "highbrow," "lowbrow," and "middlebrow" adolescents with respect to motion pictures, television, radio, and library materials. Most students will identify a range in taste in the appeal of TV programs and motion pictures from shoddy horror movies created for adolescents to serious works of art.

2. Ask a mature student to select a recent motion picture which he admires and to locate at least three reviews of the film. Then ask the student to write a composition summarizing the critics' attitudes toward the film and including his own as well. Edgar Daniels reports this to be a provocative assignment for college freshmen.[29]

3. Read criticism of radio serials derived from the content analysis by Rudolf Arnheim.[30] Ask students to study serials currently on television to see if the criticisms still apply.

4. Ask junior high students to collect advance publicity releases on a forthcom-

[28] Russell Lynes, "The Tastemakers" (N.Y., Harper, 1954), pp. 326-327.

[29] Edgar F. Daniels, "First Step in Research: The Movie Review," *Exercise Exchange*, Vol. 5, No. 2 (December 1957), p. 5.

[30] Rudolf Arnheim, "The World of the Daytime Serial," in Daniel Katz, ed., *Public Opinion and Propaganda* (N.Y., Dryden, 1954).

ing film or broadcast. Before seeing the presentation, ask each to write a brief paragraph on his expectation fostered by these advertisements and stories. Follow the viewing with a second assignment in which individuals are asked to assess the production and to offer possible explanations for its being different from his expectations.

Evaluating Growth

Increasing discrimination in reading, in viewing, and in listening to the popular arts is the ultimate goal of the program discussed in this chapter. The success can be judged only by seeking the answer to three basic questions:

Do students seem to understand the popular arts better?
Do they seem to be extending their interests in the media?
Do they seem to be developing and applying standards of critical judgment?

Many of the learning experiences described earlier will help teachers assess growth in discrimination. For example, analyses of programs written in September may be compared with analyses written in May as a way of evaluating changes in response occurring during the school year. Diagnosis and evaluation are two sides of the same coin; both occur continuously. Thus parallel forms of any tests, surveys, or questionnaires may be used by teachers who desire concrete evidence of growth.

Teachers also rely on less formal ways of noting changes in behavior. They observe students who increasingly see parallels between the art of the classroom and the art outside. They study the contributions made in impromptu discussion, the compositions, the reading of students, for evidence that individuals are learning to draw ideas from many sources. Teachers can be alert, too, to the leisure reading, listening, and viewing preferences of young people and can note changes as they mature. Evidence of growth in discrimination obtained in these ways is difficult to obtain and organize but because it reflects the out-of-class behavior of students, it is evidence in which teachers may have considerable confidence.

A few specific procedures for evaluating growth in understanding and appreciation are the following:

1. *Compare qualitative responses.* Obtain qualitative responses to programs and motion pictures to help in understanding individual points of view. Ask students to complete *open* statements about two or three TV broadcasts or motion pictures which each individual feels have been "the most engrossing" or have had "the greatest impact" on him during the previous month or semester. Such statements as the following might be used:

I remember that . . .
It made me feel . . .
I would like . . .
They should change . . .

Such completed statements offer a glimmer of insight into the causes underlying student preferences as well as occasional information on the adequacy or inadequacy of the responses. Individuals who seem to respond only to narrative and suspense may well profit from some study of characterization; others who react solely to the "effectiveness" of the presentation may be encouraged to consider content features; those who fail to discriminate beyond "feeling good" or "feeling bad" may be helped to discriminate different shades of "good" and "bad" emotion. When responses are obtained early in the year and again later, teachers have a good basis for assessing the impact of instruction and changes in the reactions of individuals.

2. *Repeat interest surveys.* Questionnaire surveys of student interests may be repeated, or new listening logs may be maintained late in a semester. (See suggested forms on pp. 398-99.) By comparing responses obtained during the final weeks of a term with those reported earlier, students, with or without teacher help, may examine whether they have extended their viewing interests.

3. *Use checklists to evaluate the range of comments.* Assess student awareness of standards for evaluating offerings in the popular arts by maintaining a checklist of elements studied against which student critiques may be compared. For example, in a ninth grade class the following aspects of dramatic art may receive some attention:

Elements of content	*Elements of production*
relation of plot and theme	photography
foreshadowing	pacing
characterization	adequacy of acting

Ask students to review motion pictures or television broadcasts. Examine the reviews to determine whether students indicate an awareness of the elements which have been studied.

4. *Encourage self-assessment at the end of the year.* Ask students to review their own viewing-listening habits in a special questionnaire which requires individuals to consider extension of interests in a number of areas. The method may be used with a class at any grade level, although questions will vary depending on the maturity of the students. Questions like the following are especially appropriate:

I have increased my understanding of three kinds of television programs during the semester. (Mention each of the three and explain the change in your attitude.)

I listened to at least one program containing a discussion of an important problem that I had not considered before. (Please describe.)

I viewed at least three dramas which emphasized characterization. (Please list titles and describe.)

I viewed at least one program which dealt with a problem similar to one about which I have been reading. (Mention the program, the problem, and the reading.)

SELECTED READINGS

Erik Barnouw, *Mass Communication: Television, Radio, Film, Press.* N.Y., Rinehart, 1956. A considered analysis of the media, particularly helpful in analyzing the psychological factors which affect both viewer and broadcaster.

Commission on the English Curriculum, National Council of Teachers of English, "Making Communication Arts Reinforce One Another," in *The English Language Arts in the Secondary School,* NCTE Curriculum Series, Vol. III. N.Y., Appleton-Century-Crofts, 1956. A summary of suggestions from teachers in various sections of America, including some helpful ideas for teaching symbolism.

John DeBoer, Walter Kaulfers, and Helen Rand Miller, *Teaching Secondary English.* N.Y., McGraw-Hill, 1951. Includes special chapters and much usable material for teaching students to evaluate motion pictures and radio and TV.

Educational Policies Commission, *Mass Communication and Education.* Washington, D.C., National Education Association and American Association of School Administrators, 1958. A statement on the impact of changes in mass communication on our educational system. Analyzes the changing role of the teacher.

Patrick D. Hazard, "The Public Arts and the Private Sensibility," in Lewis Leary, ed., *Contemporary Literary Scholarship.* N.Y., Appleton-Century-Crofts, 1958. A review of research and writing for teachers who wish to locate materials for reading.

Carl Hoveland, "Effects of the Mass Media of Communication," in Gardner Lindzey, ed., *Handbook of Social Psychology,* Vol. II. Cambridge, Mass., Addison-Wesley, 1954. Reviews of research on all mass media in social psychology. Includes summaries on comparative effectiveness of media.

Walter J. Ong, "Wired for Sound: Teaching, Communications, and Technological Culture," *College English,* Vol. 21, No. 5 (February 1960). An arresting analysis of what the shift to an oral culture may mean to teachers.

Neil Postman, *Television and the Teaching of English.* N.Y., Appleton-Century-Crofts, 1961. A helpful report by the committee on the study of television of the National Council of Teachers of English.

Bernard Rosenberg and David Manning White, eds., *Mass Culture: The Popular Arts in America.* Glencoe, Ill., Free Press, 1957. A collection of articles concerning the mass media which offer excellent background information. Teachers will be especially interested in the section called "Mass Literature." A good reference for mature students.

Wilbur Schramm, *Responsibility in Mass Communication.* N.Y., Harper, 1957. Chapter 9, "Popular Art," stresses the responsibilities of broadcasters. Chapter 12, "The Public," suggests some things that viewers may do to improve the offering of the popular arts.

Gilbert Seldes, *The Public Arts.* N.Y., Simon & Schuster, 1956. A readable analysis of the major media which will interest both teacher and student. Chapters are short and are often suitable for oral reading to classes.

Francis Shoemaker, ed., *Communication and the Communication Arts,* rev. ed. Bureau of Publications, Teachers College, Columbia University, 1957. Interesting articles explore the relationship of communication to anthropology, sociology, philosophy, and other disciplines.

Macbeth

A Unit for Grade Eleven or Twelve

Overview: Every curriculum has elements of requirement and elements of free choice. This unit is offered as an example of the former. Designed for a class of students ranging in ability from average to gifted, it is largely teacher-planned and teacher-directed. Because of the nature of the class—individuals sensitive to appreciation on different levels—and because of the teacher's purpose—to help students re-create a dramatic and a literary experience—individual projects are disregarded so that attention can be centered solely on the play. Students are not asked to read in advance; assignments are concerned with explorations to probe the depths of actions and lines *already heard in context.* Thus the necessary compression of time helps students sense the headlong rush of the action and feel the tensions the play creates. Although not as broadly based as the other units in this text, the individual experiences—reading, listening, speaking, and writing—achieve unity through the literary work. However, no teaching time is spent on any skill but reading.

Appreciation for form can be enhanced by the study of *Macbeth*—one of those desirable models Wilder might recommend for youth.[1] More than any drama widely studied at the secondary level, it gives students a chance to experience what is meant by "suspense of form—the incompleteness of a known completion." [2] This suspense, occurring not because of the reader's eagerness to discover what will happen next but because of the artistic structure in which the playwright has cast his work, creates a tension between the past and the future meeting in the present and conveys a sense of destiny. This suspense of form, rather than suspenseful development of plot or characters, accounts for the pleasure derived from repeated rereadings of this literary work.

AIMS

Understandings: To perceive the development of the major theme; to recognize how minor concepts support major.

Skills: To discover the implications of lines; to develop awareness of dramatic reasons for action; to comprehend the subtleties in the revelation of character.

Appreciations: To respond to Shakespeare's poetry—its rhythm and imagery; to sharpen sensitivity to the contribution made by symbolism; to sense the force of

[1] See p. 623.

[2] Charles Morgan, "The Dramatic Illusion," quoted by Susanne K. Langer, *Feeling and Form* (N.Y., Scribner's, 1953), p. 309.

the dramatic irony underlying the play; to heighten awareness of form in relation to content.

TIME: THREE WEEKS

FORM IN RELATION TO CONTENT

Appreciation of the esthetic form—its degree depending upon the sensitivity of the reader—is first absorbed subconsciously as the play is quickly read; the discussions following the reading can help students discover how the author has ordered his material to create the total effect.

Two perfectly integrated elements, initiated by the same act—the murder of a king—and moving simultaneously toward an inevitable conclusion: the destruction of harmonious order within a state; the disintegration of two human beings—the murderers.

The economy and logic of the sequence of events:
Presented in three stages and directed toward a destined end:

The beginning to Duncan's murder shows an established society with a good king surrounded by his loyal subjects, among them the able Macbeth, each contributing to the welfare of all; but the disorder to come is foreshadowed in the opening scene—"Fair is foul and foul is fair"—and in the discontinuity of Macbeth's speeches as soon as he actually conceives the murder.

The scenes from Duncan's death to the senseless murder of Macduff's family show the change which takes place both in a society and in an individual when disorder replaces harmony.

The final stage shows the disintegration of the two murderers as well as the restoration of harmony within the kingdom by the reinstatement of the gracious Malcolm (Act IV, scene 3 establishes his character) with the help of another good king, Edward of England.

The controversial Porter scene: not primarily a humorous interlude for audience relief, but an integral part of the play's design, heightening tension because it contrasts with the preceding world of darkness and hallucination and represents the reality the two murderers must immediately face.

The symbolism:
Planting: signifying growth, the healthy aspects of life, the future: a symbol of fertility and fruition as it pertains to Duncan, changing to one of sterility and decay in the lines of Macbeth, and returning to its original significance as used by Malcolm in the last speech of the play.

Darkness: the atmosphere of the play relieved only twice: once in the beginning when Duncan approaches Macbeth's castle and again at the end when the kingship is restored to Malcolm; between is the darkness of evil.

Masking: symbolizing the disguises assumed to hide from oneself and others, a complex interweaving of many strands: inappropriate garments, borrowed robes, drunken hope as a dress, a giant's robe stolen by a dwarf; the innocence of the flower concealing the serpent, the eye winking at what the hand does, darkness as a protective covering for crime, the smoke of hell concealing the wound from the knife: this imagery is used in the beginning in a sense complimentary to Macbeth; then for the greater part of the play, to represent his desire to mask his evil from himself and others; and finally, contemptuously by Malcolm's followers in referring to Macbeth as one unfit to wear kingly robes.

The Babe: symbolizing both the unpredictable future and those compassionate qualities in man that make him human; children appearing again and again throughout the play in various guises—as characters, metaphors, and symbols; highlighting the irony of Macbeth's attempts to control a future he believes the witches already know in order to establish a dynasty—a desire that makes him human.
These symbols, often combined in a single passage, are closely interwoven into the fabric of the drama.

The language: its discriminating rhythms and images reflecting the repose or inner conflicts of the different characters.

The above elements of form may be discussed briefly with students during the initial reading and synthesized in reviewing passages after the play has been read. Such preparation will make the artistic unity of the whole more understandable as the class finally listens to a recording of the play.

CONCEPTS

Major: the disintegration of a state by the evils resulting from the overthrow of a lawful order; Duncan, Malcolm, and Edward as symbols of that order.

Supporting: the disintegration of the human personality by the disruption of inner order and harmony, which is delineated in the story of two human beings, Macbeth and Lady Macbeth.

The conflict of good and evil forces, universal in its implications—the witches symbolizing the projection of evil already existing in the human heart.

Contrast in the *immediate reactions* of Banquo and Macbeth to the meeting with the witches:

Banquo: concerned with externals, questioning the evidence of his senses—"Were such things here . . . ?"
Macbeth: interested in what has been said— ". . . tell me more. . . . Speak, I charge you."

Contrast in the *moral predisposition* of each:

Banquo thinks of the witches as an evil influence,

"What, can the Devil speak true?"

". . . But 'tis strange.
And oftentimes, to win us to our harm,
The instruments of darkness tell us truths,
Win us with honest trifles, to betray 's
In deepest consequence."

Macbeth is psychologically and morally ready for the evil suggestion:

". . . why do I yield to that suggestion
Whose horrid image doth unfix my hair
And make my seated heart knock at my ribs,
Against the use of nature?"

"If chance will have me king, why
chance will crown me,
Without my stir."

Each time Macbeth meets the witches, he seeks not help, but assurance of success. At no time does he blame the witches or Lady Macbeth for his crimes; implicit in his every line is his belief that he acts of his own volition.

Complementary natures of Macbeth and his wife form the perfect instrument for the embodiment of the conflict which Shakespeare envisioned:

Macbeth, physically brave: shown consistently, from the first report of him in Act I to his last words to Macduff; *hypersensitive and imaginative:* the majority of his lines are the poetry of a disturbed imagination, heaping one image upon another (Act II, scene 2, lines 36-40 contain six images for sleep); always more concerned with what might happen than with things as they are,

"Present fears
Are less than horrible imaginings."

Lady Macbeth, practical: quick to "catch the nearest way"; when awake, nothing impresses her but immediate facts as she sees them; most of her lines are sharp and incisive, without the imaginative concepts that Shakespeare gives to Macbeth; *lacking in foresight and reflective powers:* ". . . we'll not fail."

"Who dares receive it other,
As we shall make our griefs and clamor roar
Upon his death?"

". . . the attempt and not the deed
Confounds us."

Shrewd: understanding her husband's nature, she hurries him along without giving him time to retreat, showing him his own arguments against the crime are really arguments for it.

LAUNCHING THE UNIT

Sensing the predominant mood: Sometime before the study of *Macbeth* begins, students, as motivation for impressionistic writing, may listen to the Richard Strauss tone poem, "Macbeth," which is not identified; although responses will vary, the mood communicated by the music is so intense that the words *war, conflict, struggle, storm, fear,* will be found in most of the papers. On the day texts of *Macbeth* are given out, several student papers—impressions invoked by the Strauss work—may be read to the class and the title of the music given; then students are told that one critic has described Shakespeare's *Macbeth* as a "tempest set to music"; the class discusses the criticism in reference to the feeling conveyed by the tone poem.

Understanding the background: To avoid stopping as the play is being read, the teacher sees that the class has the following information:

Approximate time of Macbeth's reign—1040-1058—ending shortly before the Norman invasion.

The relationship between Duncan and Macbeth—to show that Macbeth's hopes of eventually becoming king were not without foundation.

Unrest in Scotland—the revolt, the invasion—with the names of the king's generals and the opposing forces written on the board.

Two attitudes—toward war and toward witches—which have substantially changed since Shakespeare's day.

DEVELOPING THE UNIT—FIRST READING OF THE PLAY

Aims: To help students understand the action, expressed in terms of human beings and a story; see and hear each scene as theater; appreciate the gradual development of character; recognize individual images and symbols and thus prepare for their cumulative force as the play unfolds; and respond intellectually and emotionally to the poetry.

General plan: reading aloud of entire play by teacher and those students willing to give time for practice; discussion of each scene after reading; and writing of brief papers designed to probe the thinking and to spark imagination.

■ *Analyzing Act I*

The analysis of Act I calls attention to concepts the play develops; poses some of the questions students should consider as they read; suggests a procedure for conducting the first reading of the four remaining acts. Lack of space prevents giving an analysis of the entire play; teachers will find that both Brooks and Traversi, referred to at the end of the unit, give valuable help on interpretation.

Scene 1. If you were staging this scene, how would you set it? What colors? What lighting? Listen to the sound of the lines. What movement would you suggest to actors to help an audience see what it hears? What is the purpose of the scene? What is the meaning of "Fair is foul, and foul is fair"? (The purpose of such a question is to direct attention to a salient point; a definitive answer cannot be given until the play has been read.)

Scene 2. What do we learn of Macbeth and Banquo from the report of the battle? How is Macbeth to be rewarded for his support of the king? Why is he marked for honor when Banquo apparently conducted himself with equal ability and loyalty? Logical reason? Dramatic reason?

Scene 3. Notice the difference in the language used by the witches when speaking among themselves and when speaking to Macbeth. Dramatic reason? (Among themselves the witches speak as women of the lowest class, for that was the class to which they were thought to belong; to Macbeth they speak in the lofty tones and cryptic utterances commonly associated with oracles. One purpose, an element of the dramatic irony underlying the play, is to confuse Macbeth, making fair things seem foul, and foul things fair. This purpose is not clearly stated until Act III, scene v, lines 26-33.)

Macbeth in his first line uses *fair* and *foul* to describe the day, apparently referring to the outcome of the battle and to the weather, respectively. Dramatic reason? What is the significance of the effect of the witches' prophecy upon Banquo as compared with its effect upon Macbeth? What is the dramatic purpose of Macbeth's being made thane of Cawdor at this particular time? (To establish his belief in the power of the witches as supernatural beings.)

Consider the symbolism: lines 86 and 118 (these references to children are not symbolic, but should be pointed out as indicating Macbeth's concern, not yet obsessive, for the future); lines 108-109 and 144-146 (because they belong to the wearer, the clothes are not ill-fitting here, in contrast to most of the garment metaphors appearing later); lines 58-59 (planting as a symbol of the unpredictability of the future is introduced here).

Scene 4. What is the dramatic purpose of Duncan's naming Malcolm his successor at this time? Notice examples of dramatic irony: lines 11-21, lines 54-58. Consider the symbols of planting, lines 28-33, and of masking, lines 50-53.

Scene 5. How does Lady Macbeth characterize her husband? (Examine the validity of this characterization as the play proceeds, finally determining to what extent her description of her husband fits herself.) What is the meaning of Lady Macbeth's line, "I feel now the future in the instant"? (Later, determine how much of the future she was really aware of.) Another example of the masking metaphor occurs in lines 52-56.

Scene 6. Notice the example of dramatic irony in the lyrical description of the castle, contrasting with the scene of horror which preceded. Contrast Lady Macbeth's greeting to Duncan—its formality, stilted phrasing, emphasis on duty—with the warmth of Duncan's remarks. Notice how Shakespeare indicates Lady Macbeth's feelings by the labored rhythm of the lines.

Scene 7. Compare the sense of values, methods of thinking of Macbeth and Lady Macbeth. She does not foresee the consequences of the king's murder; he does, but hopes to avoid them. Notice how each uses the same facts to arrive at different conclusions. Is either more logical than the other? Is either more sensitive to the feelings of others? Analyze this scene for evidence of their somewhat complementary natures.

What is the significance of lines 51-54? Throughout this scene Lady Macbeth, as she has promised, gives an exhibition of her skill in chastising with the valor of her tongue; notice the range of the appeals by which she attempts to move her husband to act.

The symbol is further developed: the child, signifying both the humanity of man and his insurance for the future, lines 21-25 and 54-59; variants of the masking imagery, lines 32-35, lines 35-38, and lines 81-82.

■ *Writing*

As the reading of the play progresses, students may be asked to write briefly on selected topics which probe their thinking concerning the implications of lines and scenes significant to concepts being developed. Illustrations from the first two acts will serve as examples.

Act I. 1) What impression have you formed of Lady Macbeth? (The obvious one at this time is that she is a fiend, but later developments may suggest a woman, consciously steeling herself to commit an act against nature.) 2) "There is no way to partition off the continuum of time; the future is implicit in the present." [3] Explain. Do you agree with this statement? Do you think Macbeth would? Discuss in reference to his speech, scene 7, lines 1-28.

Act II. 1) Does Lady Macbeth really faint or only pretend to? (If she is a fiend, the faint may be pretense; however, the murder of the guards is evidently a surprise to her, the first evidence that she has unleashed a power she cannot control. The shock of knowing the king's murder is not the end but the beginning may

[3] Cleanth Brooks, *The Well Wrought Urn*, p. 2. (See resources for teachers at the end of this unit.)

well have caused her to faint.) 2) In scene 2, lines 73 and 74, Macbeth says, "Wake Duncan with thy knocking! I would thou could'st!" Is the wish sincere? Consider in relation to his character as portrayed thus far. 3) If you were staging the play, would you use a real dagger in scene 1, lines 33-49? Give reasons.

■ *Audio-visual activities*

After the reading of each act, it is helpful to have students listen to some of the key speeches (not the entire act) spoken by accomplished actors; the recording with Maurice Evans and Judith Anderson, still available in some schools, is ideal for this purpose; unfortunately, it is no longer available on the market; selections from the Old Vic recording might be used the same way.

After the first reading of the play, some teachers use the film, "Shakespeare's Theater," which suggests a method of staging the last act of *Macbeth.*

SECOND READING OF THE PLAY

Purpose: To help students understand the interrelation of the various elements which make up the whole.

Procedure: Using the section "Form in Relation to Content" as a guide, the teacher reads significant but *brief* passages to illustrate the interweaving of the various elements in each act; if this is to serve its purpose, it must be done quickly without belaboring points and with no effort to make *every* student see the significance of each.

CULMINATING EXPERIENCES

■ *Synthesis*

1. *Group work.* In preparation for the final discussion, the class may be divided into six committees, each to review the evidence concerning one aspect of the play. (Necessarily, since the various aspects are well integrated, the evidence of one overlaps that of the others.)

The Witches: Symbolic role in the play; the prophecies and the manner of their fulfillment.

Macbeth: The course of his crimes; his impelling motives; his increasing tension.

Lady Macbeth: Her intellectual processes in regard to the crimes to which she is accessory; the development of her emotional experiences.

The "Fair is foul, and foul is fair" Theme: Passages where it is stated, implied, illustrated.

Symbolism: Use of babes on various levels—as characters, symbols, and elements of metaphor. The garment and masking symbolism—from Macbeth's initial impulse to reject "borrowed robes" to Angus' description of him in the last act as a "dwarfish thief" trying to wear a "giant's robes." The plant symbolism, reflecting the development of the play—from the early references to seeds and planting, symbolic of the fertility surrounding Duncan, to Macbeth's lament that his life "is fall'n into the sear, the yellow leaf."

Dramatic Irony: During the reading, the Oedipus myth may be discussed in relation to similarities and contrasts with *Macbeth;* Oedipus struggled to overcome a fate which had already been decided; Macbeth, although he believed the witches possessed "more than mortal knowledge," tried to impose a plan on the future, contrary to that which they had predicted.

2. *Discussions.* Led by the teacher, the final discussion should attempt to integrate the evidence of these various elements into a unified whole.

■ *Writing*

In writing the final essay, students may be allowed to choose any one of the following topics.

The Prophecies (Highest possible grade, C). A factual account of the substance of the prophecies and of the manner of their fulfillment.

Ideal Partners in Crime (Highest possible grade, B). An analysis of the complementary natures of Macbeth and Lady Macbeth, supported by specific examples.

Dramatic Irony (Possible grade, A). Critics have compared the structure of dramatic irony underlying *Macbeth* with that of the Oedipus myth. Discuss dramatic irony as it operates in each case, noting the similarities and contrasts in the two situations.

Symbolism as an Integrating Force (Possible grade, A). Select any one of the series of symbols that run throughout the play—masking, seeds and planting, the Babe; explain its contribution to the drama; give specific examples.

■ *Final reading*

The students follow in their books as they listen to the Old Vic recording of the play.

■ *Viewing Macbeth*

The Hallmark TV production of *Macbeth* with Maurice Evans and Judith Anderson is available on loan, free of charge, from Associated Films, 347 Madison Ave., New York 17, N.Y. The Evans-Anderson 1960 TV version, filmed in Scotland, is markedly superior; undoubtedly it will soon be available to schools.

EVALUATION

Appreciations: Genuine appreciation of the play as a dramatic and literary experience cannot be evaluated exactly; the teacher has to depend upon observations of personal reactions.

Skills and understandings: The teacher has class discussions, the short papers written as the reading progresses, and the final essay which may be used for purposes of evaluation.

Brief key quotations, listed in scrambled order, to be arranged in proper sequence, prove useful in testing some of the more subtle understandings of the development of the drama; for each, a short explanation of the significance of the sequence the student selects should be required. Quotations that could be used are lines from Macbeth's speeches showing his mental and emotional states as his affairs grow progressively worse, or lines containing symbols—especially the masking and planting metaphors—which change in their application as events in the play change.

AFTERMATH

After the completion of the unit, the students may enjoy hearing one of their number read James Thurber's essay, "The Macbeth Murder Mystery."

Resources for teachers

Cleanth Brooks, *The Well Wrought Urn.* N.Y., Harcourt, Brace, 1947. See especially Chapter 2, "The Naked Babe and the Cloak of Manliness."

Robert Ornstein, *Shakespeare in the Classroom.* Urbana, Ill., Educational Illustrators, 1960. Available from National Council of Teachers of English.

James Thurber, *My World and Welcome to It.* N.Y., Harcourt, Brace, 1942.

D. A. Traversi, *An Approach to Shakespeare.* Garden City, N.Y., Doubleday Anchor, 1956. See especially pp. 150-181.

Margaret Webster, *Shakespeare Without Tears.* Original edition, 1942. N.Y., Fawcett, 1957. See especially Chapter 10, "The Tragic Essence."

Fortitude, the Backbone of Courage

A Unit for Grade Eight

Overview: This unit is designed for a heterogeneous group of eighth-graders and may be used either in a two-period combined English-social studies class or in a separate English class. The unit illustrates a way of developing a thematic unit in school situations where books are comparatively scarce. Unlike most others described in this volume, this unit requires the availability of only six to ten copies each of six different anthologies, plus whatever titles may be obtained for individual reading. The selections are suitable for readers with abilities ranging from fifth to eleventh grade; thus provision can be made for both the more and the less able. The anthologies are supplemented by individual titles from the school library and by materials read aloud by the teacher. Teachers fortunate enough to have class and group sets of books on related themes could expand the study.

Stories of courage and endurance have considerable appeal for eighth grade students who respond well to selections containing elements of adventure, heroism, and the like. This unit tries to extend this rather superficial interest in action and narrative to a probing of the impact of courageous action on individuals, the qualities of character involved, the distinction between a single act of bravery and prolonged behavior requiring fortitude. Because American literature and American history are emphasized in many eighth grade classrooms, literature dealing with American heroes and the American setting is emphasized. The unit ends with a consideration of fortitude in the modern world so that the student may grasp some sense of continuity in the development of our national character and perhaps more easily see the implications of the study for his own life.

AIMS

Concepts: Understanding the nature of human fortitude and the effect on individuals of struggling against great odds; understanding some of the patterns of behavior with which individuals respond in moments of stress; recognizing how the valor, courage, and endurance of groups and of individuals contributed to the development of America; perceiving that history is partially a heritage of the experiences of great individuals.

Skills: Varying the rate of reading in accordance with the purpose and difficulty of material; perceiving organization in fiction (special emphasis for slower readers); compressing ideas into a limited number of words; speaking clearly in group and class discussion.

Appreciations: Developing sensitivity to vividness of prose which conveys the impact of real experience; responding to simple rhythms in poetry.

TIME PLAN

Two to three weeks in a two-hour block course. About four weeks in a one-period English class.

CONTENT OUTLINE

Fortitude in Establishing America
- Determination and bravery of the pioneers
- Persistence of early Americans in clinging to their ideals
- Patience and endurance in settling the frontier

Fortitude in the World Today
- Stamina and courage in today's life
- Qualities needed to support fortitude today: hard work, courage, determination

LAUNCHING THE UNIT

1. Read aloud the selection from *The River of Wolves* by Stephen Meader, reprinted in Arbuthnot's *Time for True Tales and Almost True* (7),[1] and develop through class discussion an understanding of how the determination, bravery, and stamina of the boy—i.e., his fortitude—gradually wins the respect of the tribe. Ask students to recall other courageous acts by Americans. In a combined English-social studies class, examples may be selected from reading earlier in the year. As interest begins to develop, the teacher may suggest a unit study of incidents involving courage and stamina in America's past.

2. Mount in the classroom a number of photographs and paintings from current periodicals depicting individuals in classic adventure situations which call for fortitude, e.g., a ship capsizing, a lifeboat adrift, a fort besieged, a lonely individual fighting a snow storm. Ask students to suggest possible similarities between the depicted situations. Use the comparative approach to arouse interest in the kinds of situations requiring stamina, courage, fortitude.

3. Where library resources permit, begin with individual reading. Spread books related to the unit theme on a table and urge each student to select a title for personal reading. After several days, organize the class in small discussion groups of six persons each. Ask each group to follow these directions:

> Each group member will cite from his book an illustration of a person struggling against great odds.
>
> Following the reports, the groups will rank illustrations in the order in which the character possesses each of the following traits: stamina, strength (physical strength, strength of character), determination.
>
> Each group will note areas of agreement and disagreement and report these to the class.

[1] Here, as elsewhere in these units, teachers attempting to adapt the plan will wish to substitute similar selections from the literature available to them. The titles mentioned merely indicate the kind of literary selections which may be used. The numbers in parentheses refer to the bibliographical list at the end of the unit.

A report from each group introduces a class discussion. As disagreements, problems, and questions arise, they are written on the chalk board and serve to limit subsequent reading and study in the unit.

DEVELOPING THE UNIT

■ *Planning*

1. As a result of interest awakened by the introductory activities, the teacher and students list on the chalk board in haphazard fashion all questions about courage, endurance, or fortitude that they wish answered. The teacher then asks each student to write on a slip of paper the questions which interest him most. A committee of student volunteers groups the questions under the following headings:

Questions about *how* actions happen
Questions about *why* actions happen
Questions about how individuals are affected
Questions about results of action

In some circumstances the teacher will use the questions to guide discussion; in others, individual students may be assigned special reports designed to answer questions. Since the questions will serve as a guide throughout the unit, the class will need to copy them in notebooks.

2. Courage and fortitude having been identified as the focus of study during the introductory activities, the teacher suggests that students consider their interest or lack of interest in each of several possible areas of concentration:

True stories of fortitude in American history
Fortitude in settling the West
Strength and valor in combat
Fortitude in the world today
Stories of great adventures

Students are encouraged to offer additions to the list. Subsequent activities are modified depending on the interests expressed by the class.

3. Once content objectives are determined, discuss possible class activities with students, such as participation on a creative dramatics or graphic arts team, preparation of an individual report, writing an original story. Ask each student to volunteer for one activity.

4. Ask each individual to review his progress in skill development; studying earlier papers and tests is the most desirable method if these are filed in the room. Ask each to write a paragraph identifying the skills in which he needs the greatest help. Modify the unit to provide for individual, group, and class instruction as necessary.

■ *Literature*

1. Bring into the classroom six to ten copies each of six anthologies. Identify in each anthology the stories related to the unit theme. During each of the two phases of the unit, assign students to read two or three selections and as many recommended selections as possible. For the six anthologies used here, the following assignments provide for a variety of abilities:

Phase I: Fortitude in Establishing America

Basic readings (Required of all)

Stewart Holbrook, "America's Ethan Allen" (4) [2]; persistence in clinging to ideals.

Rose Wilder Lane, "Grasshopper Nightmare" (3); patience and endurance in establishing homes.

Honoré Morrow, "Child Pioneer" (1); determination to push to the West.

Recommended readings (Read as many as possible)

Alexander Key, "Night Hunter" (1)
Gouverneur Morris, "Growing Up" (1)
Russell Gordon Carter, "The Royal Green" (3)
Stanley Young, "Twelve Mile Creek" (5)
Albert F. Blaisdell and Frances Ball, "The Bravery of Elizabeth Zane" (6)
Freeman H. Hubbard, "Legend of Kate Shelley" (3)
Laura Ingalls Wilder, "The Long Dakota Winter" (4)
Julia Davis, "No Other White Men" (1)

Phase 2: Fortitude in the World Today

Basic readings (Required of all)

William Douglas, "Two Boys on a Mountain" (2, 3); an experience of individual stamina and courage.

Jim Scott, "Boy Meets Decision" (2); hard work and talent prepare Bob Mathias for a grueling sports event.

Recommended readings (Read as many as possible)

Chelsea Frash, "How a Woman Duplicated Man's Most Famous Flight" (3)
David Lavender, "High Victory" (4)
Russell G. Carter, "High-Climber" (4)
Katherine B. Shippen, "Desert Storm" (4, 5)
Richard Byrd, "Alone" (4)
Katherine B. Shippen, "Igor Sikorsky and His Helicopter" (4)
James C. Derrieux, "10,000 Times Under the Sea" (6)

Allow sufficient class time for reading so that the slow students will finish the basic assignment; during this interval, rapid readers may complete as many as four or five of the recommended selections. Because books will be passed from student to student during reading periods, individuals are not asked to read the selections in any particular order. Present the total assignment for each phase at one time, and allow several days for completion.

2. Ask each student to read at least one longer book related to the theme of the unit. Prepare a display of books similar to those listed in the bibliography at the end of this unit. Encourage individuals to choose one of the recommended books or to substitute a biography of an early American hero.

■ *Oral expression*

1. Basic discussion: Discuss each of the assigned stories to develop an understanding of fortitude and its key concomitants—courage, endurance, determination.

[2] The numbers in parentheses refer to the various anthologies, listed at the end of the unit, in which these selections can be found.

For each selection, consider the courses of action rejected by individuals, e.g., changing goals, compromising principles, quitting the task, moving away.

2. Discussion of stories read by individuals: Organize students in small discussion groups to consider the concepts in these books in relation to the central theme of the unit. On the day before group discussions, assign each student one of the following problems to consider:

How much a character is able to endure—physically, morally, emotionally
What human endurance accomplishes
How a person feels in a time of crisis
The thoughts which occur to a person in a moment of crisis
How actions of fortitude affect other people

Organize students into separate groups to discuss each of the topics. Later ask groups to summarize conclusions for the entire class.

3. Creative dramatics: After reading and discussing Morrow's "Child Pioneer," ask volunteers to dramatize the arrival of the Sager children at the last crest of the mountain overlooking the Columbia River Valley. Students are to depict the feelings and attitudes of the children as they imagine them to have been. Focus the subsequent class discussion on an analysis of the emotions of the group of children. Use the activity to lead into imaginative writing—"How I Would Have Felt."

4. Poetry reading: Introduce the following poems as indicated. Share copies available in anthologies for brief intervals or write the poems on the chalk board.

"Columbus," Joaquin Miller—Ask for volunteers to read it orally as a poem which says something germane to the ideas being discussed. Ask class to compare the fortitude of Columbus with that of other heroes. After considering the meaning of the poem, discuss its rhythm. Ask students to reread, emphasizing the quickened pace of each paragraph. See pp. 366-68 for arrangement for choral speaking.

"Lewis and Clark," Rosemary and Stephen Vincent Benét—Read this aloud following an oral report on Julia Davis' *No Other White Men,* a novel depicting the Lewis and Clark expedition.

"Who But A Boy—" Eleanor Alletta Chaffee—Teacher reads aloud during the discussion of Douglas' mountain climbing adventure, for the purpose of extending the discussion to a consideration of the many adventures of youth.

"Paul Revere's Ride," Henry W. Longfellow—The teacher reads first, with vigor and animation. Following a general discussion of the rhythm and mounting excitement of the poem, ask individuals in the class to express the excitement of the narrative by reading selected stanzas.

■ *Reading skill development*

1. Adjustment of reading rate to content and purpose: Present three brief, timed reading tests. For each test ask students to read with comprehension as quickly as possible and answer ten factual questions for each selection. After each trial, students compute and enter in notebooks their reading rates according to the number of words read per minute and their comprehension as measured by a percentage score. Use three diverse kinds of materials for the trials—an easy fictional selection, a passage from an encyclopedia dealing with an American hero, and a set of directions written by the teacher. Then guide students in an analysis and comparison of

the scores. In general, the analysis will reveal that those students whose comprehension remains high on all three trials tend to read directions and encyclopedia material at greatly reduced rates, whereas students whose comprehension falls considerably on the second and third trials read these materials at the same rate used for fictional materials.

Introduce a brief experience in skimming as students search for American heroes to be depicted in the mural (see p. 420). Encourage individuals to skim through their history textbooks for fifteen minutes to locate the names of as many "heroes" as possible. At the end of the period lead the students in a brief analysis of the methods which they employed in the search, pointing up the importance of relying on chapter headings, boldface type, key sentences, chapter summaries.

2. Comprehending sequence of events: Provide special help for slower readers. During the hours assigned for silent reading, meet with groups and individuals to offer needed instruction. Aid readers in comprehending sequence by using the following aids and exercises:

A simplified outline of the incidents in "America's Ethan Allen." Encourage students to refer to this guide as they read.

An exercise in rearranging events in the order in which they occur in "Child Pioneer." Permit students to reread the textbooks as they complete the exercise.

An assignment to identify at least four major shifts in the attitudes of the two boys toward each other in "Two Boys on a Mountain." Discuss the shifts with the group of slow readers, then ask these students to present them to the class during a general discussion of the selection.

■ *Written activities*

1. During the reading of pioneer stories, ask students to imagine either that they are living in a sod house suffering from hunger, trapped in a stockade surrounded by Indians, or lost on a mountain trail of the West with no hope of rescue. Given only 150 words to write messages to their families, ask students to state what they would write under the circumstances.

2. Present the motion picture, "Driven Westward," which depicts the Mormon trek to Utah. Following the showing, ask students to write paragraphs comparing the following incidents in the film and in their readings:

The emotion of the Mormons at the crest of the Rockies overlooking Salt Lake with the emotions of the Sager children crossing the Columbia River

The struggle against the locusts in comparison with the "grasshopper winter" described by Rose Wilder Lane

3. Following the discussion of "Two Boys on a Mountain," ask each student to describe "A Time When I Was Scared," explaining how he felt and the decisions he had to make.

4. Ask each student to find one example of fortitude in modern life from articles, stories, illustrations, or photographs in magazines or newspapers. Ask them to explain briefly the ways in which the example is similar to or different from those discussed in class. Plan to use these contributions in a bulletin board display.

■ *Provision for gifted students*

In addition to urging extensive individual reading from a recommended list, challenge the more able students by the following assignments:

1. Background reading for special oral reports related to selections studied by class:

For "Paul Revere's Ride"
  Esther Forbes, "America's Paul Revere" (4)
  Mildred Pace, "A Pioneer for Freedom" (5)
For "Lewis and Clark"
  Julia Davis, "No Other White Men" (1)
For "Two Boys on a Mountain"
  Library research on the life of William Douglas

2. Ask a special group to dramatize a "You Are There" presentation of an incident in American history revealing valor and fortitude. Mention such diverse examples as Washington crossing the Delaware or the battle of the Alamo, but encourage students to choose their own.

CULMINATING ACTIVITIES

1. Developing a mural on courageous incidents in American history: Select a committee of volunteers to draw on heavy wrapping paper a suitable background for a large mural to extend over an entire wall. The background, vaguely suggesting the geography of the United States, may include an ocean, mountain ranges, a great plains area, and an extensive river network resembling the Mississippi, or any combination of these. Ask for volunteers to prepare small colored figures representing the personages about whom the total class has studied, e.g., Paul Revere, the Minutemen, Ethan Allen, the Sager children, Daniel Boone. Mount each figure at an appropriate place on the mural.

Ask each student to select from his reading one incident revealing fortitude, to obtain special information on the person involved, and to prepare for the mural a colored representation of the person's actions. The incident may be taken from the individual reading book or from reading in the history book supplemented by other information. In placing the figure on the mural, ask each student to present a brief explanation of the significance of the episode and its relation to the unit theme. In particular, each is to discuss the importance of the experience, how it affects the person involved, and how it affects others. Among the "heroes" to consider for inclusion are the following:

Peter Zenger	Jane Addams
Commodore Perry	Walter Reed
Kit Carson	F. D. Roosevelt
Booker T. Washington	Dwight Eisenhower
John Fremont	Pony Express Riders
Susan B. Anthony	Sam Houston

2. Read aloud to the class "When Hannah Var Eight Yar Old" by Katherine Peabody Girling. Ask students to identify similarities between the character traits of the girl in the story and those of heroes studied throughout the unit.

EVALUATION

1. In a summary discussion, review with students the major experiences of the unit and list the qualities and characteristics which seem to enable men to meet great tests. This discussion offers the teacher one way of assessing the effectiveness

of the unit in developing understanding of the basic concepts. Among the ideas which should be contributed by students are the following:

Faith in something greater than oneself (John Sager, Brigham Young)
A surge of great energy which permits physical endurance (Douglas, boy in "Night Hunter")
Abandonment of petty differences (Douglas)
Hard work (Mathias)
Ability to concentrate on immediate purpose (John Sager)

2. Ask students to write paragraphs in their regular notebooks explaining how a character or characters in their individual reading illustrate one or more of these traits. Evaluate the extent to which each student's perception of fortitude embraces considerations beyond those involved only in obvious physical ordeal.

3. Evaluation of progress in skill development occurs continuously throughout the developmental activities. No final test is needed.

Materials and resources for students

LITERATURE TO BE PRESENTED ORALLY

Stephen Meader, "Captured by the Abenaki," from *The River of Wolves* (7). A captured youth's determination and bravery wins the respect of his Indian captors.

Katherine Peabody Girling, "When Hannah Var Eight Yar Old" (8). A small girl faces her mother's death.

Poetry: Recreating courageous experience—Joaquin Miller, "Columbus," Henry W. Longfellow, "Paul Revere's Ride." Praising valorous actions—Ralph Waldo Emerson, "Concord Hymn," Alfred Guiterman, "The Oregon Trail." Suggesting the significance of actions—Eleanor Alletta Chaffee, "Who But A Boy—" (2).

ANTHOLOGIES FROM WHICH COMMON READINGS ARE SELECTED

1. Luella B. Cook, Walter Loban, George Norvell, William McCall, eds., *Challenge to Explore.* N.Y., Harcourt, Brace, 1941.
2. William J. Iverson and Agnes McCarthy, eds., *Prose and Poetry: Adventure.* Syracuse, N.Y., Singer, 1957.
3. Wilfred Eberhart, Irma Swearinger, Bernice Leary, eds., *Reading-Literature, Book II: Your Country.* Evanston, Ill., Row, Peterson, 1955.
4. Paul Witty, Mariam Peterson, Alfred Parker, eds., *Reading Roundup, Book One.* Boston, Heath, 1954.
5. Elizabeth Bennett, Mabel B. Bowse, and Mary D. Edmons, eds., *High Roads to Glory.* Morristown, N.J., Silver Burdett, 1947. (Easy)
6. Marquis E. Shattuck, ed., *Beacon Lights of Literature, Book Six: Toward Pleasant Shores.* Columbus, Ohio, Iroquois, 1949. (Easy)
7. May Hill Arbuthnot, ed., *Time for True Tales and Almost True.* Chicago, Scott, Foresman, 1953 (7).
8. Luella Cook, Walter Loban, Ruth Stauffer, and Robert Freier, eds., *People in Literature.* N.Y., Harcourt, Brace, 1957 (8).

SUGGESTED BOOKS FOR INDIVIDUAL READING

Claire H. Bishop, *The Big Loop.* N.Y., Viking, 1955.
Vivian Breck, *Hoofbeats on the Trail.* Garden City, N.Y., Doubleday, 1950.
Henry Steele Commager, *America's Robert E. Lee.* Boston, Houghton Mifflin, 1951.

James Daugherty, *Daniel Boone.* N.Y., Viking, 1939.
———, *The Landing of the Pilgrims.* N.Y., Random, 1950.
———, *Of Courage Undaunted.* N.Y., Viking, 1951.
Julia Adams Davis, *No Other White Men.* N.Y., Dutton, 1937.
Jeanette Eaton, *Narcissa Whitman.* N.Y., Harcourt, Brace, 1941.
John Floherty, *Men Without Fear.* Phila., Lippincott, 1940.
———, *Search and Rescue at Sea,* Phila., Lippincott, 1953.
Thomas Galt, *Peter Zenger, Fighter for Freedom.* N.Y., Crowell, 1951.
Shannon Garst, *Amelia Earhart, Heroine of the Skies.* N.Y., Messner, 1947.
Charles Boardman Hawes, *Dark Frigate.* Boston, Little, Brown, 1934.
Edgar Buell Hungerford, *Forge for Heroes.* Chicago, Wilcox & Follett, 1952.
Helen Keller, *The Story of My Life.* N.Y., Grosset & Dunlap, 1947.
James Kjelgaard, *Rebel Siege, Story of a Frontier Riflemaker's Son.* N.Y., Holiday House, 1953.
Lois Lenski, *Indian Captive.* Phila., Lippincott, 1941.
Cornelia Meigs, *Call of the Mountains.* Boston, Little, Brown, 1940.
Armstrong Sperry, *Call It Courage.* N.Y., Macmillan, 1940.
Katherine B. Shippen, *Passage to America; the Story of the Great Migration.* N.Y., Harper, 1950.
Arthur D. Stapp, *Escape on Skis. N.Y.,* Morrow, 1949.
———, *Mountain Tamer.* N.Y., Morrow, 1948.
Hildegard Hoyt Swift, *The Railroad to Freedom.* N.Y., Harcourt, Brace, 1932.
Laura Ingalls Wilder, *Little House in the Big Woods.* N.Y., Harper, 1932.

PART FOUR

Communication

9. Oral Language
10. Written Expression
11. Grammar and Usage

UNIT: Meeting a Crisis

Chapter Nine

Oral Language

Let your speech be always with grace,
seasoned with salt that ye may know
how ye ought to answer every man.
—ST. PAUL TO COLOSSIANS 4:6

PERSPECTIVE

Writers from Solomon's day to the present have testified to the power of the spoken word; dictators have paid their tribute by attempting its suppression. In man's development of Western civilization, speech has been an important tool; today it is a significant instrument in making possible the cooperative activity necessary in the complex society this civilization has created.

The teacher of oral communication One who attempts to teach students to speak effectively must himself have a deep respect for the force that can be unleashed by those who use this power skillfully. He knows that the right of free speech implies the obligation both to use language with integrity and to discriminate among the many voices clamoring for attention. The teacher himself must have savored the pleasure which comes from the ability to say exactly what he means, to express the appropriate thought or feeling with telling effect. For only one who understands the complexity of communication appreciates the difficulties—intellectual, emotional, and technical—which confront his students.

Two approaches In daily life the context of oral communication is usually the give and take of conversation, only occasionally the speaker-audience situation. In planning learning experiences, teachers use both contexts. To insure the most practice for the greatest number, they use discussion to develop skills needed for informal speaking; they use small groups as the setting for prepared talks demonstrating the principles underlying effective speech. All procedures suggested in this chapter are variants of these two methods. Both place the reluctant pupil in a situation where he can operate more successfully; both allow all students to perform according to their respective abilities; both save time and permit integration with other areas of

English. Since similar principles govern effectiveness in discussion and in more formal speaking, skill in one reinforces skill in the other. Thus, using a combination of the two approaches, the teacher can provide sufficient practice to help students speak better in the many informal situations of daily living.

The social situation

Oral communication takes place in many different kinds of situations, each with its own particular aura. The pervading atmosphere may be genial or strained, favorable or antagonistic, but language is used for saying something to someone—and for valid reasons. When the exchange is between two persons, either what is said or the way it is said may inject a discordant or harmonious overtone; so too may the entrance of a third individual. The social situations in life resemble what the dramatist calls *scenes.* Even a one-act play with only two characters is made up of numerous scenes, the atmosphere changing as disclosures made by one or the other bring relief or create tension. The climate in which oral communication takes place has direct bearing on its effectiveness, and each participant has a stake in creating that climate.

Communicate means literally *to give to another as a partaker.* All communication requires a sender, a receiver, and something shared. With speech the relationship of the three is immediate and apparent; every social situation must have a speaker, a listener, and spoken language—the medium of exchange between the two. Control of this medium is equally important to both speaker and listener, for speech can serve either as a bridge or as a barrier between ourselves and others. Our command of language, with all that phrase implies,[1] determines in part how well we can function in the various social situations, no two identical, of which we are a part. This emphasis on communication rather than on language in isolation pervades all instruction in English.

The climate A flexible situation where participants are relaxed and self-confident is essential for effective communication. Thus, maintenance of a classroom climate conducive to learning is nowhere more important than in the teaching of oral skills. The desire and the ability to use language honestly takes root only when conditions are favorable; they will not flourish unless carefully nurtured over a long period of time. In the main it is the teacher's attitude toward himself, toward others, and toward ideas that determines whether he can create an environment to stimulate growth. If the student feels that the subject being discussed strikes at the heart of his world, if he knows that any opinion he can support will be treated with respect, if he is assured of an interested response, he will learn to speak. Even the slow and inarticulate has demonstrated repeatedly that, given subjects on his own level and interested listeners, he can learn to discuss with enthusiasm and a fair degree of skill. He

[1] See Chapter 1, "Language as Dynamic Process," and the statement on the significance of communication in "Teacher and Learner," p. 9.

is reluctant only when he has no desire to communicate or is beyond his depth—and who isn't?

The teacher can create a favorable atmosphere by providing a classroom where students know they can say what they think; where it is not only their right but their duty to have opinions and to defend them; where the ideas will not, however, be accepted automatically but will be examined impartially and critically. Yet, even such an atmosphere will fail its purpose unless the teacher starts with content at the level of the interests and abilities of his students. In the beginning they should be asked to discuss only matters of particular concern to them—the only ideas about which they can be expected to have convictions that merit defense.

Although introduced by topics sure to challenge response, the oral program does not stop there. The teacher begins gradually and consistently to broaden the base of the content, attempting to widen and deepen the interests and to increase the abilities. In this way he can help young people develop the characteristics which seem desirable for those who are to realize their potential in the kind of society to which they belong.

What qualities do we hope the oral skills program will foster in students? The reader will probably not quarrel with the characteristics selected as desirable. His response is more likely to be, "Sounds fine! Now tell me *how!*" As he well knows, no tricks or gimmicks will perform this miracle. The habit of using language with integrity is formed, if at all, over a long period of time as students practice principles of effective communication in environments which build confidence and stress the responsibility for straight thinking and honest communication. Nor does honest communication imply saying what one thinks in any way one pleases; the effect on the listener has to be considered; no instruction and no skill are required if the purpose is to antagonize. This chapter is concerned with a program that gives emphasis both to honesty in the use of language and to the skills necessary to make that honesty function.

The speaker Speech and personality are related. Over two thousand years ago Aristotle in his *Rhetoric* extolled the persuasive power of the "man of honesty" in contrast to the one of "sharp argument." Today too we select *integrity* as the basic requirement for the speaker; we must be convinced he speaks the truth as he sees it. We require a degree of *authority*, a certainty that in the limited field of the moment he knows what he is talking about. We want him to show a healthy *respect* both for himself and for others, admitting their rights to their own opinions but not relinquishing his own unless convinced of his error. We are likely to admire the man with *courage*, one who will not curry favor by evading unpleasant truths that must be stated to clarify the issue; one who, with unfailing good humor and tact, voices honest opinions he knows are unpopular with the majority. We expect *vitality*, that the speaker's manner will convey his belief that he is saying something of importance to both himself and his listener. Lastly, we want *intelligibility*, evidence that the speaker realizes his obligation to make his ideas comprehensible, to hew to the line of his argument with directness and economy of words. Students can be helped to develop these qualities in classrooms where they deal with increasingly complex problems in an atmosphere which encourages tactful and critical appraisal of independent thought and expression.

The listener The listener needs the same qualities as the speaker. He is equally important; without him there would be no communication. Even when he is in a situation where he cannot interrupt with questions and where his rebuttal must be silent, his mind is active, accepting this fact, rejecting that conclusion. He shows his *vitality* by remaining alert; his *integrity,* by weighing honestly opinions at variance with his own; his *authority,* by marshaling facts to confirm or refute and by following the line of argument to detect sound or fallacious reasoning. He shows his *respect* for himself and others by quiet admission that the question may have more facets than he had anticipated and by an earnest effort to relate the new facts to his previous understanding of the problem; his *courage,* by changing his opinion when the evidence seems conclusive. In all this he is using his ability for *intelligent expression as an aid to straight thinking,* for the two are inseparable. The listener is neither a complacent sponge ready to absorb heedlessly everything he hears; nor is he a stone wall, bristling with preconceived notions, automatically rejecting ideas without giving them a chance to penetrate. He never plays a passive part; his is the role of active collaborator.[2]

The speech In the ordinary affairs of life most oral communication is brief, fragmentary, and impromptu. These qualities are evident in conversation where the speaker, with no time for specific preparation, must determine quickly the relevancy of his remarks to the context. Knowing the complexity both of language and of man forces the realization that effective speaking on all occasions is impossible even for the most brilliant. Human nature is limited.

The most adept speaker, although he may possess unusual natural ability, has not acquired his great skill by chance. Usually he is a man of lively curiosity and varied interests. His expertness in speech is based upon a store of information and upon discriminating judgment of human beings. Although he may never have enrolled in a speech course, somehow he has learned to speak by speaking; he has done a lot of it and he has been doing it a long time. He has developed certain characteristics of mind, and has made certain methods of procedure more or less habitual. His expert control is a mark of his maturity.

Being realistic, we cannot expect a high degree of competence from all those enrolled in our English classes. We can, however, give the student specific methods for attacking the problems of oral communication; if the principles and practices are sound, those motivated to perfect the skill can, over the six-year period, acquire a reasonable degree of effectiveness in the use of oral language.

[2] For suggestions for teaching listening, see Chapter 4, pp. 182-211.

The communication

An effective communication—whether a long speech or a contribution to a conversation—has certain characteristics. The speaker has an *idea* important to him and, he hopes, important to the listener. This idea, whether expressed in one sentence or in many, is *ordered in intelligible form.* Automatically, the competent speaker uses and the listener expects the patterns inherent in the language. However, a well-ordered idea is not yet communication. If thoughts and feelings are to be shared, the listener's needs and the skills of expression assume importance. The gifted but inarticulate employee with an idea the head of the firm would welcome; the learned specialist, world famous but unable to hold an expectant audience—these are individuals equipped with ideas and probably able to organize them but lacking the power to *communicate.* These factors of communication, as they pertain to the classroom, are considered in the following sections: selecting material, organizing material, communicating the ideas.

SELECTING MATERIAL [3]

The student is often convinced he has nothing worthwhile to say. Sent forth on his own to try to find material, something with the dignity and the importance the classroom seems to demand, he will go directly to a magazine, or worse yet to an encyclopedia, and come back with a poorly digested, pallid imitation of the original. Reports based solely on library research have their place, but the teacher cannot depend upon them to develop oral skill—certainly not with beginners. Unless the reporter is proficient in speaking, his attention will be on content rather than on *communicating ideas.* Students, within the storehouses of their own experience, have a wealth of subjects on which they can speak; they need help in selecting suitable ones. The teacher must let them know he is not necessarily expecting from them accounts of world shaking events or opinions on international problems. The things he likes to hear from them concern themselves—what they have done, what they would like to do, what pleases them, what annoys them, what frightens them; in short, what they know, think, and feel about this, that, and the other as it impinges upon their lives.

General sources of material Most pupils can be taught to make brief, carefully prepared speeches. However, such learning should operate as a means to a larger end; the ultimate aim is to acquire attitudes and skills which will make communication effective in the impromptu situations of most daily speaking. On such occasions, as well as on those allowing preparation for an organized speech, the material comes from the same general sources—thinking, listening, observation, personal experience, and reading. One characteristic of the expert speaker is his awareness of the worth of all experience as possible grist

[3] See Chapter 10, pp. 485-541.

for the conversational mill. In finding topics suitable for classroom work, the teacher helps students tap those sources, helps them realize that all facets of both direct and vicarious experience furnish the raw material one adapts to one's own purpose in using language.

Material for the classroom One cannot learn to speak effectively without some writing; precision in diction and in organizing ideas demands the use of pencil and paper. One cannot generate and clarify ideas if he depends solely on direct experience; he must read. Conversely, discussion aids both writing and comprehension. Thus, the teacher is being realistic and economical in directing learning when he fuses these activities in the classroom. The literature studied and the books for individual reading offer many ideas to challenge students; both are indispensable for teaching oral skills. In addition, students should have a chance to explore problems of vital concern which they themselves choose. These three sources furnish ample material to teach both the skills needed for orderly discussion and the techniques required for organized speech.

ORGANIZING MATERIAL

The principles of organizing material are the same whether one is taking part in a discussion or a conversation, preparing a speech, or writing expository prose. Identical for the novice and for the expert, they are controlled by three basic rules: Make assertions capable of development, support adequately assertions made, create an over-all design by arranging assertions in a meaningful pattern.* In informal communication, although no one individual makes the over-all pattern, his sensitivity to its need helps him contribute to it. Repetitions, irrelevancies, and belated references to points already covered cannot be avoided. Ideas do not come strait-jacketed and in military precision; too close adherence to any pattern dampens spontaneity and restricts the flow of thought. However, sensitivity to order, an aim of most classroom instruction, is a characteristic both of the good conversationalist and the effective platform speaker. In conversation, as in more formal types of oral communication, all three principles apply.

Making assertions Before we are ready to make a statement we intend to support, we have to be sure the scope of the topic is narrow enough to be covered in the time at our disposal. For the student in the ordinary English class this always means a small area, whether he is to speak for a minute in discussion or longer before a group. Situations in daily life—interviews, committee meetings, sustained conversations—demand the same directness and economy. The give-and-take of informal communication implies that the speaker states a fact or expresses a point of view to which he expects a response; if chal-

* Students understand the need to apply these rules in organizing a speech; they require help in perceiving the relevancy of all, and especially of the third, to discussion and conversation.

lenged, he should be ready to give evidence—cite events, incidents, reasons—to win the listener's acceptance. Moreover, anyone aware of the nature of communication is sensitive to the danger of monopolizing, to the need for giving everyone a chance to speak. Practice in making significant statements capable of support in a short time prepares the student for much of the oral communication he uses in daily life.

Supporting assertions The student tends to rely too heavily on generalizations, on bald statements of opinion, often confused in his mind with fact. He must learn that support is needed for assertions in any form of communication. He can see the need for amplification most easily in speech, where the listener must keep pace with the speaker; where an idea, to be understood, accepted, and remembered, must be built up with the specific. The support of single assertions is the most useful aspect of organization to teach all pupils. Indeed it is the only one possible with those strictly limited in the capacity for sensing more complex relationships.

The necessity for concreteness in developing statements, for helping the listener visualize, is an important idea for pupils to assimilate. Therefore, the use of illustrations and examples to amplify ideas should receive considerable stress. The more capable students, however, should attempt to secure variety in the kinds of material used for support; most of the problems they themselves select to explore demand the ability to discriminate between facts and alleged facts; between sound, unbiased authority and incompetent or prejudiced.[4] Using different kinds of material—facts, illustrations, testimony—in their own communications teaches students the difficulties involved in assessing each and the contribution each can make to the total context.

The accomplished speaker is discriminating; he seeks to vary his material, using just enough of each kind to accomplish his purpose—facts to give substance, illustrations to enliven, and testimony to add emphasis.

Creating the design To create an over-all design, the speaker must arrange assertions in a meaningful pattern. The ability to see correct relationships among ideas underlies all forms of purposeful communication and of sustained thought.[5] Because a speech appears to the student less tangible than an essay, he is likely to accept the need for a preliminary outline as more imperative here than in his written compositions. In preparing for oral work he has an opportunity to practice outlining step by step, eventually persuading himself of its usefulness in both speaking and listening. This knowledge can then be applied to his writing and reading.

Building the outline for a speech is somewhat similar to building the framework for a house. First, the central idea sentence (CIS),[6] the foundation which

[4] See Chapter 1, pp. 37-45 and Chapter 2, pp. 97-98.

[5] See "Teaching a thinking skill within a unit," pp. 667-71.

[6] These names are arbitrarily assigned to the statements representing the three steps to be recommended in teaching the plan for a speech: The central idea sentence (CIS) controls

defines the form and the limits, is constructed. After that come the topic sentences (TS), the skeleton framework for the entire structure. Finally, the subtopic sentences (STS), the details of each section, are fashioned. The completed design of a speech and that of a house are also similar, for both have a psychological as well as a logical aspect. Logically, the plan of each shows the relation of parts to each other and that of each to the whole. Psychologically, both take into account that the finished product is being designed for human beings whose particular needs and interests must be considered. Therefore, the best plans are made by speakers or architects who, aware of the demands of the material and of the persons for whom the structure is intended, create both logical and psychological designs.

Although pupils have had experience with outlining in elementary school, they must receive instruction throughout the secondary school years as well. As thinking grows more complex, outlining becomes more difficult. Each outline presents a fresh problem in the organization of thought. The *form*—the conventions of numbering and lettering—can be reviewed in very little time. The student needs to know, first, that the visual outline is made to help the memory after the reasoning process has determined the logical relationship of ideas, hence the form is important because it shows these relationships quickly. Numbers and letters are guideposts and should be placed so they can be seen at a glance. If cluttered with words above and below, they are no more use to the reader than are traffic signs obscured by weeds to the motorist. Secondly, the student needs to know that an outline, made for any one of many purposes, is always as brief as is consistent with usefulness; it contains a great deal in a little space. In short, the student should see the outline primarily as an exercise in thinking, and after that as a succinct and helpful recording of the thought.

After students understand the principles governing organization, learning experiences should consist of making written plans for most prepared talks. The plan then becomes not an isolated activity but a means of organizing thought for a definite objective—effective speech.

COMMUNICATING THE IDEAS

The aspects of expression previously discussed are concerned with preparation—having something to say and organizing it to have meaning for the listener. The ideas still have to be communicated. The teacher can aid the student best by placing him in a situation in which he feels reasonably secure; by letting him know that the aim is not to make a perfect speech each time but to acquire gradually skills to improve his control in all social situations; by helping him realize that the ultimate objective of this instruction is to develop a command of language enabling him to speak effectively without specific preparation—to use language on those many occasions when he is called

the organization of the entire speech; the topic sentences (TS) state the main ideas used to support CIS; the sub-topic sentences (STS) are statements of the facts, illustrations, testimony, used to amplify TS. The teacher will use whatever terminology will aid the student.

upon to answer questions, give directions, engage in the informal talk so much a part of daily living.

Extempore method of delivery The extempore method of delivery—a method where content and order of ideas have been prepared, but the words and sentence patterns come "out of the time"—gives the best practice for impromptu speaking. Speaking extemporaneously, one may or may not use notes; that too depends upon circumstances. If at all possible, it is better from the very beginning to accustom the student to speaking without this prop, for sooner or later it has to be removed. If the teacher maintains the right atmosphere and gives time for adequate preparation of a limited idea, notes should not be needed.

Qualities of delivery What qualities of delivery should be stressed? In the beginning with most classes they should be non-technical and minimal. Since he can acquire skill only by speaking, the first objective is to get the student to like to speak; once that is accomplished, it is comparatively easy to guide him in attaining higher standards. If attention is kept mainly on content, suggestions for improvement in delivery can be postponed. Examples of good practices should, however, be pointed out. Young people might well concentrate on these desirable traits: audibility, intelligibility, directness, and vitality. A simple guide helps both listener and speaker.

- Can the speaker be easily understood?
  - Does he use the necessary volume?
  - Does he enunciate clearly?
- Can his speech be easily followed?
  - Is his plan apparent?
  - Does he omit extraneous details?
- Is his manner direct?
  - Does he meet the eyes of the listener?
  - Does he seem to be talking *with* the audience?
  - Does he seem straightforward and sincere?
- Does he show vitality?
  - Does his voice have sufficient energy?
  - Does he seem to think what he is saying is important both to him and to his listener?

Only after the student has gained a degree of assurance—and sometimes not even then—should his attention be called in private conference to distracting mannerisms of body, voice, and expression. Moreover, many nervous habits disappear as soon as the speaker is sure of himself. When progress is discernible, additional objectives may be added.

Practice in finding, organizing, and communicating ideas for specific purposes should help the student gain confidence. But even more, it helps him acquire skills preparing him for those informal social situations where his only allies are his general background of information, his knowledge of human nature, and his habitual ways with language.

Discussion

The oral skills program stresses *communication* and therefore *consecutive* discourse. In daily classroom discourse the teacher should distinguish sharply between the oral quiz and discussion. In the first the student speaks not because he wishes to communicate but because he must present evidence that he remembers items the teacher already knows. His contributions consist for the most part of disconnected words, phrases, or sentences. In discussion, *ideas* are important, and the participant has a chance to develop those he favors and to challenge those he thinks untenable. His information and opinions do not drop into a void, but elicit response. Even though in large classes lack of time prevents a single participant's making lengthy remarks, he should in any well-conducted discussion see the unity and development of the whole. The oral quiz has its place in the classroom, but both teacher and student should see its purpose as other than the promotion of oral skill.

Discussion defined Continued experience throughout the secondary school years should help students see discussion for what it is—a learning device through which everyone contributes a little and where each learns from all. They should see it, first, as a means of thinking together to bring out the facts, the possible interpretations, and the different points of view on any particular question; second, as a process of reasoning to determine what tentative conclusions can be drawn from these facts and judgments.

Discussion is not a debate where the speaker sets out to prove he is right and those who disagree with him are wrong. It in no way resembles a lecture or a monologue. It is not quibbling over facts; they can be verified. It is not the bald statement of opinions without support. The aim of discussion is not always to find an answer; it may be merely to explore the various aspects of a topic. Often, however, the purpose is to find a solution to a problem or to reach a decision affecting all members. Although the result may not be entirely satisfactory to anyone, and some may completely disapprove, consideration of the issues as a preliminary to formulating plans for group action is the recognized mode of operation for free men in a free society.

Role of discussion leader A discussion is an experience in group thinking. If it is to accomplish its purpose, the leader must assume a twofold responsibility—to help the participants explore the implications of the content and to conduct this exploration so the result will represent the best thinking of the entire group. If students are to learn the requisite skills, they must be concerned with more than tacit acceptance of the conclusions reached; they must be aware of the procedure used and play their individual parts in making that procedure effective. In leading, the teacher strives for both interplay of ideas and involvement of as many contributors as possible—throwing opinions of one participant to another for reaction, calling for summaries at strategic points, tactfully halting one disposed to talk too long, encouraging the reluctant with appropriate questions. In evaluating discussions, he calls attention to procedures demonstrated. Thus he helps students understand that both process and product are important, that both logical and psychological aspects are significant.

Transfer of skills The principles of effective speaking can perhaps best be taught through short talks prepared individually. Teachers must then help students see that the same rules apply to discussion; after students have learned the importance of the controlling sentence in their own speeches, let them determine a governing sentence for a discussion just completed; after they have studied support of assertions, ask them for examples of statements which have been adequately developed. Before starting a discussion, briefly review the concepts taught through individual speeches and suggest that students try to put them into practice. In evaluating, try to draw from the class ways individuals have used effective speech, whether in selection of content, awareness of organization, or clear and forceful presentation.

The similarity between discussion and conversation may not be apparent to pupils. The teacher should help them realize that skills of oral communication can serve them in places other than the classroom. Questions similar to the following may act as springboards for discussions emphasizing the desirability of capitalizing on abilities being developed. Has anyone used an illustration to amplify a point made in conversation? Heard a statement which the speaker when challenged could not support? A conversation where misunderstanding arose because of imprecise use of language? Do you know anyone who refuses to stick to the point? Anyone who bores a listener with unimportant details? In some such way, teachers can keep re-emphasizing the idea that the same principles underlie effectiveness in formal and informal speech.

The group process

Today the interdependence of men demands that each person participate in many groups; productive participation requires of him the ability to work with those groups of which he is a member as well as to accept the coexistence of others to which he does not belong. Experience in the English classroom can aid him in developing the necessary insights and skills. On the first day of almost any class the student finds himself in a large group; he may be associated with one of several cliques or sub-groups; he may be completely isolated. One of the teacher's first tasks is to weld the class into something resembling solidarity—necessary both for morale and for learning. With widely heterogeneous classes this welding process can rarely be accomplished except through the formation of many small units within the class as a whole, the personnel of each group periodically changing. Thus, the teacher can make it possible for the contribution of each student to be recognized, for him to be accepted as a participating member of the class. Through group efforts, as students learn the content of the course, they can improve the skills needed for working in any social group.[7]

From the student's viewpoint Most students recognize the desirability of becoming more adept in group participation. Some, highly grade-conscious, may at first be fearful their contributions will not receive due credit; they will be reassured if they understand that individual learning is still the focus, although accomplished through group effort. During adolescence, a time of confusion and ambivalence, the student is trying to learn his role both as an individual and as a group member; peer approval is probably more important now than at any other period of his life. Classroom experience can help him find himself as he gains skill in working with others; consideration of divergent viewpoints can deepen his understanding of those whose backgrounds differ from his own. Thus, he becomes more aware of the social significance of the group process. He knows or can learn that most of the world's problems, if they reach solution, are solved around the conference table—the importance of the committee work of congressional leaders, the significance, in settling labor disputes, of discussion among representatives of various factions. The realization that he is learning skills to use not only in the classroom but in life convinces him of the practicality of learning better ways of working with others.

From the teacher's viewpoint The advantages for the teacher in using the group method are far-reaching in their import. Since each member can contribute according to his capacity, this type of instruction allows teachers to take care of particular interests and needs, to accept the student as he is and to help him progress at his own rate toward his potential goals. Moreover, the interaction of minds, one of the salient characteristics of group work, provides a stimulation that can be gained in no other way.[8] Above all, because this plan creates a situation comparable to those met in life, it lends itself to many of the objectives in education. Working in small groups, the more capable need not adjust his pace to the less competent; the slowest, the most diffident, the most inarticulate, can be placed in an environment where he can be taught to function. Group work gives experiences in leading and following; it affords opportunities to think through problems under peer and teacher guidance; it furnishes small, realistic audiences for the student's attempts at expression, where he may learn to evaluate his own opinions and those of others. Teachers who use the group method find it pays big dividends.

Helping young people acquire oral skills asks from the teacher a hard head and a soft heart. In an atmosphere of free inquiry where students know they

[7] Jean D. Grambs, *Group Processes in Intergroup Education* (N.Y., National Conference of Christians and Jews, n.d.), pp. 9-24.

[8] See, in T. M. Newcomb and E. L. Hartley, eds., *Readings in Social Psychology* (N.Y., Holt, 1947): Marjorie E. Shaw, "A Comparison of Individual and Small Groups in the Rational Solution of Complex Problems," pp. 314, 315; and Ronald Lippitt and R. K. White, "An Experimental Study of Leadership and Group Life," pp. 315-329.

can say what they think but realize their opinions require support; where they recognize that proficiency demands practice over a long period of time; where both speaker and listener accept responsibility for making communication effective—in such an atmosphere the individual can develop both the habit of using language honestly and the skills for using it effectively.

THE TEACHING PROBLEM

Because oral communication is so frequent, because it pervades everyday experience, a multitude of situations exist for teaching. This very multiplicity presents both an opportunity and a problem: an opportunity, because as soon as students understand the purpose of instruction, most see the desirability of becoming more adept in handling a tool they use so widely; a problem, because a program must be devised to encourage transfer of attitudes and skills developed in the classroom to the varied social situations the individual encounters daily.

Organizing Instruction

In organizing instruction, the teacher asks himself questions similar to these: What problems can be anticipated? What content is appropriate? What particular skills are to be emphasized? What methods will produce the best results? These questions are not discrete, nor can the suggested answers be; all interact with one another. However, problems of organizing instruction are considered in the following sections: establishing a climate to promote growth; selecting content; emphasizing principles underlying effective speaking; using discussion; using the group method.

Establishing a climate to promote growth

Several basic problems, inherent in the nature of oral communication and thus pertaining to a climate conducive to the development of appropriate attitudes and skills, require initial consideration.

Finding the necessary time Students cannot learn to speak without speaking; if the skills of this week are to build on those of last, practice must be continual. Thus, if the teacher is dedicated to a program stressing individual speeches to which the whole class listens, he is defeated before he starts. Time is not available to build the necessary attitudes and skills in this way. Two time-saving methods have been proposed—discussion and group work. The teacher has to convince himself he can provide instruction enabling pupils to speak better if he places them in situations where they can gain confidence; although he divides his time as best he can, he does not have to listen to every speech and every group discussion.

Using the course content as the major source of material also saves time. For instance, ideas gleaned from the study of several short stories can provide practice in applying the principles of effective speaking if process, as well as content, is emphasized in discussion. Likewise, skills demanded for making a speech plan can be used in writing if students are helped to effect the transfer. Integration of all areas of instruction, helping students see the unity and relationship among the various aspects of the English program, not only promotes learning but is economical of classroom time.

Providing practice for all In apportioning time to give the most practice to the greatest number, the teacher considers the problems of both the glib and the unwilling. Instruction stressing improvement through genuinely motivated communication, in contrast to aimless talk, is basic to solving the problems of each. The excessively vocal must learn what communication means; he must be taught to channel his fluency—a real asset—for conciseness and pertinence; he must recognize that for him cultivating responsiveness as a listener may be more important than speaking upon every question.

The shy and unwilling presents a greater problem. The teacher tries to discover the reasons for his attitude. Undoubtedly, individuals differ in degree of articulateness and in the pleasure they derive from conversation; however, all have the need to communicate. If placed in situations where this need can be satisfied, they will acquire the necessary skills. The seeming aversion to speech *in the classroom* cuts across all levels of maturity and intelligence. Fear of exposure is one cause; the individual may have been conditioned in classrooms giving sole importance to the right answer and to correct usage. Reluctance may be induced by a feeling of superiority, often unconscious; the situation may seem so purposeless as to make meditation more profitable than attempts to contribute. Placing those inclined to talk too much and those forever silent in situations where they have the desire and opportunity for honest communication is crucial. Use of discussion in small groups offers a partial solution; allowing students some voice in selecting content helps; finally, the correction of mistaken ideas concerning *purposes* of the program and methods of evaluating improvement and thus of *determining grades* promotes a climate conducive to growth.

Explaining purpose and scope Failure to recognize the purpose and scope of the oral skills program partially accounts for the attitude of those unconvinced of its value. The first weeks of any English course, when needs are diagnosed, goals explored, and standards agreed upon, provide opportunity to promote desirable understandings. The student is likely to equate speech as taught in the classroom with that of the accomplished speaker addressing an audience. Perhaps he has been in classes where the only oral work considered grade-worthy consisted of reports based on research and given for "extra credit." Unaware of any objective except expertness in "public" speaking, he may reject the program because he cannot see himself as a platform speaker.

One of the first discussions in any school year might well be concerned with leading students to realize that one major purpose of oral communication is to help the individual exercise a degree of control in the social situation. What follows is a skeletal plan for such a discussion, with irrelevancies and digressions omitted.[9] Although many discussions result in tentative or alternate conclusions, here the teacher has decided beforehand what the result is to be, but only because it seems so obvious as to be inescapable. Even with only one conclusion possible, helping students think through the steps increases their understanding of the problem and prepares for acceptance of the inevitability of the conclusion.

In this abridged version the minor ideas leading to the major conclusion are italicized. As each is reached, it may be written on the board. This teaching device helps students see that each discussion has purpose and pattern.

A discussion leading to an understanding of the purpose and scope of the oral skills program might go something like this:

> How have you used speech recently?
>
> Talking with friends, shopping, meeting in committees, explaining to the repairman what's wrong with the TV, talking with my family around the dinner table, asking my father for an increased allowance, planning a party, asking for a date . . .
>
> How have you used writing?
>
> Note to a friend, letter to my aunt, list for the laundry, assignment in English . . .
>
> Which do most people use more, writing or speaking?
>
> Speaking.
>
> Yes, most people speak more than they write. This has always been true. There are many things we don't know about the origins of language, but one thing scholars agree upon is that it appeared first in its spoken form and existed in only that form for centuries. Today *spoken language is the most widespread form.*
>
> In telling how you used speech, no one mentioned a type of experience I've had many times—speaking before a group. Has no one had that experience? Is it so uncommon?
>
> Yes and no. It depends upon the person, his situation, and his work.
>
> Certainly, by far *the greatest part of our speaking takes place in informal situations.* But even if you're sure you'll never stand before a group and speak, is there anything we can learn from practice of more formal speaking that might help us use speech effectively even on informal occasions? What are some of the things you'd like your speech to tell about you?
>
> That I'm not afraid, that I know what I'm talking about, that I can make people understand, that I'm a person worth knowing, that I'm able to express my own opinion . . .

[9] Other examples of discussion sequence are given in this text. See *Johnny Tremain,* pp. 76-78.

Is it enough just to express your opinion? Don't you have to do more than that? What if your listener differs? What do you do then?

Tell him why I think the way I do.

You've mentioned self-confidence, poise, clarity and effectiveness of the statement, impression on the listener, support of an idea . . . Are these much different from the characteristics of an effective speaker and speech on more formal occasions?

No, *similar principles underlie effective use of language in both formal and informal situations.*

All the speech occasions we've mentioned have concerned more than one person, as they always do. In other words they're social. What elements do we find in every social situation?

Speaker, listener.

Isn't there another, equally important? How do speaker and listener get together, if they ever do?

By speech.

We can agree that *any social situation has three elements: speaker, speech, and listener.* This is true whether the communication is formal or informal; speech is the instrument which allows sender and receiver to understand each other. In attempted communication does understanding always result? Have you ever asked directions for reaching a certain place, received them, and then found you couldn't follow them? What was wrong?

The speaker did not know or did not explain clearly; the listener did not listen carefully or did not interpret correctly.

Yes, the fault may lie with either or both. When language creates confusion—when you can't follow directions—speech does not accomplish its purpose. Besides confusion, what other unpleasant effects can language have?

It can irritate, antagonize, arouse contempt, make a person unsure of himself . . .

Then we could say, couldn't we, that *speech may either bring persons closer together or drive them farther apart?* If two persons in any situation really want to establish satisfactory contact, what must each do? For instance, I'm giving an assignment, you're talking to a friend. What must each of us do?

The speaker considers the listener, presents ideas clearly, watches the reaction, adds additional explanation when necessary; the listener remains alert, tries to understand, responds actively.

We'll come back to this point often during the semester. Now let's leave it and see if we can pin down the speaker's purpose a little more exactly. What were you trying to do on those occasions you gave as examples of speech used recently?

To get the TV fixed, to make the date, to enjoy our friends, to persuade my father . . .

In every social situation there is something we are trying to do. Let's try to find a general statement that will cover all purposes of speech on all occasions. Help me fill in this sentence: The purpose of speech is to help us ______ the social situation. We're looking for verbs now. Suggest some. We'll find out what they mean and which is more exact.

Dominate, control, govern, adapt to, change, adjust to, withdraw from . . .

We might want to do any one of these on some particular occasion, but have we any words here which include some of the others?

Control, adapt to.

If we qualify "control" and use instead "exercise a certain degree of control," would that help? What is the difference in the connotation of the two terms? For now, let's accept *the purpose of speech is to help us exercise a degree of control in the social situation.* You check all the work we do in speech against this purpose; if later we find it doesn't fit, we'll change it.

In the above illustration, the teacher definitely tried to direct the thinking toward one certain conclusion. However, the framework given is not the discussion, which would never proceed with such clockwork precision; it would not be a discussion if it did. A teacher's integrity demands that he drive for one certain decision only when no other seems possible. Presumably, he would not lead such a discussion if he did not think the conclusion broad enough to include all forms of oral communication and, therefore, any specific example a student could give. If he had encountered any unforeseen evidence that did not fit, he would have had no choice but to qualify his preconceived conclusion. A procedure that brings out all phases of a topic and admits objections and counter arguments, even if it leads to one inevitable result, is an expression of a democratic principle. It is the duty of the teacher to lead students through the thinking that will convince them of its inevitability.

Establishing bases for grading A second misunderstanding arises because in many classrooms progress is evaluated mainly on ability to write and to pass tests proving knowledge. Thus when a student returns after absence and is moved to ask if he has missed anything, he is not disparaging the teacher's ability to maintain a scintillating classroom. What he really wants to know is whether there has been a written assignment, now represented by a blank space after his name in the record book. Grades may not represent a worthy motive for learning. However, they do indicate to both learner and teacher—and to parents, colleges, and employers—an estimate of individual accomplishment. They cannot be ignored; while the teacher avoids using them as incentives, they are facts that must be faced. Students in each particular classroom have a right to know on what bases the grades for the course will be determined. Because of the fluid nature of oral communication, the need for understanding is perhaps greater here than in other areas of English instruction.

Understanding the general purpose of oral communication will prepare students for the many aspects needing emphasis. As each is singled out for instruction, practice, and evaluation, the student comes to realize that his grade depends, not upon his ability to make a finished speech each time, but upon how well he has met specific requirements. In order to help pupils appreciate the firm basis for grading, the teacher should assure them that first assignments will be concerned with only one or two principles—for immature pupils, audibility, or conversational tone, or meeting the eyes of the listener. He must then give them a chance to use these skills in speaking and help them evaluate the results. He should let them know that skill in speech is cumulative, that they will be given time to consolidate their gains.

Fusing with total program In fusing the oral experiences with other phases of instruction, the teacher fits method to content. In general, either problems chosen by students or ideas emerging from books read individually offer the most practical material for teaching the principles governing effective speech and for providing practice for their application in small groups; the content here is largely individual and thus lends itself to short talks. Ideas from the literature studied and synthesis of experiences with either the selected problems or personal reading furnish material for class discussions. Here a mutuality of experience supports the give-and-take of informal communication. No arbitrary division is intended; each teacher experiments to find the methods most suitable for teaching the course content with a particular class.

The teacher also considers the timing of oral work, usually trying to combine speaking with reading and writing so that one experience flows naturally into another. Thus reading may provide ideas for discussion, which in turn gives incentive for writing. The illustrative units furnish many examples. However, when it seems desirable, oral work can be inserted without interrupting the continuity of other curricular activities; the teacher uses a split schedule. By careful planning, he can devote portions of several class hours to experiences stressing oral skills, the rest of the time being spent on other aspects of instruction. (An illustration appears on p. 659.) Several days at the beginning of the year, when teacher and students are exploring the potential of the course, or short interludes at the completion of units offer other possibilities for brief instruction and practice. Oral communication is so much a part of life that opportunities to help students develop the necessary skills present themselves continually.

Selecting content

The problems students face and the information they possess form the foundation upon which skill in oral communication can be built. However, it is often unwise to begin by asking outright what subjects merit discussion. Suspecting a snare presaging dire things to come, some will deny interest in anything. An oblique approach helps counteract this difficulty. Teachers, taking a tip from the pollsters, have found an indirect way to discover what students feel deeply about. The following example will show how one teacher of an eleventh grade class used an opinion poll to find suitable topics and to introduce the techniques of discussion with the aid of group work.

An opinion poll From his observation of the class and from his knowledge of problems that were disturbing faculty and students, although often for different reasons, the teacher made up a list of provocative statements similar to the following:

Opinion poll

Directions: If you strongly agree with the statement, circle SA; agree, A; are undecided, U; disagree, D; strongly disagree, SD.

SA A U D SD 1. Students usually do better work in school when there is close relationship between parents and teachers.
SA A U D SD 2. Too few students in this school have an opportunity to participate in student government.
SA A U D SD 3. High school clubs encourage snobbishness.
SA A U D SD 4. Students should have a part in determining regulations governing student conduct.
SA A U D SD 5. This class should be so organized that homework will be unnecessary.
SA A U D SD 6. School parties and dances cost so much that many students are unable to attend.

The teacher introduced the subject by saying he knew certain problems connected with school affairs seemed of concern to many. Thus he was temporarily assuming the role of Mr. Gallup to determine how the class as a whole felt about them. As in all such surveys the identity of the participant was unimportant; no names were to be signed. He gave no hint that the exercise was more than a slight detour to satisfy the curiosity of an eccentric instructor.

The returns seemed to indicate many of these controversial questions were of vital concern to students. Probably because the community was being agitated by some parents who wanted an increase of homework, this topic provoked the most decided reactions. The students, however, were disinclined to make any concessions to unreasonable adults; over two-thirds said they believed the class should be conducted so that no homework would be necessary.

When the class arrived the next day, they found the statement concerning homework on the board with a tabulation of the opinions expressed; fifteen strongly agreed; ten agreed; eleven disagreed; no one was undecided. The teacher said that since this was a question affecting all of them, it had better be discussed; that although he could make no promises, he would consider seriously any conclusions reached by the class. Accordingly, he was dividing them into groups for the purpose of discussion.

Bringing his knowledge of his students to bear, he had previously determined the personnel of the groups, placing, as he thought, two dissident members in each. Before taking their places the students were asked to jot down reasons for their opinion, not to hand in but to use to help group thinking. The written reports from the secretaries were to indicate the number advocating each point of view and the reasons accepted as valid support. They were allowed ten minutes. Wishing to leave the student free to express himself honestly without fear of incrimination, the teacher ignored the discussions, a procedure which cannot often be employed with group work.

As was to be expected, the reports were similar; all indicated that the students had difficulty finding support for their opinions. Substantiation for both viewpoints was based on lack of time, but with a difference. Those favoring homework did so because there was not time in class to complete assignments; those opposing, because there was not time outside of class.

Both opinions seemed to have a basis in fact. Previous estimates of the average time per day spent outside the classroom in preparing for English ranged from two who spent none to three who spent over an hour and a half. The teacher's records showed that about one-fourth of the students were employed in part-time jobs, about one-half were carrying heavy academic loads, about one-third were active in the extracurricular program; a few could be placed in all three categories.

Taking into consideration the caliber of his students and trying to anticipate objections, the teacher prepared carefully for the next day's discussion. His purpose was twofold: to devise a practical plan for accomplishment of the essential aims of the course and to lead students to see their responsibility for facing facts honestly. The problem seemed to revolve around the following questions: To what extent are the reasons given for the opinions valid? What do we need to know before we can come to a decision which will affect the group? Where can we get additional information?

The teacher wished students to realize the demands imposed by the course, the necessity for considering their own problems as individuals, the need for evaluating their study habits and for budgeting their time. He therefore attempted to find the questions and examples which would help him direct the thinking along lines logically and psychologically sound—facts he hoped would lead to the conclusion that everyone, in school or out, faced the responsibility of planning for himself a realistic program.

The next day he began by reviewing quickly the aims of the course and what had been accomplished to date. He then read a news item in which a representative of a labor union, currently negotiating for certain benefits, tried to justify the demands. The reliability of the writer as an authority was briefly discussed, the class deciding that he could be accepted only with reservations as bias had to be suspected. Most of the students were, of course, well aware where such an admission was leading.

After these preliminaries, the teacher proceeded with the discussion, selecting questions from the following, *when and if they seemed pertinent:*

Previous assignments

Have they been excessive? Suggestions for curtailment?

Should a teacher always give identical assignments for all students? Why?

What type of work for English do you prefer to do in class? Outside?

What are the advantages of long-term assignments? Difficulties?

Study habits

According to your own estimates, the amount of time spent in preparation for this class varies widely. How do you account for this?

Is it possible for two students, equally intelligent, to spend the same amount of time and produce results of different quality? Reasons?

What are some of the characteristics of a study period if the time is to be spent profitably?

Does the time that you reported spending on English represent that much time in concentrated effort?

How many of you know specific ways that you could improve your study habits?

Budgeting time

How many are taking subjects that require less preparation time than English? More? How many feel that their general schedule is too heavy?

How do you apportion your time among several assignments? Let's say you have problems to work and turn in for mathematics and a story to read for English. You think the two should take an hour; you have only half that time. How do you proceed?

Some people with charge accounts at several stores, finding at the end of the month they can't take care of all of them, pay a little on each in order to maintain credit. What do you think of this plan? Is there any similarity between maintaining credit at the store and at school?

You may have read articles which express alarm at the credit situation in the country as a whole. Some writers seem to think that too many people, buying on time, contract debts which they will never be able to pay. Suppose for the moment this is true. Why do you think people become so involved? Is it unavoidable? Under what circumstances?

In planning your schedule, do you have any responsibility for seeing that it is one you can handle?

Summary of tentative conclusions

Preparation for final discussion

Magazines have devoted quite a bit of space recently to the question of homework. Would some of you be willing to consult the *Reader's Guide,* look up an article, and report?

Do any of you know someone whose opinion on homework—reasonable amount of time, system, etc.—might be worth having? A teacher who is able to organize his course so that all the work can be done in class? A student who has a good plan? How about getting the opinion of your counselor? Parents? Do you know anyone in no way connected with the school—a business or professional man—you could consult?

Assignment: This day next week we'll finish discussing this problem and see if we can come to some sound conclusions. At that time we'll hear reports from volunteers; there will also be time for other information anyone else may find either from reading or interviewing.

As a result of the final discussion, the teachers and students arrived at the following conclusions:

Two hours a week was not an excessive amount of time to devote to homework for English.

Long-term assignments would help, especially if some system of intermediate checking were devised to insure that work was progressing at an acceptable rate.

The most desirable type of homework was that connected with reading and individual projects.

There should be two types of assignments—one required of all, the other where the student had some choice.

Although, most assuredly, not all students will comply with regulations set up in this way, the fact that they have followed the argument step by step makes them more ready to accede to demands which have seemed reasonable to the majority.

The entire experience required little class time; it showed that many kinds of learning may take place concurrently. In less than three periods the teacher had given all a chance to talk, both in group and class discussion, had helped them face and think through a problem of vital concern, had made provision for volunteers to interview, to read, and to report the results; he had, without mentioning oral skills, laid the foundation upon which a sound program for developing oral skills could be built.

Furthermore, the poll seemed to indicate that other subjects on the list might be worth investigating. The results of the poll were, therefore, given to a student committee to discover which of the five remaining topics had aroused most vigorous response. Their report follows:

	SA	A	U	D	SD
1	0	0	0	20	16
2	10	5	9	2	10
3	12	10	2	2	10
4	14	3	0	11	8
6	0	6	20	10	0

Through class discussion, the first topic was immediately discarded. The other four seemed to have something in common. With some rewording and organization, the teacher and class arrived at the following plan. If students could make their own regulations what would they suggest should be done about 1) securing wider participation in student government? 2) putting membership and activities of clubs on a more democratic basis? 3) planning parties and dances to appeal to greater numbers? The class was divided into three groups, each to investigate one aspect of the problem. The procedure followed was substantially the same as in the preceding experience. The discussion resulted in an editorial written by a student committee and published in the school paper. However, the greatest benefit probably derived from the fact that these young people were able to consider all phases of the problem and both participants and non-participants in school activities had a chance to see themselves through the eyes of the other.

A simple questionnaire The above plan can be used in many junior high classes; even seventh-graders who have had similar experiences in elementary school may be capable of the sustained attention such procedures demand; however, many immature pupils are not. For these, a simpler form of questionnaire with fewer follow-up activities is suggested.

Directions: Please check in the proper column; do not sign your name. Have you recently discussed with any member of your family or any of your friends

Yes______ No______ 1. Grades you've received in school subjects?
Yes______ No______ 2. Your choice of friends?
Yes______ No______ 3. Time you have to be in at night?
Yes______ No______ 4. Length of your telephone conversations?
Yes______ No______ 5. Number and selection of movies you are permitted?
Yes______ No______ 6. Choice of or time spent on television programs?
Yes______ No______ 7. The books you are reading?
Yes______ No______ 8. Comic books?
Yes______ No______ 9. Time spent on homework?
Yes______ No______ 10. Your allowance?

Since younger pupils often cannot sustain the continuity of discussions over an extended period, two other methods allowing for more immediate follow-up of the questionnaire will be illustrated. Both methods—role playing and demonstration—should be preceded with a brief discussion to bring out the facts fundamental to the problem.

Role playing Role playing is a term applied to an extemporaneous dramatization of a social situation involving conflict, with an attempt to suggest a solution.[10] It differs from similar dramatizations made from stories children have read in that here the plot is not ready made; the situation delineates a problem students face and for which they try to find alternative answers. Scripts are not written; a general plan of presentation is agreed upon—the main ideas, the role of each character, the direction the dialogue will take, etc. After the general plan is agreed upon, lines are spoken impromptu.[11]

Suppose the television problem has been selected for dramatization; the following situations might be chosen.

Three children with different interests, each wanting priority with the TV, discuss their respective claims.

[10] See also Chapter 3, "Imaginative Thinking," pp. 143-44.

[11] See George Shaftel and Fannie R. Shaftel, *Role Playing the Problem Story* (N.Y., National Conference of Christians and Jews, 1952). Although many examples concern elementary pupils, the principles underlying the approach apply to the secondary level as well. See also Hilda Taba, *Curriculum in Intergroup Relations for Secondary Schools* (Washington, D.C., American Council on Education, 1949), an analysis of sociodrama enlivened with concrete examples.

Four parents discuss crime programs, giving different points of view regarding the effect on young people.

Several students evaluate different kinds of programs, assessing their value as entertainment.

The same situation is used by several groups and the solutions compared. The discussion of the various interpretations of the problem is often the most significant part of the experience, pointing up, as it may, examples of straight thinking, tact, or thoughtful consideration of opposing viewpoints.

In preparing for role playing, the participants should answer such questions as: What is the attitude of each character? What are the reasons for this attitude? What action follows logically from this attitude? What are the effects of the action on the other characters? What changes are to occur as the dramatization unfolds? How are these changes to be brought about?

For the first experience in role playing it is well for the teacher to lead the class through the preliminaries—helping pupils define the problem, select the situation to be used, analyze possible attitudes and action—and then to accept volunteers for the performance.

Demonstrations Sometimes the facets of a subject lend themselves to individual demonstrations. Pupils, working in pairs, give their versions of both the correct and incorrect procedure. Since young people can often profit by some attention to telephone manners, such a topic is ideal for demonstrations. List on the board as many examples as students can give of different uses they have made of the telephone. With pertinent questions draw out others that are common. The list might look something like this:

Chatting with a friend
Taking a message for another
Sending a telegram
Placing an emergency call—ambulance, fire department, police
Making a complaint about a mistake in delivery
Ordering several items from a department store
Asking information about planes, trains, and buses
Accepting an invitation
Declining an invitation
Asking for release of party line in order to make a call

Both the demonstrations and the discussions following can emphasize the desirability for clarity, brevity, and courtesy in the use of the telephone.

The use of some kind of poll offers a quick and effective way of discovering some topics of concern to students. Followed by instruction and by practice in applying the principles of effective speaking, such devices provide a basis for extending interests as well as developing attitudes and skills. So too do ideas generated by the literature studied and by the books individuals read. From these three sources the content of the oral communication program may be derived.

Emphasizing principles of effective speaking

In selecting principles of effective speaking to emphasize, the teacher remembers he is trying to develop attitudes toward speaking and habitual methods of procedure. Instruction and practice may focus now on one aspect of content, organization, or delivery, and now on another; thus skills are gradually built.

Graphic presentation of sequence As instruction in oral communication proceeds, graphic presentation can help students concentrate in practice on the various principles studied. They may keep in their notebooks a chart listing each emphasis as it is introduced. Items may first be recorded in their own words; as standards are periodically reviewed, teacher and pupils may reword and reorganize. The completed chart for any class will represent only those aspects of effective speech students have had an opportunity to practice. The one below offers a sample of the beginning of such a chart for a class with little previous instruction. Each of the three horizontal blocks represents the focus for a single assignment. In addition, the individual should try each time to apply all the principles previously listed. Thus in the review speech no new idea would be injected, giving time for synthesis of various skills.

Sequence of emphases

Content	*Organization*	*Delivery*
Interesting to speaker		Easily heard Easily understood
	Beginning that interests Conclusion that clinches idea	
Controlled by purpose		Eye contact with listeners
	Governed by a central idea sentence	Conversational tone

Review speech, demonstrating application of all principles studied

The suggested sequence of emphases—indicated by horizontal blocks—is not intended to dictate an arbitrary order. Since sequence depends upon the experience and the maturity of the class, the order cannot be determined far in advance. Above all it must be flexible, starting with simple objectives students may be expected to achieve in a few attempts and continuing with others added one or, occasionally, two at a time. The teacher proceeds slowly; time is not lost, even if no new principle is introduced, because each repetition builds confidence, which in turn aids in the development of skills. After the teacher has drawn from students what they believe to be the characteristics of effective speaking, the class can decide what to strive for first. With some students, attaining only a few elementary goals may be enough to expect even after six years' practice. With others, each assignment may emphasize several objectives. Even with the capable, however, skill is acquired gradually. Many brief speeches, each concentrating on one or two points, produce better results than a few longer ones trying to incorporate everything.

Additional objectives The chart below suggests further objectives, some of which certainly should be added for many classes or suggested for individuals at the teacher's discretion.

Content	*Organization*	*Delivery*
Interesting to listener	Ideas pertinent	Is straightforward, seems sincere
Few abstractions, many concretions	Support adequate	Speaks with an air of authority without being overly aggressive
Variety in material—facts, illustrations, testimony	Sequence planned to maintain interest	Maintains a pace which makes comprehension easy
Material from several sources	Transitions clear	Maintains posture which does not call attention to itself
Facts accurate	Use of devices to begin and end other than statement and restatement of central idea sentence	Shows vitality
Evidence of originality		Is free from distracting mannerisms
		Uses language both precise and vivid

If the teacher keeps in mind that the second chart lists some objectives suitable only for the mature and gifted, he will avoid pushing pupils to the point of discouragement. If students continue to want to speak, skills can be developed.

Teaching the speech plan In the beginning, even ultimately for many pupils, three steps (I, A, 1) in the outline for the main part of the speech are enough to teach. If the student learns to apply these, he can later learn to deal with more complex material, for the principle is the same. If he cannot understand three-part relationships, it confuses him to be allowed to run the gamut of lettering and numbering denoting intricate points and sub-points; the complex outline should be reserved for the clear thinker working with complicated material. Moreover, three steps should be sufficient for the oral work most students may be asked to do in the English class.

What type of outline is most useful in teaching oral communication? Since the purpose is to help the student form the habit of perceiving exact relationships, *the sentence outline is most effective.* Only this form permits teachers to determine quickly whether the writer is precise in his thinking; the individual conference time demanded for all other types prohibits their use. It is immediately apparent that it is impractical to try to teach this difficult form to the pupil who still has trouble recognizing a sentence; teachers should spend all their efforts on helping him learn to support single assertions.

Even competent students resist making speech plans in sentence form, their chief contention being it takes too long to write the ideas as statements.[12] However, it is the thinking, not the writing, that takes the time. They are also prone to believe they know what they want to say but can't write it. Such a conclusion betrays spurious thinking. Writing gives training in exactness, and repeated practice in ordering one's ideas in a form another can follow fosters clarity of thought and precision of statement. If the student can gain facility in the thinking that even three steps in the sentence outline demands, he has acquired a valuable tool, which becomes more useful as thinking and communication grow more complex.

The beginning and the ending of the prepared talk are difficult for the inexperienced; therefore the student should formulate his introduction and conclusion rather carefully. Because first impressions are likely to either quicken or deaden interest, the first sentence is important. The experienced speaker gets into the main part of his speech as rapidly as the occasion permits, avoiding apologies and details that seem to discredit the listener's intelligence. The ending is equally significant, for it must, by drawing the threads together, leave the listeners with a sense of completeness. The speaker avoids inserting new ideas, drawing out his material, giving repeated warnings of closing. Although a long speech may require recapitulation of the points covered, a general statement clinching the central idea is sufficient for the short talk.

The student, after becoming proficient in building both introduction and conclusion around the restatement of the central idea, may experiment with other types. If pressure of time makes such experimentation impractical, variations can be tried in the writing experiences, for problems of speaker and writer are similar. A series of questions, a pointed anecdote, a vivid description of an apt situation, arouse interest and help lead into the development of speech or essay. A quotation, a word picture strong in sensory appeal, an impressive illustration—anything epitomizing the central idea—make effective conclusions.

Using discussion

Several major problems in using discussion to teach content and develop skills will be considered: preparing to lead, starting effectively, arriving at conclusions democratically, securing variety through different patterns.

PREPARING TO LEAD A DISCUSSION

Guiding group thinking through discussion requires understanding of the implications of content and insight into characteristics of group members.

Considering content Significant questions in a significant order are essential if students are to think their way through content to logical conclusions.

[12] The topical outline is usually sufficient for expository *writing*, since student and teacher can examine the thinking in the complete communication as it assumes permanent form on paper.

No activity requires more careful preparation on the part of the teacher. In considering the implications of content, he must decide: What ultimate conclusions are logical? What minor conclusions build to these? What questions will help students think through each step? If the issues are identified correctly, the success of any discussion depends mainly upon the questions which guide thinking—questions that bring out the facts and probe the reasoning based on those facts.[13] Failure to ask the right questions results, after a period of perhaps enjoyable but aimless conversation, in the more capable students or the teacher telling the class what the facts seem to indicate. Such a failure is serious, for it defeats the main purpose of discussion.

How does the teacher find the right questions? It is not easy. Even when he thinks he has found them, students fail to oblige with the anticipated answers. However, most of the difficulty seems to arise from two closely allied errors: asking, too soon, questions which require an abstract rather than a concrete answer and attempting to skip links in the chain of reasoning. Both these mistakes in strategy force students to take steps for which they are not ready. Conscientious preparation on the teacher's part which, in framing questions, takes into account the students' experience will help eliminate both errors.

Considering group members Since the aim is to involve as many students as possible without detriment to the discussion, the teacher in directing questions gives some thought to the abilities of individuals. Usually the *what*, and sometimes the *how*, questions laying the groundwork for each minor conclusion can be answered by the less able. If the brilliant and vocal are allowed to volunteer this information, no contributions are left for those incapable of abstract thinking. This is not to say the pace should be slowed to accommodate the inarticulate. Teachers have, however, helped the student overcome reluctance in various ways. They have advocated to individuals the wisdom of making remarks early before fear has a chance to take hold. During preliminary study periods they have given time for specific preparation—handing to a pupil a copy of the opening question and telling him he will be called upon first; asking him to listen to initial points and to be ready to give the first summary; letting him select some phase of the topic he feels ready to discuss. Discouraging raised hands until discussion grows controversial and *always when others are speaking* helps create an atmosphere more favorable to participation. In short, considering the strengths and weaknesses of group members can insure more fruitful discussion.

STARTING THE DISCUSSION EFFECTIVELY

Sometimes the beginning of a discussion moves so slowly that most of the allotted time is spent in preliminary skirmishes. Even when students are in possession of the facts, they may not be able to marshal them quickly. Time is lost and interest wanes as participants grope their way, trying to interpret questions, searching for pertinent evidence. Often a short period spent in

[13] See pp. 438-40 for illustration.

preparation with pointed direction to stimulate thinking serves to get the discussion moving fast and purposefully.

Using preliminary groups A brief warming-up session in small groups, with questions to be used later for the entire class, gives students a chance to mobilize their thinking. Such preparatory work bolsters the confidence of the timid, who may be more ready to voice ideas they know have some support; other students whose deductions have been challenged are likely to be eager to prove their thinking correct. Illustrations of preparation for discussions with different purposes and for different levels follow.

Suppose a class of widely varying abilities has read "The Necklace," by Guy de Maupassant. The reader will recall the story of Madame Loisel, who loses a diamond necklace borrowed from a friend, finds a replica to replace it, works all her life to repay the debt incurred by the substitution—only to learn in the end that the lost jewels were paste. In the discussion the teacher's purpose is to lead the class to discover how the author reveals the total meaning by the skillful arrangement of incidents built around particular characters. The teacher prepares questions similar to those here to point the way to the concepts the author develops.

> What do we learn of the character of Mme. Loisel and of her husband from what the author tells us about their actions?
>
> What, from their respective thoughts?
>
> What courses of action were open to Mme. Loisel when she discovered the loss of the jewels? Was the course chosen consistent with her character? Explain.
>
> Would the outcome of the story have been changed if the jewels had been real? Would there have been irony in the story even if Mme. Loisel had never discovered the jewels were paste? Why does the author make the jewels paste? Consider our study of symbolism.

The teacher divides the class into groups, giving each one of the questions, assigning the third and fourth to the most capable students. In large classes two groups may be given the same problem. In the class discussion, he uses the same questions; to clinch the ideas developed and to point up the alternative meanings, he uses this quotation: "How little a thing is needed for us to be lost or saved." What "little thing" is Mme. Loisel referring to? Does the author think she has been lost by a "little" thing?

With less mature students who have read Corey Ford's "Snake Dance," the teacher's purpose might be to explore the relationship that exists between the problems presented in stories and those we meet in life. This story tells of a boy who, for what he considers the best of reasons, deceives his parents; instead of attending college as they expect, he has taken a job as a soda fountain clerk. In the preliminary work, each group may be given all the questions.

> What did the boy's parents want?
>
> Has the boy given up all chance of fulfilling the ambition his parents have for him?

Is it believable that the boy will be able to deceive his parents long? Why or why not?

What was the boy's reason for the deception?

What will happen if it is discovered? What effect do you think it will have on his mother? On his father? Could the discovery cause the very damage the boy has been trying to avoid?

Can you from your reading or from experience suggest other incidents where people have been forced to choose between what they consider two evils?

In the class discussion which follows, the motivation of the three characters can be clarified, the arguments for and against the deception weighed, and perhaps the conclusion reached that finding a totally satisfactory answer to important questions is seldom easy.

Using directed study A variation of this method may be used without recourse to group work. The teacher may list on the board questions representing the major steps planned for the discussion, and give each row of students a different question. Students are to jot down evidence to support a definite answer. After the study period the discussion proceeds as planned, the students who worked on a certain question being given the first chance at answering. This plan offers an advantage to the more capable and to those well prepared; it throws the laggards on their own resources. The effect is salutary, for students must not come to rely upon group work to save them from the penalty of faulty preparation.

Another method allows students to compose their own questions for the literature studied. Suppose all have read five chapters of a novel. The class may be divided into five groups for a study period; each individual, working on one assigned chapter, prepares two questions which touch upon the salient points. These questions are then given to a capable member of the group; he is allowed time to select two to guide him in leading the class in discussion. After the five chapters have been examined in this fashion, the teacher takes over as leader, calling attention to important aspects of the story that may have been overlooked, clarifying the ideas that this segment of the novel presents.

Not all classes nor all discussions require the impetus of preliminary work. To lend variety to the program and to tailor the oral procedures to the needs and abilities of the students, the teacher will experiment with different methods.

ARRIVING AT CONCLUSIONS DEMOCRATICALLY

Occasionally, disapproval is voiced of carefully planned and guided discussions on the grounds that they invite the authoritarian approach. Such critics seem to misunderstand the function of the teacher-leader. A leader, from lack of either integrity or perceptiveness, might drive for a predetermined conclusion which ignored both the facts and their implications as well as the sensibilities and intelligence of group members; a teacher cannot. Presumably, he is wiser than his students; he has prepared more carefully than they; he is interested in teaching them how to think, not what to think. Admittedly, all these assumptions may be false in any particular instance. However, if they are true, the teacher in preparing has considered the merits of all possible inferences and has taken pains through his questions to see that the facts which point to these conclusions are given fair play. He is morally obligated not to reveal his own opinion until the implications of the evidence and of all viewpoints have been taken into account. His aim is to guide individuals to think for themselves rather than to spend their energies trying to guess what he wants. The time has long passed—indeed it probably never existed—when secondary school pupils looked upon teachers as founts of infallibility. Continued experiences similar to those described below may convince students the teacher sees one aspect of his job as concerned with teaching thinking rather than with providing answers.

Avoiding pat responses The film, "Right or Wrong?" often used at the junior high level, presents the case of a boy under pressure to give information about an act of vandalism he has witnessed. He can exonerate himself by telling what he knows, but the price of immunity is distasteful. The last scene shows his distress as he realizes that the deadline for his decision is fast approaching. What would you do? Any honest adult will probably have to admit that he isn't absolutely sure what he would do. However, as the pupil watches the incident unfold he is likely to suspect a none too subtle attempt to underline a moral lesson. He may be willing to voice acceptance of approved attitudes—vandalism is wrong, everyone should aid the police—and finish the distasteful matter with dispatch. Obviously, the right-thinking citizen is on the side of law and order. If the purpose in showing the film is to extract this admission from the class, the enterprise seems hardly worthwhile.

The film certainly does not suggest any pat answer; it does provide material for a stimulating discussion. The basic problem does not concern juveniles nor their delinquency, but the recognized truth that all of us, often through our own lack of foresight, find ourselves enmeshed in circumstances where whatever decision we make will not please us. The roots of any problem and of the way any individual attempts to solve it go back, sometimes far back, in time.

The discussion, therefore, will be more fruitful if it centers upon the universality of the problem—the necessity of considering the consequences of behavior, the inevitability of being forced sooner or later to assume responsibility for one's own actions. It should leave the student with sharpened awareness that painful decisions are not confined to the young nor to a life of crime but are the lot of all human beings. The question as to what the boy in the film should do can be left to each individual to ponder.

Permitting alternate conclusions In interpreting levels of literary works, the teacher has another opportunity to show students he is not always sure of the answer. He can let individuals draw conclusions differing from his own. After students have presented their evidence, he can suggest some they have overlooked, but he cannot force a conclusion their experience is not ready to accept. "The Necklace" will again serve as an example. The immature student, inclined toward romanticism, will interpret the shock of the ending as the author's way of forcing the realization that the woman has been betrayed by chance. Apparently that is Madame Loisel's interpretation, as she thinks of the little thing by which one may be lost or saved. The mature reader may interpret the story more realistically; he may think the author uses *little thing* ironically. Evidence at the beginning of the story shows that this woman's whole life is guided by selfish and materialistic values; one might conclude that if she had not been betrayed by the loss of the necklace, something equally foolish would have produced the same result. The author does not state his theme; he lets the reader make up his own mind. After all the evidence has been presented, the teacher must accord his pupils the same privilege. They will take it anyway; conclusions cannot be forced. Only varied experiences with literature will lead students to interpret facts below the level of the obvious.

Not all discussions are as strictly guided as those used as illustrations in this chapter. Sometimes the teacher's purpose may be to stimulate a group of seemingly inarticulate pupils or to explore the possibilities of some topic preparatory to more intensive study; thus a definite order would be too restrictive. However, too many discussions without logical sequence are likely to frustrate the intellectually able and convince them that to the teacher *discussion* and *random talk* are synonymous. If the student is aware of the purpose of each discussion, he can recognize the relation of form to content.

SECURING VARIETY THROUGH DIFFERENT PATTERNS

Useful as discussion is as a way to learning, too much repetition of the same pattern blunts its effectiveness. Teachers, in planning with students the oral program for a year—or a semester—vary the approach by introducing different types.

The round table The round table, illustrated above, is probably the most satisfying way for a group to consider problems. As the name suggests, it refers to a number of persons, seated or "conceived to be seated" around a table for the purpose of discussion. At its best, this arrangement permits each member to speak several times, thus fostering informal exchange of ideas and interaction of thinking; ideally it resembles stimulating conversation. Although limited time and large numbers do not allow every student to contribute orally, nevertheless class discussions follow the round table pattern. To meet the problems posed by the far from ideal classroom situation, teachers supplement class discussions with those of small groups. Although for most occasions the round table may be preferable, panels and symposiums, both highly adaptable to student interest and need, also have their place in the classroom.

The panel The panel, similar in some respects to the round table, is composed of a chairman and from two to six members who sit before an audience and discuss a question. In preparation, the issues are decided and the manner of presentation planned. No set speeches are made; the exchange is informal, no one talking much more than a minute at a time. The chairman steers the discussion according to the outline agreed upon by the members. Usually about half the time should be reserved for audience participation. Occasionally, a listener may ask for clarification or make a suggestion before the panel has finished. As a rule, this is postponed until the chairman makes a brief summary and invites comments. The panel, characterized by flexibility and spontaneity and thus requiring some degree of ability in impromptu thinking and speaking, is difficult for the less confident; it should be tried first with students not easily daunted by such demands. The chairman's job is particularly difficult, since he must fit the pieces into the over-all design. Sometimes the teacher is the only person competent to act in this capacity, as, for example, in discussions of several books with which no one student can be expected to be familiar. However, as often as it can be done without harm to either content or class, a student assumes the role.

The symposium The symposium, like the panel, consists of a chairman and several members. Here, however, speeches are prepared; presentation is more formal, adhering more rigidly to a preconceived plan. The subject chosen will suggest different ways in which the responsibility for its exploration may be divided. Sometimes it is more effective if the speakers represent divergent points of view; at others, each may give a certain aspect of the topic. In any case, the purpose is the same as that of the panel—to provoke discussion. Therefore, information must be given, issues clarified, pertinent questions raised. Then the audience, under leadership of the chairman, takes part. Since the speakers are presumably experts on the subject, the symposium lends itself to classroom experiences where intensive research is necessary and can be delegated to a few. However, the more knowledge the class has acquired on the subject previously, the more stimulating is the discussion likely to be.

The various approaches to discussion have been used to good effect on both radio and television. Over the years programs such as "America's Town Meeting" and "University of Chicago Round Table" have aroused and sustained nation-wide interest on important questions. Investigation of worthwhile programs should be suggested to students with special interests. At times groups may volunteer to listen and to report to the class.

Books from the guided reading program provide an abundance of material for panels and symposiums:

> Several mature students who have read biographies might comprise a teacher-led panel built upon criteria devised by a committee for judging the medium, such as the following, the product of a class of eleventh-graders: 1) Is the biography historically accurate in that it depicts the individual in relation to his times? 2) Does it present not a type but a human being, showing the gradations of hu-

man character? 3) Does the author bring both incidents and characters to life? To include all students, the class discussion might center on how well the criteria for judging biographies apply to the evaluation of works of fiction being read.

Any grouping of stories—pioneer, teen-age, adventure, sports—with student-chosen or teacher-suggested items for comparison can be used. When several have read the same book, either panel or symposium makes a satisfying manner of presentation.

Problems in which students have evinced interest [14] can be handled as a series of panels or symposiums prepared by groups who plan the attack, do the necessary research, design the arguments, and select members to represent them as speakers.

Any topic which adds informational spice to other class work may be used in the same way: A group of ninth grade pupils attempted to trace similarities in ideas in the folklore of widely separated locales as a contribution to the class study of folk literature. Seventh-graders, combining story telling with appropriate background material, entertained with American tall tales from Davy Crockett to Superman.

The variations to which either the panel or the symposium lends itself are numerous.

Material for discussion, whatever the type and however initiated, abounds in any well-integrated English course. Teacher and students may pick and choose; the problem is really one of elimination.

Using group process

Group work within the classroom is a common activity for elementary school children; in addition, many pupils have had such practice in youth organizations. In planning work for secondary school students, the teacher will build on this experience. Even those who have had little previous practice can learn with guidance to work effectively in small units within the class.

GUIDE LINES FOR THE TEACHER

Forming the groups The teacher's purpose will guide him in deciding upon the personnel of groups.[15] Those that are to be maintained over a period of some weeks are usually composed of students of somewhat similar needs, interests, or abilities; groups may be formed for those who need to learn certain points of grammar or usage, for those seeking to eliminate particular errors in sentence structure, for those whose reading skills are below par for the class. They may be made up of students interested in preparing a bulletin board, in presenting a play or a panel, in studying a literary work. For such long-term activities, the size of the group may be comparatively large; more often than

[14] See pp. 441-46, 465.

[15] The teacher who wishes to establish criteria other than those derived from observation may consult Helen H. Jennings, *Sociometry in Group Relations* (Washington, D.C., American Council on Education, 1948).

not it is led by the teacher while the rest of the students are quietly engaged with individual work.[16]

However, dividing the entire class into small units to work at the same time on identical or similar problems is also advantageous. This is especially true in teaching oral communication. These groups meet only for a few times, occasionally only once. Student-led, they should be limited to no more than six members. Here the purpose is to aid the handling of any of the day's activities—to warm up for class discussion, to provide a small audience for those reading poetry, to give the student a chance to secure face to face response for his original work.

The teacher may use almost any plan he wishes in selecting those to make up each group. His choice, even though the result of much thought, should at first seem casual, the make-up of groups changing frequently to give each student a chance to work with as many different individuals as possible. Often planned heterogeneity in group formation during the early weeks will contribute substantially to the socialization of the class. Until he is sure of his students, the teacher will proceed cautiously, trying to place individuals where they can function most easily. He is usually careful to separate those who seem antagonistic to each other; to place special friends together only when he thinks it will help rather than hinder; to divide both the shy and the talkative among the groups; to include in each at least one person who shows potentialities for leadership. Even if pupils have had experience with group work in elementary school or in preceding classes, the teacher cannot take skill for granted. Behavior may change with different environment and with different group personnel; each class needs a period of orientation.

After students have developed some skill in working together, a less careful selection of groups may be possible. Students may be grouped alphabetically or according to their position in the room. Even placing the very slowest, as if by accident, all in one group often brings out unexpected initiative. Occasionally, pupils may form their own groups. If they know of the plan in advance, it can be put into effect without commotion and waste of time. Experimentation will point the way to many effective groupings.

Dominating the physical set-up Unquestionably, movable furniture and extra space are desirable in group teaching; however, it is a mistake to think them essential. The method has been used successfully in overcrowded rooms with narrow aisles and with seats screwed inexorably to the floor. To make listening easy and to avoid bothering others, groups should be as compact as possible. Since the time to be spent in such formation is short, participants will not be unduly uncomfortable even when sitting two in a seat. Because the question of suitable arrangement in crowded space has been asked so often by prospective teachers, the following diagram—showing how a room filled to

[16] See also the units "Fortitude, the Backbone of Courage," p. 415, "Consequences of Character," p. 633, "Meeting a Crisis," p. 592; and "Establishing a usage habit," p. 674.

capacity may be used for this type of work—is included, even at the risk of being overly explicit.

A classroom with 48 seats and 48 pupils

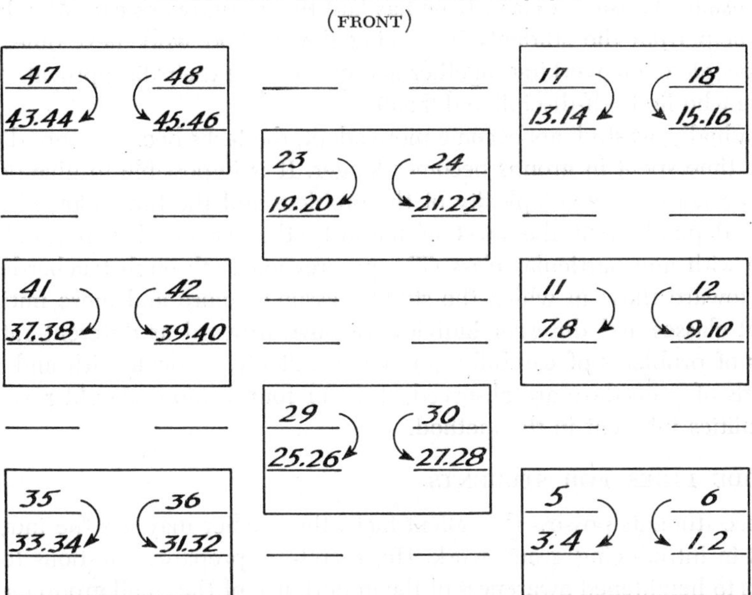

Each block of four seats will take care of six pupils, leaving sufficient space between groups so that one need not disturb the other. For teacher-led discussions, nine seats in any corner of the room will accommodate eighteen students, over one-third of the class; this leaves nine vacant desks to provide insulation for those working on their own. Teachers have made the groups even more compact by using stools placed in the aisles.

Planning increasingly complex experiences Realizing he is trying to teach skills demanding a degree of intellectual and emotional maturity, the teacher will be careful not to push students into experiences for which they are not prepared. Initially, he plans simple tasks with the help of the class, moving slowly, avoiding problems that invite conflict. He starts with very short meetings of no more than ten minutes, perhaps only five. In order to discourage dilatory practices, he errs on the side of allowing too little time rather than too much. Alert to evidence he may have misjudged the readiness of students, he is prepared to turn to a more formal type of activity at the first sign of possible disintegration of groups. Any flagrant disregard of standards,[17] even if only on the part of a few, should mark an end of group work for the day. He avoids being influenced by the pleas of those who have been working conscientiously; the method has to work for all groups or not at all. At this point the teacher can rarely be too strict. He is careful, however, not to make writing or reading

[17] See pp. 462-63.

sound like a punishment for disorder. He may tell the class calmly that since this doesn't seem to be a good day for group work, it will be postponed, as there are many other things to do. Since this obvious truth promises a second trial, it usually satisfies a class. If he has laid the groundwork carefully, he can expect help from the students in making the method work next time. Most young people enjoy working together and often bring their disapproval to bear on those who find self-discipline difficult.

Gradually, as students become more adept, the tasks become more difficult and the time spent in groups becomes longer. It is impossible to give definite rules; necessarily, the complexity of the problem and the time allowed for its solution depend upon the level of maturity the teacher has been able to achieve with any particular class. The progression is through teacher-led activities toward those in which the student assumes more and more initiative; different classes and different individuals move forward at different rates. If a series of problems of carefully graduated difficulty is dealt with and if the standards of procedure are observed, three or four sessions should reveal the potentialities inherent in the method.

GUIDE LINES FOR STUDENTS

Since students possess the salient facts, the teacher may use the inductive method in introducing group work. He, therefore, prepares questions to lead students to heightened awareness of the importance of the small group meeting in conducting everyday affairs, to fuller understanding of the nature of guided discussion and of the standards governing its effectiveness.

Introducing the group process Any day the teacher wishes to introduce the group process to a class, he will have no difficulty finding current examples to illustrate its extensive use. With some classes, a reference to a previous discussion of a school problem is the best approach. Teachers have used such varied topics as ways of securing wider student participation in assemblies, the possibility of providing music during lunch hour, the responsibility for keeping halls and classrooms neat, the prevention of vandalism on Halloween, conduct worthy of a sportsmanship award. The practice in many schools of publicizing the results of such class discussions by a report to a school-wide committee, an editorial for the school paper, a letter to the principal, or items on a central bulletin board emphasizes for students the significance of their own contribution. If a class is fortunate enough to be familiar with similar procedures, reference to such experiences will stress the importance of any group to the whole and will show pupils the practicality of using small group discussions as a help in arriving at class decisions.

With more mature students a community, national, or international event may provide greater incentive. The morning paper will furnish material. Teachers have used such current happenings as negotiations to settle a steel strike, a youth conference in the national capital, a meeting of the Security Council of the UN, planning committees for a world fair, a national conference of scientists meeting nearby. Since the purpose of the discussion is not, for example, to help settle the strike but to understand the procedure used in trying to bring it to a satisfactory conclusion, the selection of such a topic does not presuppose any great amount of technical knowledge on the part of either students or teacher.

The questions will be general: What is happening in the steel industry? How many factions are interested? Do you think it probable that any one faction will get all it wants? Why? What usually happens in such disputes? How do the different factions communicate with each other? What is the responsibility of the representative of each? The responsibility of each individual concerned to understand the basis for the demands? To make his opinions known? What can any large group do if it wants to insure the right of every man to speak for himself? How satisfactory is a plan using a hierarchy of committees in giving everyone a chance to voice his ideas? To take advantage of it, what must a person be able to do? Can such skills be gained here in class? Whatever example is selected to illustrate group process, the student himself can supply others; instances from his own experience will support the fact that small group meetings to explore problems and to seek solutions represent an important aspect of oral communication.

Anticipating difficulties Before even the simplest type of group work is launched, it may be helpful for students to consider the difficulties they may encounter. Any guided discussion tries to arrive at the approximate truth through consideration of various points of view; it may attempt to reconcile divergent opinions in order to bring about desired action. Therefore, one can be sure of meeting disagreement and conflict; he can expect his opponents to cling as tenaciously to their opinions as he does to his own. What must he do then if he wants to work effectively with others? Is it enough to believe he is right? How does he handle opposition? Of what significance are his own mood and motives? Those of the rest of the group? Of what importance are tone of voice and choice of words? Consideration of the obvious truths that living with others has already taught students leads to the conclusion that sensitivity to the total situation, tact, and patience are needed if one is to develop group skills. Such a conclusion sets the stage for understanding the role of participants and for devising standards for the group work to follow.

Understanding role of participants Since results of discussion should represent the best thinking of the group and not merely that of the brilliant or the vocal, the most significant concept for students to assimilate is *all participants are important.* This will follow logically if class members agree on the desirability of everyone's learning to exercise a degree of control in the social situation.[18] Students, familiar with most of the roles of group members, may list the duties of each. Tell students that one of the aims of group work is that each person should try many roles and that for a time these roles will be given

[18] See pp. 438-40.

to volunteers. When the personnel of groups changes often, it is a waste of time to allow students to go through the process of election. The *chairman,* impartial to individuals and to ideas, coordinates the efforts of all by maintaining an atmosphere conducive to participation, by keeping the discussion on the question, and by asking for a summary whenever necessary. He calls for clarification of facts and tries to help the group reconcile conflicting opinions. But all this should not be left to him; the rest should realize he is neither a disciplinarian nor an authority; he is a leader. Every member, alert to his own responsibilities, should be willing to assume any of these tasks when it seems necessary. The *secretary* keeps an account of the arguments given and the tentative conclusions reached; if a written report is required, he takes care of it. His notes assist the *reporter* in preparing an oral résumé of the results. At times, in mature groups, when it seems desirable to focus more directly on process, an *observer* may be added. He takes no part in the discussion; his job is to discover and to report specific practices which have facilitated or obstructed the performance. It is important that his report concern these and not personalities.[19] *All participants* try to state their views briefly so all may have a chance, to ask for amplification of obscure points, to consider the evidence objectively, to think for themselves.

All these requirements cannot be gleaned from students; therefore, take only what the class thinks essential as a guide for the first group meetings. Others, discovered as the work progresses, can be added. Try to leave the class with one idea—if each fulfills his role, the resulting interaction of minds insures cooperative group thinking.[20]

Setting standards In guiding students in setting standards, the teacher should first draw from them the difficulties they see in their particular situation—restricted space, nearness to other classes, necessity for six or seven groups working at the same time. He may show students a chart giving the best seating arrangement he has been able to devise, calling attention to the compactness of groups and his attempt to separate one from the other. Why? He will probably assure them in the beginning he will give exact directions and an exact time limit for the completion of the work. Again, why? A series of questions—What must you know before you get into groups? How can forty persons move into and out of groups without disturbing classes under us or next door? When you are in a group what is your responsibility if the method is to work? What is the teacher's responsibility?—will result in a set of simple standards suitable for beginners working on simple tasks.

[19] To develop oral skills students must constantly keep in mind that communication is a two-way process; it can be aided or hindered by both logical and psychological factors. Reports of observations—a suitable task for gifted students in the beginning and later for the less gifted—can be used to lead students to generalize on the nature of communication and on practices which foster its effectiveness.

[20] See, in Bert Strauss and Frances Strauss, *New Ways to Better Meetings* (N.Y., Viking, 1951), "Salvaging Problem Members," pp. 64-75, and "The Group Learns to Produce," pp. 76-83.

Make the necessary preparation. This would usually mean doing the assignment; for impromptu groups it may mean only being familiar with the directions, assuming a cooperative attitude.

Get into groups quickly and quietly. Before the class separates into groups, every student should know with whom he is to work and in what part of the room.

Follow the directions given. Directions must be specific; if they are not very simple, they should be written. They may be placed on the board if all are engaged on the same problem; if not, the chairman of each group may be given a copy.

Ask for help just as soon as needed. The teacher moves from group to group, giving what help he can; he is careful not to let the more aggressive students monopolize his attention.

Keep the work within the group. That each group must work without disturbing other groups cannot be overemphasized. Whispering can be as distracting as noise; help students see that talking in a low conversational tone is best.

Be willing to contribute. Willingness to express one's own views, to consider those of others, to ask pertinent questions, to allow everyone to speak, is a minimum requirement.

Return to seats quietly and quickly. In the interests of control, work should usually be planned so that students assemble as a class before dismissal. Too, an immediate discussion of the work undertaken by the groups is often helpful.

The standards may be copied in the pupil's notebook where he can refer to them in evaluating his own work. Although other requirements may be added, these usually refer to the material rather than to methods of procedure. These simple standards give enough emphasis on *process* to serve the purpose with most classes.

Teachers adept in using groups within a class find the method, since it permits the student to function at his ability level, conducive both to the improvement of morale and to the promotion of learning.

In organizing instruction, the teacher tries to plan a program economical of classroom time, designed to motivate individuals of varying interests and abilities. Central to such a program is helping students realize that the acquired skills will serve them in the demands of everyday life.

Suggested Learning Experiences

For purpose of emphasis, skills required for responsive and critical listening and those needed for effective speaking have been discussed separately in this text. In practice such division is unrealistic. The teacher, in planning the oral skills program, will consider the two as a unit, selecting from each chapter those experiences most meaningful for particular students at any particular time. Too, since all communication has much in common, he will realize that many of the suggestions for oral and written communication are interchangeable; one can be used to supplement the other.

To acquire skills for informal social situations

■ *Recognize that school situations demand oral skill*

1. Talk over with students the importance of making classroom visitors feel welcome; let different students assume the role of host or hostess, greeting these visitors, supplying them with books, explaining the work being done.

2. Ask the most outgoing students to take responsibility for making new students feel at home.

3. Use social events such as open houses, father-son dinners, teas for parents, as occasions for review of simple forms of introduction. Discourage any practice that smacks of formula and rigidity. Since the aim is always to put those who do not know each other at ease, explain the importance of giving a conversational lead to the two introduced. Students will be less self-conscious if asked to devise leads for fictional characters—e.g., let them decide what one statement about Tom Sawyer or David Copperfield would best serve as a lead in introducing him to a boy his own age, to a girl, to an adult.

After the review with the class, let students, working in groups, practice making introductions, acknowledging them, starting conversations. For example, an individual may introduce two classmates to his father, the principal to his parents, an out-of-state cousin to his friends.

■ *Discover some qualities of effective conversation*

Discuss in small groups quotations concerning various aspects of conversation:[21]

I don't like to talk much with people who always agree with me. It is amusing to coquette with an echo for a little while, but one soon tires of it: Carlyle

Never hold anyone by the button in order to be heard out; for if people are unwilling to hear you, you had better hold your tongue than hold them: Chesterfield

It is wonderful that so many shall entertain those with whom they converse by giving them a history of their pains and aches: Steele

For good or ill your conversation is your advertisement. Every time you open your mouth, you let men look into your mind: Barton

The tongue is only three inches long, yet it can kill a man six feet high: Japanese Proverb

Know how to listen and you will profit even those who talk badly: Plutarch

It is good to rub and polish your brain against others: Montaigne

As we must render an account of every idle word, so we must of our idle silence: Ambrose

Not only to say the right thing in the right place, but far more difficult, to leave unsaid the wrong thing at the tempting moment: Sala

Those who have finished by making all others think with them have usually been those who began by daring to think for themselves: Colton

Ask members of each group to interpret the author's meaning, to decide to what extent they agree, to give examples from experience to support their opinions; summarize the conclusions through class discussion.

[21] These quotations, reprinted with the permission of the publisher, are taken from *The New Dictionary of Thoughts* (N.Y., Standard, 1954).

■ *Practice conversational skills in interviews*

Ask each student to hand in one subject he enjoys discussing with his friends and upon which he feels reasonably well informed. Divide the class into groups, each to select the person with the subject most interesting to them; later other group members are to interview him. Ask each interviewer to prepare questions to ask the speaker and to select, from his own information on the subject, items he might be able to introduce to enliven the conversation.

On the following day, groups meet and conduct the interviews; one member acts as observer. Observers report to the class, noting the general tone, examples of good transitions, tactful questioning, extent of participation, and the like. Teacher and class compile a list of characteristics marking the good conversationalist.

To select content

■ *Find out what is likely to interest*

1. Give students a week to notice subjects being discussed in other classes, at home, among their friends, in newspapers and magazines, on radio and television. Ask them to hand in a brief list of those they find most stimulating; to star those profitable for class work. Duplicate the list of starred topics and give a copy to each student; ask him to make a first, second, and third choice. After a student committee has tabulated results, discuss with class and make selections for a tentative program.

2. Use an opinion poll to discover problems (pp. 442-46).

■ *See relationships among topics*

If several have chosen aspects of medicine and a few science, they may be willing to combine, selecting such topics as implications of the Hippocratic oath, recent scientific discoveries applicable to the medical field, possibility of using atomic energy in medicine, quackery in the name of medicine. One ninth grade class, combining topics handed in by several members, arranged programs under these topics: Moments to Remember, Moments to Forget, I Wish Parents Wouldn't, My Parents Wish I Would, I Would Like to Know Why.

■ *Consider appropriate ways of presenting ideas*

Discuss how interest of listeners, number of speakers, nature of the subject matter, may affect the method of presentation. Tentatively select subjects which might be better presented in prepared talks to small groups, to the class by panelists, through general class discussion, and so on. This procedure is applicable to any class and usually nets more ideas than can be used for oral work in any one semester, since the literature studied and the books read in the guided reading program will furnish many more. The initial selection of subjects, however, should not be considered final. As interests expand, some topics may be discarded and others added.

To widen and deepen interests

■ *Exchange recommendations for reading*

1. Ask each of the more capable students to assume responsibility for reading one certain magazine a month and for recommending its best article to others; post the list in the library or in the classroom; arrange time for those who have read the same article to discuss it.

2. Have a class committee accept students' recommendations of books worth

reading; keep such a list posted on the bulletin board; when several have read the same book, plan a group discussion or a presentation for the class.

■ *Form the habit of collecting conversational bait*

1. Encourage individuals to clip from newspapers and magazines short items of wide appeal; place these on a table in the rear of the room where students who finish work early may browse. If there is no space for a table, the material may be kept in large envelopes and made available to those who want it.

2. Let volunteers who maintain personal files meet occasionally in a small group for ten minutes to give one member a chance to start a conversation which will allow introduction of ideas suggested in his file.

■ *Become an expert on several subjects*

It has been said that the good conversationalist knows a little about many things and a lot about a few. Using students' original lists of topics, encourage individuals to become authorities in one or two areas that interest them. Then arrange for a series of interviews called "The Expert Speaks."

To learn to consider recipients in communications

■ *Study the significance of impersonal questions as means of starting conversations*

1. Introduce by discussion: Why impersonal? Why questions? Why questions requiring more than one-word answers? Since openers grow out of particular situations, ask students to consider the English classroom on this particular day and to suggest questions which might serve to start conversations.

2. Each student lists on a card three ideas he enjoys talking about; students exchange cards. Working in pairs, each composes several questions suitable for starting conversations on topics suggested by the other; they agree on one example to be reported to the class; the class evaluates these according to the criteria set.

■ *Plan a communication to interest one particular person*

Each student writes on a slip of paper his name and a topic. Students exchange slips; each is to write for the other a composition on the given topic which will arouse and hold interest. The two read their papers to each other; the listener decides whether or not the purpose has been accomplished and determines reasons for the writer's success or failure.

Teacher and students explore means successful writers have used, trying to discern similarities which may indicate some things likely to create interest—suspense, conflict, unusual details, strange facts, humor, illustrations, colorful language.

To learn that ideas form the core of communication

■ *Recognize ideas capable of development*

Ask students to decide which sentence in each of the pairs below expresses an idea the speaker might prefer "to leave with his listeners."

We started for Yellowstone early in the morning. Our Yellowstone trip had several highlights.

Our class officers will meet after school. After school our class officers will meet to transact important business.

Madame Defarge spent a lot of time knitting. Madame Defarge's knitting proved to be more than an innocent pastime.

After Caesar's death Antony addressed the mob. Antony showed his knowledge of mob psychology in his speech over Caesar's body.

I just finished reading *Treasure Island.* *Treasure Island* is an exciting story.

This exercise should take very little time, as the controlling sentences are easy to recognize. The difficulty will come later when the student tries to construct a plan for a talk controlled by one sentence. If a student selects the first one of any pair, ask how he would develop it; e.g., I just finished reading *Treasure Island.* If his purpose is to tell something unusual about the finish of the book, he can compose a better sentence. Let him try.

■ *Construct sentences expressing a point of view capable of development*

Ask students to write a sentence which could be developed into a one-paragraph talk, and to exchange with his neighbor, who is to write a brief statement as to what he would expect from a communication so controlled. Move about the room, trying to discover examples which deserve the attention of the class. After the papers are returned to the owners, hold a brief discussion to correct misunderstandings. Even though all students may not have written satisfactory sentences, it is better not to belabor the point at this time. Since it is central to organization, it will recur repeatedly in later work.

To learn to support assertions

■ *Learn to support with illustrations*

1. Read a short anecdote, parable, or joke. Ask students to construct sentences which it might be used to support. Discuss.

2. Duplicate several of the less well-known fables of Aesop, omitting the moral. Give each student a copy of one. Have him write a controlling sentence. Divide the class into groups according to the fable read; ask each to select the best sentence and to choose one member to read the fable to the class, concluding with the sentence chosen.

3. Ask each student to choose a favorite anecdote or joke, compose a controlling sentence, and prepare as a short talk to be given to a group.

4. Read Kipling's "If." Let each student select one statement as a controlling sentence, support it by a factual or fictional detailed example, and prepare as a short talk.

5. Ask each student to select a proverb or aphorism—A penny saved is a penny earned; one man's meat is another man's poison—to support it with one specific example developed in detail, to restate the proverb in other words to clinch the idea, and to prepare to give the paragraph orally.

6. Teach capable students to develop assertions by a list of examples briefly stated. Such an assignment presents an interesting problem in control of language, much more complex than it may appear to students; that is, the difficulty comes not in finding examples, but in so stating them that they carry the full charge of meaning in as few words as possible. Therefore, the student will be more successful at first if he writes out his paragraph and prepares to read it aloud. Since teaching this principle troubles the inexperienced, a detailed illustration of the way it was introduced by a tenth grade teacher follows:

First the teacher told the class for their next assignment he was going to ask them to do something difficult—to support a statement by using several specific examples concisely stated; that before they tried it on their own, the class would work out a sample. Taking from volunteers statements appropriate for paragraph control, he helped the class select those that might be developed by a list of examples:

Several interesting personalities headline the news.
Our record in basketball this season has been outstanding.
The National Safety Council suggests a code of ethics for drivers.
Union High School offers the student a variety of experiences.

In amplifying general statements by a list of concise examples, the speaker is assuming that the listener's background is such that a reminder will be sufficient to call up latent knowledge; thus, the illustration given below would be appropriate only with a group knowing Shakespeare's plays well enough to fill out the picture hinted at in the allusions.

Shakespeare has given us a gallery of distinctive portraits.
- In Cassius we meet the wily, scheming politician, eager for power
- In Hamlet, the sensitive, vacillating individual, tortured by the agony of making the right moral decision
- In Falstaff, of the shrewd mind and gross body, an entertaining companion but an untrustworthy friend

However, the illustration was used with these tenth-graders to point up the care that must underlie both choice of examples and their wording if they are to suggest more than they say. The students could appreciate the reference to Cassius because they knew *Julius Caesar*, but those to Hamlet and Falstaff carried little weight.

Then the teacher, taking the controlling sentence selected by students, listed the events the class gave in support.

Our record in basketball this season has been outstanding.
- Winning from Morton High School
- No game lost
- Two players chosen for the all-city team
- Award of the sportsmanship plaque

Next he took each example, listing the facts that described each event:

- Winning from Morton
  - Opponents previously undefeated
  - Game decided championship
  - Best scorer of home team ill

He asked students to take a few minutes to write a statement that included all these items. Combining bits from the work of several students, the class arrived at this statement:

> The brilliant work of our team, deprived though they were of Johnson's extraordinary skill in connecting with the basket, trounced the undefeated Mortonites and placed us first in the league.

Assignment: Take a general statement; develop by three concise specific examples. Write a paragraph to be handed in after being read in a group. *Follow-up:* Ask each group to select one or two examples, vividly worded, to read to the class, giving the statement each supports.

7. Suggest an assignment based on books from the guided program. Use as a controlling sentence an opinion you've formed concerning a character in the book you are reading. Support with three specific examples briefly stated. Conclude with a sentence which will clinch the idea in the minds of your listeners: "(Character) in (title) by (author) shows great bravery," or "is too perfect to be credible," or "overcomes many obstacles," or "meets defeat through his own fault." Prepare a short talk.

For the follow-up, students meet in groups to give talks; after each member speaks, questions like these are considered:

Was there a controlling sentence, either stated or implied?
Were illustrations well chosen? Brief? Did they give enough information to be meaningful?
Did the conclusion clinch the idea?

The group chooses one member to give his talk before the class.

8. Take general statements applicable to work previously studied for either oral or written work. Use statements like:

Treasure Island provides many exciting moments.
Dickens in *A Tale of Two Cities* makes the hatred of the commoners for the aristocrats comprehensible to the reader.
The short stories studied represent many different locales; present various problems; help us understand human nature . . .

■ *Learn to support with facts*

1. To help students become aware of the use of facts in differing kinds of contexts, ask them to:

Select an article from the daily paper or from a weekly news magazine. List the facts; give the sentence which they are used to support.
Choose an editorial; state its proposition in one sentence; list the facts given. Does the writer use any other type of supporting material?
Write a sentence which will give the reader an impression of the setting for the book being read. List the facts the author gives in creating this impression.
Choose a fictional character. What details does the author give to help the reader visualize him? Summarize the general effect in one sentence.

2. Let each student list three or four statements of fact pertinent to some general topic he chooses—Open House is held every year; it is on November 17; parents are invited to the school; exhibits are up in many rooms; demonstrations are to be given in classrooms; a program is being arranged in the auditorium. Working in pairs, each student makes up a controlling statement which the facts supplied by his partner might be used to support; the two compare results. Ask for volunteers to read a few examples; discuss. The teacher may need to remind students that the items are to be used as facts, not as specific examples. Therefore the controlling statement does not state these facts but makes their inclusion possible in development, e.g., At Open House parents can become better acquainted with their school.

3. Ask students to prepare a one-paragraph talk, supporting a controlling sentence

by facts. Let them make their own choices but suggest some easy subjects: explanation of how something is made, description of a pet, the rules for playing some game, the reasons for a person's being featured in the news.

4. Give students a week to become aware of interesting facts that come to their attention. Then ask them to select the most unusual; give them a minute to prepare; take the reports as rapidly as possible. After all facts are given, ask the class to select two or three of the most stimulating. Discuss their value in a talk where the information would be pertinent.

■ *Learn to support with testimony*

1. To call attention to the different purposes for which testimony is used, suggest that students:

Find an ad which uses testimony. Is it convincing? Give reasons.
Select a news item which contains a quotation; read the quotation, stating the idea it supports.
Select a current happening which has aroused conflicting comments; clip or compose statements representing different viewpoints; discuss in groups.

2. The following experience is suggested only for able students; however, it has proved successful in grades from eight through twelve.

Assignment: Choose the most interesting character in the book you are reading. Consider the facts given about him from the point of view of a lawyer who has accepted this person as a client. Imagine you are defending him on a specific charge. (If you'd prefer, you may act as prosecutor.) What other characters would you subpoena as witnesses? Has the author given any explanation which would make his testimony desirable? Present the evidence you think would acquit (or convict) the defendant of the charge made against him.

If two students have read the same book, they may like to take opposite sides, presenting the evidence for and against. Another variation allows a class, after study of a short story, novel, or play, to dramatize an imaginary courtroom situation dealing with one of the characters. In giving such an assignment, the teacher can illustrate with examples suggested by the literature studied:

You are defending Aunt Polly as a suitable guardian for Tom Sawyer.
Antony is charged with willfully inciting a mob to violence. You are prosecuting attorney.
You are defending Lady Macbeth as an accessory to murder.
You are prosecuting Barsad for perjury.
You are defending Miss Pross on a charge of manslaughter.

■ *Learn to support by combining the three types of material*

1. Let students work in groups of six to select a subject for which they are to find the three types of material, two members to bring in each particular type. Since the research problem should not be formidable, the teacher suggests easy topics and calls the first group meeting a few days in advance of the follow-up.

Follow-up: The groups meet, compose controlling sentences for which they have support, disregarding irrelevant material; one member reports to the class. (The problem of interesting but non-pertinent material at times troubles all speakers—and writers. Students should learn there are only two choices—elimination, or reorganization to permit inclusion. Class and teacher can often suggest a change in the controlling sentence that makes such items apt.)

2. Ask each student to make a statement concerning the book he is reading and to prepare to support it with the three types of material. For example, (Author) in (title) gives a picture of intrigue in eighteenth-century England; fails to provide sufficient motivation for behavior; tells an hilarious story; develops suspense; has created unforgettable characters . . .

To learn the preliminaries to speech planning

■ *Break down a broad subject into logical parts*

Take an easy subject to which all can contribute as it is worked out on the board, e.g., Union High School.

I. Academic Education
II. Vocational Education
III. Social Education
IV. Physical Education
  A. Class work
  B. Intramural sports
  C. Interscholastic sports
    1. Basketball
    2. Baseball
    3. Track
    4. Football
      a. Team
      b. Coaching system
      c. Season's program
        1′ Upsets
        2′ Our next game

This process is not always necessary; some minds leap automatically through several steps at once. Younger or slower students, however, may profit by following the procedure with several topics; with some pupils it is necessary to start with a much narrower one, for example, football.

■ *Decide upon a point of view*

1. Consider the effect of the speaker's interest. In a talk on our next football game what might be the viewpoint of the business manager? The coach? A member of the rally committee? A member of the team? One interested in the fine points of the game? One interested only in being a member of the crowd? Help students formulate assertions capable of development and expressing different viewpoints:

You should enjoy our next football game.
We have a good chance of winning our next game.
The team needs your support at the next game.
Our next game will be a colorful spectacle.
We face stiff competition in our next game.
Our next game is the most important one of the season.
Certain changes are promised for our next game.

Any of these assertions could serve as the controlling sentence of a short talk; it may or may not appear in the talk itself, but both speaker and listener should be aware of it. If the communication has unity, they will be.

2. Study the implications of the controlling sentence. Discuss questions similar to the following: What development does each suggest? Can one be used to support another? Is there any one which does not take the listener into account? What possible concerns of listeners are stressed? Which appeals would be most likely to move *you*? Help students see that the controlling sentence converts a topic into an

idea suggested by the topic; this important concept–ideas, not topics, govern the communication–needs continued emphasis.

To learn how to make a speech plan

■ *Reduce outlining to a three-step formula*

Construct a controlling sentence (CIS) asserting an idea that expresses your point of view toward the subject.

Construct topic sentences (TS) which when developed will support CIS.

Construct sub-topic sentences (STS), to be amplified by facts, illustrations, testimony, to support each topic sentence.

Use hypothetical material which, having no restrictions, allows attention to psychological as well as logical aspects of communication.

1. Review the first step (CIS). If students have been supporting assertions in their oral work, they will have many examples of appropriate central idea sentences to offer. Let the class select assertions formulated on a topic studied in preliminary work–in this case, our next football game.

2. Learn the second step by formulating topic sentences (A, B, . . .) to support the central idea sentences selected. Two examples devised by one class follow:

CIS: You should enjoy our next football game.
  A. It will be a colorful spectacle.
  B. It is the most important one of the season.
  C. We have a good chance of winning.
CIS: Certain changes are promised for our next football game.
  A. Jim Smith will be tried out as quarterback.
  B. Reports of a new play have the fans guessing.

3. Learn the third step–the construction of sub-topic sentences (1, 2, . . .) to support the topic sentences–using one of the partially developed examples and identical procedure. After the class has selected the plan to be completed, the secretary writes the skeletal plan on the board. Let the class think of facts, examples, or testimony which may be used to amplify the topic sentences. Give students time to select items and to compose sentences; then the class chooses those seeming to offer the most interesting development, deciding on the arrangement likely to hold the attention of listeners; the secretary inserts the sentences in the plan:

CIS: Certain changes are promised for our next football game.
  A. Jim Smith will be tried out as quarterback.
    1. Jim's track performance last spring caught the coach's eye.
    2. In practice Jim has shown keen understanding of football strategy.
  B. Reports of a new play have the fans guessing.
    1. Some predict a new aerial offense.
    2. Others foresee a different blocking arrangement.

Such a plan emphasizes both logical and psychological aspects of communication. The proper relationship of the various statements has been indicated, and the nature of the audience has been taken into account. The planners have assumed that the majority will be interested in something affecting their school; they have made use of at least one of the basic wants–the desire for new experiences. In ordering this material they have placed the stronger point last, trying to develop suspense through climactic arrangement. They have attempted to devise a psycho-logic structure.

■ *Try a simple plan*

1. Help the intellectually limited compose assertions which express a personal point of view. Even a factual talk given by a seventh-grader governed by "there are three steps in making a kite" presumes he is familiar with the procedure and has determined it has three aspects; he is not merely reporting on an article he has read.

2. Use topics rather than sentences in developing the idea. Ask pupils to think of one adage which experience has taught them contains a kernel of truth; let the class choose one for development. List on the board, in the order given, illustrations and details volunteered by pupils. Experiment with different groupings, combining some items and eliminating others. Help students compose topical headlines for major groups; consider advantages of different sequences, agreeing on one to be used. Then arrange in outline form, using pupils' own words; this should result in proper relationship of ideas although the language usually needs revision. Leave the original outline on the board for later comparisons; help students rewrite co-ordinate ideas in parallel constructions.

The procedures demonstrated for class teaching are intended to show ways of attacking the problem initially; group and individual teaching must be continual as pupils make plans for actual talks they are to give.

To increase skills for impromptu communication

■ *Develop awareness of all experience as the source of material for talks, discussions, and conversations*

1. Discuss the reasons professional writers and speakers carry notebooks to jot down observations.

2. Encourage students to collect brief interesting items that may be useful in oral work—anecdotes, jokes, quotations, vivid comparisons, startling facts. Ask each to contribute an item a week to a class file of ideas.

■ *Welcome opportunities to practice inpromptu speaking*

1. Help students briefly review the concepts of controlling idea, support, and clinching sentence. Limit impromptu speaking to one or two paragraphs. Speakers should aim at poise, directness, clarity, clear-cut organization. It is too much to expect *adequate* support.

2. Give students a formula: Start with the controlling sentence, support with an illustration or not more than two detailed facts, restate the controlling sentence to clinch the idea.

3. Provide time for practice. Let each volunteer draw one item from the idea file to use as the basis for a talk. Occasionally arrange for a few spare minutes; ask if anyone within the last week has observed or read anything he'd like to tell the class. Give him a minute to organize before he speaks impromptu. Or, let not more than six students practice impromptu speaking in a group. Each member can announce a topic and call on another for a one-paragraph talk.

To learn to give and to take criticism

The ability to criticize tactfully and honestly is important in the classroom, but especially so in daily living; it smooths the relationships between parent and child, husband and wife, employer and employee. Every human being has to accept, and probably feels inclined to give, his share. The classroom offers no better occasion for practice than in experiences concerned with the improvement of oral skills.

■ *Learn the purpose and meaning of criticism*

Study remarks sometimes made in discussing classroom speeches. Give students a list of statements; these should illustrate the completely adverse and the completely favorable, the concrete and the general, tactful and aggressive tone, acceptance and rejection of responsibility for listening.

He has a good voice.

He made three mistakes in grammar.

He said, "_______"; that's not true.

You said, "_______"; I wonder if that's always true?

Your beginning story made us want to listen, but when you began to talk about _______, I became confused.

You just mixed me all up.

He should have told us why _______ is so wonderful if he expects us to believe him.

You chose an interesting subject and had good material, but you hesitated so often I found it hard to follow.

I was bored.

It was a wonderful speech.

He kept looking out the window and he mumbled and kept shifting around, but it was a good speech.

Mr. J., will you explain *come* again. I'm not sure he used it correctly.

That's the best speech I've heard him give.

I noticed an improvement over his last speech. This time he looked at us more and had a better conclusion, but he needs to keep working on directness.

I'd like to know what makes you think . . . ?

Ask students, assuming the statements true, which ones they would most willingly accept as criticisms of their own speeches, and to divide the statements into two groups, the most helpful and the least; to then check those in the first group which they think most constructive. Give to a committee to tally.

Before presenting the results to the class, return the papers to the owners; ask them to try to discover the basis on which they made the division and then to determine why they checked the items they did. Through discussion—"When *you* make a speech what do you want to know about it?"—lead students to see that the purpose of classroom criticism is to help the one receiving it to improve, and that criticism implies evaluation—the judging of *strengths* as well as weaknesses. (This might be the time for a brief lesson on language—connotation and denotation, tone.)

■ *Develop constructive attitudes toward criticism*

1. As the sender, keep in mind the purpose—to help someone else improve. Establish a formula: greatest strengths; greatest weakness; offer specific suggestions for overcoming weakness. Remember that the way criticism is given is as significant as what is said.

2. As the receiver, keep in mind the purpose—to improve. Try to receive graciously. Try to weigh impartially, keeping attention on what is said, disregarding favorable or unfavorable opinion of the critic or the way he has expressed himself.

Developing the skill of giving apt and helpful criticisms and the habit of subordinating the personal element in those received demands from students the utmost in communication skill—ability to listen accurately, to fashion a communication which will accomplish a particular purpose with a particular listener, to interpret rationally statements which may seem highly personal and critical in a situation likely to be emotionally charged. Students know, but perhaps should be reminded, that no adult ever consistently maintains this ideal. The mature person does, however, strive for these skills in communication. Teachers who have worked with students trying to develop healthy attitudes toward criticism find such experiences contribute much to the oral skills program.

Evaluating Growth

Perhaps the chief reason the teaching of oral communication is neglected—and it is when attention is confined to the individual speech to which all must listen—is that there is no mathematically exact way of determining a grade for the product. However, the same holds true for many of the less tangible benefits teachers hope will accrue from instruction in English. Students, if given a chance in situations which foster communication, will learn to speak even if the teacher does not hear every word they say. Just as continued practice in writing, with regular periods of instruction and evaluation, develops facility with the pen, so too does a similar procedure increase facility with spoken language. Understanding, practice, evaluation—all three are essential. If the student thinks of classroom speech as communication, understands the purpose of instruction, is given time for practice of the individual principles, and is helped to evaluate progress, the plan of organizing instruction suggested here makes sense to him. In some small way it helps him discriminate between learning as a goal and fulfilling a series of assignments with his accomplishment identical to the total of the individual grades assigned. The final grade is unlikely to be any more subjective than grades in other areas of learning where the retention of factual information is not the sole aim.

EVALUATING THE INDIVIDUAL SPEECH

The problem of tactfully and helpfully handling impromptu evaluations of speeches at times worries the inexperienced teacher. However, with any new class even the skilled teacher feels his way. Before individual evaluations start, usually a period of work passes with comment only on the most elementary principles involved. Therefore, the first evaluations, used primarily for teaching, will not be designed for any one student but for the class as a whole. Such a procedure allows the teacher to set an impersonal tone with no direct reference to appraisal of individual work. He does this by his casual acceptance of speaking as a common daily experience, by focusing upon specific examples of effective communication made by students, by emphasizing content first and, only after that, form and delivery. Thus he begins to build acceptable standards. Eventually, some students will want to know how they are progressing. This is the time to begin appraisal of individual performances.

Much of the teaching in reference to *particular* oral skills is accomplished by impromptu evaluations given before the class. The situation is often emotionally charged. It is necessary, therefore, for the teacher to establish a flexible guide for his remarks. A good evaluation has three characteristics: It provides motivation, it is concerned only with immediate and essential problems, and it is specific enough to help the pupil with the next step.

Providing motivation An evaluation should convince the student that he has already shown potential and that he is capable of doing the next assignment. If an attitude conducive to gains in oral skill is to be fostered, the order in which the points in evaluation are given is important. If the student is to feel that further effort will be worthwhile, he must first know that his current offering has had some merit; only after he has been told in what way he has succeeded will he be receptive to adverse comment. Beginning speeches for some individuals may well be so inadequate that the teacher must exercise his utmost ingenuity to find anything favorable; however, it is there, and find it he must. Perhaps he seizes upon a bit of original thinking, a vivid expression, a good beginning, asking, "Did you notice . . . ?" He gives the speaker time to recover from his sense of failure, probably acute. The rule that favorable remarks come first holds good, however excellent the speech and however confident the speaker. Inadvertently recognizing the frantically waving hand of one eager to contribute the devastating statistics that the speaker used "and-uh" fifteen times is likely to spoil the triumph of all but the most resilient. Although his nonchalance may seem to belie the fact, the good speaker too needs encouragement.

Once the strengths have been pointed out, the student may be told of one weakness he should try to overcome first. In making suggestions for improvement, the teacher tries to fit the task to the individual. For one, he may pick a fault difficult to correct; for another, something comparatively easy. He gives concrete ways for attacking these weaknesses.

Stressing only the essential Evaluations, when given orally, should be as concise as possible. Much classroom time can be wasted in discussing goals which lie so far ahead they frustrate rather than encourage. Too, the student can be hampered rather than helped when attention is called to trivial faults which will be almost automatically eliminated when he gains more confidence. The class should realize the teacher knows that acquiring any skill takes time. Some students will remember their first fumbling attempts at a sport in which they are now fairly proficient. Neither the athletic coach nor the English teacher expects the impossible; neither begins with a list of requirements only a professional could meet.

Since the aim of the oral skills program is never perfection in any one endeavor but an over-all record of improvement, every assignment should stress a principle of effective speaking which needs to be taught or retaught: Not the vague, "Tell us something interesting you did over the weekend," but "Give one opinion you've formed about a character in the book you are reading; furnish enough evidence in support so we may decide whether your opinion is justified." In fulfilling each assignment, the student tries to exemplify not only the new principle but, whenever possible, the ones previously discussed. The evaluation, therefore, after brief mention of ways in which the speech has illustrated concepts with which the class is reasonably familiar, centers on the current problem. This practice is effective because it provides for a brief review and directs attention to only one new point. Such a procedure, consistently followed, emphasizes the cumulative nature of any skills program.

Being specific If the class is to profit from the work of each individual, and if the student himself is to work purposefully, the approach to evaluation must be positive and the comments specific enough to point the way in preparing future work. Such generalities as "good," "interesting," "excellent voice," give very little enlightenment or help. For example:

> To the student who speaks too fast: "Next time, try to think of your speech as a succession of ideas; pause between them to give us a chance to digest each one and get ready for the next."
>
> To call attention to a good introduction: "You caught our interest immediately by a reference to an experience we have all shared."
>
> To one seemingly unprepared: "After you've thought through your next speech, make out a list of key words to aid your memory as you practice."

Specific advice gives the student direction for his next attempt and makes all more aware of the fact that purposeful speaking is governed by well-defined principles.

Not only is it essential that the evaluation be specific and geared to the needs and capabilities of the individual, but it is equally important that the teacher remember the advice previously given to each student. The practice of keeping for each class member a card on which appraisals are noted will help both teacher and student evaluate progress.

If the evaluation leaves the student convinced he has strengths upon which he can rely; if he feels the next step is within his capabilities; if he knows exactly what to work for next, it represents good teaching.

EVALUATING DISCUSSION

To help students recognize the dual purpose of discussion, evaluations should direct attention to both process and product. At first this can be done informally with the teacher guiding the class in appraisal. When some degree of skill has been attained, individual evaluations should be made. Since in many classes the initial concern is to get everyone to take part, some students may think a premium is being placed on talking for the sake of talking. They need to be reassured that pertinence, not quantity, is what counts; that time does not always permit an oral response from everyone; that often attentive listening is the most helpful contribution at any one particular time. Especially, they need to know that grades are recorded not for each discussion but for several; thus sufficient evidence will be accumulated to assess values more accurately.

Using rating sheets Since in discussion the teacher is trying to give students practice both in purposeful speaking and in the use of group skills, any evaluation will necessarily be based on the principles governing both. A simple rating sheet serves the purpose for beginners.

Check list for self-rating as a speaker

Number of discussions included in rating________

A. Content
   1. Were my facts correct?
   2. Were my opinions supported?

B. Organization
   1. Were my comments immediately clear?
   2. Were my comments concise?
   3. Were my comments pertinent?

C. Delivery
   1. Did I speak so all could hear?
   2. Did I enunciate clearly?
   3. Was my tone always courteous?

My chief contributions have been____________________________

The following brief check list was prepared by a tenth grade class. The teacher first asked each pupil to list practices of listeners which aided him as he spoke as well as those which hindered. These lists were given to a committee which summarized the responses for the class. Then teacher and students prepared the guide.

Check list for self-rating as a listener

I can help a speaker by	*Yes*	*No*
Appearing interested: do I		
Look at him as he speaks?		
Try to attend even if the subject seems dull?		
Avoid distracting movements?		
Refrain from comments and questions until he has finished?		
Reacting intelligently to his ideas: do I		
Try to accept or reject ideas on their own value rather than on personality of the speaker?		
Try to consider impartially both statements I'd like to believe and those I'd like to reject?		
Evaluating honestly: do I try to		
Help the speaker rather than impress with my cleverness?		
Comment on strengths as well as matters needing improvement?		
Make my remarks concise and specific?		
Maintain an impersonal tone?		

I notice the following improvements in my ability to evaluate:______________

The value of using rating sheets lies in their repetition. The reiteration of desirable qualities serves as a guide to the pupil not only as he evaluates his past performance but also as he prepares for those that are to come.

Securing variety Use of various means of evaluating lends interest, provides different viewpoints, and involves more students in this important aspect of learning. The following suggest methods teachers have found effective:

Before the discussion, pair students, each to write an informal evaluation of the other.[22]

After the discussion, give students five minutes to analyze the performance of the one person who has contributed most. It is good teaching to discuss the papers, selecting the two or three persons most often chosen and evaluating their contributions. This should be done without identification of the individuals. The specifics given will stress the qualities of good participation—the aim of such an activity.

Assign students to act as observers, each to note a different aspect. This is ideal work for those who contribute little orally. They may be asked to find examples of questions that helped clarify an issue, information that supported or refuted a point made by another, logical or faulty reasoning. They may note when and how digressions arose, how the discussion was brought back into focus, the extent and quality of participation. The use of such an evaluation method implies some degree of skill and confidence on the part of students. The teacher should, of course, add the items gradually, starting with only one and asking several pupils to act as observers. To the extent suggested here, it is suitable only for the mature and capable.

Ask several students to observe the discussion and to pool their finding for a general evaluation.

Whatever form the evaluation of discussion takes, it should be specific; it should be concerned with only the most pressing problems; it should leave students confident of the progress they have made and of their ability to take the next step.

EVALUATING GROUP EXPERIENCES

Evaluating the group process has much in common with evaluating discussion since both involve communication among many participants. Here, too, both process and product are essential; the teacher provides frequent means for evaluating both.

Evaluating process The process can be evaluated as formally or as informally as the situation warrants. It can be done in a variety of ways. Perhaps if the results have exceeded the teacher's hopes, a general discussion will be sufficient to elicit reasons why certain groups have been able to accomplish more than others; to highlight practices that have helped, disregarding for

[22] Such an assignment presupposes that students have had instruction in giving and receiving criticism. See pp. 473-75.

the time those that have hindered. To make it as easy as possible for individuals who find it difficult to speak, the teacher can call attention to examples of attentive listening, to an instance when the right question helped clarify the issue. If the analysis leaves the students ready and willing for the next attempt, if it excites rather than quenches, the teacher has accomplished his purpose.

Suppose though the teacher discovers he has expected too much from this first venture. Then his task is to discover something, however small, which augurs well for the future, to enlarge upon it, to review the steps that should have been taken. Were the directions clear? Did the group have the necessary facts? Did the leader understand his duties? The teacher assumes a share of the blame. This may be the time to ask the student to make a written evaluation of his own participation. The appraisal can be very simple. He may be asked to mention his own contribution and to think of one thing he might have done to insure smoother operation. If a more complete evaluation seems desirable, the teacher can review the standards and ask for a comment in reference to each item. Sometimes it is well for the teacher to tell the class he too is writing an evaluation of his own performance. The very act of writing down first impressions sometimes has a wholesome effect on both students and teacher.

True, in our classes it is often the most hardened sinner who can review his actions and say with disarming candor just what he must do to improve. His confidence in his ability to effect a complete reversal of form is often one of the most beguiling, if the most frustrating, of his charms. Lack of belief in his promises should not, however, blind us to the possible therapeutic value of the device. Save these flights of fancy; later, confront the author with his series of evaluations, all containing the same diagnoses and the same glib predictions of better things to come. At times such accumulated evidence has made a slight chink in the armor of even the most persistently wayward. Self-evaluation is not a magic wand either for adolescents or adults; it carries no guarantee of immediate transformations. However, it has so often demonstrated its effectiveness that it is well worth trying.

A rating sheet, based upon the objectives previously agreed upon, often helps each group diagnose its own difficulties and evaluate its own accomplishments. The same holds true for the individual. The first two forms may prove useful with beginners.

Group's self-rating

Purpose:______________________________

1. Did we get to work promptly?
2. Did we stick to the point?
3. Did we work quietly?
4. Did all contribute?
5. Did we ask for help as soon as it was needed?

What did we accomplish?______________________________

Such a reaction sheet, filled out by the group, serves as impetus for a class evaluation which re-emphasizes the purpose of the experience and the means used for its accomplishment.

Beginner's check list for self-rating

Subject:________________________________

1. Had I prepared sufficiently?
2. Did I follow directions?
3. Did I make the best use of my time?
4. Did I work without disturbing other groups?
5. My chief contribution to my group was____________________

After several meetings let students draw names to rate one other member.

Evaluation of a group member

1. What was his chief contribution?
2. What factor should he first try to improve?
3. Evaluation by____________________________

With an experienced group, a more complete rating is possible. In making up a form, select only the items in which instruction has been given and ask the student to select several aspects of his performance to evaluate in a brief essay.

Check list for self-rating by more mature students

1. Did I assume the responsibility the group wished?
2. Did I listen alertly?
3. Did I willingly express my own point of view?
4. Did I try to understand the viewpoint of others?
5. Did I attempt to assess the strengths and weaknesses of all opinions expressed?
6. Did I encourage those who seemed reluctant to speak?
7. Did I help the chairman maintain a friendly, businesslike atmosphere? Keep the discussion moving purposefully?
8. Did I subordinate my own wishes to further the aim of the group?
9. My greatest contribution to the group was____________________

After the importance of group solidarity has become an accepted tenet of the thinking of the majority, it is often beneficial to have students rate all members. The following form has been used for that purpose. It is more appropriate for groups keeping the same personnel for several meetings.

Check list for rating group members

Number the names of members alphabetically.

1. Adams, Ruth	4.
2. Harris, John	5.
3.	6. Swenson, Sandra

Use the corresponding number for the check list. Rate from 1, excellent, to 5, poor.

	Group members					
	1	*2*	*3*	*4*	*5*	*6*
1. Carries out responsibilities	5					
2. Cooperates in discussion	1					
3. Expresses himself clearly	1					
4. Considers all viewpoints	2					
5. Encourages others	2					
6. Shows interest in the group's success	5					

Focusing on the evaluation of process can, of course, be overdone. It is useful, at first, as a teaching device to emphasize standards. When students become more adept, it may be needed only rarely.

Evaluating product In one respect, evaluation of the work produced by a group does not differ from that of the same work done by an individual. The result, weighed against the purpose, is judged by the completeness with which that purpose has been fulfilled. Has the subject been adequately handled? Has a possible solution which accords with the facts been offered? Have the results been presented in an intelligible form? This aspect of the problem is comparatively simple—if evaluation ever is.

When it comes to assigning a grade, however, we may run into difficulties. This matter of grading worries students as well as teachers. Some teachers believe the product of each group should be assessed and all members should receive the same grade. We have seldom found this practice successful. The conscientious student, working with laggards or absentees, justly resents being penalized. Group stimulation often produces amazing results from individuals who lack the purpose or the initiative of producing on their own, but it is unrealistic to expect this always. We know which pupils we find hard to motivate; we should not demand from students what we have been unable to do ourselves. We believe it is wiser and fairer to grade on an individual basis.

Groups require continual guidance if they are to work at maximum capacity. Therefore, it is not difficult, as we move from one to another, to be aware of those pupils who produce and of those who do not. It is always wise to discuss the method of grading with a class, and never more essential than in those instances where the student is likely to think the situation so nebulous as to defy accurate appraisal. Constant supervision while work is in progress—private hints to the dilatory as well as judicious praise for the conscientious, suggestions that those who have achieved certain proficiencies devote themselves to more fruitful experiences—will disabuse the student of the idea that the individual performance is being submerged in the general.

We can avoid possible recriminations by periodically letting the student know where he stands. The task is neither arduous nor time-consuming. After several group meetings, the teacher may tell the class he wants them to know the grades recorded for individual contributions. He wants everyone to be sure of the basis on which evaluations have been made. Therefore, he is asking each to assess his own work and decide what grade he thinks he deserves. The sole purpose is that teacher and student understand each other before it is too late to do anything about it; if there are discrepancies in ratings, individual conferences will be arranged. Then he passes out dated slips of paper on which students are to record the grades they believe they deserve. The next day he returns the slips with his estimate; he asks for signatures and collects the slips to be filed. He then plans a study hour so that he will have time to talk with individuals. Usually there are not many; for the most part, students are fair judges of their own performances. Those who underestimate themselves need encouragement; those who value their work too highly need to face the facts.

Such periodic reports on progress will prepare the student for the final assessment from which there is no recourse. The practice of keeping for each class member a separate folder for all written work is extremely valuable. A dated and signed record of evaluations of his group skills should also be included. The essential thing here, as in all grading, is that the student know the teacher is keeping a record which is available to him and that his final grade is not determined by the whim of the moment.

SELECTED READINGS

Jean D. Grambs, *Group Processes in Intergroup Education.* N.Y., National Conference of Christians and Jews, no date. A delineation of the principles pertinent to the group process as well as explanation of various techniques for group involvement.

Jean D. Grambs, William J. Iverson, and Franklin K. Patterson, *Modern Methods in Secondary Education,* rev. ed., N.Y., Dryden Press, 1958, pp. 229-252. Suggestions for handling groups in the classroom.

Irving Lee, *How to Talk with People.* N.Y., Harper, 1952. A discussion of the understandings and practices necessary for effective communication.

James H. McBurney and Kenneth G. Hance, *Discussion in Human Affairs.* N.Y., Harper, 1950. A presentation planned primarily for college students but valuable for teachers interested in deeper understanding of the principles governing discussion and the techniques of leadership.

Louise Parrish and Yvonne Waskin, *Teacher-Pupil Planning.* N.Y., Harper, 1958. A brief account with many specific examples designed to help teachers plan instruction with pupils and to work with groups within the class.

Florence M. Santiago, *Inexpensive or Free Materials Useful for Teaching Speech.* Ann Arbor, Mich., Braun-Brumfield, 1959. A paperbound book with annotated bibliography of materials for teaching fundamentals, discussion, dramatics, oral interpretation, radio, television, and speech correction; non-selective but useful.

Bert Strauss and Frances Strauss, *New Ways to Better Meetings.* N.Y., Viking, 1951. A lively presentation of the problems of discussion as they pertain both to the leader and to group members.

Commission on the English Curriculum, *The English Language Arts in the Secondary School,* NCTE Curriculum Series, Vol. III. N.Y., Appleton-Century-Crofts, 1956. See pp. 203-227, 236-246, suggestions for planning a program to include all pupils and for integrating speaking experiences with the other aspects of English instruction.

Leland P. Bradford and Gordon L. Lippett, "The Individual Counts." *NEA Journal,* Vol. 43, No. 8 (November 1954). Principles operative in effective group learning form the basis for an analysis of a demonstration showing that group work enhances individual development.

Pearl Spinks, "Life Brought to Literature Through Group Work." *English Journal,* Vol. 39, No. 4 (April 1950). A discussion of the effect of group work on increasing appreciation of literature.

Chapter Ten

Written Expression

> *The very nature of writing indicates it must be learned through actual experience in putting words together to express one's own meaning. One does not learn how to create a sentence by adding or subtracting words and punctuation marks in a sentence someone else has created. Composing a paragraph or an essay is a closely knit operation, and playing with the pieces will not substitute for making the whole.*
>
> —LOU LA BRANT [1]

PERSPECTIVE

The nature of writing

To write clearly, students must think clearly. To write competently, they must think competently. To write with power or imagination, they must think with power or imagination. Think . . . write . . . write . . . think . . . these processes cannot be disjoined. When a student has learned to write better he has learned to think better. This is a law. "There is no way around, only through." [2]

In writing as in gardening, placing vigorous roots in fertile soil is more important than spraying or pruning a plant's foliage. Too much emphasis on pruning spelling or punctuation—especially in writing that is half-hearted or perfunctory—may undermine the aims of instruction. Distracted from the heart of the matter, the learner is led to focus on subsidiary features. These fundamental aspects have already been presented in the first three chapters of this text, "Language as Dynamic Process," "Logical Thinking," and "Imaginative Thinking." Those chapters presented power over language as dependent upon disciplined reason, creative imagination, and an awareness of how language works. To write well, students must grapple with their own thought, and the more aware they are of language in relation to purpose, the more readily they will impose order on their expression.

[1] Commission on the English Curriculum, *The English Language Arts in the Secondary School,* NCTE Curriculum Series, Vol. III (N.Y., Appleton-Century-Crofts, 1956), p. 297.

[2] The quotation is borrowed from a different context in Ibsen's *Peer Gynt.*

Writing as communication But thinking is not writing. The thought must manifest itself in written word-symbols and be arranged in single-file order, for "language is not like an army marching abreast, but like an army forced to go through a mountain pass single file, with one soldier emerging from the pass first, then another and then another." [3] However, the reflective reader may note also that there is a caution required here. One does not always think first and then, subsequently, translate the thought into word-symbols to be written. In actuality, the process probably never so sharply divides but instead proceeds as an interplay of all that comprises thought and symbol-making.

In most cases when we write our thoughts, we intend to communicate, and therefore we must use those systems of arranging word-symbols that have become accepted modes of communication in our culture. As has been emphasized in earlier chapters, *communication* is a key word because it focuses attention upon making ideas available to someone else. Thus, this understanding of the importance of *communication* supports the teacher in rejecting any tendency to teach writing in a vacuum. Having something to say, a desire to say it, and *someone to whom to say it* are as important in learning to write as in learning to speak. Whereas composition is skill in arranging words to form sentences, paragraphs, or verses in larger units, communication is the capacity to make one idea the property of two or more persons. Successful communication, of course, requires efficient skills in composition. One need not make an either-or choice; both concepts are necessary to excellence in writing just as they are to power over oral language.

Writing and speaking But, one might ask, does writing really differ in any fundamental way from speaking? Since the foundations of teaching writing and speaking converge on the point of effective thinking, why not emphasize speech in almost all lessons in expression? Even without the evidence of research, we realize that most human beings talk far more than they write. Why not grant that power over the spoken word is of paramount importance? Why teach anything about writing, other than spelling, capitalization, and punctuation?

The answer is clear. Writing, whenever human beings resort to it, usually conveys relatively crucial meanings in situations where sender and receiver are separated. Love letters, applications for jobs, communication between scattered families and friends—these, like most writing, relate deeply to the needs of human beings. Furthermore, the act of writing, by virtue of its permanence and especially *its separation from the reader,* demands much more careful attention than speech. In his daily talk, a speaker can easily modify his presentation, shift to a new approach, or elaborate points that appear to mystify his listener. In writing, where the receiver of thought is absent during the writing and the creator absent during the reading, such spontaneous modification of the communication is impossible. Unless sentences as well as paragraphs reveal

[3] Thomas Clark Pollock, *The Nature of Literature* (Princeton, N.J., Princeton U. Press, 1942), p. 19.

a sure grasp of concepts and their relationships, a reader may become confused or discontinue reading entirely. Thus, the two considerations of cruciality and the separation of the communicants explain why writing cannot be taught solely through speaking. Properly taught, writing becomes another valuable way to clarify thought, a way that puts a particular premium upon precision and clarity, and therefore a significant part of the curriculum for all pupils.

Writing is also a technique of thinking. Through writing, one comes to know more fully what has heretofore been incomplete and confused thought. The writer explores his thinking, struggles to discriminate among the various feelings and concepts which swirl about in his mind, uses words on paper to control, tie down, and find the most fruitful relationships among his ideas. Because writing is one of the ways of *coming to know,* it is also one of the ways of becoming an educated person.

Keystones of communication The three keystones of effective communication—whether oral or written—are clear thinking, the desire to communicate, and the skills needed to make communication effective. Instruction in writing, it follows, must emphasize the effective organization and expression of thoughts and feelings for others. Such an emphasis places mechanics and conventions where they properly belong as means to an end, not as ends in themselves. Whenever methods of teaching writing are wisely chosen, the learner will feel a concern for his reader. Since unconventionalities of spelling or punctuation distract a reader's attention from the ideas a writer seeks to communicate, he should strive to avoid them. Nevertheless, careful organization of significant thoughts and feelings should remain uppermost in his mind. Dull, lifeless prose, no matter how perfect the spelling or punctuation, is even more to be feared than genuine thought and feeling written without a proper attention to the conventions. If the three keystones of communication are firmly placed in classroom instruction, neither extreme needs to prevail.[4]

Ferment of ideas

The futility of methods which neglect the learner's own thought and feeling cannot be overstressed. "Persons who have read little and thought less will find the writing of an acceptable essay somewhat beyond their powers. But . . . those who have learned to recognize the meaning and significance of personal experience will have the material out of which an acceptable essay may be constructed."[5] What teachers do in advance of writing to help students develop thought often proves as valuable to writing as instruction about the actual composing or perfecting of the manuscript. Instruction in writing can

[4] Fred Joyce Schonell, in his *Backwardness in the Basic Subjects* (London, Oliver and Boyd, 1949), Chapters 17 and 18, reports an investigation in which the structural and mechanical aspects of writing improved automatically as students' interest and ideas improved.

[5] Report of the Board of Admissions and Relations with Schools, C. W. Jones, Chairman, University of California, Berkeley, April 8, 1958.

never evade Henry Seidel Canby's dictum: "Writing is like pulling the trigger of a gun; if you are not loaded, nothing happens."

Curiosity and imagination flourish in the years of youth, but without direction, adolescents often waste these attributes on shallow or trivial matters. The teacher who loses heart when he discovers that "my hobby is sending for pictures of television singers" has not yet accepted the realities of taking adolescents as they are and guiding their growth toward wisdom and maturity. Yet to deepen students' interests, to help them evaluate those interests in terms of a comprehensive set of standards, is entirely possible.

Ideas for writing, just as for speaking, come from all of experience. Students observe the world around them and through their five senses take in the raw materials by which thought is stimulated. Because they are human, they are curious, develop interests, read books, view television, brood and daydream. They have feelings and emotions: humor, sympathy, and anger need outlets; attitudes, antipathies, and affinities need expression. Like all adolescents, they have needs: to accept their size, shape, and sex; to grow toward emotional independence of adults; to make choices in their encounters with other people and with the values in their culture. We have already, in the preceding chapter on oral language, stressed the necessity of a classroom atmosphere where students know they can say what they honestly think but where ideas will be examined impartially and critically. In that chapter, we said the teacher should start with content at the level of the interests and abilities of his students. In the beginning they communicate best matters of particular concern to them. The teacher who is growing, both in his mastery of his subject and in his understanding of adolescents, devises many ways to release this vitality of thought necessary to good writing.

The true teacher does not view adolescence as ludicrous or annoying; to him it is a part of the miracle of life, and therefore worthy of respect. Such a teacher not only provides the motivation for pupils' writing or speaking but often leaves a permanent imprint upon their lives. From his high school memories, John Steinbeck describes a teacher who exemplified these qualities:

> She aroused us to shouting, bookwaving discussions. . . . Our speculation ranged the world. She breathed curiosity into us so that we brought in facts or truths shielded in our hands like captured fireflies. . . . She left a passion in us for the pure knowable world and me she inflamed with a curiosity which has never left me. . . . She left her signature on us, the literature of the teacher who writes on minds. I have had many teachers who told me soon-forgotten facts but only three who created in me a new thing, a new attitude and a new hunger. I suppose that to a large extent I am the unsigned manuscript of that high school teacher. What deathless power lies in the hands of such a person.[6]

The English teacher then, is necessarily one who understands adolescents. He is familiar with their ambivalence between childhood and maturity, their

[6] John Steinbeck, ". . . like captured fireflies," in *CTA Journal*, California Teachers Association, Burlingame, Calif., Vol. 51, No. 8 (November 1955), p. 7.

strong drive for security, and their need to become increasingly independent of adults. He understands and respects their feelings about these and other matters, yet he views each as an individual to be taught. Drawing upon this wisdom, he helps his pupils evolve and evaluate ideas before they write, distinguishing between the essential and non-essential, between the original and the trite, between the sound and the unsound. In other words, the teacher of composition understands adolescents but he also realizes the important changes that good instruction can contribute to their thinking.

Creating a design

The teacher of writing must indeed be concerned with the ferment of ideas; he must not neglect vitality of thought, for without it expression falters or withers away completely. But the pattern and order necessary to prevent vitality from aimless overflow must also receive attention. In the natural world men harness rivers, steam, and electricity to good use; in the human world they applaud the control and form of a superb musician, a ballet troupe, a championship basketball team. Students' writing, humble though it may be, must acknowledge this universal necessity to impose pattern on thought, form on content, order on vitality. If they are to write, pupils must first release the forces of thinking and feeling, but they must not be left like the Sorcerer's Apprentice, lacking the wisdom or skill to impose order on those forces.

To many adolescents, the importance of form presents itself most clearly in team sports, dancing, or popular music. The understanding that order is one of the most significant elements in everything from a parking lot to a religious service has not occurred to them any more than it has to most adults. Consequently the value of design and form cannot be assumed; it must be consciously taught. For most students, exposition, with its inherent requirements of logical organization and clear presentation, contributes most directly to this growing awareness of form in writing. However, the subtler evocative forms of poetry and imaginative prose should not be neglected, for in almost every school some creative pupils perceive experience through these fairly complex patterns and balances.

Consciousness of form is apparently the outstanding lack in the equipment of poor writers. At Michigan State University, Barch and Wright studied the characteristics of good and poor writers among freshmen students and reported some remarkable contrasts: The good writer worries about organization, about not having anything to say, about not being specific, about having no clear-cut purpose in his writing, and about not being direct and to the point. But the poor writer worries about none of these things. Rather, he is concerned about spelling, about vocabulary, and about all sorts of mechanical matters. Moreover, poor writers, unlike the good, are unable to recognize good writing in others.[7]

[7] A. M. Barch and R. L. Wright, "The Background of Good and Poor Writers," *Journal of Communication,* Vol. 7, No. 4 (Winter 1957).

Instruction in expository writing Expository writing, in which the student may learn to discipline his thought and compose his ideas, requires a fundamental kind of clear systematic expression. The problems of instruction, however, are far from simple, for they require the teacher to help pupils with the thinking which precedes their final or even semi-final versions on paper. This is one of the most baffling and intriguing experiences in teaching, for much nebulous thinking occurs at these various levels of awareness with many stages of transition from the first level to that represented in the final ordered composition.

To come to terms with this problem, to achieve some system and progression in a maze so intricate, the teacher finds some classification a helpful guide. For exposition the process of writing can be conveniently viewed in two stages of development.

Preliminary organization

Searching for an idea; identifying a purpose and an audience; limiting the idea; planning an over-all arrangement.

Perfection of the plan

Excluding the irrelevant and extraneous; consistently sticking to the purpose and furthering it. (Unity)

Guiding the reader in an orderly manner from one stage of the subject to the next so that he sees clearly the relationships and encounters no abrupt leaps or confusing gaps. (Coherence)

Bringing out those elements that deserve to be featured and subordinating those that are merely supportive or illustrative. (Emphasis)

Presenting the content in the most effective manner: impressive beginning and ending; appropriate style and tone; acceptable usage, spelling, and punctuation. (Style and convention)

Beginning writers usually feel they must tell everything. The "interesting experience" one teacher [8] wryly describes is all too familiar. It

> starts off as the alarm rings at 5:30, proceeds through the breakfast details, the trip in the car, the first night, the stops at filling stations, the luncheon menus, until at last we get to the race for the shore on a storm-swept lake, only to find that a sentence or two has carried us through the climax, and we are lunching and filling-stationing our way home again, "where we arrived at 6:35, having had a very interesting and thrilling experience."

Whether in personal narratives or exposition of ideas, most pupils need planned instruction in learning to select what they present in terms of purpose and audience. They must find a controlling idea around which to construct the total design.

For junior high school students and even for many in senior high, the primary emphasis in writing should be the paragraph. Skill in writing effective paragraphs requires lucid thought, for every sentence should be clearly related

[8] Eric W. Johnson, "Stimulating and Improving Writing in the Junior High School," *English Journal*, Vol. 47, No. 2 (February 1958).

to the topic sentence or, lacking that, with the central idea. A paragraph should usually present both a distinct beginning and end, with the intervening sentences arranged to help readers see the connection between each sentence and those which precede and follow. A reader should never wonder, even subconsciously, if a sentence is out of place. Thus the principles of unity, coherence, and emphasis enter into each solution of expressing an idea in paragraph form. Such skill in writing, requiring as it does thought and time, constitutes the ultimate goal for many pupils.

Before any discussion of longer papers, the point should be made that in most cases, several short themes serve the purposes of instruction much better than a single long theme. In the junior high school, certainly, the paragraph is a sufficient challenge for the average pupil. Least valuable of all at the secondary level, the long research paper is declining in prestige. Contrary to what many high school teachers believe, college professors of English consider the research paper as inappropriate to the secondary school and wasteful of time needed for more fundamental kinds of writing.[9] However, at all levels some gifted students need help in organizing longer compositions, and occasionally most high school pupils should develop exposition of sufficient length to require guidance on the problems of relating paragraphs to one another. The planning of sequence in a six-year program of writing is very important.[10]

Instruction in imaginative writing By imaginative writing, we mean writing of the kind the *Oxford English Dictionary* defines as "literature," writing that makes "a claim to distinction on the grounds of beauty of form or emotional effect." The terms *creative, personal,* or *literary* are sometimes used to distinguish imaginative from expository writing, but exposition, too, is often creative, personal, or literary, and many arguments circle about these terms. In this text, *imaginative,* contrasting with writing which has a practical purpose, is applied to the composition of those students who find pleasure in expressing personal thoughts and feelings in forms literary writers employ.

Even though it is often the product of prolonged effort, imaginative writing seems more like quicksilver than conscious arrangement of logical thought. Certainly the unconscious enters into these acts of creating much more pervasively than it does in expository writing. Robert Frost has described the surprise of "remembering something I didn't know I knew. . . . There is a glad recognition of the long lost and the rest follows. Step by step the wonder of unexpected supply keeps growing. The impressions most useful to my purpose seem always those I was unaware of and so made no note of at the time when taken . . ." [11] But however spontaneous the result may seem, imaginative writ-

[9] For the point of view of one College English Association, see James J. Lynch, "College Support for High School Teachers," *College English,* Vol. 21, No. 2 (November 1959).

[10] For help in the problem of planning a six-year sequence, grades 7 through 12, see Clarence W. Hatch, "Needed: A Sequential Program in Composition," *English Journal,* Vol. 49, No. 8 (November 1960), pp. 536-537.

[11] Quoted by Lawrence Thompson in *Fire and Ice: the Art and Thought of Robert Frost* (N.Y., Holt, 1942), p. 31.

ing, like the expository, still requires appropriate design if either writer or reader is to realize the full import of the expression.

Helping adolescents find the best organization and form for their imaginative writing requires even more sensitivity to the purpose of the writer than does such help with expository writing. The delicate shreds of imagery, the unconscious freight of emotions, move mysteriously but not always successfully toward form. Often the teacher cannot suggest solutions without interfering with the inner process. As Hughes Mearns suggests repeatedly in *Creative Power*,[12] the teacher can really be helpful only through providing a climate of encouragement and sincere, tactful criticism based on the apparent purpose of each creation. All pupils will not respond to such opportunity. Even so, imaginative writing should not be relegated to the gifted few; all students deserve an opportunity to try writing in which they strive to capture experiences and moods for their own sakes. Teachers are often surprised at how much satisfaction and learning occur for certain pupils, hitherto quite mute and unresponsive to other parts of the English curriculum.

Perfecting the presentation

Whether organized by logical or imaginative design, thought and feeling deserve to be presented effectively. Courteous consideration for those who will read his material prompts a writer to observe conventions of spelling, legibility, and punctuation. Concern for the effect of his ideas leads him to search for the exact word or the most felicitous arrangement. Thus style as well as conventionality enters into considerations of how best to present ideas.

Conventions in presenting ideas Why do teachers want students to observe the conventions of language? Certainly not because these matters are important ends in themselves. But teachers do see language as a clear window opening to the view beyond. Like the window glass, language should be as inconspicuous as possible, permitting the communication to reach the reader or listener without distracting his attention from the idea to the manner in which it is expressed.[13] The teacher wants his students to use the conventions so they will not be denied access to any opportunities, economic or personal, that they may desire. In a democratic culture, proficiency in accepted ways of writing and speaking is an important factor in securing equality of opportunity.

Style in presenting ideas Students observe style in clothing, in automobiles, and in dancing. They are interested not only in fashions but also in the characteristic appearance or manner of these things which so fascinate them. Style commands their attention because it is related to something they care about. Style in writing must also be founded upon genuine interest. Instruction

[12] Hughes Mearns, *Creative Power* (N.Y., Dover, 1958).

[13] There are, of course, stylistic uses of language which are exceptions to the principle stated here.

is futile when pupils have no intensity of living, no depth of feeling or thinking they wish to share through writing. Assuming that the teacher has provided for this fundamental motivation, instruction in style will still be far from easy. To let meaning choose the words rather than the opposite is never simple; there is, indeed, a tyranny of words, particularly of stereotyped phrases, clichés, and imprecise expressions. Developing a personal style requires honesty and much effort; in schools, such an aim is not likely to be accomplished in a single year.

In the history of American education, English teachers have needed to close their ears to many siren calls and not a few fads and extremes. Writing, for instance, can never be improved solely through motivation and enthusiasm; it is hard work, very hard work. On the other hand, an emphasis on vigorous disciplines unaccompanied by pupil enthusiasm and interest creates permanent boredom and distaste. Thus, the goals of written expression for students should be listed in some such order of priority as this:

> The security and disposition to enjoy a wide range of experience with an awareness of the values in both the familiar and strange
>
> Heightened powers of observation and clearer perceptions as the bases for reflection and expression
>
> The habit of clear, orderly thinking about matters within the learner's own experience
>
> The power to organize and express thought and feeling effectively for others
>
> Adequate mastery and habitual use of the conventions: sentence sense, paragraphing, spelling, punctuation, capitalization, and appropriate appearance of manuscript.[14]

While the emphasis here is upon expository writing, there should also be opportunity for imaginative writing with encouragement and further instruction in artistic form available for those who respond with notable interest or give some evidence of ability.

THE TEACHING PROBLEM

Organizing Instruction

In a commendable desire to insure adequate attention to writing, teachers have sometimes allocated a semester or several days a week to composition. The disadvantages in this method—which implies separation from the other arts of language and from the stimulation of ideas in the rest of the curriculum—almost always undermine the alluring promise and simplicity of such an organization. A better plan proves to be an integrated English program, emphasizing writing throughout all six years of the secondary school. (See the Hatch article

[14] See Appendix D, pp. 692-97, for help on handwriting and Appendix C, pp. 689-92, for help in spelling.

recommended, p. 491.) Such a plan, combining writing with speaking, reading, literature, and other subjects, promotes a vitality composition cannot achieve as an isolated activity.

Basic understandings

Certain basic understandings will do much to help teachers planning instruction in written expression. First of all, what pupils write about should have a broad base; possibilities for content should be viewed as little less than everything in the world, all of life, all that the imagination and curiosity of youth can conceive. Secondly, the program in writing should distinguish between ideas and topics. In this sense, ideas are attitudes or points of view toward a topic or subject. Thirdly, provisions for genuine communication must never be neglected. Students should write for someone whom they want to persuade, entertain, inform, or convince. As often as possible, their reader should be someone interested in the ideas expressed, not merely a proofreader detecting mistakes in the conventions of writing.

Content with broad base Writing succeeds best in the classroom when it is part of a larger concern with significant ideas, no matter whether they begin in the English class, elsewhere in the school, or in life beyond the school. Writing may be related to the total English program in a number of ways. For example, during unit instruction the incubation and motivation of thought is reinforced by all the language arts. In the unit on science-fiction (pp. 257-72), a series of five compositions is used to develop the content. Writing frequently draws its vitality from the study of literature. Writing and literature complement each other so naturally that their mutual reinforcement is one of the arguments for integrating the elements of English. The culminating activity for the unit on *Macbeth* (pp. 405-13), an organized essay, is a clear example. Insofar as the teacher is alert to relationships between English and other subjects in the school, writing may also originate in shop, homemaking, school sports, or science. Some schools have unified studies in which English and social studies are closely allied to the school's program in guidance; such classes engender much of their own content for writing and speaking. Nor should the world beyond the school, especially the local community, be neglected. The more comprehensive the content in English, the more opportunities the pupil has for writing. In the main, instruction should frequently interrelate the arts of language as they are interrelated in life beyond the classroom.

None of what has been said is intended to dismiss the value of pausing in a unit or a study of short stories in order to give direct attention to skills needed in writing. A teacher may indeed pause to identify or to teach an important segment of the whole without destroying that whole, much as a coach stops a basketball practice game to inspect or improve a faulty technique of dribbling. It is precisely at this point that the integrated program reveals its advantages, for any skill—physical, mechanical, or conceptual—acquires more significance and clarity when learned in relation to some more comprehensive purpose. Taught in isolation, featured primarily as an exercise or drill, paragraph development or dribbling are usually boring matters that all too frequently waste the teachers' and students' time, not to mention the taxpayers' money.

Nor does the entire policy for student writing need to reflect such integration. No one organization should be used exclusively, and it is entirely possible to use the benefits of synthesis without excluding special separate lessons in composition. A number of such lessons appear in the Suggested Learning Experiences later in this chapter. Conditions do vary and require modified teaching designs. English teachers learn to be flexible, using many approaches but favoring those which (like integration) sustain a principle of economy.

Concern for ideas As in all the previous chapters this text stresses a concern for ideas. In writing, this means students cannot be expected to talk or write effectively about topics. They should be helped to see how an idea about a topic must be a base for their communication. For this idea, they must decide upon a point of view, an attitude toward the topic. Applying this to writing, one teacher makes a clear distinction between the organized accumulation of expanding a topic and the controlled development of an idea.[15] His distinction is illustrated in two sets of titles.

Topics	Ideas
Hamlet *or* Hamlet's Conduct *or* Hamlet's Conduct in the Scene with His Mother	Hamlet's conduct in the scene with his mother shows him to be raving mad. *or* Hamlet's conduct in the scene with his mother shows him to be extraordinarily sane.
Hobbies *or* My Hobby—Raising Prize Pigs	Raising pigs is the best way I know to make money and have fun at the same time.

This teacher suggests that supplying pupils with ideas may be a stepping stone to genuine composition. Because this method implies using someone else's ideas, the instruction should move quickly to providing only the frame of an idea, e.g., Hamlet's conduct in the scene with his mother shows him to be . . . The final achievement is to help pupils comprehend the importance of restraining their impulses to write until they have evolved an idea that can dominate their selection of content. Then they will truly compose what they write.

Writing to communicate As often as possible, students should write for someone who is to receive their ideas. There are many ways to organize in-

[15] Bertrand Evans, "Writing and Composing," *English Journal*, Vol. 48, No. 1 (January 1949).

struction by this basic principle of communication. Arrangements may be made for pupils to write to others their own age in various parts of the United States and the world. Just before Christmas many teachers present the form and spirit of thank-you letters. When a pupil is away from school for any bereavement or illness, students write letters of condolence, or get-well notes. Toward the close of school the teacher presents the letter of application in relation to summer jobs. Friendly letters may be studied at any time during the year, first drafts being written in class in order to receive suggestions and corrections, provided the student wants the teacher to read them. Special recognition might be given for letters neatly copied and brought to class in stamped envelopes ready for mailing.

The principle of communication does not always require such lifelike situations. Any teacher instructing at least two classes of the same or approximate grade levels may organize plans to accommodate a pupil's desire to express something for someone his own age. In the following paragraphs one such plan is described in detail.

The first step is to explain that students in each class will write a composition to be read and evaluated by members of the other class. The teacher first points out that it will be important that the composition and not the student be evaluated. For this reason each student is to choose a pseudonym, an alias, a *nom de plume*. Only one person in the class, someone selected by the class as a whole or someone already elected as class secretary, is to have a complete list of the names of the students in the class and the aliases chosen. Each student will report his alias to this one student, who will keep the secret. Not even the teacher will know whose compositions will have at the top such names as Jet Pilot, Methuselah, or Butterflop.

Next the students suggest topics which might be of interest to the other class. These topics are placed on the chalk board. The students and teacher discuss them, selecting four or five. The teacher then takes one of these topics and conducts a lesson on how it might be limited, reminding students of such important matters as effective beginnings, development of the main body of the composition, and effective conclusions. Any conventionalities or mechanics in which the class has been weak are called to their attention, and the students are set to writing their rough drafts. Meanwhile the same procedure is occurring in the other class; those students, too, are writing rough drafts, to be exchanged with the first class.

During the writing period, the teacher moves about the room willing to answer any questions but not reading the compositions. After the rough drafts have been completed the final polished versions are copied and the student secretary gathers all the papers, none of them identified by any name except the alias. The purpose of this, the pupils are again reminded, is to prevent students in the other class from appraising the composition in terms of its author. Each deserves to be evaluated in its own right and should stand on its own merits or weaknesses. When compositions have been completed in both classes, the student secretaries exchange them and the process begins:

Each student receives a composition from the other class.[16] Each reads the one he has drawn—reads it several times, carefully and thoughtfully. When he has completed his study, he writes at the close of that composition his own comments. The teacher has placed on the chalk board, in advance of this step, some points agreed upon by both students and teacher, points one should look for in good compositions. It is important to accent the positive, for there are few schoolroom sights more unpleasant than a group of adolescents inflamed with the fever of the chase, hunting for mistakes in spelling and punctuation. The teacher must lift their sights to more significant aspects, such as the author's intention and whether or not he was successful in carrying it out.

Next, the students move into groups of five. Now each reads aloud the composition he has drawn and also reads the comments he has written. The other members of the group discuss each paper, adding any comments they wish; the person in charge of the paper acts as secretary, making note of these contributions. Each person, in turn, follows the same procedure until all the papers in a single group have been read.

Each group chooses the best composition, or in some cases the best two, and these are read before the entire class. Comments from the class and the teacher are now added to each of these excellent papers. In many cases the student who has drawn such a composition writes as much as the original writer, viewing this as an opportunity and not a punishment. This attitude can be established if the teacher talks over the purposes of written composition and the value of experience in writing material *that is going to be read by someone else*. In this case the original owner of the paper is going to be extremely interested in reading all the comments.

Now the class affixes some kind of a symbol—a star or a seal—indicating that these five or six papers just read and discussed have been selected as the best. So far no one knows to whom the papers belong.

The papers are then returned to the authors. Now in each class the students whose papers were selected by their peer group are honored by having their real names divulged. Their compositions are read aloud, and the virtues and qualities they have exemplified are noted and praised as goals to be emulated.[17]

If the teacher has no other group with whom to exchange compositions, the plan may be used within any class taught by another teacher. In the group reading of the compositions, there is excellent opportunity for comparing and contrasting points of view on writing; students may learn from one another. For those whose papers are chosen, there is some small degree of honor and this gives the teacher an opportunity to set up models for others to follow. The disadvantage that sometimes good papers are drawn by poor readers is

[16] If there are not enough compositions to go around, two students may work together on a single composition. If there are too many compositions, some able student may be allotted two.

[17] In some instances, the teacher himself has written a composition, using a pseudonym known only to one member of the class. If the teacher does write, everybody is on his mettle to read carefully the composition he has drawn, for who knows, he may have the teacher's composition. It is considered fair in such a situation for the teacher to write a single composition to be used in both classes, and for him to have some conspirator in still another class who does the job of copying the teacher's composition twice so that no one will know the handwriting.

offset to some degree by the fact that each paper must be read aloud to a wider group and the individual reader's opinion of the paper is supplemented by that of at least four or five other students. Certainly not the least of considerations is the fact that the teacher carries on instruction but, for this one composition, does absolutely no reading. The method may be used successfully several times a semester.

Note that this method gives the teacher many excellent opportunities to teach the qualities of good writing, that the students write something for someone, and that the someone in this case is a member of their own peer group. It gives the students an opportunity to do something useful and helpful for someone else. The method may be adapted to any level from the seventh grade to the twelfth. It has been presented here as one illustration of how a teacher may use the principles of communication—having something worthwhile to express, a desire to express it, and someone to whom the pupil wants to express his ideas. Then, and only then, can there exist effective instruction in how to express ideas.

Organizing efficient routines

Instruction in writing involves such a diverse and complex strategy that a teacher must develop a system to care for all the details of filing, checking, and conference time, to mention only a few of the details making for efficiency and success.[18] Foremost in importance is a folder for each pupil, in which are kept all his compositions, other written work, lists of spelling errors, and pertinent duplicated material, everything listed cumulatively on a table of contents. A student writing chairman, working in collaboration with his teacher, may be responsible for filing and distributing the folders. This permanent file, invaluable both to pupil and teacher, determines the agenda for many pupil-teacher conferences.

Conferences with pupils may be planned for times when the class is writing or studying. If the teacher writes on the board names of students he wishes to see, and if on either side of his desk he places a chair, no time will be wasted. As the teacher finishes with one student he turns to the other while the one who is through goes to the board, erases his name, and quietly notifies the next person on the list.

During some periods when students are writing, a teacher may remain at his desk to confer with individuals on the *organization* of their writing. During this time the teacher will give no assistance on such matters as spelling, punctuation, or usage. Students receive help only on the improvement of paragraphs or the design of their total composition, including unity, coherence, emphasis, style, and tone. On the "Consultation Board,"—a chalk board clearly in view of all students—is a column where may be written the names of individuals who

[18] For many helpful organizational recommendations see the article, "Managing Student Writing," by Sarah I. Roody and Bess Lyman, *English Journal,* Vol. 44, No. 2 (February 1955).

are either requested to consult with the teacher or who wish to do so. Also on the Consultation Board questions and admonitions like these appear:

Conference Comments

Remember: Today's conferences are to help you with the *organization* of your writing. DO NOT ASK FOR HELP on spelling, punctuation, or usage.

Questions on Organization

Is the BEGINNING right for your topic? Does it catch the reader's attention? Did you plan it or just start?

Are there any confusing gaps, abrupt jumps that will leave the reader behind?

Are the most important points given the position of greatest emphasis? Or the greatest length?

Are the other parts treated in proportion to their importance?

Whenever the conferences concern papers longer than a single paragraph, teachers can work more effectively if students have underlined their topic sentence in each paragraph that contains one. Students should also have jotted down the questions and matters on which they seek help.

If they are to expect high quality work from their classes, teachers must also establish high standards. From the beginning of the school year, they must make clear that only papers which meet reasonable criteria of neatness, legibility, and content are to be accepted. Papers which do not meet these requirements may be returned for rewriting. The exact standards will of course vary with the age and maturity of the students. However, any tendency in September to overlook standards stressed during the previous June only encourages slovenly work. Like children pressing for certainty on the limits permitted them, many pupils will "try out" a new teacher—passing in something less than presentable work if they believe it will be accepted. The recurring human tendency to test limits often manifests itself in the composition program.

Evaluating compositions by the method of a double grade offers another way to establish standards for those individuals who have special problems with the conventions of expression. Some teachers use this device only with students who produce and develop ideas more skillfully than they present them. At the senior high school level, the more able learners respond quickly to the challenge of low scores on such mechanical skills.

Among the special questions students will want answered with respect to standards for composition are the following: Is there a routine heading? Margin? Form? (Some junior high school teachers post model papers on the bulletin board or display "larger than life size" models as reminders.) Which papers must be written in ink? Is typing acceptable? Under what conditions will papers be returned unread? For each of these, the teacher will want to establish a policy.

Often a rotating team is used to assist with routines. One teacher[19] recommends a secretary to keep a complete class log and assignment book

[19] Grace Daly Maertins, "Organizing the Class," *English Journal*, Vol. 47, No. 7 (October 1958), p. 416. This article, with its suggestions concerning the solution of problems of classroom management, is recommended to beginning teachers.

which may be read on any day review seems desirable. Absentees, with their inevitable question, "Did I miss anything?" are referred to the secretary and his class log. Paper monitors assume responsibility for collecting homework and distributing supplies and materials. Such assistants often have responsibility for a table or a single row of seats. They are particularly helpful when the class is meeting in groups and materials are difficult to distribute. Some teachers prefer not to introduce too formal a structure but rely upon appointed or elected student assistants for many projects.

Reading and judging compositions

All who are seriously concerned about the teaching of writing in our schools realize that finding time to read compositions and to help learners with their difficulties is the English teacher's greatest frustration. To bring even half the pupils up to a level of competence which meets the expectations of their parents or the needs of a democratic society is impossible in many schools. Practice in writing is necessary for improvement; one research study on the effects of increasing the amount of writing practice shows that doubling it reduces failures by two-thirds.[20] Overwhelmed by the impossible load of paper evaluation, teachers continue to receive public criticism. In desperate but futile efforts they sometimes resort to cram courses for seniors planning to go on to college. Yet almost everyone realizes that proficiency in writing, developing as it does only over a long period of time, requires skilled instruction from primary school through high school. Furthermore, the great numbers of pupils who do not go on to college also benefit from the most important contribution of writing instruction, the clarification of thinking. The teacher craves time to help everyone in his classes.

Yet until English teachers are assigned work loads commensurate with the task they have been set, they must continue to do the best they can under the circumstances. Dusel's study for the California Council of Teachers of English [21] shows plainly that teachers consider the amount of practice necessary to develop an average pupil's competence in written expression varies from 150 words a week for ninth-graders to 350 for seniors, with 250 words an over-all average. Many recommended that some writing be done daily. Nevertheless to read and comment constructively on these compositions would require at least 28 hours beyond the typical work week. The conscientious English teacher, if he fulfilled present expectations, would read enough pupil papers each week to equal several novels the size of *War and Peace* and would write enough incisive comments to rival the length of *Gone with the Wind.* Until our society places a greater value on education and realizes that people responsible for

[20] Virgil L. Lokke and George S. Wykoff, " 'Double Writing' in Freshman Composition—An Experiment," *School and Society,* Vol. 68, No. 1773 (December 18, 1948). Improvement also increased, by sixty per cent; however, the number of students involved in this experiment, 22, was small.

[21] William J. Dusel, "Determining an Efficient Teaching Load in English," *Illinois English Bulletin,* Vol. 43, No. 1 (October 1955).

teaching important and complex skills should be assigned only the number of pupils they can teach effectively, the situation will remain. A hopeful sign is the recommendation in the Conant report that one hundred pupils be the maximum load for English teachers.[22]

In view of this serious situation, what methods do English teachers use in order to cope with the paper load? What short cuts and strategies within the limits of integrity help to alleviate an impossible burden? [23] In classrooms where students keep their writing in folders, teachers often wait until three compositions have been written and then ask students to turn in for grading only the one they consider best of the three. The other two may be examined in conference but do not receive as thorough a scrutiny. The method of *noms de plume*, described earlier in this chapter (pp. 496-98), also relieves the teacher of reading several sets of compositions. Pre-vision—considering with the class the purpose of an assignment, what they may learn, what the teacher anticipates as a finished product—is still another strategy to reduce time wasted on futile enterprises. The most effective teacher protection, however, is planned pre-correction. Pre-correction procedures, even in a utopian schoolroom, would be sound pedagogy. In a crowded school day they become a necessity.

Establishing basic methods of pre-correction

Procedures to increase pupil responsibility Pre-correction is a method of insuring definite proofreading by the student writer before the teacher ever sees the manuscript. Two class periods, usually on successive days, are required. On the first, students write their *rough drafts*. These follow an informal outline the student has planned in order to provide his composition with some basic arrangement, but in this writing, he is free to consider his outline as tentative, modifying and changing it as his plans develop. He is also free to smudge, erase, cross out, and insert. Capturing ideas in words rather than maintaining neatness of appearance receives emphasis at this point.

During this first period the teacher moves about answering student questions, making suggestions to individuals, and advising those whose composition problems he remembers from previous assignments. Fifteen minutes before the end of the class period, he goes to the board and writes a series of questions which he and the students have evolved. For example: [24]

> Are there any *words* in my composition which may be *misspelled?* If there are, I should draw circles around each one, and look for them in the dictionary tonight.

[22] James B. Conant, *The American High School Today* (N.Y., McGraw-Hill, 1959). This is the official recommendation of the NCTE as adopted and reiterated by resolution in 1956, 1957, and 1959.

[23] The Educational Testing Service (Princeton, N.J.), with a grant from the Fund for the Advancement of Education, has experimented with a program of hiring lay readers in sixteen cities throughout the nation. See Henry Chauncy, "The Plight of the English Teacher," *Atlantic*, Vol. 204, No. 5 (November 1959).

[24] For a longer list suitable to grades 11 and 12, see the one used by Henry Fitts, Winchester, Mass., High School, in *English Journal*, Vol. 48, No. 1 (January 1959), p. 39.

Have I any *awkward sentences* reflecting muddy thinking? (Example: My greatest ambition is to be a nurse which I have had from when I was a child.) Can I revise any of my sentences to reflect clearer thinking?

Have I used any run-on sentences? (Example: The car came to an abrupt stop, in it was a stout woman and a great many children.) This is sometimes called "the baby blunder."

Have I at least one sentence beginning with a phrase, clause, or *ing* word?

The teacher may place on the board as many questions as the students will assimilate, but experience suggests it is better to focus on a few problems each time rather than to scatter efforts on a great many. Those composition errors which have appeared most often in earlier compositions should be emphasized, and as different problems of writing come to the forefront, the questions should vary.

When the questions have been listed on the board, the students should stop writing, and together with the teacher, read the questions and search their rough drafts for the problem involved in each. Unless time for this scrutiny is provided in class, some pupils will not bother to use this help. After applying the questions to their own manuscripts and asking further assistance of the teacher, the students are asked to complete and polish these rough drafts at home; they are told to bring materials for copying the *final draft* in class the next day.

At the beginning of the second class hour, the teacher discusses briefly the purpose of neatness and the elements of attractive appearance in a manuscript. Some teachers draw parallels with food attractively served or window displays in good taste. After answering any questions applying to more than a single individual, the teacher, as the class begins copying the *final draft*, writes on the board a new set of questions such as the following:

Have I remembered to use question marks and apostrophes in places requiring them?

Have I underlined three dull verbs or nouns in my rough draft and replaced them with more colorful or precise words?

After most of the students have had an opportunity to copy their manuscripts, to check for the points covered by the questions on the board, and to obtain the teacher's help on special problems, a final oral reading check is made. Many pupils need to establish this habit of looking back over their writing and of "hearing" it as it "sounds" in the mind of a reader.[25] To develop this inner ear, each pupil now reads aloud his own composition in a quiet voice. If the whole class starts at once, no one is embarrassed. Some teachers prefer to have the students sit in groups, either reading their compositions aloud to one another or exchanging compositions and pointing out the mistakes they find. One or all of these methods may be used. At their conclusion, the teacher is assured

[25] Anyone who has ever reread a personal letter is aware of the manner in which careless errors find their way into written symbols—words are omitted, or are written twice in a row, diction needs improvement, or *come* has been set down for *comes*.

of a product in which many careless errors have been caught by the writer himself.

Ideally, writing should be taught in situations providing maximum opportunity for individual instruction. Although such situations are frequently impossible, the method of pre-correction described here will enable a teacher to instruct a group and at the same time to talk with many individuals. Both groups and individuals receive help at the time when learning is most likely to occur. Errors in usage, mechanics, and form can be anticipated, thus making it possible for the teacher to read the compositions later with his attention focused on larger considerations—organization, tone, good taste, precision of thought, and other qualities of good writing. Even for this, there will not be enough time.

Clarifying purposes of correction The teacher's purpose is not so much to improve a particular composition as to help pupils become more self-critical and to improve their writing ability. Thus he needs to ask himself whether or not his correction procedures are effective. For instance, the careful and meticulous marking of every error has been rejected by almost everyone who has studied the problem. One study of compositions corrected by teachers of college freshmen showed that only twenty per cent of the comments helped the writers become more self-directive, and almost thirty-six per cent of the comments were worthless or positively false.[26] Such findings show a lack of standards or critical wisdom on the part of many who read compositions. In another study the weekly themes of two groups of ninth grade students were read and checked in two different ways. For the first group, themes were read by means of an error guide and code. All errors were checked and the themes were assigned grades. They were then returned to the pupils to be rewritten and returned to the teacher in corrected form. For the other group, writing just as frequently, only a grade was given. No errors were checked or indicated in any manner and no rewriting of corrected themes was required. Comparison of the relative improvements of these pupils showed that although the detailed theme correction was slightly more effective in eliminating technical errors, the difference was not great enough to justify such a tremendous expenditure of teacher time.[27]

In view of this and similar research, the English teacher needs to consider carefully whether or not the long hours he spends in reading and commenting on pupil compositions are paying dividends in pupil improvement. Positive criticism should often be oral during conference periods in class while other students are writing. Often more can be accomplished in this way. However, when written comments are offered, some emphases have been found to be

[26] A study of 800 themes written by college freshmen, made by an Ursuline nun of Toledo, Ohio, and reported by Augustine Confrey in "An Investigation of the Comments Made by Forty English Instructors Upon Students' Themes," *Catholic Educational Review*, Vol. 25, No. 6 (June 1927).

[27] John Ernest Fellows, *The Influence of Theme Reading and Theme Correction on Eliminating Technical Errors in the Written Compositions of Ninth Grade Pupils*, University of Iowa Studies in Education, Series 222, Vol. 7, No. 1 (Iowa City, Iowa, 1932).

helpful. Stress upon clarity of thought and stylistic elements independent of grammar were found to be effective with junior high pupils in the research of Ash; [28] emphasis upon sentence structure proved to be the major need of the pupils in his study. Even at the college level, research indicates the importance of a wealth of ideas, a discussion of those ideas, and the instructor's concern for effective organization and presentation.[29] One committee studied substandard writing among undergraduates at the University of California on the Berkeley campus and explored ways of improvement. The most conclusive of its findings: Difficulties of organization and structure are predominant; proficiency in the technique of grammatical usage seems a corollary of general ability to organize material logically.[30]

Encouraging imaginative writing

Imaginative writing succeeds best in classrooms where emphasis is on generating ideas and determining the best design for them. The essential feature of classroom organization becomes the climate of encouragement and of sincere reaction to whatever is written. The teacher's measures to secure such conditions include a preliminary class discussion of what is important to setting the stage for any creative process. He should also discuss the importance of sincerity and tact in reacting to imaginative writing, explaining that the "audience" may be the entire class, a group within the class, or an individual who might be either the teacher or a fellow classmate. Approaches that teachers have used successfully are presented here for consideration by those who wish to organize similar classroom situations.

Have a desk drawer and state that contributions may be put there at any time. Urge pupils to bring creative writing they have finished at home; criticize it honestly in terms of its apparent purpose.

Form creative writing clubs and permit students who have demonstrated good control of expository writing to present literary writing in lieu of regular assignments required of other class members. In some schools the writing club can be made a regular part of the class work.

Experiment with several verse forms, including free verse, and encourage groups of interested pupils to extend their experimentation to other verse forms. The Japanese verse form, *hokku*, serves effectively for developing creativity beyond the limerick or quatrain.

Keep a file of the students' best imaginative writing; read from it occasionally, without indicating the student-author; ask various classes to list positive points to

[28] Irvin O. Ash, "An Experimental Evaluation of the Stylistic Approach in Teaching Written Composition in the Junior High School," *Journal of Experimental Education,* Vol. 4, No. 1 (September 1935).

[29] J. D. Clark, "A Four-year Study of Freshman English," *English Journal* (college edition), Vol. 24, No. 5 (May 1935); Roy C. Maize, "A Study of Two Methods of Teaching English to Retarded College Freshmen," unpublished doctoral dissertation, Purdue University, 1952; summarized in *Review of Educational Research,* Vol. 25, No. 2 (April 1955).

[30] Committee on University Prose Standards, University of California, Berkeley, in "Report of the Committee on Educational Policy," October 29, 1957, and "Proposed Report of the Committee on University Prose Standards," September 1951.

be copied down by a pupil secretary; return these notations to the actual author.

Use some of the methods described earlier in the chapter on imaginative thinking.

Encourage individuals to keep journals with daily entries; from these journals they may draw ideas for literary writing to submit in lieu of regular composition assignments.

Nominate outstanding students for the NCTE Achievement Awards program which is based upon four compositions written by the student, standardized tests of literary awareness and composition, and supporting letters from teachers and administrators. Information about these awards is printed and available from the National Council of Teachers of English.

Without building hopes too high, encourage many pupils to submit materials for contests in the *Atlantic, Scholastic,* and other magazines.

Suggest to local school and community clubs that they offer prizes at some stated time for the best literary writing presented annually.

Teach accurate description; place before pupils some object such as autumn leaves or a piece of driftwood, gnarled and twisted; have pupils first describe the object with accurate and logical expression. Finally, ask them to describe the object imaginatively and creatively, seeing it in some new way.

To reward good writers, place their creations along with their pictures in the school showcase.

Let an art class read several superior creations and illustrate them in linoleum block, water color, and oil.

"Publish" a collection of students' best literary writings; the publication may be as humble as a collection of typewritten sheets, covered with a simple paper cover on which an appealing title is lettered; it may be a looseleaf scrapbook, covered with a brightly colored oil cloth on which has been imposed a decal design and a stenciled title. On good paper of various colors, the selections should be copied by the authors or typed by a good typist. If the teacher shows genuine enthusiasm, tells other classes about the collection, uses models from it, and places it on a special table in the library, the contributors will be gratified and the next "publication" will include a larger number of contributors. These collections of writing may be kept from year to year to serve as initiators for further literary writing.

Often, junior high pupils with creative writing interests like to use puns and malapropisms; they also like to parody juvenile books in series such as the Tom Swift and Nancy Drew titles; they like to surprise readers with unexpected endings, "the thrill that was really a dream, the dear feminine friend who turns out to be a boat, the terrible danger that proved to be merely a cat in the attic." [31]

Write plays, dialogues, and pantomimes for junior high puppet shows, for graduation exercises, and for assemblies.

Occasionally plan for a group composition, sometimes in prose and a few times in free verse; group composition often proves successful in junior and senior high school classes with many slow learners.

Discuss the earliest memories one can summon up from childhood. Early memories are often strongly related to sensory experiences. After sharing some of these, including, perhaps, one from the teacher, the class writes on the topic "A Vivid Memory from My Early Childhood."

[31] *The English Language Arts in the Secondary School,* p. 309.

Summary: Principles underlying effective instruction in composition

The bases for effective instruction in composition may now be summarized:

The best organization of writing instruction relates it to the rest of the English curriculum, to other school subjects and activities, and to pupil concerns beyond the school.

The help teachers give pupils in getting ideas and in evaluating them is as important as instruction in organizing and presenting those ideas.

Pupils must grapple with their own ideas and consciously shape them toward effective communication; mere verbalizing of principles or study of models is insufficient.

Pupils must write with a genuine sense of communication; they must have something to say, someone to say it to, and a desire to say it; only then can a teacher help them with the facility to express it.

Teachers should plan for a progression in the attainment of specific skills of composition; this progression should encompass all the grades of the secondary school.

Frequent practice in writing, usually limited to short compositions and aimed at specific problems of achievement, surpasses other plans in effecting pupil achievement.

Pupils need to be taught that a controlling idea is needed for composing any writing; thinking and writing should not be separated.

Evaluation of student writing and all revision should extend beyond a concern with mechanical correctness; the heart of the matter is clarity, forcefulness, and vitality of expression.

Expository writing should receive a heavier balance in the over-all time plan, but imaginative writing should be encouraged for those who respond with interest, ability, or both.

The complexity and difficulty of teaching writing require careful planning of routines, filing, conferences, and reading of compositions.

Suggested Learning Experiences

The suggestions which follow are intended to start readers thinking of ideas of their own. In teaching pupils to write, there is need for unlimited ingenuity; the ideas presented here are merely selected grains of sand from a vast shoreline. They are practical ways to carry out the principles which have just been presented.

In their present form, these suggestions cannot carry with them all the richness of context they would have in an actual classroom. More frequently than not, lessons like these would constitute elements of some larger plan—important adjuncts to literary study, mosaics in a unit, parts of the strategy for a core class, or preparation for a film. For instance, the first suggestion, on codes of living, actually grew out of a unit in which pupils read and discussed literary selections about characters whose choices revealed their values. Many of the other ideas presented here developed from some previous activity and evolved into further lessons not included in the description. Occasions for writing may, of course, be separately motivated, but the larger curriculum plan often provides momentum that ought not to be neglected.

Ferment of ideas

To awaken intellectual curiosity

■ *Consider codes of living*

Duplicate a list of sayings and mottoes which reflect various outlooks, from ruthlessness to unselfish altruism, and have the class check reactions anonymously. The sheet will look like this:

Nothing But the Truth

Read each statement carefully and thoughtfully. Then, after each statement, check the response with which you honestly and actually agree. There are no right or wrong answers. Do not sign your name. Write comments if you wish.

1. In this world it's every man for himself and the devil take the hindmost. You can't be too thoughtful of others or you will lose out yourself.

Strongly agree_______ Undecided_______ Strongly disagree_______

Agree_______ Disagree_______

Comment if you wish:

For the rest of the items, provide the same response framework. Other items that might be included: Do unto others as you would have them do unto you; do unto others as they would do unto you, only do it to them first; fools are made for wise men's profit; self-respect is possible only to those who do not stoop to take advantage of others; if everyone admitted the truth, we would discover that everyone is looking out for himself and for a "big deal"; honesty is the best policy; he who does not live somewhat for others does not fully live himself; the race is to the swift; I am my brother's keeper. Add others, as desired.

Because he represents an adult authority symbol in our society, the teacher may wish partly to dissociate himself from the exercise by having a small committee of students pass out the sheets, collect them after the class has completed them, and tally the results. The committee then reports back to teacher and class, leading a discussion open to all class members. The teacher will merely help pupils select a basis for limiting their ideas and an opening for writing their reactions.

If a more complete development is desired, the teacher may include selected materials from fiction and carry out a brief project called "The Choices We Make." For this purpose copies of suitable stories, biographies, and other selections are placed on a reserve table in the library or classroom. Some selections used successfully with high school students are listed here, but each teacher may have favorites of his own.

Short stories

"Too Late to Lie," Donald MacKenzie
"Glory in Bridgeville," William Wise
"I Can't Breathe," Ring Lardner
"Success Story," James Gould Cozzens

One-act plays

Two Crooks and a Lady, Eugene Pillot
Confessional, Percival Wilde
Finders Keepers, George Kelly

From class discussions of self-interest versus good will there should develop enough tension of ideas to motivate writing. The teacher will need to help pupils limit their material before they begin, these ideas being otherwise abstract and unwieldy. And of course the teacher should avoid condemning self-interest unless he wants a flood of idealistic thoughts, few of them completely sincere. One does well to make clear that honest conviction is preferable to perfunctory moralizing; otherwise these lessons may produce a crop of saints as short-lived as New Year's resolutions.

■ *Envision unfamiliar modes of living*

Assign the topic "If I were ______." The following outline indicates the main features the teacher would present in helping pupils with such a composition:

Occupations	*Races*	*Nationalities*	*Religions*
policeman	Caucasian	Japanese	Moslem
housewife and mother	Oriental	German	Buddhist
teacher	Negro	Arab	Christian
union leader	Indian	Hindu	Jew
nurse	Polynesian	Mexican	
businessman			
stenographer			
truck driver			

Ideas for development: My point of view would be ______. My loyalties and/or dislikes would be ______.

Components of "If I were": The circle below depicts rather freely some of the possible components of such a composition.

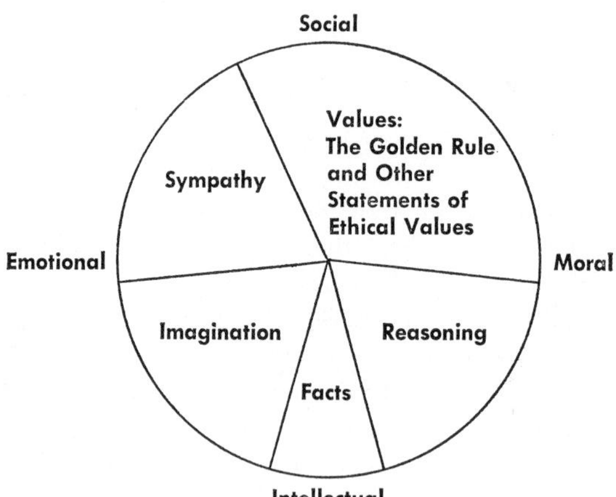

When successful, this composition may contribute to some of these desirable purposes of education: more precise observation, better understanding, more objectivity, expansion of imaginative feeling, diminished ethnocentricity, and increased sensitivity to other people.

■ *Consider the bases for making choices*

1. Some teachers may wish to compare their students' value choices with those of other adolescents. One composition, "The Person I Would Like to Be Like," has

been rather widely used in research. Havighurst's[32] directions for assigning this essay ask for the age, character, appearance, occupation, and recreations of the ideal person; results are reported for a variety of communities as well as social and age groups.

2. Similarly, a number of textbooks contain short sketches of situations involving problems of conduct and choices among values.[33] Posing such problems almost invariably starts the ferment of thought, the lively discussion, which must precede writing. For instance, the situations in these textbooks appear under titles such as "What Price Advancement?" and "The Individual Versus the Class or Group." In schools where these or similar books are not available, teachers may prepare several original case stories.

3. Pictures that raise issues also serve to stimulate discussion. Mounted on cardboard with a series of thought-provoking questions pasted beneath them or on the reverse side, such pictures become the bases of numerous compositions. Over a period of years, an excellent file of such stimulators, tested and winnowed by use, can be accumulated. In the file, also, should be clippings, headlines, poems, and quotations, all of which may be used to stimulate ideas for writing.

■ *Present two opposing points of view*

1. For either junior or senior high pupils, the tension of ideas can be created by presenting two sides of a question. Usually, the issues at stake should relate to the interests characteristic of the age group. For instance, the following lesson succeeded with a number of junior high school classes. The teacher duplicated the materials, passed them out, and read them aloud. A brief discussion, moderated by the teacher, was followed by writing.

> *General instructions:* Opinions differ as to the intelligence of animals. In the paragraphs that follow, two former students have indicated their ideas on the subject, the wisdom of dogs. Read the paragraphs carefully. After you have given thought to the matter, may we hear your viewpoint?
>
> ONE POINT OF VIEW Dogs are wiser than we think. They can foretell what is to come and they can sense the death of a beloved master, even when he is far away. A dog who was sent home from Europe by a sailor intuitively recognized his master's wife. An American dog at a concert sat through "God Save the King" but rose on all fours and stood with quiet dignity for "The Star-Spangled Banner." Some dogs do not like to see their masters drink and will get up quietly and leave the room after the second or third cocktail. Dogs are far more knowing than the average person believes them to be.
>
> ANOTHER POINT OF VIEW Popular misconceptions about dogs would fill a volume. People like to credit dogs with high intelligence and out of affection often go beyond the truth in telling about their dogs. If dogs were so faithful, wise, and skilled at detecting villains, there would be one stationed at the door of every

[32] Robert J. Havighurst and Hilda Taba, *Adolescent Character and Personality* (N.Y., Wiley, 1948); Robert J. Havighurst, M. Z. Robinson, and M. Dorr, "The Development of the Ideal Self in Childhood and Adolescence," *Journal of Educational Research*, Vol. 40, No. 4 (December 1946).

[33] H. Edmund Bullis and Emily E. O'Malley, *Human Relations in the Classroom*, course I, II, III, Delaware State Society for Mental Hygiene, Wilmington 35, Del.; Vernon Jones, *Youth Decides* (Evanston, Ill., Row, Peterson, 1952). See also Arthur Minton, "Thinking-Composition," *English Journal*, Vol. 40, No. 1 (January 1951).

store to intercept shoplifters and to bark at robbers, forgers, and other felons. Although they are intelligent animals, dogs are far less knowing than the average person believes them to be.

2. Editorials and letters to the editor in local and school newspapers provide a good source of materials for similar exercises.

■ *Discuss the nature of evil*

For classes with many gifted and/or thoughtful pupils, discussion may center on problems of a more difficult order. The nature of evil, for instance, is a topic with universal interest. What is evil, how do the religions and philosophies explain it, and how does a young person come to terms with it as he leaves the cloistered security of childhood? Such questions, a challenge to the keenest minds in any class, interest any thoughtful adolescent. Concrete illustrations may be drawn from local news and current events of the international scene. Literature, especially, will awaken thoughts on this topic.

■ *Explore puzzling issues*

Excellent discussion leading to writing often develops from topics that puzzle young people. Even if some topics prove too complex for simple answers, the discussion can reveal why some of the puzzles exist and why teachers or adults have not provided clear-cut answers. In one tenth grade class, the pupils listed twenty-three items on the blackboard. A few examples follow, phrased in the pupils' own words:

I'd Like to Know

How can people actually believe we came from monkeys? If we did, why are there any monkeys left today and why can't we watch the apes on earth turning into human beings?

Just what is Communism? What makes some American soldiers become Communists, and are they real Communists or do they just take a different attitude?

Is the age for getting a driver's license going to be increased, and if so why should all teen-agers suffer just because some are careless?

Although such questions include considerations that must be handled with care, they furnish valuable opportunities for reasoning and imaginative thinking, both in the preliminary discussion of the question and in the subsequent written compositions. Class discussion often reveals that questions are inaccurately phrased or beg the real issue. After a preliminary inspection of all the questions, the teacher might ask pupils to select two or three topics they consider particularly promising for writing. After these have been chosen, each student spends the next few days learning everything he can about one of the chosen topics, trying to discover any differing points of view, trying to assess dispassionately the ultimate problems behind each question.[34] Whenever the pupils show enough readiness of ideas, the lesson may be transferred from discussion to writing.

■ *Exploit local history*

One class invited to school old settlers who remembered the community's early days. The students recorded on tapes all the memories the older people offered, and

[34] If the topics appear to involve controversial material, the teacher should not evade the issues. He can discuss the matter with his principal or the parent's association in advance, explaining what he is seeking to do and requesting their approval for genuinely educational procedures.

from the tape recordings mimeographed *Wagon on the Trail,* a series of writings based on the reminiscences.

■ *Serialize topics suitable for several compositions*

Seventh grade students in one school wrote a continued story about a truck driver named Matt. Their writing began when a young teamster came to school at the teacher's invitation to explain his work and tell some of his adventures. The students liked him and readily followed the teacher's suggestion that they write about him. Their writing became a continued series which eventually grew into a class book. About once every three weeks the students wrote another set of stories. From each set, a superior episode was chosen for the class book, called *Matt's Miles.* The pupils learned a great deal about the world of labor, unions, and about the national economy.

■ *Take advantage of nearby building construction*

Teachers have often turned to advantage the construction of new buildings in the vicinity of the school—usually new schools or additions to the existing one. Pupils keep records of construction progress and write about the multiple aspects of building: engineering principles, bulldozers and construction equipment, the building trades unions, esthetic design, use of color, landscaping, and building materials. Modern building construction provides enough possibilities to interest every pupil, including any boys who classify English as a subject designed especially for girls. Here is an example of intellectual curiosity and increased powers of observation combining and reinforcing each other as bases to stimulate writing.

■ *Use a time machine*

Students are often intrigued by H. G. Wells's idea of a time machine for traveling backward and forward in history. The teacher may choose some year of the past such as 1295, when Marco Polo returned to Venice, and prepare several illustrative paragraphs to serve as stimulators for discussion and models for writing. For samples of the future, the teacher may read aloud "The Man in Asbestos," by Stephen Leacock or portions of E. M. Forster's *The Machine Stops.* In discussing the models, the teacher will need to recommend that students avoid an unimaginative imitation. The basic idea, however, is excellent for stimulating response.

To extend and sharpen observation

■ *Feature the five senses in descriptive observations*

1. Assign or plan with students a description in which they use words to make a reader hear, feel, taste, smell, and see. Emphasize the use of effective verbs rather than adjectives. Where adjectives are used recommend those that refer to one of the five senses: pungent smell of orange peel; salty crispness of bacon; snarling rasp of machinery in a sawmill. If duplicated, part of the assignment might read like this:

> Choose one of the following and describe the subject as exactly as possible. Ideally you should write immediately after having had the sensory experience. These are only suggestions. If you wish, choose an equally useful experience of your own.
>
> The feel of a baseball snugly caught in a mitt, a bat firmly striking a baseball, a fabric such as satin or velvet; the feel of a baby's cheek, of a baby chicken.
>
> The take-off of a jet plane.

The smells and sounds of a shop class. (Don't attempt too many. A few will be better.)

The noon rush of students down the stairs to the lunchroom. Does it remind you of something else?

The sight of a parade or school carnival from a high window. Does it look like something other than what it is?

The smell of burning leaves, roasting coffee, or tar on a hot summer day.

The sound of a high wind, noises at night, or band practice in the music room.

The world seen through gently falling snow or heavy fog.

A perfect dive. What did it look like? How did it feel?

The sight of moving traffic from a hilltop or a plane. Does it look like something else?

The taste of olives, toasted marshmallows, onions, or peanuts.

2. Like the scientist, the skilled writer has developed his powers of observation. Students who have completed one of the descriptions above could improve their writing through careful, exact observation and the practice of recording such observation in concise language. They might try some of these exercises in observation as a follow-up to the first assignment:

Students visit the shops at school or observe machinery in operation during an excursion to a factory. They record observations and compare the results.

Students draw a plan of some friend's house, listing colors, furniture, and arrangements. They take the plan with them on their next visit, as a check-up, and report their degree of success in a written statement to the teacher.

At home, students watch a dog, squirrel, or bird for ten or fifteen minutes. To this study they should bring both a sharpened alertness in observing everything that would escape the attention of most persons, and an inquiring mind in connection with what they observe.

At Christmas, the class divides into groups to describe the sights, sounds, smells, and tastes peculiar to the season, each group specializing in one sense, the final product a class composition.

A committee arranges on small paper plates or sponges a slice of lemon peel, geranium leaf, vanilla beans, fresh chewing gum, turpentine, witch hazel, coffee, moth balls, crushed lavender, or similar scents. Everyone shuts his eyes. Members of the committee carry the plates from student to student. They also distribute a score pad to be used by each student after he has identified or described the odors. Discuss the results.

Prepare similar tests for touch, taste, and hearing.

Note that our language contains more words for seeing and tasting than for smelling, hearing, or kinesthetic feeling. If dogs had a language, which sense would command the most words? Encourage a gifted or interested pupil to report on the language of smell that permeates the biography of Flush, Elizabeth Barrett Browning's spaniel.[35]

Select some person outside the class to pay an unexpected visit. Let him carry a number of different objects as well as speak and act in some surprising manner. After he has gone, have students write an account of his surprise appearance and actions.

[35] Virginia Woolf, *Flush* (N.Y., Harcourt, Brace, 1933).

■ *Present models illustrating sensory perception*

1. Effective models of writing featuring sensory appeal may be identified in literary selections studied or read aloud while students listen to note down outstandingly effective words and phrases. In such a case the models should be read several times. In the first rendition the students listen for the over-all meaning; in the others they listen to select certain words or phrases. Two that have proved effective are reprinted here.

Modern Music

. . . At that moment, everybody began clapping. The conductor, a tall foreign-looking chap with a shock of grey hair that stood out all around his head, had arrived at his little railed-in platform and was giving the audience a series of short jerky bows. He gave two little taps. All the players brought their instruments up and looked at him. He slowly raised his arms, then brought them down sharply and the concert began.

First all the violins made a shivery sort of noise that you could feel travelling up and down your spine. Some of the clarinets and bassoons squeaked and gibbered a little, and the brass instruments made a few unpleasant remarks. Then all the violins went rushing up and up, and when they got to the top, the stout man at the back hit a gong, the two men near him attacked their drums, . . . The noise was terrible, shattering: . . . walls of houses were falling in; ships were going down; ten thousand people were screaming with toothache; steam hammers were breaking loose; whole warehouses of oilcloth were being stormed and the oilcloth all torn into shreds; and there were railway accidents innumerable. Then suddenly the noise stopped; one of the clarinets, all by itself, went slithering and gurgling; the violins began their shivery sound again and at last shivered away into silence. The conductor dropped his arms to his side. Nearly everybody clapped.[36]

Earliest Memory

I was five. Already I had known the drowsy scent of red peonies in a hot corner of the garden, the friendly smell of cool apples. Taste I knew, too—the puckery, restraining taste of forbidden chokeberries, the taste of sulphur and molasses, lingering and powdery long after it should have gone. And the yellow of a floor was to me never so yellow as a great ball of dandelions which my father had once made for me and which he rolled to and fro, hither and yon, across the clipped green grass. . . .[37]

2. To vary this method, teachers sometimes present pupils with a version pared to its least evocative paraphrase. Students are to take a skeleton such as the following, develop it more fully, and finally compare their own work with the original. For example, the first paragraph in the model just above can be reduced to a version like this:

Already I had known the smell of flowers in the garden and of apples. Taste I knew, too, the taste of chokeberries and the taste of sulphur and molasses. The floor paint was not as yellow as some flowers.

[36] John Boynton Priestley, *Angel Pavement* (N.Y., Harper, 1930), pp. 234 ff. Other passages following this one may also be used. They include further descriptions of contemporary music and of the Brahms *First Symphony*.

[37] Mary Ellen Chase, "A Kitchen Parnassus," from *The Golden Asse and Other Essays* (N.Y., Holt, 1929), p. 111. The passage following this is also an excellent model.

To explore feelings

■ *Relate amusing incidents of everyday living*

All pupils have some comic anecdotes worth sharing. In order to elicit some of these in writing, the teacher may read aloud some droll account of everyday living such as "Mama and Uncle Elizabeth" from *Mama's Bank Account,* "The First Prom Is the Hardest" from *We Shook the Family Tree,* or "The Slom Season" in Selma Lagerlöf's *Marbacka.*[38] Because all story writing demands rather a stern effort from students, a teacher may wish to let this project represent more than a single composition. The story may be planned so that it falls into several parts, each representing a single composition, each part to be turned in over a period of time. For the first assignment, only the first segment is to be completed.

■ *Describe an act of generosity*

A written activity which has succeeded for a number of teachers requires, initially, an act of generosity on the part of the pupils. Each is to do or give something without expectation of money or acknowledgement in return. Students have carried out such individual projects as cleaning the house, baby-sitting, visiting some sick or aged person, helping a brother or sister with lessons, making or creating something as a gift to please someone, washing the car. The written account is usually divided into three parts; what was done, how it was received, and how the giver felt about his experience in generosity.[39]

■ *Probe feelings about school*

In "Five Ripe Pears," [40] William Saroyan tells of being punished in the first grade. He had brought to school five ripe and beautiful pears; taking them from a tree along the way, he had not realized he was stealing. His wryly amusing account will evoke students' memories of schoolday troubles. Such topics as "The Best Thing That Ever Happened to Me in School" and "The Teacher I Remember Best from Grade School" set pupils to considering positive characteristics of schooling and teachers. Students should avoid identifying individuals.

■ *Use picture strip stories*

For slow students the teacher may draw and duplicate a series of five pictures, simple and cartoon-like in nature, illustrating an incident that has recently caused deep feelings among the pupils, e.g., an April Fool prank, a happy picnic or party. The students then complete the series by drawing balloons to the mouths of the characters and writing in what each person said. After this, they may be interested in writing more "comic book" stories, in which they draw the pictures and write the stories to go with the pictures. After several of these lessons, the teacher assigns an explanatory paragraph to be placed under each picture series, thus leading these slow learners to a more conventional type of composition.

[38] Or "The Seventeen Cats," also from *Marbacka;* see also "The Marseillaise," from her *Memories of My Childhood* (Garden City, N.Y., Doubleday, Doran, 1934). Other examples of everyday comedy are "The Apricot Tree" from *The Human Comedy* by William Saroyan, as well as many of his short stories; and the chapter on the shopping expedition from Shirley Jackson's *Life Among the Savages.*

[39] Edyth W. Hadley, Youngstown, Ohio, describes such a lesson in "Techniques in Teaching High School Students to Listen," *English Journal,* Vol. 40, No. 7 (September 1951).

[40] From his book *Inhale and Exhale* (N.Y., Random House, 1936).

■ *Choose from several suggestions*

The following suggestions to be placed on the blackboard represent a list from which pupils may choose one they prefer to develop. Each title has been selected for its relation to the affective side of pupils' lives.

Controlling My Temper
The Pleasures of Being Alone
The Pleasures of Being with People
A Day I'd Like to Live Over Again
The Meanest Thing I Ever Did
The Sorrows of a Bashful Person
Sometimes I Worry About _______
I Am Happiest When _______
Things That Bother Me
When I Am Older

To increase ability to interpret

■ *Present models with a range of interpretiveness*

From a set of compositions select four ranging from exceptionally interpretive to cryptic. From these delete the names and with masking tape arrange the compositions on the front chalk board. Beside each one write comments showing how selection of details, illustrations, and word choice add expressiveness to writing. During study times invite individuals to go forward to read both compositions and comments. For a variation of this method choose a model, from student writing or from literature, and pare it to a Spartan lack of expressiveness. The original and the "skeleton" are then duplicated and compared for effectiveness.

■ *Write biographies and autobiographies*

One teacher assigns a composition called "To Every Man His Boswell." The students draw names and write the biography of the person whose name they draw. In other schools an autobiography at about the ninth or tenth grade is the major writing project of the year. Subtitles within such autobiographies may include Important "Firsts," Turning Points, My Happiest Memories, and Important Decisions. The value of detail and example in such material, where a pupil draws on his own experience, is sometimes easier to demonstrate than in more impersonal writing.

■ *Tell a whopper*

Students enjoy reading tall tales about Paul Bunyan, Pecos Bill, and Baron Munchausen. After reading and discussion each student fabricates his own tall tale, using some event in his own experience as the nub for uninhibited expansion.

■ *Try "Twenty years from now"*

1. By this method, pupils write to the adolescents who, twenty years from now, will follow them in the same school. The boys may describe sports, vocational plans, and recreational activities. The girls may write about fashions, teen-age problems, and dating. All discuss current events and personal interests. These letters may be filed in the school storeroom in a durable box labeled "To be opened by the tenth

grade class of this school on the fifteenth day of the school year 198–." The project often creates a deep interest, both on the part of the students and the community.[41]

2. In a somewhat similar project, "Letter to the Future," students in one school wrote to themselves letters to be mailed a number of years later. To care for possible inflation, each pupil provided double the amount of present postage. These letters were then stored with a label "To be mailed in January of the year 197–."

■ *Expand "personals"*

Clip items from the personal column of any newspaper and let pupils choose one from a large number. "Personals" are almost always capable of varied interpretations. If several pupils expand the same item, the less imaginative may come to see what possibilities of interpretation exist in a few words such as these:

> T. M. Kept appointment, Cougar Cafe. Displayed token at table; so may I apply for renewal? D. F.
>
> Reba, be at big tree, Lime Drive, noon, same day as before. Important information. J. F.

Sometimes grouping three or four pupils together to write an expansion permits the less imaginative in each group to observe how others set about expanding a "skeleton."

■ *Interview imaginary persons*

The students write their imaginary interviews with a person living in a communistic country, a character in a novel, or a person of the historical past. Preliminary discussion of the possibilities will lift the level of thought that goes into such a composition.

To connect writing with personal needs and interests

■ *Compile a youth guide*

Two classes list for one another some of the major problems they believe today's youth has. These lists are exchanged and used for class discussion. Usually this discussion is led by the teacher; sifting the problems and organizing them requires leadership in seeing relationships and placing items in proper categories. When the listing is completed, the most important teen-age problems are chosen for compositions which will represent the best advice distilled from class discussion. Thus, the students in each class select several problems listed by the other class. In suggesting how the problems might be handled or solved they bring to bear upon each the best wisdom they can offer. The essays may be polished and, after being read by the class raising the problems, bound for the library or for the teacher to use as models next semester.

■ *Rate and discuss handicaps*

To motivate writing, one teacher asks his students to list twelve handicaps, rating them in two different ways: first, as deterrents to success in school life, and second, as deterrents to success after school. Handicaps typically listed are lack of poise in social situations, poor looks, unattractive home, poor health, poor speaking ability,

[41] In large schools, this project may not be practical for all teachers to use. Lack of storage space could be an insuperable obstacle. However, used occasionally by a single teacher, the method is highly effective.

and lack of money. This topic usually proves deeply interesting and almost always motivates intense discussion leading to equally intense writing.

■ *Choose topics which appeal to adolescents*

Teachers frequently offer topics closely related to pupils' interests. Rather than assign a single topic to everyone, they allow choice among several. Some topics and subjects that have proved particularly effective with many classes are listed here:

The Fortunate Accident A halo, lost by a careless angel or cherub, lights on a typical young person—you or one of your classmates. He or she immediately becomes exceptionally well behaved and angelic. Tell about the situations and the surprise to various people.

Should High School Boys Play Football? To develop this topic the teacher or some student should gather the facts about injuries for several seasons.

The Future of Hunting Are the hunting grounds disappearing? Do farmers nowadays want hunters on their property? Is hunting becoming a standardized and commercialized affair, no longer a deep pleasure? Will the future population bulge eliminate hunting?

Does Honesty Pay? The teacher or some able student writes a provocative statement contending that honesty does not pay. This letter, unidentified as to author, may be read to the class or to groups in the class. Usually the letter arouses lively discussion.

Teenicide Teenicide, the death caused by automobile drivers under twenty years of age, is usually the result of recklessness or immature judgment. The facts, figures, and reasons behind high insurance rates for families with teen-age drivers are almost always a source of much interest and discussion on the part of students.

Self-Deceptive Thinking

Pull is what counts; it's a waste of time looking for a job.

There isn't time for a person to read while he is going to school. Besides you can keep up better with current events by watching television.

What good does history do you? It is a waste of time studying about events that are over.

If I Could Have Three Wishes Come True

I want my husband (or wife) to be _______

Tomorrow as I would like to spend it

A day I would like to live over again

What I expect of my teen-age son (or daughter) (Assume you are a parent)

■ *Begin the year with an exchange letter between students and teacher*

Some teachers open each school year by addressing a letter to each student, in which the teacher explains he does not know the pupil and has not consulted previous teachers nor any records. He will consult records later; now he prefers first of all to form his own individual impression of each student. In order to help in forming this impression the student is requested to write a letter in which he tells something about himself as an individual and as a student of English. First of all what are his interests, likes, and dislikes? What are his plans and hopes for the years after high school? Next, how has he fared in English up to this point? Has he been a successful student? A good or weak reader? What of writing? Speaking? Skills such as spelling? What difficulties has the student had and how does he account for those difficulties? What especially should be chosen for improvement during the coming year? How can the teacher be of the greatest assistance?

These letters, it is explained, will remain confidential and will never be placed in the files of the school. They will, however, be kept in the individual folders of the students and at the close of the semester, the teacher and the student will examine them to see whether or not the student's plans and requests for help from the teacher have received attention. Teachers who use this approach find that students respond very favorably. In addition to learning something about the characteristics of the students, the teacher gathers information on how well they write, organize their ideas, and use conventions of spelling, punctuation, and capitalization. Thus the letter is diagnostic in multiple ways.

■ *Keep daily diaries and vignettes*

Many teachers plan some writing for fifteen minutes each day, usually diaries or paragraphs of personal reflection and comment. From these vignettes the pupils copy out the best of their entries for a weekly or bi-weekly assignment. In one class the results were stored in the student's manila folders. Any amount was acceptable, one sentence or twenty, as long as the student wrote something every day. On Fridays, students received their folders at the half-hour and copied a selection from the previous week's writing. Only this portion of the writing was read and evaluated. The project started slowly. Some students, disliking English, were appalled at the prospect of daily writing. "What'll I write about?" they complained. Class discussions provided some suggestions; quiet students wrote out attitudes they would not discuss aloud; other students wrote stories, adding an episode a day; others kept diary-like records of their experiences and changing points of view. For a while the teacher wrote on the board each day five provocative ideas. Later he wrote only one and students supplied the other four. These ideas often helped pupils find content for their writing.

To write for practical and immediate uses

In order to persuade students of the importance of writing and the value the world places on it, teachers often use evidence from the business world. *Industry Views the Teaching of English* [42] is one of the best of these aids. General Electric, Schenectady, New York, publishes a most helpful bulletin, *Why Study English?* presenting the importance of writing. Other firms employ personnel officers who confer with teachers on the writing skills they seek in new employees. Students may also interview adults on the values and uses of writing and report these interviews to the class. Finally, the range of financial rewards and the deeper satisfactions writers enjoy should be occasionally emphasized as well as the amazing variety of occupations open to those skilled in writing.

■ *Correspond with youth abroad*

The experience of writing to young people, whether at home or abroad, transcends mere considerations of letter form. Although students should realize their letters become models for those learning our language, they should be even more aware of how their letters' content and tone reflect political ideals and a particular

[42] Everett C. Smith, *Industry Views the Teaching of English*, reprinted from the *English Journal*, Vol. 45, No. 3 (March 1956). Available from NCTE, Champaign, Illinois.

way of life. Some of the agencies where teachers may enroll pupils for foreign correspondence are listed here:

International Student's Society, Hillsboro, Oregon

The Swedish Central Committee of International Exchange between Schools, Storkyrkobrinken 11, Stockholm C, Sweden

Student Letter Exchange, Waseca, Minnesota. Names will be furnished of foreign students who write in English.

For letter exchange entirely in English, Miss Edna MacDonough, Executive Secretary, International Friendship League, 40 Mount Vernon Street, Boston, Massachusetts, provides names and addresses.

For information on the International Albums Program, write local Red Cross chapters. School and classroom groups enrolled in the Junior Red Cross in the United States now correspond with similar groups in sixty countries.

Letters Abroad, 45 East Sixty-fifth Street, New York 21, New York, serves students aged fifteen and older.

■ *Send letters to age mates*

One junior high school class in Minneapolis wanted to correspond with other American youngsters living in communities different from their own. They chose three towns whose names intrigued them: Horse Heaven, Washington; Cody, Wyoming; and Osceoles, Arkansas. They decided to write a letter to the eighth grade teacher in each of these three communities asking whether or not that teacher would be willing to furnish names of students who wanted to correspond. After these letters to the three teachers had been composed in rough draft, they were examined by the entire class for proper tone and completeness of information. The teacher helped plan appropriate letter form, and once such conventions had been reviewed, the final versions were neatly written and mailed.

Horse Heaven proved to be a small rural school with only three eighth-graders, but the other two towns furnished larger numbers of correspondents, and the teachers in all three schools saw value in the project. The result was that for a year the Minneapolis students corresponded with students in the other three communities. The individual writers told about themselves, their schools, families, and communities, receiving in return similar letters to be shared with the rest of the class. These became the basis for lessons, not only on letter form, but on writing in general. So many Minneapolis students became intrigued by the Horse Heaven Hills, the Rattlesnake Hills, and Lost Horse Plateau in south central Washington that letters were finally dispatched to several eighth grade teachers in larger towns located near those exciting geographical place names. Other pupils, however, retained their allegiance to Cody or Osceoles.

■ *Keep class minutes*

In some schools, minutes are kept for every class meeting, and most class hours begin with a reading of the minutes from the previous day. For many pupils this provides a sense of continuity and direction. Confused often by the multiplicity of assignments and activities in many different subject matters, they find in the minutes a sense of security. Rotating responsibility for keeping and reading the previous day's minutes provides everybody in the class with an opportunity to do some useful writing. The minutes, kept in a looseleaf notebook, include all assignments, in order to help students who are absent. Some pupils keep class logs which include also their personal reactions.

■ *Write for publication*

1. On public controversies, write letters that exhibit rational and sensible thought. Send the best of these to the local or nearest newspaper's letters to the editor column.

2. Many newspapers, like Hawaii's *Honolulu Advertiser,* devote a Sunday section to teen-age writers. Written and edited primarily by teen-agers themselves, "Hawaii's Youth" is for young people from fourteen to eighteen. The young reporters interview newsworthy teen-agers, visiting celebrities, and local officials. They report outstanding school news, express opinions in editorials, and review new books.

3. Duplicate occasional news sheets or collections of creative writing prepared by the class, to be distributed in the school.

■ *Write for other courses*

Occasionally the English classroom should become a writing laboratory for papers required in other courses such as social studies, homemaking, science, or journalism.

■ *Write self-evaluations at marking periods*

An impressively functional exercise is the self-evaluation that students write just before grades are to be made out in many schools. These compositions aid teachers in assigning grades and in some schools they are attached to the pupils' reports and sent home. A copy should certainly be filed in the pupil's writing folder. Usually these evaluations are titled, "What I Have Learned (in English) This Marking Period." Duplicate or outline on the chalk board the major goals of instruction during the period of time in question, discuss these goals, and remind the students of some ways they have worked toward them.

■ *Enter writing contests, both local and national* [43]

Service groups and other clubs in the local community sponsor writing contests, and many of these offer excellent opportunities for students to write for a genuine purpose. In cases where past contest titles have been considered too broad or vague, teachers have met in advance with representatives of the sponsoring groups. Almost always teachers have found these men and women only too anxious to phrase topics that will contribute both to instruction in writing and the intent of the sponsoring organization. Contests are offered also by *Seventeen, Literary Cavalcade,* and other national magazines.

Creating a design

To master the paragraph

■ *Build a paragraph in class*

To teach that each detail should relate to the topic sentence, ask the class to suggest a topic sentence that can be developed by the use of detail, e.g., the members of the band were tuning up; girls need a course in shop; a baby sitter does

[43] The National Association of Secondary School Principals, 1201 Sixteenth Street, N.W., Washington 6, D.C., publishes every year (usually September) in its magazine *The Bulletin* an "Approved List of National Contests and Activities for the Year ——." This organization maintains a committee which has studied contests of all kinds for over two decades.

more than sit. Have a student write the sentence on the blackboard. Class members contribute statements using details to develop the topic sentence. If the details offered have any connection with the topic thought, the secretary records them on the blackboard. The class then evaluates the relevancy of each suggested detail, giving reasons. With the assorted accepted details in full view on the board, each student writes his version of the paragraph, including the topic thought and arranging the sentences in a logical order.

■ *Use audio-visual aids*

"Building Better Paragraphs," a film lasting fifteen minutes, presents on the junior high school level basic principles of planning in relation to paragraph construction. Selection and arrangement are shown through two compositions about a prize-winning dog who jumps a hurdle at a dog show. A series of pictures illustrating the poorly written composition is flashed on the screen scene by scene, an amusing but confusing jumble to the viewer, just as the poorly planned paragraph would have been to a reader. Then the organization of a good paragraph is illustrated through selection and arrangement of a series of snapshots about the same dog. Make the transition from film to students' writing by discussing how important it is to plan what is to be written.

■ *Present strong and weak models*

1. Many composition textbooks contain examples of paragraphs which ramble from their unifying topic or fail to support a topic with sufficient detail. These models are often effective means of identifying the crucial features of strong and weak paragraphs.

2. Some teachers like a variation of this method, the selection of several superior paragraphs on topics that appeal to students. Each superior paragraph is matched with a version the teacher has distorted. The two passages are duplicated, or shown with an opaque projector. The students read the two versions, tell which is the better and why they think so. This method of spoiled versions, because it shifts the role of explanation from teacher to pupil, proves to be a highly effective method of instruction. For each paragraph identified as superior, the teacher asks the class to select the topic sentence and the key word(s) in that topic sentence. Next the pupils are asked to note the arrangement of items in the paragraph, indicating if they can, the plan of paragraph building, e.g., examples, analogy, comparisons, contrasts. Finally the pupils are asked to note the writer's manner of clinching or ending the paragraph.

3. Some teachers type the sentences of paragraphs on separate slips of paper, jumble them, and put them in envelopes. The pupils take the envelopes and assemble the paragraphs in the best order. Such exercises are helpful, but eventually the learnings involved must be proved in the pupil's actual experience of composing *his own* ideas into a unified paragraph.

■ *Learn to write different kinds of paragraphs* [44]

From class texts, assign a different paragraph to be read by each individual in the class. The problem: to determine what each paragraph does. Through class discus-

[44] For this composition idea and others, the authors are indebted to the English teachers of George Washington High School, San Francisco (Chairman, Mrs. Melanie Ainsworth). Their monograph, *Advanced English Composition*, has been further drawn upon for ideas in this text.

sion formulate the awareness that all writing is divided into narration, description, exposition, and argumentation, or a combination of these types. List these major classifications across the chalk board. Be sure students understand the purpose of each of these kinds of writing. Fill in some methods by which paragraphs in each kind of writing may be developed, but guide pupils away from any stress on nomenclature as an end in itself.

Narration	*Description*	*Exposition*	*Argumentation*
Details in time order	Details grouped by location	Definition	Reasons for
	Details grouped for emotional effect	Details	Reasons against
		Examples	
		Comparison and contrast	

Read sample paragraphs. Have the class decide into which classification each one fits and what method of development is used. Have students write and read aloud paragraphs of their own construction, afterwards checking them against the chart.

Encourage students to use variety of paragraph development in compositions.

To plan longer compositions

■ *Help students narrow a specific subject* [45]

On the board draw three columns, headed *Subjects, Topics,* and *Central Idea Sentences.* Explain that a subject, the largest of the three concepts, can be handled in a book. Obtain from volunteers suggestions as to subjects: The United Nations; The Place of Minority Groups in Today's World; Today's Youth. Have each student who makes an acceptable suggestion write it on the board in the subject column and then reduce it from a subject to a topic, e.g., Pitfalls of the U.N. Organization; Housing Restrictions in a Democratic Society; Fads of Teen-agers.

Explain that the central idea sentence governing the organization is the phase of the "topic" selected for the essay. Obtain from students suggestions as to central idea sentences derived from the topics now written in Column Two. These sentences are then written in their appropriate places in the third column.

From the beginning of the United Nations the power to veto has been a hindrance to the successful functioning of this organization.

The widely publicized ________ case was an unfortunate instance of selfishness and prejudice.

In adopting fads teen-agers find some of the security they seek.

Now that the columns have been filled out, discussion follows. Questions are asked; ideas are exchanged. The teacher makes certain the class grasps the necessity for narrowing a subject, selecting a point of view, and addressing the writing to a definite reader or audience.

Each member of the class now prepares his own chart, filling in new subjects, topics, and central idea sentences. If one of the topics on his chart pleases a student sufficiently, it may be used for his next essay.

[45] Compare this with the same problem in "Oral Communication," pp. 429-30, 471-72. Correlation of similar skills in speaking and writing reinforce the learning of skills.

■ *Teach outlining* [46]

In expository writing, outlining can prove helpful in over-all designing and in clarifying thought. To be sure, some teachers might view outlining as an end in itself. Certainly this is a danger. Furthermore, many pupil compositions are not complex enough to justify a detailed plan. But when an outline is justified and is used as a means to the purposeful designing of a composition, the teacher will probably emphasize these points:

> Express all topics of the same rank in the same form. The topics may be nouns, or phrases, or sentences, but whatever they are, they should remain parallel—e.g., if *A* under *I* is an infinitive phrase, *B*, *C*, and *D* should be the same.
>
> Single sub-topics should not occur; sub-topics are subdivisions, and if a topic cannot be divided into two or more parts, it is not susceptible to outline analysis.
>
> Avoid overlapping of topics.

■ *Conduct pupils through a complete experience in composing*

Students quite naturally find difficulty in applying generalizations like "be coherent" or "maintain unity of thought." But their learning is reasonably rapid whenever teachers actually show them how to grapple with their own ideas and how to arrange them effectively. The obstacle, however, to such desirable instruction is the sheer impossibility of penetrating the thoughts—or half-formed thoughts—of more than one pupil at a time. To solve this difficulty in large classes, teachers sometimes use one effective strategy. They select a topic of interest to as many pupils as possible and conduct the entire class through the steps of composing an essay on that topic. In his description of this method, Blumenthal [47] used the topic of military training for every boy. With younger pupils, the question of extending the American school year to twelve months is nearly always successful; in fact, on this issue student involvement is deep at any grade level.

After selecting the topic, the teacher makes an assignment. Each pupil is to write two single-sentence arguments, each one on a separate card or half-sheet of paper. For instance, here are two arguments opposing the twelve-month school:

1	2
Parents with several children in school could not plan vacations which would include the whole family.	Young people need some rest and change from school if they are not to weary of it.

Two arguments are much better than one; the teacher is seeking a variety of points for the composing about to be carried out in class, and a greater diversity appears among the students' second arguments than among their first.

Next the students read their arguments aloud and the teacher helps them find general headings for the various points. Blumenthal's students, for instance, found

[46] Outlining is presented in Chapter 9, Oral Language, pp. 430-31, 472.

[47] Joseph C. Blumenthal, "Without Form and Void, A Device for Teaching Organization in Expository Writing," *English Journal*, Vol. 35, No. 7 (September 1946).

that all their arguments against military training would fit under one or another of such headings as Ineffectiveness, International Distrust, and so forth.

These general headings are written horizontally across the chalk board and the students lay their cards or slips of paper on the chalk ledge beneath the appropriate headings. The pack of cards or slips for each general heading is then assigned to a committee which reduces the arguments by eliminating duplicate ideas. The committee is to design the best possible order for those arguments that remain and to be prepared to give a reason for the order they select. Now the committee writes the arguments, in the sequence they have chosen, under their general heading on the chalk board. One special committee, or the class as a whole, turns its attention to the best sequence for the general headings, learning that there is no one right way but several equally good ways. "The important point is that we present our ideas according to a plan, not in the hit or miss way in which they march through our minds." [48] The plan chosen should take into account the impression or conclusion the writer wants to leave in the mind of a particular reader or group of readers. The total method is an example of how a teacher may do more than assign writing. Most students, if they are to improve their writing, need to be taught how they may do so.

■ *Require an organizing blueprint*

For some compositions, if not all, require a blueprint like the following. Plans such as these often assist organization of thought better than a formal outline.

Written composition plan

Topic:
The following sentence states my central idea:
In my composition, I plan to use the following topic sentences in this order:
The following sentence states my concluding idea:
Title for my composition:

An interesting use of this plan: When essays are completed, have each pupil write his central idea on the front board. Let the class decide which ones are the most interesting to them and warrant being read aloud. The authors of these compositions then read their essays to the class. Discuss whether or not—and why—the composition lived up to the promise of its central idea.

■ *Summarize the essentials of an impressive model*

From a magazine or a non-fiction textbook choose a well-organized selection on a topic of genuine interest to most adolescents. Ask the students to submit a brief summary. Have several summaries read aloud. Probably all will be incomplete in one way or another. Refer back to the article; have students select the main idea by reference to the beginning and end of the article. Have a member of the class construct an outline on the board based on topic ideas suggested by the class. Leave space under each topic idea.

Through oral discussion have students point out subordinate ideas and documentation for each of the sections on the board. Have students find items least important to the author's thesis and draw a line through these items on the board. Stress the importance of having students rephrase the ideas in their own words. However,

[48] Blumenthal, "Without Form and Void," p. 379.

if there are words or phrases in the text that are new to the students or particularly suitable, encourage the students to discuss them. Help students see the close-knit thought that characterizes good organization and ask how they can transfer what they have learned.

To feature effective beginnings and endings

■ *Use advertising to illustrate beginnings and endings*

Almost all successful magazine ads have effective eye-catching beginnings and skillful closes. Variety shows on television illustrate the same principle. These beginnings and endings may be unusual camera shots or some skillful arrangement of acts, but inasmuch as they do illustrate the universal importance of an appropriate beginning and close, the principles may be transferred and applied to writing.

■ *Write with the pupils*

Several times each semester organize a topic on the chalk board, writing out with pupil suggestion the first two paragraphs, thinking out loud as the composing progresses. Students need more than completed models; they need the learning that can come only through observing the process and realizing the thoughts and considerations that accompany that process. After the teacher has demonstrated the initial paragraphs, students *and teacher* may complete the composition individually as a basis for discussing their strategies and the reasons for them. The first time a teacher carries out such a demonstration, he may prefer a topic he has considered in advance, but eventually he will find more challenge—and be more effective—with topics requiring him to organize from absolute zero.

■ *Feature clear thinking and planning*

After a lesson on planning has been taught and students have written some longer papers, choose two for illustration. Have their authors copy on the board the introductory and concluding paragraphs of the essays. The class is asked to speculate on what should logically be found in the paragraphs of development. The two authors will then write their other topic sentences on the board and read the missing paragraphs. The class will decide whether or not the body of the essay fulfills the promise of the introduction and accomplishes what the conclusion says it has accomplished. The class should check to insure that no new ideas are introduced in the final paragraph or formal closing material.

To improve transitions

■ *Teach transitional words and phrases*

1. To teach students the necessity for using accurate transitional devices as "bridges" in their writing, the teacher may read aloud a sample of writing overusing *and* as a connective; a sample of writing using no connectives at all. Ask the class to determine what is wrong with each of the two pieces of writing. Have the class contribute some useful substitutes for *and.* Keep the suggested words on a side board. Write on the front board the types of transition words with examples of each. If pupils develop the list, the exercise will be far more effective.

Words referring back to something already mentioned (the personal and demonstrative pronouns): he, she, it, this, that, these, those.

Words of time: meanwhile, afterward, soon, later, eventually.

Words of number: first, second, in the first place, etc.

Words continuing the same line of thought: also, furthermore, moreover, likewise, besides, similarly, for example, in fact, for instance.

Words introducing contrasting thoughts: but, then, nevertheless, still, however, yet, on the other hand, on the contrary.

Words stating degrees of certainty: certainly, undoubtedly, presumably, indeed, perhaps, possibly, probably, anyhow, anyway, in all probability, in all likelihood, at all events.

Words of consequence or result: therefore, consequently, accordingly, hence, then, thus, as a result, so.

2. Distribute mimeographed paragraphs lacking transition words. Students will fill in blanks with words they deem appropriate. Discussion of their selections will follow.

3. Choosing a composition from his own folder, each student may underline every transitional word he has used and indicate by an *x* the place where one should have been used.

To learn better subordination

■ *Teach the value of subordination*

1. Use sentences appropriate to the level of the class. For young students, for example, put on the board sentences such as the following:

Buck was a big dog. He lived on an estate.
There was a gardener on the estate. He needed money.
One day he stole Buck. He sold Buck to some men.
These men were going to Alaska.

Have the students read these aloud and offer suggestions for improving them.

2. For a period of time, ten minutes a day spent on revising a single sentence written on the board will achieve results.

■ *Use précis writing*

Précis, presented briefly in the pupil's own words, summarize the main ideas of longer materials. They can help students analyze writing for its essential ideas. Through exercises like the following, pupils can learn how shearing off illustration and repetition helps to extract the essential thought of a passage. They also experience the necessity of subordination.

Differing viewpoints

Opinions differ on the possibility of space travel. In the two selections which follow, the writers have given their respective ideas on the subject. Read the selections carefully and follow the directions below. (Here the teacher would offer two selections with differing viewpoints on the possibility of space travel as seen by a Dr. Farile and a writer who calls himself "Astrophysicist.")

Write a well-constructed paragraph in which you explain the viewpoint of either Dr. Farile or "Astrophysicist."

Write a paragraph (or two) in which you set forth your own reaction to the ideas in these two selections.

■ *Require students to write economically*

The teacher says, "You may choose one hundred and fifty words to spend. Who can get the most for his one hundred and fifty?" This method gives the teacher an opportunity to emphasize appositives, various kinds of phrases, subordination, and unity of paragraph construction. Learning to use appositives and phrases will be stressed, of course, rather than merely learning to identify them in some drill book.

To become interested in design

■ *Compile booklets of student writing*

1. Some schools publish mimeographed booklets of student writing selected for class study. Committees of teachers, sometimes augmented by student members, choose good and weak models of paragraphs for a booklet "Power Over Paragraphs," deleting the names of those whose paragraphs are presented. Longer compositions, when collected into such booklets, also become valuable aids to instruction. Although composition texts available on the market contain excellent models for such purposes, homemade booklets have two special advantages—the vitality deriving from the students' awareness that these compositions were written in their own school and the teachers' familiarity with materials they have personally selected and arranged for instruction.

2. Many colleges and universities publish statements on the quality of writing they seek, for students who continue their education beyond high school. Included in these statements are samples of student prose, varying in quality, along with analyses of the strengths and weaknesses of the samples. Such publications may be used to advantage in many senior high school classes, not only for college-bound students, but for all who need to think and write more clearly. The method when used most effectively begins with reading and discussing the samples, followed by a study of the comments of the college instructors. Typical of these aids is Kentucky's "Principles and Standards in Composition for Kentucky High Schools and Colleges." [49]

■ *Use the opaque projector*

The opaque projectors now manufactured do not singe papers.[50] They make it possible for an entire class to view a student's composition while the teacher and pupils point out positive qualities: A student has organized his material well, has made good transitions, or has established a definite point of view. For instance, it is much easier to talk about arranging ideas in the order of magnitude if an actual composition is thrown on the screen or wall before the students.

Perfecting the presentation

To establish standards

■ *Agree upon a set of error taboos*

Early in the school term, the students list conventions and mechanics they know so well that only carelessness could account for mistakes. Because students are often overzealous and optimistic about their good intentions, the teacher will need to prevent this initial list from growing too long. Once agreed upon, the list should

[49] *Kentucky English Bulletin,* Vol. 6, No. 1 (Fall 1956-57), Kentucky State Department of Education, Frankfort. Lois M. Grose, Dorothy Miller, and Erwin Steinberg, *Suggestions for Evaluating Junior High School Writing,* Pittsburgh Association of English Teachers of Western Pennsylvania, n.d. Both publications available from NCTE, Champaign, Ill.

[50] For instance, Model 3008, Vu-lyte, Beseler Company, 60 Badger Avenue, Newark 8, N.J., shows material 10″ by 10″, weighs 33 lbs.

be posted conspicuously for a period of time, additions should be made as new learnings occur, and copies should later be duplicated for all composition folders. Many groups have an agreement that whenever the teacher notes one of these errors he may, without further reading, return the paper to the student.[51] One teacher has actually purchased a rubber stamp with the word *TABOO*. Whenever one of the standards on the list is violated, the teacher merely stamps the composition *TABOO* and returns it ungraded to the student.

■ *Place reminders on the chalk board*

At the time of writing, the teacher lists examples, both right and wrong, for items which have troubled many pupils in the previous composition. For instance, in an eighth grade, a reminder like this might be helpful:

Subjects and predicates agree even though a phrase comes between them.
The *sails* (of the boat) *wave* in the breeze.
The *hands* (of the clock) *jump* forward.
One (of the boys) *is going*.

The teacher reviews the material on the board before the students start to write.

■ *Have a round-up day*

The teacher, under this plan, reads papers only for content, paying no attention whatsoever to problems of spelling, punctuation, capitalization, or even sentence construction. After each student has written five compositions, the teacher arranges at his side five or six able students, either from his class or from some student-helper club formed for this purpose. The students bring their folders and present their last five compositions to the teacher and his aides who place check marks by errors and encircle misspelled words. Checked papers are returned to their owners, who tabulate the marks, usually on a duplicated sheet provided for this purpose:

	Composition number				
Difficulties	1	2	3	4	5
capitalization					
commas in a series					
run-on sentences					
sentence fragments					
clear handwriting					
(Etc.)					

List below those words you misspelled, with red letters showing the correct spelling at point of difficulty:

Each student aide, carefully prepared in advance, looks for a single type of problem, one he has just thoroughly reviewed in a composition-grammar text. These aides become specialists on commas in a series or run-on sentences, or whatever problem they are prepared to note. In some schools, older pupils receive points toward honors for such assistance with the younger pupils. Through their help

[51] One teacher avoids using a red pencil for noting errors. Anything in red always praises effective or appropriate writing.

the teacher can reach many students in a short time. As the pupil finishes with each of the five or six student aides, he is to study his errors, tabulate them, and then consult with the teacher about steps to take toward eradicating errors and improving his control of conventional usage.

■ *Rewrite some compositions*

Parents sometimes ask whether or not compositions, after being corrected, should be rewritten by the students. Explain that a flexible approach may provide a better solution. Sometimes it is helpful to require that a set of compositions be corrected and returned in perfect form. Other times, however, such a requirement could be unwise. Students often feel the writing they have finished is cold; they have lost interest in that particular composition. Rewriting under such circumstances would be of dubious value. A wise teacher merely notes the kinds of difficulties in that set of compositions and prepares to teach better solutions just before the next writing assignment. If compositions are filed in personal folders, these errors may also be pointed out in conferences or students may tally their particular problems.

When compositions are to be corrected—not entirely rewritten—the following technique may be used. Errors marked are to be corrected on the back of the preceding page in sentences numbered to correspond with the error marked (see p. 530).

■ *Establish school-wide standards for written work*

Many schools establish basic standards for written English, standards that are applied in all departments. Each fall the principal of one high school [52] distributes to all students a bulletin which includes the following points:

> The ability to use English properly in both oral and written communication is an essential skill, in school and out.
>
> Consequently, teachers in every department will require students to adhere to proper English standards in oral and written work.
>
> (A statement of standards, the form to be used in all papers, and words to be spelled correctly may be included.)

■ *Use check lists—and use them regularly*

Provide students with check lists to be turned in, properly marked, with each composition. By regularly using check lists the students become progressively more alert to the items involved and reflect this in their writing. The example offered here is for senior high or for advanced junior high classes.

Check off each item as you examine your paper

_______ 1. Has the opening paragraph definite points to be developed?

_______ 2. Has each paragraph a topic sentence? (Occasional deviation from this standard is possible and acceptable but such deviation should be the intended exception, not the rule.)

_______ 3. Is each paragraph completely developed and unified?

_______ 4. Are there bridge words between the sentences within the paragraph wherever such words would be appropriate?

_______ 5. Does the closing paragraph embody the subject of the preceding paragraphs? (There must be no new points introduced here.)

[52] George C. Bliss, principal, Oakland Technical High School, Oakland, Calif.

①	On the river, he noticed a large rock on the middle of an island.	① ambiguous What was in the middle? the rock or the island?	On the river he noticed a large rock on an island that was in the middle. As they came closer Steve felt sure their island held the secret.
②	Ever since boyhood his greatest ambition had been to find some buried treasure	② awkward	His greatest ambition which he had had from when he was a boy was to find some buried treasure. He leaned foreward eagerly as Dave steered the launch toward a sandy beach.
③	As soon as the boat landed he leaped out and rushed to the granite rock	③ Tense	As soon as the boat landed he leaps out and rushed to the granite rock. Toward its base he found a runic carving, and just

________ 6. Does the closing paragraph conclude with a strong clinching sentence?
________ 7. Is there a run-on sentence or sentence fragment in the whole theme?
________ 8. Is there a definite, unmistakable antecedent for every pronoun used?
________ 9. Is spelling accurate?
________10. Is handwriting readable?

Check lists like this may be varied from one part of the semester to another or from one class to another, depending upon the most crucial needs of instruction. Items such as the above may be replaced by items dealing with punctuation, capitalization, letter form, or whatever the teacher wishes to emphasize.

To acquire an effective style

■ *Direct attention to the art of writing*

1. Encourage students to become interested in the craft of writing. Give dictation once every two weeks from some writer on the art of writing. Discuss and explain the ideas, and make the dictation the basis for supplementary spelling and vocabulary work.

2. Have students jot down in their notebooks brief samples of writing which impresses them as particularly forceful and effective. Have a weekly round-up of these ideas and quotations.

3. Teach Julian Cate's "A Style-ish Fable." Let students imitate the styles described in that essay.

4. Offer varied and frequent experiences with words. Use the vocabulary suggestions presented on pp. 235-39 in Chapter 5, "Reading With Comprehension." Encourage pupils to purchase and use the new pocket thesaurus arranged in easy alphabetical order.

5. Read many prose passages aloud, the students listening for the rhythms of the English sentence, for musical quality, for pleasing balances of sentence structure.

■ *Identify style and forceful expression*

1. Select a paragraph from any effective writer and substitute weak verbs; delete from it as many modifiers as possible, leaving a bare core. Present mimeographed copies of the denuded passage for reconstruction by the class. Through class discussion establish the need for the exact or vivid word and the striking metaphor. Point out the pitfalls of wordiness and flowery adjectives. From class suggestions work out the first sentence or two on the blackboard. Give time for students to comment on both good and poor suggestions. Read several of the finished student paragraphs anonymously and discuss. Then read the original passage.

2. For variations of this technique, try adding excess words, shifting the sequence of ideas, and omitting transitions in the prepared copy.

■ *Use helpful "commandments"*

To help students, whether in junior or senior high school, the teacher merely proclaims a "Helpful Commandment": No word is to be repeated within an interval of ten sentences. Certain justifiable exceptions such as *the, a* and forms of *to be* will not count, of course.[53]

[53] The intentional use of repetition for a valid purpose is not, of course, to be ignored. When students are more aware of style, the teacher may present this side of the coin.

With many pupils, another "Helpful Commandment" proves effective: None of the following words is to be used in this composition: nice, pretty, interesting, good.

■ *Present two versions of the same passage*

Begin a discussion of style by playing two or three recordings of the same song or melody. Many students are experts on the musical style of popular singers and orchestras. Then choose some author, notable for his style. Hemingway is particularly effective because he supports classroom work on selecting vigorous verbs to replace adjectives. Read passages from his short story, "Big Two-Hearted River" and discuss the style with students. Tell the students that when Hemingway was a young man learning to write, he gave his manuscripts to older and more famous writers who returned them with most of the adjectives crossed out. Put two passages on the board, or read, dictate, or duplicate them. Ask pupils which *they* consider the better:

An Escape

VERSION I

I ducked down, pushed between two men, and ran for the river, my head down. I tripped at the edge and went in with a splash. The water was very cold and I stayed under as long as I could. I could feel the current swirl me and I stayed under until I thought I could never come up.[54]

VERSION II

Furiously I pushed two big gruff, burly men away from me and ran like a streak to the swiftly flowing icy river waters. When I was in, I was able to feel the chilling, blood-curdling cold, but I remained patiently beneath the murky, pitch black water. The rapid, plunging running current brought me down the swiftly flowing stream where I was under until my paining, bursting lungs told me to come to the dangerous surface for some rapid, life-giving fresh air which made me realize how good life was and how good it was to be alive and kicking.

If any students claim they prefer the second version, accept their explanations without question or protest. Merely indicate that the first represents Hemingway's style; probably the author would say the second description distracts the reader's mind from the action and the speed with which the escape took place. Students may be taught *about* an author's style without being told they should prefer him.

■ *Stress sentence variety*

Keep model sentence "patterns" on the chalk board—compound sentences, complex sentences containing *who* and *which* clauses, sentences beginning with prepositional or adverbial phrases, sentences containing appositives, sentences with verb first, subject last; show the possibilities of sentence variety.

To learn conventional letter forms

■ *Teach letter form as fashion*

1. On the day when personal letter writing is to be introduced, discuss changing styles in clothing: Men wear or no longer wear suit vests; boys change their haircuts; an ivy league look was popular in the 1950's, now in the Sixties. . . . What will be

[54] In Hemingway, *The Viking Portable Library,* Malcolm Cowley, ed. (N.Y., Viking Press, 1944), p. 309.

the new look in the Seventies? The shrewd teacher will talk about boys' fashions, for students are more apt to supply references to the changing length in hemlines or the way girls style their hair. Fashions in architecture also change, as do the designs of cars, airplanes, and television sets. What is popular in music in one decade appears old-fashioned to another.

What then is fashionable in letter writing? The teacher reads aloud to his classes some samples of formal style in letters from the eighteenth and nineteenth centuries.[55] Next he asks, What is fashionable in letter writing today? In friendly letters how does a writer usually begin? What punctuation does he use for the salutation? What tone and manner characterize most friendly letters? Are there differences in these matters between letters to friends, letters of condolence, thank-you letters, and invitations?

Attention to the formalities of invitations and situations which students will not use for many years should be avoided. Students may be referred to library books on letter writing and etiquette which will be available if ever they encounter such situations. The main emphasis should be upon the typical kinds of letters students are writing or may soon be writing. Friendly letters, thank-you letters—taught just before Christmas holidays—and expressions of sympathy and condolence are probably their main needs.

2. Save forty or fifty business letters; or ask students to bring in letters. All these are placed in a folder and on the day business letters are introduced pass out one or several letters to each student. Then ask, What is the present style in business letters? What kind of headings do most of these use? Is there an inside address? How many students find a comma after the salutation? How many find nothing at all? How many find a colon? How many find a semi-colon? How many find something else? When it is established that at least 90 per cent of the business letters use a colon after the salutation, this point requires no further teaching. Are paragraphs indented or not? How many find a comma after the complimentary close? The advantage of this method is that students devise their own rules from the actual practices of business firms. This impresses pupils and proves a painless way to teach business letter form. Instead of being told what is convention, they tell the teacher what they find to be acceptable practice.

■ *Use a check list of qualities*

Students may compare business letters they write, usually actual letters to be mailed, with the following list of opposites:[56]

Try to be	*Avoid being*
courteous	discourteous
sincere	curt
pleasant	sarcastic
friendly	sharp
cheerful	impatient
warm	cold
helpful	peevish

[55] The school or public library will have collections of older letters.

[56] William Henry Leffingwell, in his book *A Textbook of Office Management* (N.Y., McGraw-Hill, 1932), describes these as part of the manual of correspondence used by one "large, well-conducted company."

If to each of the words in the first column, one can answer "Yes," his letters show appropriate tone. Should he answer "Guilty" to any of the points given in the other column, then he should revise the letter or letters, even if it is necessary to hold them until the next day. An unfriendly letter is often a wrench dropped into the gears of the business machine.

Evaluating Growth

In written expression, as in the other arts of language, the least critical factors are the easiest to appraise. Many standardized tests are available for measuring a pupil's ability to proofread for errors in usage, capitalization, spelling, and punctuation. But power over language, power more dependent upon thought than rules, does not lend itself so easily to objective testing procedures. To be sure some tests do go further, assessing the pupil's ability to select and organize ideas, to maintain a single point of view, and to distinguish between emotional and rational appeals to the reader.[57] Yet none of these evaluate the pupil's own thought and feeling as expressed in his own words. In judging thought and writing, standardized tests have only a very limited value.

The really significant evidence, as always, concerns the effectiveness of the pupil's thought and changes in attitudes toward writing. Most of all, teachers want to know if the pupil takes more interest in writing, is less reluctant to revise, and is expressing his thoughts and feelings with more clarity and originality than before instruction. The aims of teaching expression through writing (p. 485) include the habit of clear, orderly thinking about matters within the learner's own experience and the power to organize and express thought and feeling effectively for others. For appraising such significant aims evidence can usually be found in only one place—the pupil's composition folder with its accumulation of writing saved over a period of time. The care and pride with which the pupil has kept his folder can be estimated. Has he saved all his papers? Are they carefully arranged? Are there revisions and practice drills and vocabulary improvement lists? Do the compositions actually exemplify growth in clear, orderly thinking? Is there a decrease in hasty generalizations, prejudice, and narrowness of sympathy and understanding? Do the later compositions avoid the errors and problems of the earlier ones? No better evidence of growth in written expression is likely to be located.

[57] For instance, until the 1960 revision, the *Cooperative English Tests* included a test called "Effectiveness of English Expression." This attempted to determine a student's sense of sentence structure and style, organization, and diction. However, in preparing the 1960 revision of the *Cooperative English Tests,* the makers of this test found their attempt to revise it meaningfully so discouraging that it does not appear in the revision. Instead, there is a test called "English Expression" which includes only mechanics and choice of effective diction. Once again, the more significant aspects of written expression have eluded attempts at objective measurement, and the only valid test of a student's effectiveness in writing is his own act of expression.

Nothing said here is intended as a criticism of the attempts of test makers to help teachers with the difficult problem of evaluating written expression. Nor is this a criticism of the tests within the limits of what they can do. Teachers interested in the *Cooperative English Tests,* either the earlier version or the 1960 revision, may secure samples and information from the Cooperative Test Division, Educational Testing Service, Princeton, N.J., or Los Angeles 27, Calif.

Some of the ways to evaluate written expression, garnered from many classrooms, are presented here. An emphasis, as the reader will note, has been placed on those that take into account effective disciplined thinking.

Repeat the same check sheets at regular intervals. At the time of examining student folders, the teacher can help both himself and the pupil by using a check sheet listing the items most important to examine in the folder. These check sheets include columns for both pupil and teacher to indicate degree of success. A portion of such a check sheet might look like this:

Written expression—Pupil-teacher check sheet

Directions to the student: These ten scales can help bring out more definitely some of the really important learning you should gain from the writing we are doing this semester. For each item, rate yourself on a scale from 1 to 5. Number 1 is low and is described by the words at the left-hand side of the scale. Number 5 is high and is described by the words at the right-hand side of the scale. Numbers 2, 3, and 4 represent degrees between high and low, with 3 about average. For each of the ten scales, circle the number you honestly think describes your ability as of now.

Scale I. Organization of material

Low	High
Rambles; shows no plan or direction; thoughts just spill out as they occur; paragraphs not unified around a single idea.	Plans what is written; controls ideas and the order in which they occur; logical paragraphs built around one idea.

Student Rating	1	2	3	4	5
Teacher Rating	1	2	3	4	5

Scale II. Effective sentences

Low	High
All sentences put together the same way and of about the same length. Some sentences awkward or incomplete. Sometimes two sentences are run together with only a comma between.	Sentences varied and flexible in length. No instances of fragments, comma blunders, or long confused sentences.

Student Rating	1	2	3	4	5
Teacher Rating	1	2	3	4	5

Scale III. Originality of thought

Low	High
Tends to repeat ideas of others; does not think for himself; uses overworked words and phrases; afraid to be different from the crowd.	Thinks through to a position of his own; avoids thoughts and language that have been overworked; originates ideas of his own; independent thinker.

Student Rating	1	2	3	4	5
Teacher Rating	1	2	3	4	5

Scales IV to X, not shown here, may deal with spelling, handwriting, effective openings and conclusions, or whatever aspect of composition the teacher wishes to emphasize. Perhaps the most important point to make about such a check sheet concerns repetition. If the check sheet is used a number of times, the students begin to be more conscious of the scales in relation to their writing. Such lists serve more than the purposes of evaluation; they actually prove to be teaching devices, identifying desirable qualities and serving as levers to improve writing.

Use graphic charts to identify problems. Teachers often puzzle about the papers of students who have ideas but who make serious errors in written expression. To encourage such students—and these are often above average individuals—some teachers use double grades; others use graphic devices in evaluating each theme. Below appear reproductions of three stamps used for grading themes.

Ideas	
Organization	
Mechanics	
Appearance	
Grade	

Subject ______	Style ______
Originality ______	Mechanics ______
Organization ______	Appearance ______
Grade ______	

Content	
Organization	
Reasoning	
Style	
Mechanics	
Grade	

Use Ideaform paper. The National Council of Teachers of English prints a special composition paper prepared by the members of their High School Section Committee with the advice of teachers of college composition courses.[58] On the back of each sheet are spaces for the teacher to comment on the ideas or content of the pupil's writing, and a place to check such items as organization, spelling, and sentence structure.

[58] NCTE, Champaign, Ill.

Purchase profiles of communication skills. Scholastic magazine publishes a chart prepared by the English section of the Metropolitan School Study Council.[59] The charts for writing, speaking, listening, and reading serve as scales by which students may be rated and their needs for improvement identified.

Apply evaluation forms. Forms like the following may be duplicated. The first example features structure rather than originality, but in some classes this may be exactly what is needed. Forms such as these may always be altered to fit the aims of special situations. Junior high students require simplified variations of the forms shown here.

Form A

Theme title and length________________________________

Structure	*Excellently*	*Fairly*	*Poorly*	*Not at all*
The theme is defined and delimited.[1]				
The sequence of ideas is planned.				
Sufficient detail or evidence is presented.				
Paragraph unity is maintained.				
Transitions are smooth and appropriate.				
Sentences are well constructed and varied.				
Words are used correctly and exactly.				
Evaluation of structure:				
Grammar and usage				
Spelling				
Number of errors				
General Comment				

[1] Definition of theme may be either explicit or implicit. Key words of title and key ideas of early paragraphs control the development of the paper; there is one theme or subject; irrelevant material is omitted.

Form B

Is the purpose suited to the interests of the reader?

1 2	3 4 5	6 7
Minor degree of interest.	Probably of interest to most people.	Worthwhile purpose; arouses considerable interest.

Is there a unifying idea?

1 2	3 4 5	6 7
Paper leaves no single impression.	Attempted, but subordinate ideas detract.	One idea stands out throughout the paper.

[59] *Scholastic* magazine, 33 W. 42nd St., New York 36, N.Y.

Do the details build up and make clear the purpose?

1 2	3 4 5	6 7
Details chosen with little regard to purpose.	Majority of details clarify purpose.	All details chosen to build up purpose.

Is irrelevant material omitted?

1 2	3 4 5	6 7
Many unnecessary points.	Some wandering from point.	No effort needed to follow; smooth transitions.

Are mechanics acceptable for pupils' level of maturity? (Mechanics include spelling, punctuation, capitalization, legibility.)

1 2	3 4 5	6 7
Mechanics seriously interfere with attempt to read paper.	Average number of minor errors.	Almost perfect mechanically.

Forms such as these may be modified by the aims a teacher emphasizes. For students whom the teacher judges to be in need of heightened powers of observation and an increased awareness of the values in all experience, the last three items of the chart directly above might be replaced by others more pertinent to imaginative or descriptive writing. Similarly, in the form which follows, originality of ideas might be deemed important enough—in certain classes or during certain periods of instruction—to replace organization as described in the present form.

Form C

Scale for Characterizing Student Themes *

I. Organization

1	2 3	4 5
A. Plan not evident on careful first reading.	Plan evident but lacking in logic or suitability to the subject.	A definite and suitable plan, clear throughout.
B. Useless introduction and summary.	Simple and direct beginning and ending.	Attractive and effective beginning and ending.
C. Two or more cases of lack of continuity between paragraphs.	Two or more cases of mechanical and/or awkward transitions.	Logical and unobstrusive continuity.

* Based upon a more comprehensive scale prepared by the staff of Freshman English, University of Minnesota (Copyright 1938 by the English Department of the University of Minnesota). The total scale includes presentation, content, and mechanics in addition to organization.

D. Emphasis lost by obvious errors of proportion or position.	Adequate but not skillful use of proportion and position to secure emphasis.	Effective proportion of main point.
E. Two or more pseudoparagraphs, or ineffective paragraph fragments, or paragraphs containing irrelevant material.	Prevailingly simple, clear paragraphs but without adequate development.	Logical and effective paragraphs.

Compare student accomplishment. The teacher may compare his own students' works with the published standards of other teachers in such pamphlets as these: *Evaluating Composition in the Junior High School* (English Teachers of Western Pennsylvania); *Evaluating Ninth Grade Themes* (Illinois English Bulletin); *Evaluating Twelfth Grade Themes* (Illinois English Bulletin); *Evaluating Student Themes* (University of Wisconsin); *A Guide for Evaluation of High School Student Essays* (California Association of Teachers of English). All five of these are published by the National Council of Teachers of English, and are helpful to both teacher and students. Sample student themes clearly illustrate what the teacher hopes for in composition. Students may be led to compile a similar set of student themes, using their own compositions.

Use pupil evaluations. Read aloud a composition and ask everyone in the class to write a comment. Then collect and read aloud the comments, discussing both comments and the composition.

Try self-evaluation. At regular intervals or just before grading periods, students write self-evaluations which include a statement of errors they have learned to overcome. For the first occasion of such self-evaluation, the students will profit from an example placed on the board. One such a model, dealing with conventions, read as follows:

> I have learned that I have a tendency to run together two different sentences. For instance, in my first essay I wrote: "I jumped as if I had seen a rattlesnake then I swallowed my tooth." Now I know what I used to do that was wrong. I hurried along without thinking how the sentences would sound if I spoke them. Also I know more about subjects and predicates, and I have finished the three mimeographed exercises on run-on sentences. Also I have deliberately written, as Mr. Reagan suggested, three Horrid Examples of run-on sentences, aware all the time that I was making the mistake. I think this cured me more than anything else.

Such self-evaluation may continue, dealing with other indications of growth: organization, paragraphing, spelling, awareness of loose thinking.

Grade the same set of papers with other teachers. Evaluating the compositions of students is always a highly subjective procedure. Teachers' estimates of quality vary markedly, and although it will never be possible to standardize such evaluation, it is almost always a profitable, and sometimes a very chastening, experience for a group of teachers to read the same set of compositions and rate them separately.[60] For a secondary school teacher, one value of grading papers with several of his colleagues lies in the evidence on whether or not he tends to be an easy, typical, or overly severe grader. Quite often a grading bee of this kind results in a departmental study of the aims of composition and the standards that are reasonable to expect. Inevitably such a study brings about some improvement of instruction and evaluation.

In evaluation, the teacher tries to be comprehensive, avoiding concentration on any single aim such as the mastery of conventional mechanics. Evaluation should be continuous and flexible, taking advantage of a variety of methods, both formal and informal. Above all it should encompass the expression of both reason and imagination. Nor should there be a sharp distinction between the powers of imagination and powers of intelligence or understanding. Santayana concludes [61] that "reason is itself a method of imaginative thought" and that the figments of the imagination are "created by the same faculty that enables man to grasp the systematic relation of things in time and space, and to recognize their dependence upon one another." [62] But whether imaginative or systematic, thought is necessary for reputable written expression. Of this final principle we may truly say, "There is no way around, only through."

SELECTED READINGS

BOOKS

Roger H. Garrison, *A Creative Approach to Writing.* N.Y., Holt, 1951. The basic premise of this book: Writing begins with good thinking. Garrison considers creative writing as more than technique. "Ultimately you train the whole working of your mind."

Commission on the English Curriculum, *The English Language Arts,* NCTE Curriculum Series, Vol. I. N.Y., Appleton-Century-Crofts, 1952. This first volume of a series on the English curriculum clears away some stale items from the English curriculum. For instance, the comma after a dependent clause coming first in the sentence is no longer required except where necessary for clarity. See also the chapter on writing in *The English Language Arts in the Secondary School,* Vol. III of the same series (1956).

PERIODICALS AND PAMPHLETS

Joseph C. Blumenthal, "Without Form and Void, A Device for Teaching Organization in Expository Writing." *English Journal,* Vol. 35, No. 7 (September 1946). For the main features of this method, see p. 523 of this text.

[60] This problem occurs at the college level also. At Louisiana State University a report of the committee on academic standards tells of the same composition receiving grades from A to F.

[61] In *Dominations and Powers: Reflections on Liberty, Society, and Government* (N.Y., Scribner's, 1951), p. 463.

[62] In *The Sense of Beauty* (N.Y., Scribner's, 1936), p. 105.

Luella B. Cook, "Fundamentals in the Teaching of Composition." *English Journal,* Vol. 30, No. 5 (May 1941). Mrs. Cook distinguishes between errors that are a careless failure to put into operation what the student already knows and errors that arise from lack of knowledge or imperfect control over meaning. Fundamentals of composition are related to effective thinking rather than mechanics. See also, her articles, "Form in Its Relation to Thought," *English Journal,* Vol. 37, No. 5 (May 1948), and "Writing as Self-Revelation," *English Journal,* Vol. 48, No. 5 (May 1959).

William J. Dusel, "Determining an Efficient Teaching Load in English." *Illinois English Bulletin,* Vol. 43, No. 1 (October 1955). This valuable study shows how much time it takes to correct the same set of compositions at various levels to help the pupil. Dr. Dusel concludes, "Until English teachers are given a workable teaching load, they will continue to be forced to cut corners—and inevitably at the expense of the writing program."

Alfred Grommon, "Preparing High School Students for College Composition." *California Journal of Secondary Education,* Vol. 28, No. 2 (February 1953). Dr. Grommon recommends specific practices and notes the futility of a cram course of grammar in the twelfth grade as a substitute for twelve years of careful instruction in writing.

Clarence W. Hatch, "Needed: A Sequential Program in Composition." *English Journal,* Vol. 49, No. 8 (November 1960). This article presents a specific program for growth in composition from grade seven through twelve.

Eric W. Johnson, "Stimulating and Improving Writing in the Junior High School." *English Journal,* Vol. 47, No. 2 (February 1958). The highly specific suggestions here are useful in senior high as well as in junior high school. Mr. Johnson uses one of his five English periods each week as an independent reading and conference period when students come prepared to read silently or to confer with him about their writing.

Marguerite H. Malm, "Creative Writing in the Junior High School." *English Journal,* Vol. 28, No. 9 (November 1939). This article remains, of many that have been written, a most sensible and helpful description of how a teacher leads junior high school pupils to write and to improve their writing.

Practices in the Teaching of Composition in California Public High Schools. California State Department of Education, Bulletin No. 5, Vol. 27 (June 1958), Sacramento, California. This bulletin describes methods and assignments for the teaching of writing as reported by teachers throughout California. Hundreds of specific practices are presented.

Chapter Eleven

Grammar and Usage

There is no language apart from a speaker active in expression.
—CHARLES C. FRIES [1]

PERSPECTIVE

The study of grammar, syntax, and rhetoric—however these are identified—has as its chief end the development of power over language. Only as students learn to express their own ideas more clearly and to understand the expression of others is any program of language study worthwhile. Therefore, instruction in grammar and usage, designed to improve student thinking, must be continually applied to the processes of communication. The teacher's essential task is to relate instruction to use.

Language exists as a vehicle to transmit thought, not as an inert body of words and principles for separate study. Speakers or writers active in expression strive for increasingly effective communication of ideas; thus, they respond to studying ways of conveying precise meaning. Yet, instruction in language must be limited to necessary learnings—to those generalizations about English grammar which assist individuals in analyzing and constructing sentences. Furthermore, research indicates that use of principles in practice occurs most frequently when theoretical knowledge is learned in relation to the student's own writing and speaking, rather than when studied independently as a set of logical principles.[2] Knowing that the way in which these generalizations are learned affects their use, teachers place much stress on meaningful practice.

In recent years the discussion of ends and means in teaching grammar and usage has created an aura of ambiguity around the terms themselves. Both laymen and teachers refer to *grammar* and mean *usage*, or group all kinds of language instruction under one or the other term. So unclear are the referents that the words are used with various meanings even in scholarly publications.

[1] Charles C. Fries, *The Teaching of English* (Ann Arbor, Mich., George Wahr, 1949), p. 107.

[2] Cf. Oscar N. Hough, "Representative Research in the Communication Skills," *Education,* Vol. 42, No. 7 (March 1952); John J. DeBoer, "Grammar in Language Teaching," *Elementary English,* Vol. 26, No. 6 (October 1959); Harry A. Greene, articles on English Language, Grammar, and Composition, in W. S. Monroe, ed., *Encyclopedia of Educational Research* (N.Y., Macmillan, 1950).

For the purpose of discussion in this book the most widely recognized meanings are accepted:

> *Grammar*—The systematic study of the relationship of words, clauses, and phrases within the English sentence.
>
> *Traditional*—The Latin-based body of principles which has been taught in schools for many decades.
>
> *Descriptive, Linguistic, or Structural*—The description of English and its ways emerging from the studies of linguistic scientists.
>
> *Usage*—The established habits of an individual in using language in speech and writing, the forms he accepts and rejects, and the appropriateness of these forms to his expression.

Grammar, being a codification of principles and generalizations which describe the structure and operation of the sentence as it is used, is dependent on usage, and is thus an accepted working *guide* to the ways in which ideas are expressed.

Much of the confusion about grammar in recent years has resulted from attempts by modern linguists to substitute for traditional principles a description of English as used by educated men today. Linguistic grammar, supporting its conclusions by using scientific observation rather than authority or tradition, directs its attention to the systematic patterns of the English sentence. One of its contributions to classroom teaching may well be the stress it places on inductive thinking. In no sense does the linguistic approach require the teacher to abandon everything he has learned and taught about grammar. Rather it offers a viewpoint which will help him in modifying his procedures, his use of textbooks, and his curricular offerings in the light of new understandings. An increasing number of textbooks seem to be introducing certain insights of the linguists. The years immediately ahead promise to be a transitional period during which the new approaches are gradually tested as ways of increasing the effectiveness of instruction.

Perceptive teachers have for many years used some of the same techniques that linguists employ. Even when a definitional approach has been used to introduce parts of speech or structural elements, students' understandings have been developed through analysis of their own speaking and writing, through the study of sentence patterns, and through drills requiring substitution of similar elements in original sentences—all important attributes of a descriptive approach.

The program discussed here suggests some ways teachers, without abandoning all that seems familiar, may strengthen their present programs by introducing procedures gleaned from modern linguists. Whenever possible, familiar terminology and familiar teaching techniques are employed. Some new emphases are suggested, but so too are ways of utilizing exercises in present textbooks. These suggestions are based on experiences of successful teachers, on research in methodology, and on recent linguistic studies. A selective program is recommended. This chapter will discuss the content of such a program, key problems in organizing instruction, and related learning experiences.

An understanding of certain basic concepts about language is necessary before the teacher can select content and teaching procedures appropriate for secondary students. Since the ineffectiveness of some instructional programs stems largely from attempts to teach too much, teachers need to identify the learnings that are basic and then to set up for each level of instruction certain priorities in terms of cruciality. Often a curriculum guide will provide such leadership. This section includes a discussion of the important concepts, followed by a consideration of those learnings about structure and usage really needed by young people.

Three basic understandings about language

Normally students preparing to teach English devote some course work to the study of the language itself—its history, operation, and structure. It is from such systematic study that sound programs in grammar and usage evolve. Research of linguists has yielded many understandings having implications for classroom teaching. Perhaps the three most important are the following:

Language is primarily speech, secondarily writing.

Language changes, and the changes are not necessarily either advantageous or detrimental to effective communication.

Appropriateness is the standard for good language.

LANGUAGE IS PRIMARILY SPEECH, SECONDARILY WRITING

Spoken language is primary; writing is a symbolization which depends on the prior existence of speech. The studies of linguists are based on spoken language largely because researchers find in speech a complete signal system of the meanings conveyed in verbal communication, e.g., the employment of pitch, stress, and pause. The signal system which man uses to convey meaning in spoken language is only imperfectly approximated in writing. Understanding the distinction between the two forms of communication is basic to the scientific study of language.

Studies of spoken language reveal clearly that secondary students have for many years used in their speech the basic structures and patterns of the English sentence. Any student, no matter how poorly educated, who speaks English knows at the level of use the inflections, the sound structure, and the syntactical arrangements of English.[3] The secondary teacher's role is less to reveal new patterns and structures than to bring to the conscious level that which the student controls on another level.

Because the structures and patterns of the English sentence are employed in somewhat different ways in speech and in writing, teachers and students need to bear in mind the following distinctions:

Spoken language contains a wide range of non-verbal signals for conveying meaning; written language does not. Speakers indicate meaning and intent

[3] Donald J. Lloyd, "The Child Who Goes to School," *Elementary English,* Vol. 30, No. 7 (November 1953).

through stress and pitch and through juncture—the pauses which interrupt the sequence of speech sounds. Writers approximate these grammatical signals in other ways, usually by punctuation and capitalization, at best imperfect representations.

Spoken language frequently conveys meaning through phrases, clauses, and other fragments of sentences, because the completeness of the idea can be communicated from sender to receiver in non-verbal ways. Thus, one deer hunter murmers "on the hill" to another, points in a certain direction, and communicates perfectly that he has spotted game. A speaker conveys meaning through gesture, facial expression, and tone. Written language requires more attention to precision and completeness, hence greater dependence on modification, subordination, and word choice.

Written language, since it must stand alone in conveying meaning, demands greater clarity than does oral language.

Written language requires more attention to the conventions of language. Many colloquial terms and stylistic considerations used in speech are inappropriate in writing. Spoken language cannot, therefore, be the sole determinant of appropriate written usage; no linguist argues that teachers accept in the writing of students all forms accepted in speech.

In developing awareness of unfamiliar written structures, the teacher will draw on the student's oral language habits but will find in each form unique problems demanding separate consideration. Because speech is the primary language, teachers of grammar will search especially for methods to relate what they teach to spoken communication.

LANGUAGE CHANGES, AND THE CHANGES ARE NOT NECESSARILY EITHER ADVANTAGEOUS OR DETRIMENTAL

Because language is an instrument for communication, its nature and form are inevitably adapted to the requirements of society. As these requirements change, so does language. The English of mid-century America differs substantially from the English of eighteenth-century England, yet who can say the change is for the better? The ultimate test of any language is how it fulfills its function as social communication.[4] This is not to say that in any society or segment of society individuals will not differ considerably in their command of language.

Change occurs continually in speech, more slowly in writing because form and convention are standardized through printing. Yet many changes first accepted in speech later find their way into writing.[5] The teacher of English should be neither a harbinger of such changes nor a rigorous defender of outmoded forms. Rather he needs to steer a steady course, recognizing that changes do occur and cannot be controlled by arbitrary pronouncements. In most situations the teacher helps pupils most if he is somewhat conservative. He can

[4] For a discussion of American English in its social setting, see Donald J. Lloyd and Harry Warfel, *American English in Its Cultural Setting* (N.Y., Knopf, 1956), pp. 9-56.

[5] See Chapter 1, "Language as Dynamic Process," pp. 21-23. See also Charles C. Fries, "Linguistic Science and the Teaching of English," pp. 144, 145 in Robert C. Pooley, ed., *Perspectives on English*, N.Y., Appleton-Century-Crofts, 1960.

develop awareness of fundamental differences in the standards for speech and for writing; he can clarify reasons for these differences; he can explain why some forms used in speech are not acceptable in writing.[6] Acceptance of the fact that language changes does not necessarily mean approval or disapproval of specific changes.

APPROPRIATENESS IS THE STANDARD FOR GOOD LANGUAGE

What standard should teachers adopt as a guide? What criteria should govern choice of constructions? Most teachers recognize several levels of usage, agreeing that language is neither "correct" nor "incorrect" but rather "appropriate" or "inappropriate" depending upon the situation in which it is used. A student's "it don't" is unsuitable in the classroom, but so is overly precise usage by the teacher. Both divert attention from the meaning to the manner of expression.

Teachers of English are not interested in perpetuating false or snobbish dogmas about language. They realize that human worth cannot be measured by the speech patterns a man uses, and they know usage varies from one locality to another and from one historical period to another. But they know, also, that in the world to which their pupils go, language is a mark of social and educational status. The faculty of any school hopes that its students will never, because of language, be denied access to opportunities or entrance to the social groups they desire. The stubborn fact is that leaders of many communities are sensitive to deviations from the informal English which tends to be the accepted language of our day. Thus the teacher must be clear about two points—why he recommends changes in the pupil's language and which changes are actually important enough to merit attention.

The National Council of Teachers of English recommends that teachers accept as good English language "appropriate to the purpose of the speaker, true to the language as it is, and comfortable to the speaker and listener." The Council sees such language as "the product of custom, neither cramped by rule nor freed from all restraint . . . never fixed, but [changing] with the organic life of the language." Bad English, on the other hand, is seen as language which is "unclear, ineffective, and inappropriate to the linguistic occasion, no matter how traditional, 'correct,' or elegant." [7]

Acceptance of this touchstone means recognition of a responsibility to prepare students to evaluate the circumstances under which they are writing and speaking as well as the factors influencing appropriateness: time, social situation, and other features of the environment.[8] Many students come from homes in which the English spoken differs from that appropriate in the classroom. In teaching such students to suit language to the occasion, teachers need

[6] Teachers searching for a guide to specific changes will find useful help in A. H. Marckwardt and Fred Walcott, *Facts About Current English Usage* (N.Y., D. Appleton-Century, 1938).

[7] Commission on the English Curriculum, *The English Language Arts*, NCTE Curriculum Series, Vol. I (N.Y., Appleton-Century-Crofts, 1952), p. 277.

[8] See pp. 425-26.

run no risk of seeming to belittle the language of the students' parents. Indeed the very rejection of arbitrary standards of correctness offers teachers an opportunity to explain why usages differ and why a student may speak a different level of language in school than he does at home. Carefully avoiding judgments which may offend individuals accustomed in their personal lives to usages quite different from those encouraged in the classroom, the teacher can try to develop understanding of the criterion of appropriateness.[9]

Three understandings about language, then, are basic to any program: speech and writing differ, language changes, and appropriateness is the standard for good language. These are insights needed by the teacher in selecting and organizing instruction; they are understandings needed by the learner who must live with flexible standards and suit his speech and writing to the occasion. On this foundation a selective program may be built.

The structure of English

Although students learn to analyze language so they may have a method for studying and clarifying sentences, research so far has consistently shown that only the more able students apply the principles of grammar in evaluating oral and written expression.[10] To be sure, research has dealt almost entirely with applications of traditional grammar; the study of the effectiveness of linguistic learnings has yet to be made. It seems likely, however, that immature students, incapable of sustained abstract thinking, will experience almost as much difficulty in coping with generalizations emerging from the new grammar as with those from the old, since the difficulty lies with the level of abstraction rather than with the precise content. However, the descriptive approach possesses one advantage in that it forces the learner to concentrate on the study of usage as he strives to generalize. Even slower students may profit from concentration on specific sentences, whether or not they always relate examples to underlying principles; moreover, such an inductive approach may lead able learners to a more realistic, more lasting, and more usable understanding of English sentence structure. Certainly the new grammar's concentration on inductive method and on actual usage holds much promise.

Our program, then, needs to stress practice in using language, particularly for students who experience difficulties in handling abstractions. Emphasis on the concrete, rather than the abstract, is desirable in teaching most students in the early stages of junior high school, even many of average and above average ability, who in their comparative immaturity tend to profit more from a rigorous

[9] Teachers will find helpful discussion of "levels" in Robert Pooley, *Teaching English Usage* (N.Y., D. Appleton-Century, 1946), pp. 16-24. See also J. N. Hook and E. G. Mathews, *Modern American Grammar and Usage* (N.Y., Ronald, 1956).

[10] Greene, articles on English Language, Grammar, and Composition in *Encyclopedia of Educational Research,* and "Direct Versus Formal Methods in Elementary English," *Elementary English Review,* Vol. 24, No. 5 (May 1947). Ingrid M. Strom, "Research in Grammar and Usage and Its Implications for Teaching Writing," *Bulletin of School of Education,* Indiana University, Vol. 36, No. 5 (September 1960).

program of sentence building than from sustained grammatical analysis. Seventh- and eighth-graders may be introduced to a few grammatical concepts, such as the predicate, subject, and complement, and to a few of the concepts of expansion and modification. But most class time should be devoted to actual writing and speaking. This practice will prepare students for later generalizing concerning sentence patterns and grammatical principles.

Practice in using language should form virtually the entire program for slow learners. For these young people there is little sense in limiting the few hours of instruction to generalizations which cannot later be remembered or applied; it is better to introduce carefully planned experiences in using language.

For the older student, particularly the able learner in the ninth grade and beyond, the study of grammatical structure can offer important insights concerning the nature of English as well as a resource to which he may refer in improving the clarity of his sentences.

Recent books on linguistic grammar are proving helpful to teachers.[11] Although various methods of analyzing English are presented in such books and different terminologies advanced, all volumes stress the classification of English words according to function in the sentence. Because the English language is such a complex and variable instrument for communicating ideas, no perfect system for describing it is likely to be achieved. However, modern linguists offer us a more accurate description of our language than we have had before, and in their work teachers find several major understandings on which to base a program of instruction:

The importance of word order in determining the meaning of the English sentence. If "Bob struck Tom who struck John" conveys the intended meaning, any rearrangement of the nouns alters the intent. The position in which a word appears determines its function and its meaning.

The necessity for functional description instead of definition. The common definition of a verb as a word expressing an action or a state of being cannot be applied logically to such statements as "Running a race requires speed" or "The departure seemed imminent" where clearly action is expressed by words used as nouns. The substitution of functional description—A verb is a word used like *seems* or *requires*—implies that understanding of grammatical concepts will be developed slowly as the result of much analysis of examples and illustrations.

The value in studying common sentence patterns. The familiar Subject-Predicate-Object is a basic sentence pattern for all of the following examples even though different methods of expansion are used in each:

	John	hit	Tom	
On the way to his biology class	Rupert	saw	a rhinoceros	in the hall
The	owl (and the) pussy cat	entranced	each other	
		(and) sailed		away in a pea green boat

[11] See the annotated list at the end of this chapter.

Only several patterns need be emphasized, yet from such study students learn structures which can be applied to an infinite number of specific sentences.

The fact that students know sentence patterns on the level of use. Children use basic sentence patterns in their speech before they arrive at school.[12] Secondary students use these same patterns to express more complex ideas. The problem in teaching knowledge of structure is to develop at the conscious level understandings about structures that students are already using.

A selective study of the structure of English based on these principles will contribute substantially to improving students' communication. Some years ago Fries demonstrated that a major difference between educated and uneducated writers occurs in the former's consciously varied and flexible use of basic sentence patterns.[13] Teachers can help students improve the structure of their sentences in the same way they help them improve the content—by developing inductively, through the study of structures they presently use orally, understandings which will also apply in writing.

THE ESSENTIAL ELEMENTS

Although analysis of the English sentence begins with the understanding of the basic elements—the predicate, the subject, and the complement—stress at all times should be placed on the complete thought unit and the relationship of the word to the complete sentence. Teachers avoid asking students to "identify" nouns or verbs in lists of isolated words. Nouns are nouns because of the ways in which they are used in a statement, not because of any quality in individual words. In the statement, The *galfumps* are coming, we recognize *galfumps* as a noun because it is used as nouns are used, just as we recognize the same word as a verb in, The eebak *galfumps* his tail.

When students learn to distinguish the essential elements—subject, predicate, complement—they have a base from which to analyze the function of other words in the sentence. At least the first two of these elements, and often all three, are necessary to convey meaning in any statement. Other elements of the sentence are dispensable; not these essentials. The basic patterns involved in the subject-predicate relationships are found in every language of the world.[14] Teachers confused by conflicting discussions between traditional and linguistic grammarians can emphasize the subject, predicate, and complement with confidence. Essential to the structure of the sentence, these elements should receive top priority in teaching. In grades seven and eight, the teacher may introduce the simple terminology and begin to develop awareness of the essential elements, even while recognizing that deep understandings ripen slowly

[12] Lloyd, "The Child Who Goes to School"; also verified in unpublished research on language development by Ruth Strickland, University of Indiana, and Walter Loban, University of California, Berkeley.

[13] Charles C. Fries, *American English Grammar* (N.Y., D. Appleton-Century, 1940). See also the discussion in Byron Guyer and Donald Bird, *Patterns of Thinking and Writing* (San Francisco, Wadsworth, 1959), pp. 98-99.

[14] Edward Sapir, *Language,* 1921 (N.Y., Harcourt, Brace, Harvest Books), p. 119.

over many years as individuals continue to write and to analyze increasingly complex sentences.

No mention is made here of the classroom setting in which grammatical study is introduced. However, the principles of method presented earlier require that, insofar as possible, the sentences be those of the students; the moment grow out of the writing and speaking of class members and occur at a time when students are ready for instruction.

A basic approach One learns to know predicates in much the same way as one learns to know individuals, through repeated contact which reveals more and more about them. If the student learns to recognize the predicate in its various aspects,[15] identification of subjects and complements, the other two essential elements, is largely a matter of common sense. Predication is a difficult concept. Complete understanding of it requires intensive teaching of all aspects of the verb over a long period of time. However, the teacher begins early to build this concept with simple predicates. Using easily recognized examples, he habituates students to the following three steps in sentence analysis: [16]

1. Find the predicate:
2. Find the subject of the predicate:
   Who or what plus the predicate yields the subject
3. Find the word used as a complement:
   Subject plus predicate plus who, what, or whom yields the complement

For many pupils, this approach is almost foolproof, even with more complicated sentences.

I believe *that he is honest.*
I believe what?

Recognizing the predicate Attempts to recognize predicates may begin with the analysis of two-word sentences in the seventh grade. For example, the teacher asks the group to select the name of a student, Kevin, and to think of all the things Kevin can do. Kevin runs, grunts, climbs, dates, drives, studies, . . . The students substitute as many words as possible within the basic sentence. Soon individuals begin to see that although one word may perform the function of the predicate, the English language often demands two or three.

[15] The term *predicate* is used here to refer to the *simple predicate,* the word(s) used as a verb in the sentence without reference to the words that complete the verb's meaning. Concepts of modification will be introduced as methods of expanding the essential elements of the sentence.

[16] These steps may be introduced with simple and compound sentences in the junior high school; later, students may apply them to complex sentences involving several predicates and their subjects contained within interlocking dependent and independent clauses. The steps will be the same. Students can learn to identify all predicates, then to find the subject and possible complement of each.

Kevin *whistles.*
Kevin *can whistle.*
Kevin *has whistled* before.

The teacher explains that any word or words which can be substituted for *whistle* or *can whistle* or *has whistled* are called *verbs.* Pupils will begin to see that words like *sing* and *make* and *begin* can be substituted, whereas *song* and *maker* and *beginner* cannot. Learning experiences involving such substitutions may be repeated over several semesters with increasingly difficult sentences.

Locating the subject Attempts to identify the noun used as subject follow this introduction to the predicate, and may be introduced before linking predicates are considered. Begin discussion of the subject with the basic two-word sentence: Kevin runs, grunts, climbs, dates, drives, studies, . . . Ask students to suggest other words which can be substituted for Kevin, using any of these predicates.

Geneva runs	Geneva grunts
clock runs	he grunts
he runs	cat grunts
motor runs	cow grunts
cat runs	

Explain that a word used in this way is called the *subject* and ask students to suggest questions which individuals can ask themselves to determine the subject: Who? What? Then establish the basic formula for determining the subject:

Who or What	plus the predicate yields the subject.
Who runs?	*What* runs?

Ultimately students will discover that this method is useful in analyzing even more complex sentences. For example, sentences with more than one clause contain more than one predicate, each with its own subject.

The woman *jumped* when the trunk *fell.*
Who or *what* jumped? *Who* or *what* fell?

Then the relationship between the clauses can be examined to determine the central thought.

The students have now learned that words used as predicates are called *verbs* and those used as subjects are called *nouns.* Recognition that the part of speech is determined by the use of the word within the sentence prepares the students for recognizing phrases and clauses functioning as nouns. Pronouns are perhaps best treated as a special subgroup of nouns since they fulfill the same functions in the sentence.[17]

[17] Both Francis and Sledd suggest ways of treating pronouns as special classes of nouns despite their inflectional variations. See W. Nelson Francis, *The Structure of American English* (N.Y., Ronald, 1958), pp. 244-246; and James Sledd, *A Short Introduction to English Grammar* (Chicago, Scott, Foresman, 1959), pp. 83-85.

Identifying the complement The third essential element in many sentences is the complement. The teacher may begin instruction by aiding students in describing the function of the word changed in each of the following sentences:

Kitty eats steak.
Kitty eats lettuce.
Kitty eats cheeseburgers.

Students will supply other words to be used in this way: dinner, gooseberry pie, mincemeat, hamburgers, . . . Explain that words used as *dinner* and *pie* are called *complements* because they "complete" the meaning of the statement. Ask the class to find additional examples. Then let them suggest questions which they can ask themselves to determine the complement, and establish the formula:

Subject plus predicate plus what or who or whom yields the complement.

John wrote a *book.*	John followed the *criminal.*
John wrote *what?*	John followed *whom?*

Finally, when students indicate by their substitutions that they understand this type of complement, review the concepts established thus far:

At times the meaning of a sentence may be complete with subject and predicate only, e.g., John *runs.*

At other times subject and predicate have a complement, e.g., John *runs* a *race.*

Explain that this type of complement is called an *object* and that students will later learn other types.

Recognizing linking predicates and their complements A knowledge of linking predicates and their complements, known to some teachers as predicate adjectives and predicate nominatives, is essential to understanding certain sentence patterns. For some students the study of these elements will come later, after the basic pattern of subject-predicate-complement is understood. Normally the study of the linking predicate and its complement will not be introduced until students have considered some ways of modifying or expanding the basic sentence pattern discussed above. As methods of expansion are studied, students will begin to comprehend the function of words used as adjectives and thus more easily distinguish the predicate-adjective complement.

In introducing students to linking predicates and their complements, the teacher again uses simple examples.

Predicate nominative—if the complement is a noun.
John is *captain.* (Renames the subject)
Predicate adjective—if the complement is an adjective.
John is *handsome.* (Describes the subject)

Here again, lasting understandings are more effectively developed by using examples than by defining. Ask students to substitute other words which can be used for the predicate nominative:

John is captain, a man, a teacher, her brother.

Then for the predicate adjective:

John is handsome, tall, old, wise, crabby.

Then ask them to substitute other words for linking predicates:

John is, was, has been
The boys are, were, have been

Working initially with forms of the verb *to be* only, students can learn to recognize this sentence pattern. Later they will see that a few other verbs—seems, looks, appears—use the same pattern.

Understanding different functions of complements Ultimately students will have to learn that some verbs requiring an object take an additional complement, differing from the object in function.[18] Students use such constructions in their speech; they can easily recognize the patterns.

At times this complement, referring to a person or a thing different from the object, precedes it. It is either a noun or a pronoun. Students may call it the *inner complement.*

Examples of inner complements:

They made *Don* a costume.
The mother sang the *baby* a lullaby.
Peter gave the *dog* a bath.
They sent *Joan* a check.
The hills give the *house* protection.

Help students imitate the pattern using verbs like *teach, tell, read, write, ask, offer,* . . .

At other times the complement follows the object and is directly connected with it. It may be a noun renaming the object or an adjective referring to it. Students may call this the *outer complement.*

Examples of nouns used as outer complements:

They made Don a *chairman.*
They elected Bill *captain.*
His parents consider Paul a *genius.*
Perfect coordination makes Jack an expert *golfer.*

[18] See Hook and Mathews, *Modern American Grammar and Usage,* pp. 84-86; and Paul Roberts, *Patterns of English* (N.Y., Harcourt, Brace, 1956), pp. 171-173.

Examples of adjectives used as outer complements:

> Teasing makes the dog *irritable.*
> The class considered the explanation *foolish.*
> His teachers think Barney *talented.*

Help students compose sentences with both nouns and adjectives used as outer complements following verbs like *appoint, choose, name, find, believe,* . . .

Practice in composing sentences with both inner and outer complements will enable students to understand the conditions under which a complement, in addition to the object, may be expected.

The approach illustrated here for developing understanding of the essential elements of the simple sentence may be applied in analyzing more complicated structures, where the method is the same. Once students are introduced to the basic elements, the teacher will find many moments in the classroom when difficult or obscure sentences will yield before an analysis into their essential elements—subject, predicate, and complement. For example:

> After the moon rose, bats flew from the belfry and people bolted their doors.
> Find the predicates:
> *rose* *flew* *bolted*
> Find the subject of each predicate:
> *moon* rose *bats* flew *people* bolted
> Find the complements:
> moon rose bats flew people bolted *doors*

Teachers faced with courses of study and textbooks based on traditional grammar should see that the inductive approach recommended here will not prevent them from teaching the important understandings. For instance, the parts of speech that students need to understand, defined in terms of their use in the English sentence, may be studied at appropriate times: Verbs and nouns may be identified as students learn the essential elements (subject-predicate-complement); pronouns at the same time, whether they are considered as a separate class or a subgroup of nouns; adjectives and adverbs, when the class considers modification; prepositions as signals for a phrase modifier which will be completed by a noun. Other markers or signal words may be similarly introduced.

METHODS OF EXPANSION

Once students begin to comprehend the essential elements of the sentence, teachers can introduce methods of expansion. Both understandings can develop together as classes work with increasingly difficult examples. Speakers and writers use two basic methods of expansion—compounding and modifying.

Compounding elements The most obvious method of expanding the nucleus of a sentence is by compounding elements. Any element may be compounded—the predicate, subject, or complement.

The compounding of simple predicates and subjects may be taught as these elements are taught, or may be delayed for a special lesson. Later, students will learn that phrases, clauses, and sentences may also be compounded. Of the problems likely to occur as students compound elements of a sentence, three require attention: misuse of connectives performing coordinating functions, faulty punctuation of coordinate ideas, and failure to maintain parallel structure of identical elements. Over a period of time these three problems require much analysis and drill, with attention during junior high school years probably wisely devoted to rather obvious problems in using connectives and in punctuating. Parallelism becomes important as students try to express complex ideas, attempts which occur increasingly throughout the secondary school years.[19] For this reason special instruction on parallelism may well be delayed until grade nine and later. One of the most effective ways of working with students on such problems is to study sentences actually written in class.

Modifying ideas Modification is a second way to expand each of the essential sentence elements. If the student is to develop any basic understanding of sentence relationships, he must perceive the relationship between main and subordinate ideas. Teach him from the beginning that both single words and groups of words are used to modify, for only over a period of years will he acquire skill in recognizing and using phrases and clauses as modifiers. Relying again on description of sentence characteristics, teachers can lead students to see that noun modifiers are words used as *good* in such expressions as "The good girl" or "The girl was good," whereas verb modifiers are words used like *sometimes* or *happily* in "She skis sometimes" or "She smiled happily."

Once students possess some understanding of the essential elements, the concept of modification may be introduced by studying single-word modifiers in basic sentence patterns. Later the teacher or other teachers can build on these basic understandings. Because the complexity of sentences in student writing increases perceptibly between grades nine and ten, teachers will wish at this time to provide special instruction. Assignments involving the summarizing of discussion or the compression of an idea into a single sentence can lead to comparisons of different ways writers, by compounding and modification, vary sentence structure. From such comparisons students can glean many helpful insights into methods of expansion.

VARIETY IN SENTENCE PATTERNS

As students learn the three essential elements of the sentence and the two basic methods of expansion, they begin to perceive recurring patterns of statement. The study of these sentence patterns can emphasize ways of achieving variety within each model and give students an opportunity to apply their developing understandings of compounding and modifying.

[19] See Lou La Brant, "A Study of Certain Language Developments of Children in Grades Four to Twelve," *Genetic Psychology Monographs*, Vol. 14, No. 4 (November 1933).

Four basic sentence patterns Most English sentences can be reduced to one of four basic patterns; each is illustrated on the accompanying chart:

Pattern I: Subject–Predicate
Pattern II: Subject–Predicate–Object
Pattern III: Subject–Linking Predicate–Predicate Nominative
Pattern IV: Subject–Linking Predicate–Predicate Adjective

These four sentence patterns can be varied in an infinite number of ways, and students profit from practicing varying expression within each pattern.

Ultimately, of course, students will need to study some of the less frequently used patterns:

Pattern V: Predicate–Subject (Inverted order, common in questions)
Have you the book?
Pattern VI: Expletive–Predicate–Subject
It is easy to learn to skate.
There is a tower on the hill.
Pattern VII: (Understood Subject)–Predicate–Complement (Request or command)
Show the picture.
Pattern VIII: Subject–Predicate–First Object–Second Object (Or Adjective)
Jean gave Tom the book.
Everyone thinks Fido adorable.

However, these need not be introduced until students have grasped the four basic patterns. Moreover, these patterns are less frequently subjected to variation and embellishment than are the four basic ones.[20]

Four sentence patterns

Pattern I: Subject–Predicate

Tom	sits.
He	sleeps comfortably.
Evaluating papers	is tiring but often stimulating.
Whatever he says	is heard.
The boy who is in the third row	sits silently while the bell rings.

Pattern II: Subject–Predicate–Object

Tom	hits	Bob.
The dog and cat that were running	violently struck	the rock wall.
One of the boys	tried to reach	the swing which was just beyond his grasp.
I	know	what it means to be rich.

[20] No attempt is made in this book to suggest a complete, detailed method of patterning. Suggestions for these are presented in several books listed at the end of the chapter. However, the descriptive approach presented here will develop a point of view toward language and sentence patterns which will assist students who later study approaches recommended by Fries, Francis, Hill, Roberts, Sledd, Whitehall, and others.

Pattern III: Subject–Linking Predicate–Predicate Nominative

This	is	the place.
Behind the barn	seems	a good place to play.
This spot on the beach	appears to be	a good place to picnic.
That she is guilty	is	our final judgment.

Pattern IV: Subject–Linking Predicate–Predicate Adjective

She	is	pretty.
Sinking in the west, the sun	appeared	almost too brilliant.
The sun,	as it was sinking in the west, seemed	overly brilliant.

Modifying patterns Whether teachers wish to rely on the simplified patterning suggested here or on one described by a linguistic grammarian, they must adopt an approach which begins with the simple and moves to the complex.[21] Even young children may be asked to substitute words or sentences similar in pattern to "The cat ate the rat" or "The teacher saw the boy." Later, as students develop some understanding of the basic Subject–Predicate–Object pattern, encourage them to add word modifiers, then phrases and clauses, e.g.,

The *cat*	*saw* a mouse.
The fat old *cat*	*saw* a gray mouse.
The fat old *cat* in the chair	*saw* a gray mouse running away.
The fat old *cat* who lay comfortably in the chair	*saw* a gray mouse running away.

Through expanding such simple sentences, students begin to understand the concept of modification and to perceive basic patterns as they appear in increasingly complex statements. Ultimately, students may study the function of modifiers in the sentence and generalize concerning their position and use:

Articles precede words used as nouns and other words modifying nouns.
Single-word modifiers normally precede words used as nouns.
Phrase and clause modifiers normally follow words used as nouns.

Teachers may utilize a similar approach in introducing the modifiers of verbs and complements and, to mature students, more complex forms of modification and subordination.

Teaching students to vary expression requires prolonged and continued attention. The program outlined here for studying the structure of English can be accomplished only through intelligent, systematic study in many classrooms. The descriptions of basic structural elements and methods of expansion gleaned during junior high school years provide a foundation on which teachers later

[21] See Roberts, *Patterns of English*, pp. 56-76; Lloyd and Warfel, *American English in Its Cultural Setting*, pp. 110-151; Wallace Anderson, "Structural Linguistics: Some Implications and Applications," *English Journal*, Vol. 46, No. 7 (October 1957). See also the different analysis presented by Robert Pooley in *Teaching English Grammar* (N.Y., Appleton-Century-Crofts, 1957), pp. 87-102.

can build as students begin to demonstrate interest in expressing complex ideas and in creating more varied sentences. Throughout this program, too, such instruction in structure is accompanied by instruction in usage. Each, paralleling the other, provides opportunity for students to express ideas thoughtfully and well.

The usage of English

Once teachers accept appropriateness as the criterion for judging language, the major problems in teaching usage are those of limiting the field of coverage and applying tested instructional procedures. This section is particularly concerned with ways of identifying specific usages to be taught and basic principles to observe in teaching them.

SELECTING ITEMS FOR EMPHASIS

How do we identify the items to be taught? How do we establish priorities in order to cover a few items thoroughly and successfully? A survey of informed opinion toward language usage made by O'Rourke some years ago suggested that instruction in English usage may be divided into three phases:

> The essential elements of usage, for example, avoiding confusion between verb and noun modifiers—He does his work *well* (not *good*).
>
> Elements of secondary importance, e.g., distinguishing *who* and *which* in referring to persons and animals.
>
> Least important phases, e.g., using *so* or *as* in negative comparisons: This is not so useful as that.[22]

O'Rourke further demonstrated that in attempting to present an overly comprehensive program, schools were actually slighting essential learnings. As the accompanying table shows, graduating seniors failed to achieve even a 75 per cent mastery of the essentials. Certainly such results point to the need for a selective program concentrating on a few new items in every grade and on a continual attempt to eliminate gross errors.

Degree of mastery of English usage in grades 7 and 12

	Percentage of correct answers	
	GRADE 7	GRADE 12
Essentials such as:	35	74
He invited John and *me.* (not *I*)		
There *are* two apples on the table. (not *is*)		
Secondary elements such as:	23	56
John *may* do it if his mother agrees. (permission)		
John *can* do it if he tries. (ability)		
Least important phases such as:	12	38
He said that the world *is* round. (not *was*)		
One should be loyal to *one's* country. (not *his*)		

[22] L. J. O'Rourke, *Rebuilding the English Curriculum to Insure Greater Mastery of Essentials* (Washington, D.C., Psychological Institute, 1934).

Teachers need to consider several factors in identifying items for emphasis at any level. Prevailing language habits in the social environment may create particular problems for a school. Social conditions will sometimes create a need for instruction; at other times they will make such emphasis almost fruitless. Teachers will also need to consider research. A few of the important findings and their implications are summarized in the accompanying chart. Pooley, in a book describing research and practice in teaching usage,[23] suggests certain forms to be emphasized and others to receive no instruction at the elementary, junior, and senior high school levels. Pooley's widely used lists offer a basis for establishing priorities in usage instruction and are particularly helpful for teachers who feel the need for definite guidance in selecting items for emphasis.

Using the recommendations of Pooley and other findings reported in research, committees of teachers in many school districts have attempted to construct guides for sequential language instruction. For example, teachers in Oakland, California, worked for six years to develop and revise a usage guide to cover instruction from grades one through twelve. A sample from this guide is reprinted in "Program and Plan," p. 650.

Some implications of research for instruction in usage and language conventions *

Finding	*Implications for instruction*
VERB FORMS	
Verb errors account for between 40 and 60 per cent of all errors in usage.	Since confusion in past tense and past participle causes many errors, plan appropriate oral practice in expressing past time. Direct special attention to selecting forms of *to be* when used as an auxiliary.
A majority of all verb errors may be traced to usages of *see, do, come,* and *go.*	Provide much practice in using appropriate forms of irregular verbs.
PRONOUN FORM	
Errors in pronoun reference and agreement with antecedent are second in frequency to inappropriate verb forms.	Teach specific forms as well as the underlying rationale.
SUBJECT-PREDICATE AGREEMENT	
Errors in subject-predicate agreement are a widespread source of difficulty.	Concentrate on eliminating the following specific problems: 1) Confusion in third person singular present tense: He *don't.*

* Based on research reported in Walter Loban, "Studies of Language Which Assist the Teacher," *English Journal,* Vol. 36, No. 10 (December 1947); Orville Nordberg, "Research and the Teaching of Written Expression," *California Journal of Educational Research,* Vol. 2, No. 7 (March 1951); Pooley, *Teaching English Usage;* Martin J. Stromzand and M. V. O'Shea, *How Much English Grammar?* (Baltimore, Warwick and York, 1924).

[23] Pooley, *Teaching English Usage,* pp. 180-181, 194-198, 218-223.

Finding	*Implications for instruction*
	2) Failure to use plural verb with compound subject: The dog and cat *is* playing. 3) Confusion when subject and predicate are separated by an element with a different number: The events of the year *is* explained.
CONVENTIONS OF LANGUAGE	
Errors in capitalization of proper nouns account for a large percentage of mechanical problems. Frequent capitalization errors at the beginning of sentences result from a lack of sentence sense rather than misunderstanding of the need for initial capitalization.	Stress distinctions between common and proper nouns throughout secondary school. Avoid repetitive instruction and drill on beginning capitalization; concentrate instead on exercises which promote students' understanding of sentence completeness.

Whatever guide for instruction is established in any school, the teacher will concentrate only on necessary forms and then will insist that these be used in the writing and speaking of students.

PLANNING EFFECTIVE PRACTICE

Sound practice results from observing sound principles of learning. Purposeful drill in usage can be planned only in relation to the readiness of the learner, his interest in learning, and the range of individual differences among students in the classroom. Both research and experience help to identify certain characteristics of effective approaches.

Relate practice to the communication setting Instruction in usage cannot be presented independently of the writing and speaking of students. Only as the learner sees his classroom study of usage related to his expression of ideas will instruction be effective. By basing practice on errors in the writing and speaking of students, some teachers attempt to relate instruction to thinking. Included in "Program and Plan" is an example showing how usage skills may be taught within a unit of instruction.[24]

Plan oral practice Many studies reveal oral practice to be an effective method of improving the usage habits of students.[25] Our basic command of English is established through the spoken word; habits perpetuated in conversation and speech are often continued in writing, and forms eliminated in oral usage most certainly will disappear from written expression.

[24] Pp. 671-75.

[25] See Prudence Cutright, "A Comparison of Methods of Securing Correct Language Usage," *Elementary School Journal*, Vol. 39, No. 9 (May 1934); P. M. Symonds, "Practice Versus Grammar in the Learning of Correct Usage," *Journal of Educational Psychology*, Vol. 22, No. 2 (February 1931).

Such oral practice need not be presented through drill alone. Classroom activities in which students have an opportunity to record, listen to, and analyze their own speech and the speech of their classmates have been used to improve usage. In one study, written drills and formal exercises were abandoned and nearly all language lessons were devoted to recording and analyzing the effectiveness of the communication in the stories and reports of the learners. The results indicated that students instructed in this way did as well as others on tests of competence in use of written language and significantly better in oral composition and oral usage.[26] Many kinds of oral practice are presented among the Suggested Learning Experiences later in this chapter.

Utilize many brief, varied drills Practice, important and necessary if we are to change patterns of language usage, is most effective when it is varied, and least effective when it is repetitive. A 10-sentence drill may offer a good exercise; a twenty-five-sentence drill will not necessarily be better. The experience of many teachers, supported by research, points to the value of frequent brief drills and exercises, especially when the need for each drill and its relation to writing and speaking problems are clear to each student.

One tested approach to the teaching of language involves eight steps: [27] 1) Pretesting; 2) Explaining the problem—e.g., an appropriate pronoun form; 3) Using mimeographed drill sheets on correct forms; 4) Repeating orally each sentence five times in concert with a pupil leader; 5) Writing original sentences illustrating the usage; 6) Discussing the sentences; 7) Reviewing the drill sheets; and 8) Final testing. Such a multiple attack is more effective than an equal amount of time spent on a single kind of activity. The teacher plans the work so that no one exercise need take longer than ten or fifteen minutes. Occasionally, varied activities of this type may be introduced within a single class hour, but more frequently teachers will wish to spend only a few minutes in one day on intensive usage drill. Some find the beginning of the period offers a convenient time for such instruction.

Fundamentally, then, effective instruction in usage may be described by four characteristics—emphasis on essential items, relation of their practice to the communication setting, attention to oral practice, and reliance on many brief, varied drills.

A selective program in grammar and usage is one that concentrates on those concepts and usages needed by students at any instructional level. Too often programs are overly comprehensive, attempting to survey all elements rather than to concentrate on a few. This discussion has suggested some

[26] Haverly O. Moyer, "Can Ear Training Improve English Usage?" *Elementary English*, Vol. 33, No. 4 (April 1956).

[27] The effectiveness of these procedures is demonstrated by C. C. Crawford and Madie Royer, "Oral Drill Versus Grammar Study," *Elementary School Journal*, Vol. 35 (October 1935).

guide lines for selecting the important elements of structure and usage to be presented.

In developing a program, a teacher cannot depend solely on the text he finds in the school book room. The language needs of students will vary from community to community, influenced to a considerable degree by cultural and social factors.[28] Usages which create teaching problems in one region are not found in others. Textbooks written from a national perspective cannot offer sufficient guidance to meet local problems. In addition teachers must be wary lest they introduce so much to students in any grade, especially during the early junior high school years, that they defeat their own purpose.[29] For these reasons teachers must be discriminating in their choice of what to teach, selecting at any level a few important items for emphasis. Any attempts to present all elements of language structure and language usage will lead only to failure.

THE TEACHING PROBLEM

Organizing Instruction

No theory of learning has yet been advanced to suggest that students will learn to use English well without systematic teaching. Teachers sometimes refer to *incidental* learning of language which may occur during the exchange of ideas in social studies and science classes, but certainly students learn language best when definite time is reserved for study and practice. This is not to say that language periods can be divorced from actual experiences in communication nor that several learnings cannot occur in the classroom at the same time; but there is a need for systematic direction and organization. What is embraced by sound incidental learning is instruction in which learning experiences occur in meaningful context, with planned instruction in grammar and usage introduced as incidental to but in essential support of the student's quest for ideas. Certainly no important learning can be left to chance.

A basic method

Relating systematic instruction in grammar and usage to the communication setting in the classroom is a major problem. Most successful teaching includes the following steps:

[28] A practical discussion of ways of teaching usage to children of impoverished backgrounds can be found in Ruth Golden, *Improving Patterns of Usage* (Detroit, Wayne State U. Press, 1960).

[29] For an analysis of some of the deficiencies in language textbooks, see Pooley, *Teaching English Grammar,* pp. 45-48. Pooley's belief that heavy grammatical loading in grades 7 and 8 is introduced at the expense of extensive reading experiences, despite the knowledge that most students will read more during these years than at any other time of their lives, is quoted in Mildred Dawson, "Summary of Research Concerning English Usage," *Elementary English,* Vol. 28, No. 3 (March 1951).

Establishing areas of emphasis for each grade or instructional level
Example: Teaching uses of introductory phrases and clauses in varying sentence patterns may be assigned to the tenth grade.

Planning learning activities which require students to use the particular skill or usage to be emphasized in instruction
Example: The teacher delays instruction on ways of varying sentences until students are engaged in writing several long papers so that the need for variation is more readily apparent.

Diagnosing the needs of particular students with reference to the items to be emphasized or reviewed
Example: The teacher asks students to review three previous papers to determine the percentage of sentences differing from S–P–O pattern or the number beginning with a phrase or dependent clause.

Providing needed instruction and practice for class, groups, and individuals
Example: The class discusses the importance of variety in sentence construction. Students then review their papers. Those whose writing already shows an awareness of the principle continue with other activities. Students who need help are assigned special practice in rewriting sentences taken from their own papers, exchanging their revisions with fellow students for analysis and correction.

Maintaining the skill or usage in all communication activities
Example: After specfic instruction and practice, the teacher studies applications in student writing. Excellent examples of sentence variation are brought to the attention of the class. Students who do not attempt to vary sentences are reminded of the possibility. Grading is based on the actual use, in writing and speaking, not on results of drills.

The basic method described here is subject to much variation.[30] Even direct grammatical instruction may be presented through modifications of this method. The teacher may select areas of emphasis, use student sentences for analyses, base diagnosis on previous writing, provide instruction only for those with obvious needs, and follow through by later presenting for analysis occasional sentences taken from the students' own papers. The method is appropriate for a series of brief lessons or drills spread over several days, as well as for two or three hours of intensive study. Some teachers prefer to introduce instruction of this type after each writing or speaking activity, with brief lessons and individualized drills developed according to needs identified by analyzing student writing and speaking. Others devote the short intervals between units to the concentrated study of grammar or usage, although infrequent concentration tends to be less effective than brief, frequent practice. A few teachers like to "take time out for repairs" whenever needs so indicate, and they do not hesitate to substitute instruction and practice in language skill for other activities whenever they and their classes agree. Whatever the exact combination of procedures, the teacher will want the instruction to grow from and contribute to the actual communication activities of the class.

[30] Further illustrations of this approach are presented in the plan, "Establishing a Usage Habit within a Unit," pp. 671-75.

The textbook problem

Teachers attempting to modify their present programs to incorporate the understandings and procedures of descriptive grammar must consider ways of utilizing presently available language texts. Although the findings of linguists will undoubtedly influence to a considerable degree the texts of the future, several years may well pass before books based on the new approaches are available in all schools. At present, therefore, teachers need to consider ways of using current texts.

Most grammar books are organized logically and systematically, patterned for the most part after the organization of traditional grammar. Usually a definitional approach is used to introduce readers to each grammatical principle, with the definition followed in turn by examples, applications, and suitable exercises for the reader. It is in the exercises that the teacher of descriptive grammar will find the greatest help. The many sentences included in most texts can be used in ways other than those suggested in the book. Teachers relying on the inductive procedures recommended in this chapter will probably wish to introduce grammatical elements by analyzing sentences students themselves have written or spoken and by helping them to develop understandings of structural patterns and of parts of speech from the ways in which these elements are used. In studying structure and in searching for similar or dissimilar use of particular elements, students may use sentences and exercises from the text, disregarding the definitions and explanations. Material in current texts may thus be used in such ways as the following:

As source material in comparing elements within sentences

Students are asked to find signal words that introduce adverbial clauses in a group of sentences.

As source material in comparing sentence patterns

The teacher introduces the S–LP–PN pattern, then asks students to find additional sentences of this pattern in a list printed in the text.

As the basis for oral usage drill

The teacher divides the class into pairs or small groups to complete drills which require students to select appropriate from inappropriate usages in a sentence context, e.g., He did his work (good) (well). As each student reads a sentence aloud and selects what he believes to be the appropriate form, his companion indicates agreement or disagreement. Disputed usages are referred to the teacher.

As the basis for individual drill

The teacher maintains a series of duplicated one-page explanations of recurring problems, such as those concerned with parallel construction or sentence fragments. Accompanying each corrected composition returned to a student is an explanatory sheet reviewing a grammatical problem with which he has had difficulty. Each sheet refers him to appropriate drills which he must complete in the grammar book. Thus students in any class may be assigned different kinds of exercises at the same time. (Copies of explanatory sheets prepared for one occasion are saved by the teacher for future use.)

As material for reviewing capitalization, punctuation, and the conventions of language usage

Classes or groups needing to review the uses of capitalization in designating the titles of particular persons or the use of commas separating items in a series are assigned appropriate explanations and exercises.

As source material for diagnostic exercises and tests

The teacher uses a list of twenty-five sentences as the basis for assessing the ability of students to identify similar structural elements. For example, students may be asked to underline all words or groups of words used as *running* is used in "I believe that running is good exercise."

These are only a few of the ways in which teachers, trying to develop the understandings and procedures of descriptive grammar, may adapt the material of current texts. The exercises are used to reinforce principles after students are led initially to recognize concrete examples of these principles in their own use of language.

What research says

Effective instruction is more likely to result when the classroom approaches are similar to those tested by research. In teaching both grammar and usage, teachers can use the following tested procedures: Approach instruction positively; emphasize a thought approach; use diagnostic procedures, including self-diagnosis; use the laboratory method whenever possible.

Approach instruction positively Effective instruction focuses upon strength rather than weakness. The teacher directs attention of students to models of good writing, whether the distillation of thought in an offering by a student or the compression in a sentence by Sean O'Faolain. The teacher also encourages students by praise, so they will recognize their own achievement and will strive to even greater accomplishment. Recognizing that most individuals work to sustain real growth but become discouraged when they see little improvement, the teacher tries honestly to build positive attitudes.

Emphasize a thought approach Instruction emphasizing errors in sentence structure as problems in the thinking processes, rather than as subjects for grammatical analysis, produces improvement in writing, according to a study by Frogner.[31] Her research indicates that learning occurs through both the thought method and the grammar method but that the former produces greater improvement in sentence structure and a longer retention of the abilities involved. For students of superior intelligence, the methods were found to be about equal in effect, although the thought method was more economical of time; for students of average intelligence, the thought approach clearly resulted in greater learnings. In this approach, "Running to the rescue, the

[31] Ellen Frogner, "Grammar Approach Versus a Thought Approach," *English Journal*, Vol. 28, No. 7 (September 1939); also reported in *School Review*, Vol. 47, No. 9 (November 1939).

fire burned me" becomes a problem in communication rather than an exercise in recognizing a dangling participial phrase, with the key test being whether the sentence conveys meanings intended by the speaker. Similarly, instruction on coordination and subordination may be introduced without reference to grammatical terminology if the teacher wishes.

The approach emphasizes thinking through each idea. This method can be introduced in a number of ways. A recent study by Kraus reveals that significant gains in student learning were obtained through three variations of the approach—by presenting instruction in sentence structure in logical sequence, with appropriate sentence exercises but no related writing; by presenting instruction in the same predetermined order but assigning a weekly theme as well; by including instruction in a unit on literature and introducing it as needed in relation to errors on student composition.[32] All approaches were effective, but the results achieved by relating instruction to actual errors were achieved in only *one-third of the time.* The first method required thirty hours of instruction; the second, twenty-four; the unit based on lessons required only ten. Kraus describes the sequence for a typical unit-based lesson as follows:

> Reading a particularly effective student paper which deals with content of the unit. Discussion of ideas presented and of the effectiveness of the composition.
>
> Discussion of basic errors found in sentences taken from student papers.
>
> Division of class into groups to work on problems in sentence structure according to needs demonstrated in the compositions.[33]

All three of the over-all approaches tested by Kraus used the thought approach and showed the importance of discussing structure in relation to the ideas being presented. Under each method, too, provision was made for individual differences, with a student excused from group and individual assignments if he had demonstrated mastery of the concept.

Use diagnostic procedures Most theories of learning and almost all research in language indicate that effectiveness is increased when instruction is based on the needs of individuals. The pretest-teach-retest approach is one that has been thoroughly proved, especially when students recognize the instruction needed and the teacher avoids unnecessary drill. Since the task of improving language usage is complex and difficult, even when not considered in relation to the limited time available for instruction, teachers do well to distinguish those items which are essential from those which are desirable but unnecessary. Several ways of doing this are described in the Suggested Learning Experiences at the end of this chapter.

Use the laboratory method A completely individualized program in which many students are writing while others are completing exercises or work-

[32] Silvy Kraus, "A Comparison of Three Methods of Teaching Sentence Structure," *English Journal,* Vol. 46, No. 5 (May 1957).

[33] Kraus, "A Comparison of Three Methods," p. 280.

ing with the teacher seems visionary in today's large classrooms, yet research repeatedly shows the effectiveness of such a program. Particularly in the high school and the junior college has this laboratory approach been shown to result in permanent gain. Normally the method involves working on drills and writing papers according to individual need, with the teacher making himself available for conferences with individuals and groups. Much varied practice in writing is offered; indeed this may account for the demonstrated effectiveness of the approach. Comparisons favor the laboratory method over organizations involving extensive workbook drills, weekly themes, and classroom sessions in which instruction is presented to the total group.[34]

Teachers who are unable to organize their classes in this manner may still utilize the approach. They can avoid the assignment of endless practice for students who demonstrate reasonable mastery of a form. Such individuals may be set to writing or reading while instruction is presented to other pupils. More group teaching may be provided, so that students can obtain help without distracting the attention of the entire class. Finally teachers can provide for individual writing and drill to the greatest extent possible.

If selectivity is the crux in organizing the content of the program in grammar and usage, certainly application is the clue to determining the method of learning. The problem in teaching is to so organize instruction that it will be integrally related to the communication of young people. The approaches discussed here lead the teacher in this direction.

Suggested Learning Experiences

Research and experience have long demonstrated the futility of attempting to improve the written and oral usage of students through reliance only on fragmentary and isolated lessons on English grammar. The learning experiences which are suggested in the following pages will prove effective only as they are introduced in relation to the writing and speaking of students. Because these experiences stress inductive approaches, they can perhaps be most skillfully incorporated in class work during moments devoted to formulating concepts concerning the ways of language used by students in spoken and written communication.

To learn essential elements of the sentence

■ *Recognize signal words within the sentence*

1. Teach students to perceive articles as signals to help in locating words used as nouns. "The sign checks perfectly" differs in meaning from "Sign checks perfectly." Point up the importance of becoming aware of these distinctions by asking students to shift the article to various positions in the following sentences and note the changes in meaning.

Plan approaches slowly
Union demands increase

[34] John J. DeBoer, "Oral and Written Language," *Review of Educational Research,* Vol. 25, No. 2 (April 1955).

Witness moves carefully
Spear flounders in flight

Then ask students to rewrite sentences using possessive pronouns as signal words, *e.g., my, our, their, his,* etc.

2. Study elements which exist primarily to tie together different parts of the sentence or to point up the function of other words, *e.g.,* not only articles like *the, a,* and *an,* but intensifiers like *too* and *very* as well as prepositions and participles like *on* and *coming* which signal phrases and auxiliaries.

■ *Study the clues in word order*

1. Use the flannel board to permit quick changes in word order. Mount on individual strips of tagboard, backed with small pieces of flocking paper, such words as the following:

RUNS PLANS THE HE

Ask individuals or groups of students to rearrange these words in different patterns on the flannel board, e.g.,

HE RUNS THE PLANS
HE PLANS THE RUNS

Follow the activity by asking students to draw conclusions about the importance of a word's position in the English sentence. Help students to see that their inevitable conclusion—changed meaning or no meaning results from shifts in word order—applies to all words and groups of words in the sentence.

2. In analyzing sentences, encourage students to rely on natural clues within the sentence, such as a group of words—nouns and their modifiers, phrases, clauses—as well as specific signal words. The importance of such clues within each sentence may be emphasized by asking students to identify the predicates and subjects in such nonsense statements as the following:

The saleb tringes tributhed on the flust.
Thus arthusta was emfressed by the bibblement.

Few will have difficulty in selecting "tributhed" and "was emfressed" as predicates, "tringes" and "arthusta" as the subjects. Why? Can they tell? Encourage them to substitute familiar words for each of the nonsense words.

3. Ask students to unscramble disarranged sentences like

peacock jumped she when the screamed

Then let them unscramble parts of sentences like

funny a very fellow
complain may irrespective of you how

Later students may be asked to add the missing elements in scrambled sentences like the following:

out the green groundhog has of grass onto the

Or they may eliminate the extra word in a scrambled sentence:

swooped Quantrill's the overhead down raiders on town.

■ *Identify similarities and differences in structure*

1. Write pairs of sentences on the chalk board. Underline 1 element in the first sentence. Underline and number several elements in the second, e.g.,

A. Precious Pansybelle hit the timid boy with a stick.
B. Ed Snopes carved the carcass with an old hatchet from his woodshed.
(1: Ed Snopes; 2: carcass; 3: hatchet; 4: woodshed)

Ask students to determine which word in the second sentence corresponds in structure to the underlined word in the first sentence.[35]

2. Follow this exercise by asking students to write sentences of their own which contain words parallel in structure.

■ *Use sentence patterns to test understanding*

Ask students to maintain lists of words that may be substituted in each of the following kinds of position.

Verb	*Noun*
They ______ if they can.	The ______ was interesting.
Please ______.	I saw the ______.
Please ______ it.	He has no ______.
They ______.	Was he happy with the ______?
They will ______ next week.	Her ______ is here.
She ______s occasionally.	______s are scarce.

Similar patterns may be introduced as other elements are taught. Examples of substitution tests may be found in many modern grammars.[36]

To understand and use methods of expanding the basic sentence

■ *Use the inductive approach recommended by Pooley* [37]

Have students construct sentences lacking the element to be taught.

Example: The boys ran. The friends met.

To these sentences add the new element in such a way as to make very clear what has been added.

Example: The happy boys ran. The old friends met.

Lead students to recognize what has happened to the meaning or structure of the sentence as a result of the addition.

Have students construct many sentences making use of the new element in its normal applications. This is the point to watch for confusions and to assist the student in correcting them.

When the use of the element is familiar, when it can be recognized unmistakably in written sentences, and when the student can create sentences using the element

[35] John B. Carroll discusses how he uses this method in testing in "Psycholinguistics and the Teaching of English Composition," in Harold B. Allen, ed., *Readings in Applied English Linguistics* (N.Y., Appleton-Century-Crofts, 1958), pp. 319-326.

[36] See Roberts, *Patterns of English,* pp. 13-14; Sledd, *A Short Introduction to English Grammar,* pp. 81-91; Francis, *The Structure of American English,* pp. 235-236.

[37] Robert Pooley, *Teaching English Grammar,* p. 140. Used by special permission. Examples are added for illustrative purposes.

accurately, teach its name, and give sufficient practice in the use of the element thereafter to attach the name to the function it performs.

To test the student's grasp of the concept, call upon him to write sentences employing the named element in the various sentence patterns to which it applies.

■ *Substitute modifiers in basic sentences*

1. Present basic sentences and ask student to supply modifiers:

The boy ________ looked sick.

Supply modifier to indicate what the boy was doing. (who was sleeping, sitting on the fence, finishing his lunch)

This approach offers a useful way of developing the understanding that words, phrases, and clauses can function in the same way in a sentence:

________, Tom was startled.

Supply a modifier to show when this happened to Tom. (after reading, having closed the book, running to the door, awakened)

Or of understanding increasingly complicated sentences, e.g.,

The boy who ________ and who ________ is likely to receive an "A" grade.

Supply modifiers which tell what the boy has done.

2. Present basic sentences in which noun modifiers and verb modifiers are used and ask the student to select the appropriate forms of several from an accompanying list, e.g.,

The girl is ________.	sad	beauty
The girl sings ________.	sadness	beautiful
	sadly	beautify
	saddens	beautifully

3. Lead students to see structure signals within words which indicate how the words may be used within the sentence. List words which take different forms depending on their use, e.g., joy, beauty, sadness. Ask students to note changes which must be made in supplying words in the following sentences:

The girl's (joy) (beauty) (sadness) surprised me.
The girl (saddens) her friends; the girl (enjoyed) (beautified) it.
The girl accomplished it (joyfully) (beautifully) (sadly).
The (joyful) (beautiful) (sad) girl appeared.

To achieve variety in sentence patterns

■ *Study the concepts of subordination and coordination*

1. Pose two statements that may be related: "John saved my life" and "He shot the unicorn." Show that in this case the linking word "and," frequently used as a connector, acts as a weak tie. Ask students to suggest a better connector—one that more clearly shows the relationship between the two statements. Present some words that may be used to point clearly to possible relationships between two statements: *since, if, although, when, whenever, while, before, after, unless, as if, as though,*

provided, except that. Ask students to try various connectors between the two statements: "John saved my life" and "He shot the unicorn." Discuss the effect the choice has upon the meaning.

2. Now present the students with the following list of statements. Ask them to point out the connector and tell what kind of relationship it points to.

1. When the game starts, the crowd roars.	Time
2. Groundhogs grow where the sun is bright.	Place
3. She combs her hair as if she were a model.	Manner
4. Most football players are tall, although not so tall as most basketball players.	Degree
5. The bull charged so that it hit the cape.	Result
6. Girls study harder than boys, so that they can get better grades.	Purpose
7. Because I jumped from the thirteenth floor, I was almost certain to break a leg.	Cause
8. The rocket will hit the moon if it has sufficient thrust.	Condition
9. Although the singer is tired, he will try to entertain.	Concession

3. Ask students to divide each sentence into two statements and to arrange the statements in two lists. One group is to be listed under the heading *Statements That Can Stand Alone.* The other group is to be listed under the heading *Statements That Depend on Another Statement for Meaning.*

Statements that can stand alone	*Statements that depend on another statement for meaning*
1. The crowd roars.	1. When the game starts
2. Groundhogs grow.	2. Where the sun is bright
3. She combs her hair.	3. As if she were a model

■ *Study uses of basic patterns*

1. After students identify a basic pattern, give them an opportunity to substitute different words and phrases for the essential elements; then ask each to write five or six examples of the pattern. Explain that the exercise will require each writer to achieve considerable variety within the pattern framework:

Subject–Linking Predicate–Predicate Nominative
When speaking before the class, John becomes a real orator.
He is a speaker who is a spellbinder.
To students he is both leader and friend.
To teachers he seems to be more a future politician than a teenager.
John is a remarkable boy.

2. Study the patterns the students actually use in speech and writing. Ask each student to classify the sentences in one of his compositions according to the basic patterns studied; then summarize the findings for the entire class. Individuals may also compare the results of their personal surveys with patterns used by the entire class or outside groups. One recent survey of American writing selected from fifty publi-

cations reports the following percentages as indicating the use of basic patterns eithei as the sole sentence pattern or as the pattern of an independent clause: [38]

Pattern I	(Subject–Predicate)	30.4%
Pattern II	(S–P–O)	38.8
Pattern III	(S–LP–PN)	13.2
Pattern IV	(S–LP–PA)	13.8
		96.2%

3. Transcribe from a tape recording some selected sentences used by class members in discussion. Ask students to identify the basic patterns used in each sentence.

■ *Study variations in the writing of others*

1. Compare two translations of a single passage as evidence of the varying effects which may be achieved in expressing identical ideas in English. While studying *Cyrano de Bergerac,* for example, consider such an example as the following:

Cyrano de Bergerac by Edmund Rostand

Why you might have said—
Oh, a great many things! Mon dieu, why waste
Your opportunity? For example, thus:—
Aggressive: I, sir, if that nose were mine,
I'd have it amputated—on the spot!
Friendly: How do you drink with such a nose?
You ought to have a cup made especially.
Descriptive: It is a rock—a crag—a cape
A cape? —Say rather, a peninsula!
—(Translation by Brian Hooker)

One might make, oh, my Lord, many
Remarks, on the whole, by varying the tone,
For example. Listen:
Aggressive: Sir, if I had such a nose, I should
have it amputated at once!
Friendly: It must dip into your cup;
In order to drink you must have a goblet
made for you!
Descriptive: It is a rock. It is a peak!
It is a cape! What did I say? A cape?
It is a peninsula!
—(Translation by Helen B. Dole)

2. Ask each student to select a passage of prose he particularly admires. For practice, ask him to imitate the sentence patterns by writing an original paragraph.

3. Have students organize special sections of their notebooks in which they copy interesting sentences from their reading or paste sentences clipped from magazines and newspapers. Ask students to classify their findings according to the basic sentence patterns.

[38] Hook and Mathews, *Modern American Grammar and Usage,* pp. 76-94.

4. After studying introductory adverbial clauses, students may be asked to write without punctuation three sentences using such clauses. Then have class members exchange papers and correct and/or punctuate each other's sentences. Exercises of this type require a twofold analysis of original sentences, since students not only create examples but must analyze them.

■ *Practice compressing ideas*

1. Help students express ideas in different ways, such as by writing a single sentence to capture the basic thought of the following description:

> The title of a film, "Snow White," was listed on the theater marquee. A small candy counter was situated at a newsstand next to the theater. A woman in a brown suit was dragging a small child and stopped to make a purchase at the candy counter. She then dragged the child to the ticket office, purchased a ticket, and entered the theater.

Analyze the variations found in sentences written by students to demonstrate ways of subordinating ideas.

2. Stress at every opportunity the value of compression and economy. La Rochefoucauld stated, "True eloquence consists in saying all that is necessary and nothing but what is necessary." Place the quotation on the chalk board. Drive the point home whenever possible. Encourage students to reduce long statements by asking class members to summarize discussions, to restate the plot of a story in a single sentence, or to compress a printed paragraph into a few original words and expressions.

3. Flash student papers on a screen with the opaque projector. Direct attention not only to sentences to be rewritten but to examples of effective expression.

■ *Practice achieving variety in expression*

1. Provide exercises in which students combine two or more ideas. For example, ask students to list six events which happened to them over a weekend. Then involve them in writing original statements to illustrate the following:

Relating two ideas by using a word like *and* or *but.*
Relating two ideas by using a word like *however* or *then.*
Relating two ideas by using a word like *since* or *although.*

2. Ask students to achieve variety in expression by including examples of the following in their paragraphs:

Quotations
Questions
Inverted sentence order
Introductory sentence starting with adverb, prepositional phrase, or participial phrase
Appositives

3. When introducing the analysis of sentences by average students, encourage individuals to use their own sentences as examples. Ask them to select a particular kind; for instance, a sentence in which inverted word order is used. In some cases teachers mark appropriate sentences in the compositions of each pupil and follow the return of papers with a lesson in grammatical analysis.

To provide effective practice in usage

■ *Relate instruction to the writing and speaking of students*

1. Plan for some compositions to be written in class so that instruction may be presented to students at the time when they will both recognize the need and have opportunity for practice. Write on the chalk board any sentences on which an individual requires help. During the final ten minutes of the period, correct these sentences with the entire class.

2. Introduce pre-correction periods as a regular activity before papers are passed to the teacher.[39] Before collecting the first composition assigned after a lesson on sentence structure, ask students to scan their papers especially for glaring errors of a particular type. Some teachers ask students to attach to their papers a statement that they have engaged in pre-correction.[40] Others give students check sheets such as the following which may be attached to compositions before papers are passed to the teacher.

Sample check sheet (Grades 7-8)

I have checked my paper for the following items:

________ appropriate form, penmanship, margins, neatness
________ spelling
________ end punctuation
________ fragments
________ run-together sentences

*Signed*________________________________

3. Encourage alertness to inappropriate oral usage. Some teachers regularly ask students to identify the two or three errors which they find most common in their own speech. Special practice may be introduced to eliminate those problems which seem to be widespread.

■ *Provide oral practice*

1. Plan oral drills on appropriate forms, e.g., follow instruction aimed at establishing "This isn't a pumpkin" as more appropriate than "This ain't," with five unison readings of the desired usage.

2. In the junior high plan simple oral games or exercises. For example, to concentrate on eliminating "ain't" or the double negative, schedule five minutes of drill in which different individuals attempt to "guess" an object selected by a class and various students respond with the appropriate usage form:

Question: Is it a yo-yo?
Answer: No, it isn't a yo-yo.
Question: Is it a bloodhound?
Answer: No, it isn't a bloodhound.
Question: Is it a spaceship?
Answer: No, it isn't a spaceship.

[39] See the discussion of pre-correction in Chapter 10, "Written Expression," pp. 501-04.

[40] Teachers in high school and junior college will be interested in a device used to guide the editing of more mature writers. Albert T. Anderson and Thurston Womack, *Processes in Writing* (San Francisco, Wadsworth, 1958), pp. 142 ff.

Most teachers find that games of this type result in learning by younger pupils when the purpose is clear, when students understand the appropriate form being emphasized, and when the drill is continued for only a few minutes.[41]

3. Follow drill involving the choice of correct and incorrect forms by oral repetition of the correct responses. Through this method ask the students first to distinguish the correct forms in such sentences as:

(Him and me) (He and I) went to the show.

Then ask them to write each correct sentence five times and to recite the correct form orally in a unison reading. Here again effectiveness is increased when the forms being stressed are clearly those which pupils recognize as causing them difficulty. For example, an appropriate time for such a drill is after a lesson in which pupils have had an opportunity to check their compositions and have agreed on the usage items on which they need help.

4. Use an oral drill requiring students to indicate whether sentences read aloud by the teacher conform to appropriate usage. Usually ten sentences are presented; all concerning the same problem of usage. Five of the sentences are correct; the other five are incorrect versions of them. After preliminary explanation of the error and the appropriate form, ask students to fold their papers in half vertically and number from one to five on the first lines of the left side, from six to ten on the identical lines of the right. With each student placing only the left side of his paper before him, read five sentences aloud, being careful not to betray by voice or expression which ones are right and which are wrong. If the sentence sounds correct to the student, he is to place a plus after the appropriate number on his paper; if it sounds incorrect, he is to place a zero. After the first five sentences have been read, ask the student to turn over his paper so that only the right side shows. This time, the teacher reads the corresponding five sentences, presenting whichever form was not used earlier. The following ten sentences might be read aloud to illustrate the problems of compound subjects and objects.

Left side

1. Evelyn felt very upset about David and me.
2. Mick wouldn't speak to Barbara and me.
3. Tessie and me forgot about going.
4. My aunt and I are going to the park.
5. The swimmer said he'd give my sister and I a lesson.

Right side

6. Evelyn felt very upset about David and I.
7. Mick wouldn't speak to Barbara and I.
8. Tessie and I forgot about going.
9. My aunt and me are going to the park.
10. The swimmer said he'd give my sister and me a lesson.

Already on the board are the numbers from 1 to 10, and when the sentences have been pronounced, the teacher writes the key.

1. +	6. 0
2. +	7. 0
3. 0	8. +
4. +	9. 0
5. 0	10. +

[41] Many suggestions for oral exercises of this type are to be found in Marjorie Burrows, *Good English Through Practice* (N.Y., Holt, 1956).

Since the first five sentences parallel the second five—one of each pair presenting the correct form and the other the incorrect—students are able to see at a glance the usages which they understand. When they understand, parallel items are correctly marked; when they do not understand, parallel items are incorrectly marked; when they are confused or uncertain, only one of a pair is correctly marked. After correcting the papers and discussing the forms, conclude the drill by asking the group to recite in unison the five correct sentences. For this purpose, the sentences may be repeated after the teacher or copied on the board.

5. Encourage students to read their compositions orally for the purpose of noting awkward constructions. Occasionally divide the class into pairs or into groups for such purpose. Students with severe writing problems sometimes will recognize poor sentences more quickly by listening to their papers read by another person—preferably the teacher.

6. Teacher readings of sentences containing problems in faulty reference are often enjoyed by students. Such examples as the following may often be found in student compositions:

> After picking up the baby, Margaret placed a bottle in her mouth and walked to the crib.
>
> One neighbor, meeting another, complained that his beagle puppies were playing on his lawn among his shrubs, and that they were nearly ruined, and he had better look after them.

7. Encourage pupils to conduct oral drills by the coach and pupil method. Divide the class into pairs. One of each pair repeats sentences aloud, while the other keeps a record indicating which are correct and which incorrect. When the first student finishes the drill, the roles are exchanged. Especially useful are two books based on this method, *An Oral Language Practice Book* and *Spoken Drills in English.*[42]

■ *Utilize brief, varied usage drills*

Use the following check list as a guide in planning instruction.

A check list for varying drill in English usage

Nature of drill	*Examples*
Writing original sentences	As an exercise in punctuating conversation, students write jokes using dialogue.
Varying sentences	The teacher writes five sentences in the simple past. (I went.) Each student expresses past time in at least two other ways. (I was going, I have gone, etc.)
Adding examples	After studying the formation of the past tense with irregular verbs, each student writes five additional examples, such as: I *ring* today, and I *rang* yesterday; I *rise* today, and I *rose* yesterday.
Correcting sentences written by students	Students pass original sentences to a neighbor who rewrites, punctuates, or checks as directed.

[42] Mabel Vincent Cage, *An Oral Language Practice Book* (San Francisco, Harr Wagner, 1935), and *Spoken Drills in English* (San Francisco, Harr Wagner, 1939).

Choosing correct form	Students are asked to select the appropriate form in such sentences as: I gave it to (he) (him).
Completing a statement	Students are asked to complete a sentence: Yesterday Tillie (use form of "to sing") to me.
Replacing a word	Students substitute ten other words for "better" in the following sentence: She is better than I am.
Correcting of errors	Students rewrite sentence or paragraph marked as incorrect.
Written repetition	Students are asked to write five sentences using correct forms, such as five statements including adverbial modifiers.
Dictation	Students copy sentences or paragraphs dictated by the teacher. (Particularly useful spelling and punctuation drill.)
Proofreading	Students correct and change a paragraph which is presented without punctuation and capitalization.
Changing forms	Students are asked to reword such statements as the following to use plural subjects: The mouse runs in the house; The girl doesn't want to go; I witness the phenomenon.
Oral drill	See suggestions advanced on p. 574 of this chapter.

To approach language instruction positively

■ *Praise effective expression by students*

1. In evaluating panel discussion, respond to the ways in which ideas are presented, particularly if a statement deserves special comment. Similarly, in classroom discussion, react to concepts presented succinctly and well by commenting, for example, "Will you say that again, Roland? Notice how forcefully his idea is stated." Without being insincere or overly obvious, find opportunities for commenting on the oral expression of students.

2. Encourage students to develop sections in their notebooks called "Ideas Worth Remembering Expressed by Class Members." Whenever a particularly interesting idea is presented by a student, ask the others to add the sentence to their lists.

3. Share with the total class single sentences, words, or phrases from the written work of students. One teacher culled an entire set of compositions to list a dozen well-turned phrases. Similar lists may be made of apt descriptive terms, original images, compressed ideas, or unusual sentence patterns. From an analysis of compositions, develop a bulletin board display.

4. In correcting papers, respond to the ideas presented—whether by challenging, extending, or agreeing—and react to the way in which these ideas are expressed. The more specific the comments, the more helpful. "I like your use of colorful verbs" conveys more than the enigmatic "good," as do reactions to the effectiveness of the parallelism, the nature of the sentence structure, or the clarity of the idea.[43]

■ *Emphasize important ideas with entertaining arguments*

Whenever possible, utilize opportunities for stressing appropriate language. Use graphic examples to be found in literature or current affairs. Shaw's *Pygmalion*, for

[43] For additional suggestions on correcting student papers, see Chapter 10, "Written Expression," pp. 501-04.

example, suggests some valid arguments for increasing our command of English, as do the lyrics of the song, "Why Can't the English Learn to Speak?" from *My Fair Lady*. Introduce Victor Borge's humorous recording on punctuation to underscore the importance of separating ideas.

To use diagnostic procedures, including self-diagnosis

■ *Construct diagnostic tests*

When responsible for a list of grammatical concepts to be presented or reviewed, attempt to ascertain the students' prior understandings by constructing a special diagnostic test. If students demonstrate ability to recognize complete sentences, detect run-togethers, or classify individual words in the way desired, proceed to an analysis of language on a more advanced level. If the diagnostic test identifies fifteen students needing definite instruction in any one area, plan group assignments. Usually pretesting reveals a few individuals so deficient they will require special help. Some may be found to be extremely proficient; assign these advanced studies. Diagnosis of this type offers a way of identifying those able and gifted pupils who become bored and resentful when faced with repetitious drills on skills they have long since mastered.

The following sample test suggests a number of ways in which diagnostic tests may be constructed. Some teachers prefer to develop separate tests on each item rather than to undertake the over-all survey suggested here.

Suggested form for a diagnostic test to be administered early in the year

I. *Sentence Study*

A. In the left-hand margin write the number of sentences in each group of words. Write "O" if the group does not constitute a single sentence.

Example:

__2__ "Thank you," said Richard as the car started she reached out her hand to him. (Two is placed on the line because the group of words should be written as two sentences.)

________1. Before the work of the new day had begun.

________2. Come or you may not see the hot rods how disappointed you will be.

. . .

B. Below is a series of word groups, some written correctly as sentences and some not. Change the punctuation and capitalization of the word groups where you think it necessary in order to show clearly where sentences begin and end.

Example: Lucybelle was very silly she giggled all the time. About nothing. Don't you dislike such foolishness?

Correct: Lucybelle was very silly. She giggled all the time about nothing. Don't you dislike such foolishness?

1. Since there was no one to meet us and it was late. We went to the motel.
2. I made up my mind to study. When I failed in the last examination. I hope to finish with my class.

. . .

II. *Subject and Predicate*

A. Underline the simple subject with one line and the predicate with two lines.

1. The Martians rushed into the street.
2. In the park grew beautiful marshmallow trees.
3. Has your brother purchased a new sports car?

. . .

B. Underline the correct form and copy it on the line in the left-hand margin.

________1. I heard you (was, were) at the bowling alley.

________2. He (don't, doesn't) plan to study engineering at college.

. . .

III. *Pronouns*

Underline the correct form and copy it on the line in the left-hand margin.

________ 1. The aviator sent my brother and (he, him) on an errand.

________ 2. (Us, We) girls will go to college in three years.

________ 3. The girls met mother and (they, them) at the station.

________ 4. The teacher assigned (us, we) boys detention.

. . .

IV. *Verbs*

Fill in the blank space with the correct form of the verb in parentheses. Indicate some form of past time in every sentence.

(know) 1. The student ________ the answer to every question.

(sing) 2. The robins ________ early this morning.

(wear) 3. The rear tires had ________ well.

. . .

Note: Reread your answers to this question to see that every verb is in some form of past time, not in the present.

V. *Modifiers*

Underline the correct form and copy it in the left-hand margin.

________ 1. He went down the freeway (quicker, more quickly) than his pal in the foreign sports car.

________ 2. The patient is not so (well, good) as he was yesterday. (Applies to health)

________ 3. We were (real, very) glad to hear the final score.

. . .

VI. *Main and Subordinate Clauses*

Underline the main clauses *once* and the subordinate clauses *twice.*

1. When my father was a boy jet planes hadn't been developed.
2. James put his knife into his pocket after he had made his whistle.

. . .

VII. *Capitalization and Punctuation*

A. Underline the letters which should be capitalized in the following sentences:

1. george thompson lives in horse heaven, washington.
2. after he finished amarillo high school he went to college.
3. howard enjoyed reading the call of the wild.

. . .

B. Punctuate the following sentences.

1. Have you ever fished from a helicopter
2. Dr and Mrs Popper are in Rosebud Ark this week

3. Dr Pillgiver said he would meet you at the operating room
4. My dear Ricky

____

____

____

Very sincerely yours

. . .

VIII. *Correct Usage*

(This section is to be administered orally by the teacher. The pupil follows the printed sentences with his eyes as the teacher reads each one aloud.)

Put a *C* in front of all sentences which sound correct to you. If the sentence is incorrect, underline the wrong expression and indicate the correction on the line in front of the sentence. *Examples:*

His	That book is his'n.
C	That book is his.
omit *of*	He jumped off of the plane in his parachute.

________ 1. We could of done better if we had tried.
________ 2. We gave the child a orange.
________ 3. If he's wrong, it don't matter what he says.
________ 4. The leprechauns sang the song and then left.

. . .

■ *Collect information on usage habits*

Record information on specific usage errors observed in the speech and writing of students. Use a single card for each student and enter information as on the following sample:

Suggested teacher record of error analysis

Name *David Whitford*	Oral Usage
Fragment 𝍸 //	*"could of" 2/30, 4/5 5/15*
Run-Together Sentence ////	*"can't never" 4/5*
Dangling Modifier /	
Misplaced Modifier ///	
Reference /	
Parallelism	
Agreement 𝍸	
Spelling 𝍸 //	
Punctuation 𝍸 𝍸 ///	

■ *Ask students to record errors*

Some teachers find the recording of pupil errors to be difficult and time consuming. Heavily burdened, they are unable to maintain the recording in any but the most haphazard fashion. Often teachers encourage pupils to maintain the records, possibly by developing a cumulative file of all written work with a covering tally sheet on which the record is maintained, as in the Individual Error Record illustrated. Approaches of this kind encourage self-evaluation which can result in a heightened readiness for drill and instruction. Much of the value of this type of error analysis emanates from such motivation. Teachers find that students who identify their own problems—even through such a simple activity as examining papers—tend better to understand the intended goals of instruction and less to question the purpose.

■ *Analyze needs with students*

1. Periodically ask students to review recent compositions kept in a permanent classroom file, and report the kinds of writing problems which occur most frequently in their papers.

2. With seventh- or eighth-graders construct a Usage Traffic Signal chart based on results of a diagnostic test. (See p. 578.) Introduce the procedure early in the year when planning the semester's work. If separate sections of the test deal with basic problems—such as case forms of pronouns, agreement of pronoun and antecedent, agreement of verb with subject, forms of irregular verbs, and the choice of verb forms—then such a chart as is illustrated here may be constructed. Allow students to choose pseudonyms to avoid broadcasting information on their proficiencies to the entire student body. During a study period, ask students individually to color their own sections; place the chart at a rear table to preserve the mystery of the pseudonyms. Although the standards vary for each situation, a student with no more than one error in a single area may color the appropriate square green (for "Go"), one with three or four errors may use yellow ("Proceed with Caution"), whereas more than four errors may result in the use of red ("Stop!"). Once all scores are recorded, the teacher and students may examine the chart to find:

Areas where the total class needs instruction. These appear as almost solid red vertical lines, as for Case Forms and Irregular Verbs on the sample.

Areas where segments of the class need instruction. These are divided between green and the other two colors.

Individual

Paper	Errors			
	Spelling	Punctuation	Reference	Agreement
9/18 Essay	//	///		/
9/26 Story	///	/		
9/29 Paragraph	//	//		
10/4 "My Favorite Sport"	///			/

Individuals who need special instruction. These are represented by nearly solid red horizontal lines, as in numbers 1 and 5 on the sample.

Individuals who might be assigned advanced work. Student 6 on the sample should be excused from lessons planned for the remainder of the class.

Often a parallel form of the test is presented at the end of the school year so students may see their improvement.

■ *Analyze recorded conversation*

Divide the class into small groups and assign a topic for each group to discuss. Use questions that will appeal to students so that their language will flow easily. Limit each conversation to ten minutes and record it in the rear of the room while other students are reading. Enter the conversation only to question diffident participants. Use the recorded conversations for the following kinds of analysis:

For diagnosis of special needs. Try to identify students with problems in fluency as well as in grammatical usage. Then observe the language of these students during later in-class and out-of-class situations.

As the basis for conferences with parents. Play the recordings during parent conferences and encourage parental cooperation in improving the student's usage at home.

As a basis for assessing growth in oral language. Record one conversation in September, another at the end of the year. Use a comparison of the two as one way of estimating growth.

To provide for individual practice

Develop over a period of time a file of mimeographed drill sheets dealing with various usage items. Periodically, devote time to completing such drills with each exercise assigned according to individual need.

When each student has an individual copy of a handbook, assign needed drills in correcting papers. Those students who reveal only limited understanding of the sentence may be referred to an appropriate corrective exercise; others may study

error record

Errors				
Parallelism	Misplaced Modifier	Dangling Modifier	Run-Together Sentence	Fragment
	/			////
		/		~~////~~
				//
/				/

Usage Traffic Signals					
Student	Pn Case	Pn Ag.	Verb-Sub Ag.	Verb. Irreg.	Verb Tense
1	Red	Red	Red	Red	Red
2	Red	Red	Yellow	Red	Yellow
3	Red	Yellow	Yellow	Red	Red
4	Red	Red	Green	Red	Red
5	Red	Red	Red	Red	Red
6	Green	Green	Green	Green	Green
7	Red	Red	Yellow	Green	Yellow
8	Red	Yellow	Red	Red	Green
9	Red	Yellow	Green	Red	Red
Green	Go	0-1 error			
Yellow	Caution	2-3 errors			
Red	Stop	4 or more errors			

lessons on punctuation or variety in sentence structure. Ask individuals to file the completed drills with their corrected papers.

Some teachers identify two or three individuals with unusual problems in writing and ask each to write a paragraph a day for several weeks.

To increase individual awareness of the problems involved in communicating ideas, record on tape a reading of a paper exactly as written by a student. Ask the writer to listen carefully to the recorded material before the paper is returned for correction. A similar, less dramatic procedure involves having a paper typed exactly as it is written and returning it to the student for correction. Often problems which the writer initially failed to see become clear through such methods.

Evaluating Growth

Ultimately the test of a sound program in grammar and usage is found in the writing and speech of students. Other forms of evaluation are secondary to such evidence of achievement. Certainly there is a place for objective measurement in grammar and usage programs, but that place must be seen within a total perspective.

Nor is knowledge of technical grammar tested to any appreciable degree on college entrance examinations throughout the country, though such examinations are frequently cited to justify the teaching and testing of grammatical principles. Colleges and universities are interested in students' command and use of English. A recent study of 142 placement tests reveals that only about 2 per cent of the items on college tests deal with problems in technical grammar, such as the identification of parts of speech, clauses, and phrases.[44] Eighty-six per cent of the tests include no items on technical grammar. Almost eighty per cent of the items measure actual use of grammatical forms along with spelling and punctuation, a gain of fifteen per cent from a similar survey twenty years earlier. Where it is economically possible, institutions recognize the need for evaluating the writing of applicants and use an essay examination either as all or part of the test. Clearly the colleges believe that the emphasis in evaluation should be placed on ability to use English.

An understanding of the structure of English may well be an important secondary goal in programs of general education. If so, it is the responsibility of the English teacher both to teach and test for the desired understandings. In doing this, however, teachers must recognize that tests which assess only the student's knowledge of certain English structures, rather than their ability to write and speak, are not in themselves valid and sufficient measures of the effectiveness of a total program. Both use and knowledge must be tested in any complete assessment.

The ways of evaluation are many. Some of the more widely used are described in the section following.

Assess application of instruction to writing and speaking

Rely on conferences Personal conferences are helpful, particularly when based on a sequence of several papers. The teacher and student together can identify apparent strengths, determine weaknesses, and plan a program of study. Try planning such conferences at least at the end of every marking period. Many teachers schedule conferences during study interludes when the remainder of the class is occupied.

[44] David M. Litsey, "Trends in College Placement Tests in Freshman English," *English Journal,* Vol. 40, No. 5 (May 1956). See also Dora V. Smith and Constance McCullough, "An Analysis of the Content of Placement Tests in English Which are Used by One Hundred and Thirty Colleges and Universities," *English Journal,* Vol. 25, No. 1 (January 1936).

Maintain writing folders Permanent files of written work completed over a period of several months is perhaps the best possible source material for evaluation. Include tests in these as well as hurriedly written papers and those composed with care at home. Suggestions for organizing such folders are presented in Chapter 10, "Written Expression" (p. 498).

Sponsor school-wide essay examination Provide for assessing abilities throughout a school on a once-a-year basis by introducing an essay examination for all classes. Standards for evaluation are best established and applied by a committee of English teachers. Ask members of the English department to exchange papers for grading, with each essay read by at least two teachers.

Assess recorded samples of student speech Recorded samples of the conversation of individual students may be analyzed independently by the teacher or in a conference with students. Save recorded specimens of conversation taken early in the year to compare with later samples of speech. The recording of student speech has been used as one way of illustrating for parents the importance of sound language habits.[45]

Provide for objective measurement of particular skills

Evaluate continuously with diagnostic procedures Recognize that diagnosis and evaluation are two sides of the same coin. The procedures for diagnosing language needs suggested early in this chapter, when repeated after a period of time, provide an excellent basis for evaluation.

Construct tests to measure applications of grammatical learnings Test the kinds of understandings and practices which have been stressed. Some possible kinds of questions[46] are the following:

Write three sentences which use each of the following sentence patterns:
Subject–Predicate
Subject–Predicate–Object
Subject–Predicate–Noun Modifier–Object

Use a phrase or a clause to do the job of the single-word modifier in each of the following sentences:
The *bright* boy sat before us.
She walked *carefully* across the field.

From the following sets of statements, select the sentence which does not fit the same sentence pattern as do the other three. Rewrite the sentence to fit the pattern.
Percy and Cedric fought each other.
After going to bed, she read her book.

[45] Elizabeth J. Drake and Jessie V. Enevoldsen, "Solving the Problem of Correct Usage," *Elementary English*, Vol. 35, No. 2 (February 1958).

[46] Many other ideas for specific test questions are presented by Pooley in *Teaching English Grammar*, pp. 184-202.

Lady Fizzle wrote a sarcastic letter.
Kevin talked without asking permission.

Make judicious use of printed tests Standardized tests provide national norms with which achievements of particular groups may be compared. When the limitations of the tests are recognized, most teachers find their occasional use helpful. However, printed objective tests cannot and do not measure the students' ability to write. Most deal with ability to select appropriate forms or usages, a related skill. In addition, some older tests include sections based on Latin grammar which demand of students a definitional knowledge largely repudiated by recent research in language. In evaluating growth in the use of language, teachers need to select and use tests or sections of tests which measure the important skills that have been stressed in the classroom and to avoid those tests or sections of tests which deal with other skills. Among the widely used printed tests are the following:

Iowa Language Abilities Test, Intermediate test for grades 7-10. (World Book Co., Yonkers, N.Y., 1952-1954.) Objective. Separate sections deal with spelling, word meaning, usage, grammatical form recognition, sentence sense, capitalization, and punctuation.

Barrett-Ryan English Test Grades 7-13. (Teachers College, Bureau of Educational Measurements, Emporia, Kansas, 1948-1951.) Test limited to a survey of students' understanding of English mechanics. Several forms.

Cooperative English Tests. (Cooperative Test Division, Educational Testing Service, Princeton, N.J., 1960.) Grades 7-12, 11-16. Various forms are available. English usage is tested on the first of three sections; Parts II and III test spelling and vocabulary. Norms are given from grade 7 through college.

Iowa Tests of Educational Development: No. 3, Correctness and Appropriateness of Expression. (Science Research Associates, Chicago, Ill., 1942-1951.) Objective tests present samples of writing and require students to make appropriate changes. May be used as a self-scoring device. Senior high school.

Essentials of English Tests. (Educational Publishers, Inc., Minneapolis, Minn., 1946-1950.) Widely used for diagnosis as well as evaluation. Three forms available. Objective test of 157 items covers spelling, grammatical usage, word usage, sentence structure, and punctuation and capitalization.

Sequential Tests of Educational Progress: Writing Tests. (Cooperative Test Division, Educational Testing Service, Princeton, N.J., 1957.) Promising new test with two forms available for levels 7-9, 10-12, and college. Uses forced choice method in making students choose the most effective usages and variations. Tests ability to express ideas logically, to organize, to write appropriate language, and to use conventions of language.

Stanford Achievement Tests: Language Arts. Advanced tests, grades 7-9. (World Book Co., Chicago, 1941-1949). Reading, paragraph meaning, language usage, and spelling.

SELECTED READINGS

REFERENCES ON LINGUISTIC GRAMMAR

Harold B. Allen, ed., *Readings in Applied English Linguistics.* N.Y., Appleton-Century-Crofts, 1958.

Leonard F. Dean and Kenneth G. Wilson, eds., *Essays in Language and Usage.* N.Y., Oxford U. Press, 1959.

W. Nelson Francis, *The Structure of American English.* N.Y., Ronald, 1958.

Charles C. Fries, "Linguistic Science and the Teaching of English," in Robert C. Pooley, ed., *Perspectives of English.* N.Y., Appleton-Century-Crofts, 1960, pp. 135-155.

———, *The Structure of English.* N.Y., Harcourt, Brace, 1952.

Archibald A. Hill, *Introduction to Linguistic Structures.* N.Y., Harcourt, Brace, 1958.

Paul Roberts, *Patterns of English.* N.Y., Harcourt, Brace, 1956.

James Sledd, *A Short Introduction to English Grammar.* N.Y., Scott Foresman, 1959.

Harold Whitehall, *Structural Essentials of English.* N.Y., Harcourt, Brace, 1956.

These references offer the teacher an introduction to linguistic grammar. The books by Fries, Francis, Sledd, and Whitehall present interesting analyses of structure for the teacher. Roberts' book has been used successfully in secondary classes. The volumes by Allen and Dean and Wilson reprint selected articles.

REFERENCES WHICH AID IN SELECTING AND ELIMINATING CONTENT

John B. Carroll, *The Study of Language.* Cambridge, Mass., Harvard U. Press, 1953. Chapter 6, "Language and Education," includes a readable summary of research in linguistics which has implications for teaching.

John J. DeBoer, "Grammar in Language Teaching," in *Children's Writing: Research in Composition and Related Skills,* Champaign, Ill., NCTE, pp. 32-40.

Harry A. Greene, articles on English Language, Grammar, and Composition, in W. S. Monroe, ed., *Encyclopedia of Educational Research.* N.Y., Macmillan, 1950. A helpful and concise summary of error frequency studies.

Ingrid M. Strom, "Research in Grammar and Usage and Its Implications for Teaching Writing," *Bulletin of the School of Education,* Indiana University, Vol. 36, No. 5 (September 1960).

Meeting a Crisis

A Unit for Grade Ten

Overview: Life is characterized by a series of crises, some great and some small. Whether they seem tragic or trivial to the observer, to the protagonist they assume importance because of his emotional involvement. How we react in a crisis depends at times upon the state of our physical health, but always upon our mental and emotional maturity. Our degree of maturity, in turn, depends upon the extent to which our experience has accustomed us to examine the possible courses of action, to predict the probable consequences of each, and to exert volition to follow the course which seems wisest.

Because the short story "attempts to reach some point of vantage, some glowing center of action from which the past and future will be equally visible,"[1] and because it exists in sufficient quantities on all levels of difficulty, this literary form is featured in this unit suggested for classes where reading ability ranges from average to low. Because in the short story interest is centered on one individual in a crucial moment of his life, the less able readers can identify the problem, examine the motivation for the decision, and determine whether the outcome seems inevitable; the more highly endowed can gain subtler appreciations of this literary form.

This unit, depending as it does upon a single copy of a selection, or at most only a few, is suitable for the teacher who finds himself without enough sets of material for an entire class. At times, to give unity to the experience, the teacher may read a selection aloud; at other times, a few students may present plays and panels; the short poems may be made available to all in mimeographed form. The major portion of the time is spent on individual reading and the learning experiences growing out of this reading.

AIMS

Understandings: Recognizing that literature presents problems with universal implications admitting of no one simple solution; sharpening awareness of the influence of habitual patterns of thinking and of belief in values in determining decisions made in moments of crisis.

Skills: Improving ability to recognize similarities and contrasts among various literary works; gaining skill in supporting a general statement wth specific examples; improving ability to make pertinent contributions in discussion.

[1] Frank O'Connor, "And It's a Lonely, Personal Art," in Francis Brown, ed., *Highlights of Modern Literature* (N.Y., New American Library, 1954), p. 77.

Appreciations: Developing sensitivity to the intellectual and emotional impact of literary works; extending imagination to apply concepts to various situations; sensing the irony underlying situations in literature and in life.

TIME PLAN

Five weeks is the maximum time suggested for the unit. By eliminating some of the introductory experiences or by limiting the time for individual reading, the class may complete the unit in three to four weeks.

LAUNCHING THE UNIT

To arouse interest in some of the concepts to be developed—comparison of themes in literature, application of ideas in literature to life—introduce some of the following experiences and activities.

■ *Explore the differences between one who tries to think objectively and one whose habit of indulging in unrealistic daydreams clouds his perception.*

1. "Gold Mounted Guns," by F. R. Buckley (1, 6).[2] In order to help a boy make an important decision, the sheriff forces him to put himself in the place of the persons he has wronged. Have you ever tried to understand another by attempting to look at his problem from his point of view? What difficulties did you encounter?
2. "Mrs. Ketting and Clark Gable," by Ann Chidester (18). Mrs. Ketting, a confirmed dreamer, finds it impossible to face reality. Find in the story the evidence that proves Mrs. Ketting has been a dreamer for years; show why the choice she made was the only logical one within the framework of the story.
3. "The Road not Taken," by Robert Frost (9). The decisions we make along the way make "all the difference." Discuss the use of symbolism. Discuss the roads open to the protagonists in the two stories just mentioned; what in the situations and in the characters themselves accounts for the choice each made?
4. "Miniver Cheevey," by Edwin Arlington Robinson (15). An ironical portrait of another dreamer who avoids facing reality, and "Death and General Putnam," by Arthur Guiterman (27). An imaginative recreation of events in the life of Putnam shows why the General was able to meet death gallantly. Compare the ideas and characters in these two poems with those in the two stories. Compare the short story and the poem as media for presenting characters and ideas.

Suggestions for writing: Write of a wise, or unwise, decision you have made; give the reasons which made you decide as you did and the effect of the decision on yourself and others. Or, write of a daydream as it persists in the mind of an imaginary character; tell how this dream might affect his action.

■ *Explore blocks to clear thinking and wise action engendered by tradition, culture, and environment; discover the conflicts likely to occur when a person is not sure which of his values are most important.*

1. "England to America," by Margaret Prescott Montague (1, 6). "Lord, but English people are funny." Elicit from the class examples of preconceived notions hampering judgment.

[2] The numbers in parentheses refer to the anthologies which contain the stories mentioned; titles and full bibliographical data are given in the list of resources at the end of the unit.

2. "The Enemy," by Pearl Buck (21). A Japanese couple, born in Japan but educated in America, find the two cultures in conflict when a decision is to be made. Discuss the possibility of conflict for the individual even within a nation such as ours, where different segments of the population have different values arising from various traditions, cultural strains, and environments.

3. *Confessional,* by Percival Wilde (23). A crisis helps the members of a family see themselves and each other as they really are, not as they thought themselves to be. Discuss confusion of values as a deterrent of wise choice.

4. "Mending Wall," by Robert Frost (31). We sometimes substitute clichés for thinking. Discuss with students some of the factors which influence the formation of personal values.

5. "The Unfamiliar," by Richard Connell (32). The people of Crosby Corners discover that courage has more than one dimension.

Suggestions for writing: Investigate some value you think helps guide your behavior, trying to discover what has led you to think this value important. Or, write of one specific instance where your belief in a certain value guided, or failed to guide, your action. Describe your feelings, both as you tried to decide and as you considered the results of your action.

■ *Compare the decision of a real person with that of a fictional character*

1. "Daniel Webster," by John F. Kennedy (28). Webster is forced to choose between personal political advantage and his responsibility to the nation.

2. *Dust of the Road,* by Kenneth Sawyer Goodman (23). Through the symbolism of Judas Iscariot, the playwright portrays the remorse which often plagues one who makes an unwise decision.

Suggestions for writing: Choose a decision made by a character in a book you have read or in a selection studied in class; explain the considerations weighed in making it and its effect. Or, compare a decision you have made with one made by a fictional character, showing similarities and differences in the motivation for the decision and in its results.

DEVELOPING THE UNIT

Phase I: Teacher-pupil planning

Purpose: to help pupils understand the conditions under which they will be working; determine a focus for the unit; develop a guide which will direct the reader's attention to the values to be considered; and agree upon a plan for recommending stories, for both inclusion in the unit and for recreational reading. Before planning the unit, the pupils should know that the number of copies of each selection is limited, and that while it is desirable that several read the same story, a copy may not be available at the time the reader wishes it; therefore, while waiting, he should substitute another selection.

Reviewing concepts: Ask students to copy in their notebooks O'Connor's statement concerning the short story (quoted in the overview of the unit, p. 589). Divide the class into three groups, giving each group one of the following assignments:

Examine the stories studied thus far and determine how successful the authors have been in choosing and developing an action which suggests both the past and the probable future of the protagonist.

Review the ideas concerning human behavior brought out in the discussions of the selections studied.

Write a definition of irony as it is exemplified in the illustrations we have found in our reading. (This for top group.)

Devising study guide and title: Place students in groups to use the discussion of material already read as a guide in devising questions applicable to the stories that students will select for individual reading, and then to use the questions in finding a title for the unit.

Teacher and pupils select the best questions from each group to formulate a guide for studying stories to be read in the unit—the following was made in one class:

Study guide

1. In what conflict is the character involved?
2. What is the crisis? Could it have been prevented? If so, how?
3. Does this same crisis or a similar one occur often in life? Give examples.
4. Does the person meet the crisis successfully? Why or why not?
5. What hints do we have in his character and background which might explain the decision he makes?
6. Can you think of similar situations in which this person might be forced to make an important decision? What values would probably guide his decision?

The class then agrees upon an appropriate title for the unit. The class using the above study guide selected "Meeting a Crisis"; other classes, having devised slightly different study, have chosen "Moment of Decision," "The Best Choice," and "Conflict in Values."

Planning mechanical details: To insure that the class will run smoothly and that time will not be wasted, the teacher needs to

1. Be able to suggest the first story for each to read; therefore, the volumes in the room library must contain stories presenting problems of varying complexity, some important to girls; others, important to boys; and some important to both girls and boys. They must also offer various levels of reading difficulty. (The list of titles given at the end of the unit meets these requirements, but each teacher must compile his own from the material available and with a particular class in mind.)

2. Help students decide how to record information about stories they read which are not included in the unit. (Students, after the initial story, select the ones they wish to read; therefore, some means must be found to acknowledge reading which, because of the pressure of time or the story's failure to illustrate the theme of the unit, cannot be included.) Some classes have agreed to compile a list, with titles briefly annotated, to be posted in the library—"Recommended for Students by Students." Others have prepared lists that the teacher might use in other units or might suggest as reading for individuals. (The reader can record the information on 3 x 5 cards; the compilation can be taken care of by volunteer groups.)

3. Provide means for informing the class of recommended stories and for segregating the volumes containing those stories. A bulletin board can be kept, where the one making the initial recommendation places a 3 x 5 card with title, author, volume, and his name. Anyone who reads the story adds his name. Students use the cards in finding suggestions for reading; the teacher, in forming

groups for discussion. Or, perhaps the class can designate a shelf to which volumes containing recommended stories are returned; if the shelf is empty, the student knows he is to try to find "another first."

4. Provide a means of keeping the books circulating without waste of time. Allow students to sign up for stories they wish to read as soon as a copy is available. Give the responsibility for handling reservations to one or more of the faster readers, who can pass quietly around the room, discover the present reader, and arrange with him to pass it next to the one for whom it is reserved.

Phase II: Experiences growing out of reading

Discussion. Review the standards for discussion: the need for listening carefully to be able to make pertinent contributions, to evaluate support of generalizations, to summarize and synthesize; and the need for speaking clearly and to the point. After all pupils have read at least two stories, form groups of those who have read the same story or ones that can be related; meet with each group, while other students continue reading, helping individuals to relate the concepts and judge the skill of the author. Or, conduct a class discussion on the ideas and characters, exploring similarities and contrasts in the examples given.

Alternate between class and group discussions. Permit several students who wish to discuss a story to do so without supervision. Whenever possible, meet with a group who have read some of the more difficult stories to discuss the less obvious aspects of the author's technique.

Panels. Encourage the better readers to select stories not discussed to present to the class in the form of a panel which will point up likenesses and differences. For one such presentation the following stories were chosen:

"The Snob," by Morley Callaghan (8)
"Split Cherry Tree," by Jesse Stuart (15)
"The Piece of String," by Guy de Maupassant (11)
"Freshman Fullback," by Ralph D. Paine (16)
"Her First Ball," by Katherine Mansfield (30)

Oral reading. Some teachers like to include volumes of poetry in the classroom library; they encourage students to browse through these anthologies to find poems which seem appropriate to the concepts evolving as the unit progresses. An audience for those finding poems can be provided in small groups, who select some to be read to the class. One such choice included

"Little Things," by James Stephens (22)
"Columbus," by Joaquin Miller (24)
"I Did Not Lose My Heart," by A. E. Housman (20)
"Motherhood," by Agnes Lee (19)
"Invictus," by William Ernest Henley (25)

With some classes, it is effective to ask students to copy sentences and phrases from poems which stir their imaginations upon first reading. The responses will be varied: a particularly vivid aural or visual impression, a reminder of an experience, an illumination of a truth, and so on. Several partial class hours may be devoted to discussing these contributions, and groups may be formed for brief lessons in language study.

Expository writing. The purpose of this writing is to help students learn to support by the use of specific examples. These assignments will need to be repeated more than once, if not for the entire class, at least for individuals. For each type of assignment, work out an example with the class on the board. For the first assignment given below, use a story studied in the introduction of the unit, letting the class suggest several topic sentences before one is selected. For the second assignment, which is much more difficult, follow the same procedure; this time give the class several topic sentences from which to choose. After a choice has been made, accept examples from any stories individuals have read, helping students select salient details and secure precision of statement.[3] Assignments:

Use a statement about a character, a setting, a story, etc., as a topic sentence; develop a paragraph with one detailed example.[4]

Using a general statement as a topic sentence, develop a paragraph by a series of three specific examples, each briefly stated.

Write an essay defining *crisis* (substitute any term used in the discussion of the stories—conflict, universality, motivation of action, foreshadowing, irony); illustrate by two or three specific examples, each constituting one paragraph.

The same as the above assignment, except that the development is to be in two paragraphs, one giving a detailed example and the other a series with each item concisely stated.[5]

Imaginative writing. The purpose here is to extend the imagination by applying concepts presented in literature to life situations. Assignments:

Considering the implications of "The Road not Taken," show how the life of any one of the characters in the stories we have read might have been different if he had taken another road; consider the changes necessary in his sense of values to have made the choice of another road possible.

Select any character you have read about during this unit and place him in an imaginary crisis; show what you think he would do in such a situation.

CULMINATING EXPERIENCES

Relating literature to life: Ask students to find, in newspapers, accounts of persons in moments of crisis; let the class select the situation which seems to present the most complex problem and help them relate this to the concepts that have been developed. While one class was working on this unit, the story of a man who was attacked and beaten by a group of hoodlums appeared in the local papers; those who witnessed the scene were reported to have acted in the following ways: One stood and watched; one went to the help of the man and was severely beaten; one called the police; many ran away.[6] This episode was selected by the class and the following plan was devised by teacher and students, sparked by the question, What probable interpretations can be made to explain the reaction of the witnesses?

The students handed in questions to be used in guiding discussion; from these, with additions by the teacher, the following guide was devised:

[3] See "Program and Plan," pp. 670-71.

[4] This may be all the slowest students can master; if so, the assignments from this point should be differentiated, e.g., such individuals can move to the third assignment without achieving competence in the skills necessary for the second.

[5] See Chapter 9, "Oral Language," pp. 467-69.

[6] Norman Cousins, "The Desensitization of Twentieth-Century Man," *Saturday Review*, May 16, 1959, reports a similar incident.

Discussion guide

What was the probable motivation for each of these actions?
What kind of person might react in each of these ways?
Who made the "wisest" decision? Why?
With which one are you most in sympathy?
With which one are you least in sympathy?
Do you think any of the persons you have read about in this unit would react as any of these spectators did in this situation?
Do you know anyone who might have a reaction similar to any of these?
Why is the public disturbed by such occurrences?

Students were given the guide and time to come to their own conclusions before being placed in groups for discussion; each group, having considered the questions, selected one member to represent them in a round-table discussion in which the teacher acted as leader.

Synthesizing ideas: Organize a series of student panels which review the various aspects of the short story which have been covered in the essay assignments. Each panel member illustrates the particular concept with an example taken from one of the stories he has read. The series should be represented by as many stories as possible, with few or no duplications.

Expository writing. In preparation for writing, help students compare the traits of characters who seem to have met crises successfully with the characteristics of those who apparently failed; any similarities and contrasts? Usually students find a sufficient number of clear-cut examples to show that many who were successful had the following characteristics; in like manner, those who failed lacked these attributes:

They were able to exercise self-control.
They were able to forego a selfish advantage when the welfare of others was in question.
They were able to discount immediate advantage for future benefits.

Ask students to explain maturity and to develop their ideas with examples taken from literature and from personal experience.

Read to the class "How to Avoid Emotional Maturity" by Sylvia Wright;[7] this short article satirizes with broad humor the interest in the superficial self-probing and self-rating which some of today's magazines seem to foster. Ask students to write an essay suggested by the article (e.g., Self-Probing, Help or Hindrance?), to state a point of view, and support the opinion with specific examples. Or, ask them to write either a serious or humorous essay on a topic such as Sometimes I Think I'll Never Grow Up, or Flashes of Self-Revelation. Occasionally individual students are interested in trying to write two essays using the same ideas; one essay treats the ideas seriously, the other humorously.

Imaginative writing:

Select either "Lucinda Matlock" (15) or "George Gray" (15) by Edgar Lee Masters; show how one of the characters you have read about might develop into such a person as is described in the poem.
Write a poem which might be used as an epitaph for one of the characters studied.

[7] *Vogue* magazine, Vol. 130, No. 3 (August 15, 1957).

EVALUATION

■ *Of individual growth*

The teacher has evidence, gained from the discussions and from the writing, upon which to base an estimate of individual growth. The student may:

Examine his folder of written work to determine what improvement he has made.

Review his oral work and check progress in oral skills; a form, such as those suggested on pp. 478 and 481, including only those items pertinent to the teaching in the unit, can be used as a guide.

List the most important insights he has gained concerning one, several, or all of the following:

Motivation of behavior.
Need for considering consequences of decisions.
Universality of certain problems and ideas.
Values that energize the personality *vs.* those that enervate.

Write a paper criticizing the adequacy of the following guide for use in making important decisions:

What is the principle by which I justify this course of action?
Will this action ultimately tend to bring about what I believe to be most worthwhile?

■ *Of the plan of the unit*

Teacher and pupils may evaluate the unit as a whole to decide which experiences should be retained and which should be modified or eliminated if the unit is to be taught to another class; and to determine, on the basis of progress made, some of the learning experiences which should receive priority in the immediate future.

TITLES CHOSEN BY ONE CLASS

1. "Five Minute Girl," Mary H. Bradley (1). Judy discovers that the price for saving face comes high.
2. "Mother Knows Best," Edna Ferber (3). Sally Quail owed everything to her mother, perhaps even unhappiness.
3. "Not Wanted," Jesse Lynch Williams (2). A father finds it difficult to show his love for his son.
4. "Wife of the Hero," Sally Benson (3). Libby is confused as to a man's qualifications for a husband.
5. "Weep No More, My Lady," James Street (9). A boy has to decide whether to keep a dog he has found or return it to the owner.
6. "The Fifty-first Dragon," Heywood Broun (12). Self-confidence is gained in many ways.
7. "Blue Murder," Wilbur Daniel Steele (6). A horse is almost blamed for a murder.
8. "Four Men and a Box," Leslie G. Barnard (7). Only the promise of a clever man brought these four men safely out of the jungle.
9. "Snake Dance," Corey Ford (8). Jerry tries to play the game, but not on the football field.
10. "Prelude to Reunion," Oliver La Farge (8). Pride betrays a young college student into making a pledge he will have difficulty keeping.

11. "Tenth of the Month," Sally Benson (13). A young wife has reasons for concealing the juggling of household accounts from her husband.
12. "Basquerie," Eleanor M. Kelly (6). Emily regrets a decision.
13. "Retrieved Reformation," O. Henry (17). A reformed burglar weighs love against personal safety.
14. "Tol'able David," Joseph Hergesheimer (6). A boy wants to avenge the death of his father and brother.
15. "Sherrel," Whit Burnett (3). A boy worries that he may have been the cause of his young brother's death.
16. "The Quiet Man," Maurice Walsh (4). A man of peace wins a moral and physical victory.
17. "Barn Burning," William Faulkner (4). Sarty learns that the time has come when he must think for himself.
18. "Prelude," Albert Halper (5). Prejudice and vandalism invade the rights of the individual.
19. "Eight-Oared Crew," Harry Sylvester (14). Kep discovers what *winning* really means.
20. "After the Ball," Sally Benson (5, 14). A young girl learns that there are advantages in being sixteen.
21. "A Start in Life," Ruth Suckow (5, 14). Daisy finds that "out working for other folks" is not the delightful experience she had expected.
22. "Thank You, Dr. Russell," B. J. Chute (29). A son may prove to be a better man than his father.
23. "Bred in the Bone," Elsie Singmaster (10). A wife's decision brings about an event she is trying to avoid.
24. "Every Man for Himself," Robert Zacks (7). Jimmy faces the last test to qualify him for membership in the submarine crew.
25. "Traffic Incident," Edward Doherty (8). Grampa Jerry finally gets a traffic ticket that can't be fixed.
26. "One Throw," W. C. Heinz (7). Manari considers throwing the game in order to get even with the manager.
27. "Molly Morgan," John Steinbeck (4). Molly avoids discovering the truth because she prefers keeping her illusions.
28. "Pilot's Choice," Hunt Miller (7). Brady has to decide whether to risk the lives of his crew in a desperate attempt to effect a rescue.
29. "The Cub," Lois D. Kleihauer (7). A boy in his victory learns one of life's truths—a poignant discovery.
30. "The Last Lesson," Alphonse Daudet (26). The last lesson is an emotional experience for teacher, pupils, and townspeople.

Materials and resources for students

1. Great American Short Stories: O. Henry Memorial Award, 1919-1934. Garden City, N.Y., Doubleday, Doran, 1935.
2. Howard Francis Seely and Margaret Roling, eds., *Recent Stories for Enjoyment.* Morristown, N.J., Silver Burdett, 1937.
3. William Robert Wunsch and Edna Albers, eds., *Thicker Than Water.* N.Y., D. Appleton Century, 1939.
4. Frank G. Jennings and Charles J. Calitri, eds., *Stories.* N.Y., Harcourt, Brace, 1957.

5. Maureen Daly, ed., *My Favorite Stories.* N.Y., Dodd, Mead, 1949.
6. Edwin Van Berghen Knickerbocker, ed., *Notable Short Stories.* N.Y., Harper, 1929.
7. Eric Berger, ed., *Best Short Stories.* N.Y., Tab Books, 1958.
8. William R. Wood and John D. Husband, eds., *Short Stories as You Like Them.* N.Y., Harcourt, Brace, 1940.
9. Egbert N. Nieman and George E. Salt, eds., *Pleasure in Literature.* N.Y., Harcourt, Brace, 1949.
10. Elsie Singmaster, *Bred in the Bone and Other Stories.* Boston, Houghton Mifflin, 1925.
11. Rewey Belle Inglis and William K. Stewart, eds., *Adventures in World Literature.* N.Y., Harcourt, Brace, 1936.
12. Abraham Harold Lass and Arnold Horowitz, eds., *Stories for Youth.* N.Y., Harper, 1950.
13. Emma L. Reppert and Clarence Stratton, eds., *Modern Short Stories.* N.Y., McGraw-Hill, 1939.
14. Ernestine K. Taggard, ed., *Twenty Grand.* N.Y., Bantam Books, 1947.
15. Rewey Belle Inglis, John Gehlman, Mary Rives Bowman, and Norman Foerster, eds., *Adventures in American Literature.* N.Y., Harcourt, Brace, 1941.
16. Rosa Mary Mikels, ed., *Short Stories for English Classes.* N.Y., Scribner's, 1926.
17. C. Alphonso Smith., ed., *Selected Short Stories from O. Henry.* Garden City, N.Y., Doubleday, 1922.
18. Herschel Brickell, ed., *Prize Stories, 1950.* Garden City, N.Y., Doubleday, 1950.
19. Harriet Monroe and Alice Corbin Henderson, eds., *The New Poetry.* N.Y., Macmillan, 1924.
20. Oscar Williams, ed., *A Little Treasury of Modern Poetry.* N.Y., Scribner's, 1950
21. Luella B. Cook, Walter Loban, Oscar James Campbell, Ruth M. Stauffer, eds., *The World Through Literature.* N.Y., Harcourt, Brace, 1949.
22. Gerald De Witt Sanders and John Herbert Nelson, eds., *Chief Modern Poets of England and America.* N.Y., Macmillan, 1943.
23. George Goldstone, ed., *One Act Plays.* Boston, Allyn & Bacon, 1926.
24. Louis Untermeyer, ed., *This Singing World.* N.Y., Harcourt, Brace, 1926.
25. ———, *A Treasury of Great Poems.* N.Y., Simon & Schuster, 1942.
26. Bernadine Kielty, ed., *A Treasury of Great Stories.* N.Y., Simon & Schuster, 1947.
27. Arthur Guiterman, *Death and General Putnam.* N.Y., Dutton, 1935.
28. John F. Kennedy, *Profiles in Courage.* N.Y., Harper, 1956; N.Y., Pocket Books, 1957.
29. Simon Certner and George H. Henry, eds., *Short Stories for Our Times.* Boston, Houghton Mifflin, 1950.
30. Whit Burnett, ed., *Time To Be Young.* Phila., Lippincott, 1945.
31. Louis Untermeyer, ed., *Robert Frost's Poems.* N.Y., Pocket Books, 1953.
32. Luella B. Cook, H. A. Miller, Jr., and Walter Loban, eds., *Adventures in Appreciation.* N.Y., Harcourt, Brace, 3rd ed., 1950.

If time permits, any one of these films may be included in the unit:

"The Story that Couldn't Be Printed"
"Story of Dr. Carver"
"Mahatma Gandhi"
"Due Process of Law Denied"

Teachers wishing to try a unit similar to this should consider the rich source of inexpensive material—both short stories and poetry—available in paperback editions. The purchase of several copies of each title allows one to remove appropriate stories and poems, staple them individually or by groups in heavy paper covers, and thus promote wider circulation.

PART FIVE

Values

Chapter Twelve

Discovery of Values

Excellent performance is a blend of talent and motive, of ability fused with zeal. Aptitude without aspiration is lifeless and inert.

And that is only part of the story. When ability is brought to life by aspiration, there is the further question of the ends to which these gifts are applied. We do not wish to nurture the man of great talent and evil purpose. Not only does high performance take place in a context of values and purpose but if it is to be worth fostering, the values and purpose must be worthy of our allegiance.

—THE PURSUIT OF EXCELLENCE [1]

All life is a search for meaning, a continuing struggle to impose reason and order on the fragmented moments of experience. The wisdom of the choices made determines to what degree the search will be satisfying and the striving productive. Edgar Lee Masters uses a boat with a furled sail at rest in a harbor to symbolize the life of one who, through fear of disillusionment, refused to grapple with the challenge of the unpredictable. George Gray, the subject of Masters' portrait, realizes too late that if life is to have meaning, one must

. . . lift the sail
And catch the winds of destiny
Wherever they drive the boat.
To put meaning in one's life may end in madness,
But life without meaning is the torture
Of restlessness and vague desire—
It is a boat longing for the sea and yet afraid.[2]

At the opposite extreme, Masters presents a woman whose lifted sail caught the winds of destiny—a woman who for over ninety years reached out to life with understanding and purpose. Lucinda Matlock accepted the eternal tension between the forces that sustain life and those that destroy as the price one pays for being human. Decrying flabbiness and discontent, she leaves as

[1] Rockefeller Brothers Fund, Inc., *The Pursuit of Excellence: Education and the Future of America* (Garden City, N.Y., Doubleday, 1958), p. 45.

[2] Edgar Lee Masters, *Spoon River Anthology* (N.Y., Macmillan, 1931), p. 65.

her legacy a statement epitomizing her own faith and courage, "It takes life to love Life." [3]

Little more than half a century separates us from the world Lucinda Matlock knew. During that short time technological advancement has had an impact on our culture which could scarcely have been envisioned fifty years ago. Changes have been great, and there is no reason to believe that change will not continue. One thing, however, remains constant—man's deep-seated struggle to develop values which will guide him toward self-realization. In a "Seminar of Basic Ideas" concerning the purposes of education, Viktor Frankel of the medical faculty of the University of Vienna selects man's search for meaning as the truest expression of the state of being human. He suggests that each individual, although he may begin by questioning life, must eventually realize that "it is he who is being questioned—questioned by life. It is he who has to answer—by answering life." He commends the wisdom contained in Nietzsche's words, "He who knows a Why of living surmounts almost every How," as an appropriate motto for all education.[4]

What the student accepts as the Whys of living serves as the foundation for his values; this, in turn, determines the choices he will make. Making intelligent choices involves almost everything of importance in the education of young people in a free society, for decision-making implies not only the ability to select wisely among many competing interests but also acceptance of personal responsibility for the choices made. In any time or place, adherence to one's code, with its inevitable conflicts, requires conviction and stamina; but the youth of Lucinda Matlock's generation were at least spared the confusion of trying to determine what their culture prized. In the relatively stable life of that day, there seems to have been fairly general agreement as to what was worthwhile. In contrast, young people in contemporary America are confronted by a bewildering array of conflicting values, each sanctioned by various segments of society. "The principal causes of our adolescents' difficulty," Margaret Mead concludes, after contrasting our young people with Samoan youth and their serene way of life, "are the presence of conflicting standards and the belief that every individual should make his or her own choice." [5] If we agree with Mead, we must conclude that our schools should grant more attention to the considerations underlying wise decisions and to the significance of choice as the inevitable consequence of freedom.

Role of English teacher unchanged In our culture, with its ever-accelerating change, the role of the English teacher in helping students develop values perhaps becomes more difficult than in the past but basically remains unchanged. For those of us who teach language and literature, the decision to

[3] Masters, *Spoon River Anthology,* p. 229.

[4] *Saturday Review,* Vol. 41, No. 37 (September 13, 1958), p. 20.

[5] Margaret Mead, *Coming of Age in Samoa,* 1936 (N.Y., New American Library, 1949), p. 154.

deal with values is by no means a new urgency.[6] Our material has always led us to a concern with both the ethical and the esthetic aspects of life. Literature cannot be taught apart from the morality of humanity; speaking and writing unrelated to truth can become twisted and debased, a threat to the very basis of communication. Nor is it a mere quirk of legalistic minds that perjury is so seriously regarded in the courts. The need for sincerity and integrity in everyday use of language, the power of literature to illuminate choices among values—we have always accepted these as basic in the teaching of English. Cultural change has only made more apparent the importance of the liberal arts.

Balance essential In the pressures resulting from society's concern with the need for helping youth acquire values, we must maintain our balance. Literature, unlike propaganda, is not intended to secure immediate, practical results. It is not a poultice to be applied to weaknesses in moral perception. Between *Macbeth* and *Mein Kampf* a difference exists, and that difference is immense. The precarious harmony of any work of art is a balanced structure of innumerable tensions, qualities, and relationships. To view literature as a formula for moral action is to mistake its nature and to miss its rewards. However, because it can enlarge our awareness of values and refine our discrimination among values, literature is a force of tremendous potential for education. Literature can disclose for the reader wider and deeper perceptions and organizations of experience. Literature can lift that reader above the petty or narrow concerns that usually consume his time. No one who has appreciated a play by Shakespeare or a poem by Li Po is left unchanged. To whatever extent the good life is dependent upon discrimination among the values in experience, literature can contribute to the liberal education our civilization seeks for as many human beings as possible.

Values, a major concern The point of view throughout this book has been concerned with the discovery of values. The over-all aim has been to suggest ways to help the pupil build a solid core of integrity that will resist attrition in the pressures of everyday existence. Implicit in the underlying philosophy is the belief that "comfort" is unsatisfying as a final goal, that the zest of living comes from the struggle—the pursuit of values the individual considers worthwhile. Therefore, the ideals our students choose are important, for without durable values the learner will always fall short of true power with language and literature. But on one point there must be no doubt; we cannot "teach" values, although students learn them in our classrooms. They learn them from our attitudes and actions which derive from our own beliefs as to what shall receive top priority in our teaching. They learn them through ex-

[6] For a discussion of the relation of literature to moral attitudes, the authors recommend Louise M. Rosenblatt, *Literature as Exploration* (N.Y., D. Appleton-Century, 1938). For a discussion of the role of the English teacher in a changing society, see Committee on National Interest, *The National Interest and the Teaching of English*. Champaign, Ill., NTCE, 1961.

periences planned with the long-range aim of stimulating and guiding individuals in *self-discipline* and in *self-development*. Hence the emphasis throughout this text on the necessity for helping the student set standards for achievement and for behavior, for making self-evaluation an integral part of learning, for developing understanding of the resources of literature and the power of language—both of which lead to the discovery of values.

Harmony basic to all values Although for the purpose of emphasis two aspects of personal values—the ethical and the esthetic—are discussed separately in this chapter, in reality both are inextricably fused in the balanced personality. Moral and esthetic values have an identical foundation; the good and the beautiful, traced to their ultimate considerations, dissolve into a single principle—the law of harmony. Vicious and destructive behavior may be viewed as discord and productive living as harmony. In *Spoon River Anthology*, George Gray's withdrawal from life strikes a discord because it destroys his human potential; Lucinda Matlock's acceptance of all that life offers creates a harmony which makes living an adventure. We are concerned here with choices such as wise men and women make in their search for harmonious lives.

UNDERSTANDINGS CONCERNING VALUES

A value expresses the essence of experiences the race has found to be worthwhile. Over the centuries Man, guided by the forces of instinct and of intelligence, has groped slowly but steadily toward the humanitarian ideal. The student, in the disciplined forms of literature, discovers these same forces at work; here he finds bared the restless, searching human spirit. The literary artist, highlighting now one aspect of experience and now another, is concerned with the mystery of Man.[7] Thus literature, embracing as it does the accumulated conscience of the race, provides a medium which allows the student to grapple on his own level with the ideas and values that have guided Man in his long struggle from the twilight cave toward the light.

Whether or not a teacher should help any particular group formulate principles concerned with values must remain at the discretion of that teacher. Certainly he will not do so unless the concepts can be arrived at inductively, until he has helped students examine motivation for behavior in many concrete situations, and until he has helped them probe their thinking concerning some of the beliefs they think they hold. All this presupposes a mature class. It presupposes students who have formed opinions of the worth of many ideals, who have discovered some of the difficulties in determining the basis for beliefs

[7] Cries James Joyce's Stephan Dedalus in pledging himself to art: "Welcome, O life! I go to encounter for the millionth time the reality of experience and to forge in the smithy of my soul the uncreated conscience of my race." *The Portrait of the Artist as a Young Man*, N.Y., Modern Library, 1928, p. 299.

and in making those beliefs function in action. Granted these conditions, two understandings may help students become more realistic in assessing problems concerned with values: Values are guides, not prescriptions, for conduct; values are a balance of rational thought and controlled emotion.

VALUES AS GUIDES

A value merely points the way, directs the course. Although we have the experience of humanity to guide us, we have no chart that all may follow. We can see similarities among the ideals chosen by men and women of both fact and fiction in building harmonious lives. But each individual must choose his own, for it is to his own life he must give meaning.

Principles guide action Students can more readily comprehend the function of a guiding principle if they see that function impersonally in the perspective of time. An example, of which they are at least dimly aware, is close at hand—the manner in which through the years our own nation has tried to implement the belief, first stated in 1776, that "all men are endowed by their Creator with certain inalienable rights." Recalling with a class some of the steps we as a nation have taken to insure any one of our personal rights will help young people appreciate how a value acts as a guide toward any goal.

In the classroom the necessity for redefinition of values has been highlighted by means of a discussion on the right to vote, initiated by citing the case of Susan B. Anthony, who was arrested for voting in the presidential election of 1872.

The Fourteenth Amendment (1868) stated, "All persons born or naturalized in the United States and subject to the jurisdiction thereof are citizens . . ." The Fifteenth Amendment (1870) stated, "The right of the citizens of the United States to vote shall not be denied or abridged . . . on account of race, color, or previous condition of servitude." On what grounds could Miss Anthony be tried, found guilty, and fined one hundred dollars? (A fine which was never paid.)

Call attention to the fact that *men* of the Declaration of Independence has been translated to *persons* in the amendments. What meaning did Miss Anthony give to these two words? What did those who arrested her think they meant?

Some students may be surprised to learn that not until 1920, when the Nineteenth Amendment gave women the right to vote, was Miss Anthony's interpretation of these words accepted.

Understanding the struggle required to secure privileges we now take for granted will show that the evolution of our rights, based on belief in the worth of the individual, has been slow; that gradually the meaning of these rights has become clearer as official documents, each in terms of its own era, have tried to define the essentials that permit men to maintain their dignity as human beings.

Critics of our culture point to examples of discrimination against individuals and groups as a contradiction of democracy. Such criticism betrays its authors' failure to recognize the gap which will always exist between ideals and attainment. Margaret Mead in answer to one such critic stresses the need of "recognizing that in the tension between ideals and practice which must fall behind those ideals, lies the dynamic of American democracy—that the whole point of hitching one's wagon to a star lies in the tension on the rope." [8]

Values provide direction The tension on the rope serves as well for the individual as it does for the nation. Belief in a certain value will pull him in the direction he thinks will help him attain it; the more firmly rooted the belief, the more forceful the pull and the greater his chance of approaching his ideal. But it is approximation only, never complete realization. Those who profess faith in the perfectibility of man speak in relative terms—they believe that inherent in man is the urge and the capacity for moving toward perfection. The student should understand that it is the *pursuit* of worthwhile values, not their perfect attainment, that will characterize his efforts; that intermediate successes keep him on the right road but that the ultimate goal will always lie ahead. For, as Whitehead says, "When ideals have sunk to the level of practice, the result is stagnation." [9]

Understanding the progress his nation has made toward the ideal first stated nearly two centuries ago helps the student realize that a value acts as a guide, not as a prescription, for conduct; it makes him aware of the relationships ideals bear to practice; it helps him see values as flexible in operation, continually tested in specific situations, constantly reassessed and redefined in the light of greater knowledge and widening experience. As with a people, so with the individual; his values are guides providing direction but giving no pat formula for conduct. Each person must determine for himself what behavior at any particular time is consistent with the belief he professes, what line of action will help him approximate his goals.

What constitutes *kindness* in any particular instance? To allow a friend to copy from one's paper in a test? To allow a friend to use one's name in obtaining parental permission to remain out later than usual when one is not involved in the situation? Was Jerry in "The Snake Dance" being kind, as he thought, in deceiving his parents?

What constitutes *loyalty* to friend or duty? Does loyalty to Tom Brown, a member of *my* club demand I vote for him in the school election, even though I think his opponent better qualified for the job? Has Javert in *Les Miserables* become so emotionally involved in his sense of duty to his job that his pursuit of Jean Valjean has become an obsession?

VALUES AS A BALANCE OF THOUGHT AND EMOTION

Personal values are the result of an individual's reflective experience, in both its intellectual and emotional aspects. Both elements—and they are rarely

[8] Margaret Mead, *New Lives for Old* (N.Y., Morrow, 1956), p. 158.

[9] Alfred North Whitehead, *The Aims of Education*, 1929 (N.Y., New American Library, 1949), p. 40.

separable—must correspond to the reality to which they refer. That is, if there is no thinking or only confused thinking, if there is too little or too much emotion, a value lacks the force needed to make it a guide for action. Thus, we try not only to determine a reason for the importance of any ideal we hold but also to become alert to the complexities of its application as a guide to behavior. We try to develop discrimination in the degree of our emotional involvement with any certain value, desirable as it in itself may be.

A perfect balance of rational thought and controlled emotion is impossible to maintain; its approximation is a mark of maturity. In trying to achieve equilibrium, everyone has difficulty. Understanding the ways thought and emotion operate in developing values will prepare the student for some of the complexities involved in making important choices.

When emotion rules The first sense of values is acquired in an emotionally toned, either-or world; the child is taught by verbal commands and exhortations to conform to the demands of his immediate environment. His world is small, his choices limited. Reactions of adults quickly inform him that one type of conduct wins approval; its opposite, the reverse. His conflicts arise not in determining the right course of action but in summoning volition to obey the dictates of the person he wishes to please. Failure brings discomfort, even a sense of guilt. When he begins to reason, to ask why, he is met with either circular reasoning ("That's the way nice little boys act." "We want you to grow up to be a good man.") or appeals to external pressures ("When you go to school, you'll have to behave." "No one will want to play with you if you're going to lose your temper.") [10] Thus, first values, never the product of reasoning, carry an emotional load, vestiges of which remain throughout life.

Such an orientation makes it difficult to eradicate the idea that all choices are between the good and the bad, each easily identifiable, the belief that the path is well defined and leads straight to the goal. Gradually one learns that each particular situation may present its own problem; that values are sometimes in conflict; that many choices are concerned with several "goods," each desirable in its own right, or with several "evils," making a completely satisfactory course of action impossible. Individual progress toward belief in and understanding of a multi-valued world is slow and painful.

The child, learning rules of conduct by rote, accepts the words without the necessary experiential basis to give the language meaning; consequently, the abstract statement becomes for him the reality. The formula, embedded in his emotions, admits of no question until further experience subjects the

[10] Students should see these examples of parental guidance as a *description* of the child's introduction to values, not as an indictment of the way parents train children. Charged with responsibility for the child, parents can do no other than try to inculcate the values they themselves hold. That they cannot supply cogent, universally accepted reasons, even if the child could understand them, is not surprising. Even perceptive observers concerned with the study of modern man and his spiritual needs, although they agree on the highest human values, define them differently and have different reasons for their judgments. See Abraham H. Maslow, ed., *New Knowledge in Human Values* (N.Y., Harper, 1959).

value to the searchlight of reason, reinforcing, modifying, or negating it. For example, as the child's world enlarges, he may notice that others win popularity by methods he has been taught are unacceptable. Then his conflicts begin as he tries to square teaching with practice. What adolescent, unless he has been wisely and continually guided in examining the basis for his values, has not at times been shocked to discover that a principle he has long accepted as valid—and which of course may well be—has no roots in his thinking, only in his emotions?

After viewing such a film as "Right or Wrong," or reading such a story as "Bill's Little Girl," students may be asked to write on a topic similar to the following:

> Tell of a decision you were forced to make between two courses of action which seemed either almost equally desirable or almost equally distasteful; what was the compelling factor leading you to decide as you did?

When intellect rules As adults we sometimes encounter the problem in reverse. Our first contact with statements of democratic values probably occurs in the elementary school when we memorize portions of the Declaration of Independence. "All men are created equal. . . ." Each time we hear the words we may respond to the moving language; we may even experience a vague feeling of pride in the nobility of our political heritage. Almost automatically we have accepted the values as our own, but rarely do we think of them in reference to our own conduct. When we are first conscious of meeting the test in action, we may discover we have fooled ourselves. What we have is an intellectualized concept, not a value; it lacks the emotional involvement needed to give it vitality.

Admittedly, stating a value may be verbalization only—that is, it may lack either the reasoned acceptance or the emotional involvement sufficient to commit one to action; it may lack both. Must we then conclude that because verbalisms sometimes betray us, students should never be helped to formulate the principles underlying a series of experiences planned to stress certain values? Certainly not. Understanding the relationship between the concrete and the abstract is as desirable in studying values as in developing concepts in science. We must, however, lead students to see that the formulation of a personal code is important only if it influences conduct. We cannot doubt that our national ideals have had such influence. Nor can we doubt that our privileges as individuals would have been curtailed if more autocratic principles had been selected to guide the nation. Admittedly, the expressed ideals are not incorporated into the behavior of every citizen. However, their acceptance in individual thinking means they are part of the nation's thinking; their violation nags at the nation's conscience. The danger lies, not in putting our beliefs about values into words, but in deceiving ourselves by thinking that the language and the values are synonymous.

The Slave with Two Faces illustrates how the verbalization of a value may be accepted as the reality. This symbolic play contrasts the attitudes of two girls toward life. The firm belief that a person should show no fear guides the conduct of one girl. Her companion, verbally accepting what the other has "taught" her, discovers that the ideal lacks the necessary roots in her thinking and in her emotions to serve as a guide for action when the test comes.

Continued and varied approaches are necessary in the consideration of ethical values; but fundamental to the effectiveness of both content and method is the maintenance of a climate encouraging growth. Admittedly, the search for standards to give meaning to life is an important part of the education of the adolescent, but the school is only one factor in his environment and experiences in the English classroom only one aspect of the school. The educational problem is at heart the problem of helping young people select from their culture all constructive values, all striving for wholeness, and of helping them subdue or convert those tendencies that are destructive, negative, wasteful, or smugly complacent. The learning experiences within the English classroom may be placed in the balance that is tending toward this aim. The clear-sightedness and the integrity of the teacher will be the significant factor in this dynamics of forces. Not always will the teacher succeed, but success comes often enough to justify the effort.

ETHICAL VALUES

To deal with moral concepts and values requires tact and wisdom. Does it need to be said that a heavy-handed frontal attack does more harm than good? That literature converted into a group of homilies to illustrate Goodness loses its power as literature? We assume wiser readers than this. We also assume readers who realize that literature cannot be sharply separated from consideration of ethics any more than it can be divorced from an awareness of beauty. We assume readers who know that both written and oral communication is the man himself and that "no amount of practice in composition courses will draw anything but a cheap style out of a cheap person." [11]

We need no prescriptive maxims in our study of values in the classroom. All we need is awareness of the experience of the human race. Any belief that man is manipulated solely by his environment or by a blind fate contradicts the inner consciousness of the healthy segments of humanity. Any mode of thought that reduces man to the status either of a machine or of an animal, any mode of conduct that uses man as a means to an end, is an affront to his essential dignity. The literature we teach offers numerous studies both of harmony—Cather's Neighbor Rosicky, Eliot's Dolly Winthrop, Dickens' Joe Gargery—and discord—Macbeth and his wife, Huck Finn's father, Madame Defarge. Literature gives an illumination to the study of values which prescriptive maxims lack. So too do the methods we use to teach that literature and the ways we devise to help students gain power over language.

[11] Howard Mumford Jones, *American Humanism* (N.Y., Harper, 1957), p. 91.

A student may gain some of his most valuable insights into the meaning of "respect for the individual" through six years practice in the *form,* not necessarily the *content,* of discussion. Here as teacher and pupils practice the courtesies of disagreement, the student can acquire the attitude of welcoming opposition to his own ideas, a sense of responsibility for expressing minority opinions, a realization that he can preserve his integrity while at the same time maintaining respect for the person whose values he cannot accept.

After students have had some experience with discussion techniques, a teacher may stimulate thinking by giving out copies of questions, for *reflection only:*

> Has opposition to one of your pet ideas ever given you fresh insights which caused you to modify your opinions?
>
> Is there anyone you know whose values differ greatly from your own but who, nevertheless, commands your respect?
>
> Can you remember any time when your integrity forced you to voice an objection or to support an opinion although it would have been "safer" and more pleasant to keep still?

Occasions when students may be allowed some choice occur often in our classrooms. Through a sequence of experiences similar to the following, students, practicing decision-making over a six-year period, can assimilate the ideas that freedom has limitations; that it carries its own responsibilty; that a degree of freedom is possible for all only when controversial issues are settled in disciplined ways.

Recently, a student teacher of thirty-five eighth-graders helped them plan a mural which was to culminate a unit on poetry. From the preparatory work for the mural to its completion, the principle of choice operated. These young people were being involved in consideration of ethical and esthetic values without, of course, being burdened with the distinction—without, in fact, hearing *value* mentioned.

Early in the planning they saw that choice has practical limitations, that the size of a mural is dictated by the spaces available; that, in turn, its size and placement bear a relationship to the number and the size of the illustrations. They preserved their *right of dissent* while they saw personal choices subjected to the will of the majority, as poems and symbols sponsored by different individuals were eliminated.

They considered esthetic values as they decided what effect the color of the walls would have on the color scheme chosen for the mural, as they evaluated rough over-all sketches submitted by volunteers, as they weighed the significance of symbols to choose the one best expressing the literary experience, and as they reluctantly eliminated poems whose essence would be distorted by visual representation.

Finally, they considered ethical problems as the teacher helped them choose the type of contribution each could make. Patiently, with skillful questions on the day of final choice, the teacher led the class to see the difficulties and requirements of each type of work—abilities needed, probable amount of time demanded, necessity for working as an individual or as one of a group, the inevitable deadlines. Wisely, she postponed decisions to give students time to determine what they had to offer and how much time they were willing to give. Setting the class to work, she provided time for conferences with those asking for guidance. The choice was important to all, for it was personal and irrevocable; each student realized his obligation to complete the work he chose as his contribution.

To understand both what we can and what we cannot expect to do with our students, we need to consider how young people discover values. Many elements in one's background and environment assume significance—home, friends, church, school, community, all aspects of the culture of which one is a part. Influences in one area may fortify or nullify those in another. Thus classroom experiences must, if they are to have any effect, generate cumulative force over the six secondary school years. Commendable traits cannot be implanted directly in another; personal values are built slowly over a long period of time out of the totality of individual experience.

Our purpose is to teach students the considerations involved in making wise choices, not to teach them the choices that must be made. Translated into terms for the classroom, our purpose is to give students continued experience in appraising the effect of different beliefs on conduct and the influence of habitual conduct on the destiny an individual creates for himself. Our purpose, if understandings are to bear fruit in behavior, is to place the student as often as possible in situations where he is allowed to make his own decisions and where he must assume responsibility for the choices he makes. Such a program throughout the six secondary school years, although it cannot insure volition, does provide the necessary practice and understandings. It takes much traveling in "goodly states and kingdoms" to discover for oneself even a few of the Whys of living.

Selecting values for emphasis

If we keep in mind just what we can do in helping students discover values, we may be less reluctant to come to grips with the problem in the classroom. We realize that the emphasis on free choice within the American culture militates against imposing, even if we would or could, any particular values; we realize too that the condition of freedom itself offers the most compelling argument for education for choice. Yet even in our society, which encourages wide deviation in thought, we find a certain community of belief and, especially, widespread approval of the values inherent in democratic practices. During recent years we have seen several important statements of values which might be emphasized during twelve years of public schooling:

Humanist Values in American Culture [12]—knowledge, creativity, experimentation, man as the measure of things, the intelligent ordering of life as based on knowledge, sense of responsibility to self and others, living as an essentially cooperative venture.

American Ideals [13]—human rights and freedoms, equality of opportunity, social responsibility, and discipline.

[12] H. Otto Dahlke, *Values in Culture and Classroom* (N.Y., Harper, 1958), p. 66.

[13] James C. Stone, "A Curriculum for American Ideals," unpublished doctoral dissertation, 1949, a contribution to the American Ideals Project of Stanford University, Palo Alto, Calif.

Moral and Spiritual Values in the Public Schools[14]—human personality, moral responsibility, institutions as the servants of man, common consent, devotion to truth, respect for excellence, moral equality, brotherhood, the pursuit of happiness, spiritual enrichment.

Such statements, which have much in common, are helpful in pointing direction but are too general for direct application to the classroom. However, they do illustrate the extent of agreement possible in our society. That they are stated in general terms merely underlines the necessity for each school to translate them into specifics applicable to its own pupils.

How can such broadly stated ideals be used as guides for learning experiences? Ideally, the teaching staff in each school should determine the focus for instruction in terms of students' needs. In one school where many members of different racial and cultural backgrounds enter the seventh grade, *North Fork,* a novel by Doris Gates in which a boy finds himself a member of a minority group in an American Indian community, is read by all students. Indian-Caucasian relations present no problem in this particular school; thus, the study of such a work provides a not too specific but yet pertinent experience designed to increase understandings among those of divergent backgrounds. *North Fork* is, for pupils of this age, a good literary experience. Moreover, the issues and concepts implicit in the novel point up and reinforce basic values needed at this time by these seventh-graders. Thus, as pupils consider the difficulties likely to be encountered by minorities in any group, the broadly stated ideal "respect for the individual" is translated into concrete terms of particular cogency.

In some such way each school can select content which, while fostering insights that seem necessary for its students at particular times, will still provide a well-rounded experience with literature and communication.

Influence of the curriculum However, too much must not be expected from the teaching of a single book or a single unit. Selection of content for such a specific purpose would represent only one phase of instruction and in no sense should such emphasis dominate the curriculum. The way in which values are discovered, the multitude of choices offered in our culture, preclude such restriction.

Teachers of English desiring to develop a systematic approach to encourage the discovery of values might first choose broad areas for emphasis, then be alert for ways to permit the recognition and appreciation of values to take their appropriate place within the context of literature and communication. A systematic approach will assist the teacher in choosing content. The values needed by students might well be the determining reason for selecting *Great Expectations* instead of *Wuthering Heights,* or for directing written expression to an honest exploration of the difficulties involved in avoiding self-deception or in practicing disciplined ways of settling difficulties. Students

[14] Developed by the Educational Policies Commission of the National Education Association, Washington, D.C., 1951.

themselves provide a guide by their concern with significant values involved in the problems they themselves select to investigate. Both the content and the way instruction is organized contribute to the climate of the classroom and provide the setting for the discovery of values through the study of language and literature.

Influence of the teacher The design of any curriculum represents only a few choices among the multiplicity offered; so too does that of any course within that curriculum. Both present guide lines toward goals the planners think desirable; both direct attention to the general needs of adolescents. Within each classroom, however, the teacher is the motivating force; daily he makes his own choices with particular students in mind. Through his selection of content and method, he emphasizes values; more especially he does so as he reveals his own values in actions reflecting his conviction—or lack of it—as to the importance of using language honestly and of recognizing literature as one of the props which can help man "endure and prevail."

Focusing on values

Since, in providing learning experiences, the content teachers select and the methods they use will influence the effectiveness of attempts to help students discover values, examples of both aspects of instruction follow.

Using the comparative approach The method of teaching two or more selections having parallel themes or points of view often proves an effective way for later discussion of ethical values. For instance, "The Bishop's Candlesticks" by Victor Hugo and "The Rat Trap" by Selma Lagerlöf deal with the redeeming influence of true charity. In the French story Jean Valjean is influenced by a priest who believes in the moral worth of each individual; in the Swedish story a tramp is reformed by a girl who treats him as a human being.

Each story is considered on its own merits, the students being led to recognize its ethical and esthetic elements. After each has been taught, the comparable themes are noted. Perhaps after teaching several selections, the teacher asks, Do you see anything in common between any of these stories? It is from such questions that the focus on the value—in the case of the two stories cited above, the significance of love in helping a person maintain human dignity—can be established.

Selections with parallel themes

Family cohesiveness	*The Happy Journey* Thornton Wilder
	The Car Dorothy Thomas
	The Ten-dollar Bill Richard T. Gill
Unselfish courage	*Granny* André Birabeau
	When Hanna Var Eight Yar Old Katherine Peabody Girling

Need for love and affection	*Yours Lovingly* Eugene Courtright
	Not Wanted Jesse Lynch Williams
	A Mother in Mannville Marjorie K. Rawlings
Scapegoating and human dignity	*The Horse* Marian Hurd McNeely
	The New Kid Murray Heyert
	Prelude Albert Halper
	The Lottery Shirley Jackson
Response to good will	*The Kiskis* May Vontver
	The High Hill Mary Deasy
Integrity	*Glory in Bridgeville* William Wise
	Most Valuable Player D. Tracey

Teaching by organizing experiences around topics or themes is only an extension of teaching by parallels.[15] The same challenge to discern similarities and relationships among selections is present. During each school year a few units of instruction, featuring the particular emphasis desired, may be shaped rather directly toward a concern with ethical values. The illustrative unit "Meeting a Crisis" uses in part this approach.

Using the classics When a teacher is dealing with one of the classics, attention to moral values falls into place among consideration of the many other important facets of the literary work. *Macbeth, The Tale of Two Cities, John Brown's Body*—each exhibits a rich composition of many elements. There is always the danger of emphasizing one aspect to the detriment of the others; there is likewise the danger of examining parts at such length that the unity of the whole breaks down. As a great philosopher has pointed out,

> Every poem is meant to be read within certain limits of time. The contrasts, and the images, and the transition of moods must correspond with the sway of rhythms in the human spirit. These have their periods, which refuse to be stretched beyond certain limits. You may take the noblest poetry in the world, and, if you stumble through it at a snail's pace, it collapses from a work of art into a rubbish heap.[16]

Whitehead's comment concerning poetry is equally applicable to any literary work; the teacher aims first to help students see it as a whole; he avoids overemphasis on either the ethical or esthetic values, trusting that later consideration of both will clarify and intensify first impressions.

However, when the first reading has been completed, the classic may be examined from various points of emphasis; one may well be concerned with the ethical values implicit in its context. Both fiction and drama offer noteworthy examples not only of characters who have values in accord with the ultimate order of the universe—Captain Dobbin, Joe Gargery, Cordelia—but also of those whose lack of unity and harmony creates imbalance in their lives —Becky Sharp, Miss Havisham, Goneril and Regan. Within the limits of litera-

[15] See pp. 284-85 for discussion of this method of organization.
[16] Whitehead, *Aims of Education*, p. 79.

ture it is possible to study values as they are being developed over a period of time; to see what happens when the lives of persons, each governed by fully integrated but conflicting values, impinge upon each other; to understand how a person of soundness and integrity, or one twisted and debased, can influence some lives greatly but have no apparent effect on others; these are all significant ideas for students. Moreover, since the author through his characters presents various philosophies, many literary works permit the selection of key statements expressing ideas pertinent to life; students can be helped to apply these to their own experience.[17] Thus, the complex texture and rich scope of great literary works, if they are wisely selected for the right students at the right time, have an unparalleled force and vitality in their impact upon adolescents.

Using biography For stressing the universal need for a personal code, biography is an excellent vehicle. The idealism of many adolescents leads them to admire excellence whatever its source. Through study of our own leaders of the past and present, students can become aware of the premium our heritage has always placed on moral values. Enlarging that study to include the lives of men and women of integrity who represent diverse origins and cultures will strengthen the belief that no nation, race, or creed has a monopoly on high courage and spiritual stamina. Noble men of all countries, whether Juarez of Mexico, Gandhi of India, or Nansen of Norway, exemplify the desirable qualities all human beings share. Admirable men of various faiths, whether Schweitzer, Damien, or Tensing, command respect. Stories of the lives of real people have for some pupils at certain times a greater impact than do stories of imaginary characters; for all students, biography is a necessary complement to fiction. Especially is this true in focusing on moral values which flourish regardless of boundary lines.

Using guided reading Experiences planned in connection with the guided reading program offer opportunities for consideration of problems concerning values.[18] In organizing topics for discussion for readers of many diverse works, teachers can sometimes select rather restrictive questions which will channel attention toward the decisions and judgments that are made.

Any question similar to the following offers an appropriate guide for groups of five or six students who have read different titles:

Select one situation in your book in which a character must make a decision that will affect someone else. How does he act? To what extent does the knowledge that others will be affected influence his decision?

Find an incident in your book in which a person either fails to live up to one of his ideals or fears that he will fail. How does he respond in this situation? Why?

How many examples can be found where a character is confronted by a

[17] See "Applying the Ideas," p. 249.

[18] For discussion of the guided reading program, see pp. 292-94, 627-30.

situation in which two rights are in conflict, making a completely satisfactory solution to a dilemma impossible?

Discussions of this type can lead groups to explore and appraise many different kinds of behavior and the similar and contrasting values which motivate each.

Using problem situations By presenting problem situations and by encouraging students to make appropriate decisions, teachers can approximate the conditions under which individuals learn through making actual choices. Reactions to such situations can touch adolescents deeply only if problems seem real and responses honest and valid.

Such questions as the following are not easily answered:

If a group project breaks down, what is my personal responsibility? Should I do more than my share even if another shirks?

What is each participant's responsibility to the group? What is his responsibility to himself?

Suppose he disagrees with a decision?

Suppose he is uninterested?

How should the group react to one who is shirking responsibility?

Films, magazine illustrations depicting conflicts, flat pictures such as those in the Focus collection[19]—any of these may elicit sufficient interest to initiate the exploration of a problem through discussion, writing, or role playing.[20]

Once presented, a problem will need clarification. Teachers can encourage students to review what is known about the persons involved, the issues facing them, the prevailing feelings and attitudes. The next step is for students to suggest solutions; much give-and-take occurs when classes are divided into small groups to allow for exchange of opinion and for exploration of the effect of different courses of action. Productive too are assignments requiring each class member to examine the conflicting motives, predict probable outcomes, and select an appropriate solution. Role playing, if students learn to share the feeling of the roles they assume and if reversal of roles allows them to compare the contrasting feelings resulting from differing circumstances, is especially effective with junior high school pupils.

Whatever the form of exploration, the culmination of the experience should represent an evaluation of the solutions considered. In role playing, for example, both the cast and the audience should examine the validity of the different solutions, the effect of each on the attitudes and actions of the characters. Similarly, in following up composition and group discussion assignments, the teacher can provide opportunities for students to share and evaluate ideas; selected papers can be read, or representatives from each group can join an informal panel discussion of the probabilities involved in each situation. Whatever means the evaluation takes, students should have had a

[19] *Focus on Choices Challenging Youth,* A Discussion Kit, National Conference of Christians and Jews, New York.

[20] See pp. 143-44 and 446-47 for discussion of role playing.

chance to see the ramifications of the problem and be left to draw their own conclusions; we must refrain from trying to impose ours.[21] We have to trust to our faith not only in the power of reason but in the capacity of human beings to display, more often than not, the qualities that make them human.

ESTHETIC VALUES

Since the laws of harmony form the basis for esthetic as well as for ethical values, the two cannot easily be separated, nor is it desirable that they should be. However, just as we may, for purposes of emphasis, concentrate in our teaching on the ethical aspects of the art of living, so too, by directing attention to aspects of beauty, we can help students understand some of the principles underlying the esthetic experiences that enrich life. The aim here, therefore, is to suggest a simple framework within which esthetic values may be studied in their own right.

Selecting values for emphasis

Few adolescents are indifferent to beauty. Even less than anyone else do they wish to be told that they are homely, that their voices are unpleasant

"Sea shells, lady?"

Drawing by George Price; Copr. © 1933 The New Yorker Magazine, Inc.

or their teeth crooked. Like all human beings they respond to music, color, pageantry, dancing; they prefer some kind of law to chaos. The problem is not to initiate an awareness of esthetics but rather to educate their discrimina-

[21] See pp. 453-54 for a specific illustration.

tions. Here, the aims of the teacher, quite simply, fall into two parts: to increase awareness and, by clarifying standards, to decrease confusion.

How do teachers include these desirable aims in their teaching? How, aside from transmitting by contagion their own aliveness and balance, do they teach these esthetic considerations to their pupils? In general, one acquires a taste for the best in the realm of esthetics in somewhat the same manner one establishes habits which foster ethical values. Both develop slowly; both demand discipline of the intellect and the emotions; both require continued evaluations—in experiences of gradually increasing complexity—of models of the excellent contrasted with the inferior. Here, as well as with the ethical, if students are not to confuse verbalizations of acceptable standards with genuine appreciation of the esthetic qualities of life, time must be allowed for internalization and synthesis. Esthetic values cannot be implanted directly in another any more than can the ethical; both are highly personal, growing out of the individual's experience.

Although this entire book is intended to describe the strategy of teachers who exalt vitality and disciplined control of that vitality, this section will feature a special emphasis on esthetic choices. In the paragraphs that follow, experiences to support the two aims of *awareness* and *orderliness* are described.

AWARENESS

To be aware, to be vitally alive, is one of the most important of all choices, an essential ingredient of all productive living. It is what Lucinda Matlock had, what George Gray lacked. Erich Fromm, in a context dealing with ethical values, writes, "Man is gifted with reason; he is life being aware of itself." [22] It is this awareness of living that teachers want to help students cultivate as a base for the esthetic values.

In *Our Town,* when Emily determines to return to life for a day, the dead urge her not to choose one of her happiest days. "No," says one. "At least, choose an unimportant day. Choose the least important day of your life. It will be important enough." At the close of that return visit, Emily says, "I didn't realize. So all that was going on and we never noticed. . . . clocks ticking . . . and Mamma's sunflowers. And food and coffee. And new-ironed dresses and hot baths . . . and sleeping and waking up. Oh, earth, you're too wonderful for anybody to realize you." It is then she asks, "Do any human beings ever realize life while they live it—every, every minute?" And the answer is. "No. The saints and the poets, maybe—they do some."

Beauty of the everyday To make students aware, to lead them to realize and to respond more fully to the beauty of life as it exists around them, is the first aim of the teacher concerned with esthetic choices. This aim implies a concern first of all with the everyday experiences of life, with new-ironed dresses and the feel of a baseball smacking snugly into a mitt. Too hasty a preoccupation with Brahms, Dante, or Cézanne can be as disastrous for an

[22] Erich Fromm, *The Art of Loving* (N.Y., Harper, 1956), p. 8.

adolescent as can a ride on a bicycle for a two-year-old child. The foundation for appreciating art lies first in a heightened awareness of the wonder and beauty of the familiar.

The teacher plans an initial lesson based on one of the many poems celebrating delight in the familiar things of life; depending upon the age and abilities of the pupils, the choice of poems ranges from "Autumn" by Emily Dickinson and "A Vagabond Song" by Bliss Carmen in the seventh grade to passages from *A Stone, A Leaf, A Door* by Thomas Wolfe and "Pied Beauty" by Gerard Manley Hopkins in the senior high school.

The students prepare a list of everyday pleasures they have appreciated; these are grouped into categories—sights, sounds, odors, tastes, physical feelings, emotional satisfactions, etc. Committees representing each category prepare free verse catalogues of pleasures.

Individuals read aloud appropriate passages, such as "I Hear America Singing" by Walt Whitman or the dramatic lines from Emily's celebration of life in the final scene of *Our Town*.

The class concludes the series of lessons by reading "God's World" or parts of "Renascence" by Edna St. Vincent Millay.

Audio-visual materials to support the theme of familiar beauty are numerous:

"Begone Dull Care"—color and line take momentary shapes before merging into new forms.

"Nature's Half Acre"—time-lapse photography portrays nature's way with birds, plants, and insects.

"Ansel Adams, Photographer"—nature studies, insightful portraits, and examples of industrial design reveal the beauty of the everyday aspects of life.

"And Now Miguel"—the film on which Joseph Krumgold's Newbery Prize novel for young people is based uses camera techniques which point up esthetic values in familiar things.

Beauty in the arts We can make our students aware of some of the esthetic principles underlying all the arts. At the very least we can help them understand how artists in every medium, stimulated by their environment, select and organize elements of their intellectual and emotional experience to create moments of beauty accessible to all. In addition we can perhaps encourage our more sensitive students to educate their eyes, ears, intellects, and emotions, in order to respond more fully to the vision of experience the artist provides; to cultivate awareness of the arts as a chief means of clarifying and interpreting individual experience.

Discussion arising from the study of Helen Keller's essay, "Three Days to See," forms an effective bridge from awareness of the beauty of the everyday to sensitivity to the beauty revealed by the artist.[23] A bulletin board for which students collect material featuring the sculptors and painters mentioned in the essay provides initial stimulus for increasing awareness. An appropriate quotation for the bulletin board taken from the essay might be:

[23] A recording of this selection and of the poems mentioned is available on *Many Voices* (N.Y., Harcourt, Brace, 1958).

> Artists tell me that for a deep and true appreciation of art one must educate the eye. One must learn through experience to weigh the merits of line, of composition, of form, of color. If I had eyes how happily I would embark upon so fascinating a study! Yet I am told that, to many of you who have eyes to see, the world of art is a dark night, unexplored and unilluminated.

A committee of students interested in the visual arts may agree to keep the display "up to date"—to search for illustrative material, to call attention to local art exhibits and expertly illustrated articles in magazines, and, finally, to preserve the most effective material in a scrapbook to be used with future classes.

To underscore Helen Keller's awareness of beauty and its meaning, permit students to choose one musical recording to which they are to listen as if they are to be struck deaf thereafter; call attention to some esthetic element of the music—its variations in tone color, its appropriate rhythms, its diversity within a pattern, and so on.

Play recordings of poetry or prose read by an expert reader. Good choices are "To Helen" and "The Bells," read by Alexander Scourby, or Ullman's "Behind the Ranges," read by Arnold Moss.

Audio-visual materials:

"The Photographer," to emphasize the principle of selectivity.

"Art in Our World," to stress environmental sources of inspiration to artists.

"Art and Motion," to show how artists make use of motion in painting, mobiles, camera techniques.

"The Rime of the Ancient Mariner"; occasional animation and camera techniques give movement to reproductions of the Doré engravings used to accompany the reading of Coleridge's poem.

Since awareness is based on intellectual curiosity and imaginative insight, both essential for the balanced individual, we need to do all we can to help young people develop these characteristics. J. Christopher Herold, editor-in-chief of the Stanford University Press, in commenting upon the danger of passivity says, "Without an active imagination there can be no curiosity, no sympathy or love, but only passive acceptance and complacency. And these are the true dangers to our civilization." [24]

ORDERLINESS

The second aim, to decrease confusion by clarifying esthetic standards, is to foster the search for order and harmony that goes on in every life. The universal yearning for a dynamic order partially explains why adolescents like to dance; the fluid movements of the body are patterned; there is the same vitality under control that we recognize in the music of Mozart and in the poetry of Shelley or Pope. This wonder of form inextricably interrelated with meaning is also what the teacher wants students to achieve in a written essay or in a panel discussion; it is what delights all who sincerely enjoy Frost's "Stopping by Woods on a Snowy Evening" or Debussy's "Images."

Absolute chaos is incompatible with life. Upon each fleeting moment in

[24] Quoted by Charles Einstein, San Francisco *Examiner,* May 3, 1959.

the flux of experience, impulse, habit, or reason imposes some kind of order; automatically, we organize, into some coherence and form, the multitudinous impressions constantly impinging upon us; at the very least, *conventional* patterns of response are essential to bare existence. This need for order is so insistent that it represents a danger to productive living; one who is to live creatively for himself and for society must maintain a precarious balance between too little and too much. A highly organized society has its rewards and its penalties. At the one extreme, the individual, either because he is resentful of any conformity or because he is unable to so order his personal experience as to give meaning to his life, may settle for anarchy and confusion; at the other, he may accept a rigid order, often not of his own making, as the ideal pattern. Students need help in developing two concepts concerning the role of order in the art of living: order as necessity and order as controlled vitality.

Order as necessity Students are aware of the manifestations of order within the school—the requirements for graduation, the scheduling of classes, assignment of rooms, regulations governing behavior in the halls, in assemblies, on the playground. They are also aware of the need for order within each classroom if learning is to take place, although the teacher must help them first recognize and then maintain the balance between too much rigidity and too much flexibility. A school so organized as to permit students to have a degree of genuine participation in determining some of the regulations that come within their province—and they are as wise as are adults in recognizing what that province is—makes a real contribution to the development of the individual. It gives the student the opportunity not only to understand the necessity for order but also to realize that segments of his life are within his own control if he develops the necessary wisdom and volition. The English classroom so organized as to permit some choice within the limits of the curriculum is making a similar contribution. As teachers we have a responsibility to help students discover that the need for order inherent in human nature is manifested in all aspects of living.

Using Pope's line, "Order is heaven's first law," as a theme, the teacher elicits examples which support the idea; appropriate questions will insure a wide variety of illustrations:

Order in nature

Movements of the planets, seasons, tides, darkness and light, heart beat, breathing, waking and sleeping, planting and harvesting. . . .

Man-made order

Dictionary, telephone directory, arrangement of books in a library, of parts of a book, and so on.

Traffic regulations—streets and highways, water and air routes, train and bus schedules.

Organization of events—track meet, golf tournament, crowds at a football game, preparation for a school dance.

Business—newspaper, grocery store, cafeteria serving counter.

The recording "Rhythms of the World" dramatizes the universality of order.

With an opaque projector the teacher shows pictures of order and disorder in a wide variety of situations: store windows, traffic jams, landscaping, flower arrangement, architecture, advertising, clothing; inclusion of photographs of children abandoned in squalid homes and of the shambles in which certain eccentrics live will be helpful for later emphasis on the relationship of disordered thinking to living. These pictures can be related to an example of disordered writing similar to the following:

"Do you know of any *personal* reason why she might want to leave home?"

Drawing by George Price; Copr. © 1938 The New Yorker Magazine, Inc.

For a competive sport, fansy diving is wanna most difficult for a Boy. I have notice lotsa kids shiver when they Get near the bored and he ain't cold on such warm days as we had last summer the sun was so hot that you could scarcely help but *boil* an egg if we hapen to drop it on sidewalk. My sister says that when I dive, I have manage to poise perfectly. You were always in danger of making a flop the diver takes three steps up the Board and then they made a final leap, she says a diver hasta be born with a sense of balance. Not that anyone cares. The water—the French call it *L'eau* and there are some who say aqua *however* Bud who is my pal from Bodal, a town near where they give watermelons *away* free everry Fourth July is the best competer in all kindsa sport, including diving, which is my favarit.

Next the teacher shows several examples of clear, ordered writing, if possible from compositions the students have recently written; he identifies outstanding illustrations of unity, coherence, and planned emphasis.

A series of lessons similar to these will help students assimilate the idea that order is a necessity of life, not only for a society but for an individual as well.

The teacher helps students relate outer disorder to inner imbalances which enervate human beings; for this purpose, fictional characters are most useful in furnishing commentary on problems of personal living. Junior high school favorites like *Lou Gehrig, A Quiet Hero,* and mature plays like *Craig's Wife* and *Death of a Salesman* chart the distance between order and confusion in the art of living.

Discussions centering upon the price individuals pay for confused values may grow out of the study of any literary work depicting a character whose lack of inner order creates his failure to find satisfaction in human relations: Many of Ring Lardner's stories—"Haircut," "I Can't Breathe," "Travelogue"—feature a character whose penalty for inability to appraise action in terms of standards is the confusion in which he lives.

Literature the students have studied earlier in the year and in previous years, as well as examples from the guided individual reading, should be recalled to support the concept.

> In junior high school, *Only Child, Johnny Tremain,* and *Bennett High* are novels suitable for this purpose; Scrooge in *A Christmas Carol,* the bogus duke and king in *Huckleberry Finn,* and the launch thief in *Smugglers' Island* are characters whom some pupils know and in whose lives the unfortunate results of confused values can be demonstrated.
>
> In senior high, some students may be familiar with the sons of Wang from *The Good Earth,* Eliza Gant from *Look Homeward, Angel,* Willy Loman from *Death of a Salesman,* Alice Adams from the novel of that title, Captain Bligh from *Mutiny on the Bounty,* and Clyde Griffiths from *An American Tragedy.*
>
> In these discussions, the appeal to ethical standards need not be introduced; the uncertainty of lives out of balance, in contrast to those that achieve equilibrium, is sufficient ground for instruction; like lopsidedness in a deformed tree, imbalance in the art of living may be viewed as an esthetic flaw.

An assignment to follow such discussion might be to locate in newspapers and magazines accounts of persons whose failure to make distinctions in the realm of values has plunged them into trouble. One tenth grade class brought in clippings concerning teen-age groups who crashed parties to which they had not been invited. The students found no difficulty in X-raying the protests of one delinquent who asserted he had a right to "protect" himself when the father of the young hostess tried to expel the intruders.

With junior high school pupils, films are effective for conveying the values of a well-ordered life; "Make Your Own Decisions" and "Understanding Your Ideals" are two short films dealing with the ingredients of that personal harmony that characterizes self-reliant, psychologically mature individuals.

Order as controlled vitality Order, to be effective, must be flexible and vital, not mere routine which dulls the senses and deadens response to life. It is this vitality, expanded in striving toward self-fulfillment and controlled by intelligence, that we would wish for our students. Although it is in the contemplation of great art that we can most easily recognize an ordering of forces which intensify and clarify experience, we can create such moments in our everyday existence. Irwin Edman, discussing the universality of esthetic principles, writes, "So far from having to do with statues, pictures, and symphonies, art is the name for that whole process of intelligence by which life, understanding its own conditions, turns them to the most interesting and exquisite account." [25] Literature is the most powerful ally of the teacher's own disciplined vitality in helping the student acquire sufficient discrimination among values to use this noblest faculty and thus to turn more and more conditions of life to exquisite account.

All literature can in some way enlarge and enrich the idea of the need for a vital order; a few examples:

The Scarlet Letter, a novel showing the restrictions imposed by society and the effect on two persons reacting differently to the impact of those restrictions.

"Mending Wall," a poem which presents the dangers of routine patterns of reaction, either due to ignorance or indolence, which evade the need for independent thinking.

Macbeth, a tragedy depicting the effects of the overthrow of order both on the state and on the human personality.

Acquiring discrimination in awareness and in appreciation of the characteristics of a necessary but flexible order requires a series of experiences growing in depth and breadth over a long period of time. A carefully planned program of the six years of secondary school should give students both a basis for evaluating the multi-hued facets of life and a realization of the significance of the esthetic qualities which enrich one committed to the search for harmonious living.

Focusing on values

The English teacher has an important role to play in directing pupil attention to the critical aspects of esthetic merits in literature, for this is an appreciation few achieve on their own but that can be cultivated through able instruction. Although critical analysis, concerning itself with gradually deepening complexities, is needed, appreciation is never a wholly conscious process. Also necessary is what Thornton Wilder calls "the admiration of a series of admirable examples—a learning that takes place in the subconscious." And, Wilder adds, "Beware of what you admire when you are young." [26] Appreciation for what is best in literature evolves most surely from a careful developmental program beginning in the first grade with, for example, *East of the Sun and West of the Moon* and building toward *Ethan Frome* in grade twelve or *Victory* in junior college. Through such a program, the teacher identifies and illuminates two important esthetic standards: the concept of form in the literary work and the concept of the integrity of the literary artist.

[25] Irwin Edman, *Arts and the Man* (N.Y., W. W. Norton, 1939), p. 10.

[26] Quoted by Ross Parmenter in "Novelist into Playwright," an interview with Thornton Wilder, *Saturday Review,* Vol. 28, No. 7 (June 11, 1938), p. 11.

FORM IN THE LITERARY WORK

Students need help to see that all elements of a literary work of art are combined into a design conveying balance and wholeness. This is not a matter solely of technical elements—climax, rhyme, or point of view; it most certainly does not rest primarily upon mechanical identification of narrative devices, sonnet patterns, or figures of speech. It includes also recognition of the balancing and unification of human feelings, ideas, and attitudes. Form is the organic relationship of many elements—emotions and ethical values as well as symbols and foreshadowing; teaching these esthetic elements of form requires attention to the harmony of the total artistic structure. The examples below illustrate form in fiction and poetry.[27]

Fiction Because of the length and complexity of most novels, it is often difficult for students to see the total design; however, even readers inexperienced with this literary form can be taught to recognize some of the esthetic elements. Such recognition, gathering force as different fictional works are studied, finally results in the ability of synthesis—the appreciation of individual factors culminating in an understanding of the logic of the whole. Two novels, the first usually recommended for the tenth grade and the second for the eleventh or twelfth, have been selected for analysis.

Silas Marner

The unusual passivity of the central character, comparable, as far as significance to the plot is concerned, to an axis around which the events revolve. Things happen to Silas; he does not make them happen.

The balancing of various elements around that center.

- The simple humor of the village characters, contrasting with the deadly seriousness of Silas.
- The gold and the child, each serving a twofold purpose:
  - As a link between the two main groups of characters, because of Dunstan's theft and Godfrey's child.
  - As a symbol of a way of life, one leading to the stunting of the human spirit; the other, to happiness and fulfillment.
- The sincerity and wholesomeness of Dolly Winthrop, contrasting with the hypocrisy of William Dane.
- At a deeper level, the pervasive influence of these two characters as essential links in the account of a human being's gravitation between isolation from mankind and integration into the community of man.

Even these few understandings will give students some feeling for literary form on a significant level.

Ethan Frome

The harmony existing among

- The characters—dignified, inarticulate, repressed.

[27] Answers to questions on "The Necklace," p. 452, should lead to an understanding of form as it is achieved in this short story; a discussion of form in drama can be found on p. 406, in the *Macbeth* unit.

The setting—grim, barren, bleak.
The events—inexorably tragic.

The story

Told, without sentimentality or emotionalism, by an observer remote from the actual happenings.

Given body and vitality as details are gleaned gradually from Herman Gow and Mrs. Hale, each revealing an individual interpretation of the events.

Given dramatic compression in recounting events spanning a generation by the use of the flashback technique.

The crushing irony of the climax, making the ending unexpectedly dramatic.

The unadorned style, as stark and uncompromising as the events it describes.

No false notes are struck in this literary work; it is a particularly effective vehicle for teaching the combination of all esthetic elements into a seemingly inevitable design.

Poetry With poetry, as with other literary forms, an understanding of artistic entity grows slowly, from pleasure in the rhymes of *When We Were Very Young* to deepening appreciation of the complicated tensions and organic structure of the great poems of the English language. We cannot hurry this process in our students, even if we would; we can, however, nurture its growth. We teach poetry on the secondary level by a constant use of concrete examples; in the early years we use poems requiring little or no analysis, trusting to the lure of rhythm and rhyme, story and sentiment, to create a desire for more. Starting in the tenth grade, or perhaps with sensitive ninth-graders, and still working with many individual poems rather than with explanations of the mechanics of poetry, we can begin to help students inductively build the foundations for an appreciation of esthetic form.

Lord Randal

For immature pupils, the ballad permits an effective introduction to the study of organic form in poetry. The following procedure has been used successfully with *Lord Randal.*

Reading of the poem to the class by the teacher with any discussion necessary to make the details of the ballad clear.

Second reading of the poem.

Perhaps a comparison of the impact of the ballad with that of a hypothetical news item based on the facts given.

The study of organic form presupposes that pupils have at least slight knowledge of some of the individual qualities that characterize poetry—rhythm, rhyme, clarity of image, precision of language; with appropriate questions the teacher will help students discover the artistic structure of the whole:

The story

A dramatic moment, revealed entirely by dialogue, presented in five steps without the customary devices of explanation and transition used in narration.

The transitions effected by form: rhythm, rhyme, repetition; the first four stanzas composed of questions and answers; the last by statements, but with other elements keeping the form consistent with that of the other four.

Compression and precision gained by selectivity and economy of concrete details.

The movement

Within the stanza, rapid in the first two lines but slowing in the last two; within the whole, not a steadily flowing smoothness but five successive waves as the pause between stanzas provides a slight break in momentum.

The significance of variations in the last stanza

Because the mother has led the reader, almost without his being aware, to make the same series of inferences she herself has made, the finality of statements in contrast to questions gives a sense of completeness. "I'm sick at the heart" replaces "I'm weary wi' hunting." Why sick at the *heart?* The answer is in the poem.

Encouraging speculation on the true love's motive, or probing for reasons to explain the mother's ready suspicion, is a mistake because it takes us outside the poem.

The emotional response

Evoked by the tension and balance of all elements, emotion mounts gradually from the first seemingly commonplace question to a realization of the hints at tragedy in those that follow; the irony of the situation is made explicit as the young man admits that his spirit as well as his life has been destroyed.

Final reading of the ballad—always necessary after attention has been directed to its parts—gives students an opportunity to synthesize intellectual and emotional response and restores the poem to its significance as a literary experience.

INTEGRITY OF THE LITERARY ARTIST

The study of the artist's integrity profits from negative examples as well as positive models. The corrupt brightness of much that appears in print, if it is to be seen for what it is, requires the searching ray of light a teacher can provide; the ways in which some authors violate their material in order to spawn situations and manipulate outcomes to attract readers deserve attention. The inconsistencies of these writers are such that they can echo an easy morality about the unimportance of material possessions, yet reward their heroes with unexpected inheritances or their heroines with contrived marriages to wealth. In their books simple causation is substituted for multiple causation, and life's most difficult problems yield to simple formulas. By comparing the excellent with the inferior, teachers can help students appreciate integrity as an indispensable quality of the literary artist.

Study through literature Through comparisons of the author's method of expression with that which might have been used by one less skilled and less conscientious,[28] and through demonstrations of consistency among the various elements of a literary work, teachers can help students acquire respect for the integrity of the writer. This quality of genuineness announces itself in freedom from clichés, stock characters, easy generalizations evoking stereotyped responses, non-sensory prose strait-jacketed into conventional metrical patterns—all those devices by which pseudo-literature seeks to contrive stories and poems to entice the reader. The genuine artist, in contrast to those writers

[28] For examples see pp. 363-64.

whose sole aim is to exploit the shifting demands of the market, seeks to give us the image of life that stirred his imagination, and is uncompromisingly patient and exact in devising the best form to capture this inner world he attempts to shape into artistic expression. The exactness of the descriptions and their use for more than one purpose, the inevitability of action, the relationship among all the elements of the literary work—character determining plot, setting establishing mood, rhythm fortifying meaning, diction evoking the associations required by the content—all this economy of means combines to create the esthetic pleasure we find in literature.

Study through guided reading However, the desire to choose the writer of integrity in preference to his opposite is not an easy one to foster in a culture where sensationalists rate as top favorites among authors. Repeatedly in specific works we can direct attention to instances where integrity is maintained or where it is violated; repeatedly we can demonstrate, compare, and contrast, to the point of exhaustion; but if students themselves do not read widely enough to give an appreciation for the best a chance to develop, the seed falls on stony ground. It seems fairly obvious that nothing but a developmental program in guided individual reading, where the literature studied is supplemented by intimate acquaintance with books of all kinds, can insure for as many young people as possible not only recognition of the importance of this standard of integrity but also its acceptance as a guide for personal living. Only such a program permits the student to see the relation between the principles of literary art taught in the classroom and their presence or absence in the books and television programs he selects for himself. The non-reading television addict will readily admit that the ease with which the slim young detective, surprised by several husky thugs, fells them with a series of knock-out punches, finishing the performance slightly disheveled but still intact, is incredible. But what of it?

Another aspect of the problem of helping the student make the connection between integrity in art and integrity in life deserves mention; here the ground is treacherous. What of the integrity which excludes from the classroom all portrayals of violence and sordidness except those stamped with classical approval? Of the too rigorous control of books students are allowed to read for "credit"? Charles Calitri, in a discussion of this problem, writes,

> Until we can allow a boy to come to us with *God's Little Acre* saying "Can I read this?" and nod to him, suggesting that his report answer the question, "Why did Caldwell put the word God in the title . . . and what does he say about man's relationship with God?" we must silently suffer the knowledge that he is going to read that book anyway, hidden, on his own, with no chance of guidance and with no opportunity to see past the sordidness and the perversion of the life of the people it depicts.[29]

[29] Charles Calitri, "Macbeth and the Reluctant Reader," *English Journal,* Vol. 48, No. 5 (May 1959), p. 260.

Is this a plea to provide students with the strongest fare they can take? Certainly not. It is a plea for a realism in the classroom which will enable teachers to help students understand life; it is a plea for the wisdom of discrimination in guiding the reading of the sensitive young girl and of the boy who, at first hand, already knows more about the seamy side of life than his teacher ever wants to learn. Certainly, it is not the business of the English teacher to suggest to adolescents books which parents will be horrified to find their children reading; neither is it his business to ignore the books known to be passing surreptitiously from locker to locker, from desk to desk. Impartial examination of such books with the help of a wise teacher dissipates the lure of the forbidden and lessens the possibility of the young reader's gaining a warped impression. If not all teachers are wise, one can only point out that this dilemma has been raised before.

> If we were to suspend all religious activities until we found the perfect leaders, churches would soon close; if we were to suspend all medical activity until we found perfect doctors, the death rate would rise alarmingly. Complete mastery may well be an idealistic goal of our instruction; happily it has never been a prerequisite to teaching.[30]

In senior high school the dissection of an unworthy novel has been used to establish many important touchstones of good taste. In some communities, the teacher has planned the lessons in advance with parent groups and school administration; in other schools, mature teachers have presented for student organizations dignified reviews of salacious books students are known to be reading. In many classrooms, the problem is handled through individual conferences or through discussion in small groups. Whatever the method chosen, avoidance of sanctimonious horror and assumption of reasonable maturity on the part of students can do much to establish a situation in which principles of esthetic judgment become clearer.

In the junior high school also, where the comic book is much more likely to need the attention of the teacher, direct attack and condemnation will do less good than an examination of the *varying* quality among the comics. Teachers of seventh-graders have used a study of literary supermen—Hercules, Paul Bunyan, Stormalong—as a springboard for analysis, first, of favorite comic strips and then of favorite television programs. In suggesting books as likely competitors for more stereotyped fare, teachers should remember that

> Books must be easily accessible in classroom libraries, frequently changed.
>
> Books assume importance when the teacher gives them a central position in the curriculum, providing time for discussing and sharing the enjoyments of reading.
>
> Books must be supplied in sufficient variety to appeal to the interests of the individual reader and satisfy some of the needs that draw children to the comics. For many young children, such books as *Homer Price, Box Car Children, Smugglers' Island, Henry Huggins,* have proved effective lures. For slower readers, *The Five Hundred Hats of Bartholomew Cubbins, Mr. Popper's Penguins,* and *Deep Sea Adventure* have been keys to turn the lock.

[30] Robert Hogan, "Education for Wise Choice," *California Journal of Secondary Education,* Vol. 33, No. 4 (April 1958), p. 240.

One eighth grade class keeps a large scrapbook called "Distinguished Books"; each page is fifty inches high and twenty-five inches wide; at the top of each page is the title of some book enthusiastically recommended by a petition signed by at least five members of the class. Only by petition can a book acquire enough fame to be listed, and each entry must include a review of the book written by the petitioners. After a book has been chosen, each pupil who reads it adds his comment, being careful not to reveal elements later readers should discover. In the course of several years, the pages for such books as *No Other White Men, Ginger Pye, Little Vic,* and *On To Oregon* fill up and become the reading guides for new groups of eighth-graders. The teacher often chooses a superior book like *Call It Courage* and compares it with some weaker title for such esthetics as naturalness of conversation or growth of the main character during the course of the story.

Whatever means the teacher provides for sharing the pleasures of reading—book courts, panels, discussions, written recommendations—if he takes every opportunity to focus attention on such basic esthetic qualities as originality of humor, consistency of character delineation, inevitability of action, use of description to contribute to plot, he will be helping pupils acquire effective standards for judging integrity in literature.

The need for integrity in the writer and belief in the indestructibility of the qualities that make men human have never been more eloquently stated than by William Faulkner in his speech accepting the Nobel award for literature. Expressing his desire to share the acclaim accorded him with "all those who work not for glory and least of all for profit, but to create out of the human spirit something which did not exist before," he contrasts such writers with those who write "not of the heart but of the glands." Teachers have used, with mature classes, these quotations as a theme for a final review of literature, as students recall the literary works they have studied and the books they have read in an effort to illuminate the ideas with specific examples. Testifying to his faith in the nobility inherent in humanity, Faulkner charges the literary artist with the responsibility for helping man nurture the best that is in him:

> I believe that man will not merely endure: he will prevail. He is immortal, not because he alone among creatures has an inexhaustible voice, but because he has a soul, a spirit capable of compassion and sacrifice and endurance. The poet's, the writer's, duty is to write about these things. It is his privilege to help man endure by lifting his heart, by reminding him of the courage and honor and hope and pride and compassion and pity and sacrifice which have been the glory of his past. The poet's voice need not merely be the record of man, it can be one of the props, the pillars to help him endure and prevail.[31]

The essence of the help we can give the student in discovering values, both ethical and esthetic, lies in our ability to create in a six-year program a sequence of learning experiences which may foster integrity in communication and a desire to explore the vast resources of language and literature. We can

[31] Reprinted in *Saturday Review Reader,* Vol. I (N.Y., Bantam, 1951), p. 68.

only trust that such experiences, providing some choice and much evaluation, will make him somewhat wiser in the decisions he makes outside the classroom, where the most crucial tests come. With a faith in the invincibility of the human spirit equal to Faulkner's, we must believe that although the effect of our influence is rarely revealed to us, the help we give may tip the balance away from a life as disillusioned and futile as that of a George Gray toward one marked by the vigor, the fortitude, and the high purpose of a Lucinda Matlock.

The Consequences of Character

A Unit for Grade Twelve

Overview: The study of a long literary work by a class heterogeneous in intellectual and esthetic potential often proves an unrewarding experience for many students. The answer to the problem need not be a single novel aimed at either the best readers or the average; nor need it be a program depending entirely on guided reading to meet individual needs. One solution may be found in teaching several novels to groups of varying ability; another, in the study of a work offering insights on several levels of appreciation. With the latter, however, unless the work is comparatively short, allowing the teacher to present the most difficult parts orally (see the unit on *Macbeth*), appreciation on even the most elementary level proves an unrealistic goal for some students. An incompetent reader may gain from the discussions based on the ideas in the literary work; he misses direct experience with the literature.

This unit illustrates the use of both recommended methods. Conrad's *The Secret Sharer* (others used have been *Ethan Frome* and *The Old Man and the Sea*) offers on the lowest level of awareness the suspense and excitement of plot; it gives more capable readers an opportunity to appreciate ramifications of theme, and insights into symbolism and irony. The study of different novels in groups allows the student enough intellectual and esthetic stretching to stimulate growth.[1]

MATERIAL REQUIRED

The plan requires three groupings of material: a fictional work long enough to show character development and to increase understandings of novelistic techniques; six or seven novels from which the groups may make selections; many novels for individual reading. The guided reading program, always important, is essential here

[1] See Margaret Ryan, "Achieving Unity with Diversity," *The English Journal*, Vol. 40, No. 10 (December 1951). This article describes the method in greater detail, using different material.

to provide additional materials for the faster readers. A simple diagram helps a class comprehend the organization.

The plan has the following advantages:

It allows the teacher to adapt the learning experiences to the abilities of the students, to provide for the gifted and the less competent.

It allows the teaching of each novel as a distinct experience; therefore, the temptation to distort the literary work to fit a preconceived theme is eliminated.

It can be used even if the teacher decides to omit any unifying ideas in the various novels selected, allowing each group to be concerned with only one novel.

This unit, therefore, is designed to give the teacher help in teaching any form of literature by groups; in preparing a novel for teaching; and in helping students see relationships among literary works of the same genre.

The plan suggested here may sound formidable to the inexperienced teacher; the amount of preparatory work required for teaching one class for a period of four to five weeks may seem unjustifiable. The answer to such objections is simple; the beginning teacher should not attempt it. He should postpone its use until he has had time to experiment with the method—perhaps trying it first with short stories or essays in several classes—and until experience with teaching several novels has provided a backlog of study guides which can be adapted to particular groups within a class. Since the guides are designed to help students discover the values the teacher discerns in the literary work, they may be used with slight change for successive classes. Often, members of English departments in large schools build up a central file of such guides; a single English teacher in a small school can gradually collect his own. Many novels printed as texts for high school use include study questions which can be adapted for this purpose. The inexperienced are reminded also that the guided reading program must be well under way before the teacher can be freed to teach several novels concurrently.

AIMS

To understand and appreciate a particular novel; to increase awareness of devices used in fiction; to see how the writer's purpose influences form in relation to content.

To realize similarities and contrasts among literary works.

TIME: APPROXIMATELY FOUR WEEKS

LAUNCHING THE UNIT

The Secret Sharer

Purpose: to develop awareness of possible levels of meaning in a literary work; to become more familiar with novelistic techniques.

■ *Reading for the story*

1. A brief introduction by the teacher, stressing Conrad's fascination with the sea and the East as settings for his stories.
2. Reading of approximately first ten pages aloud by the teacher, followed by discussion to insure understanding of setting and initial situation.
3. Silent reading, with the teacher available to answer individual questions as students finish the story.
4. Writing in class the next day on one of these topics:

Throughout the story the captain links himself with Leggatt, stressing they are both strangers on a ship with which all other crew members are familiar. Would *The Two Strangers* serve as well for the title as the one Conrad chose? Why or why not?

Who is the protagonist, the captain or Leggatt? Give reasons for your answer.

■ *Individual study*

1. Divide the class into four groups and the story into four parts, approximately ten pages each. Allow fifteen minutes for students, working individually, to find in the assigned section as many different ways as they can in which the captain identifies himself with Leggatt; to find any instances where the author implies a similarity between the two men which the captain does not mention.
2. Conduct a discussion leading students to see points of comparison.

■ *Group study*

Divide the class into heterogeneous groups, each to explore the answers to questions similar to these:

1. Explain why the author makes
   - the captain see Leggatt first as an indistinct form, then as a man without a head.
   - the fugitive first to appear "as if risen from the bottom of the sea" and at the end disappear into the sea again. (Why is the reader not allowed to see him reach land?)
   - the fugitive come and leave under cover of darkness.
   - the captain provide a sleeping garment rather than a daytime suit.
   - the captain insist Leggatt take his (the captain's) hat.
2. Consider these two statements:
   - "None whatever" (p. 41) *
   - "And suddenly I rejoiced . . . singleness of its purpose." (p. 21)

   What literary device do they illustrate? Are they both on the same level of significance? Why or why not?
3. Review the ending:
   - Why does the reader never learn the name of the captain?
   - Why was it "a matter of conscience" for the captain to "shave the land as close as possible"? (p. 52) Why did he think Leggatt would be able to understand this feeling? (p. 54)
   - Why, at the end, is attention centered on the captain and his ship?

* Page references are to texts listed on page 646.

Compare these thoughts of the captain:

About himself— "Nothing! No one in the world . . . the perfect communion of a seaman with his first command." (p. 55)

About the fugitive— "A free man, a proud swimmer striking out for a new destiny." (p. 56)

■ *Final synthesis*

Without trying to provide categorical answers and without making conclusions a matter for testing, the teacher leads the class to discern relationships among plot, possible themes, the irony, and the possible symbols.

■ *Final paper*

Choose either subject:

One critic has called *The Secret Sharer* "a powerful *fable* of the *mystery* man must *know* and *master* before he can . . . *save himself from himself*." [2] Explain, paying particular attention to the italicized words.

If you have changed your mind since writing your paper after the first reading, or if you can more fully substantiate the opinion expressed then, use the subject chosen at that time for your paper.

DEVELOPING THE UNIT—THE STUDY OF NOVELS IN GROUPS

■ *Choosing the novels*

1. Bring into the classroom sets (ten to fifteen copies) of six or seven novels on different levels of ability; introduce the novels to the class, telling something of the nature of each and its degree of reading difficulty. Tell students that no more than five, preferably four, groups will be formed. (More than five prolong the study unduly—bad for both the class and the novel.)

2. Allow time for students to examine the novels and to make a choice. Place titles on the board, leaving space for students to write their names under each as soon as they have reached a decision. The groups need not be equal in size; often it is worthwhile to teach a difficult novel, or an easy one, even though it is suitable for only a small group. Usually at the end of the hour enough interest in two or three novels warrants forming groups; let those in groups too small to be maintained take other novels overnight and reconsider their decisions.

3. Allow students to change. Those with a novel much too difficult offer no problem; they will "not like it" and will change quickly to another. Those with a novel too easy will usually change to one more suitable to their ability if they understand the purpose of the group study and if their first choice is accepted as part of their individual reading.[3]

In one class in which this plan was used, *Vanity Fair* was chosen by the more able students; *Rain on the Wind*, by the least competent; *Great Expectations* and *The Bridge of San Luis Rey*, by two more heterogeneous groups. These four novels, as studied in this class, will be used to illustrate the method.

■ *Preparation of novels for teaching*

In preparing a novel for instruction, the teacher must first decide what values the work offers both as an artistic achievement and as a record of human experience.

[2] Morton Dauwen Zabel, *The Portable Conrad* (N.Y., Viking, 1947), p. 607.

[3] Occasionally as the work progresses, fast readers may wish to join a second group. Such interest should be encouraged.

After such an analysis he then selects the emphases most meaningful to his students, assigning priority to the elements most essential to foster appreciation and including as many others as time and the particular group allow. He calls attention to these points in a study guide to help students discover significant aspects of content and forms as they read. Both aspects of preparation—analysis and study guide—will be illustrated.

1. Analysis of a novel: the most difficult of the four novels has been chosen as an example.[4]

Vanity Fair

The *subject* is the world of well-to-do Britain at the beginning of the nineteenth century—a world seen in terms of specific human relationships among characters placed in concrete social situations.

The *central problem* concerns marriage and the difficulties of personal relationships in marriage at this time and in this society.

The *method* is "panoramic," in that Thackeray surveys a broad field and does not allow the reader to get "inside" the characters; the reader knows all about them although he is not directly involved in their feelings. The term panoramic misleads if it suggests anything of the documentary or implies that the characters are not important.

Plot and Development of Major Characters

Becky and Amelia complement each other—the one, "bad" and active; the other, "good" and passive; their careers parallel each other in contrasting curves of development—Becky's low at the beginning, then gradually rising, but falling again at the end; Amelia's, the opposite.

Becky	*Amelia*
Childhood of poverty; despised position at Miss Pinkerton's	Protected childhood; apparently idyllic childhood romance with George
Disappointment over failure to get Jos to propose; governess at Queen's Crawley	Bankruptcy of old Mr. Sedley; break with George enforced by his father
Marriage and prospect of happiness with a reformed Crawley; failure to effect a reconciliation with Miss Crawley	Marriage, and fright at how little she means to George
"Affair" with George, Becky's most pointless cruelty	Prostration over George's death; slavish devotion to an unrealistic image of the late "saintly" George
Living in grand style on "nothing a year"; affair with Lord Steyne	Life of self-abnegation in lodgings with her parents and her little boy
Descent into a Bohemian life of degradation	Loss of son Georgy to old Mr. Osborne
Depredations on Jos	Return of Jos and Dobbin; reunion with Georgy; re-entry into society
Final equivocal re-entry into society as a "reformed" woman	Awareness of past selfishness toward Dobbin, marriage

[4] Courtesy of Robert Holloway, Cubberley High School, Palo Alto, Calif.

Thematic Relationships

PRINCIPAL CHARACTERS

Becky	*Amelia*
In Becky is satirized the vanity of the social climber; for her nothing exists *but* social position.	In Amelia is satirized the vanity of romantic love, for whose practitioners social class and position are at most delightful obstacles to be overcome.
Becky, seldom mistaken about a person's character or motives, always falls prey to her crucial defect of the heart.	Amelia, often fooled about character and motives, is able to redeem the most flagrant errors through her generous sympathy.

Many readers feel that much of the novel's interest stems from the vitality of Becky. Amelia after fifteen years of self-deception certainly cannot be expected to command our unqualified sympathy. Becky wins not our approval but a certain human fellow-feeling; a woman of spirit and intelligence, she rebels openly and consistently against a life of subservience. She uses systematically all the weapons society has reserved for men, plus a few of her own; her way leads to moral degradation. Amelia, "the little parasite," chooses the way approved by society; she is rewarded at the end, but not until even Dobbin sees her as she is.

Thackeray's tone is ambiguous: Is he pronouncing a moral judgment? Does he approve of Amelia? Is he condemning Becky? Or is he presenting two women, both products of their individual temperaments, characters, backgrounds, social environments?

Are the themes of the novel applicable only to the early nineteenth century?

Is the novel primarily, as has been said, "a comedy of manners" or an exploration of human nature?

MINOR CHARACTERS

Through these the author: *Satirizes particular vanities*—Jos, person and dress; Miss Crawley, "enlightened" free thinking; George Osborne, "gentlemanly honor"; old Mr. Osborne, dynastic ambition—"family tyrant"; Mr. Sedley, commercial ambition; Dobbin, excessive humility. *Praises particular virtues*—Dobbin, personal loyalty and steadfastness to an ideal; Colonel O'Dowd, faithfulness to duty; Mrs. O'Dowd, kindliness; Miss Briggs, personal loyalty.

Possible Symbols

Thackeray is not a "symbolic novelist" but passages similar to the following may be suggested as having a significance beyond or aside from the immediate revelation of character or exposition of plot.

The "Dixionary" episode. Spurning this book, Becky not only expresses her resentment of Miss Pinkerton but foreshadows her rejection of life in the subservient position of a woman who must earn her own living.

The frontispiece representing Isaac and Abraham in the family Bible from which old Mr. Osborne strikes his son's name. The symbolism here is ironic—

Abraham was reluctantly ready to sacrifice his son to God; Osborne sacrifices George merely to Mammon and his own angry pride. (p. 233)

The "great funereal damask pavilion in the vast and dingy state bedroom" which serves as Amelia's bridal chamber—note especially *funereal* (p. 264). The symbolism is again ironic—Amelia had envisioned her love match as a thing of sweetness and light, quite apart from the sordid cares of mankind; however, the weight of commercial motives entering into a marriage contract, even though defied by George, makes itself felt in this image.

The pastoral pictures Amelia paints and tries to sell may be taken as types of the romantic conception of love with which she still deludes herself; the paintings, significantly, are unsalable.

Becky's secret desk in which over the years she hides money from Rawdon may be suggested as a symbol of that inner core of her being which is never touched and which never participates genuinely in any ennobling human relationship.

Historical Background

The years covering the novel are especially eventful; one might consider them as showing, broadly, a movement toward democracy within nations and self-determination among nations.

2. Study guides: The teacher trusts to a guide to do some of his teaching for him; these guides, in the method suggested here, are divided into no more than five parts, each part representing a segment of the novel and each used as the basis for one discussion. Since the time the teacher can spend with each group is necessarily limited, the guide will include more points than can be discussed. In this way attention is called to significant details requiring little or no explanation but which careless readers might overlook.

Here are four excerpts from the complete study guides covering the four novels chosen by the students. These particular segments have been chosen to show different aspects of the study of any novel.

1) The first, for *Vanity Fair,* is included to show the teacher's attempt to translate his understandings of the values of the novel, as shown in the analysis, into questions which will lead students to discover these values for themselves.

Vanity Fair

First Discussion—Chapters 1-14

What purposes do you see in the "Dixionary" episode?

Contrast Becky and Amelia in as many ways as possible. What do they have in common?

Although each treats her differently, Becky reacts to Miss Jemina and Miss Pinkerton in the same way. What purpose may the author have in presenting this? What are Becky's reasons for her actions?

Analyze Becky's technique for ingratiating herself with persons she wants to impress. How does this work for and against her?

What were the consequences of Dobbin's victory? Do they seem logical? Why or why not?

Chapter 11 introduces Bute Crawley and his wife; what impression do you get of each?

What seems to be the attitude of Becky and George toward each other? Support your opinion.

Can you find any evidence of irony in Chapter 12? If so, at what or whom is it directed? If not, what is the purpose of the chapter? What does Thackeray mean (p. 112), "This was not . . . time should come." Why use *good* three times in one sentence?

Why were Becky's tears *genuine*? (p. 144)

Be prepared to comment on the following quotations:

"Say a bouquet . . . genteel." (p. 1)
"All the world . . . of his own face." (p. 9)
"Are not there . . . rest of the history?" (p. 49)
"I'm a liberal . . . my own station." (p. 57)
"Whatever Sir Pitt . . . disguise of them." (p. 68)
". . . there is always such a lady in a coach . . ." (p. 70)
"And, as we bring . . . which politeness admits of." (p. 79)
". . . and if Harry the Eighth . . . this season?" (p. 81)
"Miss Crawley . . . made her beloved anywhere." (p. 85)
"And it's to this man's son . . . unchristian." (p. 101)
"She's faultless . . . play for it." (p. 117)
"Whenever he met . . . Briton can do." (p. 123)

Notice the references to historical and social background, pp. 8, 52, 61, 82, 111.

2) For *Rain on the Wind* the guide for the third discussion has been selected. For the reluctant reader the middle section of a novel often represents a crucial point. The teacher, by taking time to review significant past happenings and to stress more explicitly details which foreshadow future events, may rescue the discouraged and create greater zest for completing the reading.

Rain on the Wind

Third Discussion—Chapters 10-14

In clarifying the situations covered by the following questions, the teacher may need to review these points from previous discussions:

Attitude of the people of Connemara toward Mico's birthmark
Peter's interest in helping "the poverty stricken"
Effect of Peter's injury on the other characters
Attitude of members of the family toward Tommy and Mico
Attitude of Tommy and Mico toward each other

Why did Mico choose the life of a fisherman? Why didn't he quit when he discovered it wasn't always romantic and adventurous?

In Chapters 9-12 Gran and Peter are put "out of the running" because each can no longer function as he used to do. Both men voluntarily remove themselves. Is there any similarity in the reasons each gives himself for quitting?

Why does Gran announce his retirement in the way he does? Does he deceive Micil? Mico? Does he think they are deceived? Give reasons for your answer.

In Chapters 10-12 how does the author build suspense and concern in the reader for Peter? When does the reader know definitely there is something wrong with Peter? When does Peter know?

Why does Micil propose to take Mico to see Uncle James? What special reason does Mico have to want to go?

Has the author prepared the reader for the family quarrel centered around Tommy and Mico? Do the members of the family act as you would expect them to from the events in Chapters 1-3?

Can you account for the mysterious boat in Chapter 14? Why does the author have Uncle James think he sees Coimín in the boat? How has the author prepared for the way the other fishermen interpret this story?

Be prepared to comment on the following quotations:

"It was the way . . . no cure for it." (p. 145)
"Money never did . . . you stand with it." (p. 149)
"Like accepting the fact . . . would be eternal." (p. 150)
"Maybe they even thought . . . relaxed limbs." (pp. 152, 153)
"Times had changed . . . things like granite?" (p. 154)
"Why, oh, why, . . . out loud." (p. 171)
"There was so much . . . of it all." (p. 175)
"So much he could say . . . on Tommy." (p. 179)
"It doesn't do . . . from a fist." (p. 184)

3) The next two partial guides prepare for the final discussions of two novels of contrasting patterns. Dickens through novelistic techniques presents a closely woven tapestry in which recurring motifs are important; Wilder, on the other hand, depends upon a stark undergirding structure to create the basic design.

Great Expectations
Final Discussion

Examples of the devices used to weave plot, characters, and themes into a unified whole.

Developing mystery and suspense

Pip's fears of what will happen, p. 13.
The stranger with the file, p. 73.
The pain Estella was to cause, p. 78.
Jaggers at Satis House, pp. 78, 79.
Pip's realization of why he made Biddy a confidant, p. 92.
Wemmick's telling Pip to notice Jaggers' housekeeper, p. 193.
Estella's troubling resemblance to someone, p. 228.
The stranger crouching on the dark staircase, p. 313.

Developing characters and themes

Pip's feelings of guilt and remorse
 Stealing the food, p. 14.
 Being ashamed of his home, p. 102.
 Providing the iron with which his sister is injured, p. 116.
 Rejecting his home and Joe, pp. 139, 311, 404, etc.
 Undeserving his wealth, p. 238.
 Being responsible for Magwitch's possible capture, p. 328.
 Being "misremembered" after death, p. 408.
 Intending to desert Magwitch, p. 442.
Gentlemen and working men—the rich and the poor

Joe and "his honest old forge"
His contentment with his lot, pp. 67-68, 142.
His explanation to Pip of "common," p. 67.
His reaction to Miss Havisham, p. 96.
His burning the identure papers, p. 141.
His pride, pp. 143-144.
His constraint with Pip and his understanding of their relative positions, pp. 214-215.
Pip and his life of ease
Reference to the rich man and the kingdom of Heaven, p. 141.
First deference shown him by Trabb and Pumblechook, pp. 145-147.
Herbert's unrealistic ideas of gaining wealth, pp. 175-176.
Pip's belief his money was not good for him, p. 261.
Magwitch's telling Pip that one man's hard work enables another to become a gentleman, p. 307.
The rich and the poor before the law, pp. 335-336.
Pip's content with his life at the end, p. 462.
Pip's need for the security and love parents can give
Pip's forming his impressions from the engravings on the tombstones, p. 1.
Pip's rejection of his sister as a suitable parent, p. 59.
Pip's connecting Magwitch's footsteps with those of his dead sister, p. 302.
Magwitch's claiming him as a son, p. 307.
Pip's rejection of dependence on Magwitch, his preference for a lifetime of work at the forge, p. 328.
Pip's realization that Magwitch is Estella's father, p. 391.
Pip's final understanding and acceptance of Magwitch.
Pip's relationship with Joe.

Any novelistic devices the teacher thinks important for a particular group would be referred to in appropriate places in the study guide and reviewed after the completion of the novel.

The Bridge of San Luis Rey

Final Discussion

Exploration of the relationship between form and meaning

Does the use of parallel episodes add or detract from the impact of the novel? Explain.

Analyze the role of the Abbess in the novel—her relation to plot, characters, themes.

Do the five who die have anything in common? Do any of those who remain after the tragedy—Brother Juniper, Don Andres, Alvarado, the Abbess, the Perichole—have anything in common?

Explore the meaning of the comments Wilder makes about:

literature and the readers of literature, p. 15; the art of biography, pp. 108, 109. Are these comments particularly relevant to this novel? Why?

Does Wilder *directly* answer the question the novel poses? If so, what is his answer? If not, why doesn't he? Does he suggest a solution, complete or partial, to the difficulties which cause human beings to ask the same question?

How are the separate stories linked to create a unified design?

Writing

1. As the novel is being read: It is essential that reading and clarification through discussion should continue at the fastest pace the group can maintain while at the same time acquiring the necessary understandings; however, some novels are longer or, even if shorter, more difficult than others; individuals within each group will also differ. Therefore, the writing program should be flexible:

The same number of writing assignments need not be given to all groups. Under ordinary circumstances, those reading *The Bridge of San Luis Rey* should finish before other groups do; the teacher and students must decide whether writing or some of the reading and discussion activities suggested will be more profitable.

Writing experiences (suggested by topics from the study guide) should be brief; [5] the teacher's purpose is to probe for deeper meanings suggested in the novel, not to teach particular writing skills. Those students who have difficulty maintaining the pace set by the group should not be asked to write.

2. After the reading has been completed: An essay to which students bring all their skill in interpreting the novel, in organizing, and in precise expression, serves as a good culminating and evaluative device. Students should have time for preparation (see time schedule) before writing the final draft in class; they should have some choice as to topic—one, where understandings developed through the discussions will enable them to do an acceptable job; another, which demands insights the discussions may have touched upon but have not fully probed. Examples of both kinds of topics follow:

Vanity Fair

Thackeray says his novel is without a hero; has it a heroine? If so, who is it? Define "heroine" and substantiate your opinion. If you think the book contains no heroine, why do you think so? What might be the author's purpose in writing a novel without a hero? With neither hero nor heroine?

Conrad in *The Secret Sharer* is concerned with an individual's struggle to attain maturity. Does any one of the characters in the Thackeray novel embody the same struggle? If so, who? Explain. If not—since *Vanity Fair* covers a considerable portion of the life span of his characters—why does the author omit such an important aspect of individual human development? Give evidence to support whichever point of view you choose.

Rain on the Wind

Is it characteristic of Mico to burst in upon Mauve unannounced? Why does he go out into the storm in his boat after his visit? Why does he finally turn back? Does this final episode in any sense epitomize his life? Give evidence from the novel to support your opinion.

Compare Mico and the captain in *The Secret Sharer* as to the essence (not the detailed events) of the total experience of each; does Mico in any sense have his Leggatt too? Explain.

Great Expectations

You will remember we agreed that *gentleman* used today in a complimentary sense means "a man of fine feelings or instincts—irrespective of social position and

[5] See the writing assignments for *Macbeth,* pp. 410, 412.

training—as shown by his behavior and especially by his generous consideration of others." Select the character in the novel that best exemplifies these qualities; give specific examples to support your choice.

Compare Pip and the captain in *The Secret Sharer* as to the essence of the total experience of each; does Pip in any sense have his Leggatt too? Explain.

The Bridge of San Luis Rey

The *major* theme of the novel concerns "the justification of the ways of God to man." Is this statement true or false? If true, support your belief with evidence from the novel; if false, state what you consider the theme to be and provide evidence to support your opinion.

In *The Secret Sharer* the captain says, "I wondered how far I should turn out faithful to that ideal conception of one's own personality every man sets up for himself secretly." Apply this statement to any one of the principal characters of the Wilder novel, showing what the ideal conception is, the obstacles hindering its attainment, and the final degree of success achieved.

■ *Time schedule*

Each student received a copy of the schedule; another was posted on the bulletin board. The class hour was fifty-five minutes, allowing approximately twenty-five minutes for each discussion. Thus while the teacher was working in one corner of the room with those studying *Vanity Fair*,[6] all others were reading. One student from each group was asked to take care of signing slips, receiving messages—all those "emergencies" likely to interrupt a class.

A glance at the schedule shows the need for thorough understanding of procedural routines before discussions start; a well-established guided reading program with many novels available on various levels; and a class with sufficient experience in assuming responsibility for self-guidance.

Monday	*Tuesday*	*Wednesday*	*Thursday*	*Friday*
Discussion 1 Group 1 * Group 2	Discussion 1 Group 3 Group 4	Reading, discussion, conferences	Discussion 2 Group 1 Group 2	Discussion 2 Group 3 Group 4
Reading, discussion, conferences	Discussion 3 Group 1 Group 2	Discussion 3 Group 3 Group 4	Discussion 4 Group 1 Group 2	Discussion 4 Group 3 Group 4
Reading, conferences discussion,	Discussion 5 Group 1 Group 2	Discussion 5 Group 3 Group 4	Study period to prepare for writing	Final writing

* 1—*Vanity Fair* 2—*Rain on the Wind* 3—*Great Expectations* 4—*The Bridge of San Luis Rey.*

As the above schedule indicates, class time should be allowed between some of the discussions; the slower students may need it to complete the assigned reading; others may use it for writing or for student-led discussions on the books in the guided reading program. The teacher also needs the time—usually to confer with

[6] See p. 459.

absentees, and occasionally to confer with those who may require more help than the discussions give.

■ *Over-all designs of the four novels*

These diagrams, worked out with each group, were used to show the different basic designs; the bulletin board committee—a volunteer from each group—prepared legends, using illustrations from the novel to make the diagram concrete.

Vanity Fair

The author at the core of story—observing, commenting, interpreting—standing between the reader and the characters.

Rain on the Wind

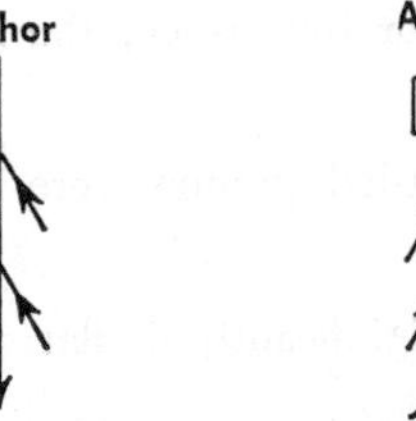

The omniscient author, allowing the reader to "get inside" the characters and thus become involved in their thoughts and feelings.

Great Expectations

The story told through the impression persons and events make on the principal character, allowing the reader to become involved to the extent Pip is involved.

The Bridge of San Luis Rey

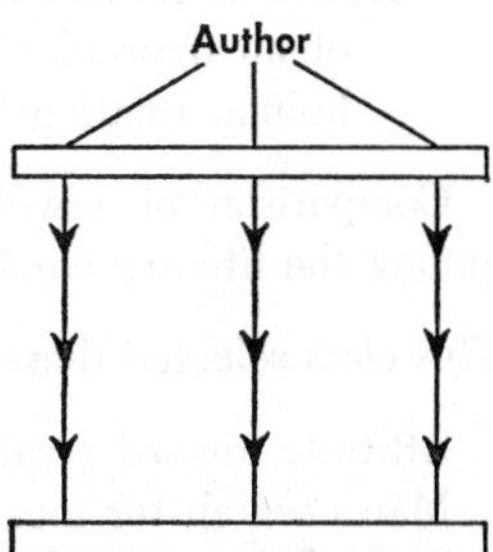

Again the omniscient author, allowing his readers to become involved with his characters but working out his ideas in parallel episodes, linked through characters, events, and themes.

CULMINATING EXPERIENCES

Ideas and characters: Student-led groups were asked to select ideas and characters from each novel, using specific criteria. First, each student, in preparation, was to select the three characters most essential to the novel, and prepare to defend his choice; to select no more than three important ideas the novel emphasizes, submitting evidence to support his opinion. Then, students met in groups to agree upon characters and ideas, a list of both to be handed in. The following were selected: [7]

Vanity Fair
- Becky, Amelia, Dobbin
- Attitude toward social position; effect of social inequalities.

Rain on the Wind
- Mico, Gran, Tommy
- Search of characters for meaning in unexplainable events; need for and difficulty

[7] The problem in selecting ideas is one of elimination, since all of any importance will have been stressed in the discussions; certain characters, too, are inevitable choices, but usually the third and sometimes the second demands a rather close look at the novel.

in attaining maturity; problem of the individual who finds his usefulness at an end.

Great Expectations

Pip, Joe, Estella

A child's need for security and wise guidance in becoming a worthy adult; attitude of the individual and of society toward wealth and social position; the poor in relation to the social institutions of the time.

The Bridge of San Luis Rey

The Abbess, the Marquesa, Uncle Pio

Desire of human beings to discover whether the events in their lives are part of an over-all plan or occur by chance; the need for courage and love in human relationships.

Comparison of novels: Student-led groups were asked to discover similarities among the literary works.[8]

This class selected these ideas as significantly similar:

Attitude toward wealth and social position. (Novels 1 and 3)
Man's search for meaning of the unexplainable. (2 and 4)
The needs and difficulties of the individual in reaching maturity. (2 and 3)
The need for courage and love in human relationships. (Applicable in some respects to all four.)

The class chose these characters as having something in common:

Amelia, Mico, Pip, the Marquesa (Not all the readers of *Vanity Fair* agreed that Amelia should be included.)
Dobbin, Gran, Joe, the Abbess, Uncle Pio
Becky, Tommy, Estella

Final presentations: Students in original groups were to suggest ways of handling the final presentation, their suggestions to be given to a committee to devise plans. This committee made the following decisions regarding final presentations.

A series of oral reports, each followed by contributions from the class:

Two students to compare Pip and Mico in their attempts to achieve maturity.

Two students to present the social climate of the times as represented in *Vanity Fair* and *Great Expectations.*

Two students to present the circumstances in *Rain on the Wind* and *The Bridge of San Luis Rey* which caused the people to ask questions concerning the meaning behind the events.

One student to present the need for courage and love as portrayed in *The Bridge of San Luis Rey,* amplified by illustrations from the books read individually.

[8] The teacher planning to use this method should not try to select literary works which fit a preconceived theme; the important thing is to have novels which challenge each group. The study of each individual work reveals its unique values. Since all are records of human experience, they will have points of similarity—sometimes as basic as here; at other times, relatively minor—which students can discover for themselves (see footnote, p. 631). The probing takes place in the study of each work; recognition of likenesses in the various works should come spontaneously if it is to be worthwhile.

A panel which would consider the characters chosen.

The groups met once more to select members to represent them in the final presentations. The time allowed: two periods for the first four, one period for the panel.

4. For a final assignment, the teacher asked the class to consider all the work that had been done on the novels and to try to suggest a suitable title for the unit. All titles growing out of the ideas discussed were immediately rejected as being too limited. Many concerned with character were considered, but most were eliminated because examples from one or more novels seemed to invalidate them. Finally only two remained—"Character Makes the Man" and "The Consequences of Character"; the latter was selected.

EVALUATION

Evaluation is continual and ways for evaluating are inherent in the methods suggested for teaching.

Teacher evaluation

1. Through discussion—Does the student show increasing ability to detect motives in the actions of characters? Is he growing in ability to see relationships among characters? Is he able to connect the events and characters in the novel with those in life? Is he becoming more aware of the methods and devices used by the novelist to create a unified impression?

2. Through writing—Does the student always select the "safest" topic for writing, the one for which the discussion has prepared him? If so, does he show understanding of the concepts being developed? Is he at times willing to try the more difficult of the two assignments? If so, does his writing show deepening insights into the literary works? How does his final writing on the group novel compare with that done on *The Secret Sharer*?

3. Through comparisons with books read individually—An assignment similar to the following will test the student's understanding of design in the novel:

> Keeping in mind the over-all designs of the four group novels, consider others you have read; does any one conform in general to one of the four designs of the novels studied? If so, give title and author; discuss, showing similarities. If not, explain the design of the novel you have selected.

Student evaluation

Assignments similar to the following (not to be used for grading) will give the teacher some insight into what students think of content and method:

> If such a unit were to be taught to similar classes, should the novel studied by your group be included? Why or why not? From the impression you have gained of other group novels, do you think any one should be omitted? Why or why not?
>
> Do you see any advantages in studying a novel in groups rather than with the entire class? Any disadvantages?
>
> What did you gain, if anything, from the culminating experiences? If you consider your gains slight, why do you think so?
>
> Do you consider *The Secret Sharer* a good novel for high school seniors? Defend your point of view.

EDITIONS OF NOVELS

Paperbound editions were used for all novels except *Rain on the Wind,* which is available only in hard covers. Inexpensive editions of the many literary works continually appearing on the market allow teachers to experiment with fresh material to supplement, or perhaps eventually replace, that already in the curriculum. Thus, a more flexible program can be maintained.

Joseph Conrad, *The Secret Sharer.* N.Y., New American Library (Signet edition), 1957.

William Makepeace Thackeray, *Vanity Fair.* N.Y., Random House (Modern Library, College edition), 1950.

Walter Macken, *Rain on the Wind.* N.Y., Macmillan, 1951.

Charles Dickens, *Great Expectations.* N.Y., Pocket Books, 1956.

Thornton Wilder, *The Bridge of San Luis Rey.* N.Y., Pocket Books, 1955.

Program and Plan

Good planning of many kinds is crucial to good teaching. Without sound planning, instruction is haphazard, and what students learn depends mainly on chance. A basic curriculum pattern for six or twelve years influences many classroom decisions. So too do the requirements of particular courses. Thus, planning of work before students arrive is as necessary as adapting plans prepared in advance to the class that does appear. Occasional lessons may bear little direct relationship to those that precede or follow. Others are integral steps in a developing unit and can be considered only in relation to over-all objectives. It is not possible, then, to predict the sequence in which every teacher will engage in various planning activities. Consequently, the diverse stages of planning are discussed here in separate sections so they will be accessible to each reader as needed: Planning a Six-Year Program; Planning a Year Program; Planning a Single Unit; and Planning a Single Lesson.

Planning a six-year program

Through the directed study of significant values and concepts students grow in ability to receive and to communicate ideas. Increasingly teachers of English are recognizing that a value-centered or idea-centered curriculum contains a basic content which prevents the study of language skill from becoming isolated, apathetic, and sterile. In values and ideas teachers of English find the *content* of their curriculum. As the Rockefeller report on education makes clear,

> Education is not just a mechanical process for communication to the young of certain skills and information. It springs from our most deeply rooted convictions. And if it is to have vitality both teachers and students must be infused with the values which shape the system. No inspired and inspiring education can go forward without powerful undergirding by the deepest values of our society.[1]

If the development of values, the development of understandings, and the development of skills are important parallel goals in our English curriculum, through what organizational framework can these be achieved? The pattern varies with school size and organization, but certain characteristics are common to many programs. Usually the six-year secondary English curriculum includes a balanced general program for all students during grades seven

[1] Rockefeller Brothers Fund, Inc., *The Pursuit of Excellence* (Garden City, N.Y., Doubleday, 1958), p. 49.

through ten, with some literary study, much reading, and considerable work on basic skills of communication introduced in every classroom. Increasingly in later secondary years, however, schools tend to emphasize the study of literature and specialized interests in writing, speech, and dramatics. This basic pattern, illustrated in Chart A, is fairly common throughout America, although little agreement is to be found concerning the titles of courses or the grade placement of books, materials, and other specific learning experiences. A recent survey in the state of California alone revealed 217 separate course titles.[2] Then, too, some schools require only five years of secondary English, with individuals permitted to substitute an elective in drama, journalism, business English, or creative writing during the senior year.

CHART A

A possible organization of the English curriculum in grades 7-12

<table>
<tr><td>Grades 7 8 9 10
General English
Balanced program for all: reading, writing, oral English, spelling, literature; often organized around units of instruction.</td><td>11
American Literature
Emphasis on American ideals. Continued stress on skills.</td><td>12
Special Programs
Advanced Composition
Advanced Literary Study: English, World, Modern
Drama
Journalism
Public Speaking
Creative Writing
Business English
General English for Those Needing Review</td></tr>
</table>

Special Courses for Individuals Available throughout Program

1. Remedial reading
2. Individual speech work, sight-saving instruction
3. Directed reading; library study
4. Exploratory courses for gifted students
5. Special class for the severely retarded
6. English as a second language

Common Variations

1. Core or Common Learnings Programs. English-social studies combinations in grades 7, 8, 9.
2. Some elective courses in grades 7, 8, 9: journalism, drama.
3. Advanced placement programs in grades 10–12.

Grouping in secondary English The requirement that students complete five or six years of English does not necessarily suggest a common standard of achievement for all. Schools have learned to expect great variation of ability in any single group and have attempted to meet those differences in many ways: by providing multiple copies of books and learning materials at varying levels; by sectioning students into average, advanced, and slow-

[2] *English Language Arts in California Public High Schools,* Vol. 26, No. 7 (September 1957), California State Department of Education, Bulletin No. 26, p. 10.

learning classes; by organizing "opportunity" classes for those who need special help or reveal special talents. Many teachers prefer to work with homogeneous classes in which an attempt is made to reduce the range of differences in ability; others just as conscientiously believe that the wide variation in student abilities and the diversity of student backgrounds contribute to learning by providing important experiences in communication between students from all social and cultural groups. For every class the important question to be considered is the educational purpose to be served. On this depends the wisdom or shortsightedness of both rigid and flexible patterns of sectioning. Probably different kinds of sectioning may be introduced to achieve special purposes, but almost surely these should include at times a planned heterogeneity which brings together students with many kinds of backgrounds and abilities.[3] As experienced teachers know, a range of differences in the classroom continually poses a challenge to the ingenuity of teachers, regardless of the type of sectioning used.

Grade level—age level emphases Given some underlying framework, many school programs provide for continuity in student learning by designating skills or experiences for emphasis at each age level or grade level. An over-all pattern gives some guarantee of cumulative learning. Moreover, textbooks normally offer only limited help in identifying and establishing continuing goals. Such books are prepared to assist, not to control, teachers. Only a few years ago Pooley examined eight series of language textbooks and found only two of 179 grammar-usage items to be common to all series and almost no agreement on grade allocation.[4] Clearly the task of providing continuity must be faced in every program.

To minimize haphazard learning, schools use different approaches. From experience and the evidence of modern research beginning with Sir Thomas Galton, teachers know that youngsters in a classroom at any grade level will vary considerably in language proficiency no matter how the students are selected. Consequently, the once familiar pattern of basing an instructional program on rigid grade standards has yielded to approaches which neither restrict the advanced nor penalize the slow. Two examples illustrate this trend.

Emphasis within grade level cycles In the schools of Oakland, California, secondary teachers met for six years with elementary teachers to devise a workable language arts guide for skills to be taught within each grade level cycle: K-3, 4-6, 7-9, 10-12. For each skill to be taught, the guide indicates

[3] Readers familiar with recent sociological studies of education know that rigid sectioning procedures tend to discriminate against students from lower socio-economic groups. See Allison Davis, *Social Class Influences on Learning* (Cambridge, Mass., Harvard U. Press, 1952); Robert Hollingshead, *Elmtown's Youth* (N.Y., Wiley, 1949); Robert Havighurst and Bernice Neugarten, *Society and Education* (Boston, Allyn and Bacon, 1957). Often those who protest against ability grouping do so because they believe that true ability is obscured by our present methods of assessing intellectual power.

[4] Robert C. Pooley, "Language Arts Survey in Wisconsin Elementary Schools," *Elementary English Review*, Vol. 13, No. 1 (January 1946). See the discussion of this point in Chapter 11, "Grammar and Usage," p. 562.

concrete objectives to be stressed within each cycle, as illustrated by Chart B. Exact grade placement of individual items is determined by the teachers in schools of the district, who interpret the framework with relation to their particular class.

CHART B

Example of allocating skills by grade level cycles *

Areas of emphasis for teaching clarity and variety of single-word modifiers

K-3

Develop the use of single-word modifiers to express a clearer, more vivid idea. *Example:*

I see a flower. I see a *pretty* flower.
I see a *pretty red* flower.

4-6

Compose oral, then written sentences by using fresh, vivid picture-making words and by avoiding overworked words. *Example:*

It was a fine day so I got up bright and early. (rather than) It was a *pretty* day so I got up pretty early.

7-9

Use words with sensory appeal. Search for words to express ideas more precisely. *Example:*

A *kind* person (rather than) a *nice* person

Tasty food (rather than) *Good* food

Learn to place modifiers to make clear what words they modify. *Example:*

He found only two errors.
He had eaten almost the whole pie.

10-12

Expand vocabulary to include words with various shades of meanings; to help find the precise word to express an idea. *Example:*

The S.S. United States is an *enormous* ship. (rather than) The S.S. United States is a *monstrous* ship. (Since the ship is not frightening and is not a monster.)

* Adapted from "A Chart of Skills in Written Expression," Rev. ed., Oakland Public Schools, Oakland, Calif., p. 3.

Identifying sequences of experiences Concentrating on the sequence of learning experiences leading toward proficiency in skill or in depth of understanding is a second useful approach. Schools adapting this method identify the steps through which the learner must be guided, often without assigning definite instructional responsibilities to a particular grade or even a particular level of development. A description of a sequence of dramatic experiences from the Florida State Guide illustrating this approach is presented in Chart C. Teachers use such guides to identify ultimate goals and are charged with the responsibility of determining the developmental levels of their own students and planning appropriate experiences. This approach to curriculum planning requires teachers to use sound diagnostic methods to identify specific needs.

Providing for common and diversified experiences A still different consideration in developing a six-year program involves identifying the instruction which all students need in common as well as that possible for the academically advanced or the academically limited. Often this is done with reference to plans for a particular school grade, as in Palo Alto, California, where classes are divided into *A* and *B* sections. In eleventh grade classes in American literature, for instance, thematic emphases are held common for both groups, but certain related sub-themes are taught to particular groups. An example adapted from the course of study is presented in Chart D. Literature selected in relation to the designated themes reflects the abilities of the students. Thus, *A* lane students may approach considerations of "Freedom, Individualization, and Acceptance" by reading *Arrowsmith* and *The Scarlet Letter, B* lane students by reading *The Caine Mutiny* or *The Big Sky*. Like other plans used here as examples, the Palo Alto approach reflects the attempt of English teachers to provide sound sequence and continuity in learning within the context of the great diversity which they continually experience in public school classrooms.

Providing for a balanced program Schools rely on various ways of assuring a sound balance of learning experiences in English. For example, Oakland's identification of areas of emphases for each cycle level helps to avoid unnecessary duplication, as does Palo Alto's identification of concepts to be taught. In like manner, the South Bend, Indiana, English program is organized by units of instruction, with different kinds of units assigned to each grade.

Chart E illustrates the South Bend approach to providing balance in the junior high schools. This chart is given to each new teacher in the system and to curriculum committees above and below junior high. A preliminary statement points out that some units contribute to personal development, some to human relations, some to social and civic attitudes, and several to economic-vocational competence, adding, "While there are several units on each grade level devoted to the enjoyment of literature for its own sake, teachers will find many opportunities throughout all the units for emphasizing pleasure in literature." Such varied fare as is indicated here is characteristic of many two-hour courses in the junior high school which present content from both English and social studies. In a class devoted solely to English, many teachers would not introduce the units on social attitudes and concerns. Many of the units are tentative and experimental; after further trial they may be modified or eliminated. Other units, based upon careful experiences and revisions, are checked as permanent. Through the master chart, grade level allocations are maintained.

An intelligent six-year program provides for continuity and balance from grade to grade, yet permits each teacher sufficient flexibility to care for varying interests and needs. Overly rigid requirements penalize the slow student who may learn language at capacity rate and still be far less proficient than his peers; they also penalize the talented who are often restricted by doctrinaire attempts to enforce minimal learnings for all. Teachers of English are

CHART C

Sequence of development of language skills *

In the following chart an attempt has been made to show the sequence of development of certain language arts skills through kindergarten, elementary, and secondary levels. Because not all individuals reach the various stages at the same age but progress according to their maturity and experience, there has been given no identification of specific stages of development with any particular age or grade group. By visualizing a sequence of development, the teacher can take the child where she finds him, ascertain what stage he is in, and guide him so that he will make the next step successfully.

Sequence in development of dramatic interpretation

Individual or solitary play reflecting life in the intimate home environment: little girl rocks her dolly, small boy drives a make-believe car. Response to music: little child dances to music, responding with whole body.	Dramatic play in small groups, often portraying home, school, and neighborhood relationships: playing house, school, firemen, etc. Beginning of dramatic interpretation of literature by acting out bits of favorite stories or jingles, e.g., Humpty Dumpty climbs up and falls over with much laughter; no costumes, much action, simple objects for properties; little, if any, dialogue, often mostly sound effects. Dramatic response to music: individual spontaneous response to rhythm and mood. Singing games, such as dancing dolls, sleepy flowers, or the Mulberry Bush.	Dramatic play in larger groups, reflecting broader interests: cowboys and Indians, cops and robbers, giving a neighborhood show or circus. Interpreting literature by dramatizing a favorite story: planning, choosing characters, and interpreting the story through that character with some attention to dialogue; a few more properties; still little staging. Dramatic response to music, suggesting circus animals, etc., singing games, and folk dances.	Interpreting literature by dramatizing longer stories, through organization of story into acts and scenes, planning and making simple stage properties, making of marionettes, writing the story in play form, writing original plays as individuals and as group projects, and/or presenting the original plays.

* From *Experiencing the Language Arts,* Bulletin No. 34, Florida State Department of Education, Tallahassee, 1948, pp. 122-123.

learning to expect seventh-graders to arrive from elementary schools with varying capacities and abilities. By the time these students finish six years of secondary English the range of differences should increase. Because of the tremendous variation in students' rates of learning, good program planning and good teaching result in an extension rather than a narrowing of differences in achievement. The examples of six-year programs reproduced here suggest ways of organizing to make such extension possible.

		Cumulative skills
Dramatizing a myth or legend. Dramatizing tense moments in selections read, using dialogue or pantomime. Dramatizing short stories, an episode from a biography. Planning a series of dramatic readings, or a radio script. Writing and producing a play. Producing a long play.	1. Wider range of dramatic interpretation: a. Dramatizing passages from literary selections, such as ballads, plays, novels. b. Dramatizing through pantomime. c. Dramatizing interviews after reading biographies. d. Dramatizing social situations, such as receptions, school dances, teas, introductions, etc. e. Dramatizing conversation at club or home gatherings, demonstrating how to include everyone in conversations, how to incorporate reactions to books, radio, and news of the moment. 2. Refinement of language through presenting a full-length play: a. Improving ability to work through committees; studying plays and reporting to the group; studying costumes, properties, and staging; advertising; selling tickets; preparing programs; selecting ushers; producing the play (prompter, director, etc.). b. Improving ability to work in total group when choosing the play; selecting characters by means of "tryouts"; deciding questions regarding time, place, price of admission, etc. c. Improving ability through individual activities, enunciation, voice modulation, etc., in order to qualify in tryouts.	Observing and thinking before talking or writing. Reading rapidly for what happened. Rereading for sense-appealing words which will assist dramatic interpretation. Learning to read for ear-appealing words, arrangements of sentences, etc. Using card catalog, indexes to dramatic selections, to locate dramatic materials for specific occasion. Using vivid words in the expression of ideas. Interpreting character through appropriate diction, voice modulation, gestures, bodily posture, costume. Using creative imagination, developed through dramatization, to help the individual get along better with the people with whom he associates.

Planning for a year

Just as English departments need over-all curriculum plans to encourage reasonable continuity in instruction, so individual teachers need long-range plans for a semester or a year to set the direction for a class. Some work must be planned in advance, before students arrive; some is best planned with students. But while assessing the needs and interests of particular groups of

CHART D

Example of allocating themes for study by ability groups *

Thematic area	*To be studied by all students*	*To be studied by* *A lane students*	*To be studied by* *B lane students*
1. Freedom, Individualization, and Acceptance	Conflicting forces which limit and extend the freedom of the individual	American Revolution	Acceptance of Self and Others
Representative literary selections:	"The Outcasts of Poker Flat" "The Eagle That Is Forgotten"	Lincoln's Gettysburg Address "The People, Yes" (selections)	*The Caine Mutiny*
2. Moral, Spiritual, and Aesthetic Values	America's attitudes toward nature and life	Puritanism	American Family Life
Representative literary selections:	"Young Man Axelbrod" "Death of the Hired Man"	*The Scarlet Letter*	*Our Town*
3. Opportunity and Success	The Pioneer Spirit	Materialism and Idealism	Finding One's Place in Life
Representative literary selections:	*Giants in the Earth* "Under the Lion's Paw"	*Rise of Silas Lapham*	*So Big*

* Based on material in *English Language Arts Resource Workbook,* No. 2, Grade No. 11, Palo Alto Unified School District, Palo Alto, Calif.

CHART E

Chart indicating areas of pupil needs and English units now available according to grade level *

AREAS OF PUPIL NEEDS	7TH GRADE	8TH GRADE	9TH GRADE
Boys and girls need to discover through reading, discussion, observation, and other experiences those values which are of the most worth	Thinking Straight	Making Choices (Revised)	Propaganda: Its Influences and Techniques
Boys and girls need to understand and use language effectively	Enjoying Poetry	Rhythm All Around Us World Languages: A World of Many Tongues Sensing the Beautiful	Using American English
Boys and girls need to understand themselves and how they are changing	Understanding Myself	You and Your Abilities [2]	You and Your Ideals [1]
Boys and girls need to understand themselves in relation to others	Let's Get Acquainted (Orientation) [2] Patterns of Family Life Learning to Make Friends	Living With Brothers and Sisters Belonging to Groups	Cues for Teen-Agers Teen-Agers and Their Parents Dating Days
Boys and girls need to learn to function in the world around them	My Time and I Manners for Moderns [1] About Owning Property Leisure Time [1, 2]	Work Patterns in a Community (Revised) [2] Money and You Looking Toward High School [1, 2]	My Job and I

The topics listed below have been suggested around which to organize additional new units. We will be happy to have teachers offer to develop one or several of these. Also, we will welcome additional suggestions for new units.

	7TH GRADE	8TH GRADE	9TH GRADE
	Flights of Fancy	Young People Around the World Teachers and Pupils Our American Heritage	Mass Media Humor in Literature Making the Most of Our Opportunities The Study of the Meaning of Words (Semantics)

[1] New units
[2] Required units

* Based on a chart entitled *English Units Available by Grade Level,* South Bend, Indiana Public Schools [undated].

young people, the teacher must consider each course in relation to the total school program, the community setting, and the resources available. The first task of any teacher is to study the context in which learning will occur.

The Total School Program

Is a course of study or guide available?

What is the relation of each class to the total program? To classes which precede and follow?

Are there certain skills or concepts to be stressed in the particular class?

Resources Available in School or School District

What arrangements may be made for use of books, records, and other learning materials?

What services are available from librarians? Curriculum supervisors? Department heads? Counselors? Others?

Resources in the Local Community

What special resources are available in community? Libraries? Theatres? Television stations? Others?

Are there opportunities for worthwhile field trips pertinent to the course aims? For consultant help? For relating classroom activities to the work world outside?

What knowledge about the community will assist in understanding the young people in the classroom?

Involving students in planning Not until the teacher has met and studied each class can detailed procedures be developed. No two groups are exactly the same; general plans formulated in advance must be adapted to satisfy needs, interests, and abilities of each. With over-all purposes in mind, the teacher considers with students their personal interests and needs for improving communication skills.

The attitudes students bring into the English class may be important determinants of what can and cannot be first attempted. Students' interests may suggest problems or topics for consideration. Even when faced with a seemingly inflexible course of study, teachers will encourage greater motivation and involvement if students share in planning some activities. Among the useful approaches are the following:

Encouraging students to express personal concerns. The attitudes of students must be considered in selecting reading material and units for study. Compositions written during the opening days, for example, "Why I Hope This Class Will Be Different," offer one way of assessing predispositions. Some teachers meet regularly with a steering committee of students who are elected to represent class members in planning. Others give each student an opportunity to express his opinion and to help plan class activities by discussing suggestions in total class or small group sessions.[5]

Giving pupils opportunity to choose. If the literature to be studied or the units to be organized are drawn from a preplanned list, students may be asked to

[5] A helpful reference for teachers venturing into cooperative planning for the first time is Louise Parrish and Yvonne Waskin, *Teacher-Pupil Planning* (N.Y., Harper, 1958).

indicate the selections or topics which interest them the most. Choices may be presented within clearly prescribed limits. Thus the teacher explains that the class definitely will study *Abe Lincoln in Illinois*, *Our Town*, and the popular arts in America, but that the reading for the initial six weeks may be drawn either from the literature of the frontier or the literature of social criticism. Before making a decision, students will need time to investigate the possibilities inherent in each choice.

Involving parents in the planning. Teachers can capitalize on the concern parents express by inviting the mothers and fathers to voice opinions. Junior high school pupils may write letters home explaining the nature of a course and asking for comments. Older students may interview their parents. Sometimes classes may prepare a special questionnaire for parents. From the considered involvement of parents in thinking through the objectives of English with their sons and daughters may emerge greater cooperation between home and school.

Diagnosing language needs In a well-organized classroom, diagnosis and evaluation operate continually, but at the opening of a school year the task requires special attention. Detailed suggestions for assessing needs in particular areas are included in appropriate chapters of this book. Here, however, the discussion concentrates on approaches to use during the initial weeks of school before long-range plans are organized.

A helpful preliminary step is the establishment of individual folders in which data on students may be collected. Some teachers summarize information on note cards; others use large envelopes into which clippings and comments may be dropped. On some occasions students may maintain folders themselves; on others the teacher will wish to preserve confidential records. Whatever the method, the teacher needs to

Begin with the type of activity in which the class is involved: If literature is important, assess students' ability to interpret; if understanding of grammatical generalizations is a goal, plan an appropriate task to check the understandings students already possess.

Be specific in diagnosing language needs. Recognize that the primary purpose of large group surveys is to identify first those individuals who may need special study and help. Later diagnoses permit refinement.

Involve students in appraising their own needs. Remember that self-identification of problems may offer motivation for subsequent learning.

The suggestions for evaluation presented at the end of every chapter in this book may be used for diagnosis and continual appraisal. Teachers interested in certain areas need only consult the appropriate section.

Designing the pattern of a course Once the teacher knows the demands of the curriculum, the resources available, and the particular attitudes and needs of his students, he must consider the flow of class activities during the semester or year. Each course must be organized to allow for an intelligent pattern in the study of ideas, for the sustained development of student skills, and for reasonable variety in class activity.

The unifying concept, as the organizing center of study, has many important advantages. It provides for concentration on a few ideas or skills for a period of several weeks. It avoids excessive reliance on day-to-day lessons which, however carefully designed, can lead only to fragmentized, unrelated learning. Most skills and concepts develop slowly over a period of time. A division of long-range goals into objectives which can be accomplished in a few weeks is necessary; those established for the entire semester or year are so broad they must be delimited to have a realistic impact on planning. A unit of work organizes instruction for several weeks around a core of ideas and pertinent activities and includes instruction in all language skills. The unit as a means of organization need not be the sole approach to classroom planning, but its value cannot be overstated.

Kinds of English units A unit may run for a week or for six weeks, depending on the complexity of the learnings. Among the more familiar kinds of units in English, eight may be readily identified:

1. *The thematic*—"Dimensions of Courage"; "Freedom's Ferment"
2. *The topical*—"Boys and Girls in Faraway Lands"
3. *The typological*—"Great Poetry"
4. *The project-oriented*—"Producing a Play"
5. *The skill-oriented*—"Analyzing the Language of Propaganda"
6. *The problem-oriented*—"Making Choices"; "Overcoming Obstacles"; "Foreseeing Consequences"
7. *The study based on a single classic*—"Macbeth"; "Tom Sawyer"
8. The study of the work of an author or of a group of authors—"Mark Twain"; "Six Modern Poets"

Normally, units are organized around concepts and themes presented through literature. Whatever the basis of organization, opportunities are provided for significant experiences in thinking, reading, writing, speaking, and listening. Certain units, such as those that are problem-oriented, may feature more writing than reading. Others, such as thematic units, draw more heavily on literature than on other aspects of English. The reader should also note that the thematic unit, with its sharper focus on a basic idea, tends to be more suitable for senior high school, whereas the topical unit is clearly appropriate for serving the exploratory function of the junior high school.

Values in unit study The unit approach lifts teacher and students above the restrictions of day-to-day planning so that they see present work in relation to past experiences and future plans. Division of the semester's work into several units, each varying in length, permits the teacher to plan a series of related lessons designed to accomplish goals which can be achieved only over long periods of time, such as those involving the development of complex understandings or the refinement of important skills. Moreover, in well-planned units students become so interested in communicating ideas that language instruction may be introduced at moments when learners are highly motivated. Since all the skills—thinking, reading, speaking, writing, listening—are brought into play in a unit, the student's growth in one area of language development tends to reinforce his command in another. Thus the words which he adds to his reading vocabulary during the unit will frequently be used in his speaking and writing as well.

The unit approach offers the teacher a manageable way of meeting individual needs. With the entire class concerned about certain key ideas, each individual can engage in related tasks within his grasp which permit him to contribute to the thinking of the entire class. Even students reading very easy books may discover interesting insights on a problem, insights not reported by other class members. During a unit, projects and activities usually become increasingly diversified to accommodate the interests and needs of individuals and groups. This diversification frees the teacher from immediate responsibilities to guide the entire class; thus he is able to work with individuals. Illustrations of such procedures are included in units in this volume.[6] Finally, a unit lends itself to the emphasis of relationships among ideas rather than to the less challenging classification of information. The brighter student—indeed all students—may profit from this approach to organizing instruction.

Blocking out a year One problem teachers and students must consider early in the year is that of blocking out areas of emphasis. Usually the teacher needs to reserve books in advance, to plan unit-related skill lessons, to arrange for films and speakers; hence an over-all framework is necessary.

Chart F illustrates the plan for a semester's work in one eighth grade

CHART F

Plan for eighth grade English class *

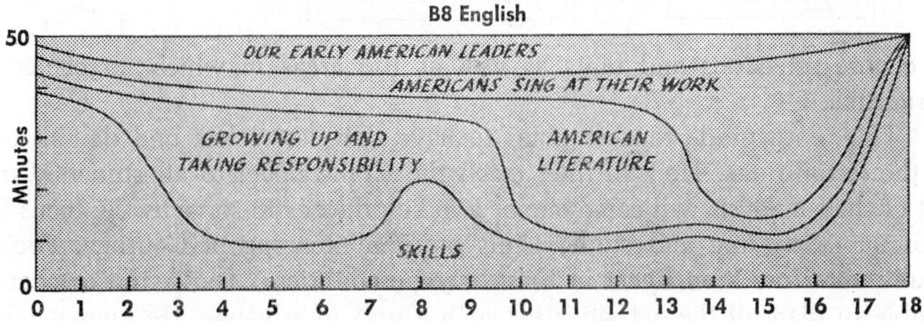

Note: Numbers on the left-hand vertical represent the minutes in the class hour devoted to each topic. The units along the bottom suggest the division of emphasis during an eighteen-week semester.

* From filmstrip "Good Methods of Teaching English," produced by the Division of Secondary Education and the Audio-Visual Section, Division of Instructional Services, Los Angeles City Schools.

English class in Los Angeles. Three major units are studied during the period, although the discussion of the ideas in each unit tends to overlap with the

[6] See the Palo Alto plan, p. 654, and the South Bend plan, p. 655.

others. The chart suggests also that individual reading about American leaders continues throughout the semester. The areas of emphasis are sufficiently broad to permit considerable teacher-pupil planning should the development of class activities warrant. For example, depending upon the problems expressed by students and upon the library selections available, the initial unit on Growing Up could concentrate on moral decisions facing youth, on problems related to the assumption of adult responsibilities, or on similarities and differences in the social situation. The second unit, generally titled "American Literature," is planned as a study of a few standard literary selections, but this may mean *Tom Sawyer* for some groups and "Old Ironsides," "The Concord Hymn," and "Paul Revere's Ride" for others. Language skills are taught throughout the semester as indicated.

One tenth grade teacher blocks out a semester's work for a general class as is shown in Chart G. He identifies those areas where students are permitted

CHART G

Sample plan for tenth grade semester

Lost Worlds Unit
or
Science-Fiction Unit
or
Literature of Travel

Thematic Unit: Developed from reading and discussion of Crane's The Red Badge of Courage. Perhaps a further analysis of courage, war, crisis.

Poetry

Julius Caesar

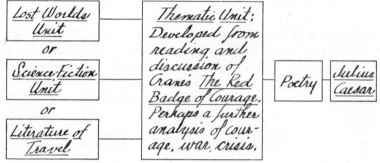

to choose selections and units as well as the areas in which no choice is permitted.

This tenth grade teacher plans to have the class select and delimit one of the initial units. He will then teach the Crane novel to all students, and out of their analysis will come one or two key themes to serve as the focus for subsequent reading and study. Units on The Meaning of Courage, Facing Reality, or How Men React in Crises are possibilities. Clearly, the teacher is unable to plan all the activities for such a unit in advance. He knows, however, that ultimately the class will study poetry and *Julius Caesar*.

Thus, teachers necessarily plan ahead but they do so only in general terms. The specific activities of each unit—indeed many of the specific readings—may vary depending on the student group. Although in blocking out a semester's work some teachers rely on other methods than the unit approach—on separate long-range programs for teaching vocabulary, spelling, and composition, for example—many find that the organization of learning activities around a unifying problem or idea provides a stimulating and manageable context for language learnings.

Achieving balance in long-range planning The content of English is so diversified and the goals so numerous that teachers constantly face the danger of overemphasizing one particular aspect of the program. Dora V. Smith once became so concerned over this problem of balance that she shocked the profession by protesting that "More students are conjugating English verbs in six tenses than are engaged in all oral activities combined." [7] Certainly one objective of long-range planning is to see that all phases of instruction receive adequate emphasis. A check list provides a useful frame of reference from which to evaluate a total course.

A check list for evaluating long-range planning in English

General

Is the course so planned as to attempt

to stimulate both the imagination and the critical thinking of the students?

to integrate the teaching of the four skills—reading, writing, speaking, and listening—so that learning in one reinforces learning in the others?

to explore varied approaches to learning?

to involve students in planning?

Literature

Literary works studied

Is the course planned to include some of the "best" of both the old and the new? A variety of types—poetry, fiction, drama, essay?

Is the literary work taught so as to preserve its integrity as a work of art, as an ordered presentation of human experiences?

Is the teaching of the literary work correlated with others studied and with the student's experiences with life?

Individual reading

Is this an *organized, guided* program, with students in the beginning reading books on their own level, but with the teacher attempting to lift that level gradually with specific recommendations of "better" books?

Is an attempt being made to help the student, through his choice of books, both to deepen his understanding and to widen his horizons?

Is provision made for some discussions of books being read?

Is a cumulative record being kept of books read by each student?

Is this individual reading one of the bases for evaluating the student's work in English?

Oral Communication

Are the principles which govern effective speaking and oral interpretation being taught and practiced with standards being built gradually?

Do students and teacher differentiate between discussion and the oral quiz or recitation?

Is the class so organized that most of the individual oral work occurs in small groups rather than before the class?

Are drama and poetry being approached orally, with students receiving some instruction in the art of oral interpretation?

[7] Dora V. Smith, *Evaluating Instruction in Secondary English*, Monograph No. 11 (Champaign, Ill., National Council of Teachers of English, 1942), p. 148.

Listening

Is the teaching of listening an integral part of the classroom experience?

Is the laboratory method—direct teaching through exercises of increasing complexity—used?

Is listening stressed as a necessary complement to all oral work?

Writing

Is there planned progression in the attainment of specific skills? Is the progression planned for all six years?

Is provision made for *revision,* not only for correctness, but for greater clarity, forcefulness, and vitality of expression?

Does the teacher provide time and help for *pre-correction?*

Is a file of each student's papers kept in the room?

Reading

Are the basic comprehension skills given proper emphasis?

Is there a consistent and varied plan for promoting growth in vocabulary skills?

Is there awareness of adapting reading speed to the nature of the material and the purpose of the reader?

Is attention given to depth reading—connotative force of words, metaphorical language, irony, paradox?

Language

Are students being helped to see language, not as a product of grammarians, but as a living, complex organism, to the growth of which all contribute?

Are they aware that

it is always necessary to determine the purpose behind the language?

words change their meaning with context, time, the individual, etc.?

statements may be factual, judgmental, normative, etc.?

Grammar and Usage

Are individual needs determined by diagnosis and specific items taught only to those who show a need for such instruction?

Is emphasis placed on the student's grappling with his own thought and on application of principles rather than on learning rules, definitions, classifications, etc.?

The Popular Arts

Are motion pictures, television, and radio being studied and wisely used?

By analyzing the commentary on contemporary life presented in these media?

By using ideas and situations suggested by programs popular with students to motivate writing, speaking, and individual reading?

By correlating suitable programs with the literature being studied?

Are students being helped to develop standards for judging the quality of various types of programs as to their entertainment value? Their artistic worth?

Planning a single unit

The kinds of units are many; they vary also in the ways they are planned. Those based on a systematic study of content—"Conceptions of Love," for example, in which the class studies in turn chivalric, Renaissance, and romantic ideals—are usually preplanned in detail by the teacher. Those growing out of concerns and problems of students—such as "Adjustment to New Situations" for a seventh grade class—usually develop cooperatively as the work progresses. However planned, effective units emphasize important subject learnings, yet satisfy significant social and emotional needs of young people.[8] Whatever the approach, the planning of any unit involves three fundamental tasks: identifying goals, planning activities to accomplish these, and evaluating the extent of the accomplishment. Once these are clear in the teacher's mind, he is able to choose teaching materials and to determine specific procedures.

Identifying goals Learning objectives are of three types—those involving the concepts and understandings which students are to explore, those involving specific skills to be acquired and refined, and those involving attitudes, appreciations, and similar affective outcomes. The conceptual objectives usually govern the flow of activities, since these are often regarded as the content or subject matter of a unit. For example, if understanding the effect of frustration on the human personality is a conceptual goal, the class will be drawn into an exploration of facets of behavior as revealed in situations of stress; on the other hand, such a content objective as recognizing the chief characteristics of the short story writing of Hawthorne, Poe, and O. Henry points toward a comparison of fictional selections with an emphasis on literary method. Several kinds of conceptual goals may be identified for a single unit.

Skill objectives usually influence less the organizational design of the unit than the stress within particular lessons. Identification of a few basic skill objectives permits the class to concentrate on a limited number of pressing needs rather than on all aspects of communication. Thus in one unit the class concentrates on certain organizational abilities, such as the expansion of the topic sentence, and in a later unit, work in other skills is introduced. By concentrating on only a few new learning goals, the students more readily achieve some degree of mastery. Of course, teachers also try to maintain standards by requiring students to use effective, appropriate language at all times.

Attitudes and appreciations are sometimes considered as concomitant learnings rather than as clearly identified goals, yet here particularly teachers need to distinguish between the goals of the students and the goals of the teacher. The teacher may hope to increase a student's inclination to turn to reading as a recreational activity or to improve his attitude toward Shakespeare, yet seldom are such aims explicitly identified by students, nor do they always need to be. The learner is motivated to find information or to solve a problem (conceptual objective) or to develop or improve a particular ability (skill objective). The teacher recognizes, however, that the most permanent

[8] Assistance in building units is available from many sources. Among the more useful references in this area are the following books: Isaac James Quillen and Lavone Hanna, *Education for Social Competence* (Chicago, Scott, Foresman, 1948); Jean Grambs, William J. Iverson, Franklin K. Pattersen, *Modern Methods in Secondary Education*, Rev. ed. (N.Y., Dryden, 1958); Thomas M. Risk, *Principles and Practices of Teaching in Secondary Schools*, 3rd ed. (N.Y., American Book, 1958), pp. 151-174; William H. Burton, *The Guidance of Learning Activities* (N.Y., Appleton-Century-Crofts, 1952), pp. 388-457.

learning outcomes of a unit may be affective changes in the student. Perhaps concern for attitudes and appreciations is of greater importance in English than in other curricular areas because of the English teacher's unique responsibility for developing permanent reading habits.

To be of real assistance to the teacher in planning, objectives must be:

Concrete, practical, realizable, and suggestive of definite learning experiences, e.g., "to be able to write sentences free from the error of misplaced modifiers."

Within reasonable grasp during the time available for study, e.g., "to distinguish between main and supporting statements," rather than generalized objectives like "to improve reading," a problem for the entire twelve years of education.

Identified in terms of desired changes in the students' knowledge, behavior, or skills, e.g., "to learn certain characteristics of poetry" rather than "to present the characteristics . . . ," an outcome which will be accomplished whether students learn anything or not.

Setting unit goals The extent to which the teacher should preplan the goals of any unit will vary with each situation. Whenever possible, there are important advantages in letting students help to choose specific goals within the over-all framework established by the teacher. The extent of pupil participation will depend, of course, upon the ability and maturity of the students as well as their insight and degree of self-discipline. Teachers have used such methods as the following to engage the class in planning experiences:

Ways of involving pupils in delimiting content goals

Following a teacher-led class discussion of a general topic, such as problems in family relationships, ask each student to discuss five key problems in written composition. Later they may compare papers in class and select the most persistent or interesting problems for further study.

Ask a student committee to sample opinion concerning the unit theme by preparing an Agree–Uncertain–Disagree questionnaire. In the introduction to a unit on the Dignity of Work, such statements as the following could be included:

A U D 1. Individuals who work with their hands (like stevedores and miners) contribute less to society than do most office workers.

A U D 2. Line play in a football game is more "play" than "work."

Those statements eliciting the greatest disagreement may form the basis for subsequent study.

Ask the class to elect a steering committee to meet with the teacher during noon hour or before school to develop plans for study.

Record ideas for unit study which emerge from a discussion of reading; for instance, concepts regarding permanence and change from a consideration of *How Green Was My Valley,* may be later used as topics for individual or group research.

Ways of involving pupils in delimiting skill objectives

Return diagnostic tests and/or folders of writing to students for analysis. Each student identifies his own areas of need. Skills of concern to all are to be studied by the total class; others, by groups or individuals.

Divide the class into committees to consider oral skills, reading, writing, grammar and usage. Each committee is charged with the responsibility of identifying standards to guide students in language activities. One group prepares "guidelines" for written work, another "suggestions" for group discussion.

Refrain from introducing specific skill objectives during the initial phase of the unit. However, lessons are introduced later at times when special skills are needed to accomplish goals important to pupils. Thus when individuals become interested in writing letters to obtain information, the teacher presents a lesson on letter writing. In such circumstances, the learner accomplishes the teacher's goal (learning how to write letters) as he satisfies his own (obtaining the desired information by writing a letter).

Planning learning activities At the heart of any unit are activities designed to accomplish the learning goals. Many kinds of experiences are introduced to satisfy the diversity of interests and needs found in thirty or forty boys and girls, some being planned for small groups and individuals and others for the total class. Since most units involve instruction in language and literature, experiences involving speaking and listening, reading, and writing flow naturally one into the other. The purpose of each activity, however—the relationship between content and skill objectives and the learning experiences—must be continually clear to both teacher and pupils. As an aid in planning, some teachers consider three distinct phases in the development of each unit.

1. *Introductory activities,* usually involving the entire class; the purpose is to challenge interest, to establish with students the objectives and scope of the unit, and to give students an opportunity to suggest activities which help accomplish objectives. *Example:*

   After seventh grade students agree to study a unit on animals, the teacher asks them to list stories they believe will interest others in the class, e.g., *Lassie Come Home, Silver Chief.* The students then begin compiling their own individual reading list. Later the teacher and librarian add titles to the list.

2. *Developmental activities,* planned for groups and individuals as well as for the total class; the teacher, guiding students from a consideration of the simple to the complex and from the concrete to the abstract, tries to help each student achieve the general goals agreed upon by the group. *Examples:*

   To develop interest in a unit on American literature, a unit planned to involve a study of creative imagination expressed in stories of suspense and fantasy, the teacher begins with a word association test. Students are asked to record the first thoughts which occur to them upon hearing such words as "ballad," "terror," "beauty," "impact," "image," and the like. A discussion of reactions to the words awakens interest in exploring the selections.

   In a seventh grade unit students select a folklore hero for intensive study, e.g., Captain Stormalong, Pecos Bill, John Henry. Later, groups are organized to share impressions and report findings to the class.

   As part of a study of family relationships, ninth grade students survey the treatment of families in current periodicals, films, television presentations, and the like. Ultimately, findings are shared concerning popular stereotypes of the American father, mother, kid brother, older sister, etc.

3. *Culminating activities,* usually involving the entire class; concepts are

clinched and skills reviewed, leaving the class with a sense of unity in the work accomplished. *Examples:*

An eighth grade study of Modern Communication culminates in the publication of a newspaper. The class elects an editor, an assistant, an editorial steering committee, and others with roles patterned after those observed at a local newspaper—copy writers, rewriters, typesetters, reporters. Each student is required to submit one story for publication.

After reading and discussing many books and articles on revenge, each eleventh grade student selects one important idea and writes an essay in which he applies the idea to a related book which he has selected from a specially prepared list of readings.

A junior high school study of great adventures culminates in the preparation of a mural on which each student mounts a figure to represent an adventurer about whom he has been reading. The symbols include a raft (*Kon Tiki*), a mountain climber (*Conquest of Everest*), Arctic igloos (*Nanook*), jungle figures (*I Married Adventure*), and many others. In a final discussion, each student interprets his symbol to the class.

A tenth grade consideration of seeing life from different points of view emerges from the reading of *A Tale of Two Cities*. As a culminating activity, three groups are formed to prepare newspapers reporting the events in France from different points of view—one paper for the revolutionaries, one for the aristocrats, and a third for the onlookers in London. In discussing the problems of writing, the class becomes interested in the problem of bias and perspective.

Evaluating growth Providing for continuous evaluation throughout a unit is as important as measuring cumulative growth at the end of the study. Through the former, teachers assess immediate needs and problems so that they may better plan daily instruction; through the latter, growth and accomplishment over a longer period of time. When unit goals are clearly identified, a teacher may use various ways of measuring progress toward each objective. Methods may be informal, such as in observing behavior in discussion, or may rely on prepared tests and similar instruments. Frequently, pupils can identify their own progress. In considering both continuing and final evaluation within each unit, the teacher must see a relationship between the objective, the methods of achieving it, and the devices to evaluate progress.

Learning objective	Activities	Method of evaluation
Select and develop a topic sentence.	Dry-run organizational exercise asking students to classify miscellaneous data under the pertinent topics.	Evaluation of individuals during work period.
	Recognizing topic sentence in selected paragraphs.	Brief quiz requiring students to identify sentences.
	Developing a topic sentence presented by the teacher.	Evaluation of individual papers.
	Writing an original paragraph based on a sentence selected by the individual student.	Evaluation of papers.

Choosing learning materials Special problems frequently arise in locating textbooks, reading materials, audio-visual equipment, graphic supplies, and other learning materials needed in each unit of instruction. In planning any unit, teacher and students must consider the availability of material, just as they consider the time required, the work space, and the other conditions affecting learning. Where library facilities are limited, for example, teachers cannot introduce much diversified reading until, by arranging for the shipment of books from the public library or for the purchase of paperbound volumes, they are able to surmount the problem.

In organizing units in advance, many teachers prepare annotated lists of resources which they use or not, depending on the classroom situation that develops. Over a period of time, teachers are able to build personal files of resources and bibliographies for use in units. The units described in this volume suggest ideas for teachers with sparse resources [9] as well as for those who enjoy access to many materials.

Teaching skills within a unit Ways of achieving skill objectives within a unit require special attention. Because most units are organized around concepts, teachers sometimes experience difficulty in planning for skill development within a framework of interrelated activities. For these reasons two detailed illustrations of how skills may be taught within a unit are presented here.

As long as teachers perceive the achievement of a skill as an end in itself, they cannot logically present instruction in such a skill within a unit context. Once they see that such competence is a step toward improved communication, they can more easily identify the place of such instruction. Students need specific skills to accomplish particular tasks, and they learn these most effectively when striving to accomplish definite goals. The goals which motivate classroom activities of students are many—to explore career possibilities in the field of atomic energy, to find out why students act as they do in desegregation controversies, to detect the logic of the symbolism in "Ethan Brand" in preparation for a test. To accomplish any one of these goals, the students need certain skills. In a unit the teacher's task is to present the appropriate instruction as closely as possible to the time when students will recognize the need for help; often this means carefully introducing special experiences within each unit to serve as significant settings for this necessary instruction. Clearly, therefore, planning for skill development can neither be left to chance nor be unrelated to the ongoing work and interests of the class. Two ways of introducing such specific instructions are illustrated in the following examples.

Teaching a thinking skill as an integral part of a unit

Name of unit: "Meeting a Crisis," a unit for grade ten.

Purposes of unit: [10] To gain insight into motives for human behavior by examining the decisions of individuals, both real and fictional, in moments of crisis; to

[9] See especially the unit "Fortitude, the Backbone of Courage," pp. 414-22.

[10] See pp. 589-98 for the complete unit design.

try to discern, in the light of the information we have concerning their backgrounds, the emotional and thought patterns brought into play when people are presented choices of action.

Specific purposes of writing lessons: To support a general statement with specific examples taken from literary contexts and life situations and to develop such a statement in expository writing.

Procedures in teaching the thinking skill: This series of exercises was designed to guide the student in his understanding of the skill from the simple to the more complex. In introducing the unit, the teacher assigns the following selections to provide common reading experiences and to introduce, in a sequence desirable for the unit, the analysis of characters in situations of stress.

Stories	*Poems*	*Plays*
1. Gold Mounted Guns	4. Miniver Cheevy	7. Confessional
2. Mrs. Ketting and Clark Gable	5. Mending Wall	8. Dust of the Road
3. The Unfamiliar	6. Death and General Putnam	

■ *To consider the problem of understanding a particular character.*

1. Students choose a character or cluster of characters from one of the assigned selections; they are divided into eight groups, each with a different selection and with all selections represented. For the character chosen students are asked to write:

the facts enabling the reader to understand him.
the nature of his problem.
the solution presented.
the explanation of the solution in terms of the character's background.

Before beginning the assignment, the class discusses these points: The first three items call for factual information given in the literature; in explaining the solution, individuals use their own judgment, but in forming opinions they may use only the evidence which the author gives.

2. The groups discuss the characters chosen for each selection and decide upon the one whose problem offers the most interest for the total class. After discussion, class and teacher record on the blackboard the information concerning the chosen characters.[11]

Background information	*Problem*	*Solution*	*Logic of solution*
1. Will			
Young, bored with his job, believes the outlaw's life glamorous and exciting.	To join the outlaw's gang when he has a chance or to risk possible danger by offending with his refusal.	He refuses to join the gang.	Seeing the problem from the viewpoint of those victimized makes him change his mind.

[11] In the chart the characters are listed under the same numbers as those of the selections in which the characters appear.

2. Mrs. Ketting			
Middle-aged, slovenly, tries to impress people, apes the movie stars, neglects her son, longs for a life of ease without responsibility.	To give up her dream world and become a real mother to her son.	The lure of her own pleasures is irresistible.	The habit, long persisted in, of living in a dream world makes change improbable.
3. The people of Crosby Corners			
Prejudiced against foreigners, inclined to be contemptuous of what they do not understand; think Velvet Pants, the foreigner, is a coward.	To readjust their estimate of Velvet Pants in the light of his later action.	The action of Velvet Pants in a situation in which they themselves had shown fear makes them realize he is not a coward.	Preconceived notions of the inferiority of foreigners required a dramatic concrete example to enable the townspeople to judge an individual foreigner fairly.
4. Miniver Cheevy			
Has no job; scorns the commonplace, romanticizes past ages, blames fate for his lack of accomplishment; tries to find solace in drinking.	To face reality.	He continues to evade reality.	The habit has become so deeply ingrained that change is difficult.
5. The neighbor			
Believes "Good fences make good neighbors."	To re-examine an opinion which has long been accepted.	He refuses to consider another viewpoint.	Habit of accepting unthinkingly ideas from those we respect.
6. General Putnam			
Has lived continually with danger, often close to death.	To face death courageously.	He goes to his death without fear.	Events of his life prepared him to meet death bravely.
7. The family			
Worried about their financial situation, anxious to keep up appearances, each believing the other's protestations of honesty.	To discover the importance of values to which they give lip service.	The large amount of the bribe leads each to find reasons why it should be accepted.	Never having been so severely tempted, they had not realized that they might be dishonest.

Background information	Problem	Solution	Logic of solution
8. The man and his wife			
Holding money in trust, they wish to keep it, since their dishonesty will not be detected.	To keep the money or give it to the rightful owner.	They decide to give up the money.	Judas, appearing to them as a tramp, convinces them that the mental anguish likely to accompany betrayal destroys the value of material gain.

■ *To illustrate flexible methods of selecting examples to support an idea.*

1. Students are asked to group the above characters, placing in the same group those in any way similar—e.g., in type of problem encountered, in motivation for action, in behavioral or thought patterns, etc. Each character may be used as many times as desired.

2. After completing the assignment individually, the class, under the teacher's direction, works out on the chalk board various categories, such as those that follow. The aim of the teacher in this exercise is to help the students discover the possibility of using the same character to illustrate different concepts, depending upon a writer's emphasis.

Wishful thinking
Mrs. Ketting

Judging from insufficient evidence
People of Crosby Corners
Will
The neighbor

Misinterpreting evidence
The family
People of Crosby Corners

Materialistic values
Mrs. Ketting
The family

Rigid thought pattern
Miniver Cheevy
The neighbor
Mrs. Ketting

Willingness to change
The man and wife
People of Crosby Corners
Will

Consistent attitude
Miniver Cheevy
General Putnam
Mrs. Ketting

Failure to judge oneself objectively
The family
Mrs. Ketting
Miniver Cheevy

■ *To realize the necessity of a writer's establishing a definite point of view; to help students apply the principle—supporting a generalization with examples—to other literary works and to life situations*

1. The teacher asks students to select three examples which may be used to illustrate a general statement. Two are to be from the literature discussed above; the other, either from personal experience or from other stories. Each individual is then to compose a statement to be used as the controlling sentence for an expository essay.

The teacher points out that the purpose of this essay is to explain an idea, and since students are not to recommend a course of conduct, they need to avoid such words as "should" and "ought" in their controlling statements. They may be permitted to use a category already suggested or one of their own.

2. The students, under the teacher's direction, work in groups evaluating the plans for the essays, using the following questions as a guide:

Is there a statement, i.e., a sentence, not a topic?

Will the proper development of this statement result in an essay that sets forth and sustains the idea?

Will the illustrations support the controlling statement?

3. After the group work, papers upon which the students cannot agree are given to the teacher for conference with the individual pupil. Each group chooses one model plan to be written on the board. For example:

People sometimes believe what they want to believe.

Mrs. Ketting

Miniver Cheevy

Characters in *The Ivory Door* by A. A. Milne, a play which had been read earlier.

Failure to secure all the evidence is a common cause of biased thinking.

Will

People of Crosby Corners

The reader who accepts one newspaper as gospel.

■ *To write an essay from a previously constructed plan*

1. The student is asked to come to class prepared to write the first draft of an essay using the plan he has written.

2. The final draft is written as an outside assignment. The essays are then read in groups where certain ones are selected to be read to the entire class.

■ *To discover how the material here can be further combined to support a broader concept; to learn how ideas developed in each of these short papers may be used as a portion of longer essay*

(In a slow class of immature students this may be omitted.) Representative ideas from the papers are written on the board; similarities and parallels are discussed; the teacher guides the class to group them under representative thesis sentences:

There are various causes for biased thinking.

The evidence may be misinterpreted.

The facts may not all be known.

A person may refuse to admit evidence with which he disagrees.

The support of statements by specific examples receives additional emphasis throughout the unit as writing and discussion demand its use.

Establishing a usage habit within a unit

Name of unit: "Power Over Language,"[12] a unit for the seventh grade.

Purpose of unit: To study the nature of communication, to improve understanding of the operation of language.

[12] See pp. 162-79.

Specific purposes of usage lessons: To use the appropriate form of the past tense in oral and written communication.

Procedure in establishing a usage habit: Early in the unit each student is to observe difficulties others have in communicating with him during a period in which he speaks as little as possible. The experiences are discussed in a lesson called "Silence is golden . . . and difficult."

At the beginning of the school year, long before the unit was introduced, the teacher established a basic plan for language instruction. Ability to use the appropriate tense to convey meaning was only one of several skills slated for emphasis during the seventh year by the scope and sequence guide for the department. Other usages to be mastered were agreement of verb and subject, correct pronoun forms of subject and object.

To diagnose needs: As one way of determining the items on the list needing intensive study, the teacher presented a simple diagnostic word-usage test of the following type:

Diagnostic Word-Usage Test

Directions: Read the following sentences carefully since many contain errors in word usage. If you think a sentence is incorrect, place a large X before it. After you have finished reading all sentences, rewrite each incorrect sentence so that it is expressed in desirable English. You will find it helpful to read the sentence aloud in a quiet voice.

1. Them was going.
2. He did it.
3. I drunk it all.
4. He brung the lunch.
5. One of the boys goes to the store.

. . . .

This survey aided the teacher in determining those usages causing students few problems and those not understood. The expression of past time, being one of the latter, was scheduled for study during a subsequent unit. However, during the first months of the year, emphasis was placed on the elimination of certain gross errors in student speech and writing, e.g., "He don't," "Don't have none."

■ *To familiarize students with the problem so that they recognize the appropriate forms and the need for instruction and practice*

These three activities are introduced within a single hour and require about twenty-five minutes.

1. The teacher writes on the chalk board five sentences containing errors in forming past time spoken by individuals during discussions occurring in the past few days.

John seen me but didn't speak.
She brung it to me.
We begun the unit on Monday.
They gived it to me.
I drunk some coke.

The class is asked to substitute desirable forms in each sentence, then to note the similarity of the five problems. To emphasize the major idea, individuals are asked to express the concept of past tense in their own words.

2. The teacher writes five verbs on the board and asks students to write an original sentence using each in describing an event occurring in the present:

is	The teacher *is* talking.
do	I *do* the assignments.
climb	Henry *climbs* out of his seat.
go	I *go* to social studies now.
see	I *see* the problem.

The students exchange papers and rewrite each other's sentences to express the events in past time. A review of the verb forms results in listing appropriate forms of the simple past for each verb.

3. Students open their notebooks to cumulative usage charts maintained since the opening of the semester and used as a way of recalling specific instruction. Here the student enters a record of errors in those items of usage which have been taught. As each item is taught for the first time, he adds a new column and the date. Thereafter he records the frequency of such errors as well as any dates on which supplementary drill has been assigned.

Cumulative usage error chart

How Well Do I Remember?

	9/20	9/26	9/31	10/8	10/15	10/20	11/3*
1. Complete Sentence	(9/20) ///	(9/26)** ///	/	////	//	//	///
2. Beginning Capitalization			/	///	/	/	
3. Pronoun Form —Subject				//	/	(10/20)** //	
4. Pronoun Form —Object					////	//	///
5. Past Tense							///

* Dates of returned papers.
** Dates on which additional drill is assigned.

After "Past Tense" is added to the charts as the most recent usage form studied, the teacher returns the paragraphs written on the previous day and the students record and correct their errors.

■ *To establish appropriate forms of past tense through brief and varied drill*

During the next few days, the teacher introduces several brief ten-minute drills on uses of the past tense. These are presented at the beginning of class hours or during interludes between other activities.

1. For oral practice, the teacher divides the class into two teams and writes the following verbs on the chalk board:

do	begin	have	climb
come	give	bring	drink
is	see		

A student on Team 1 is asked to express a statement in the present tense using one of the verbs; immediately thereafter the corresponding student on the second team repeats the statement as if it had happened the day before. Anyone who falters or uses the wrong form continues for a second or even third round, whereas the others are permitted to sit down. *Example:*

Student 1: He climbs the tree.
Reply 1: Yesterday he climbed it. (pupil sits)
Student 2: Mary has many gifts.
Reply 2: Yesterday Mary–uh–had many gifts. (pupil remains standing)

2. A brief newspaper article, related to the unit and describing an event in the present tense, is copied on the board. Students are asked to rewrite the article for a monthly newsmagazine which summarizes recent past events.

3. Students are asked to select the appropriate forms of *climb, drink, begin, bring,* and *give* for ten sentences like these:

John ________ to watch television an hour ago.
He ________ some lunch and I did too.
When I finished, John ________ the stairs.

A review of the sentences clarifies questions concerning appropriate usages, and the practice ends with the teacher leading the group in unison reading of the sentences in an attempt to fix oral usage through sound patterns. Throughout this phase of class work the teacher continually directs attention to effective ways of expressing past time, calling attention to ways used in selections studied in the unit and to usages of students themselves. These reminders are most likely to be effective if they occur just before an activity in the unit when pupils use speaking or writing.

■ *To provide for individual differences in proficiency by planning assignments for those with particular needs*

1. After three short drills on different days, the teacher introduces a pretest designed to measure progress in using appropriate verb forms. The test involves selecting correct forms in a series of statements like: I (brought) (brung) the helicopter. The exercise is followed by a unison reading of the correct sentence.

2. Five individuals who have perfect papers on the test and no difficulties expressing tense in their speaking and writing are excused from subsequent lessons. This procedure is followed regularly for lessons on skills. These individuals continue their activities for the unit, "Power Over Language." During writing periods, they sometimes function as special helpers offering assistance to other students. The five meet together to prepare a final test, patterned on the pretest, which they administer later to the class.

3. During study activities in the unit, the teacher presents needed supplementary explanation to four individuals whose scores on the pretest and whose writing reveal continuing confusion about tense. After reviewing the basic principles and discussing several examples, the teacher assigns to these students some special exercises from a language textbook or workbook.

■ *To clinch and maintain desirable habits once learning is established*

1. A final test, prepared by the five special students and checked by the teacher, is presented and reviewed as the final class activity dealing with past tense.

2. Before collecting the next set of compositions in the unit, the teacher provides for a fifteen-minute pre-correction period. During this period, the students are asked to read paragraphs aloud in small groups and listen specifically for problems in tense. The class is advised that errors in tense will be weighed heavily in evaluating compositions.

3. The teacher continually notes any special problems in uses of the past tense which appear in the writing and speaking of students. Individual problems are discussed in brief conferences held during class study periods. Problems shared by many persons are reviewed with the entire class. Students continue to maintain records of their written errors on the cumulative chart. When a review of the charts later in the semester reveals four individuals who still have repeated difficulties in expressing past tense, the teacher arranges for special supplementary instruction in a small group situation.

These two examples illustrate in detail how a series of lessons designed to achieve skill objectives may be incorporated within the context of a unit. The need for careful planning by teachers is emphasized throughout as is the value of much pupil involvement in shaping and evaluating learning. Certainly the planning of class work in units extending over an interval of several weeks gives teachers an opportunity to place in a communication setting a sequence of activities designed to encourage skill development.

Planning a specific lesson

If the unit plan provides an over-all guide for maintaining continuity in learning over an interval of several weeks, the individual lesson plan offers the teacher a detailed guide for accomplishing specific learning goals. A lesson may be concluded during a single hour or it may be shorter or longer, the length of any plan being determined by the nature of the learning experience itself. A lesson on a single short story like "To Build A Fire" may require class time on three separate days. On the first, fifteen minutes may be devoted to preparation for reading; on the second, the entire hour to a discussion of the story; ultimately time may be spent on a related writing assignment. On the other hand, a brief lesson dealing with a single language skill may be concluded in thirty minutes.

Individual lessons are normally related, one to another, through a basic sequence in the over-all plan. Thus a unit on the American short story may include separate lessons on ten short stories, one on structure, and perhaps a final cumulative lesson which attempts to draw together all the learning in the unit.

Plotting lessons How does the teacher plan a sequence of lessons? One effective way is to plan on a weekly basis, with the unit plan offering guidance in continuity and purpose. A weekly schedule for a junior high school class is presented on the following chart. To teach certain reading skills, the teacher

Weekly schedule for junior high school class working on reading skills

		Group I *slow*	*Group II* *average*	*Group III* *accelerated*
Monday	*50 min.*	Class goes to library to exchange individual books, to browse, and to review new periodicals. Teacher uses time for individual conferences to guide reading selections.		
Tuesday	*10 min.*	Rate of comprehension test, using separate material for each group.		
	20 min.	Guided oral reading of story in reader. (T)*	Silent reading to answer questions on chalk board.	Exercise on context clues.
	30 min.	Work on new assignment.	Teacher guided discussion based on these questions. (T)	Individual reading.
Wednesday	*25 min.*	Finish Tuesday's assignment. Individual reading.	Work on comprehension assignment made Tuesday.	Review of context clues. Instruction on reading "Rip Van Winkle." Application of context clue skills. (T)
	25 min.	Teacher-led discussion and instruction on word-attack skills. (T)	Individual reading.	Silent reading of story.
Thursday	*10 min.*	Brief skimming drill using same material for all groups.		
	20 min.	Direct teacher instruction on vocabulary development, etc. for Groups I and II. (T)		Complete Wednesday's assignment.
	20 min.	Individual reading.	Individual reading.	Preparation for audience reading Friday. (T)
Friday	*20 min.*	Class meets together listening to prepared audience reading by Group III.		
	20 min.	Informal dramatizations of scenes from reading, Groups I and II.		
	10 min.	Writing in notebooks: summary of week's activities.		

* (T) shows where the teacher will be during each interval.

has divided the class into three ability sections; the plotting of a weekly schedule assists him in identifying those lessons to plan in detail for each group. This chart does not present the lessons themselves; rather it presents an agenda of lessons, many of which would be developed in great detail.

Variation in lessons Some lessons are routine and require little special attention; others require much teacher preparation. Discussions usually are of the latter type, since teachers must necessarily prepare a series of questions to guide student participation. In the weekly schedule illustrated in the chart, such class hours as the library reading period on Monday and the Friday program presentations depend less on instructional plans prepared specifically for each day than on continuing class standards and routines adopted long before. By organizing classes to rely on sound regularized activity, the teacher, who has little enough time for preparation, may devote his major energies to preparing necessary lessons. The lesson on word attack skills for Group I, however, and Group III's study of "Rip Van Winkle" call for plans requiring careful attention. Through advance organization the teacher frees himself to prepare the needed lessons.

Considering a total schedule Teachers need to devise some way of maintaining a master schedule of preparation for all classes if they are to balance the demands on their time and energies. Carrying as many as five classes, few secondary teachers are able to prepare more than two detailed plans for any single day. An intelligent solution to the problem calls for scheduling activities so that those requiring advance planning and much energy and leadership execution are spaced throughout a week. Thus, discussions for period one and period three classes are scheduled on Tuesday when other groups are reading, but on Wednesday when tests are presented during periods one and three, special lessons are presented to other groups. In this manner teachers can provide equitably for all groups.

Guide for lesson planning A helpful lesson plan reveals what is to be accomplished and how. It is a tool to assist the busy teacher. Criteria for evaluating a useful lesson are suggested by the following questions:

Are learning goals clear and limited to those which may be accomplished during the time interval?

Are activities planned to lead to the accomplishment of goals?

Does the plan provide guidance in how both teacher and students will move toward accomplishment of goals?

Is reasonable consideration given to availability of materials?

Is provision made for variety in learning experiences as needed by the student group?

At the end of the lesson are important learnings summarized and clinched?

What provision is made for checking the effectiveness of the lesson?

Good lesson plans are more easily seen than described. The following, although not considered perfect by their creators, illustrate different organizational approaches and suggest kinds of planning that may be adapted in many classes. Both are more elaborate than the lesson plans teachers will normally have time to create. However, both are for particularly crucial lessons in the total teaching design, and they do represent English teaching as it should be more often. Careful planning helps to lift teaching to an art.

Lesson on response to mood [13]

Class: Grade eight
Unit: "Responding With Imagination"
Previous activity: Students had been engaged in various speaking and writing experiences in which they had attempted to respond to sensory impressions.
Time: Approximately two hours
Objectives: To develop the desire to write interestingly and descriptively; to increase powers of observation and imagination; to improve effective use of adverbs, adjectives, sensory detail, and the precise word to convey meaning and mood.

Comments	Activities
Preparation of the class is important. Here the teacher summarizes what she plans to say.	A. Introduction to experiment in "Mood." 1. Today we are going to conduct an experiment in which each of you will play a vital part. It is important that each of you listen to directions and follow them carefully if the experiment is to be successful.
Notice the specificity.	2. We are going to listen to a record. While the record is playing, shut your eyes and ask yourself, What does this music make me think of? What words express the mood I feel, or the mood of the record?
	3. After you have listened to the record for five minutes, begin to write on a clean sheet of binder paper—not to be handed in—the words and phrases which come into your mind as you listen to the music. a) At this point, do not worry about spelling, punctuation, sentence structure, or even process. b) Think only of the music and the idea which it brings to mind. B. Listening to recording of "Spellbound." Discussion of responses to record.
Here teacher relies on established groupings of students.	1. Listen carefully to the following directions: a) Each chairman is to ask each person in his group to read aloud the responses he made to the record.

[13] Adapted from a plan developed by Mrs. Carol Jensen, formerly of Bancroft Junior High School, San Leandro, Calif.

The activity provides variation from listening and gives all students an opportunity to share ideas.

b) The chairman will also ask each to select at least three responses he considers most interesting.

Note that this teacher lists on her plan any item she wishes to emphasize—a sound practice for beginners.

c) A recorder should write down five words or phrases which the group selects as the most descriptive, appropriate, and interesting.

d) In ten minutes each recorder will be asked to read the responses selected by his group. Remember to talk quietly, to work quickly and efficiently.

Less detailed directions may be appropriate in many classes. This class tended to be difficult to control and the teacher found the reminders to be helpful.

2. Recitation of responses by recorders:
Will the recorder for Group I please stand and read so that everyone can hear the responses selected?

3. Each of you has participated in the creation of mood. The record "Spellbound," like *beauty,* may mean something different to each of us. Whatever it may mean, we must admit that it creates a "mood" for each of us. That is why music like "Spellbound" is called "mood music."
   a) Who can define the word "mood"?
   b) Mood implies a "particular state of mind, especially one affected by emotion—as *to be in the mood to work.*"

Teacher tries to pull together and summarize responses. Note that teacher has general conception of ultimate understanding desired although response is to be elicited from students.

C. Moods created in pictures.

Second phase of lesson begins with allusion to earlier writing. This phase may be introduced during a second hour.

1. You all remember the picture shown you earlier in this unit.
   a) What was the mood in that picture? (Unhappiness.)
   b) What elements created this mood? (Expressions, color.)
2. Now will each of you choose one word or phrase from the following list which you think best describes the picture which I am now holding. (A foggy harbor.)

Comments	Activities
Here in her planning teacher attempts to predict student response. However, she must be ready to deal with additional ideas contributed by the class.	a) mysterious b) calm, still, undisturbed, tranquil c) gloomy and depressing d) death-like
	3. How many of you selected mysterious? Why? How many calm, still . . . ? Why? Etc. 4. What elements create mood in this picture? a) stillness, lack of life and motion b) water is still and without a ripple c) the fog lends a hushed quality
	D. Moods created in writing 1. (Distribute copies of poems.) Follow along with me while I read how two writers give different moods to the same element—fog. a) "It lies cold on the eyeballs and thick in the throat; it is an intangible blanket saturated with the stillness and the heaviness of death." b) Sandburg's "Fog"
Use of printed text as a listening aid reduces distraction and might be desirable here.	2. Listen and react to the way Poe creates a mood for a knock on the door in this poem, "The Raven." (Play recording of Poe's "The Raven," interpreted by Basil Rathbone.) a) What words set the stage for a knock on the door? b) Midnight dreary, weak, weary, napping, bleak December, dying ember, wrought its ghost. What do these words describe?
Again teacher predicts reasonable responses but is prepared to "fish" for exact answers if necessary.	1) time 2) mood of the subject 3) activity 4) season—time of year 5) weather
	E. Assignment. 1. Now for the assignment. Tonight you are to describe a knock on the door, too. Create three different moods:
Papers will give teacher opportunity to evaluate effectiveness of total lesson.	a) Write to show it's a desperate fugitive. b) Write to show it's a girl's boyfriend. c) Write to show it's a messenger boy.
	2. Listen carefully to the knock on our door. Who want to try knocking in different ways? (Volunteers.) Pay careful attention to describing. (See C above.)

Materials I plan to use

A. Recordings
   1. "Spellbound"
   2. Edgar Allan Poe—Basil Rathbone
B. Photograph: Foggy harbor from *Holiday* magazine
C. Copies of poetry anthology
   1. "Fog" page 41
   2. "The Raven" page 67

Lesson on the short story [14]

Class: Grades 11 and 12, advanced group.

Previous assignment: The assignment for this lesson, given the preceding day, was as follows: Read "The Fall of the House of Usher" and answer the following questions: 1) How does Poe achieve perfect tone throughout the story? 2) How does he hold you in suspense? 3) How does he achieve a single emotional effect?

Objective: To discuss the story and arrive, through questioning, at a complete characterization of Poe's method.

Procedure: The use of the following questions to start and guide discussion.

Comments	Activities
The teacher has carefully organized this lesson in three parts and each in turn contributes to the ultimate understandings desired.	A. Questions to draw out the meaning of *perfect tone,* and how it is used:
Teacher attempts to clarify terms and relate them to something familiar to students.	1. The use of the word "how" suggests "by what means" or "with what tools." Therefore, what are the tools Poe uses to achieve perfect tone? First, let us decide what this term means. 2. What do we mean by "tone of voice," "tone of a musical instrument," and "tone of a poem"? (Mood, feeling, atmosphere, spirit, dominant emotion, etc.)
Note specificity. With guidance, students are asked to pick out concrete words. The teacher has previously noted where words occur so that he may aid students if such help is needed.	3. Point out some phrases on the first page that seem to establish the tone. (Dull, dark and soundless day, oppressively low, dreary track, melancholy House of Usher, insufferable gloom, bleak walls, decayed trees, utter depression of soul, bitter lapse, hideous dropping, etc.) 4. Which adjectives in particular seem to describe the tone? (Gloomy, oppressive, depressive, sickening of heart, etc.)

[14] Adapted and used with permission of Henry C. Meckel, San Jose State College, San Jose, Calif.

Comments	Activities
Note that this question suggests a need for summarizing. The teacher would hope to obtain a response similar to the one here.	5. What would you say, then, is Poe's first tool? (Choice of words.)
	6. Read the opening sentence of various paragraphs. Does the author maintain this tone? Is there any change whatever? Do any of the sentences express any other emotion?
Second summary made by students.	7. Therefore, what would you say is another tool by which perfect tone is achieved? (Unity.)
	B. Questions to draw out the meaning of suspense and how it is achieved:
	1. What does suspense mean, even outside literary terminology? (Concern about what is going to happen next.)
	2. Pick out some phrases or sentences that arouse your curiosity but leave you in suspense. (. . . but many years had elapsed since our last meeting . . . a mental disorder which oppressed him . . . a very singular summons . . . yet I really knew very little of my friend . . . a barely perceptible fissure . . . a valet of stealthy step . . . an expression of low cunning . . . I must perish in this deplorable folly . . . I dread the events of the future . . . I regarded her with an utter astonishment not mingled with dread; and yet I found it impossible to account for such feelings. That lady, at least while alive, would be seen by me no more.)
	3. Which of these seem to point forward to something disastrous?
	4. How does Poe deliberately phrase these so as to put a question in your mind?
	5. Point out the questions that arise as you read the first paragraph. (Where is the man going and why? Why is anyone living in such a house? What's going on inside? What will happen to the narrator?) Second paragraph. (Why is he going to stay there? Why did Usher send for him? What is his mental disorder?)
Third summary made by students.	6. How would you say, then, that suspense is achieved? (By arousing the reader's curiosity or suspicion by putting questions in his mind and leaving only vague hints as to their answer.)

Here again note how identification of concrete detail and analyses of detail are used to build understanding of the desired concept. The teacher has a sequence of questions to guide the discussion and he is able to call attention to specific paragraphs in the selection if students do not locate these themselves.

C. Questions to draw out the meaning of single emotional effect and how it is achieved:
   1. What emotion is in your mind when you finish the story?
   2. Is it mixed with any contrary emotion? (For instance, fear and horror are difficult to define but experience tells us that they are akin; but joy (or humor) is obviously their opposite.)
   3. Can you find any words, phrases, sentences, or paragraphs in the story that do not contribute to this emotion?
   4. Can you find any other effect, such as humor, philosophy, sympathy, morality, logic, human interest, love?
   5. What, then, is the object of omitting these?
   6. Would you conclude that *unity* again is a tool?
   7. What other tools are used? What about *tone* as a tool in achieving single effect?
   8. What does *constant suspense* do to the total effect?
   9. Is the effect stronger at the end if your emotions have been allowed to accumulate? Pick out a passage that seems to build up, accumulate, or lead to a crescendo.
   10. What does the crescendo lead to? Is it the same in music? Suppose we call it a *final impact.* Does it help to achieve the single effect?
   11. Do you think that Poe devised a plot first and strove for effect, or decided upon a certain effect and then found a plot that would carry it?
   12. Would you say, then, that the element of *plot* was important?
   13. How about the characters? Is any attempt made to acquaint the reader with them?
   14. Is the setting important? In what way? (In that it sets the mood but not because it matters where the story takes place. The House of Usher could be in any country in any gloomy marsh.)

This is the understanding toward which the teacher has been leading the class throughout the sequence of questions. In clinching the idea, he would ask individuals to summarize.

   15. Would you say, then, that *subordinating* the other elements *to total effect* was a tool?

Comments	Activities
The teacher plays the musical selections; such an experience provides variety and helps establish the point.	16. Imagine that you had to choose music as background in a television play of this story. What kind of music would you pick? Would slow and mournful music do? Why not? Does there have to be a note of accumulating excitement or impending disaster? (Compare Grieg's "Ase's Death" with Sibelius' *Finlandia.*)
	Generalizations (the desired conclusions):
What are the major understandings that lesson is planned to achieve? Clearly every question and every sub-point leads toward these understandings. With less mature groups, the teacher would probably attempt less.	1. Poe's main technique is achieving perfect tone, suspense, and single emotional effect. 2. Perfect tone is achieved by choice of words and by unity, that is, by not allowing any note other than the desired one to enter the piece. 3. Suspense is achieved by arousing curiosity or suspicion and leaving vague hints concerning the outcome. This is accomplished by phrasing in such a way as to leave a question in the reader's mind as to what will happen next. 4. Single emotional effect is achieved by unity, tone, suspense, crescendo, final impact, and subordinating every other element to that of total effect.

The over-all pattern of the English program and the detailed plan of the various segments necessarily complement each other. Both require imagination and vitality on the part of planners. Not all lessons can be as thoroughly developed as the two just presented, nor can curricula like those of Oakland, South Bend, and Palo Alto rise spontaneously from a few teachers' meetings. But if instruction is not to be opportunistic, impulsive, and haphazard; if what pupils learn is not to be left to chance, some strategy must be devised to relate means to ends, to reduce to an ordered design the complexity and multiplicity of English teaching.

APPENDIX A

Periodicals and Resource Materials for Teachers of Secondary English

SELECTED PERIODICALS

Publications of the National Council of Teachers of English, 508 South Sixth St., Champaign, Ill. NCTE membership includes subscription to one of the following journals:

The *English Journal,* official journal of secondary section; monthly, September–May. The most useful single magazine for teachers of English in grades 7 to 12. Contains articles on content and methods, reviews of new teaching materials, information on professional activities.

Elementary English, official journal of elementary section; monthly, October–May, Contains many discussions of method of interest to junior high school teachers, as well as readable summaries of recent research in English methodology.

College English, official journal of college section; monthly, October–May. Although contents stress college literature and composition, some articles will interest eleventh and twelfth grade teachers.

College Composition and Communication, official journal of the Conference on College Composition and Communication; quarterly. Many readable articles on composition and language study are presented. Senior high school teachers will find much that is adaptable to secondary classrooms.

Studies in the Mass Media, a monthly magazine for teachers and high school students on films, television, drama, recordings, and periodicals. Study guides are included.

Publications of state English associations

Many state or regional associations, like Illinois, Michigan, Kentucky, Iowa, and New England, publish a regular bulletin, journal, or yearbook. Teachers will find such publications a convenient way of informing themselves on the thinking of fellow teachers, as well as a source of announcements of regional curriculum developments and professional meetings.

Publications dealing with special aspects of English, useful for reference and for teachers working in the areas of concern

The Reading Teacher, official publication of the International Reading Association, 5835 Kimbark Ave., Chicago 37; quarterly. Readable articles, columns, summaries of recent research designed for classroom teachers at all levels of instruction.

Journal of Developmental Reading, Department of English, Purdue University, Lafayette, Indiana; quarterly. Articles on recent research in reading and on curriculum projects. Designed to satisfy varying interests at all levels of instruction.

Exercise Exchange, Holt, Rinehart & Winston, 383 Madison Ave., New York 17; quarterly. Brief, readable reports of successful lessons in college classrooms, many of which are usable with eleventh and twelfth grade students.

Publications for general readers which contain material of special interest to teachers of English

Audio-Visual Instruction, National Education Association, 1201 16th St., N.W., Washington 6, D.C.; monthly.

TV Guide, Triangle Publications, Inc., 400 North Broad, Philadelphia, Penn.; weekly. Both are useful occasionally in locating audio-visual materials for the classroom.

Saturday Review, 25 West 45th St., New York 36; weekly. Discussions of contemporary events, reviews of books, motion pictures, television, plays, recordings, special issues on books for children and adolescents.

SELECTED BIBLIOGRAPHIES

Resources for Teaching English, a series of circulars prepared by Arno Jewett in the United States Office of Education, mimeographed, revised frequently. Among these are:

Circular 412, *Teaching Guides and Courses of Study in High School Language Arts*
Circular 450, *Aids for Knowing Books for Teen-Agers*
Circular 401, *References for Teachers of English as a Foreign Language*

SELECTED CURRICULUM GUIDES IN ENGLISH

"A Program in English, Guide for K–12," Denver, Colorado, Public Schools, 1953. In addition to special chapters on language skills, contains sample resource units for various grade levels.

"English, a Guide for Junior High School," Board of Education, Los Angeles, California, City Schools, 1957. Units of instruction carefully related to goals and to the books and other resources listed for the teacher.

"Language Arts: Planning for Effective Learning," Superintendent's Committee on Curriculum and Instruction, Maryland State Department of Education, Baltimore 1, 1956. In addition to helpful material on reading and the language skills, includes charts to suggest continuity of development of skills.

"Communication: A Guide to the Teaching of Speaking and Writing," Minneapolis, Minnesota, Public Schools, 1953. Suggests content and activities for instruction in various grade levels. An ingenious device of half pages against full pages silhouettes skills against the background of larger activities.

"A Guide for Instruction in the Language Arts, Grades 7–12," Curriculum Bulletin No. 18, Minnesota State Department of Education, St. Paul 1, 1956. Useful material on the nature of unit planning and its relationship to the development of skills. Contains an interesting series of units for use in grades 7 through 12.

"Reading, Grades 7-8-9," Board of Education, New York City, 1959. A comprehensive program for teaching reading skills and literary appreciation.

"The Language Arts Guide, Fourth Progress Report, Grades 7 through 12," Oakland, California, Public Schools, 1957. Establishes basic aims in various skill areas and offers suggested classroom activities. Contains a useful section on planning and some interesting material on the teaching of language and listening.

English Language Arts Resource Workbooks (separate books for various grade levels), Palo Alto, California, Public Schools. Very specific course of studies for various grades, divided into *A* and *B* lanes in high school. Literary selections are analyzed and suggestions made for units. Concrete help is included for the teaching of composition.

"Teaching the Language Arts in the Secondary Schools," Curriculum Bulletin No. 2, Part II, Seattle, Washington, Public Schools, 1952; and "Unit Plans for the Language Arts," Seattle, 1954. Contains detailed list of purposes for each grade level and supplementary series of resource units for various grade levels.

Also helpful is "We Teach Spelling," Seattle, Public Schools, 1958. "Let's Teach English," School City of South Bend, Indiana, 1958. A manual for junior high school teachers, this guide is especially helpful on unit planning.

APPENDIX B

Alleviation of Speech Disorders

Stuttering is the name given all those rhythmic speech disorders characterized by repetition, hesitation, or prolongation of sounds. Although considerable research has been made, no single cause and no single remedy have yet been found for this crippling disability. When we discover a stutterer in our classes, we can be almost certain that the disorder represents an emotional block of long standing. The fact that speech is a response of the whole organism (see Chapter 1) indicates how profound a change must take place in the individual if he is to alleviate the problem. No remedy should be suggested by one who has not been trained to make a sound diagnosis of the cause; this means most teachers. The correction of speech disorders needs the attention of a qualified therapist.

Although as classroom teachers we cannot give technical help, we do have a part in the correction program. It is our responsibility to understand the basic nature of the disorder, to detect it in our students, to seek professional help, and to maintain a classroom that will not aggravate the problem.

Basic nature of the disorder Severe speech disorders may be either the cause or the effect of serious psychological impairment. If in the initial stages of stuttering the child has the help of a speech clinician, his chances of overcoming the handicap are greater. In the beginning he is unaware that his speech differs from that of others; therefore, he is not emotionally involved in his efforts to speak. However, if he senses concern or amusement in his listeners, he may develop anxiety; tension mounts, causing more pronounced blocking. Speaking then becomes a task requiring all his physical and emotional energy. Experiments have shown that the actual physical blocking lasts probably less than a second; the intensity of the emotional reaction to the blocking determines the seriousness of the case. Therefore, the habits acquired in trying to conceal or overcome the blocking, rather than the blocking itself, cause the greater interference with communication.

Psychological blocks may interfere with any activity. A star basketball player may become emotionally upset because he seems to have lost his skill at scoring. Physical aspects are probably unchanged; his eyes, his muscles, and the basket remain the same; but the fear of failure sets up tension that disturbs coordination, making every throw a hazard. How much more intense the fear must be when it strikes at something as near to the core of our being as speech. Admittedly, this is an oversimplified explanation of an extremely complex problem. The thing we as teachers must remember is that we do not try to correct the handicap; we try to relieve the emotional strain.

Detection of disorders That anyone should have difficulty detecting stuttering might seem ironical to one so afflicted. To him it is the most noticeable aspect of his behavior. However, immediate recognition before adverse environmental elements have a chance to cause harm is essential. Because the stutterer suffers so from the dread of exposure, he may have become adept in the use of covering-up techniques. His speech may be characterized by lengthy pauses—pauses not to emphasize meaning or to find the right word, but to mobilize energy for the attack. To fill the silence he indulges in mannerisms —gasping breath, swallowing, facial contortions, meaningless gestures; first a deliberate means of distracting attention from his disability, they later become habitual. He may look ahead in order to dodge words that mean trouble, substituting others or shifting the line of thought; lack of clarity and of continuity results. Finally, and more crucial to his personality, he is likely to withdraw to activities where he can avoid speech. Awareness of the means stutterers take to disguise their handicap will make us more alert in detecting it.

Seeking professional help After detection, the next step is referral to a speech therapist. This may prove difficult because the responsibility of society for maintaining clinics has not been as widely recognized here as it has in other areas of disability. However, the teacher must find out what sources of help are available. City school systems usually have their own speech therapists; in smaller communities, referral may be to county or state boards or to clinics in neighboring colleges. If all these fail, advice may be obtained from the American Speech Correction Association.[1] If moved by the crusading spirit, the teacher might interest local and state teachers' organizations in exploring the possibilities of establishing a clinic. An adequate program for helping the handicapped in speech requires patience, time, and money, and it demands an enlarged force of trained personnel; but it is vital to a great enough segment of the population to merit widespread support.

Role of the classroom teacher Whether we obtain professional help or must rely solely on our own resources, it is most important that we maintain a classroom free from tension. To be sure, this is desirable for all pupils, but the stutterer's need is more urgent. Many students can profit occasionally by working against time; with the stutterer this results only in strain and worry. We must try to relieve all pressures.

Therefore, treat the disability casually, as differing only in kind from those of others. Bring the problem out in the open: It cannot be concealed; it should not be ignored. Talk it over with the student in conference, showing understanding but not exaggerated sympathy. Perhaps tell him how fatigue slows

[1] Wayne State University, Detroit 1, Michigan.

your own tongue, how certain fears hamper everyone. Help him plan a program, in class and without, that eliminates hurry. Do not intimate that correction is easy; it isn't. However, try to make him see that it is not the stutter that hinders communication but his emotional reaction to it. *He can learn to control this reaction.* Let him know that he will not be forced to speak, but encourage him to do so. We have found choral speaking and group work helpful to those with speech disorders.

As soon as possible, send the student on an errand while you talk the matter over with the class in the same casual manner you would discuss any problem. Explain the psychological basis for speech disorders and let them give you examples of how emotion affects their own actions. You may mention how common the affliction has been all through history; if the names mean anything to them, tell them of famous men who have suffered from the handicap–King George VI, Somerset Maugham, Charles Lamb, Charles Darwin. They will see that the only way they can help is to allow the student to build confidence in himself as a person. Ask for suggestions as to how this can be done.

If the work in one class is to be reinforced elsewhere, all teachers of the stutterer, as well as the parents, should agree on concerted action. If there is no speech correctionist assigned to the school, the English teacher may be the logical person to initiate such a program, discussing its desirability with counselor or principal. Mobilization of all favorable elements in the student's environment is necessary if his deeply rooted problem is to be alleviated.

APPENDIX C

Improving Spelling

What is the importance of spelling? Acceptable spelling is like all conventions in using language. If a persons says, "I ain't got none of them new kinda cameras," other people notice the way he speaks rather than the thought he intends to communicate. Similarly, if a person writes "Happy Ester," the attention of the reader is distracted from the thought itself to the medium of expression. All such distractions interfere with communication and tend to irritate other people. Thus good spelling, like appropriate use of spoken language, becomes not only a measure of one's education but also a measure of his sensitivity to the reactions of other people. To spell accurately is to show consideration for the person who will read what has been written.

The three key words in spelling improvement are *individualize, attack, care.*

Drill is based upon individual lists of spelling difficulty.
The teacher helps each pupil find a method of attacking his difficulties.
The learner develops a spelling conscience.

IDENTIFY INDIVIDUAL DIFFICULTIES

By the time pupils are in junior high school, spelling lists identical for all class members are seldom economical. Students vary so much in their spelling difficulties that if progress is to occur, provisions for individualization become imperative. Those who spell competently should be released from many lessons to concentrate on more appropriate learnings. Exceptionally weak spellers need to be grouped together for review of word analysis and lessons in methods of attacking new words. Average spellers should keep lists of their own problem words in their composition folders and work on these during spelling periods. Junior high school pupils enjoy Blair's medical analogy: Each pupil is a doctor who has three groups of "patients," or words needing the doctor's care. Some patients are very ill and need frequent attention; others are convalescent, requiring only occasional appointments; the largest number, it is hoped, have been ill but are now hale and hearty, functioning in compositions without the slightest malaise.[1]

To carry out such a method, teachers often have the pupils keep each "patient" on a separate card so that they may be transferred from the emergency ward to the infirmary before they are released from the hospital. Although such a method is too juvenile for senior high pupils, the same basic principle of individualization needs to operate in the word lists filed in each pupil's writing folder.

Emphasize spelling on composition days Whenever the entire class is writing, whether the subject be a planned composition or an essay test over some period of work, the teacher places reminders about spelling on the chalk board. For instance, the names of everything on a *Saturday Evening Post* cover may be listed and examined before using the picture as stimulus for a composition; baseball words or ice carnival words may be appropriate for other occasions or assignments. During a unit on science fiction, still another list may appear. Often a brief drill on using the dictionary precedes actual writing. At other times the teacher may review the spelling of certain phonetic word families or teach several demons like *separate, necessary,* or *friend,* using colored chalk to call attention to the troublesome spots.

Rules and devices Special devices, such as the phrase "Never *believe* a *lie,*" should not be overdone lest they become cumbersome. A few of them, such as associating *t(here)* with *here,* or station*e*ry with pap*e*r, may assist a learner with some particularly troublesome word, but too many of these special associations overburden the memory and prove to be inadequate substitutes for an effective method of learning.

Similarly, too many spelling rules will also confuse a learner, especially if there are many exceptions to the rule. Memorizing rules is of no value if one does not understand the principle involved; understanding makes memori-

[1] Glen M. Blair, *Diagnostic and Remedial Teaching in Secondary Schools* (N.Y., Macmillan, 1940).

zation superfluous. Some of the principles which do help many people in spelling are listed here:

Drop the final *e* before a suffix beginning with a vowel.
Keep the final *e* before a suffix beginning with a consonant.
When a word ends in *y* preceded by a consonant, change the *y* to *i* before adding a suffix (unless the suffix begins with *i*).
Use *i* before *e* except after *c* or when sounded like *a* as in neighbor and weigh.

TEACH A METHOD OF ATTACK

The difference between good spellers and poor spellers often hinges on an effective method for learning to spell. Good spellers have solved the problem. They have a sequence for studying words they want to learn. Poor spellers merely look at a new word helplessly, and when they do try, use hit and miss methods which are ineffective and seldom the same from one time to the next.

Why, then, shouldn't everyone adopt the ideal method of learning used by the best spellers? The answer is easy: Good spellers do not all use the same method. However, almost all of them use *some method,* and by studying their various ways of learning to spell, each pupil can work out an habitual procedure suited to his own individuality. Among the steps used by good spellers, at least ten are often listed: looking at the word, copying the word, visualizing the word, listening to the pronunciation of the word, pronouncing the word, dividing the word into syllables, saying the letters in sequence, writing the word with large muscle movements (in the air or on a chalk board) to get the feel of the word, analyzing the difficult places in the word, and using the word in a meaningful sentence. In addition, most competent spellers write their words in a careful, neat fashion. Sloppy, careless handwriting often results in a confused image of the word and uncertainty about its spelling.

Anyone who wants to improve his spelling should seriously consider which combination of the ten steps best suits his learning habits. No one would use all ten, but a combination of those which really assist an individual is all-important. Once the combination has been chosen and after a trial period to test its efficiency, the student should establish this thumb-rule as a regular and habitual method of learning. Probably visualizing the word should be a part of the combination for almost everyone, although oral or kinesthetic cues may claim first place for some pupils.

Dr. James A. Fitzgerald, an authority on spelling, has often recommended the method summarized here: [2]

Understand the use, meaning, and pronunciation of the word.
Visualize the word.
Note the spelling of the word.
Write the word carefully and neatly.
Check the spelling of the word.
Use the word as often as possible *in writing.*

[2] James A. Fitzgerald, *The Teaching of Spelling* (Milwaukee, Wisc., Bruce, 1951), p. 38.

This combination of methods may not be best for some individuals, but for many learners these steps, carefully followed, prove to be an effective method of study. By devoting less time to drill and more time to teaching a method of learning, a teacher can improve spelling in most classes.

One teacher provides time for the students to experiment with the various approaches and then, on a day labeled The Most Significant Day in our Spelling Year, each pupil writes down the method he has chosen as most suitable to his way of learning. These Method Testimonials are filed in students' writing folders, and from time to time the teacher asks each one to write a statement beneath his testimonial. These statements are dated and indicate whether or not the student is finding the chosen method appropriate, as evidenced by his degree of improvement in functional spelling situations. This teacher spends much more time *teaching* spelling, studying words, and identifying effective ways of attacking words than he does testing words.

AWAKEN A SPELLING CONSCIENCE

Just as there are Sunday Christians, so are there Friday Spellers, persons of limited vision who do not transfer into practice the intention of the ritual. It is the considered opinion of many teachers that little progress in spelling will be made so long as the practice persists of giving grades for spelling drills. If the spelling grade is to foster any carry-over from spelling lessons to application, it must be assigned for actual proficiency in written work. Several times each marking period the teacher should sample his students' papers, both in their writing folders and, if time permits, in written assignments for other courses. Only when pupils really comprehend the importance of applying what they learn will they develop a spelling conscience. To the extent that it is possible, even this use of grades should be replaced by the students' own pride in their spelling skill. Internal pressures such as pride are always more effective than external pressures.

APPENDIX D

Developing Legible Handwriting

Untidiness in handwriting and errors in spelling often keep company with one another, but even an infallible correctness in spelling cannot sustain a reader's attention if he must struggle to decipher a writer's handwriting. A teacher can do much to maintain good penmanship if he holds students to reasonable standards of legibility. Additionally, he can improve handwriting if he helps pupils identify specific difficulties. As in spelling, instruction in handwriting is least wasteful when adapted to the needs of individuals.

There should be a parable of the foolish teacher who persisted in teaching general skills of handwriting to his entire class. The parable would conclude with the teacher's happy realization of how inefficient his procedure had been and his resolution to teach only what was needed to those pupils who lacked specific skills. In carrying out this resolution, this happier and wiser teacher would discover the twin goals of handwriting instruction, legibility and fluency—legibility as a social courtesy to the reader and fluency as a matter of ease and speed for the writer. The teacher in our parable would discover also that research has identified the few handwriting errors which constitute the major proportion of all illegibility. For instance *a, e, r,* and *t* are the first four letters in importance to teachers searching for specific trouble spots,[1] and good letter formation is more important than slant, spacing, alignment, or weight of line.[2] Finally, if this teacher read the research of Lehman and Pressey,[3] he would be convinced that by directing teaching effort at specific faults, not only will legibility be strikingly increased but so also will be speed and quality of handwriting. In conclusion, the reformed teacher would be convinced of the individual nature of handwriting problems and the need for a direct attack on these problems.

For teachers who already accept principles of economy in teaching and avoid blanket instruction to all alike, the problem is one of locating the best methods of individualizing instruction and improving specific skills. The suggestions that follow, all drawn from actual teaching situations in which handwriting has been improved, are intended to represent such ways.

Organize a legibility campaign To carry out this method the teacher illustrates good and poor handwriting by holding up or passing around the class varied samples of pupil handwriting from which names have been removed. He drives home the point by placing on the chalk board the next day's assignment, in handwriting so difficult to read that students complain. Next, he asks each student to write a specimen paragraph—this may be copied or dictated—and to assign himself a score on the *Ayres Measuring Scale for Handwriting*[4] or the *Freeman Handwriting Measuring Scale for Grade 7, 8 and 9.*[5] These charts may be placed around the room at convenient spots or passed from student to student. "Can we identify the main characteristics of good handwriting?" the teacher asks. Through analysis and discussion, the students may be led to identify the elements which make for legibility:

Careful letter formation. Because this is the most important factor in legibility, it deserves the greatest emphasis.

Spacing.

Alignment.

[1] T. Ernest Newland, "An Analytical Study of the Development of Illegibilities in Handwriting from the Lower Grades to Adulthood," *Journal of Educational Research,* Vol. 26, No. 4 (December 1932).

[2] Leslie Quant, "Factors Affecting the Legibility of Handwriting," *Journal of Experimental Education,* Vol. 14, No. 4 (June 1946).

[3] Hilda Lehman and Luella C. Pressey, "The Effectiveness of Drill in Handwriting to Remove Specific Illegibilities," *School and Society,* Vol 27, No. 697 (May 5, 1928).

[4] Department of Education, Russell Sage Foundation, 505 Park Ave., New York 22, N.Y.

[5] Zaner-Bloser Co., 612 North Park St., Columbus 8, Ohio.

Consistent slant. The research of Quant, cited above, found regularity of slant to be fairly important, also, in creating legibility.

Quality of line. Light, average, or heavy weight of line needs to be discussed but not stressed.

The teacher reiterates the importance of careful letter formation, with concern for the other four elements only as contributors to letter formation. He urges the use of simplified efficient letter forms free from flourishes and eccentricities, as well as attention to good posture and freedom of arm movement. The two characteristics of good writing—legibility and fluency—are written on the board, and the teacher asks, "Now, what could we do to improve our handwriting?" A list of suggestions is added to the purposes already on the chalk board. If no one else makes the suggestion, the teacher proposes that teams and team leaders be formed to operate for a period of time. The team leaders will check the efforts of their team members, help them identify their difficulties, and furnish them with suitable drills. In junior high classes, recognition should be given to the teams making the most progress. Frequent expressions of pleasure and praise from the teacher are often effective. If the poorest penmen keep charts of drills completed and draw their progress on a graph, they will make greater efforts and show more improvement.

Prepare handwriting charts and related drills With the help of good penmen, the teacher can prepare charts on large sheets of cardboard. One chart might discuss, for instance, the matter of slant and the need for shifting the paper to the left often enough to keep the writing directly in line with the eye. Then might follow samples of regular and irregular slant as revealed in samples pasted to the cardboard chart. In a pocket at the foot of the chart should be placed exercises for students having difficulties with slant. Similar charts should be prepared for letter formation, spacing, alignment, and quality of line.[6]

The teacher asks the student to see whether or not he can determine which difficulties he is having in handwriting. Once difficulties have been diagnosed, the child selects drills from the appropriate chart and works on these.[7] It is important that such drills be followed soon by some regular writing in which someone is to receive the communication of ideas. These compositions are studied and become the basis for further remedial work, each student practicing on drills appropriate to his specific difficulties.

To assist in diagnosing the difficulties in handwriting, teachers and their student assistants will find especially helpful the large, well-organized *Chart for Diagnosing Faults in Handwriting* prepared by Frank N. Freeman.[8] Equally

[6] Similar helpful materials may be secured from the Handwriting Foundation, 1426 G St., N.W., Washington 5, D.C., and Zaner-Bloser Co., Columbus 8, Ohio.

[7] Teachers must remember, in all this activity, that some pupils will be left-handed. The hazards in pressing left-handed children to write with the right hand are very great. Instead, they will need special drills for left-handed writing and individual attention. Very frequently, they need to feel secure with the teacher.

[8] Houghton Mifflin Co., 2 Park St., Boston 7, Mass.

helpful is the chart called *Handwriting Faults and How to Correct Them.*[9] Both of these can be displayed in the room and the pupil may go to them with his own handwriting, holding it alongside the charts to determine the specific problems he has. Drill materials, if the teacher does not have time to prepare them, might include the *Courtis Standard Practice Tests in Handwriting*[10] and the large *Classroom Perception Strips,*[11] ten very large strips of handwriting practice which would be particularly helpful to pupils who learn best through kinesthetic methods and need, at the beginning, to practice large arm movements before refining their writing through drills on standard sized sheets of paper. *The Handwriting Training Manual,*[12] also, is an effective aid to have in the hands of each pupil.

Train "technicians" to give specialized assistance In some schools teachers instruct five or six helpers to give specialized assistance to class members who need help. These "technicians" may be either responsible students in class, members of Future Teachers of America, or older pupils receiving credit or pay for in-school work experience. Each technician specializes in a single aspect of writing—posture, word formation, general neatness and appearance, or consistent slant.

Where teachers' aides cannot be drawn from these sources or from service clubs in the school or community, teachers might use the method employed by a school in San Lorenzo, California. In grades seven and eight, handwriting receives emphasis. Captains are selected to meet with the teacher and to help plan out the needs and the program. From time to time, samples of handwriting are taken from each captain's team, papers are scored by the teacher and turned over to the captains for verification. After this, typical examples, both superior and weak, are posted without names, and plans for remedial help are organized. At six-week intervals, rechecking of samples takes place. In these subsequent checks of samples, each student writes a score on his paper. All papers which show students performing at a level below their first scores are returned to them for rewriting. By the end of the year students show a great deal of improvement.

Share research with the class The teacher may explain to students what has been discovered about handwriting. For instance, he may place on the chalk board and discuss these facts:

Rogues' Gallery for Our Post Office Wall

The "closed e" is the greatest offender.[13]

The next "most wanted" offenders on the FBI (For Banishing Illegibility) list are these:

[9] Zaner-Bloser Co., Columbus 8, Ohio.

[10] World Book Co., Tarrytown-on-Hudson, New York, or 2126 South Prairie Ave., Chicago 16, Illinois.

[11] Zaner-Bloser Co., Columbus 8, Ohio.

[12] The Handwriting Foundation, Washington 5, D.C.

[13] Newland, *An Analytical Study.*

d written like *el*
r written like *i*
i not dotted
h written like *li*
n written like *u*

Poor letter formation is usually due to one of these faults: [14]

Failure to close letters
Top loops closed (*l* like *t*, *e* like *i*)
Looping non-looped strokes (*i* like *e*)
Using straight upstrokes rather than rounded strokes (*n* like *u*, *c* like *i*, *h* like *li*)
End stroke difficulty (not brought up, not brought down, not left horizontal) (*a* like *o*, *u* like *v*)

Concentration on the items above should eliminate seventy-five per cent of the illegibility problem.

Emphasize the ten commandments of good handwriting Place on the chalk board and, from time to time, call attention to the ten commandments of good handwriting: [15]

The Ten Commandments of Good Handwriting

Here are ten important points that make the difference between legible handwriting and a mediocre scrawl:

1. Uniform but not excessive slant.
2. Properly closed *a*, *d*, *g*, *p*, *q*, and *s*.
3. Well-crossed *t* and neatly dotted *i*.
4. Loops on *f*, *g*, *l*, *k*, *b* and *g*, *j*, *y*, and *z* kept small to prevent intertwining with loops on line above or below.
5. Good spacing of letters in each word and between words.
6. Arched *m* and *n* so that they can be clearly distinguished from *w* and *u*.
7. Looped *e*.
8. Slight point on *r* so that it does not look like an *n*.
9. Good alignment.
10. Simplicity. Overelaboration is always bad form.

Present the cost of illegibility In "The Moving Finger Writes—But Who Can Read It?" Robert O'Brien [16] offers some statistics: a million letters a year in the dead-letter office, a million dollars a week in business losses due to scrambled orders, lost time, mis-sent deliveries. Teachers will find his article to be valuable ammunition in defeating illegibility.

[14] *Ibid.*

[15] In the *Teacher's Guide to Handwriting*, the Handwriting Foundation, Washington, 5, D.C.

[16] Robert O'Brien, "The Moving Finger Writes—But Who Can Read It?" *Saturday Review*, Vol. 42, No. 29 (July 18, 1959).

APPENDIX E

School Publications

Schools cannot always hire teachers or allocate extracurricular responsibilities in such a way that every assignment represents a perfect fusing of talent, preparation, and position. This sometimes means that teachers of English are assigned or choose the sponsorship of the school newspaper or yearbook. The teacher may have little or no experience or training in journalism or other aspects of publication.

Although a new sponsor in such a situation may learn by some mistakes, he need not lack for sources of help and advice. As soon as possible, he will examine any files of the school publication he is to direct, looking for traditions and features worthy of continuation. For preliminary decisions, he will seek the advice of the last faculty member to fill the position. When this is not possible, a local printer is often one of the most helpful persons to visit, for a printer can in a very short time clarify standards and regulations that are difficult to understand from textbooks. At the same time, a visit to a Multilith office in the community or a nearby city may open up possibilities not realized at first. Another helpful beginning, well worth the time expended, is a series of visits to publication advisers in nearby schools. The articles listed immediately at the end of this appendix are recommended as another resource; each of them addresses teachers lacking in experience with publications. Selective reading in a recent text will still further reduce bewilderment. Enrollment in one or several of the national or state organizations such as those listed below will add sources of help through counseling services and materials especially written to assist the new sponsor.

SCHOLASTIC PRESS GROUPS

These are national scholastic press groups. Two, the Columbia Scholastic Press Association and the National Scholastic Press Association, open their rolls only to school publications. The third, Quill and Scroll Society, emphasizes individual activity. The Catholic Press Association serves parochial schools under the jurisdiction of the Roman Catholic Church.

The National Scholastic Press Association The National Scholastic Press Association is sponsored by the University of Minnesota. Its address is School of Journalism Building, University of Minnesota, Minneapolis 14, Minnesota. The purpose of NSPA is to improve school publications by offering guidance. Membership entitles a school publication to a thorough criticism by professional journalists, who use elaborate scorebooks which in themselves prove helpful to staffs. Publications—newspapers, magazines, and yearbooks—are rated yearly. NSPA also 1) sponsors a national student press conference each year, with professional journalists to address and advise student and adviser delegates; 2) makes available specimens of model student publications through a loan service; 3) publishes bulletins and booklets; 4) provides special services for schools without trained journalism advisers.

Scholastic Editor, a magazine published nine months of the academic year, is the official organ of the association. NSPA will send you, as a member, the following: *Newspaper Guidebook, Yearbook Guidebook,* and copies of *Scholastic Editor.* An independent but affiliated organization for advisers supplies help in setting up a class in journalism and also provides short summer courses for inservice training of advisers. The organization also publishes four pamphlets the experienced or inexperienced adviser may find helpful: *Helpful Aids for the Journalism Teacher, The Yearbook Theme, A Course of Study in High School Journalism,* and *Visual Aids in Journalism.* This group is also affiliated with the National Education Association and with Quill and Scroll.

The Columbia Scholastic Press Association This organization is open to newspapers, magazines, and yearbooks of elementary schools, junior high schools, senior high schools, junior colleges, normal schools, and teachers' colleges. It has a publication for advisers with articles written by teachers in the field. The group also maintains a yearbook loan service. Annual contests are held in various grades, and the publications are criticized and rated. Individual awards are given for outstanding writing. Professional journalists and publishers speak and advise delegates at the annual convention on the campus of Columbia University. The association publishes booklets and bulletins prepared by committees of faculty advisers. The official journal is the *School Press Review,* published eight times during the school year. The address is Columbia University, New York 27, New York. The group offers such items as style books, proofreader's cards, books on fundamentals, and booklets in advertising, humor, and sports writing.

The Quill and Scroll Society Quill and Scroll, the international honorary society for high school journalists, is connected with no school or university. Because chapters are widely scattered, no national convention is held. To be eligible for a chapter, a high school must publish a newspaper, yearbook, or magazine considered of sufficient merit by Quill and Scroll's executive council. The address is Executive Secretary, Quill and Scroll Society, 339 East Chicago Avenue, Chicago 11, Illinois. To be eligible for admission to a chapter, students must 1) be of at least junior standing; 2) be in the upper third of their class in general scholastic standing; 3) have done superior work in some phase of journalism, or "creative endeavor"; 4) be recommended by a faculty adviser or committee; 5) be approved by the executive secretary.

The Society provides a critical service, issues frequent publications, and conducts contests throughout the school year. *Quill and Scroll,* the society's magazine, is published every other month during the school year. Other helpful publications are *Chapter Manual, Handbook on School News, Principal's Guide to High School Journalism, Do's and Dont's for Staff,* and *Newspaper Management Book.* All of these are included with membership. The society annually awards a $500 scholarship to an outstanding high school journalist.

Catholic Press Association The purpose of this group is to stress the diffusion of Roman Catholic thought and to promote Catholic activity as well as service to the school and community. It provides bi-annual critical rating, a style book, and awards. The address is Marquette University, 1131 West Wisconsin Avenue, Milwaukee 3, Wisconsin.

A policy on entering contests should be considered. Many schools resist such contests, preferring to avoid pressures which could lead to a transcendence of the local purposes of using publications as a part of the pupils' education. However, the school can take advantage of the critical services without entering its publications in active competition.

Some schools have prepared yearbooks or issues of newspapers to represent the pupils' concept of American life and have sent these as gifts to schools in foreign countries.

The English teacher who sponsors a school publication finds many opportunities to integrate journalism and English. He can, for instance, stimulate the reading of excellent books about newspapers and publishing, books like the autobiographies of William Allen White and Lincoln Steffens. The writings of Ernie Pyle and Will Rogers are also excellent choices for almost every pupil, and for the less mature reader, books like *Get that Story: Journalism—Its Lure and Thrills* are in most libraries. The English teacher in charge of publications can also bring newspaper style sheets and the guide sheets used in the classroom into closer conformity than they now are in many schools. Journalistic writing can be related to classroom instruction in composition except that in journalism certain restrictions are added, along with an even stricter emphasis on accuracy, observation, and clarity of expression. An understanding of the press, its control, and its function in promoting the welfare of citizens may belong to the social studies class, but the ability to read newspapers and magazines in an intelligent and analytical manner is the concern of an English class.

The issue of the exact place of publications deserves a brief comment. They may be either a curriculum offering or an extracurricular activity. However, if journalism appears in the curriculum, publications should not be projects of the English classes nor should it be possible to elect journalism in lieu of English. The crucial importance of English in the curriculum cannot be overemphasized. There is all too little time to accomplish the aims of English without whittling time from literature to make room for layout, dummies, count and column inches, even though other aspects of journalism do contribute to learning in composition. Journalism can be a valuable course offering, but it is not a substitute for English.

Four final cautions for beginning sponsors of publications:

Let the newspaper and yearbook genuinely represent the entire school rather than a clique. A small group may do most of the work, but they should see their role as one of service rather than domination.

Set up standards at the very opening meeting of the staff, standards which will preclude the callow and often harmful gossip columns. Parents and others interested in the schools often react adversely to items in such columns.

Recognize the amateur nature of school sports writers. Encourage a style suitable to school sports and avoid direct imitation of sports writers in newspapers with large circulations.

Remember that school publications are passed from student to parent to friends, sent to advertisers, placed in business offices, and, in relation to their size, widely read. They are the most active representative of a school and are often influential in establishing community opinions.

ARTICLES

Clark Green and Jerry Wergeland, "So You've Been Elected to Teach Journalism." *The Pacific Slope Student and Publisher* (September–October and November –December, 1956). This magazine is published by School of Communications, University of Washington, Seattle 5, Washington.

Harold Hainfield, "Developing an Offset School Newspaper." *School Activities* (November 1957). "Just starting a school newspaper? Consider offset printing," advises Mr. Hainfield. Not only does photo-offset give a school an attractive and neat newspaper at low cost, but it also allows more student participation and strengthens school-community relations.

James W. Olson, "Directing the School Paper." *English Journal,* No. 6 (September 1958). Practical advice and wisdom, both obviously the distillation of experience.

BOOKS

J. Kenner Agnew, *Today's Journalism for Today's Schools,* rev. ed., Syracuse, N.Y., Singer, 1960. The problems of copy writing, editing, layout-makeup, and proofreading of the high school newspaper are handled practically and directly.

Columbia Scholastic Press Association, *Guide to 16mm Educational Motion Pictures That Relate to Journalism and Newspapers.* N.Y., Columbia U. Press, 1952.

Curriculum Division of Whittier Union High School District, *Cub Reporting, Students' Manual.* Whittier, Calif., 1954.

Harry E. Heath and Lou Gelford, *How to Cover, Write, and Edit Sports.* Ames, Iowa, Iowa State College Press, 1951.

Lederer, Street, and Zeus Company, *Yearbook Production–What To Do and When.* 2121 Allston Way, Berkeley 4, Calif.

Frederick W. Maguire and Richard M. Soong, *Journalism and the Student Publication.* N.Y., Harper, 1959. Written to the student himself, this book ties together into a comprehensive whole the techniques of good writing, make-up, organization and functions of the staff, advertising, printing, and handbook material such as headline point categories and proofreader's marks. All along, the workings of a big commercial paper are paralleled in treatment with school paper techniques. The book is well organized and illustrated, and is not as detailed or advanced in study as other texts.

C. J. Medlin, *School Yearbook Editing and Management.* Ames, Iowa, Iowa State College Press, 1956.

Carl G. Miller, *Modern Journalism.* N.Y., Holt, 1955. Recommended by Green and Wergeland (see articles list) as the most useful text for beginning sponsors.

National Press Photographers Association, *Complete Book of Press Photography.* N.Y., 1950.

DeWitt C. Reddick, *Journalism and the School Paper.* Boston, Heath, 1958.

Geraldine Saltzberg, *Knowing Your Newspaper.* Yonkers, N.Y., World Book, 1953.

Harold Spears and C. H. Lawshe, *High School Journalism.* N.Y., Macmillan, 1956. This text relies almost entirely on sample illustrations instead of written instruction. An excellent guide for prize-winning goals in writing and page-planning, it is particularly helpful to a school with a large staff and paper.

BIBLIOGRAPHY

Titles, Films, Filmstrips, and Recordings Referred to in the Text

The following bibliography is included to assist teachers who wish to obtain selections and audio-visual aids mentioned in this book. Whenever possible, references are to publications available in print. Sources likely to be easily accessible to teachers have frequently been used rather than the original publication. Inasmuch as only one source is cited for each title, teachers who wish to look further should consult some of the reference tools listed here.

Books in Print, edited by Sarah L. Prakken. N.Y., Bowker, 1960. Revised yearly.

Short Story Index, compiled by Dorothy E. Cook and Isabel S. Monro. N.Y., H. W. Wilson, 1953. Supplements bring this volume up to date.

Granger's Index to Poetry, 4th ed., indexing anthologies published through December 31, 1950. N.Y., Columbia U. Press, 1953.

Play Index, compiled by Dorothy Herbert West and Dorothy Margaret Peake. N.Y., H. W. Wilson, 1953.

Index to Plays in Collections, by John H. Ottemiller. 3rd ed., rev. and enl. N.Y., Scarecrow Press, 1957.

An Index to One-Act Plays for Stage, Radio, and Television, by Hannah Logasa. 4th supplement. Boston, F. W. Faxon, 1958.

Index to Full Length Plays, 1926-1944, by Ruth Gibbons Thomson. Boston, F. W. Faxon, 1946.

Essay and General Literature Index, edited by Dorothy Herbert West. N.Y., Wilson, 1960. Supplements issued periodically.

Biography Index, edited by Bea Joseph and Charlotte Warren Squires. N.Y., Wilson, 1953. Quarterly supplements.

FICTION

Paul Annixter, *Swiftwater.* N.Y., A. A. Wyn, 1950.

Victor Appleton (pseudonym). *Tom Swift and His Great Searchlight;* or *On the Border for Uncle Sam.* N.Y., Grosset & Dunlap, 1912 (part of a series of novels).

Richard Armour, *Twisted Tales from Shakespeare.* N.Y., McGraw-Hill, 1957.

Harriette Arnow, *The Dollmaker.* N.Y., Macmillan, 1954.

Peter Asbjörnsen and Moe Jorgen, *East of the Sun and West of the Moon.* Eau Claire, Wisc., Cadmus, 1958.

Richard and Florence Atwater, *Mr. Popper's Penguins.* Boston, Little, Brown, 1938.

Jane Austen, *Emma.* N.Y., Grove, 1950.

———, *Pride and Prejudice.* N.Y., Coward, 1953.

Enid Bagnold, *National Velvet.* N.Y., Morrow, 1949.

Edwin Balmer and Philip Wylie, *When Worlds Collide.* Phila., Lippincott, 1950.

Nancy Barnes (Helen S. Adams), *The Wonderful Year.* N.Y., Messner, 1946.

J. Bédier, *The Romance of Tristan and Iseult,* trans. by H. Belloc. N.Y., Doubleday Anchor, 1953.

Edward Bellamy, *Looking Backward.* N.Y., Harper, 1959.

Ludwig Bemelmans, *Madeleine's Rescue.* N.Y., Viking, 1953.

Arnold Bennett, *The Old Wives' Tale*. N.Y., Modern Library, 1935.
James Boyd, *Drums*. N.Y., Scribner's, 1936.
H. D. Boylston, *Sue Barton, Student Nurse*. Boston, Little, Brown, 1936.
Charlotte Brontë, *Jane Eyre*. N.Y., Oxford U. Press, 1954.
Emily Brontë, *Wuthering Heights*, Mark Schorer, ed. N.Y., Rinehart, 1950.
Carol Ryrie Brink, *Caddie Woodlawn*. N.Y., Macmillan, 1935.
Pearl Buck, *The Good Earth*. N.Y., Day, 1949.
E. G. Bulwer-Lytton, *The Last Days of Pompeii*. N.Y., Dodd, Mead, 1946.
Samuel Butler, *Erewhon*. N.Y., Modern Library, 1927.
Erskine Caldwell, *God's Little Acre*. N.Y., Grosset and Dunlap, 1957.
Dorothy Canfield, *Understood Betsy*. N.Y., Henry Holt, 1946.
Willa Cather, *My Antonia*. Boston, Houghton Mifflin, 1932.
Edna Walker Chandler, *Cowboy Andy*. N.Y., Random House, 1959.
Florence Choate, *Linda Takes Over*. Phila., Lippincott, 1949.
Walter Van Tilburg Clark, *The Ox-Bow Incident*. N.Y., Random House, 1940.
Beverly Cleary, *Henry Huggins*. N.Y., Morrow, 1950.
James C. Coleman, *The Sea Hunt*. San Francisco, Harr Wagner, 1959.
———, *Treasure Under the Sea*. San Francisco, Harr Wagner, 1959.
James C. Coleman, Frances Berres, Frank N. Hewett, and William Briscoe, *Deep Sea Adventure Series*. San Francisco, Harr Wagner, 1959.
Joseph Conrad, *Heart of Darkness*. From *Tales of Land and Sea*. Garden City, N.Y., Doubleday, 1953.
———, *Lord Jim*. N.Y., Rinehart, 1957.
———, *The Secret Sharer*. Garden City, N.Y., Doubleday, 1953.
———, *Victory*. N.Y., Doubleday Anchor, 1953.
Stephen Crane, *The Red Badge of Courage*. N.Y., Modern Library, 1951.
Maureen Daly, *Seventeenth Summer*. N.Y., Dodd, Mead, 1948.
Charles Dickens, *David Copperfield*. N.Y., Modern Library, 1950.
———, *A Christmas Carol*. N.Y., Grosset & Dunlap, 1958.
———, *Great Expectations*. N.Y., Rinehart, 1951.
———, *Oliver Twist*. N.Y., Dodd, Mead, 1946.
———, *Pickwick Papers*. N.Y., Coward-McCann, 1955.
———, *A Tale of Two Cities*. N.Y., Harcourt, Brace, 1950.
Marguerite Dickson, *Bennett High*. N.Y., Longmans, Green, 1953.
———, *Only Child*. N.Y., Longmans, Green, 1952.
Feodor Dostoyevsky, *Crime and Punishment*, trans. by Jessie Coulson. N.Y., Oxford U. Press, 1953.
Theodore Dreiser, *An American Tragedy*. Cleveland, Ohio, World, 1925.
Alexandre Dumas, *The Count of Monte Cristo*. N.Y., McGraw-Hill, 1946.
George Eliot, *Silas Marner*. N.Y., Grove, 1954.
Anne Emery, *Mountain Laurel*. N.Y., Putnam, 1948.
Elizabeth Enright, *The Saturdays*. N.Y., Rinehart. 1941.
Helen Worden Erskine, *Out of This World*. N.Y., Putnam, 1953.
Eleanor Estes, *Ginger Pye*. N.Y., Harcourt, Brace, 1951.
———, *The Hundred Dresses*. N.Y., Harcourt, Brace, 1944.
———, *The Moffats*. N.Y., Harcourt, Brace, 1941.
Henry Gregor Felsen, *Hot Rod*. N.Y., Dutton, 1950.
———, *Street Rod*. N.Y., Random House, 1953.
Edna Ferber, *Giant*. Garden City, N.Y., Doubleday, 1952.
Esther Forbes, *Johnny Tremain*. Boston, Houghton Mifflin, 1943.
Kathryn Forbes, *Mama's Bank Account*. N.Y., Harcourt Brace, 1943.
Henry Willard French, *The Lance of Kanana*. N.Y., Lothrop, Lee & Shepard, 1932.
Wanda Gag, *Millions of Cats*. N.Y., Coward-McCann, 1939.
Doris Gates, *Blue Willow*. N.Y., Viking, 1940.

Doris Gates, *Little Vic.* N.Y., Viking, 1951.
———, *My Brother Mike.* N.Y., Viking, 1948.
———, *North Fork.* N.Y., Viking, 1945.
———, *River Ranch.* N.Y., Viking, 1949.
———, *Sensible Kate.* N.Y., Viking, 1943.
Theodor Geisel (Dr. Seuss), *The 500 Hats of Bartholomew Cubbins.* N.Y., Vanguard, 1937.
Fred Gipson, *Old Yeller.* N.Y., Harper, 1956.
Rummer Godden, *The Mousewife.* N.Y., Viking, 1951.
Oliver Goldsmith, *The Vicar of Wakefield.* N.Y., Macmillan, 1947.
Alfred Bertram Guthrie, *The Way West.* Boston, Houghton Mifflin, 1950.
Thomas Hardy, *The Return of the Native.* N.Y., Rinehart, 1950.
Nathaniel Hawthorne, *The House of the Seven Gables.* N.Y., Dodd, Mead, 1950.
———, *The Scarlet Letter.* N.Y., Modern Library, 1950.
Thomas Heggen, *Mr. Roberts.* Boston, Houghton Mifflin, 1946.
Ernest Hemingway, *The Old Man and the Sea.* N.Y., Scribner's, 1952.
Marguerite Henry, *King of the Wind.* N.Y., Rand McNally, 1948.
John Hersey, *A Bell for Adano.* N.Y., Knopf, 1944.
James Hilton, *Lost Horizon.* N.Y., Morrow, 1936.
Alice Tisdale Hobart, *The Peacock Sheds Its Tail.* Indianapolis, Bobbs-Merrill, 1945.
Victor Hugo, *Les Misérables.* N.Y., Dodd, Mead, 1925.
William Bradford Huie, *The Execution of Private Slovik.* N.Y., New American Library, 1954.
Evan Hunter, *Blackboard Jungle.* N.Y., Pocket Books, 1954.
Aldous Huxley, *Brave New World.* N.Y., Harper, 1946.
James Joyce, *Portrait of the Artist as a Young Man.* N.Y., New American Library, 1948.
Harold Keith, *Rifles for Watie.* N.Y., Crowell, 1957.
Carolyn Keene, *Nancy Drew Mystery Series.* N.Y., Grosset & Dunlap, circa 1940-1960 (35 books published).
Rudyard Kipling, *Captains Courageous.* N.Y., Grosset & Dunlap, 1954.
———, *Jungle Book.* Garden City, N.Y., Doubleday, 1946.
Clarissa Kneeland, *Smugglers' Island* or, *The Devil Fires of San Moros.* N.Y., New Voices, 1958.
Eric M. Knight, *Lassie Come Home.* Phila., Winston, 1940.
Joseph Krumgold, *And Now Miguel.* N.Y., Crowell, 1953.
Selma Lagerlöf, *The Ring of the Löwenskölds.* N.Y., Doubleday, 1931.
E. S. Lampman, *Rusty's Space Ship.* Garden City, N.Y., Doubleday, 1957.
Margaret Landon, *Anna and the King of Siam.* N.Y., Day, 1944.
Walter Savage Landor, *Imaginary Conversations and Poems.* N.Y., Dutton, 1933.
Rose Wilder Lane, *Let the Hurricane Roar.* N.Y., Longmans, Green, 1933.
Munro Leaf, *The Story of Ferdinand.* N.Y., Viking, 1936.
Lois Lenski, *Strawberry Girl.* Phila., Winston, 1932.
Sinclair Lewis, *Arrowsmith.* N.Y., Harcourt, Brace, 1925.
———, *Babbitt.* N.Y., Harcourt, Brace, 1922.
Mina Lewiton, *The Divided Heart.* N.Y., McKay, 1947.
Richard Llewellyn, *How Green Was My Valley.* N.Y., Macmillan, 1940.
Jack London, *The Call of the Wild.* N.Y., Arcadia House, 1950.
———, *White Fang.* N.Y., Grosset & Dunlap, 1933.
John P. Marquand, *Point of No Return.* Boston, Little, Brown, 1949.
Robert McCloskey, *Homer Price.* N.Y., Viking, 1943.
Stephen Meader, *Down the Big River.* N.Y., Harcourt, Brace, 1924.
———, *Red Horse Hill.* N.Y., Harcourt, Brace, 1930.
Herman Melville, *Moby Dick.* N.Y., Grosset & Dunlap, 1956.

James A. Michener, *The Bridges of Toko-Ri.* N.Y., Random House, 1953.
Sir Thomas More, *Utopia.* N.Y., Heritage Press, 1959.
Ralph Moody, *Little Britches.* N.Y., Norton, 1950.
———, *Man of the Family.* N.Y., Norton, 1951.
Honoré Willsie Morrow, *On to Oregon.* N.Y., Morrow, 1946.
John Muir, *Stickeen.* Boston, Houghton Mifflin, 1909.
Charles B. Nordhoff and James N. Hall, *Mutiny on the Bounty.* Boston, Little, Brown, 1932.
Mary Norton, *The Borrowers.* N.Y., Harcourt, Brace, 1953.
Jack O'Brian, *Return of Silver Chief.* Phila., Winston, 1940.
———, *Silver Chief.* Phila., Winston, 1933.
George Orwell, *Animal Farm.* N.Y., New American Library, 1956.
Alan Paton, *Cry, the Beloved Country.* N.Y., Scribner's, 1948.
Howard Pease, *The Dark Adventure.* Garden City, N.Y., Doubleday, 1950.
Marjorie Kinnan Rawlings, *The Yearling.* N.Y., Scribner's, 1939.
Kenneth Roberts, *Boon Island.* Garden City, N.Y., Doubleday, 1956.
———, *Northwest Passage.* Garden City, N.Y., Doubleday, 1937.
Ole E. Rolvaag, *Giants in the Earth.* N.Y., Harper, 1927.
S. M. Russell, *The Lamp Is Heavy.* Phila., Lippincott, 1950.
Antoine de St. Exupéry, *The Little Prince.* N.Y., Harcourt, Brace, 1943.
J. D. Salinger, *Catcher in the Rye.* Boston, Little, Brown, 1951.
William Saroyan, *The Human Comedy.* N.Y., Harcourt, Brace, 1943.
Jack Schaefer, *Shane.* Boston, Houghton Mifflin, 1954.
Kate Seredy, *The Good Master.* N.Y., Viking, 1935.
———, *The White Stag.* N.Y., Viking, 1937.
Samuel Shellabarger, *Captain from Castille.* Boston, Little, Brown, 1945.
Irving Shulman, *The Amboy Dukes.* N.Y., Avon, 1946.
Henryk Sienkiewicz, *Quo Vadis.* Boston, Little, Brown, 1943.
Ignazio Silone, *Bread and Wine.* N.Y., Harper, 1957.
Armstrong Sperry, *Call It Courage.* N.Y., Macmillan, 1940.
———, *Storm Canvas.* Phila., Winston, 1944.
John Steinbeck, *The Pearl.* N.Y., Viking, 1947.
Augusta Stevenson, *Nancy Hanks: Kentucky Girl.* Indianapolis, Bobbs-Merrill, 1954.
Robert Louis Stevenson, *Treasure Island.* Chicago, Rand McNally, 1954.
George Stewart, *Earth Abides.* N.Y., Random House, 1949.
———, *The Years of the City.* Boston, Houghton Mifflin, 1955.
James Street, *Goodbye, My Lady.* Phila., Lippincott, 1954.
———, *Tap Roots.* N.Y., Dial, 1942.
James L. Summers, *Operation A.B.C.* Phila., Westminster, 1955.
Booth Tarkington, *Turmoil.* N.Y, Grosset & Dunlap, 1918.
———, *Alice Adams.* N.Y., Grosset & Dunlap, 1921.
William M. Thackeray, *The History of Henry Esmond.* N.Y., Dodd, Mead, 1945.
———, *Vanity Fair.* N.Y., Modern Library, 1950.
M. W. Thompson, *Blueberry Muffin.* N.Y., Longmans, Green, 1942.
James Thurber, *Many Moons.* N.Y., Harcourt, Brace, 1943.
———, *Thirteen Clocks.* N.Y., Simon & Schuster, 1950.
Leo Tolstoy, *War and Peace.* N.Y., Simon & Schuster, 1942; N.Y., Grosset & Dunlap, 1956.
Pamela L. Travers, *Mary Poppins.* N.Y., Harcourt, Brace, 1934.
John Tunis, *All-American.* N.Y., Harcourt, Brace, 1952.
———, *Yea! Wildcats!* N.Y., Harcourt, Brace, 1944.
Mark Twain, *A Connecticut Yankee in King Arthur's Court.* N.Y., Harper, 1943.
———, *Adventures of Huckleberry Finn.* Boston, Houghton Mifflin, 1958 (Riverside edition).

Mark Twain, *The Adventures of Tom Sawyer*. Phila., Winston, 1952.
Hendrick W. Van Loon, *Van Loon's Lives*. N.Y., Simon & Schuster, 1942.
Jules Verne, *20,000 Leagues Under the Sea*. Chicago, Rand McNally, 1954.
Gertrude Chandler Warner, *Box Car Children*. N.Y., Scott, 1950.
H. G. Wells, *The Time Machine*. N.Y., Berkley, 1957.
Jessamyn West, *Cress Delahanty*. N.Y., Harcourt, Brace, 1953.
Edith Wharton, *Ethan Frome* N.Y., Scribner's, 1938.
E. B. White, *Charlotte's Web*. N.Y., Harper, 1952.
William Lindsay White, *Lost Boundaries*. N.Y., Harcourt, Brace, 1948.
Phyllis Whitney, *Willow Hill*. N.Y., McKay, 1947.
Kate Douglas Wiggin and Nora A. Smith, eds., *The Arabian Nights, The Best Known Tales*. N.Y., Scribner's, 1933.
Thornton Wilder, *The Bridge of San Luis Rey*. N.Y., Grosset & Dunlap, 1927.
Thomas Wolfe, *Look Homeward, Angel*. N.Y., Scribner's, 1929.
Herman Wouk, *The Caine Mutiny*. Garden City, N.Y., Doubleday, 1951.
J. D. Wyss, *Swiss Family Robinson*. Cleveland, World Publ., 1947.

SHORT STORIES

Sara Addington, "Clodhopper." In Luella B. Cook, Walter Loban, Ruth M. Stauffer, and Robert Freier, eds., *People in Literature*. N.Y., Harcourt, Brace, 1957.
Aesop, *The Fables of Aesop*, Walter L. Parker, ed. N.Y., Little and Ives, 1931.
Hans Christian Andersen, "The Nightingale." In *Six Fairy Tales by the Danish Writer Hans Christian Andersen, Published on the Occasion of the 150th Anniversary of His Birth*. Copenhagen, Det Berlingske Bogtrykkeii, 1955.
———, *Andersen's Fairy Tales*, trans. by Mrs. E. V. Lucas and Mrs. H. B. Paull. N.Y., Grosset & Dunlap, 1937.
Sherwood Anderson, "I'm a Fool." In Bennett A. Cerf, ed., *Great Modern Short Stories*. N.Y., Modern Library, 1942.
———, "Stolen Day." In Jacob M. Ross, Mary Rives Bowman, and Egbert W. Nieman, eds., *Adventures for Readers*, Book I, Mercury ed. N.Y., Harcourt, Brace, 1951.
Stephen Vincent Benét, "By the Waters of Babylon." In Luella B. Cook, Walter Loban, Ruth M. Stauffer, and Robert Freier, eds., *People in Literature*. N.Y., Harcourt, Brace, 1957.
André Birabeau, "Granny." In Luella B. Cook, Walter Loban, Oscar James Campbell, and Ruth M. Stauffer, eds., *The World Through Literature*. N.Y., Harcourt, Brace, 1949.
Heywood Broun, "The Fifty-First Dragon." In Howard Francis Seeley and Margaret Roling, eds., *Recent Stories for Enjoyment*. Morristown, N.J., Silver Burdett, 1937.
Walter C. Brown, "The Puzzle Knot." In William R. Wood, ed., *Short, Short Stories*. N.Y., Harcourt, Brace, 1951.
Morley Callaghan, "All the Years of Her Life." In Simon Certner and G. H. Henry, eds., *Short Stories for Our Times*. Boston, Houghton Mifflin, 1950.
———, "The Snob." In Luella B. Cook, Walter Loban, Ruth M. Stauffer, and Robert Freier, eds., *People in Literature*. N.Y., Harcourt, Brace, 1957.
Willa Cather, "Paul's Case." In Bennett A. Cerf, ed., *Great Modern Short Stories*. N.Y., Modern Library, 1942.
Anton Chekhov, "The Bet." In H. C. Schweikert, ed., *Short Stories*. N.Y., Harcourt, Brace, 1934.
Ann Chidester, "Mrs. Ketting and Clark Gable." In Herschel Brickell, ed., *Prize Stories of 1950: The O. Henry Awards*. Garden City, N.Y., Doubleday, 1950.

Walter Van Tilburg Clark, "The Portable Phonograph." In Luella B. Cook, Walter Loban, Ruth M. Stauffer, and Robert Freier, eds., *People in Literature*. N.Y., Harcourt, Brace, 1957.

Robert Coates, "The Need." In Martha Foley, ed., *The Best American Short Stories, 1953*. Boston, Houghton Mifflin, 1953.

Richard Connell, "The Most Dangerous Game." In Herbert A. Wise and Phyllis Fraser, eds., *Great Tales of Terror and the Supernatural*. N.Y., Modern Library, 1944.

Eugenie Courtright, "Yours Lovingly." In Luella B. Cook, Walter Loban, and Henry H. Miller, Jr., eds., *Adventures in Appreciation*, 3rd ed. N.Y., Harcourt, Brace, 1949.

James Gould Cozzens, "Success Story." In William R. Wood, ed., *Short Short Stories*. N.Y., Harcourt, Brace, 1951.

Maureen Daly, "Sixteen." In R. J. Cadigan, ed., *September to June*. N.Y., Appleton-Century-Crofts, 1942.

Mary Deasy, "The High Hill." In *Harper's* magazine, Vol. 196, No. 1173 (February 1948).

Arthur Conan Doyle, "The Adventure of the Bruce-Partington Plans." From *The Complete Sherlock Holmes*. Garden City, N.Y., Doubleday, 1936.

William Faulkner, "Barn Burning." In Robert Penn Warren and Albert Erskine, eds., *Short Story Masterpieces*. N.Y., Dell, 1954.

Michael Fessier, "That's What Happened to Me." In Walter Loban, Dorothy Holmstrom, and Luella B. Cook, eds., *Adventures in Appreciation*. N.Y., Harcourt, Brace, 1958.

Corey Ford, "The Snake Dance." In Frank G. Jennings and Charles J. Calitri, eds., *Stories*. N.Y., Harcourt, Brace, 1957.

E. M. Forster, "The Machine Stops." From *The Eternal Moment and Other Stories*. N.Y., Harcourt, Brace, 1928.

Mary E. Wilkins Freeman, "The Revolt of Mother." In Luella B. Cook, Walter Loban, and Susanna Baxter, eds., *Adventures in Appreciation*, Mercury ed. N.Y., Harcourt, Brace, 1952.

Zona Gale, "Bill's Little Girl." In Frank G. Jennings and Charles J. Calitri, eds., *Stories*. N.Y., Harcourt, Brace, 1957.

Richard T. Gill, "The Ten-Dollar Bill." In Elizabeth C. O'Daly and Egbert W. Niemann, eds., *Adventures for Readers*, Book I. N.Y., Harcourt, Brace, 1958.

Katherine Peabody Girling, "When Hanna Var Eight Yar Old." In Luella B. Cook, Walter Loban, Ruth M. Stauffer, and Robert Freier, eds., *People in Literature*. N.Y., Harcourt, Brace, 1957.

Albert Halper, "Prelude." In Maureen Daly, ed., *My Favorite Stories*. N.Y., Dodd, Mead, 1948.

Nathaniel Hawthorne, "The Great Stone Face" and "Ethan Brand." In *Complete Short Stories of Nathaniel Hawthorne*. Garden City, N.Y., Hanover House, 1959.

Ernest Hemingway, "Big Two-Hearted River." In Malcolm Cowley, ed., *The Portable Hemingway*. N.Y., Viking, 1944.

———, "A Day's Wait." In Whit Burnett, ed., *Time to Be Young*. Phila., Lippincott, 1945.

Murray Heyert, "The New Kid." In Marian Lovrien, Herbert Potall, and Prudence Bostwick, eds., *Adventures in Living*. N.Y., Harcourt, Brace, 1955.

Marjorie Holmes, "Reflections of Luanne." In Mary Dirlam, ed., *Hit Parade of Short Stories*. N.Y., Scholastic Corp., 1953.

Langston Hughes, "One Friday Morning." In Simon Certner and G. H. Henry, eds., *Short Stories for Our Times*. Boston, Houghton Mifflin, 1950.

Victor Hugo, "The Bishop's Candlesticks." From *Les Misérables*. N.Y., Norton, 1959.

Shirley Jackson, "Charles." From *Life Among the Savages.* N.Y., Farrar, Straus, & Young, 1953.

———, "The Lottery." From *The Lottery.* N.Y., Farrar, Straus, & Young, 1949.

William W. Jacobs, "The Monkey's Paw." In Herbert A. Wise and Phyllis Fraser, eds., *Great Tales of Terror and the Supernatural.* N.Y., Modern Library, 1944.

James Joyce, "Araby." In Charles Neider, ed., *Great Short Stories from the World's Literature.* N.Y., Rinehart, 1950.

Mackinlay Kantor, "The Boy in the Dark." In William R. Wood and John D. Husband, eds., *Short Stories As You Like Them.* N.Y., Harcourt, Brace, 1940.

Selma Lagerlöf, "The Rat Trap." In Luella B. Cook, Walter Loban, Oscar James Campbell, and Ruth M. Stauffer, eds., *The World Through Literature.* N.Y., Harcourt, Brace, 1949.

Ring Lardner, "Haircut." In Bennett A. Cerf, ed., *Great Modern Short Stories.* N.Y., Modern Library, 1942.

———, "I Can't Breathe." In Luella B. Cook, Walter Loban, Ruth M. Stauffer, and Robert Freier, eds., *People in Literature.* N.Y., Harcourt, Brace, 1957.

———, "Travelogue." From *Round Up.* N.Y., Scribner's, 1929.

Stephen Leacock, "The Man in Asbestos." From *The Laugh Parade.* N.Y., Dodd, Mead, 1940.

Jack London, "The Heathen." In Walter Loban, Dorothy Holmstrom, and Luella B. Cook, eds., *Adventures in Appreciation.* N.Y., Harcourt, Brace, 1958.

———, "To Build a Fire." In *Best Short Stories of Jack London.* N.Y., Permabooks, 1949.

George Loveridge, "The Cruise." In *Yale Review,* Vol. XLI, No. 1 (Autumn 1951).

Donald MacKenzie, "Too Late to Lie." In *Collier's,* Vol. 126, No. 25 (December 16, 1950).

Katherine Mansfield, "A Cup of Tea." In Harry Shaw and Douglas Bennett, eds., *Reading the Short Story.* N.Y., Harper, 1954.

———, "Miss Brill." In Bennett A. Cerf, ed., *Great Modern Short Stories.* N.Y., Modern Library, 1942.

Guy de Maupassant, "The Necklace" and "The Piece of String." From *The Great Short Stories of Guy de Maupassant.* N.Y., Pocket Library, 1958.

Marian Hurd McNeely, "The Horse." From *The Way to Glory and Other Stories.* N.Y., Longmans, Green, 1932.

Honoré Willsie Morrow, "Child Pioneer." In Jacob M. Ross, Egbert W. Nieman, and Mary Rives Bowman, eds., *Adventures for Readers,* Book I, Mercury ed. N.Y., Harcourt, Brace, 1953.

H. H. Munro (Saki), "The Lumber Room." In Luella B. Cook, Walter Loban, and Susanna Baxter, eds., *Adventures in Appreciation,* Mercury ed. N.Y., Harcourt, Brace, 1952.

———, "The Open Window." In Walter Loban, Dorothy Holmstrom, and Luella B. Cook, eds., *Adventures in Appreciation.* N.Y., Harcourt, Brace, 1958.

Frank O'Connor, "The Duke's Children." From *Domestic Relations.* N.Y., Knopf, 1957.

Lucile Vaughan Payne, "Prelude." In Bryna Ivens, ed., *The Seventeen Reader.* Phila., Lippincott, 1951.

Edgar Allan Poe, "The Cask of Amontillado." In Bernardine Kielty, ed., *A Treasury of Short Stories.* N.Y., Simon & Schuster, 1947.

———, "Descent into the Maelstrom," and "The Tell-Tale Heart." In Philip Van Doren Stern, ed., *Edgar Allan Poe.* N.Y., Viking, 1945.

———, "The Fall of the House of Usher." In Dudley Miles and Robert Pooley, eds., *Literature and Life in America.* Chicago, Scott, Foresman, 1943.

William Sydney Porter (O. Henry), "The Gift of the Magi." In Walter Loban,

Luella B. Cook, and Dorothy Holmstrom, eds., *Adventures in Appreciation.* N.Y., Harcourt, Brace, 1958.

William Sydney Porter (O. Henry), "A Municipal Report." In M. E. Speare, ed., *Short Stories.* N.Y., Pocket Books, 1950.

Marjorie Kinnan Rawlings, "A Mother in Mannville." In Whit Burnett, ed., *Time to Be Young.* Phila., Lippincott, 1945.

William Saroyan, "Five Ripe Pears." From *Inhale and Exhale.* N.Y., Random House, 1936.

———, "Locomotive 38." In B. A. Heydrick, ed., *Americans All.* N.Y., Harcourt, Brace, 1941.

———, "The Pheasant Hunter." From *The Assyrian and Other Stories.* N.Y., Harcourt, Brace, 1950.

Mark Schorer, "The Dead Dog." In William R. Wood, ed., *Short Short Stories.* N.Y., Harcourt, Brace, 1951.

Wilbur Daniel Steele, "Footfalls." In H. L. Shaw, ed., *Americans One and All.* N.Y., Harper, 1947.

John Steinbeck, "The Affair at 7, Rue de M___." In Walter Loban, Dorothy Holmstrom, and Luella B. Cook, eds., *Adventures in Appreciation.* N.Y., Harcourt, Brace, 1958.

Carl Stephenson, "Leiningen Versus the Ants." In Walter Loban, Dorothy Holmstrom, and Luella B. Cook, eds., *Adventures in Appreciation.* N.Y., Harcourt, Brace, 1958.

Robert Louis Stevenson, "The Sire de Maletroit's Door." In Bennett A. Cerf, ed., *Anthology of Famous British Stories.* N.Y., Modern Library, 1952.

Frank Stockton, "The Lady or the Tiger?" In A. G. Day, ed., *Greatest American Short Stories.* N.Y., McGraw-Hill, 1953.

Martin Storm, "A Shipment of Mute Fate." In Luella B. Cook, Walter Loban, George W. Norvell, and William A. McCall, eds., *Challenge to Explore.* N.Y., Harcourt, Brace, 1941.

Jesse Stuart, "As Ye Sow, So Shall Ye Reap." In William R. Wood, ed., *Short Short Stories.* N.Y., Harcourt, Brace, 1951.

———, "The Split Cherry Tree." In Albert B. Tibbets, ed., *Youth, Youth, Youth.* N.Y., Watts, 1955.

Dorothy Thomas, "The Car." In Luella B. Cook, Walter Loban, Ruth M. Stauffer, and Robert Freier, eds., *People in Literature.* N.Y., Harcourt, Brace, 1957.

James Thurber, "The Secret Life of Walter Mitty." In A. G. Day, ed., *Greatest American Short Stories.* N.Y., McGraw-Hill, 1953.

———, "The Macbeth Murder Mystery." In *My World and Welcome To It.* N.Y., Harcourt, Brace, 1942.

D. Tracey, "Most Valuable Player." In Leo Margulies, ed., *Baseball Round-Up.* N.Y., Cupples & Leon, 1948.

Mark Twain, "Blue Jays." (Originally titled "Jim Baker's Blue Jay Yarn.") In Walter Loban, Dorothy Holmstrom, and Luella B. Cook, eds., *Adventures in Appreciation.* N.Y., Harcourt, Brace, 1958.

May Vontver, "The Kiskis." In Luella B. Cook, Walter Loban, George W. Norvell, and William A. McCall, eds., *Challenge to Grow.* N.Y., Harcourt, Brace, 1947.

L. Waller (C. S. Cody), "The Restless Ones." In *Collier's,* Vol. 133, No. 3 (February 5, 1954).

Hugh Walpole, "The Ruby Glass." From *All Souls' Night.* Garden City, N.Y., Doubleday, Doran, 1933.

Jessamyn West, "The Hat." From *Cress Delahanty.* N.Y., Harcourt, Brace, 1953.

Jesse Lynch Williams, "Not Wanted." In Luella B. Cook, Walter Loban, George W.

Norvell, and William A. McCall, eds., *Challenge to Understand.* N.Y., Harcourt, Brace, 1950.
William Wise, "Glory in Bridgeville." In Herbert Potell, Marian Lovrien, and Prudence Bostwick, eds., *Adventures for Today.* N.Y., Harcourt, Brace, 1955.

NON-FICTION, BIOGRAPHY, ESSAYS

Mortimer Adler and William Garman, eds., *The Great Ideas—A Syntopicon of Great Books of the Western World.* 2 vols. Chicago, Encyclopaedia Britannica, 1952.
Sir Francis Bacon, *Essays and The New Atlantis.* N.Y., Van Nostrand, 1942.
Robert Benchley, "Now That You're Tanned—What?" In Egbert W. Nieman and George N. Salt, eds., *Pleasure in Literature.* N.Y., Harcourt, Brace, 1949.
Rachel Carson, *The Sea Around Us.* N.Y., Oxford U. Press, 1951.
Julian Cate, "A Style-ish Fable." In Walter Loban, Dorothy Holmstrom, and Luella B. Cook, eds., *Adventures in Appreciation.* N.Y., Harcourt, Brace, 1958.
C. W. Ceram (Kurt W. Marek), *Gods, Graves, and Scholars.* N.Y., Knopf, 1951.
Julia Adams Davis, *No Other White Men.* N.Y., Dutton, 1937.
Clarence Day, *Life with Father,* N.Y., Knopf, 1935.
Paul DeKruif, *Microbe Hunters.* N.Y., Harcourt, Brace, 1932.
Hildegarde Dolson, *We Shook the Family Tree.* N.Y., Random House, 1946.
John H. Floherty, *Inside the F.B.I.* Phila., Lippincott, 1943.
———, *Get That Story: Journalism—Its Lore and Thrills.* Phila., Lippincott, 1952.
Anne Frank, *Diary of a Young Girl.* Garden City, N.Y., Doubleday, 1952.
Benjamin Franklin, *Autobiography.* Mount Vernon, N.Y., Peter Pauper Press, 1945.
Frank Graham, *Lou Gehrig, A Quiet Hero.* N.Y., Putnam, 1942.
Anna Gertrude Hall, *Nansen.* N.Y., Viking, 1940.
Richard Halliburton, *Richard Halliburton's Second Book of Marvels.* N.Y., Bobbs-Merrill, 1938.
John Hersey, *Hiroshima.* N.Y., Knopf, 1946.
Maurice Herzog, *Annapurna.* N.Y., Dutton, 1952.
Thor Heyerdahl, *Kon-Tiki: Across the Pacific by Raft.* Garden City, N.Y., Garden City Books, 1950.
Lancelot T. Hogben, *The Wonderful World of Mathematics.* Garden City, N.Y., Doubleday, 1955.
David A. Howarth, *We Die Alone.* N.Y., Macmillan, 1955.
Richard Hubler, *Lou Gehrig, Iron Horse of Baseball.* Boston, Houghton Mifflin, 1941.
Sir John Hunt, *The Conquest of Everest.* N.Y., Dutton, 1954.
Shirley Jackson, *Life Among the Savages.* N.Y., Farrar, Straus, and Young, 1953.
Osa Helen Johnson, *I Married Adventure.* Phila., Lippincott, 1940.
Helen Keller, *The Story of My Life.* Garden City, N.Y., Doubleday, 1954.
———, "Three Days to See." In Robert V. Jameson, ed., *Essays New and Old.* N.Y., Harcourt, 1955.
Selma Lagerlöf, *Mårbacka.* Garden City, N.Y., Doubleday, 1938.
Charles Lamb, "Dissertation Upon Roast Pig." In Luella B. Cook, Walter Loban, Oscar James Campbell, and Ruth M. Stauffer, eds., *The World Through Literature.* N.Y., Harcourt, Brace, 1949.
Margaret Landon, *Anna and the King of Siam.* N.Y., John Day, 1944.
Willy Ley, *Engineers' Dreams.* N.Y., Viking, 1954.
Look's Editors, *The Story of the FBI.* N.Y., Dutton, 1954.
John Bartlow Martin, *Why Did They Kill?* N.Y., Ballantine, 1953.
John Milton, "Areopagitica." In Robert P. Tristram Coffin and Alexander M. Witherspoon, eds., *Seventeenth-Century Prose and Poetry.* N.Y., Harcourt, Brace, 1946.

H. A. Morris, *Digging in Yucatan.* Garden City, N.Y., Doubleday, 1931.
Farley Mowat, *People of the Deer.* Boston, Little, Brown, 1952.
Russell Owen, *Conquest of the North and South Poles.* N.Y., Random House, 1952.
Plato, *The Republic.* Cleveland, World Publ., 1946.
Ernie Pyle, *Home Country.* N.Y., Sloane, 1947.
———, "I Meet Walt Disney." In Egbert W. Nieman and George N. Salt, eds., *Pleasure in Literature.* N.Y., Harcourt, Brace, 1949.
Will Rogers, *Autobiography.* Boston, Houghton Mifflin, 1949.
Antoine de St. Exupéry, *Wind, Sand, and Stars.* N.Y., Harcourt, Brace, 1943.
———, *Night Flight.* N.Y., New American Library, n.d.
Carl Sandburg, *Abe Lincoln Grows Up.* N.Y., Harcourt, Brace, 1928.
Katherine Binney Shippen, *The Bright Design.* N.Y., Viking, 1949.
Lincoln Steffens, *Boy On Horseback.* N.Y., Harcourt, Brace, 1935.
———, *The Autobiography of Lincoln Steffens,* N.Y., Harcourt, Brace, 1931.
Irving Stone, *Sailor on Horseback, Biography of Jack London.* Boston, Houghton Mifflin, 1938.
Jesse Stuart, "My Father Is an Educated Man." In Luella B. Cook, Walter Loban, and Ruth M. Stauffer, eds., *People in Literature.* N.Y., Harcourt, Brace, 1951.
James Thurber, *Fables for Our Time.* N.Y., Harper, 1940.
René Vallery-Radot, *The Life of Louis Pasteur.* N.Y., Knopf, 1958.
George H. Waltz, *Jules Verne, The Biography of an Imagination.* N.Y., Holt, 1943.
E. B. White, "Afternoon of an American Boy." From *The Second Tree from the Corner.* N.Y., Harper, 1954.
William Allen White, "Mary White." In Robert J. Cadigan, ed., *September to June.* N.Y., Appleton-Century-Crofts, 1942.
———, *The Autobiography of William Allen White.* N.Y., Macmillan, 1946.
Eric Ernest Williams, *The Wooden Horse.* N.Y., Harper, 1949.
Edmund Wilson, *Scrolls from the Dead Sea.* N.Y., Oxford U. Press, 1955.
Paul Witty, *It's Fun to Find Out* (film-story books). Boston, Heath, 1953.
Thomas Wolfe, *A Stone, a Leaf, a Door.* N.Y., Scribner's, 1950.
Jade Snow Wong, *Fifth Chinese Daughter.* N.Y., Harper, 1950.
Frank Lloyd Wright, *Modern Architecture.* Princeton, N.J., Princeton U. Press, 1931.

DRAMA

Zoë Akins, *The Old Maid.* N.Y., Samuel French, 1935.
Maxwell Anderson, *Elizabeth the Queen, High Tor, Mary of Scotland,* and *Winterset.* In *Eleven Verse Plays, 1920-1939.* N.Y., Harcourt, Brace, 1940.
———, *Lost in the Stars.* N.Y., Sloane, 1950.
Anonymous, *Everyman.* In Barrett H. Clark, ed., *World Drama,* Vol. I. N.Y., D. Appleton-Century, 1933.
Enid Bagnold, *The Chalk Garden.* N.Y., Random House, 1956.
James M. Barrie, *The Admirable Crichton, The Old Lady Shows Her Medals, Peter Pan, The Twelve Pound Look, What Every Woman Knows,* and *The Will.* In *Plays.* N.Y., Scribner's, 1928.
Philip Barry, *Holiday.* In Montrose J. Moses and Joseph Wood Krutch, eds., *Representative American Dramas.* Boston, Little, Brown, 1941.
Rudolph Besier, *The Barretts of Wimpole Street.* In Bennett Cerf and Van H. Cartmell, eds., *Sixteen Famous British Plays.* Garden City, N.Y., Garden City Books, 1942.
Karel Čapek, *R. U. R.* In John Gassner, ed., *A Treasury of the Theater.* N.Y., Simon & Schuster, 1950.

Marc Connelly, *The Green Pastures.* In John Gassner, ed., *A Treasury of the Theater.* N.Y., Simon & Schuster, 1950.

Mary Carolyn Davies, *The Slave with Two Faces.* In Frank Shay and Pierre Loving, eds., *Fifty Contemporary One-Act Plays.* N.Y., 1920.

Harry Denker and Ralph Berkey, *Time Limit.* In *Theatre Arts,* Vol. 41, No. 4 (April 1957).

Mathurin Dondo, *Two Blind Men and a Donkey.* In Frank Shay, ed., *Appleton Book of Holiday Plays.* N.Y., D. Appleton Co., 1930.

Edna Ferber, *The Eldest.* In Luella B. Cook, Walter Loban, Ruth Stauffer, and Robert Freier, eds., *People in Literature.* N.Y., Harcourt, Brace, 1957.

Walter Ferris, *Death Takes a Holiday.* N.Y., Samuel French, 1930.

Rachel Field, *The Fifteenth Candle.* In Irwin J. Zachar and Rodney A. Kimball, eds., *Plays As Experience.* N.Y., Odyssey, 1944.

Lucille Fletcher, *Sorry, Wrong Number.* In Abraham Lass, E. L. McGill, and Donald Axelrod, eds., *Plays from Radio.* Boston, Houghton Mifflin, 1948.

Anatole France, *The Man Who Married a Dumb Wife.* In Bennett Cerf and Van H. Cartmell, eds., *Thirty Famous One-Act Plays.* N.Y., Modern Library, 1949.

Esther Galbraith, *The Brink of Silence.* In Milton Smith, ed., *Short Plays of Various Types.* N.Y., Bobbs-Merrill, 1924.

Zona Gale, *Uncle Jimmy.* In LeRoy Phillips and Theodore Johnson, eds., *Types of Modern Dramatic Composition.* Boston, Ginn, 1927.

John Galsworthy, *Justice, Loyalties, and The Silver Box.* In *Plays.* N.Y., Scribner's, 1928.

Susan Glaspell, *Trifles.* In John Gassner, ed., *Twenty-Five Best Plays of the Modern American Theater.* N.Y., Crown, 1949.

Johann Wolfgang von Goethe, *Faust,* Parts 1 and 2. N.Y., Oxford U. Press, 1952; *Faust,* Part 1. Baltimore, Penguin, 1958.

Walter Goldschmidt and Lester Sinclair, *A Word in Your Ear.* In Margaret Mayorga, ed., *Best Short Plays of 1953-1954.* N.Y., Dodd, Mead, 1954.

Oliver Goldsmith, *She Stoops to Conquer.* In Barrett H. Clark, ed., *World Drama,* Vol. 1. N.Y., D. Appleton-Century Co., 1933.

Kenneth Sawyer Goodman, *Dust of the Road.* In George A. Goldstone, ed., *One-Act Plays.* Boston, Allyn & Bacon, 1926.

———, and Ben Hecht, *The Wonder Hat.* In Margaret Mayorga, ed., *Representative One-Act Plays by American Authors.* Boston, Little, Brown, 1937.

Lady Gregory, *Spreading the News.* In George Jean Nathan, ed., *Five Great Modern Irish Plays.* N.Y., Modern Library, 1941.

Holworthy Hall and Robert Middlemas, *The Valiant.* In Bennett Cerf and Van H. Cartmell, eds., *Thirty Famous One-Act Plays.* N.Y., Modern Library, 1949.

Lorraine Hansberry, *A Raisin in the Sun.* N.Y., Random House, 1959.

Moss Hart and George S. Kaufman, *You Can't Take It with You.* In Barrett H. Clark and Thomas R. Cook, eds., *Nine Modern American Plays.* N.Y., Appleton-Century-Crofts, 1951.

Lillian Hellman, *The Little Foxes.* In Allan Gates Halline, ed., *Six Modern American Plays.* N.Y., Modern Library, 1951.

Sidney Howard, *The Silver Cord.* In Arthur Quinn, ed., *Representative American Plays from 1767 to the Present Day,* 7th edition. N.Y., Appleton-Century-Crofts, 1953.

———, *They Knew What They Wanted.* In John Gassner, ed., *Twenty-Five Best Plays of the Modern American Theater.* N.Y., Crown, 1949.

———, *Yellow Jack.* N.Y., Harcourt, Brace, 1939.

Henrik Ibsen, *An Enemy of the People.* N.Y., Modern Library, 1945.

Robinson Jeffers, *Medea.* In John Gassner, ed., *Best Plays of the Modern American Theater,* 3rd series. N.Y., Crown, 1952.

George Kelly, *Craig's Wife.* In John Gassner, ed., *Twenty-Five Best Plays of the Modern American Theater.* N.Y., Crown, 1949.

———, *Finders Keepers.* In Francis J. Griffith and Joseph Mersand, eds., *Modern One-Act Plays.* N.Y., Harcourt, Brace, 1950.

Sidney Kingsley, *Dead End.* In John Gassner, ed., *Twenty Best Plays of the Modern American Theater,* 1st series. N.Y., Crown, 1939.

Howard Lindsay and Russel Crouse, *Life with Father.* In John Gassner, ed., *Best Plays of the Modern American Theater,* 2nd series. N.Y., Crown, 1947.

———, *State of the Union.* In John Gassner, ed., *Best Plays of the Modern American Theater,* 3rd series. N.Y., Crown, 1952.

Frederic Garcia Lorca, *Blood Wedding.* Trans. by John Garrett Underhill. In E. Bradless Watson and Benfield Pressey, eds., *Contemporary Drama, Fifteen Plays.* N.Y., Scribner's, 1959.

G. Martinez-Sierra, *The Cradle Song.* In Bennett Cerf and Van H. Cartmell, eds., *Sixteen Famous European Plays,* Garden City, N.Y., Garden City Books, 1943.

Norman McKinnel, *The Bishop's Candlesticks.* In Esther R. Galbraith, ed., *Plays without Footlights.* N.Y., Harcourt, Brace, 1945.

Arthur Miller, *Death of a Salesman.* N.Y., Viking, 1949.

A. A. Milne, *The Ivory Door.* N.Y., Putnam, 1928.

Ferenc Molnár, *Liliom.* In Bennett Cerf and Van H. Cartmell, eds., *Sixteen Famous European Plays.* Garden City, N.Y., Garden City Books, 1943.

Eugene O'Neill, *Ah, Wilderness.* In Bennett Cerf and Van H. Cartmell, eds., *Sixteen Famous American Plays.* Garden City, N.Y., Garden City Books, 1941.

———, *Beyond the Horizon.* In Harlan H. Hatcher, ed., *Modern Dramas.* N.Y., Harcourt, Brace, 1948.

———, *The Emperor Jones* and *The Great God Brown.* In Saxe Commins, ed., *Nine Plays.* N.Y., Random House, 1954.

———, *Long Day's Journey into Night.* New Haven, Conn., Yale U. Press, 1956.

———, *Where the Cross Is Made.* In Helen Louise Cohen, ed., *More One-Act Plays by Modern Authors.* N.Y., Harcourt, Brace, 1927.

Louis N. Parker, *A Minuet.* In Bruce Carpenter, ed., *A Book of Dramas.* N.Y., Prentice-Hall, 1929.

John Patrick, *The Hasty Heart.* In John Gassner, ed., *Best Plays of the Modern American Theater,* 2nd series. N.Y., Crown, 1947.

———, *Teahouse of the August Moon.* N.Y., Putnam, 1954.

Josephine Preston Peabody, *The Piper.* In Montrose J. Moses and Joseph Wood Krutch, eds., *Representative American Dramas.* Boston, Little, Brown, 1951.

Eugene Pillot, *Two Crooks and a Lady.* In Edwin Van B. Knickerbocker, ed., *Short Plays.* N.Y., Holt, 1931.

Terence Rattigan, *The Winslow Boy.* N.Y., Dramatists Play Service, 1948.

Mary K. Reely, *The Window to the South.* Boston, Walter H. Baker, 1924.

Lennox Robinson, *The Far Off Hills.* In Frank Wadleigh Chandler and Richard Albert Cordell, eds., *Twentieth Century Plays.* N.Y., Nelson, 1939.

Edmond Rostand, *Romancers.* In George R. Coffman, ed., *A Book of Modern Plays.* N.Y., Modern Library, 1925.

———, *Cyrano de Bergerac.* Trans. by Brian Hooker. N.Y., Holt, 1923.

William Shakespeare, *Hamlet, Henry IV, Julius Caesar, King Lear, Macbeth,* et al. In Thomas Marc Parrot, ed., *Twenty-Three Plays and the Sonnets.* N.Y., Scribner's, 1953. (Well-edited paperbound editions of individual plays available from Dell, and Pocket Books, both New York.)

George Bernard Shaw, *Pygmalion.* In *Selected Plays,* Vol. I. N.Y., Dodd, Mead, 1948.

———, *Saint Joan.* In *Selected Plays,* Vol. II. N.Y., Dodd, Mead, 1948.

R. C. Sheriff, *Journey's End.* In John Gassner, ed., *A Treasury of the Theater.* N.Y., Simon & Schuster, 1950.

Robert E. Sherwood, *Abe Lincoln in Illinois.* In Barrett H. Clark and William H. Davenport, eds., *Nine Modern American Plays.* N.Y., Appleton-Century-Crofts, 1951.

Sophocles, *Antigone.* In Barrett H. Clark, ed., *World Drama,* Vol. I. N.Y., D. Appleton-Century Co., 1933.

August Strindberg, *The Father.* In John Gassner, ed., *A Treasury of the Theater.* N.Y., Simon & Schuster, 1950.

John Millington Synge, *Riders to the Sea.* In George Jean Nathan, ed., *Five Great Modern Irish Plays.* N.Y., Modern Library, 1941.

Booth Tarkington, *Beauty and the Jacobin.* In Helen Louise Cohen, ed., *One-Act Plays by Modern Authors.* N.Y., Harcourt, Brace, 1934.

Althea Thurston, *Exchange.* In Roland B. Lewis, ed., *Contemporary One-Act Plays.* N.Y., Scribner's, 1922.

Frank Tompkins, *Sham.* In George A. Goldstone, ed., *One-Act Plays.* Boston, Allyn & Bacon, 1926.

Don Totheroh, *The Stolen Prince.* In Francis J. Griffith and Joseph Mersand, eds., *Modern One-Act Plays.* N.Y., Harcourt, Brace, 1950.

John Van Druten, *I Remember Mama.* In John Gassner, ed., *Best Plays of the Modern American Theater,* 2nd series. N.Y., Crown, 1947.

Sutton Vane, *Outward Bound.* In Bennett Cerf and Van H. Cartmell, eds., *Sixteen Famous British Plays.* Garden City, N.Y., Garden City Books, 1942.

Charlotte R. White, *The Wooden Horse.* In Robert Haven Schauffler, ed., *Plays for Our American Holidays,* Vol. IV. N.Y., Dodd, Mead, 1928.

Percival Wilde, *Confessional.* In George A. Goldstone, ed., *One-Act Plays.* Boston, Allyn & Bacon, 1926.

———, *The Finger of God.* In Frank Shay and Pierre Loving, eds., *Fifty Contemporary One-Act Plays.* N.Y., D. Appleton Co., 1920.

———, *Salt for Savor.* In Margaret Mayorga, ed., *Best Short Plays, 1953-1954.* N.Y., Dodd, Mead, 1954.

Thornton Wilder, *The Happy Journey to Trenton and Camden.* In Francis J. Griffith and Joseph Mersand, eds., *Modern One-Act Plays.* N.Y., Harcourt, Brace, 1950.

———, *Our Town.* In John Gassner, ed., *A Treasury of the Theater.* N.Y., Simon & Schuster, 1950.

Emlyn Williams, *The Corn Is Green.* In Bennett Cerf and Van H. Cartmell, eds., *Sixteen Famous British Plays.* Garden City, N.Y., Garden City Books, 1942.

Tennessee Williams, *The Glass Menagerie.* In John Gassner, ed., *Best Plays of the Modern American Theater,* 2nd series. N.Y., Crown, 1947.

POETRY

William Allingham, "A Swing Song." In Alice G. Thorn, ed., *Singing Words.* N.Y., Scribner's, 1941.

Anonymous, "Chevy Chase" and "Sir Patrick Spens." In Delmar Rodabaugh and Agnes L. McCarthy, eds., *Prose and Poetry of England.* Syracuse, N.Y., Singer, 1955.

———, "Lord Randal" and "The Raggle Taggle Gypsies." In Elinor Parker, ed., *100 Story Poems.* N.Y., Crowell, 1951.

Richard Armour, "Mother Tongue." From *Nights with Armour.* N.Y., McGraw-Hill, 1958.

———, *Light Armour.* N.Y., McGraw-Hill, 1954.

Herbert Asquith, "Skating." In Lillian Hollowell, ed., *Book of Children's Literature.* N.Y., Farrar and Rinehart, 1939.

W. H. Auden, "O What Is That Sound?" In Walter Loban, Dorothy Holmstrom, and Luella B. Cook, eds., *Adventures in Appreciation.* N.Y., Harcourt, Brace, 1958.

Katherine Lee Bates, "America, the Beautiful." In Oliphant Gibbons, ed., *A Book of Poems.* N.Y., American Book, 1938.

Thomas L. Beddoes, "Dream Pedlary." In Louis Untermeyer, ed., *Yesterday and Today.* N.Y., Harcourt, Brace, 1926.

Rosemary Benét, "Nancy Hanks." In Alexander Woollcott, ed., *As You Were.* N.Y., Viking, 1943.

Stephen Vincent Benét, "Invocation." From *John Brown's Body.* N.Y., Rinehart, 1941.

———, *John Brown's Body.* N.Y., Rinehart, 1941.

William Rose Benét, "Jesse James." In Louis Untermeyer, ed., *A Treasury of Great Poems.* N.Y., Simon & Schuster, 1942.

———, "The Skater of Ghost Lake." In Robert C. Pooley, Irvin C. Poley, Jean Cravens Leyda, and Lillian J. Zellhoefer, eds., *Exploring Life Through Literature.* Chicago, Scott, Foresman, 1957.

William Blake, "The Tiger." In Rewey Belle Inglis and Josephine Spear, eds., *Adventures in English Literature.* N.Y., Harcourt, Brace, 1958.

F. W. Bourdillon, "The Night Has a Thousand Eyes." In Catharine Connell, ed., *Love Poems, Old and New.* N.Y., Random House, 1943.

Rupert Brooke, "The Great Lover." In Luella B. Cook, Walter Loban, Oscar James Campbell, and Ruth M. Stauffer, eds., *The World Through Literature.* N.Y., Harcourt, Brace, 1949.

Robert Browning, "Cavalier Tunes." In Charles W. Cooper, ed., *Preface to Poetry.* N.Y., Harcourt, Brace, 1946.

———, "Childe Roland to the Dark Tower Came" and "Soliloquy of the Spanish Cloisters." In Walter Blair and W. K. Chandler, eds., *Approaches to Poetry.* N.Y., Appleton-Century-Crofts, 1953.

———, "How They Brought the Good News from Ghent to Aix" and "The Pied Piper of Hamelin." In Elinor Parker, ed., *100 Story Poems.* N.Y., Crowell, 1951.

———, "My Last Duchess." In Rewey Belle Inglis and Josephine Spear, eds., *Adventures in English Literature.* N.Y., Harcourt, Brace, 1958.

———, "The Patriot." In Louis Untermeyer, ed., *A Treasury of Great Poems, English and American.* N.Y., Simon & Schuster, 1955.

Bliss Carman, "A Vagabond Song." In Louis Untermeyer, ed., *Modern American Poetry.* N.Y., Harcourt, Brace, 1942.

Lewis Carroll, "Jabberwocky." In Walter Loban, Dorothy Holmstrom, and Luella B. Cook, eds., *Adventures in Appreciation.* N.Y., Harcourt, Brace, 1958.

Gilbert K. Chesterton, "Lepanto." In Elinor Parker, ed., *100 Story Poems.* N.Y., Crowell, 1951.

Elizabeth Coatsworth, "Daniel Webster's Horses." In Walter Loban, Dorothy Holmstrom, and Luella B. Cook, eds., *Adventures in Appreciation.* N.Y., Harcourt, Brace, 1958.

———, "Swift Things are Beautiful." In Miriam B. Huber, ed., *Story and Verse for Children.* N.Y., Macmillan, 1940.

Robert P. Tristram Coffin, "Hound on the Church Porch." From *Collected Poems.* N.Y., Macmillan, 1948.

Samuel Taylor Coleridge, "The Rime of the Ancient Mariner." In Louis Untermeyer, ed., *A Treasury of Great Poems.* N.Y., Simon & Schuster, 1942.

Nathalia Crane, "The Blind Girl." In Elias Lieberman, ed., *Poems for Enjoyment.* N.Y., Harper, 1931.

Adelaide Crapsey, "November Night" and "The Warning." In Louis Untermeyer, ed.,

Modern American and Modern British Poetry, mid-century ed. N.Y., Harcourt, Brace, 1950.

William Crittendon, "Neptune's Steeds." In Harriet M. Lucas, ed., *Prose and Poetry of Today.* Syracuse, N.Y., Singer, 1941.

Walter de la Mare, "The Listeners." In Luella B. Cook, Walter Loban, Oscar James Campbell, and Ruth M. Stauffer, eds., *The World Through Literature.* N.Y., Harcourt, Brace, 1949.

———, "Silver." In Louis Untermeyer, ed., *Modern American and Modern British Poetry,* rev. ed. N.Y., Harcourt, Brace, 1955.

———, "The Song of the Mad Prince." In Janet Adam Smith, ed., *The Faber Book of Children's Verse.* London, Faber & Faber, 1953.

Emily Dickinson, "Autumn," "I Had No Time To Hate," and "Much Madness Is Divinest Sense." In Mabel Loomis Todd and T. W. Higginson, eds., *Emily Dickinson Poems,* 1st and 2nd series. Cleveland, World Publ., 1948.

———, "There Is No Frigate Like a Book." In John Gehlmann and Mary Rives Bowman, eds., *Adventures in American Literature.* N.Y., Harcourt, Brace, 1958.

T. S. Eliot, "Macavity: the Mystery Cat" and "The Waste Land." From *The Complete Poems and Plays of T. S. Eliot.* N.Y., Harcourt, Brace, 1952.

Ralph Waldo Emerson, "Concord Hymn." In Louis Untermeyer, ed., *A Treasury of Great Poems.* N.Y., Simon & Schuster, 1942.

John Gould Fletcher, "The Skaters." In Louis Untermeyer, ed., *Modern American and Modern British Poetry,* mid-century ed. N.Y., Harcourt, Brace, 1950.

Anatole France, "A Roman Senator." In Luella B. Cook, Walter Loban, Ruth M. Stauffer, and Robert Freier, eds., *People in Literature.* N.Y., Harcourt, Brace, 1957.

Robert Frost, "Birches," "Mending Wall," "Stopping by Woods on a Snowy Evening," and "Two Tramps in Mud Time." In Louis Untermeyer, ed., *Modern British and Modern American Poetry,* rev. ed. N.Y., Harcourt, Brace, 1955.

———, "The Death of the Hired Man." In Luella B. Cook, Walter Loban, Ruth M. Stauffer, and Robert Freier, eds., *People in Literature.* N.Y., Harcourt, Brace, 1957.

———, "Dust of Snow." In Louis Untermeyer, ed., *The Road Not Taken.* N.Y., Holt, 1951.

———, "The Freedom of the Moon." In Elias Lieberman, ed., *Poems for Enjoyment.* N.Y., Harper, 1931.

Ethel R. Fuller, "Wind Is a Cat." In Blanche J. Thompson, ed., *More Silver Pennies.* N.Y., Macmillan, 1938.

Johann Wolfgang von Goethe, "The Erl King." In Rewey Belle Inglis and William K. Stewart, eds., *Adventures in World Literature,* rev. ed. N.Y., Harcourt, Brace, 1958.

Thomas Gray, "Elegy Written in a Country's Churchyard." In Rewey Belle Inglis and Josephine Spear, eds., *Adventures in English Literature.* N.Y., Harcourt, Brace, 1958.

Kahlil Gibran, *The Prophet.* N.Y., Knopf, 1923.

Arthur Guiterman, "Death and General Putnam." In Elinor Parker, ed., *100 Story Poems.* N.Y., Crowell, 1951.

Heinrich Heine, "The Lorelei." In Luella B. Cook, Walter Loban, Ruth M. Stauffer, and Robert Freier, eds., *People in Literature.* N.Y., Harcourt, Brace, 1957.

Roy Helton, "Old Christmas Morning." In Walter Loban, Dorothy Holmstrom, and Luella B. Cook, eds., *Adventures in Appreciation.* N.Y., Harcourt, Brace, 1958.

William E. Henley, "Invictus." In Louis Untermeyer, ed., *Yesterday and Today.* N.Y., Harcourt, Brace, 1926.

Robert Herrick, "To Daffodils." In Louis Untermeyer, ed., *A Treasury of Great Poems.* N.Y., Simon & Schuster, 1942.

Oliver Wendell Holmes, "Ballad of the Oysterman" and "The Deacon's Masterpiece." In Elinor Parker, ed., *100 Story Poems.* N.Y., Crowell, 1951.

———, "The Chambered Nautilus." In John Gehlmann and Mary Rives Bowman, eds., *Adventures in American Literature.* N.Y., Harcourt, Brace, 1958.

———, "Old Ironsides." In Louis Untermeyer, ed., *Anthology of New England Poets.* N.Y., Random House, 1948.

Homer, *The Odyssey.* Trans. by Barbara L. Pickard. N.Y., Walck, 1952.

Thomas Hood, "Past and Present." In Elizabeth O'Daly and E. W. Nieman, eds., *Adventures for Readers,* Book I. N.Y., Harcourt, Brace, 1958.

Gerard Manley Hopkins, "Pied Beauty." In Louis Untermeyer, ed., *A Treasury of Great Poems.* N.Y., Simon & Schuster, 1942.

Lady Horikawa, "How Can One E'er Be Sure." In Elias Lieberman, ed., *Poems for Enjoyment.* N.Y., Harper, 1931.

A. E. Housman, "Loveliest of Trees." In Luella B. Cook, Walter Loban, Ruth M. Stauffer, and Robert Freier, eds., *People in Literature.* N.Y., Harcourt, Brace, 1957.

———, "To An Athlete Dying Young." In Louis Untermeyer, ed., *A Treasury of Great Poems.* N.Y., Simon & Schuster, 1942.

———, "When I Was One-and-Twenty." In Walter Loban, Dorothy Holmstrom, and Luella B. Cook, eds., *Adventures in Appreciation.* N.Y., Harcourt, Brace, 1958.

Richard Hovey, "The Sea Gypsy." In J. N. Hook, Blanche E. Peavey, Miriam H. Thompson, Vesta M. Parsons, and Frank M. Rice, eds., *Literature of Achievement.* Boston, Ginn, 1957.

Langston Hughes, "African Dance." In Blanche J. Thompson, ed., *More Silver Pennies.* N.Y., Macmillan, 1938.

———, "April Rain Song." In May Hill Arbuthnot, ed., *Time for Poetry.* Chicago, Scott, Foresman, 1952.

———, "Mother to Son." In Arna Bontemps, ed., *Golden Slippers.* N.Y., Harper, 1941.

Robinson Jeffers, "To His Father." In Carl Withers, ed., *The Penguin Book of Sonnets.* N.Y., Penguin, 1943.

James Weldon Johnson, "The Creation." In Arna Bontemps, ed., *Golden Slippers.* N.Y., Harper, 1941.

John Keats, "La Belle Dame Sans Merci." In Elinor Parker, ed., *100 Story Poem.* N.Y., Crowell, 1951.

———, "The Eve of St. Agnes." In Luella B. Cook, Walter Loban, Oscar James Campbell, and Ruth M. Stauffer, eds., *The World Through Literature.* N.Y., Harcourt, Brace, 1949.

———, "Upon First Looking into Chapman's Homer." In Rewey Belle Inglis and Josephine Spear, eds., *Adventures in English Literature.* N.Y., Harcourt, Brace, 1958.

Omar Khayyám, *The Rubáiyát of Omar Khayyám.* Trans. by Edward Fitzgerald. In Louis Untermeyer, ed., *A Treasury of Great Poems.* N.Y., Simon & Schuster, 1942.

Charles Kingsley, "The Old Song." In Elias Lieberman, ed., *Poems for Enjoyment.* N.Y., Harper, 1931.

Rudyard Kipling, "Ballad of East and West" and "Recessional." In Rewey Belle Inglis and Josephine Spear, eds., *Adventures in English Literature.* N.Y., Harcourt, Brace, 1958.

———, "Boots" and "If." In Herbert Potell, Marian Lovrien, and Prudence Bostwick, eds., *Adventures for Today.* N.Y., Harcourt, Brace, 1955.

———, "Danny Deever." In Walter Loban, Dorothy Holmstrom, and Luella B. Cook, eds., *Adventures in Appreciation.* N.Y., Harcourt, Brace, 1958.

Sidney Lanier, "Song of the Chattahoochee." In John Gehlmann and Mary Rives Bowman, eds., *Adventures in American Literature.* N.Y., Harcourt, Brace, 1958.

Edward Lear, "The Owl and the Pussy-Cat." In Elinor Parker, ed., *100 Story Poems.* N.Y., Crowell, 1951.

Richard Le Gallienne, "I Meant to Do My Work Today." In Horace J. McNeil, ed., *Poems for a Machine Age.* N.Y., McGraw-Hill, 1941.

Vachel Lindsay, "The Bronco That Would Not Be Broken." In Elizabeth C. O'Daly and Egbert W. Nieman, eds., *Adventures for Readers,* Book I. N.Y., Harcourt, Brace, 1958.

———, "General William Booth Enters into Heaven." In Louis Untermeyer, ed., *Modern American and Modern British Poetry,* rev. ed. N.Y., Harcourt, Brace, 1955.

———, "The Potatoes' Dance" and "The Santa Fe Trail." From *Collected Poems.* N.Y., Macmillan, 1930.

Henry W. Longfellow, "King Robert of Sicily." In Elinor Parker, ed., *100 Story Poems.* N.Y., Crowell, 1951.

———, "Nature." In J. N. Hook, Mildred Foster, Nell M. Robinson, Charles F. Webb, and Miriam H. Thompson, eds., *Literature of America.* Boston, Ginn, 1957.

———, "Paul Revere's Ride." In Louis Untermeyer, ed., *A Treasury of Great Poems,* N.Y., Simon & Schuster, 1942.

John Gillespie Magee, "High Flight." In Olga Perschbacher and Dorothy Wilde, eds., *America Speaking.* Chicago, Scott, Foresman, 1943.

Edwin Markham, "Lincoln, the Man of the People." In Louis Untermeyer, ed., *Modern American and Modern British Poetry,* mid-century ed. N.Y., Harcourt, Brace, 1950.

———, "The Man with the Hoe." In Luella B. Cook, Walter Loban, Ruth M. Stauffer, and Robert Freier, eds., *People in Literature.* N.Y., Harcourt, Brace, 1957.

John Masefield, "Cargoes," "Sea Fever," and "A Wanderer's Song." In Louis Untermeyer, ed., *Modern American and Modern British Poetry,* rev. ed. N.Y., Harcourt, Brace, 1955.

———, "Tewkesbury Road." In Mary Gould Davis, ed., *The Girl's Book of Verse.* Phila., Lippincott, 1952.

Edgar Lee Masters, "Petit, the Poet." In Louis Untermeyer, ed., *Modern American and Modern British Poetry,* mid-century ed. N.Y., Harcourt, Brace, 1950.

———, *Spoon River Anthology.* N.Y., Macmillan, 1931.

John McCrae, "In Flander's Fields." In Louis Untermeyer, ed., *Yesterday and Today.* N.Y., Harcourt, Brace, 1926.

Phyllis McGinley, "Reflections Dental." From *The Love Letters of Phyllis McGinley.* N.Y., Viking, 1954.

Irene Rutherford McLeod, "Lone Dog." In Horace J. McNeil, ed., *Poems for a Machine Age.* N.Y., McGraw-Hill, 1941.

Mildred P. (Merryman) Meigs, "The Pirate Don Durk of Dowdee." In Helen F. Daringer and A. Eaton, eds., *The Poet's Craft.* N.Y., World Book, 1935.

Edna St. Vincent Millay, "God's World." In John Gehlmann and Mary Rives Bowman, eds., *Adventures in American Literature.* N.Y., Harcourt, Brace, 1958.

———, "Justice Denied in Massachusetts." In Louis Untermeyer, ed., *Modern American Poetry,* mid-century ed. N.Y., Harcourt, Brace, 1950.

———, "Renascence." In Louis Untermeyer, ed., *Modern American and Modern British Poetry,* rev. ed. N.Y., Harcourt, Brace, 1955.

Joaquin Miller, "Columbus." In Elinor Parker, ed., *100 Story Poems.* N.Y., Crowell, 1951.

A. A. Milne, *When We Were Very Young.* N.Y., Dutton, 1924.

Angela Morgan, "Work: A Song of Triumph." In Alice Cooper, ed., *Poems of Today.* Boston, Ginn, 1930.

Alfred Noyes, "The Barrel Organ." In Louis Untermeyer, ed., *Modern American and Modern British Poetry,* mid-century ed. N.Y., Harcourt, Brace, 1950.

Alfred Noyes, "The Highwayman." In Elinor Parker, ed., *100 Story Poems.* N.Y., Crowell, 1951.

James Oppenheim, "The Slave." In Elias Lieberman, ed., *Poems for Enjoyment.* N.Y., Harper, 1931.

Bonaro Overstreet, "Unlost." From *Hands Laid Upon the Wind.* N.Y., Norton, 1955.

Edgar Allan Poe, "Annabel Lee." In Louis Untermeyer, ed., *The Magic Circle.* N.Y., Harcourt, Brace, 1952.

———, "El Dorado." In Walter Loban, Dorothy Holmstrom, and Luella B. Cook, eds., *Adventures in Appreciation.* N.Y., Harcourt, Brace, 1958.

———, "The Raven." In Elinor Parker, ed., *100 Story Poems.* N.Y., Crowell, 1951.

Edwin Arlington Robinson, "Miniver Cheevy" and "Richard Cory." In Louis Untermeyer, ed., *Modern American and Modern British Poetry,* rev. ed. N.Y., Harcourt, Brace, 1955.

Christina Rossetti, "A Birthday." In Rewey Belle Inglis and Josephine Spear, eds., *Adventures in English Literature.* N.Y., Harcourt, Brace, 1958.

———, "Lullaby." In Lillian Hollowell, ed., *A Book of Children's Literature.* N.Y., Rinehart, 1950.

———, "Uphill." In Louis Untermeyer, ed., *A Treasury of Great Poems.* N.Y., Simon & Schuster, 1942.

———, "Who Has Seen the Wind?" In Harold H. Wagenheim, Elizabeth Voris Brattig, and Matthew Dolkey, eds., *Our Reading Heritage, Ourselves and Others.* N.Y., Holt, 1956.

———, "The Wind Has Such a Rainy Sound." In May Hill Arbuthnot, ed., *Time for Poetry.* Chicago, Scott, Foresman, 1952.

Archibald Rutledge, "Lee." In Harriet Lucas and Elizabeth Ansorge, eds., *Prose and Poetry of Today.* Syracuse, N.Y., L. W. Leigee, 1941.

Carl Sandburg, "Chicago." In Oscar Williams, ed., *A Little Treasury of Modern Poetry.* N.Y., Scribner's, 1950.

———, "Fog" and "Four Preludes on Playthings of the Wind." In Luella B. Cook, Walter Loban, Ruth M. Stauffer, and Robert Freier, eds., *People in Literature.* N.Y., Harcourt, Brace, 1957.

———, "Jazz Fantasia." In Conrad Aiken, ed., *A Comprehensive Anthology of American Poetry.* N.Y., Random House, 1944.

———, "Primer Lesson." In Louis Untermeyer, ed., *Modern American and Modern British Poetry,* mid-century ed. N.Y., Harcourt, Brace, 1950.

Lew Sarett, "Four Little Foxes." In Adolph Gillis and William Rose Benét, eds., *Poems for Modern Youth.* Boston, Houghton Mifflin, 1938.

———, "Indian Sleep Song," "Marching Pines," "Sweetwater Range," and "Wind in the Pine." From *The Box of God.* N.Y., Holt, 1922.

Alan Seeger, "I Have a Rendezvous with Death." In Louis Untermeyer, ed., *Yesterday and Today.* N.Y., Harcourt, Brace, 1926.

William Shakespeare, "Blow, Blow, Thou Winter Wind." In Rewey Belle Inglis and Josephine Spear, eds., *Adventures in English Literature.* N.Y., Harcourt, Brace, 1958.

Percy B. Shelley, "Ode to the West Wind." In Louis Untermeyer, ed., *A Treasury of Great Poems.* N.Y., Simon & Schuster, 1942.

———, "Ozymandias." In Norman C. Stageberg and Wallace C. Anderson, eds., *Poetry as Experience.* N. Y., American Book, 1950.

———, "To Night." In Luella B. Cook, Walter Loban, Oscar James Campbell, and Ruth M. Stauffer, eds., *The World Through Literature.* N.Y., Harcourt, Brace, 1949.

———, "To ———." In Elias Lieberman, ed., *Poems for Enjoyment.* N.Y., Harper, 1931.

Robert Southey, "How the Waters Come Down at Lodore." In Luella B. Cook,

Walter Loban, Ruth M. Stauffer, and Robert Freier, eds., *People in Literature.* N.Y., Harcourt, Brace, 1957.

Stephen Spender, "The Express." In Oscar Williams, ed., *A Little Treasury of Modern Poetry.* N.Y., Scribner's, 1950.

Robert Louis Stevenson, "Requiem." In Walter Loban, Dorothy Holmstrom, and Luella B. Cook, eds., *Adventures in Appreciation.* N.Y., Harcourt, Brace, 1958.

———, "Where Go the Boats." In May Hill Arbuthnot, ed., *Time for Poetry.* Chicago, Scott, Foresman, 1952.

———, "The Wind." In Miriam B. Huber, ed., *Story and Verse for Children.* N.Y., Macmillan, 1940.

Sara Teasdale, "Barter," "The Falling Star," "Stars," "There Will Come Soft Rains," and "Wood Song." From *Collected Poems.* N.Y., Macmillan, 1937.

Alfred, Lord Tennyson, "Break, Break, Break," "Bugle Song," and "Ulysses." In Rewey Belle Inglis and Josephine Spear, eds., *Adventures in English Literature.* N.Y., Harcourt, Brace, 1958.

———, "The Charge of the Light Brigade." In Egbert W. Nieman and Elizabeth C. O'Daly, eds., *Adventures for Readers,* Book II. N.Y., Harcourt, Brace, 1958.

———, *Idylls of the King.* N.Y., Heritage, 1939.

———, "Sweet and Low." In Luella B. Cook, Walter Loban, Oscar James Campbell, and Ruth M. Stauffer, eds., *The World Through Literature.* N.Y., Harcourt, Brace, 1949.

Ernest L. Thayer, "Casey at the Bat." In Elinor Parker, ed., *100 Story Poems.* N.Y., Crowell, 1951.

Dylan Thomas, "The Force that through the Green Fuse Drives the Flower." In Oscar Williams, ed., *A Little Treasury of Modern Poetry.* N.Y., Scribner's, 1950.

———, "The Hand that Signed the Paper Felled a City." In Louis Untermeyer, ed., *Modern American and Modern British Poetry,* rev. ed. N.Y., Harcourt, Brace, 1955.

Francis Thompson, "To a Snowflake." In Louis Untermeyer, ed., *Modern American and Modern British Poetry,* rev. ed. N.Y., Harcourt, Brace, 1955.

Francis O. Ticknor, "Little Giffin." In George W. Norvell and Carol Hovious, eds., *Conquest,* Book II. Boston, Heath, 1947.

Walt Whitman, "Beat! Beat! Drums!" and "I Hear America Singing." In John Gehlmann and Mary Rives Bowman, eds., *Adventures in American Literature.* N.Y., Harcourt, Brace, 1958.

———, "O Captain! My Captain!" In Adolph Gillis and William Rose Benét, eds., *Poems for Modern Youth.* Boston, Houghton Mifflin, 1938.

———, "Pioneers! O Pioneers!" In Luella B. Cook, Walter Loban, Tremaine McDowell, eds., *America Through Literature.* N.Y., Harcourt, Brace, 1952.

Dixie Willson, "The Mist and All." In Matilda M. Elsea, ed., *Choice Poems for Elementary Grades.* N.Y., Edwards Press, 1944.

William Wordsworth, "Composed upon Westminster Bridge." In Rewey Belle Inglis and Josephine Spear, eds., *Adventures in English Literature.* N.Y., Harcourt, Brace, 1958.

———, "It is a Beauteous Evening, Calm and Free." In J. N. Hook, Mildred Foster, Nell M. Robinson, and Charles F. Webb, eds., *Literature of England.* Boston, Ginn, 1957.

Elinor Wylie, "Pretty Words" and "Velvet Shoes." In Rewey Belle Inglis and Joseph Spear, eds., *Adventures in English Literature.* N.Y., Harcourt, Brace, 1958.

William Butler Yeats, "The Song of Wandering Aengus." In Louis Untermeyer, ed.,

Modern American and Modern British Poetry, rev. ed. N.Y., Harcourt, Brace, 1955.

One No Yoshiki, "My Love." In Elias Lieberman, ed., *Poems for Enjoyment.* N.Y., Harper, 1931.

AUDIO-VISUAL MATERIALS

Films and Filmstrips Mentioned in the Text

A.B.C. of Puppetry (B)
Ansel Adams, Photographer (Daw)
Art in Our World (Darby)
Build Your Vocabulary (Cor)
Captains Courageous (TFC)
The Cinematographer (TFC)
Driven Westward (TFC)
Fiddle-De-Dee (IFB)
Four Ways to Drama (UCE)
The Good Loser (Cor)
The House of Rothschild (TFC)
How Honest Are You? (Cor)
Introduction to Shakespeare (YAF)
Johnny Appleseed (SVE)
Macbeth—TV Production (AF)
Mahatma Gandhi (EBF)
Master Will Shakespeare (TFC)
Newspaper Story (EBF)
The Photographer (UWF)
The Public Life of Abraham Lincoln (Nu-Art)
Right or Wrong? (Cor)
The River (UWF)
The Screen Director (TFC)
The Suicide of Society (Net)
And Now Miguel (UWF)
Art and Motion (EBF)
Begone Dull Care (IFB)
Building Better Paragraphs (Cor)
Do Words Ever Fool You? (Cor)
Due Process of Law Denied (TFC)
Getting the World's News (CA)
The Great Heart (TFC)
How Green Was My Valley (TFC)
How to Judge Facts (Cor)
The Literature of Freedom (PS)
The Loon's Necklace (EBF)
Magazine Magic (Curtis)
Make Your Own Decisions (Cor)
Nature's Half Acre (Disney)
Oliver Wendell Holmes (EBF)
The Prairie (Barr)
Radio, Television, Motion Pictures (YAF)
The Rime of the Ancient Mariner (UCE)
Rumor Clinic (ADL)
The Story That Couldn't Be Printed (TFC)
The Story of Dr. Carver (TFC)
The Story of Louis Pasteur (TFC)
The Tell Tale Heart (McGraw-Hill)
Thomas Jefferson (EFC)
Understanding your Ideals (Cor)
What Do You Think? (CBR)
Words: Their Origin, Use, and Spelling (Long)
Yours Is the Land (EBF)
Understanding Movies (TFC)
Washington Irving (EBF)
Whispers (TFC)
You and Your Newspaper (PS)

The films listed exemplify teaching aids used in specific situations. No attempt will be made to furnish additional titles. Each year the number increases so rapidly that even the most selective list soon becomes out of date. The solution to the problem of finding effective audio-visual material lies in the continual search by individuals, each seeking the best for his particular purpose with his particular students. Producers are more than willing to keep interested teachers informed of current releases. For instance, those whose names are on the mailing list of Encyclopaedia Britannica Films have probably received information concerning "An Introduction to the Humanities." This series of twelve motion pictures in color, each twenty-eight minutes in length, focuses on three historical periods—Modern, Elizabethan, and Greek. The four films devoted to each period present scenes from dramatic literature —*Our Town, Hamlet, Oedipus the King*—together with commentary which helps the student appreciate both the cultural heritage of the theater and the timeless universality of the individual dramatic works. The complete series offers a stimulating introduction to the significance of the humanities. This production, made possible by a grant from the Fund for the Advancement of Education, is only one example of the excellent material which is continually being made available for classroom use.

SOURCES

ADL: Anti-Defamation League, 212 Fifth Ave., N.Y. 1, N.Y.
AF: Association Films, 347 Madison Ave., N.Y. 17, N.Y.
B: Baily Films, Inc., 6509 De Longpre Ave., Hollywood 28, Calif.
Barr: Arthur Barr Films, 1265 Bresee Ave., Pasadena, Calif.
CBR: Canadian Board of Review, 221 Victoria St., Vancouver, B.C.
Cor: Coronet Films, Coronet Bldg., Chicago 1, Ill.
CA: Current Affairs, Films Division, Key Productions, 18 East 41st St., N.Y. 17, N.Y.
Curtis: Curtis Publishing Co., Philadelphia 5, Penna.
Darby: Darby Films, 6509 De Longpre Ave., Hollywood 28, Calif.
Daw: Larry Dawson Productions, 611 Howard St., San Francisco 15, Calif.
Disney: Walt Disney Productions, 2400 West Alameda, Burbank, Calif.
EBF: Encyclopaedia Britannica Films, 5625 Hollywood Blvd., Hollywood, Calif.
IFB: International Film Bureau, 57 East Jackson St., Chicago 4, Ill.
Long: Long Filmslide Service, 7505 Fairmount Ave., El Cerrito, Calif.
McGraw-Hill: Text-Film Dept., McGraw-Hill, 330 West 42nd St., N.Y. 36, N.Y.
Net: Net Film Service, Indiana University, Audio-Visual Center, Bloomington, Ind.
Nu-Art: Nu-Art Films, 112 West 48th St., N.Y. 19, N.Y.
PS: Popular Science Publishing Co., 355 Lexington Ave., N.Y. 17, N.Y.
SVE: Society for Visual Education, 1345 Diversey Parkway, Chicago 14, Ill.
TFC: Teaching Film Custodians, 25 West 43rd St., N.Y. 36, N.Y.
UWF: United World Films, 1445 Park Ave., N.Y. 29, N.Y.
UCE: University of California Extension, Educational Film Sales, Los Angeles 24, Calif.
YAF: Young America Films, 18 East 41st St., N.Y. 17, N.Y.

Recordings Mentioned in the Text

America Was Promises (Ling)
The American Dream (IDE)
Ase's Death (Columbia AL-35)
The Changing English Language (FW)
The Changing Literary Style (FW)
Danse Macabre (Capitol P-8296)
Down in the Valley (RCA Victor DM 1367)
Finlandia (Columbia AL-9)
Green Christmas (Capitol 4097)
I Can Hear It Now (Columbia ML 4095, 4261, 4340)
Images (Columbia ML 4979)
In the American Tradition (D:AE)
Macbeth—tone poem (Westminster 18078)
Macbeth—drama, Old Vic (Victor LM 6010)
Many Voices: Six volumes to accompany *Adventures in Literature,* grades seven to twelve (HBC)
"Irtnog" by E. B. White, read by Hiram Sherman
"Three Days to See" by Helen Keller, read by Nancy Wickwire

"To Helen" and "The Bells" by Edgar Allan Poe, read by Alexander Scourby
"Behind the Ranges" by James Ramsey Ullman, read by Arnold Moss
Mark Twain Tonight—Holbrook (Columbia OL 5440)
No Man Is an Island (D:AE)
Paul Revere (Stud)
Rhythms of the World (FW)
Saint Joan, read by Siobhan McKenna (RCA Victor 6133)
Sorry, Wrong Number, read by Agnes Moorehead (Decca 9062)
Spellbound (Capitol T-456)
Splendid Legend (SG)
Stories to Remember (IDE)
Tales from the Olympian Gods (Decca DA 475)
When Greek Meets Greek: A Study in Values—thirteen records (NAEB)
A Word in Your Ear (NAEB)
The Young Person's Guide to the Orchestra (Westminster 18372)

Recordings to Supplement the Study of Literature

Drama

Maxwell Anderson, *High Tor*—TV Production (Decca 8272); *Lost in the Stars* (Decca DL 8028)
Anonymous, *Everyman*—Meredith (Caedmon 1031) NCTE
ANTA, Album of Stars—Hayes, Le Gallienne, Gielgud, et al (Decca DL 9002 and 9009)
Stephen Vincent Benét, *John Brown's Body*—Power, Anderson, Massey (Columbia OSL-181)
Rudolf Besier, *The Barretts of Wimpole Street*—Cornell, Quayle (Caedmon 1071)
Christopher Fry, *The Lady's Not for Burning* (Decca DX-110)
Robinson Jeffers, *Medea*—Anderson (Decca DL 9000)
Arthur Miller, *Death of a Salesman*—Mitchell (Decca DX 102); Discussion by the author of attitudes toward character portrayal, with readings from *Death of a Salesman* and *The Crucible* (SA 704)
Ferenc Molnár, *Liliom-Carousel* (Decca 9020)
Richard Rodgers and Oscar Hammerstein II, *The King and I* (Decca DL 9008)
Edmund Rostand, *Cyrano de Bergerac*—Ferrer (Capitol S-283)
William Shakespeare
"Ages of Man"—Gielgud (Columbia OL 5390)
As You Like It—Cambridge University, Marlowe Society (London A 4336)
Hamlet—Gielgud (Victor LM 6007)
Immortal Scenes and Sonnets—Evans, Redgrave (Decca 9041)
Julius Caesar—Cambridge University, Marlowe Society (London A 4334)
Julius Caesar, highlights—Brando, Gielgud, Mason (MGM E 3033)
A Midsummer Night's Dream—Dublin Gate Theater (SW A5 131-133)
Othello—Cambridge University, Marlowe Society (London A-4414)
Romeo and Juliet—Old Vic (RCA Victor LM 2064)
Soliloquies, *Henry IV* et al.—Rogers (SA 723)
The Taming of the Shrew—Dublin Gate Theater (SW A-7 151-153)
Twelfth Night—Dublin Gate Theater (SW A-3 116-118)
George Bernard Shaw, *Pygmalion-My Fair Lady* (Columbia OL 5090)
Sophocles, *Antigone*—McGill University Players (FW 9861); *Oedipus Rex*—Stratford Players (Caedmon 2012)
John Millington Synge, *Riders to the Sea*—Dublin Radio Eireann Players (SA 743)
Oscar Wilde, *The Importance of Being Earnest*—Gielgud, Evans (Angel 3504-B)

Poetry

America Listens to Literature; to accompany *America Reads,* grades seven to twelve (SFC)
Appreciation of Poetry (NCTE RC-90-1)
Beowulf (NCTE RS-80-2)
Robert Browning–Mason (Caedmon 1048; NCTE) *
Lord Byron–Power (Caedmon 1042; NCTE)
Chaucer, "Canterbury Tales" (NCTE RS-80-1)
Lewis Carroll and Edward Lear, "Nonsense Verse"–Lillie, Ritchard, Holloway (Caedmon 1078; NCTE)
John Ciardi, "As If Poems"–Ciardi (FW 978; NCTE)
Samuel Taylor Coleridge–Richardson (Caedmon 1092)
E. E. Cummings–Cummings (Caedmon 1017)
Dante, "The Inferno"–Ciardi (FW FL9871; NCTE)
Early English Ballads–Read (FW FL9881; NCTE)
T. S. Eliot–Eliot (Caedmon 1045; NCTE)
Famous Poems That Tell Great Stories (Decca 9040)
Robert Frost–Frost (Caedmon 1060; NCTE)
Great Themes in Poetry (NCTE RC-90-3)
Hearing Poetry (Caedmon 1021, 1022; NCTE)
John Keats–Richardson (Caedmon 1087; NCTE)
Omar Khayyám, "The Rubáiyát"–Drake (Caedmon 1023; NCTE)
Vachel Lindsay–Lindsay (Caedmon 1041; NCTE)
Archibald Macleish–Macleish (Caedmon 1009)
Many Voices: Poetry and Prose (HBC)
Edna St. Vincent Millay–Anderson (Caedmon 1024; NCTE)
Edgar Allan Poe, Poetry and two short stories–Rathbone (Caedmon 1028; NCTE)
Percy Bysshe Shelley–Price (Caedmon 1059; NCTE)
Stephen Spender–Spender (Caedmon 1084)
Dylan Thomas–Thomas (Caedmon 1002, 1018, 1043; NCTE)
Treasury of Modern Poets (Caedmon 2006; NCTE)
Walt Whitman, "Leaves of Grass"–House, Gardner, Buckridge (FW FL9750)
William Wordsworth–Hardwicke (Caedmon 1026) NCTE
Worlds of Literature (ABC WL 1, 2, 3)
William Butler Yeats–McKenna, Cusack (Caedmon 1081)

Fiction

Arabian Nights–Melchior (Decca 9013)
Stephen Crane, *Red Badge of Courage*–O'Brien (Caedmon 1040)
Charles Dickens–Williams (London A-4221)
Dickens Duets–Pettingell (SA 741)
Don Quixote–Crocker (FW 9866)
William Faulkner, Author reads from his novels and Nobel Award Speech (Caedmon 1035; NCTE)
Paul Gallico, *The Snow Goose*–Marshall (Decca DL 9066)
Bret Harte, "Outcasts of Poker Flat" and "Luck of Roaring Camp (FW 9740)
James Hilton, *Lost Horizon*–Colman (Decca 9059)
O. Henry, "Gift of the Magi" (United Artists 4013)
Rudyard Kipling, *Jungle Book*–Karloff (Caedmon 1100)
Plato, "On the Death of Socrates" (FW 9979)

* Double listing indicates that records are available to members at discount from the National Council of Teachers of English; interested teachers should write for a current list.

Edgar Allan Poe, "The Pit and the Pendulum"—Highet (NCTE RL-20-3)
Ride with the Sun: Folktales of Many Lands (FW FC 7109)
Robert Louis Stevenson, *Treasure Island* (Mercury MSB 60018)
Stories from Irish Mythology—Susan Porter (Carmel)
Jonathan Swift, *Gulliver's Travels* (Caedmon 1099)
Tales from Ivory Towers: *Caddie Woodlawn, Silver Chief, The Good Master,* et al. Seven records (WBS)
Mark Twain, *Huckleberry Finn* (Mercury MSB 60021); Stories (Caedmon 1027); *Tom Sawyer* (Mercury MSB 60020)
Jules Verne, *Twenty Thousand Leagues under the Sea* (Mercury 60026)

SOURCES

ABC: American Book Co., 55 Fifth Ave., N.Y. 3, N.Y.
Carmel: Carmel-by-the-Sea Recording Co., P.O. Box 572, Monterey, Calif.
D:AE: Decca: Audio Education, 55 Fifth Ave., N.Y. 3, N.Y.
FW: Folkways Records and Service Corp., 117 West 46th St., N.Y. 36, N.Y.
HBC: Harcourt, Brace and Co., 750 Third Ave., N.Y. 17, N.Y.
IDE: Institute for Dramatic Education, 212 Fifth Ave., N.Y. 10, N.Y.
Ling: Linguaphone Institute, 30 Rockefeller Plaza, N.Y. 20, N.Y.
NAEB: National Association of Educational Broadcasters, 119 Gregory Hall, University of Illinois, Urbana, Ill.
NCTE: National Council of Teachers of English, 508 South Sixth St., Champaign, Ill.
SA: Spoken Arts, Inc., 95 Valley Road, New Rochelle, N.Y.
SFC: Scott, Foresman & Co., 433 East Erie St., Chicago 11, Ill.
SG: School Guild-Allied Recording Co., 3232 Greenpoint Ave., Long Island City, N.Y.
Stud: Studidisc:Audio-Visual Division, Popular Science Publishing Co., 355 Lexington Ave., N.Y. 17, N.Y.
SW: Spoken Word-Folkways, 117 West 46th St., N.Y. 36, N.Y.
WBS: World Broadcasting System, 488 Madison Ave., N.Y. 20, N.Y.

Records with familiar commercial labels may be ordered through regular dealers. The W. Schwann Catalog, 137 Newbury St., Boston 16, Mass., lists current releases monthly.

Other Producers of A-V Materials

Audio-visual materials suitable for classroom use are being produced continually. Teachers may keep themselves informed about current releases by having their names placed on the mailing lists of the firms mentioned above and of others such as the following:

Academic Film Co., 516 Fifth Ave., N.Y. 36, N.Y.
British Information Services, 30 Rockefeller Plaza, N.Y. 20, N.Y.
Stanley Bowmar Co., 12 Cleveland Place, Valhalla, N.Y.
Brandon Films, Inc., 200 West 57th St., N.Y. 19, N.Y.
Churchill-Wexler Films, 801 North Seward St., Los Angeles 38, Calif.
Dynamic Films, Inc., 112 West 89th St., N.Y. 24, N.Y.
Eastin Pictures Co., Putnam Bldg., Davenport, Iowa
Educational and Recreational Guides, Inc., 10 Brainerd Road, Summit 1, N.J.
Enrichment Records, 246 Fifth Ave., N.Y. 1, N.Y.
Eye Gate House, Inc., 2716 41st Ave., Long Island City, N.Y.
Film Images, Inc., 1860 Broadway, N.Y. 23, N.Y.
Filmstrip House, 347 Madison Ave., N.Y. 17, N.Y.
Ford Motor Co., Film Library, 15 East 53rd St., N.Y. 22, N.Y.

James A. Fitzpatrick's Travel Pictures, 8624 Sunset Blvd., Hollywood 46, Calif.
Fleetwood Films, Inc., 10 Fiske Place, Mount Vernon, N.Y.
Films of the Nations Distributors, Inc., 62 West 45th St., N.Y. 36, N.Y.
Gateway Productions, Inc., 1859 Powell St., San Francisco 11, Calif.
Ideal Pictures, Inc., 58 East South Water St., Chicago 1, Ill.
Informative Classroom Pictures Publishers, 31 Ottawa Ave., Grand Rapids, Mich.
Life Magazine, Inc., Filmstrip Division, 9 Rockefeller Plaza, N.Y. 20, N.Y.
E. L. Morthole, 8855 Lincolnwood Drive, Evanston, Ill.
Museum Extension Service, 10 East 43rd St., N.Y. 17, N.Y.
National Association of Secondary School Principals, 1201 16th St., N.W., Washington 6, D.C.
New York Times, School Service Department, 229 West 43rd St., N.Y. 18, N.Y.
Pictorial Events, 597 Fifth Ave., N.Y. 17, N.Y.
Training Aids, Inc., 7414 Beverly Blvd., Los Angeles 24, Calif.
Trans-World Airlines, Advertising Dep't, 380 Madison Ave., N.Y. 17, N.Y.
Unusual Films, Bob Jones University, Greenville, S.C.
United States Office of Education, Federal Radio Education Commission, Washington 25, D.C.
Yale University Press Film Service, 386 Park Ave. South, N.Y. 16, N.Y.

INDEX